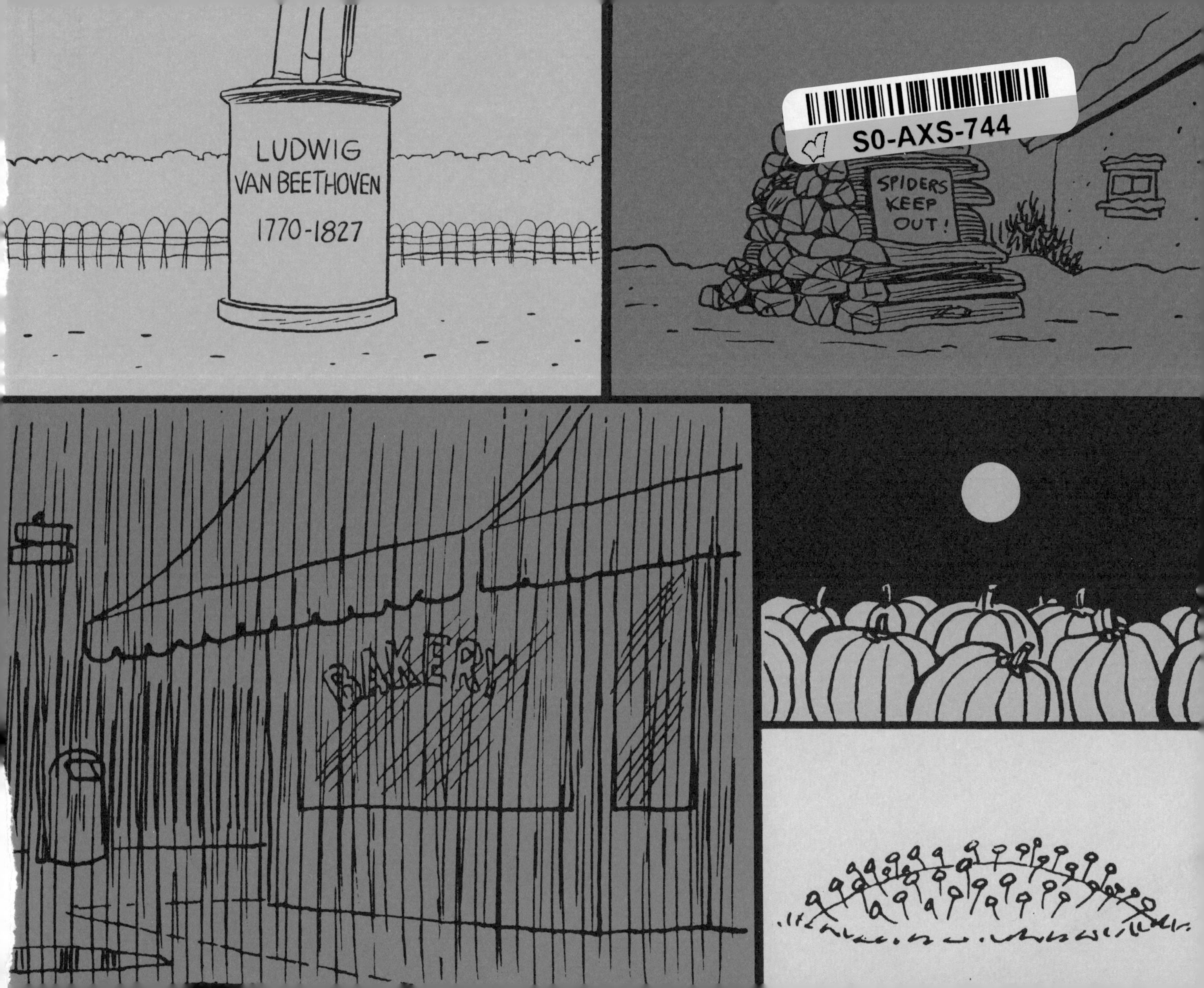
LUDWIG
VAN BEETHOVEN
1770-1827
SPIDERS KEEP OUT!
BAKERY

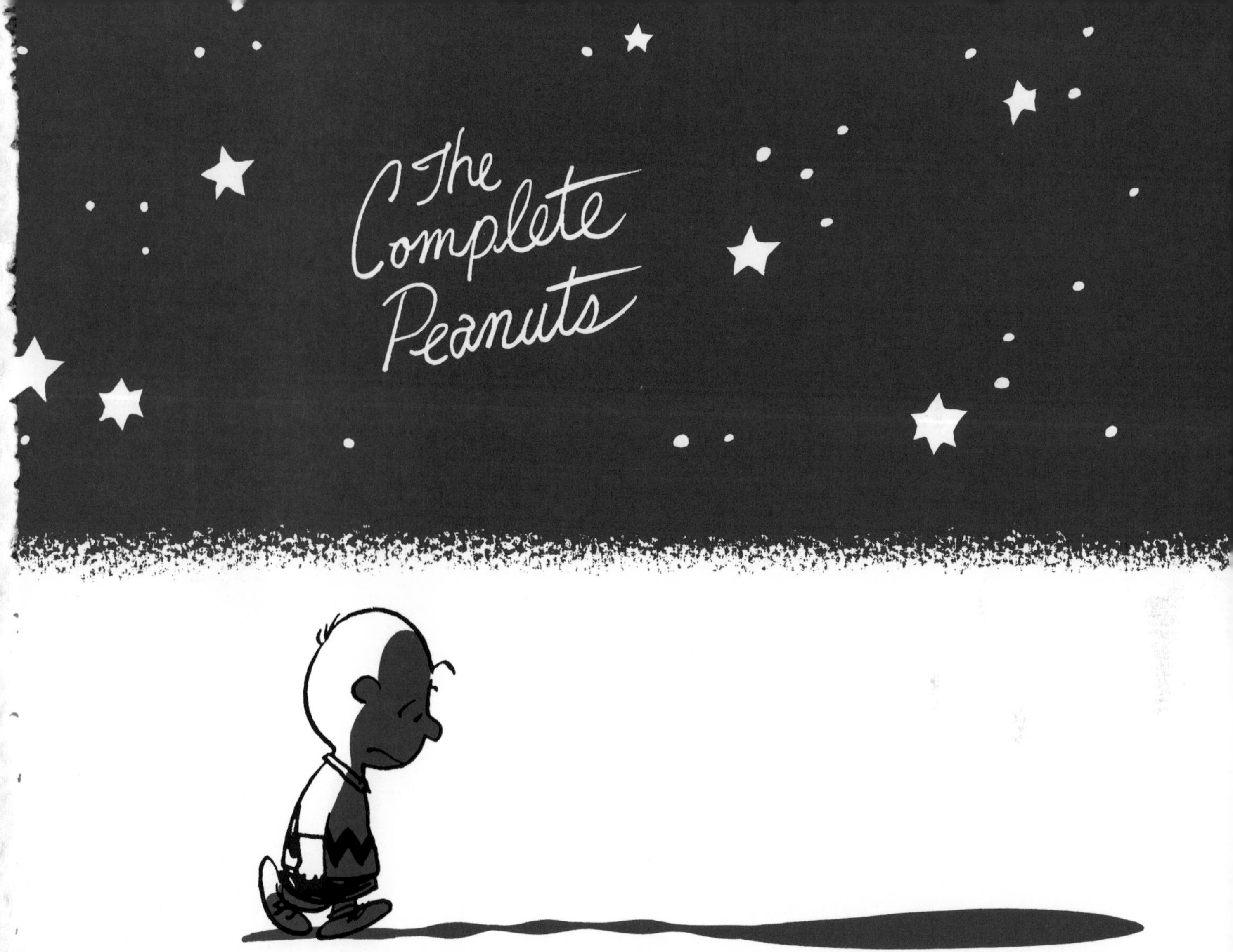
The Complete Peanuts

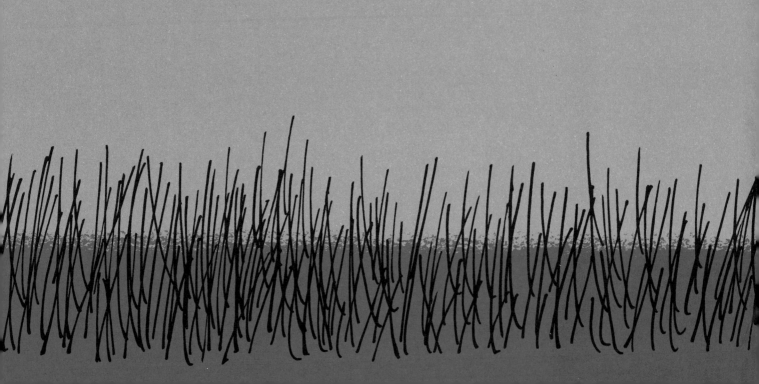

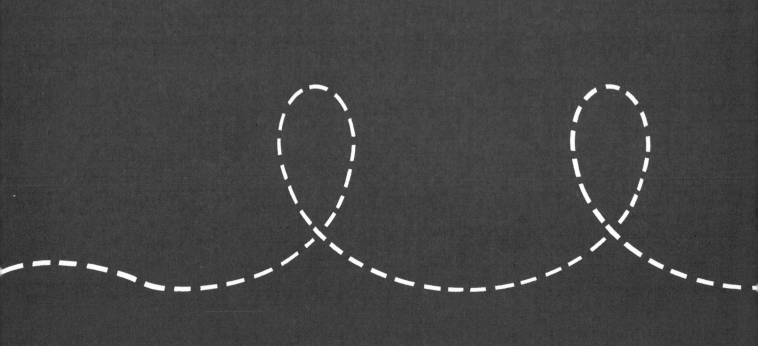

THE COMPLETE PEANUTS
by Charles M. Schulz
published by
Fantagraphics Books

Editor: Gary Groth
Designer: Seth
Production Manager: Kim Thompson
Production, assembly, and restoration: Paul Baresh and Adam Grano
Archival and production assistance: Timothy Chow, Marcie Lee, Peter H. Vollman & Janelle Anderson
Index compiled by Kevin Kepple
Promotion: Eric Reynolds
Publishers: Gary Groth & Kim Thompson

Special thanks to Jeannie Schulz, without whom
this project would not have come to fruition.
Thanks also to the
Charles M. Schulz Creative Associates,
especially Paige Braddock and Kim Towner.
Thanks for special support from United Media.

Fantagraphics Books, 7563 Lake City Way, Seattle, WA 98115, USA. For a free full-color catalogue of comics,
call 1-800-657-1100. Our books may be viewed on our website at www.fantagraphics.com.

Distributed to the book trade by:

USA: W.W. Norton and Company, Inc.
500 Fifth Avenue, New York, NY 10010
212-354-5500
Order Department: 800-233-4830

CANADA: Raincoast Books
9050 Shaugnessy Street, Vancouver, British Columbia V6P 6E5
Customer Service: 800-663-5714

ISBN: 978-1-56097-826-8
First printing: February 2008   Printed in China

CHARLES M. SCHULZ

THE COMPLETE PEANUTS

1967 TO 1968

"MY ANXIETIES HAVE ANXIETIES."

FANTAGRAPHICS BOOKS

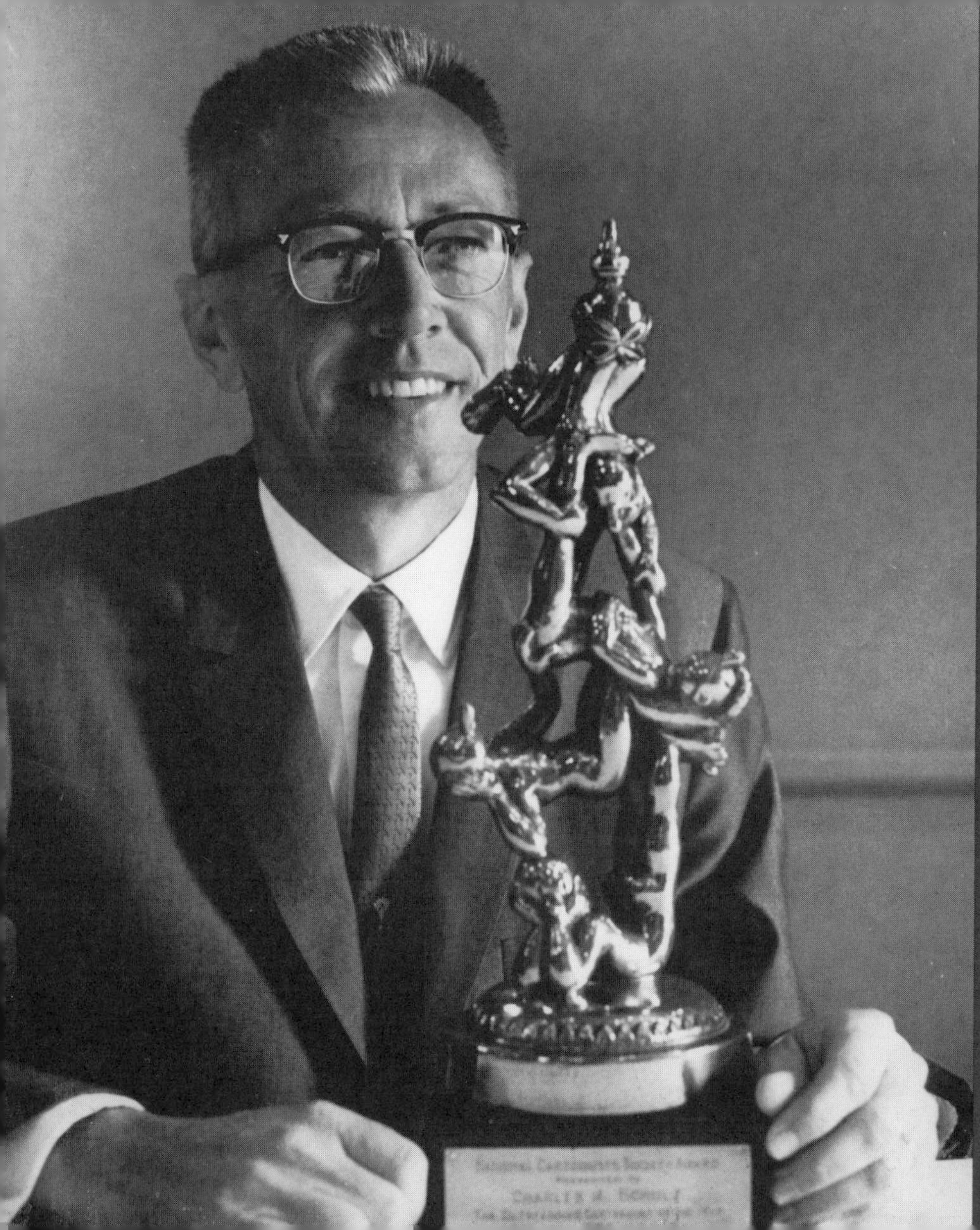

Charles Schulz with his second Reuben award, circa 1964.

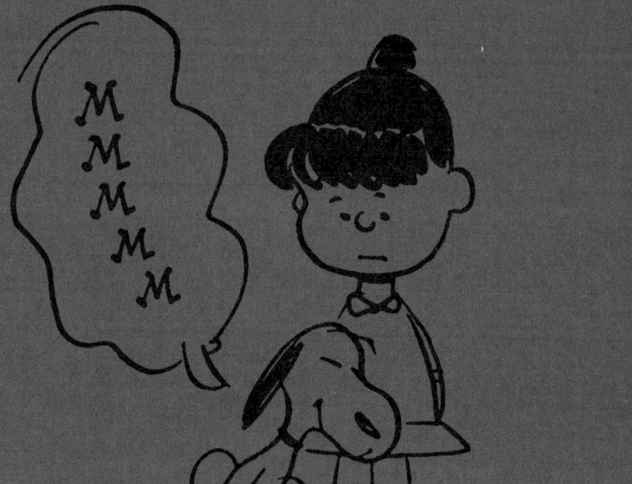
MMMMM

FOREWORD by JOHN WATERS

I first became obsessed with *Peanuts* when I lay in bed recovering from mononucleosis in the sixth grade. I had read the comic strip daily in the *Baltimore Sun* but, lo and behold, my Mom had found me a book with early collected *Peanuts* strips and finally I could spend quality time with my outsider friends. And all the characters in *Peanuts* were outsiders all right; kids who never fit in — just like me. They suffered depression (would parents give Charlie Brown Prozac today?), paranoia (even a bug on a tree could bite you if you weren't careful), holiday delusions ("The Great Pumpkin"), despair about growing older ("Who wants to be

nine?" Sally moans), and even perversity ("room temperature thumb sucking tastes best").

But of course it was all about Lucy. I *still* love Lucy and I'm not talking about the one on TV married to Desi. If I ever wanted to get in a good mood I would just look at Lucy's mean scowl (page 9, bottom strip) and suddenly I'd be ready to face the world. I like Lucy's politics ("I know everything!," "Little brothers should stand when big sisters enter the room."), her manners ("Get out of my way!," "All right, switch channels. Get up so I can sit there."), her narcissism ("Why don't you just come right out and admit that every move I make fascinates you?") and especially her verbal abuse rants ("I'll yell at you *when* I feel like it, *where* I feel like it, *how* I feel like it, and *why* I feel like it and as *often* as I fell like it!"). And just to be more obnoxious, Lucy is perfect at jumping rope, never missing a step ("Ten thousand. Ten thousand and one. Ten thousand and two," she counts). In other words, a girl after my own heart.

I have a real niece named Lucy and I'm not sure if my sister named her after the comics character or not but there are certain similarities. When I was first around little Lucy as a child, I tried to be nice, but as I held out my arms, like a good uncle should, beckoning her to come to me, she froze in her tracks and spoke her first words to me, "No!" Look at the face on Schulz's Lucy on page 61 saying the same dialogue and  you'll experience the amazement I felt at being rejected so wholeheartedly for, well... I'm not sure what. Maybe the Lucys of the world don't need a reason. They're just crabby on principle and I've learned to respect that.

Charles Schulz sure can draw. As R. Crumb's work is finally being shown today in top contemporary art galleries, and being sold for big bucks, so should Mr. Schulz's. Look at the "smoke of despair" (last panel, middle strip, page 27). If that isn't art I don't know what is. Lucy's "total warfare frown" (last panel, page 9) is just as iconic to me as Mona Lisa's smirk. Linus's concussion expression and tremors (page 31) and Lucy's "stiff upper lip" (bottom strip, page 79) are equally as stunning. Schulz is an amazing craftsman. I especially love how he draws hair; Lucy's struggle for physical strength sends her classic hairdo into full beauty parlor anarchy (page 20). Linus' thin hair, like mine, seems especially prone to emotional extremes — reacting badly to aggression (middle strip, page 80) and fear (middle strip, page 47).

To be honest, I'm reading some of the strips for the first time now because the years included (1965-1966) were probably my wildest and even though I was following Timothy Leary and not Charles Schulz at the time, I never felt *Peanuts* had sold out or was on the wrong side of the generation gap no matter how huge or broad the appeal.

Schulz's humor doesn't date either even though you can spot the late '60s subject matter as it creeps in; "I hate your generation," Sally screams to her slightly older brother Charlie Brown. "Help Stamp Out Things That Need Stamping Out" reads a picket sign that Linus carries to no notice except rude comments from his sister Lucy. There are weird mentions of the CIA and even '60s fashion model Twiggy's name is dropped. Leave it to Lucy to shout "police brutality!" to a school crossing guard doing his job. And of course Linus' "blanket withdrawal" sub-plot that goes on for several pages was rehab way before it became Hollywood tabloid fodder. One wonders if Michael Jackson's son's nickname "Blanket" is stolen directly from *Peanuts*.

Minority characters are introduced (José Peterson from New Mexico and Franklin, an African-American) and it's amazing to imagine Schulz was criticized for this at the time, rather than for not having enough minorities as he would be today. I also am fascinated by characters like Roy (page 229) who are rarely if ever heard. I like to obsess over the *Peanuts* characters who never caught on, the ones that couldn't claw their way up to stardom in Charles Schulz-land, the forgotten lost faces of *Peanuts*.

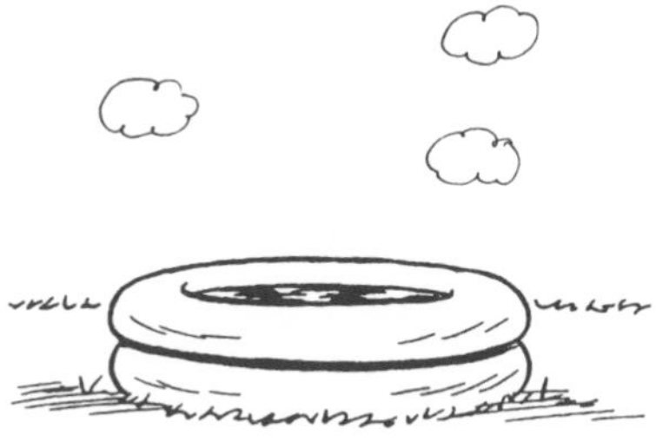

Of course, many of the characters in these strips have been influential in my own films. Pig-Pen certainly was the model for Dingy Dave in *A Dirty Shame* but in a *much* darker way. Charlie Brown's humiliations over sports reflect my childhood experiences (see top strip, page 74 for a brutal reminder) and led to my defiance that enabled me to star in a commercial in Baltimore for a local sports announcer where I got to bark "I hate sports!" "So do I!" people would yell to me in supermarkets in solidarity and I thank Charlie Brown for this opportunity. Divine cutting up her defiant daughter Taffy's jump rope when she refused to stop jumping in *Female Trouble* certainly reflects Lucy's obnoxious jump rope mania. Schroeder's obsession with Beethoven may have influenced Edie the Egg Lady's love of eggs in *Pink Flamingos* and Lucy's tone certainly influenced every word Divine shrieked in my early underground movies.

Charles Schulz is, plain and simple, a great artist and philosopher. He never shows his hand politically, understands both the horror and joy of childhood and never puts the blame on parents. You are dealt a hand. Deal with it. But most importantly, he teaches all ages that if you can learn to laugh at the things that cause you the most pain you will be the strongest of all. *Peanuts*: a real way of life. For me at least.

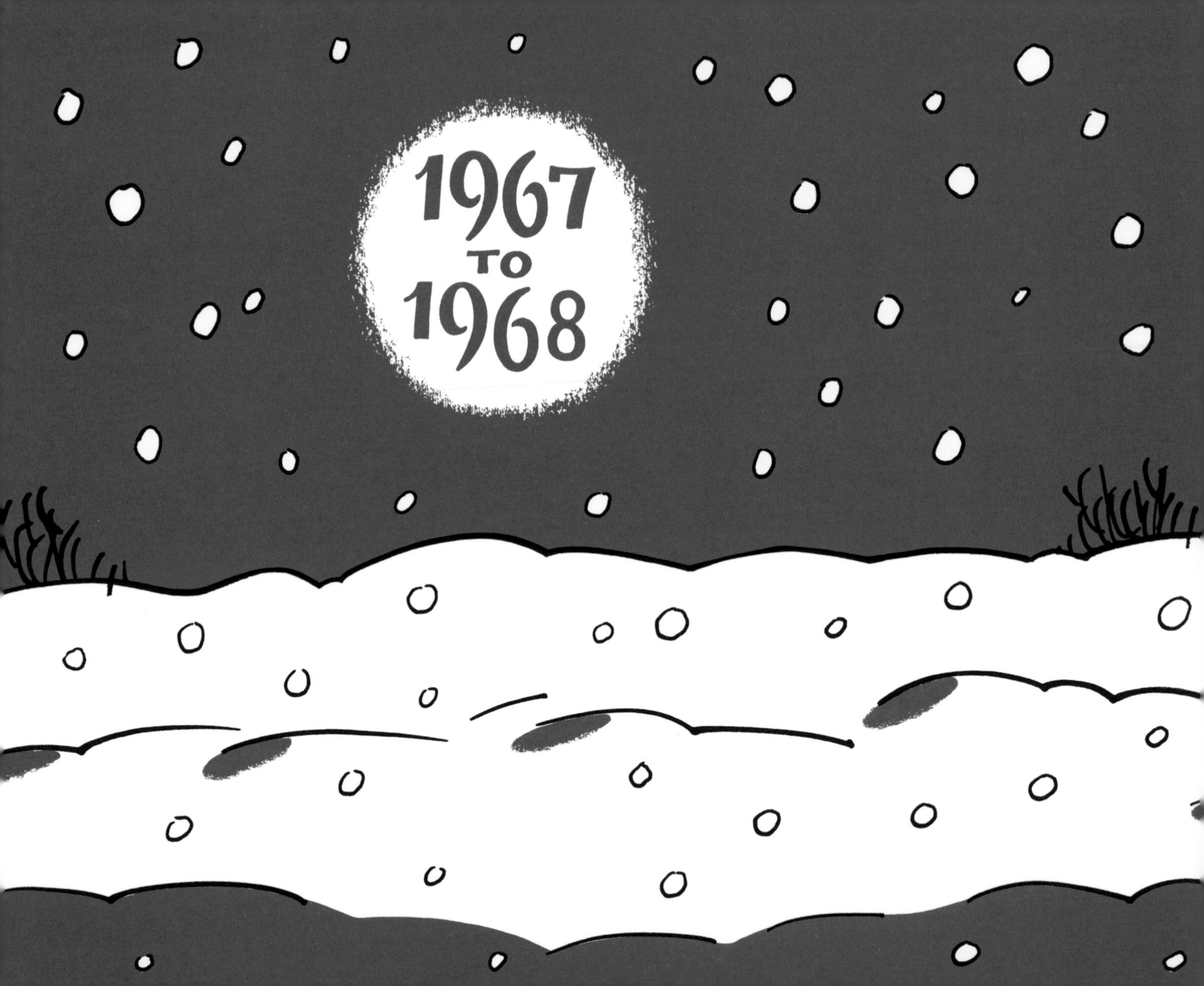
1967
TO
1968

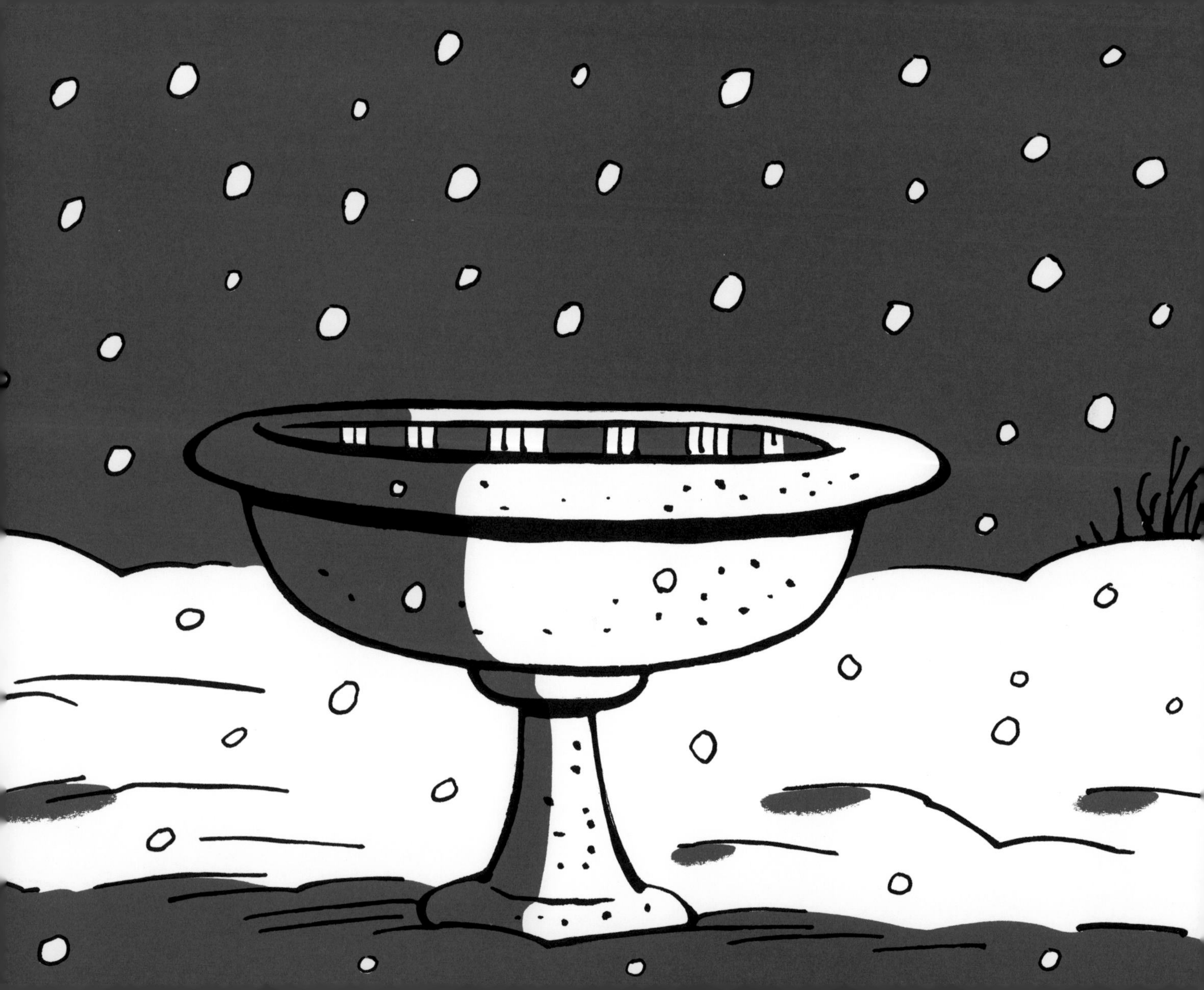

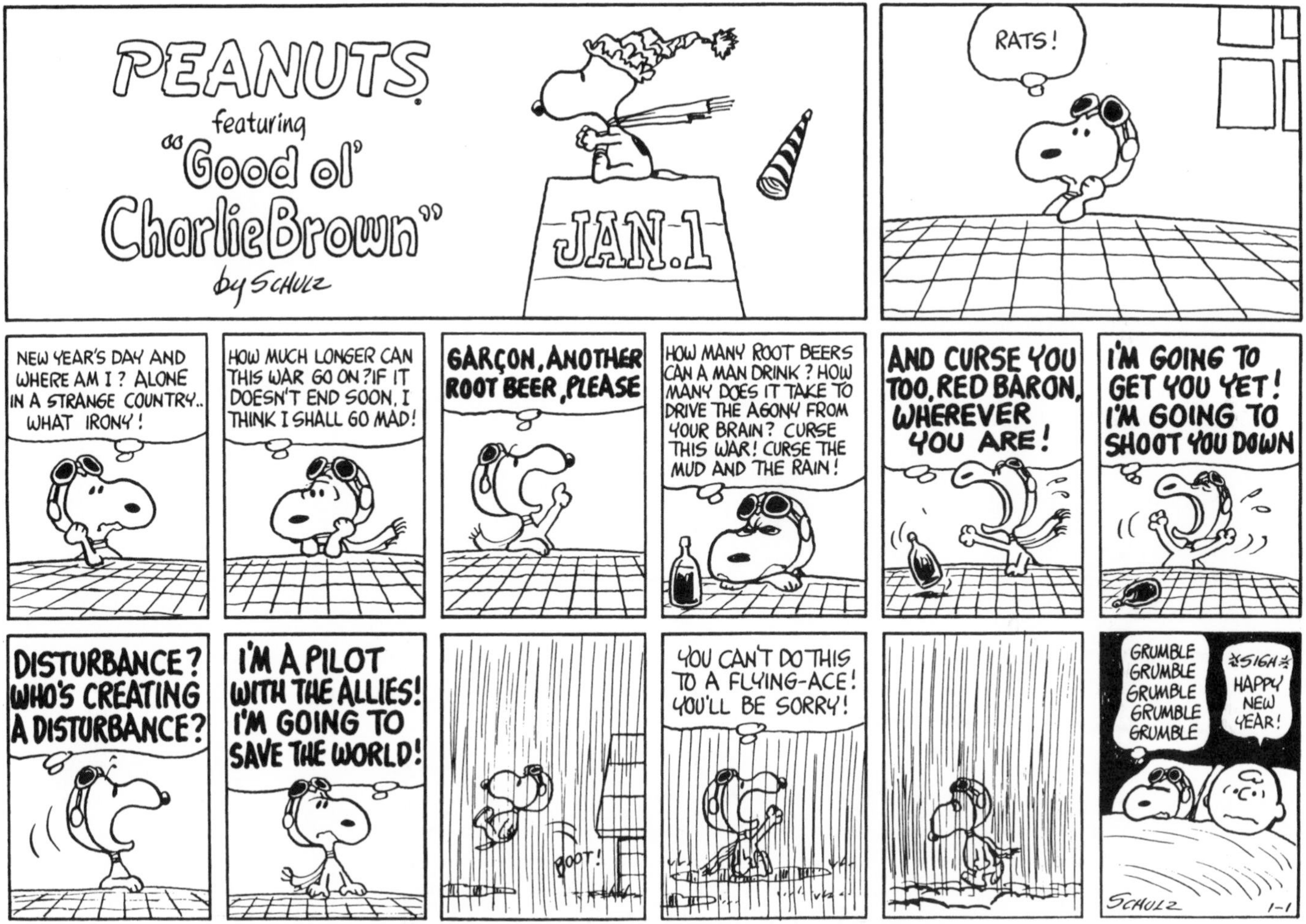
PEANUTS
featuring
"Good ol' CharlieBrown"
by SCHULZ
JAN.1
RATS!
NEW YEAR'S DAY AND WHERE AM I? ALONE IN A STRANGE COUNTRY.. WHAT IRONY!
HOW MUCH LONGER CAN THIS WAR GO ON? IF IT DOESN'T END SOON, I THINK I SHALL GO MAD!
GARÇON, ANOTHER ROOT BEER, PLEASE
HOW MANY ROOT BEERS CAN A MAN DRINK? HOW MANY DOES IT TAKE TO DRIVE THE AGONY FROM YOUR BRAIN? CURSE THIS WAR! CURSE THE MUD AND THE RAIN!
AND CURSE YOU TOO, RED BARON, WHEREVER YOU ARE!
I'M GOING TO GET YOU YET! I'M GOING TO SHOOT YOU DOWN
DISTURBANCE? WHO'S CREATING A DISTURBANCE?
I'M A PILOT WITH THE ALLIES! I'M GOING TO SAVE THE WORLD!
BOOT!
YOU CAN'T DO THIS TO A FLYING-ACE! YOU'LL BE SORRY!
GRUMBLE GRUMBLE GRUMBLE GRUMBLE GRUMBLE
SIGH HAPPY NEW YEAR!
SCHULZ
1-1

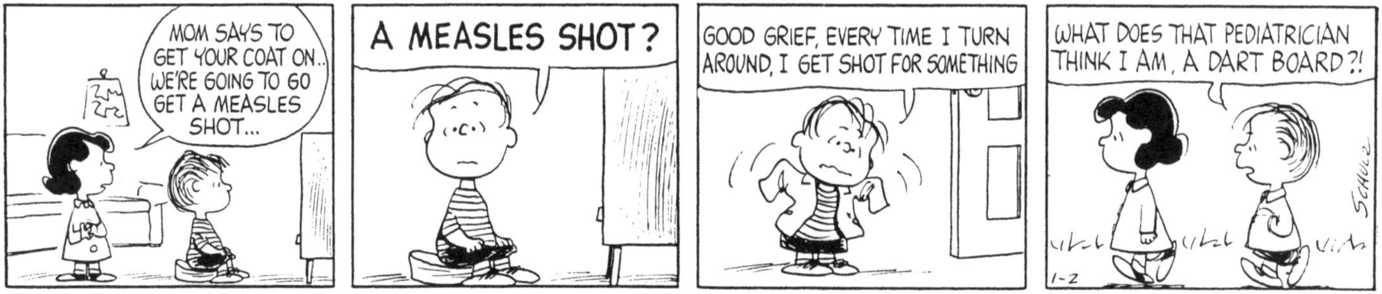
MOM SAYS TO GET YOUR COAT ON.. WE'RE GOING TO GO GET A MEASLES SHOT...
A MEASLES SHOT?
GOOD GRIEF, EVERY TIME I TURN AROUND, I GET SHOT FOR SOMETHING
WHAT DOES THAT PEDIATRICIAN THINK I AM, A DART BOARD?!
1-2
SCHULZ

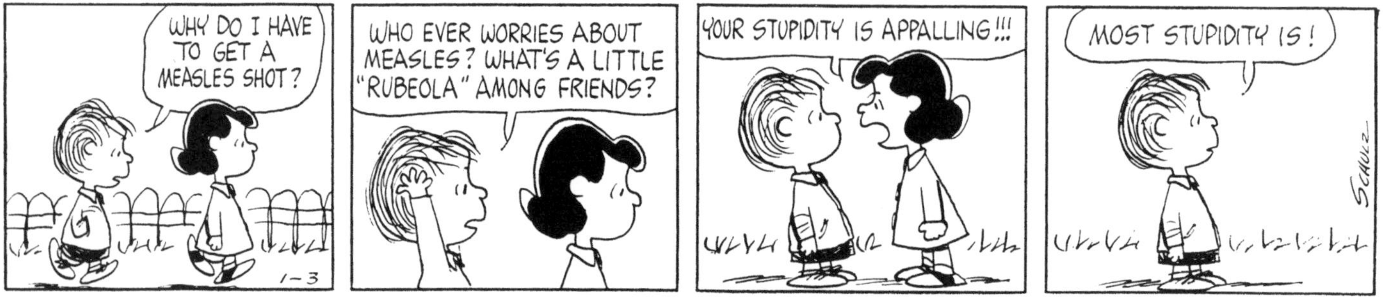
WHY DO I HAVE TO GET A MEASLES SHOT?
1-3
WHO EVER WORRIES ABOUT MEASLES? WHAT'S A LITTLE "RUBEOLA" AMONG FRIENDS?
YOUR STUPIDITY IS APPALLING!!!
MOST STUPIDITY IS!
SCHULZ

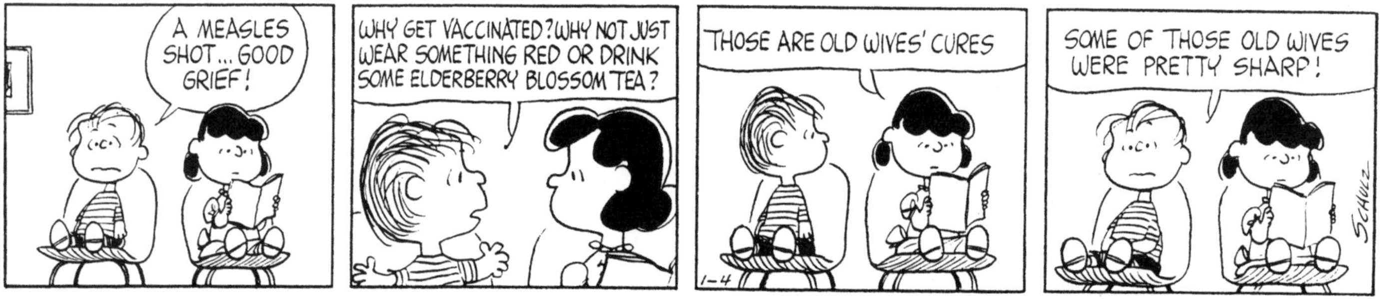
A MEASLES SHOT... GOOD GRIEF!
WHY GET VACCINATED? WHY NOT JUST WEAR SOMETHING RED OR DRINK SOME ELDERBERRY BLOSSOM TEA?
THOSE ARE OLD WIVES' CURES
1-4
SOME OF THOSE OLD WIVES WERE PRETTY SHARP!
SCHULZ

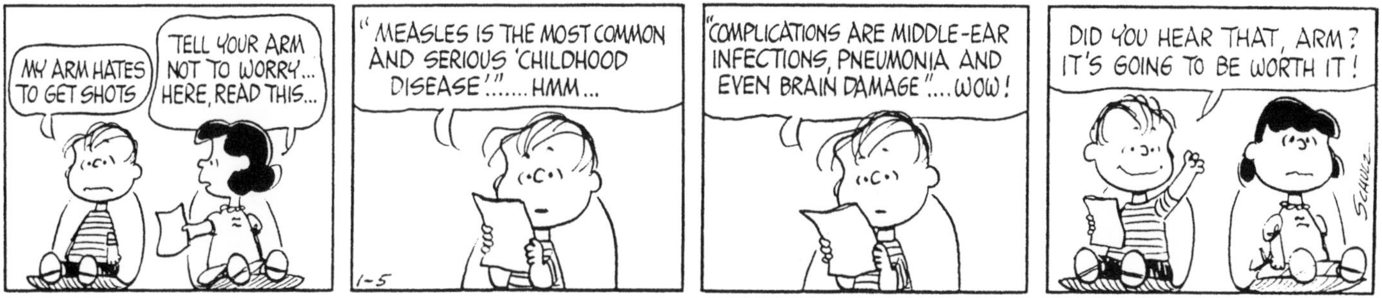
MY ARM HATES TO GET SHOTS
TELL YOUR ARM NOT TO WORRY... HERE, READ THIS...
" MEASLES IS THE MOST COMMON AND SERIOUS 'CHILDHOOD DISEASE'."...... HMM...
"COMPLICATIONS ARE MIDDLE-EAR INFECTIONS, PNEUMONIA AND EVEN BRAIN DAMAGE"....WOW!
DID YOU HEAR THAT, ARM? IT'S GOING TO BE WORTH IT!

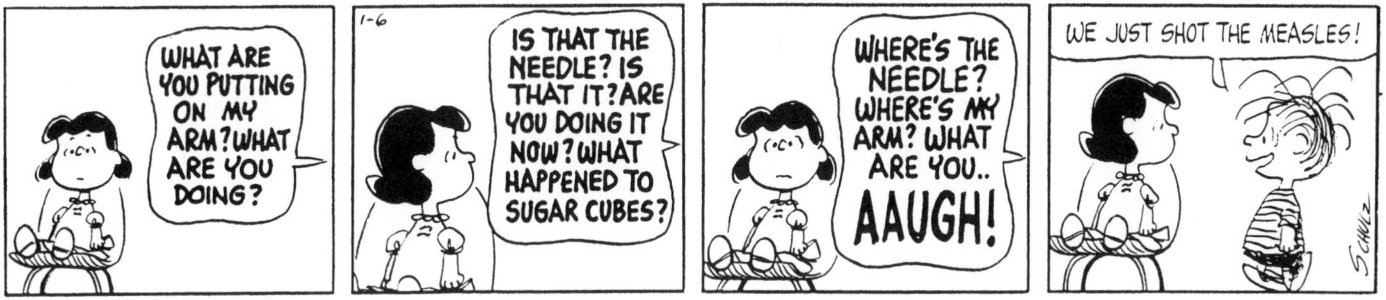
WHAT ARE YOU PUTTING ON MY ARM? WHAT ARE YOU DOING?
IS THAT THE NEEDLE? IS THAT IT? ARE YOU DOING IT NOW? WHAT HAPPENED TO SUGAR CUBES?
WHERE'S THE NEEDLE? WHERE'S MY ARM? WHAT ARE YOU.. AAUGH!
WE JUST SHOT THE MEASLES!

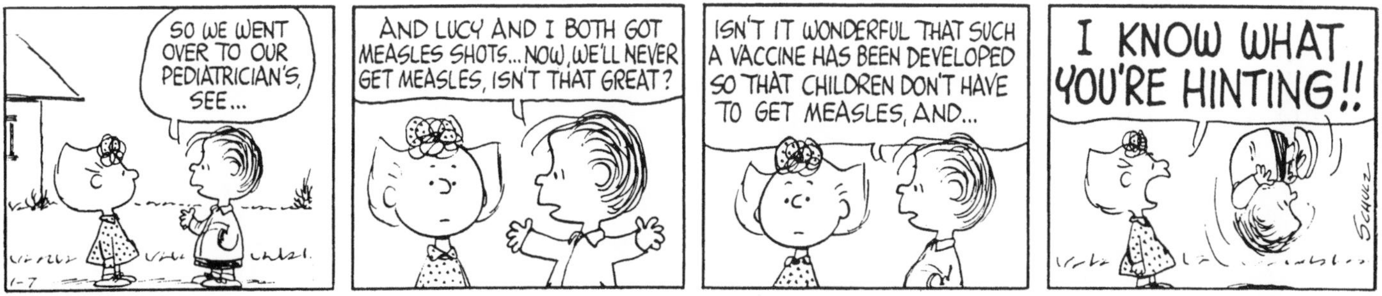
SO WE WENT OVER TO OUR PEDIATRICIAN'S, SEE...
AND LUCY AND I BOTH GOT MEASLES SHOTS... NOW, WE'LL NEVER GET MEASLES, ISN'T THAT GREAT?
ISN'T IT WONDERFUL THAT SUCH A VACCINE HAS BEEN DEVELOPED SO THAT CHILDREN DON'T HAVE TO GET MEASLES, AND...
I KNOW WHAT YOU'RE HINTING!!

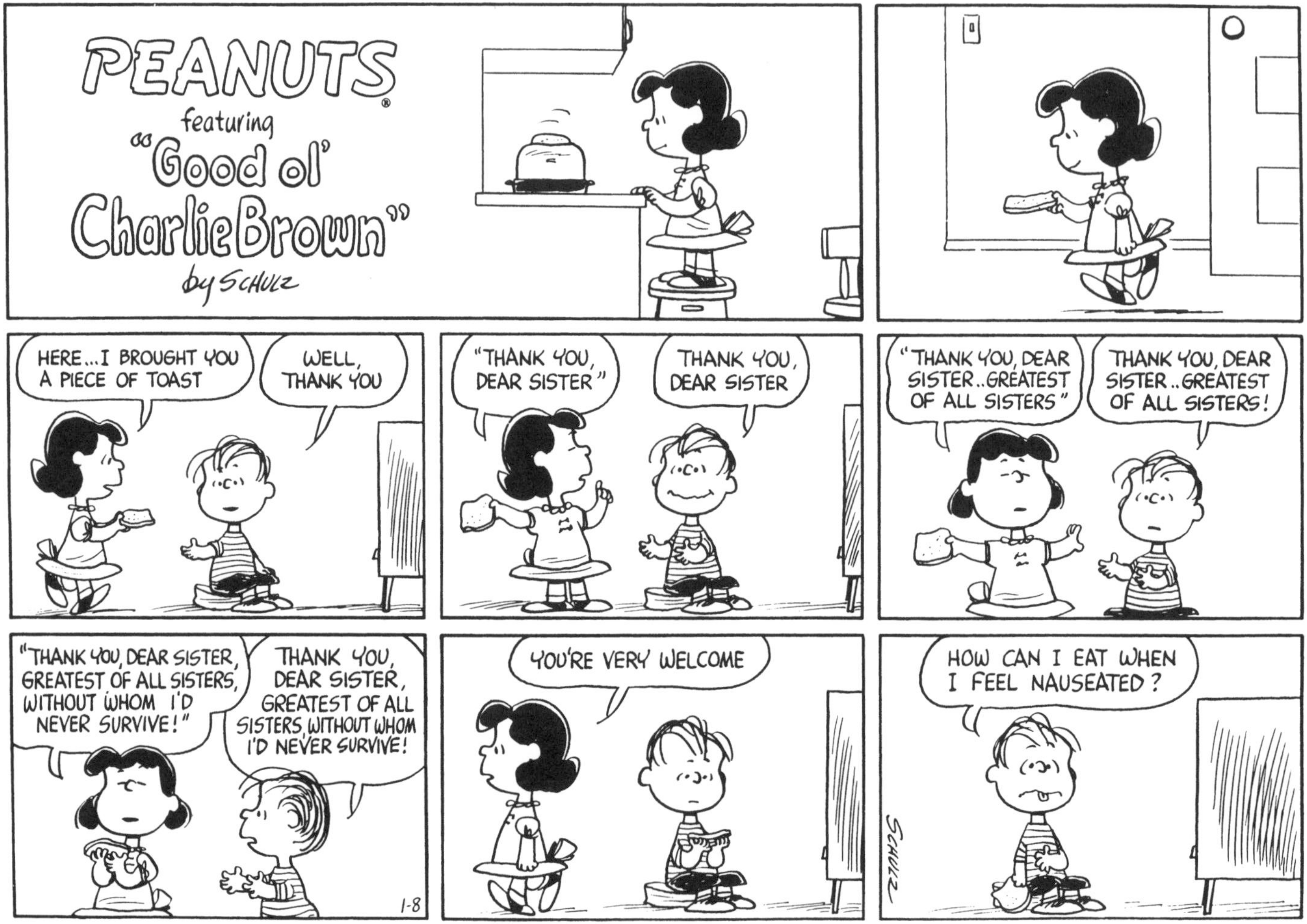
PEANUTS®
featuring
"Good ol' CharlieBrown"
by SCHULZ
HERE...I BROUGHT YOU A PIECE OF TOAST
WELL, THANK YOU
"THANK YOU, DEAR SISTER"
THANK YOU, DEAR SISTER
"THANK YOU, DEAR SISTER..GREATEST OF ALL SISTERS"
THANK YOU, DEAR SISTER..GREATEST OF ALL SISTERS!
"THANK YOU, DEAR SISTER, GREATEST OF ALL SISTERS, WITHOUT WHOM I'D NEVER SURVIVE!"
THANK YOU, DEAR SISTER, GREATEST OF ALL SISTERS, WITHOUT WHOM I'D NEVER SURVIVE!
1-8
YOU'RE VERY WELCOME
SCHULZ
HOW CAN I EAT WHEN I FEEL NAUSEATED?

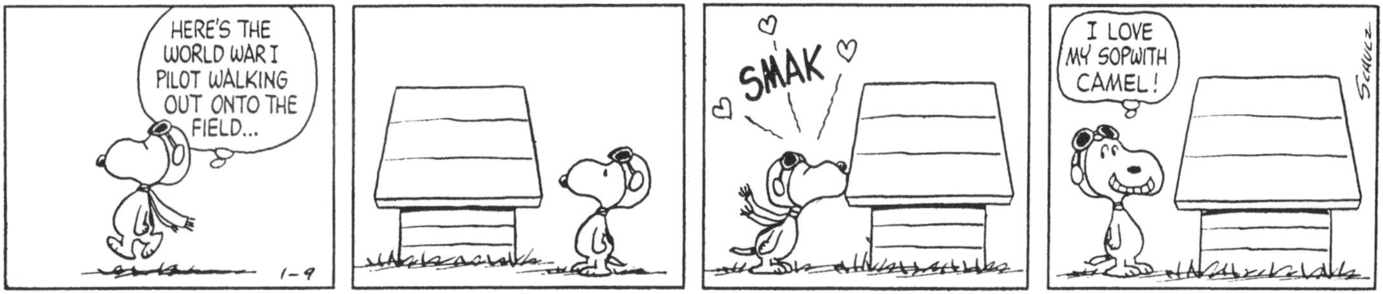
HERE'S THE WORLD WAR I PILOT WALKING OUT ONTO THE FIELD...
SMAK
I LOVE MY SOPWITH CAMEL!

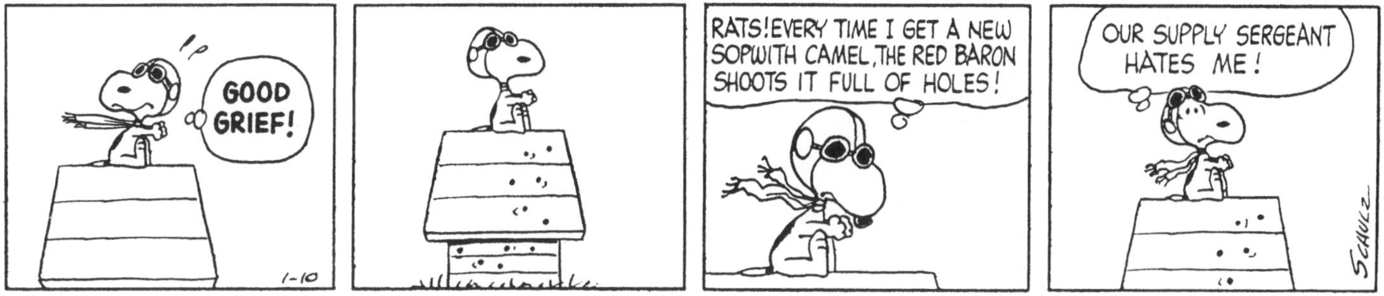
GOOD GRIEF!
RATS! EVERY TIME I GET A NEW SOPWITH CAMEL, THE RED BARON SHOOTS IT FULL OF HOLES!
OUR SUPPLY SERGEANT HATES ME!

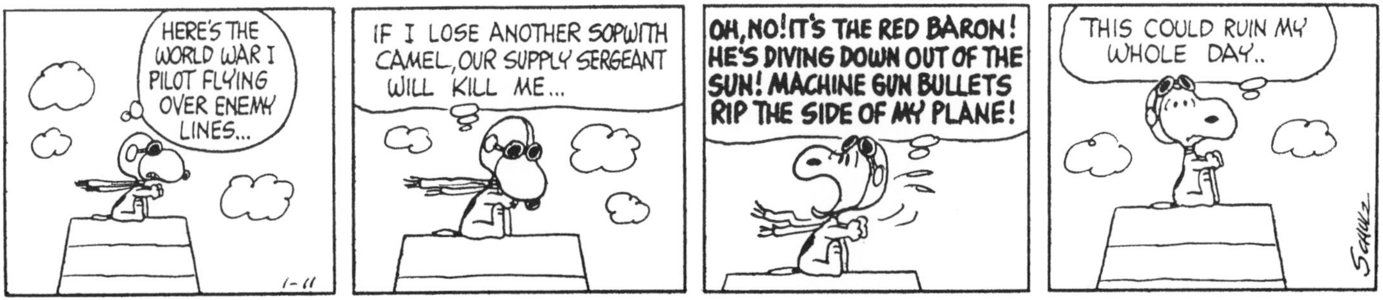
HERE'S THE WORLD WAR I PILOT FLYING OVER ENEMY LINES...
IF I LOSE ANOTHER SOPWITH CAMEL, OUR SUPPLY SERGEANT WILL KILL ME...
OH, NO! IT'S THE RED BARON! HE'S DIVING DOWN OUT OF THE SUN! MACHINE GUN BULLETS RIP THE SIDE OF MY PLANE!
THIS COULD RUIN MY WHOLE DAY..

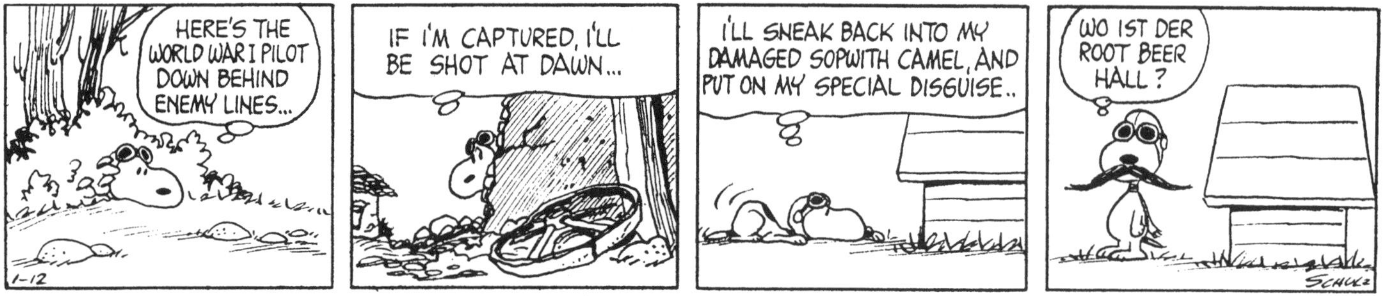
HERE'S THE WORLD WAR I PILOT DOWN BEHIND ENEMY LINES...
1-12
IF I'M CAPTURED, I'LL BE SHOT AT DAWN...
I'LL SNEAK BACK INTO MY DAMAGED SOPWITH CAMEL, AND PUT ON MY SPECIAL DISGUISE..
WO IST DER ROOT BEER HALL?
SCHULZ

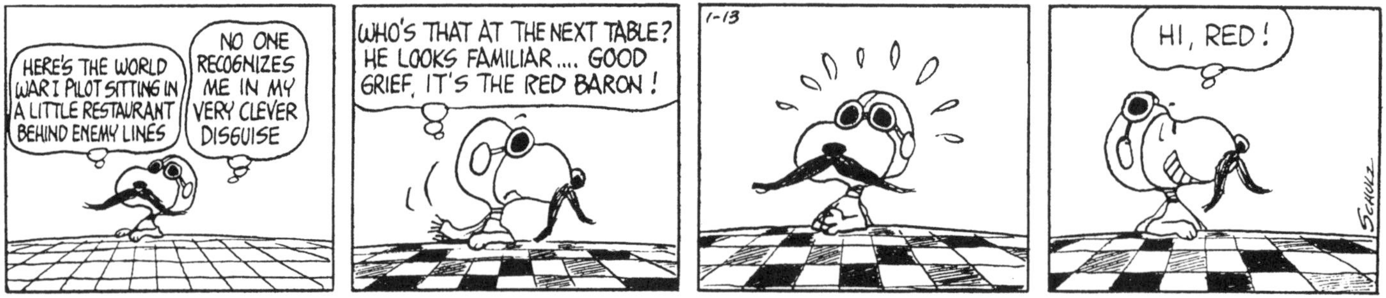
HERE'S THE WORLD WAR I PILOT SITTING IN A LITTLE RESTAURANT BEHIND ENEMY LINES
NO ONE RECOGNIZES ME IN MY VERY CLEVER DISGUISE
WHO'S THAT AT THE NEXT TABLE? HE LOOKS FAMILIAR.... GOOD GRIEF, IT'S THE RED BARON!
1-13
HI, RED!
SCHULZ

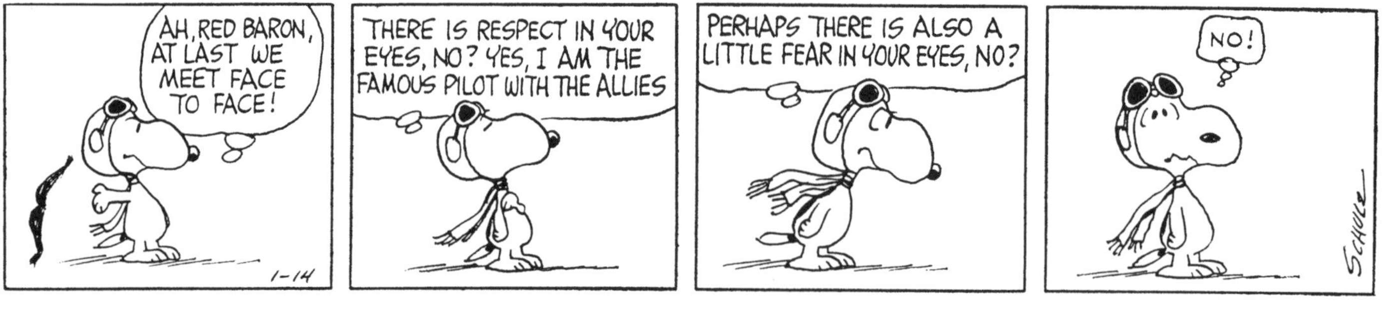
AH, RED BARON, AT LAST WE MEET FACE TO FACE!
1-14
THERE IS RESPECT IN YOUR EYES, NO? YES, I AM THE FAMOUS PILOT WITH THE ALLIES
PERHAPS THERE IS ALSO A LITTLE FEAR IN YOUR EYES, NO?
NO!
SCHULZ

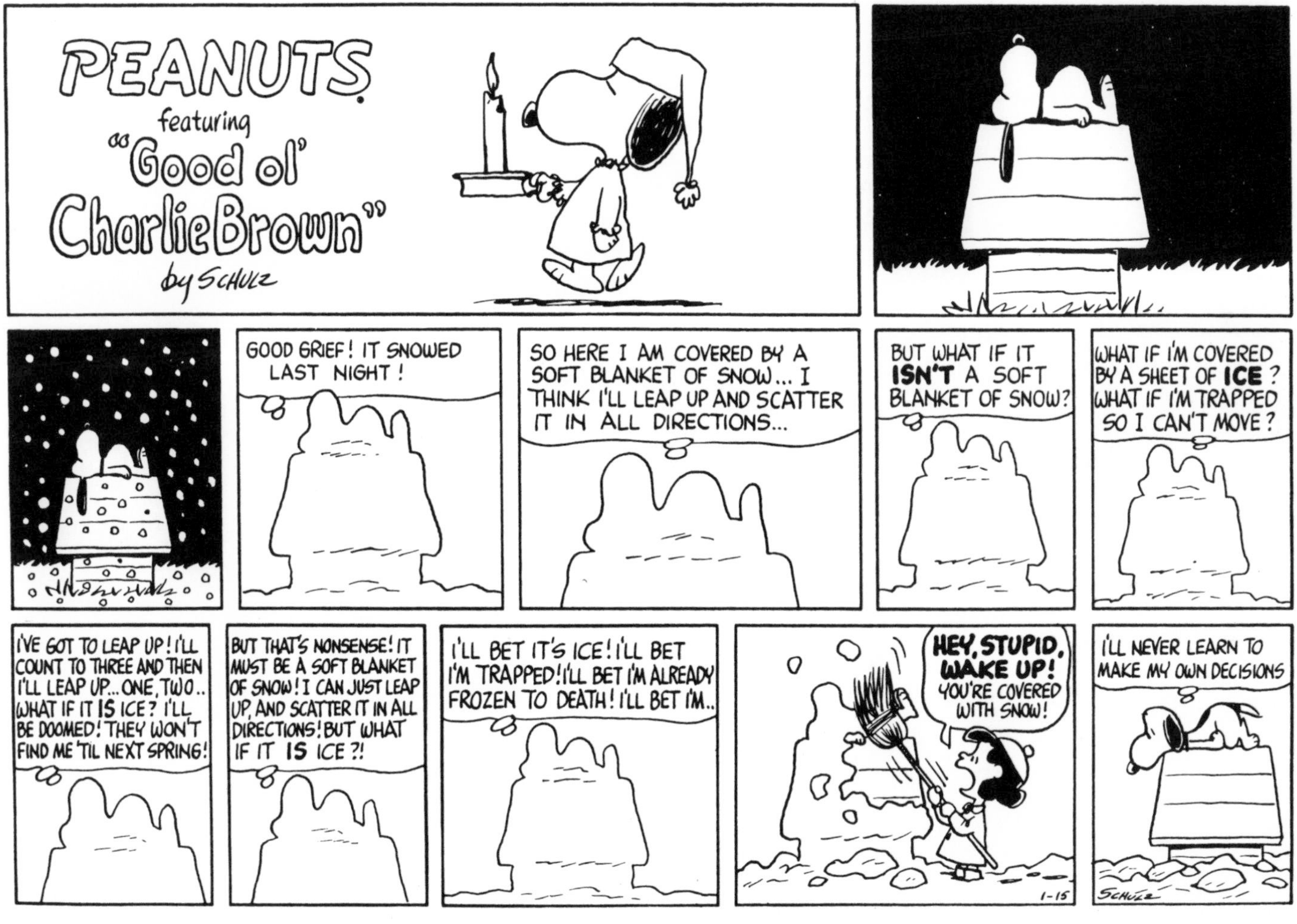
PEANUTS
featuring
"Good ol' Charlie Brown"
by SCHULZ
GOOD GRIEF! IT SNOWED LAST NIGHT!
SO HERE I AM COVERED BY A SOFT BLANKET OF SNOW... I THINK I'LL LEAP UP AND SCATTER IT IN ALL DIRECTIONS...
BUT WHAT IF IT **ISN'T** A SOFT BLANKET OF SNOW?
WHAT IF I'M COVERED BY A SHEET OF **ICE**? WHAT IF I'M TRAPPED SO I CAN'T MOVE?
I'VE GOT TO LEAP UP! I'LL COUNT TO THREE AND THEN I'LL LEAP UP... ONE, TWO.. WHAT IF IT **IS** ICE? I'LL BE DOOMED! THEY WON'T FIND ME 'TIL NEXT SPRING!
BUT THAT'S NONSENSE! IT MUST BE A SOFT BLANKET OF SNOW! I CAN JUST LEAP UP, AND SCATTER IT IN ALL DIRECTIONS! BUT WHAT IF IT **IS** ICE?!
I'LL BET IT'S ICE! I'LL BET I'M TRAPPED! I'LL BET I'M ALREADY FROZEN TO DEATH! I'LL BET I'M..
HEY, STUPID, WAKE UP! YOU'RE COVERED WITH SNOW!
1-15
I'LL NEVER LEARN TO MAKE MY OWN DECISIONS
SCHULZ

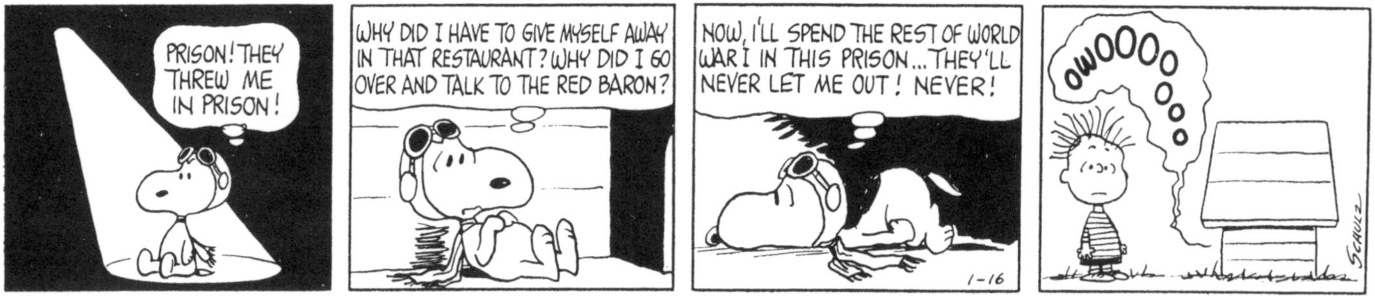
PRISON! THEY THREW ME IN PRISON!
WHY DID I HAVE TO GIVE MYSELF AWAY IN THAT RESTAURANT? WHY DID I GO OVER AND TALK TO THE RED BARON?
NOW, I'LL SPEND THE REST OF WORLD WAR I IN THIS PRISON... THEY'LL NEVER LET ME OUT! NEVER!
1-16
OWOOOOOOO
SCHULZ

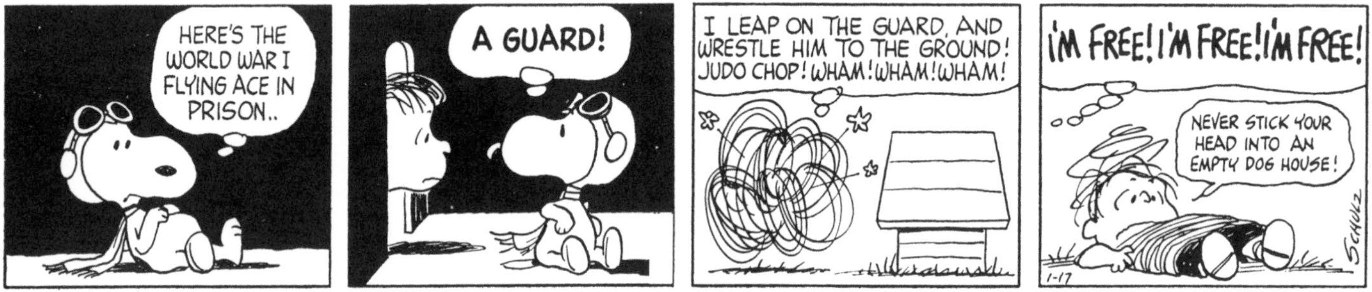
HERE'S THE WORLD WAR I FLYING ACE IN PRISON..
A GUARD!
I LEAP ON THE GUARD, AND WRESTLE HIM TO THE GROUND! JUDO CHOP! WHAM! WHAM! WHAM!
I'M FREE! I'M FREE! I'M FREE!
NEVER STICK YOUR HEAD INTO AN EMPTY DOG HOUSE!
1-17
SCHULZ

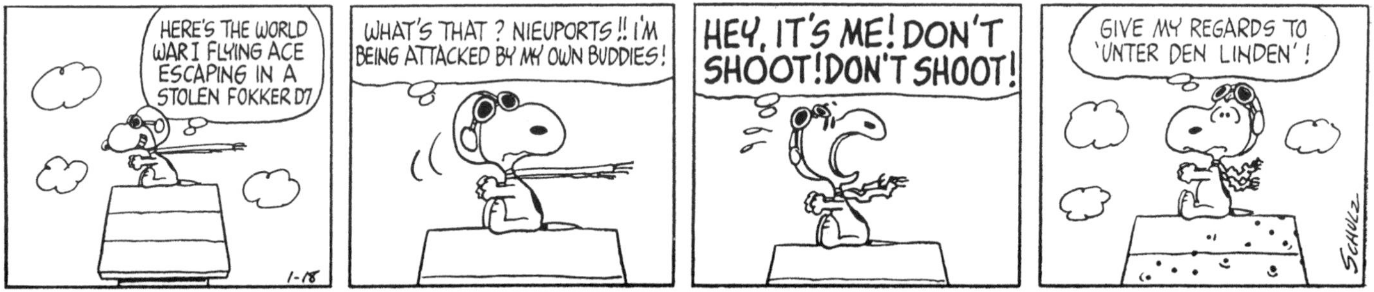
HERE'S THE WORLD WAR I FLYING ACE ESCAPING IN A STOLEN FOKKER D7
1-18
WHAT'S THAT? NIEUPORTS!! I'M BEING ATTACKED BY MY OWN BUDDIES!
HEY, IT'S ME! DON'T SHOOT! DON'T SHOOT!
GIVE MY REGARDS TO 'UNTER DEN LINDEN'!
SCHULZ

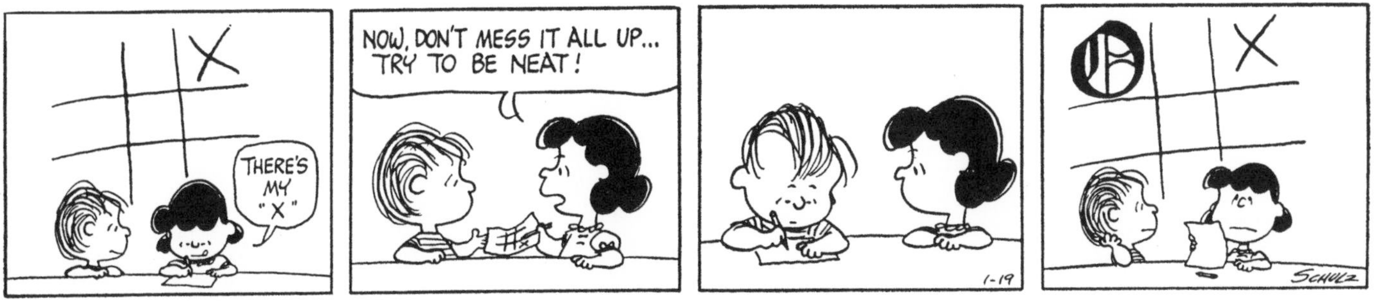
THERE'S MY "X"
NOW, DON'T MESS IT ALL UP... TRY TO BE NEAT!

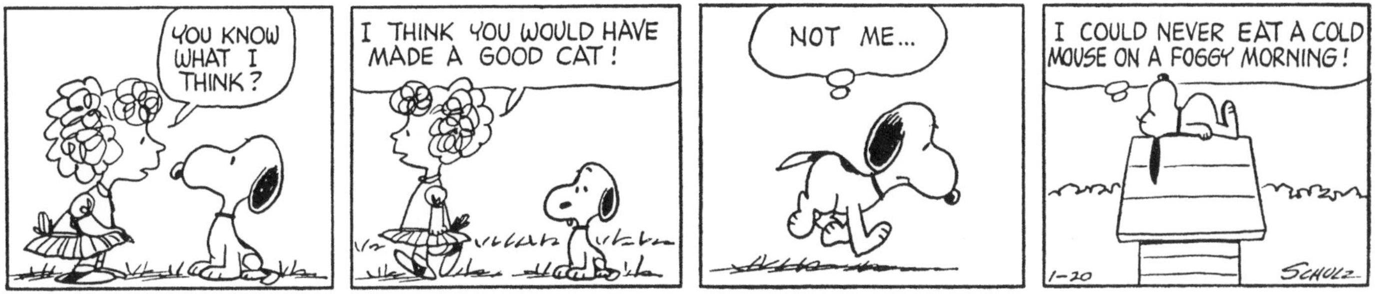
YOU KNOW WHAT I THINK?
I THINK YOU WOULD HAVE MADE A GOOD CAT!
NOT ME...
I COULD NEVER EAT A COLD MOUSE ON A FOGGY MORNING!

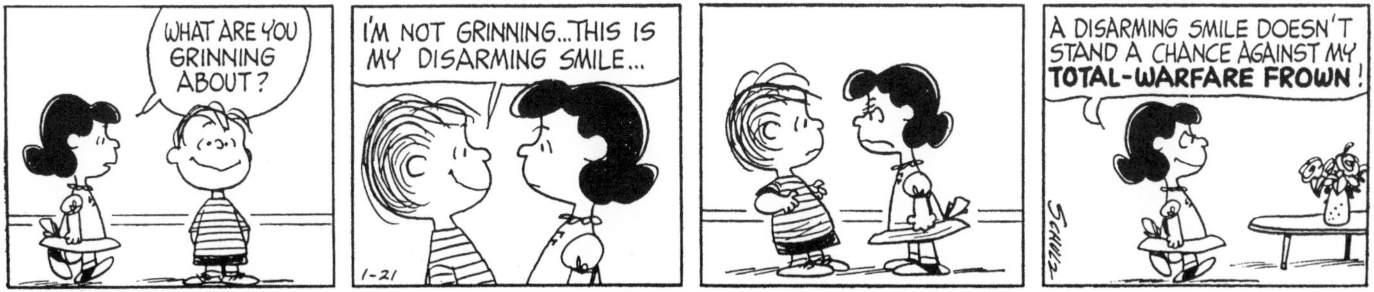
WHAT ARE YOU GRINNING ABOUT?
I'M NOT GRINNING...THIS IS MY DISARMING SMILE...
A DISARMING SMILE DOESN'T STAND A CHANCE AGAINST MY **TOTAL-WARFARE FROWN**!

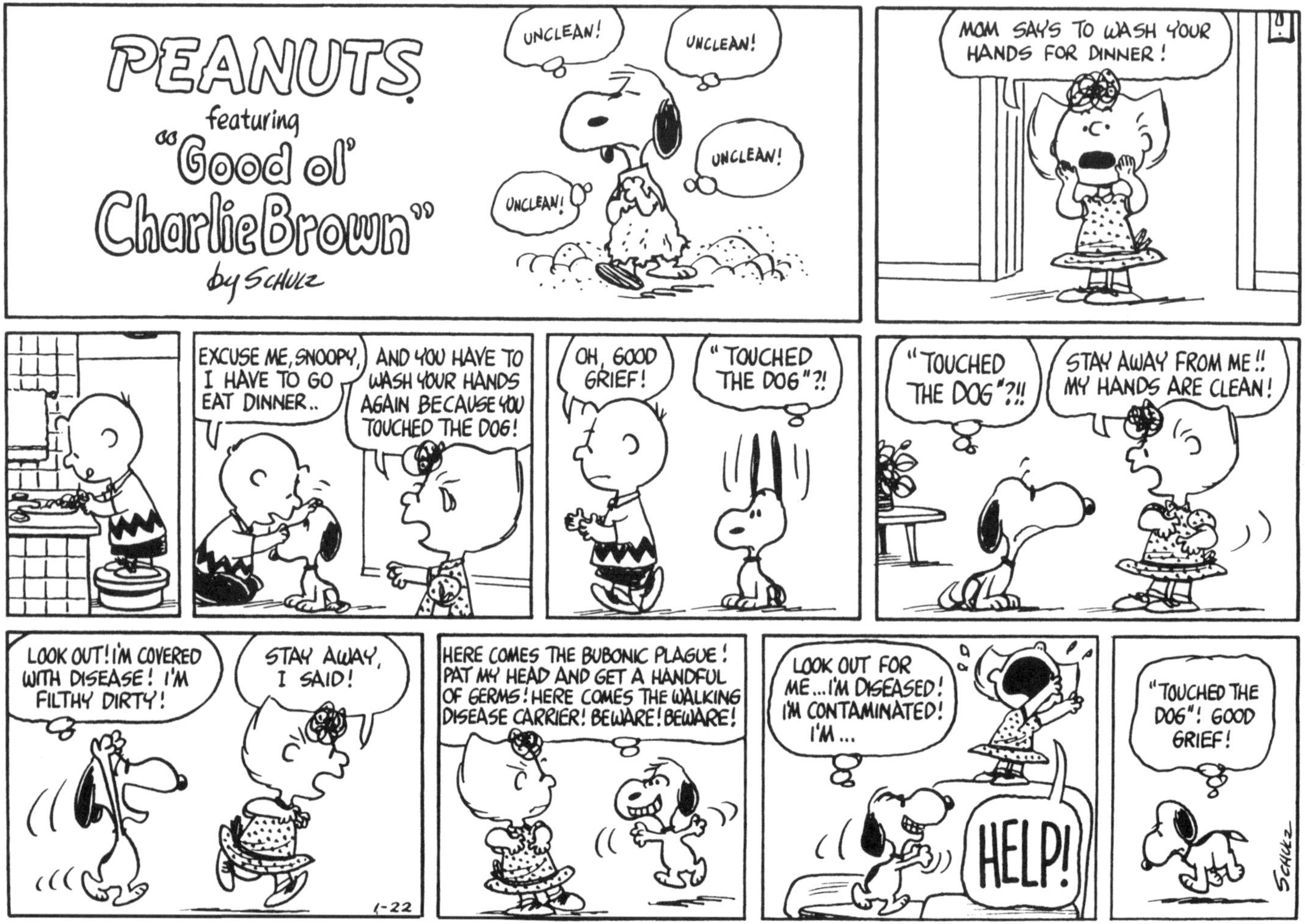
PEANUTS
featuring "Good ol' Charlie Brown"
by SCHULZ
UNCLEAN!
UNCLEAN!
UNCLEAN!
UNCLEAN!
MOM SAYS TO WASH YOUR HANDS FOR DINNER!
EXCUSE ME, SNOOPY, I HAVE TO GO EAT DINNER..
AND YOU HAVE TO WASH YOUR HANDS AGAIN BECAUSE YOU TOUCHED THE DOG!
OH, GOOD GRIEF!
"TOUCHED THE DOG"?!
"TOUCHED THE DOG"?!!
STAY AWAY FROM ME!! MY HANDS ARE CLEAN!
LOOK OUT! I'M COVERED WITH DISEASE! I'M FILTHY DIRTY!
STAY AWAY, I SAID!
1-22
HERE COMES THE BUBONIC PLAGUE! PAT MY HEAD AND GET A HANDFUL OF GERMS! HERE COMES THE WALKING DISEASE CARRIER! BEWARE! BEWARE!
LOOK OUT FOR ME...I'M DISEASED! I'M CONTAMINATED! I'M ...
HELP!
"TOUCHED THE DOG"! GOOD GRIEF!
SCHULZ

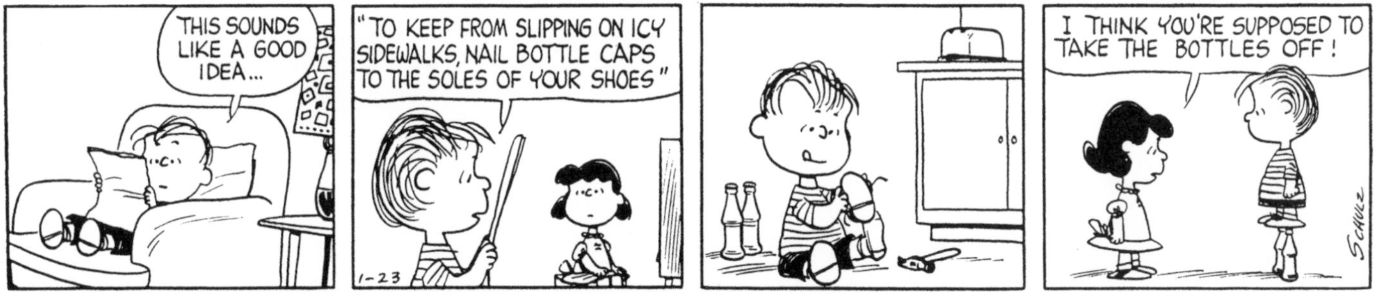
THIS SOUNDS LIKE A GOOD IDEA...
"TO KEEP FROM SLIPPING ON ICY SIDEWALKS, NAIL BOTTLE CAPS TO THE SOLES OF YOUR SHOES"
I THINK YOU'RE SUPPOSED TO TAKE THE BOTTLES OFF!

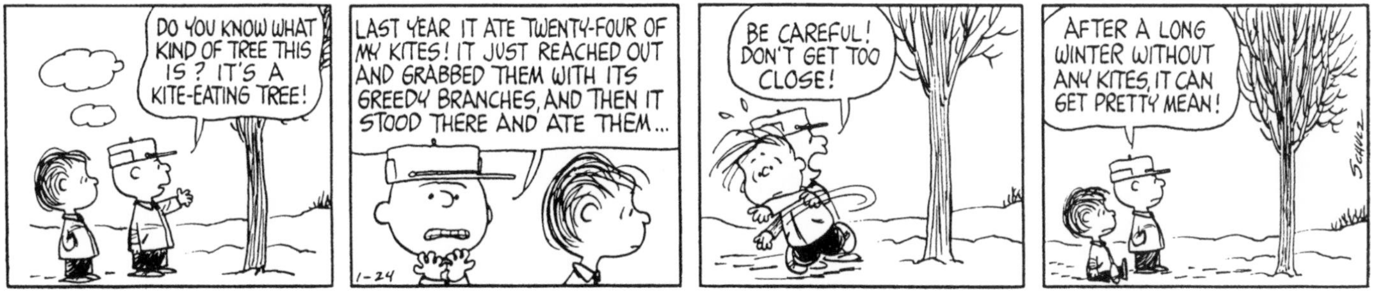
DO YOU KNOW WHAT KIND OF TREE THIS IS? IT'S A KITE-EATING TREE!
LAST YEAR IT ATE TWENTY-FOUR OF MY KITES! IT JUST REACHED OUT AND GRABBED THEM WITH ITS GREEDY BRANCHES, AND THEN IT STOOD THERE AND ATE THEM...
BE CAREFUL! DON'T GET TOO CLOSE!
AFTER A LONG WINTER WITHOUT ANY KITES, IT CAN GET PRETTY MEAN!

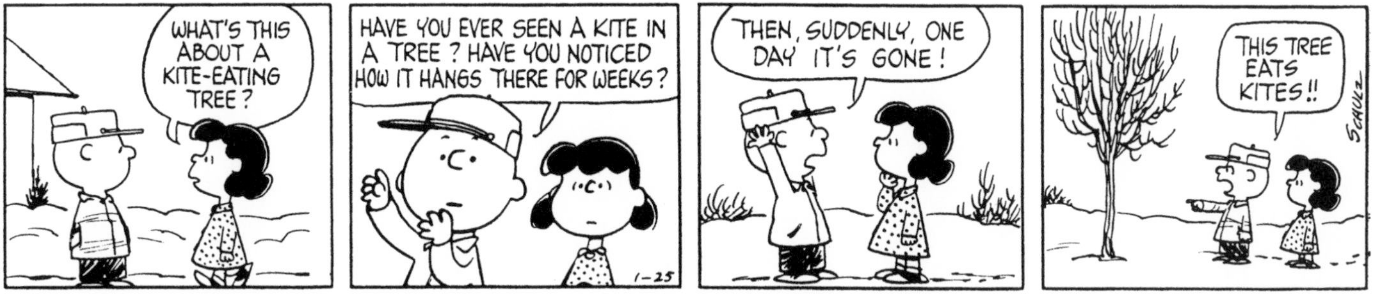
WHAT'S THIS ABOUT A KITE-EATING TREE?
HAVE YOU EVER SEEN A KITE IN A TREE? HAVE YOU NOTICED HOW IT HANGS THERE FOR WEEKS?
THEN, SUDDENLY, ONE DAY IT'S GONE!
THIS TREE EATS KITES!!

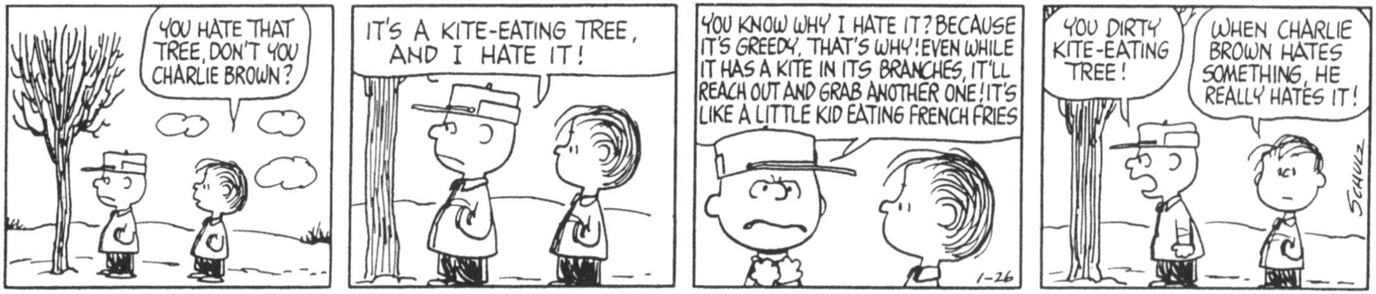
YOU HATE THAT TREE, DON'T YOU CHARLIE BROWN?
IT'S A KITE-EATING TREE, AND I HATE IT!
YOU KNOW WHY I HATE IT? BECAUSE IT'S GREEDY, THAT'S WHY! EVEN WHILE IT HAS A KITE IN ITS BRANCHES, IT'LL REACH OUT AND GRAB ANOTHER ONE! IT'S LIKE A LITTLE KID EATING FRENCH FRIES
1-26
YOU DIRTY KITE-EATING TREE!
WHEN CHARLIE BROWN HATES SOMETHING, HE REALLY HATES IT!
SCHULZ

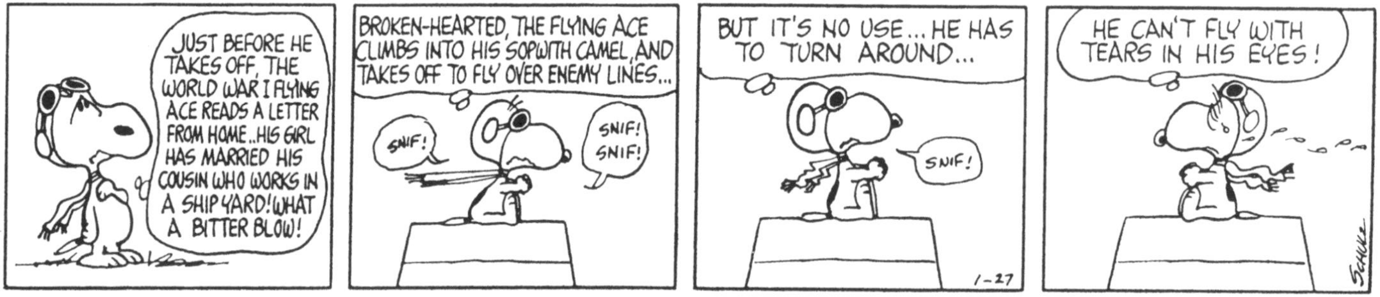
JUST BEFORE HE TAKES OFF, THE WORLD WAR I FLYING ACE READS A LETTER FROM HOME..HIS GIRL HAS MARRIED HIS COUSIN WHO WORKS IN A SHIP YARD! WHAT A BITTER BLOW!
BROKEN-HEARTED, THE FLYING ACE CLIMBS INTO HIS SOPWITH CAMEL, AND TAKES OFF TO FLY OVER ENEMY LINES...
SNIF!
SNIF! SNIF!
BUT IT'S NO USE... HE HAS TO TURN AROUND...
SNIF!
1-27
HE CAN'T FLY WITH TEARS IN HIS EYES!
SCHULZ

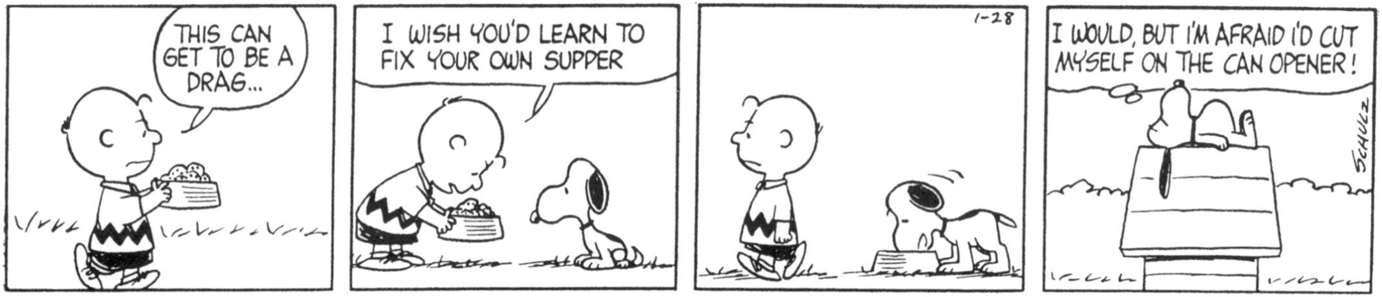
THIS CAN GET TO BE A DRAG...
I WISH YOU'D LEARN TO FIX YOUR OWN SUPPER
1-28
I WOULD, BUT I'M AFRAID I'D CUT MYSELF ON THE CAN OPENER!
SCHULZ

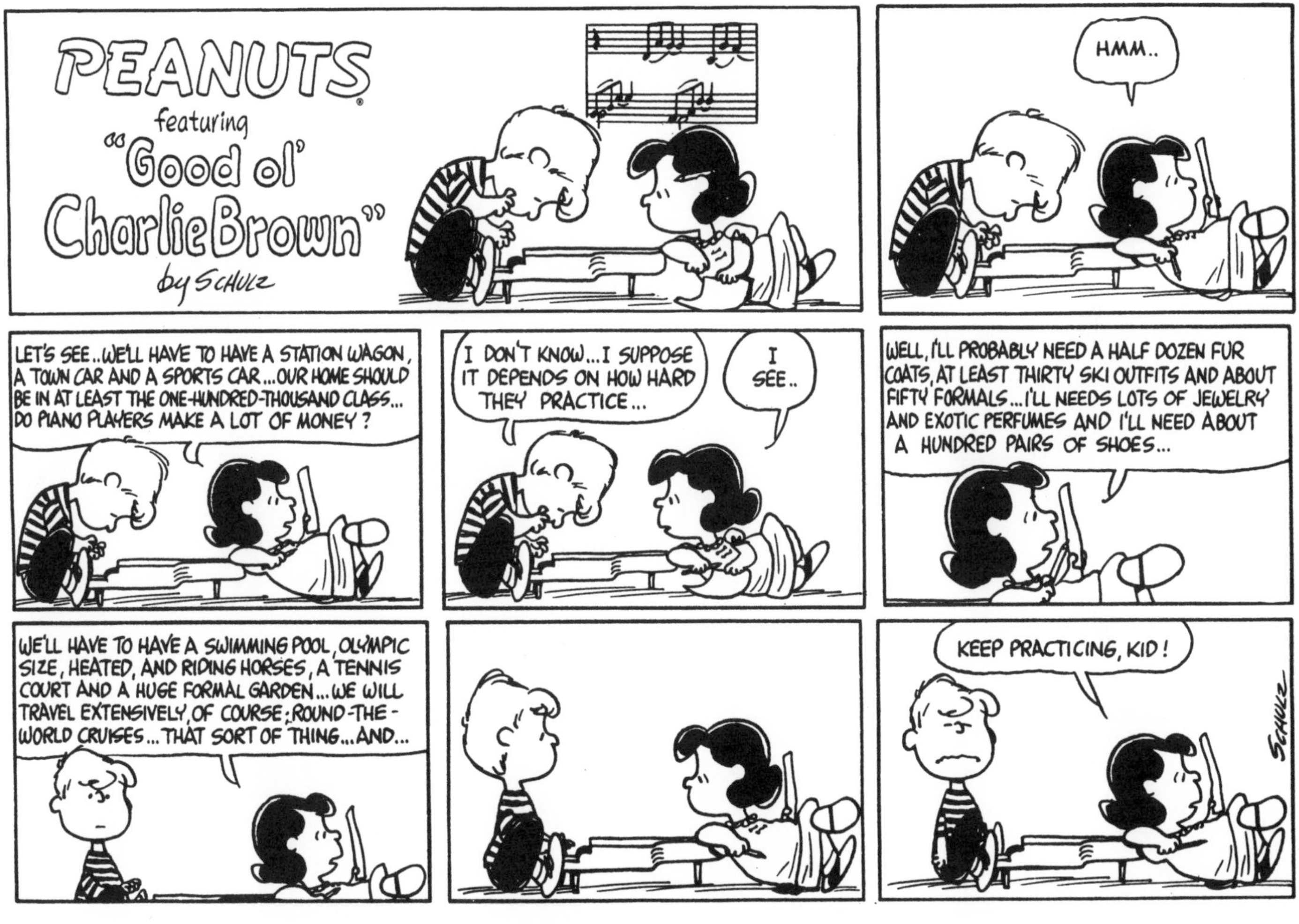
PEANUTS
featuring "Good ol' Charlie Brown"
by SCHULZ
HMM..
LET'S SEE..WE'LL HAVE TO HAVE A STATION WAGON, A TOWN CAR AND A SPORTS CAR...OUR HOME SHOULD BE IN AT LEAST THE ONE-HUNDRED-THOUSAND CLASS... DO PIANO PLAYERS MAKE A LOT OF MONEY?
I DON'T KNOW...I SUPPOSE IT DEPENDS ON HOW HARD THEY PRACTICE...
I SEE..
WELL, I'LL PROBABLY NEED A HALF DOZEN FUR COATS, AT LEAST THIRTY SKI OUTFITS AND ABOUT FIFTY FORMALS...I'LL NEEDS LOTS OF JEWELRY AND EXOTIC PERFUMES AND I'LL NEED ABOUT A HUNDRED PAIRS OF SHOES...
WE'LL HAVE TO HAVE A SWIMMING POOL, OLYMPIC SIZE, HEATED, AND RIDING HORSES, A TENNIS COURT AND A HUGE FORMAL GARDEN...WE WILL TRAVEL EXTENSIVELY, OF COURSE; ROUND-THE-WORLD CRUISES...THAT SORT OF THING...AND...
KEEP PRACTICING, KID!
SCHULZ

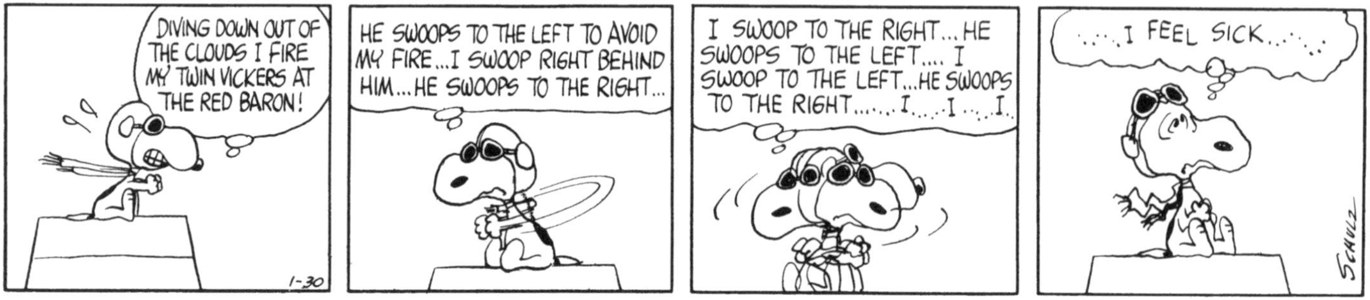
DIVING DOWN OUT OF THE CLOUDS I FIRE MY TWIN VICKERS AT THE RED BARON!
HE SWOOPS TO THE LEFT TO AVOID MY FIRE...I SWOOP RIGHT BEHIND HIM...HE SWOOPS TO THE RIGHT...
I SWOOP TO THE RIGHT...HE SWOOPS TO THE LEFT.... I SWOOP TO THE LEFT...HE SWOOPS TO THE RIGHT.......I.....I.....I..
......I FEEL SICK.........

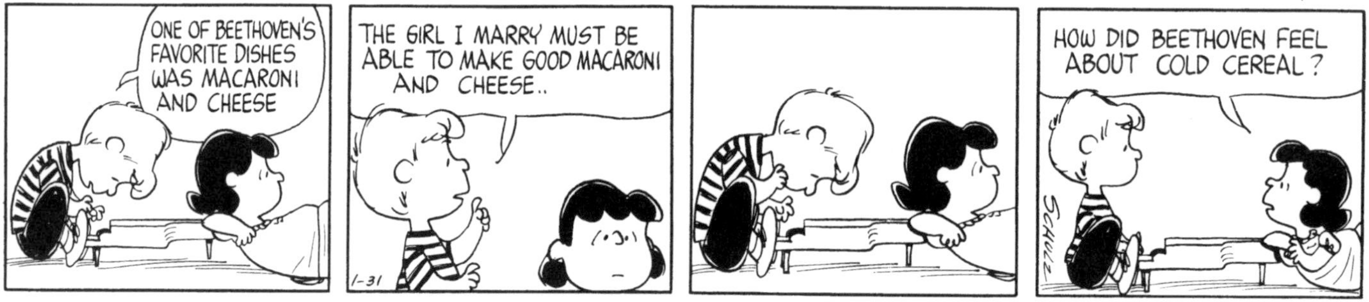
ONE OF BEETHOVEN'S FAVORITE DISHES WAS MACARONI AND CHEESE
THE GIRL I MARRY MUST BE ABLE TO MAKE GOOD MACARONI AND CHEESE..
HOW DID BEETHOVEN FEEL ABOUT COLD CEREAL?

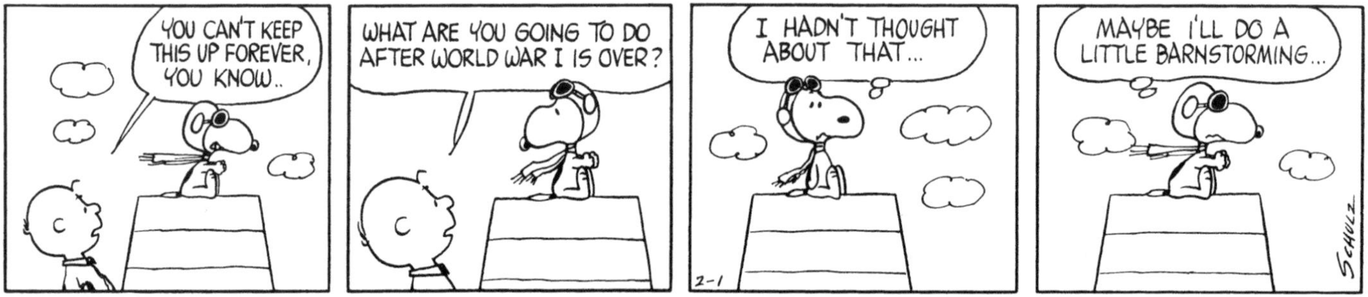
YOU CAN'T KEEP THIS UP FOREVER, YOU KNOW..
WHAT ARE YOU GOING TO DO AFTER WORLD WAR I IS OVER?
I HADN'T THOUGHT ABOUT THAT...
MAYBE I'LL DO A LITTLE BARNSTORMING...

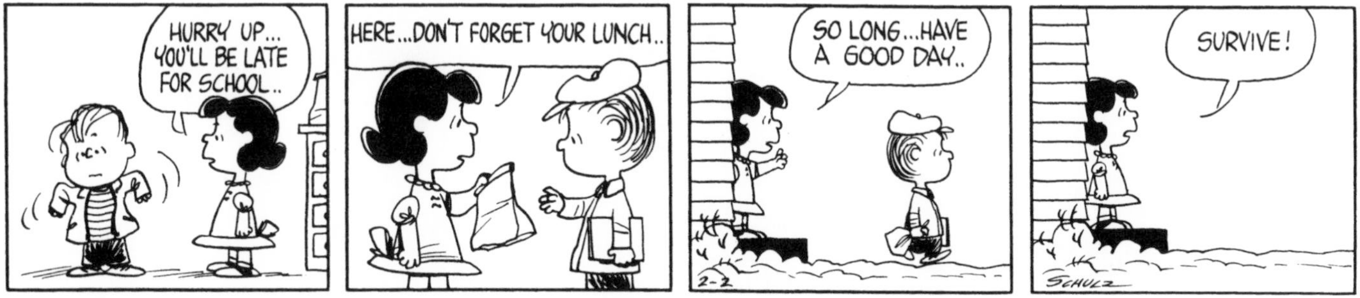
HURRY UP... YOU'LL BE LATE FOR SCHOOL..
HERE...DON'T FORGET YOUR LUNCH..
SO LONG...HAVE A GOOD DAY..
2-2
SURVIVE!
SCHULZ

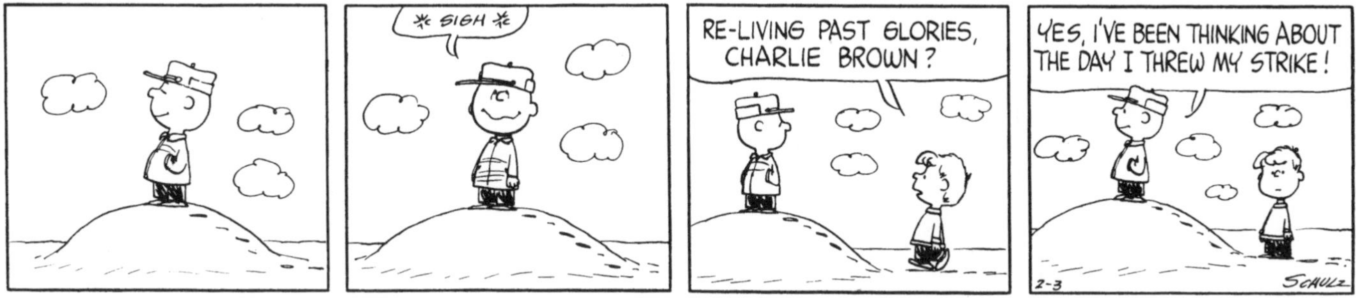
* SIGH *
RE-LIVING PAST GLORIES, CHARLIE BROWN?
YES, I'VE BEEN THINKING ABOUT THE DAY I THREW MY STRIKE!
2-3
SCHULZ

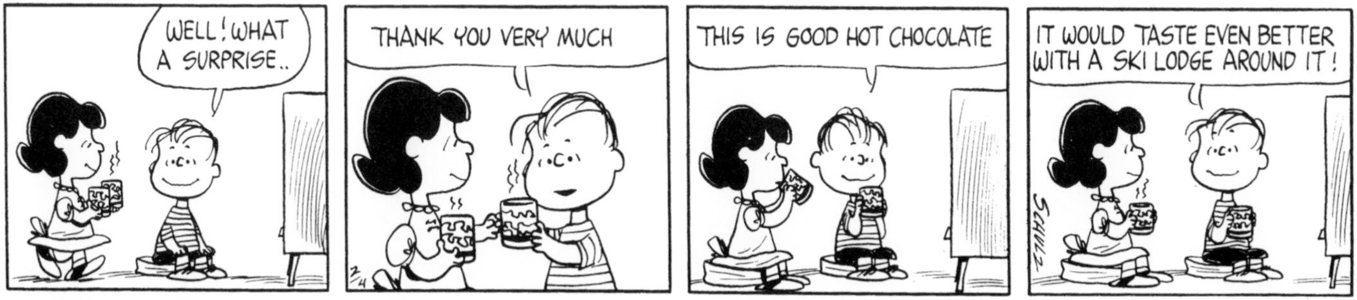
WELL! WHAT A SURPRISE..
THANK YOU VERY MUCH
2/4
THIS IS GOOD HOT CHOCOLATE
IT WOULD TASTE EVEN BETTER WITH A SKI LODGE AROUND IT!
SCHULZ

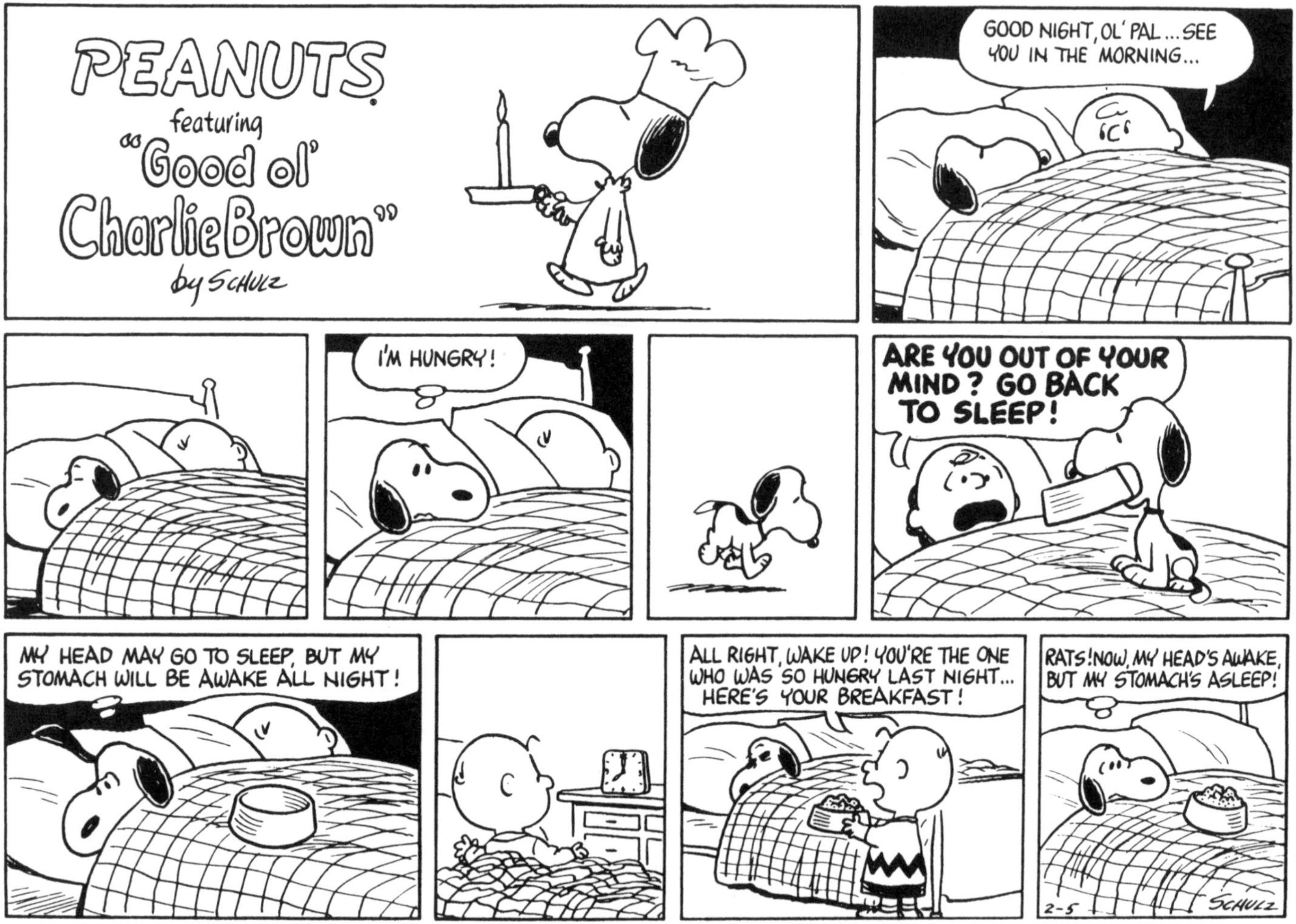
PEANUTS
featuring
"Good ol' CharlieBrown"
by SCHULZ
GOOD NIGHT, OL' PAL...SEE YOU IN THE MORNING...
I'M HUNGRY!
ARE YOU OUT OF YOUR MIND? GO BACK TO SLEEP!
MY HEAD MAY GO TO SLEEP, BUT MY STOMACH WILL BE AWAKE ALL NIGHT!
ALL RIGHT, WAKE UP! YOU'RE THE ONE WHO WAS SO HUNGRY LAST NIGHT... HERE'S YOUR BREAKFAST!
RATS! NOW, MY HEAD'S AWAKE, BUT MY STOMACH'S ASLEEP!
2-5
SCHULZ

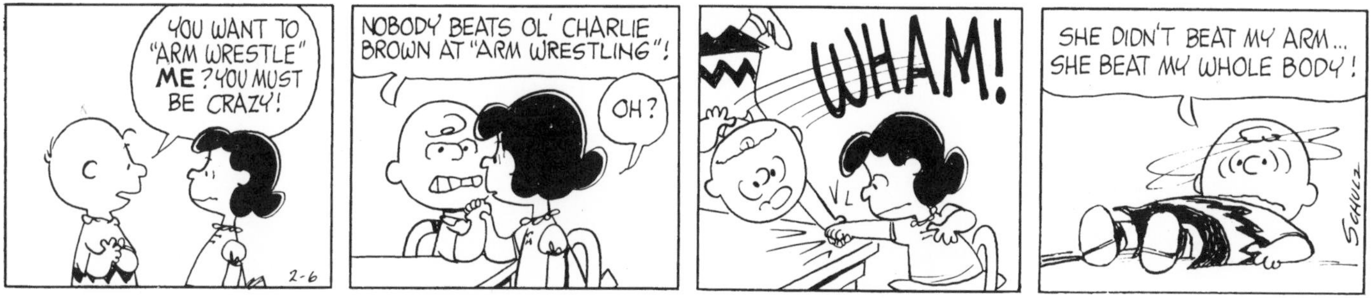
YOU WANT TO "ARM WRESTLE" **ME**? YOU MUST BE CRAZY!
2-6
NOBODY BEATS OL' CHARLIE BROWN AT "ARM WRESTLING"!
OH?
WHAM!
SHE DIDN'T BEAT MY ARM... SHE BEAT MY WHOLE BODY!
SCHULZ

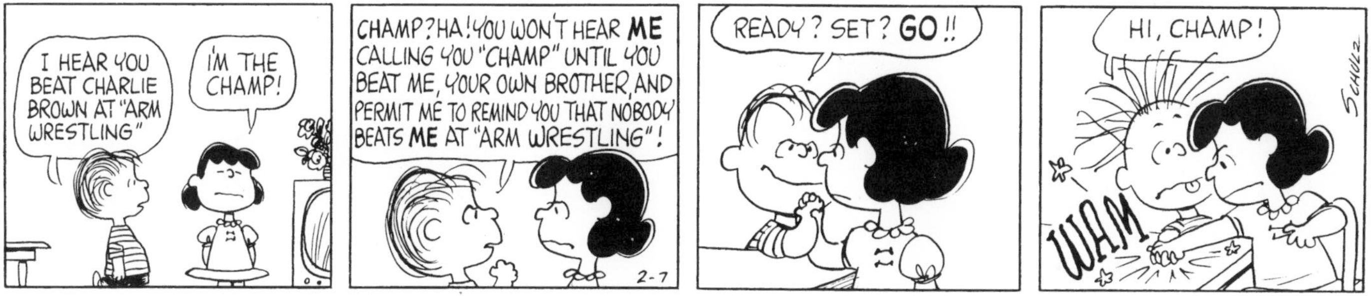
I HEAR YOU BEAT CHARLIE BROWN AT "ARM WRESTLING"
I'M THE CHAMP!
CHAMP? HA! YOU WON'T HEAR **ME** CALLING YOU "CHAMP" UNTIL YOU BEAT ME, YOUR OWN BROTHER, AND PERMIT ME TO REMIND YOU THAT NOBODY BEATS **ME** AT "ARM WRESTLING"!
2-7
READY? SET? **GO**!!
HI, CHAMP!
WAM
SCHULZ

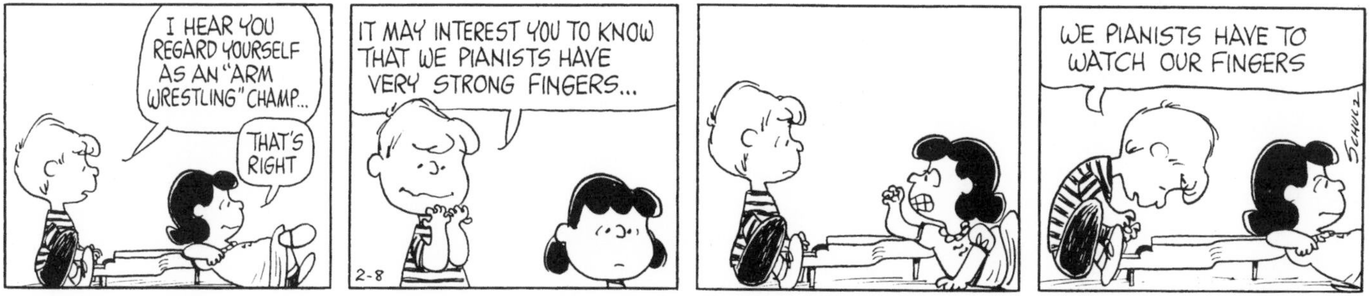
I HEAR YOU REGARD YOURSELF AS AN "ARM WRESTLING" CHAMP...
THAT'S RIGHT
IT MAY INTEREST YOU TO KNOW THAT WE PIANISTS HAVE VERY STRONG FINGERS...
2-8
WE PIANISTS HAVE TO WATCH OUR FINGERS
SCHULZ

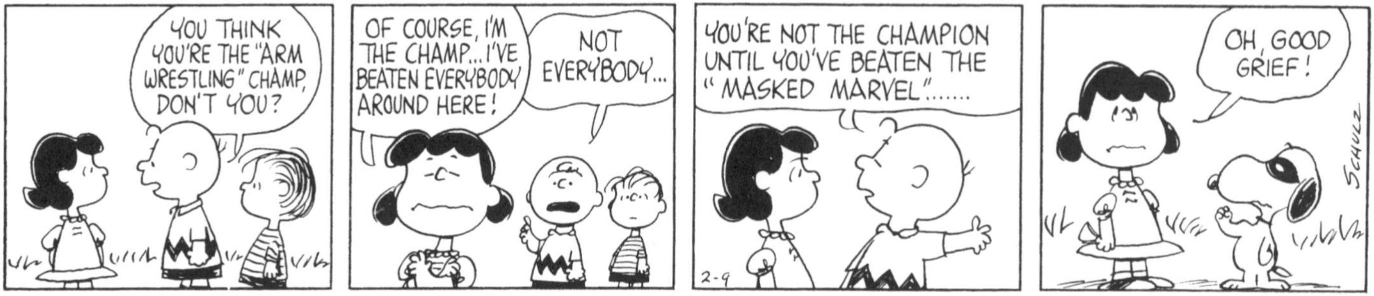
YOU THINK YOU'RE THE "ARM WRESTLING" CHAMP, DON'T YOU?
OF COURSE, I'M THE CHAMP... I'VE BEATEN EVERYBODY AROUND HERE!
NOT EVERYBODY...
YOU'RE NOT THE CHAMPION UNTIL YOU'VE BEATEN THE "MASKED MARVEL"......
2-9
OH, GOOD GRIEF!
SCHULZ

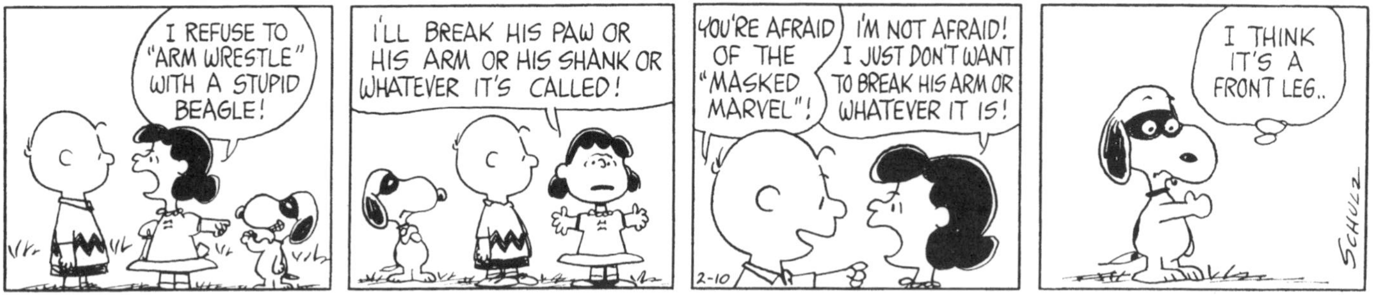
I REFUSE TO "ARM WRESTLE" WITH A STUPID BEAGLE!
I'LL BREAK HIS PAW OR HIS ARM OR HIS SHANK OR WHATEVER IT'S CALLED!
YOU'RE AFRAID OF THE "MASKED MARVEL"!
I'M NOT AFRAID! I JUST DON'T WANT TO BREAK HIS ARM OR WHATEVER IT IS!
2-10
I THINK IT'S A FRONT LEG..
SCHULZ

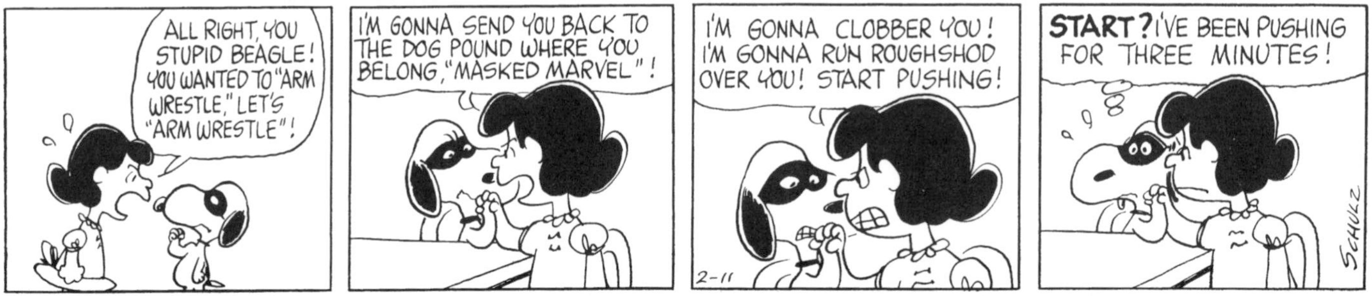
ALL RIGHT, YOU STUPID BEAGLE! YOU WANTED TO "ARM WRESTLE," LET'S "ARM WRESTLE"!
I'M GONNA SEND YOU BACK TO THE DOG POUND WHERE YOU BELONG, "MASKED MARVEL"!
I'M GONNA CLOBBER YOU! I'M GONNA RUN ROUGHSHOD OVER YOU! START PUSHING!
2-11
START? I'VE BEEN PUSHING FOR THREE MINUTES!
SCHULZ

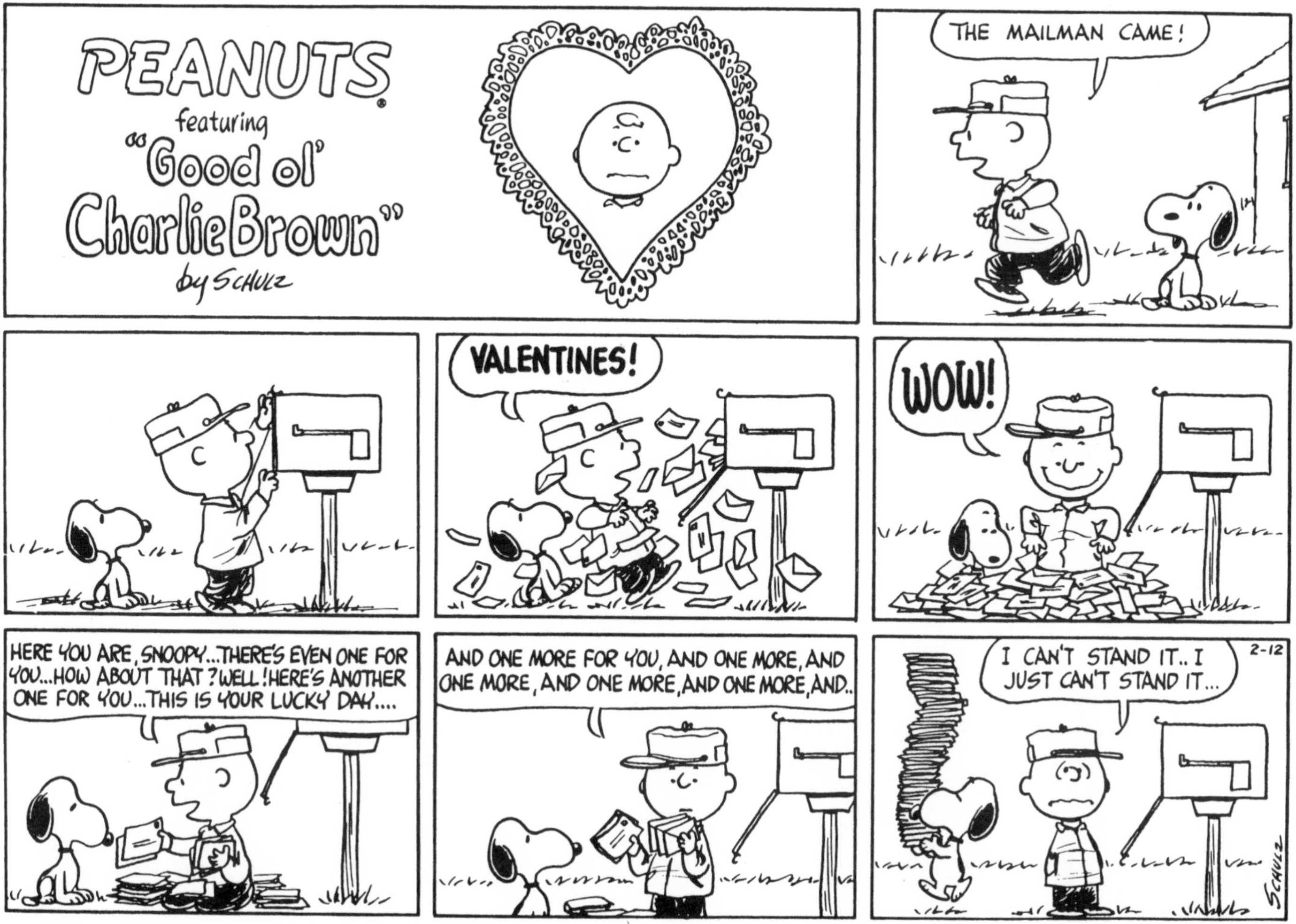
PEANUTS
featuring
"Good ol' Charlie Brown"
by SCHULZ
THE MAILMAN CAME!
VALENTINES!
WOW!
HERE YOU ARE, SNOOPY...THERE'S EVEN ONE FOR YOU...HOW ABOUT THAT? WELL! HERE'S ANOTHER ONE FOR YOU...THIS IS YOUR LUCKY DAY....
AND ONE MORE FOR YOU, AND ONE MORE, AND ONE MORE, AND ONE MORE, AND ONE MORE, AND..
I CAN'T STAND IT.. I JUST CAN'T STAND IT...
2-12
SCHULZ

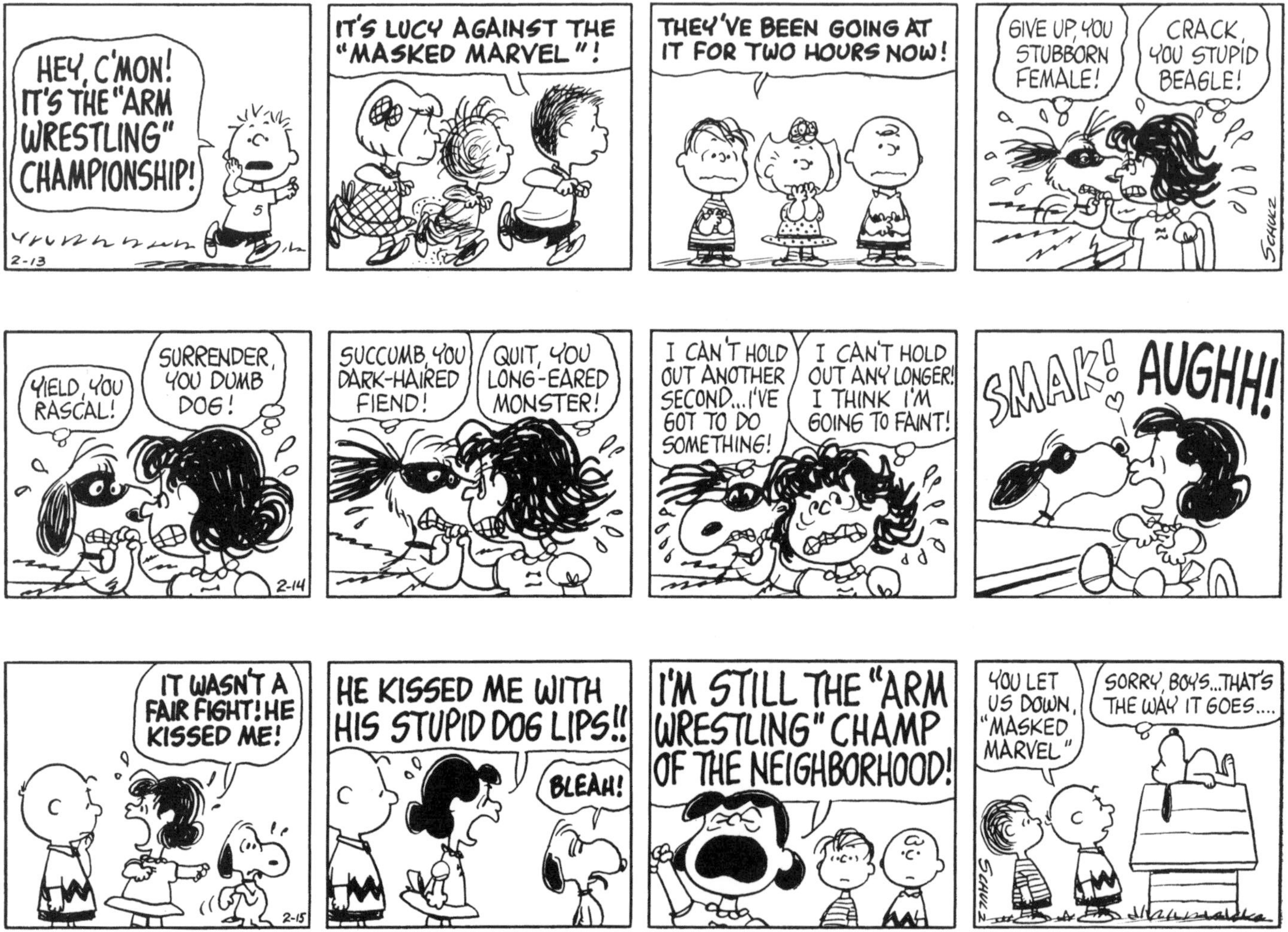
HEY, C'MON! IT'S THE "ARM WRESTLING" CHAMPIONSHIP!
2-13
IT'S LUCY AGAINST THE "MASKED MARVEL"!
THEY'VE BEEN GOING AT IT FOR TWO HOURS NOW!
GIVE UP, YOU STUBBORN FEMALE!
CRACK, YOU STUPID BEAGLE!
SCHULZ
YIELD, YOU RASCAL!
SURRENDER, YOU DUMB DOG!
2-14
SUCCUMB, YOU DARK-HAIRED FIEND!
QUIT, YOU LONG-EARED MONSTER!
I CAN'T HOLD OUT ANOTHER SECOND...I'VE GOT TO DO SOMETHING!
I CAN'T HOLD OUT ANY LONGER! I THINK I'M GOING TO FAINT!
SMAK!
AUGHH!
IT WASN'T A FAIR FIGHT! HE KISSED ME!
2-15
HE KISSED ME WITH HIS STUPID DOG LIPS!!
BLEAH!
I'M STILL THE "ARM WRESTLING" CHAMP OF THE NEIGHBORHOOD!
YOU LET US DOWN, "MASKED MARVEL"
SORRY, BOYS...THAT'S THE WAY IT GOES....
SCHULZ

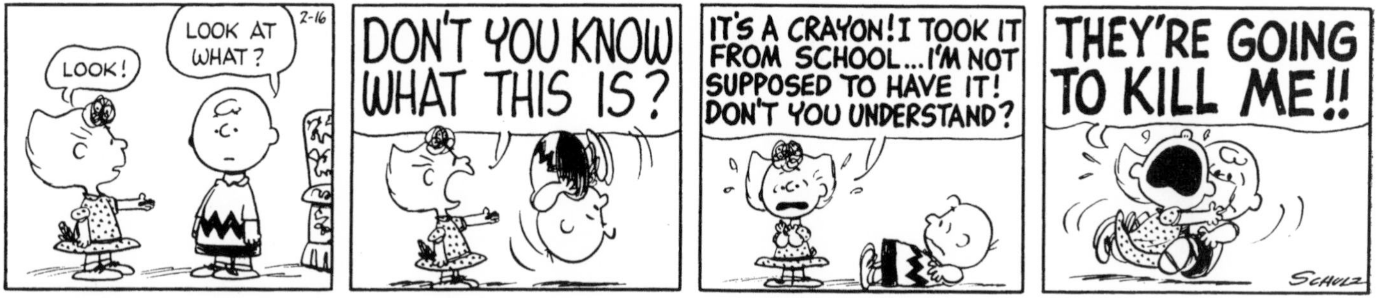
2-16
LOOK!
LOOK AT WHAT?
DON'T YOU KNOW WHAT THIS IS?
IT'S A CRAYON! I TOOK IT FROM SCHOOL...I'M NOT SUPPOSED TO HAVE IT! DON'T YOU UNDERSTAND?
THEY'RE GOING TO KILL ME!!
SCHULZ

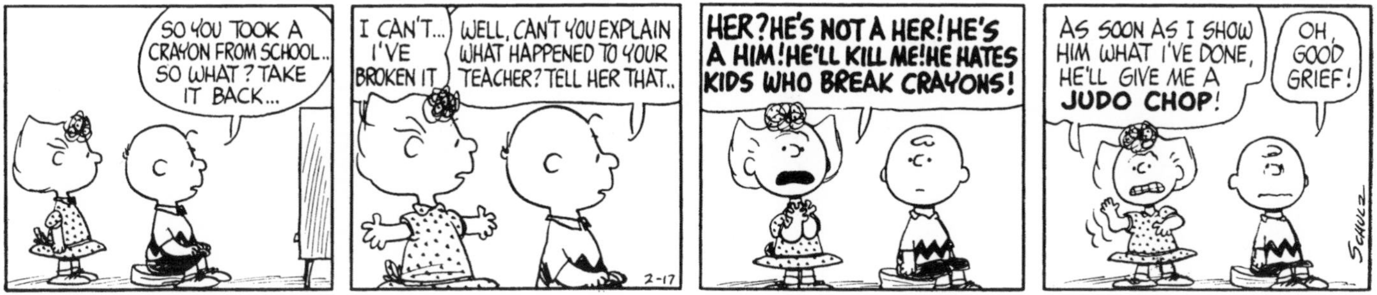
SO YOU TOOK A CRAYON FROM SCHOOL.. SO WHAT? TAKE IT BACK...
I CAN'T... I'VE BROKEN IT
WELL, CAN'T YOU EXPLAIN WHAT HAPPENED TO YOUR TEACHER? TELL HER THAT..
2-17
HER? HE'S NOT A HER! HE'S A HIM! HE'LL KILL ME! HE HATES KIDS WHO BREAK CRAYONS!
AS SOON AS I SHOW HIM WHAT I'VE DONE, HE'LL GIVE ME A JUDO CHOP!
OH, GOOD GRIEF!
SCHULZ

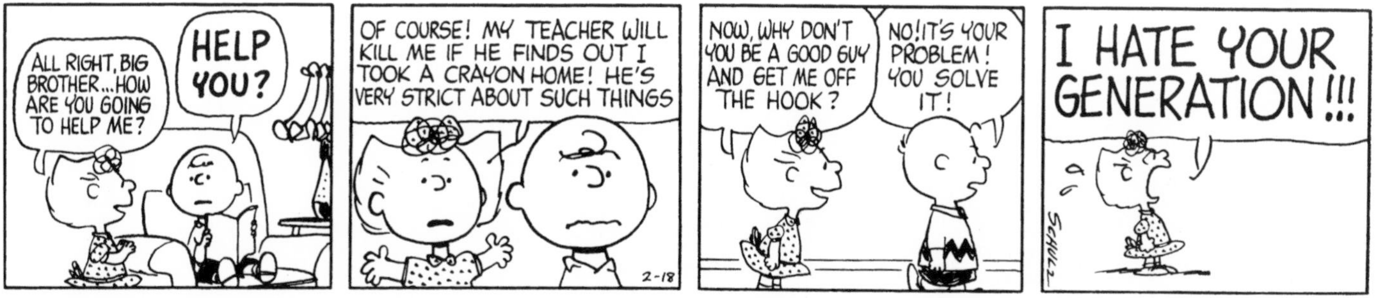
ALL RIGHT, BIG BROTHER...HOW ARE YOU GOING TO HELP ME?
HELP YOU?
OF COURSE! MY TEACHER WILL KILL ME IF HE FINDS OUT I TOOK A CRAYON HOME! HE'S VERY STRICT ABOUT SUCH THINGS
2-18
NOW, WHY DON'T YOU BE A GOOD GUY AND GET ME OFF THE HOOK?
NO! IT'S YOUR PROBLEM! YOU SOLVE IT!
SCHULZ
I HATE YOUR GENERATION!!!

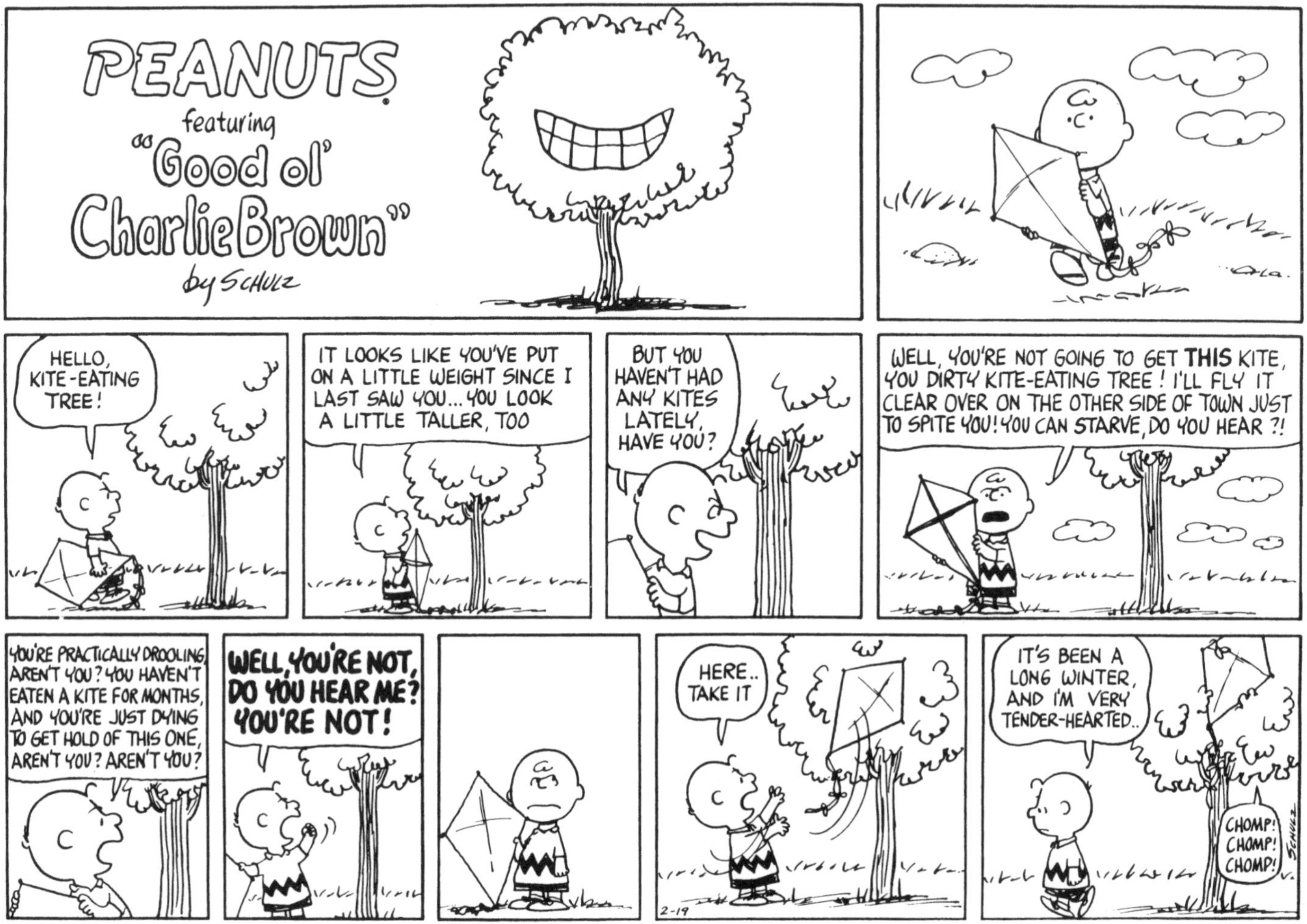
PEANUTS
featuring "Good ol' Charlie Brown"
by SCHULZ
HELLO, KITE-EATING TREE!
IT LOOKS LIKE YOU'VE PUT ON A LITTLE WEIGHT SINCE I LAST SAW YOU... YOU LOOK A LITTLE TALLER, TOO
BUT YOU HAVEN'T HAD ANY KITES LATELY, HAVE YOU?
WELL, YOU'RE NOT GOING TO GET THIS KITE, YOU DIRTY KITE-EATING TREE! I'LL FLY IT CLEAR OVER ON THE OTHER SIDE OF TOWN JUST TO SPITE YOU! YOU CAN STARVE, DO YOU HEAR ?!
YOU'RE PRACTICALLY DROOLING, AREN'T YOU? YOU HAVEN'T EATEN A KITE FOR MONTHS, AND YOU'RE JUST DYING TO GET HOLD OF THIS ONE, AREN'T YOU? AREN'T YOU?
WELL, YOU'RE NOT, DO YOU HEAR ME? YOU'RE NOT!
HERE.. TAKE IT
2-19
IT'S BEEN A LONG WINTER, AND I'M VERY TENDER-HEARTED..
CHOMP! CHOMP! CHOMP!
SCHULZ

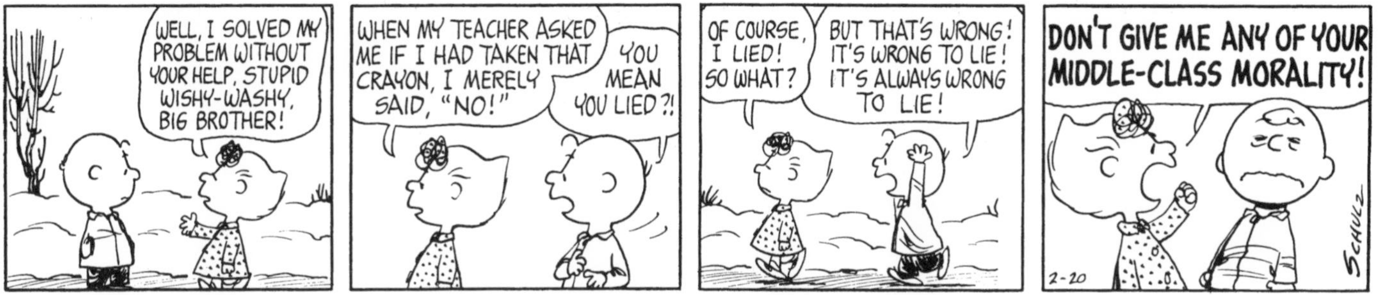
WELL, I SOLVED MY PROBLEM WITHOUT YOUR HELP, STUPID WISHY-WASHY, BIG BROTHER!
WHEN MY TEACHER ASKED ME IF I HAD TAKEN THAT CRAYON, I MERELY SAID, "NO!"
YOU MEAN YOU LIED?!
OF COURSE, I LIED! SO WHAT?
BUT THAT'S WRONG! IT'S WRONG TO LIE! IT'S ALWAYS WRONG TO LIE!
DON'T GIVE ME ANY OF YOUR MIDDLE-CLASS MORALITY!
SCHULZ
2-20

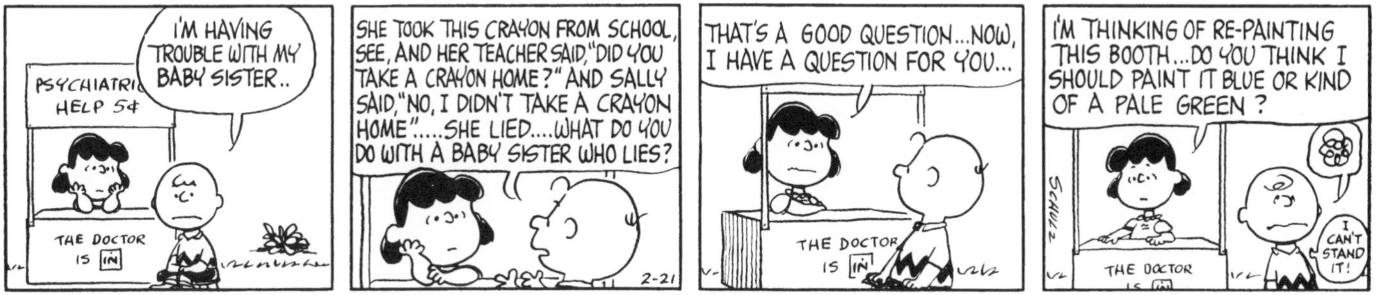
I'M HAVING TROUBLE WITH MY BABY SISTER..
PSYCHIATRIC HELP 5¢
THE DOCTOR IS IN
SHE TOOK THIS CRAYON FROM SCHOOL, SEE, AND HER TEACHER SAID,"DID YOU TAKE A CRAYON HOME?" AND SALLY SAID,"NO, I DIDN'T TAKE A CRAYON HOME".....SHE LIED....WHAT DO YOU DO WITH A BABY SISTER WHO LIES?
2-21
THAT'S A GOOD QUESTION...NOW, I HAVE A QUESTION FOR YOU...
THE DOCTOR IS IN
I'M THINKING OF RE-PAINTING THIS BOOTH...DO YOU THINK I SHOULD PAINT IT BLUE OR KIND OF A PALE GREEN?
SCHULZ
I CAN'T STAND IT!
THE DOCTOR

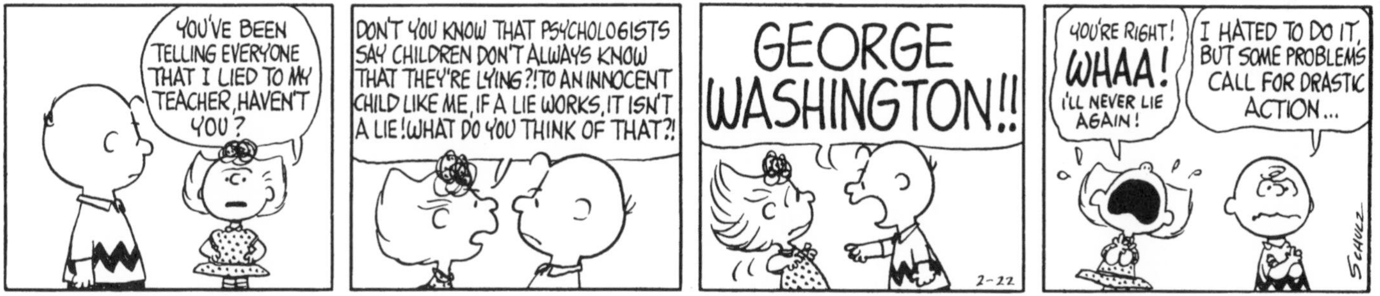
YOU'VE BEEN TELLING EVERYONE THAT I LIED TO MY TEACHER, HAVEN'T YOU?
DON'T YOU KNOW THAT PSYCHOLOGISTS SAY CHILDREN DON'T ALWAYS KNOW THAT THEY'RE LYING?! TO AN INNOCENT CHILD LIKE ME, IF A LIE WORKS, IT ISN'T A LIE! WHAT DO YOU THINK OF THAT?!
GEORGE WASHINGTON!!
2-22
YOU'RE RIGHT! WHAA! I'LL NEVER LIE AGAIN!
I HATED TO DO IT, BUT SOME PROBLEMS CALL FOR DRASTIC ACTION...
SCHULZ

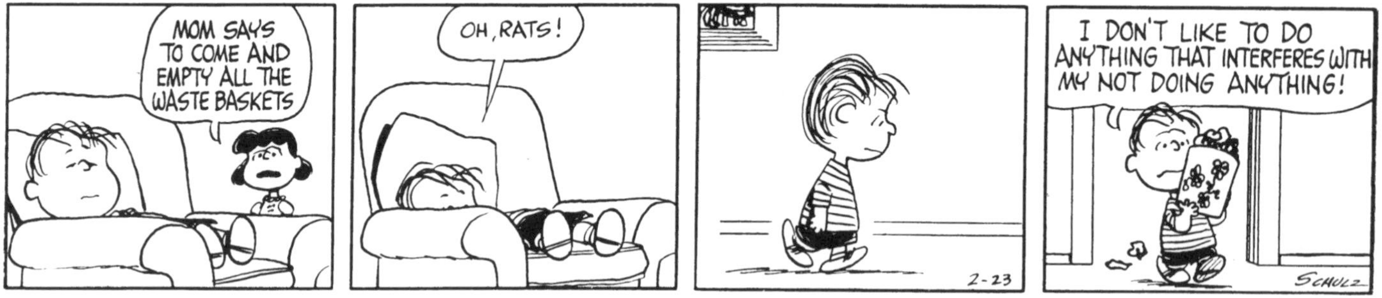
MOM SAYS TO COME AND EMPTY ALL THE WASTE BASKETS
OH, RATS!
2-23
I DON'T LIKE TO DO ANYTHING THAT INTERFERES WITH MY NOT DOING ANYTHING!
SCHULZ

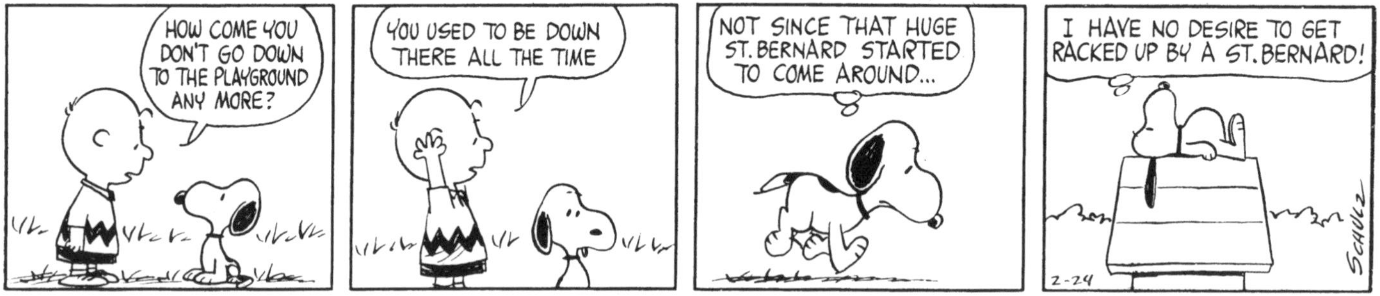
HOW COME YOU DON'T GO DOWN TO THE PLAYGROUND ANY MORE?
YOU USED TO BE DOWN THERE ALL THE TIME
NOT SINCE THAT HUGE ST. BERNARD STARTED TO COME AROUND...
I HAVE NO DESIRE TO GET RACKED UP BY A ST. BERNARD!
2-24
SCHULZ

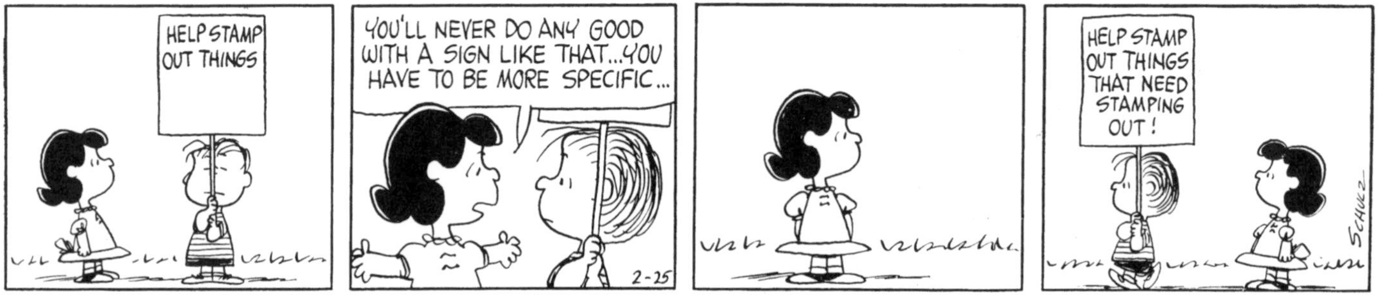
HELP STAMP OUT THINGS
YOU'LL NEVER DO ANY GOOD WITH A SIGN LIKE THAT...YOU HAVE TO BE MORE SPECIFIC...
2-25
HELP STAMP OUT THINGS THAT NEED STAMPING OUT!
SCHULZ

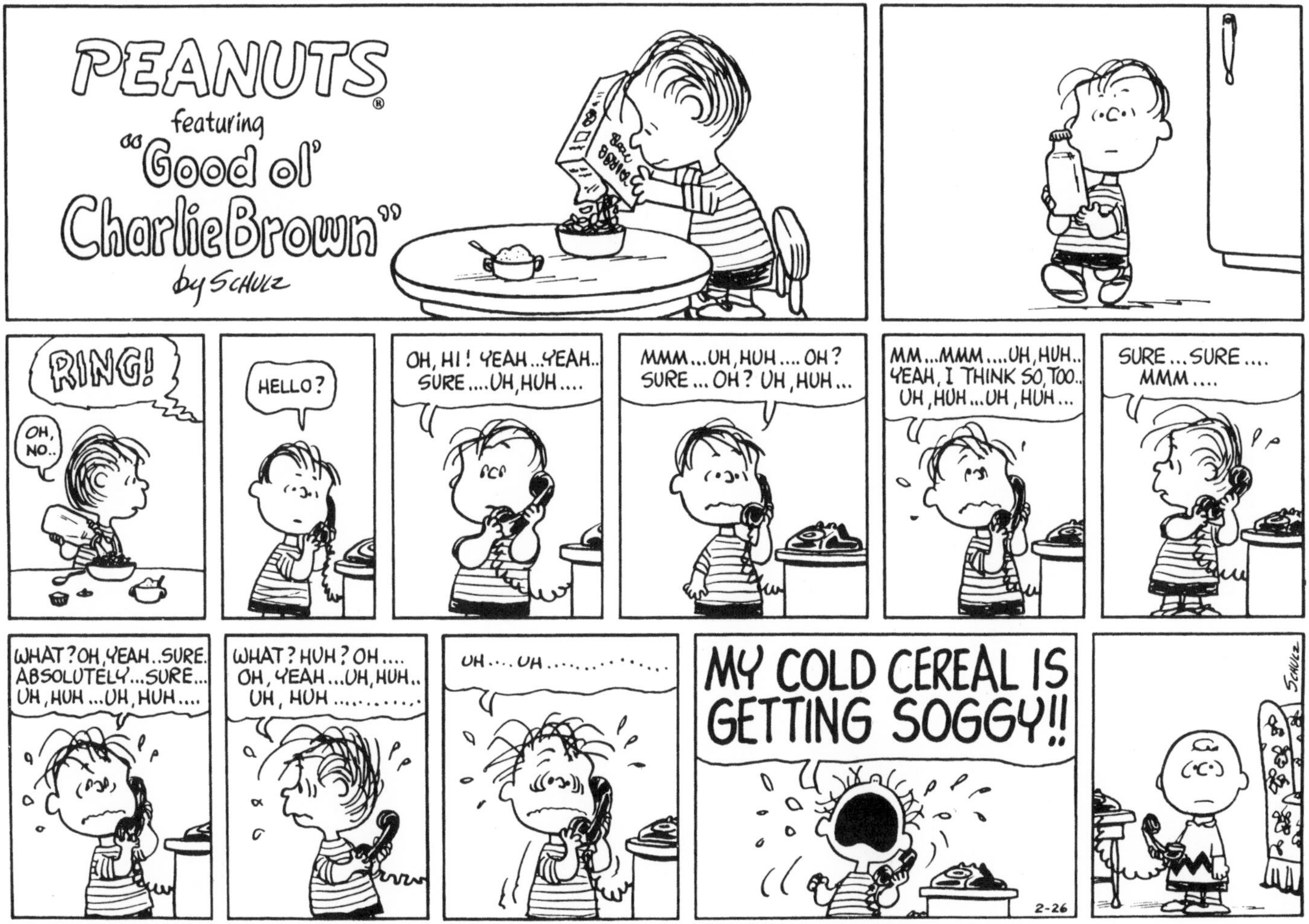
PEANUTS®
featuring
"Good ol' Charlie Brown"
by SCHULZ
RING!
OH, NO..
HELLO?
OH, HI! YEAH...YEAH.. SURE....UH, HUH....
MMM...UH, HUH.... OH? SURE...OH? UH, HUH...
MM...MMM....UH, HUH.. YEAH, I THINK SO, TOO.. UH, HUH...UH, HUH...
SURE...SURE.... MMM....
WHAT? OH, YEAH..SURE. ABSOLUTELY...SURE... UH, HUH...UH, HUH....
WHAT? HUH? OH.... OH, YEAH...UH, HUH.. UH, HUH..........
UH....UH..............
MY COLD CEREAL IS GETTING SOGGY!!
2-26
SCHULZ

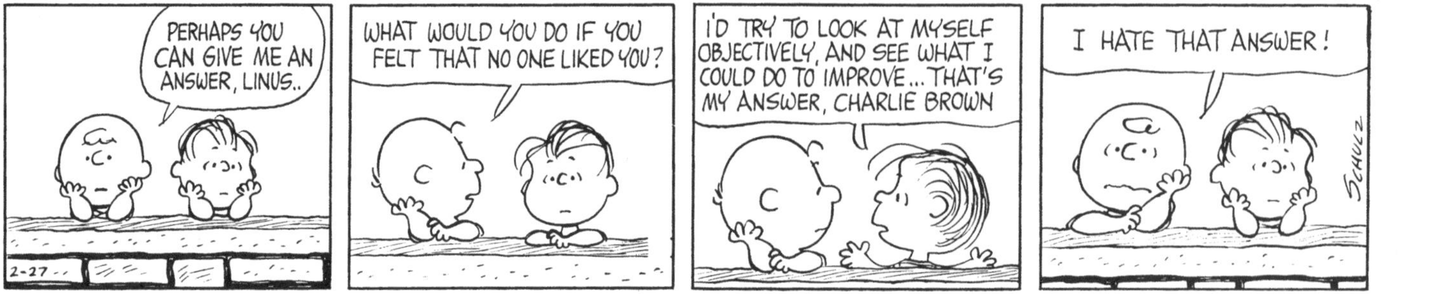
PERHAPS YOU CAN GIVE ME AN ANSWER, LINUS..
2-27
WHAT WOULD YOU DO IF YOU FELT THAT NO ONE LIKED YOU?
I'D TRY TO LOOK AT MYSELF OBJECTIVELY, AND SEE WHAT I COULD DO TO IMPROVE... THAT'S MY ANSWER, CHARLIE BROWN
I HATE THAT ANSWER!
SCHULZ

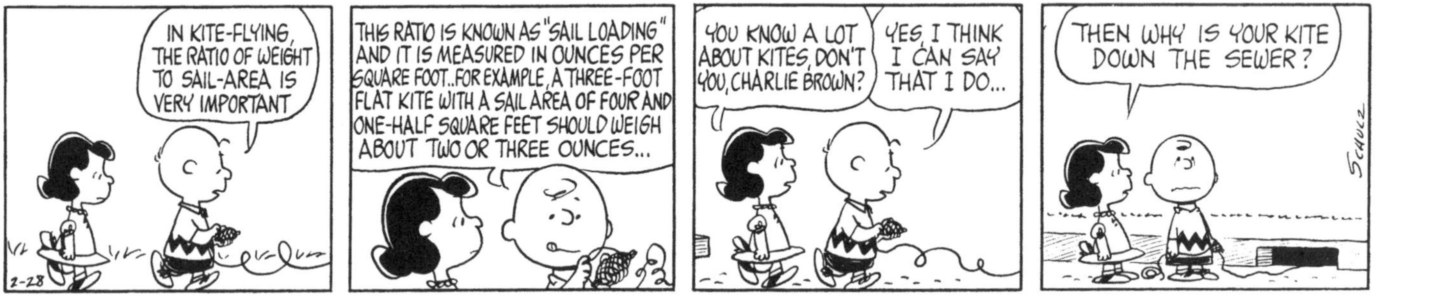
IN KITE-FLYING, THE RATIO OF WEIGHT TO SAIL-AREA IS VERY IMPORTANT
2-28
THIS RATIO IS KNOWN AS "SAIL LOADING" AND IT IS MEASURED IN OUNCES PER SQUARE FOOT..FOR EXAMPLE, A THREE-FOOT FLAT KITE WITH A SAIL AREA OF FOUR AND ONE-HALF SQUARE FEET SHOULD WEIGH ABOUT TWO OR THREE OUNCES...
YOU KNOW A LOT ABOUT KITES, DON'T YOU, CHARLIE BROWN?
YES, I THINK I CAN SAY THAT I DO...
THEN WHY IS YOUR KITE DOWN THE SEWER?
SCHULZ

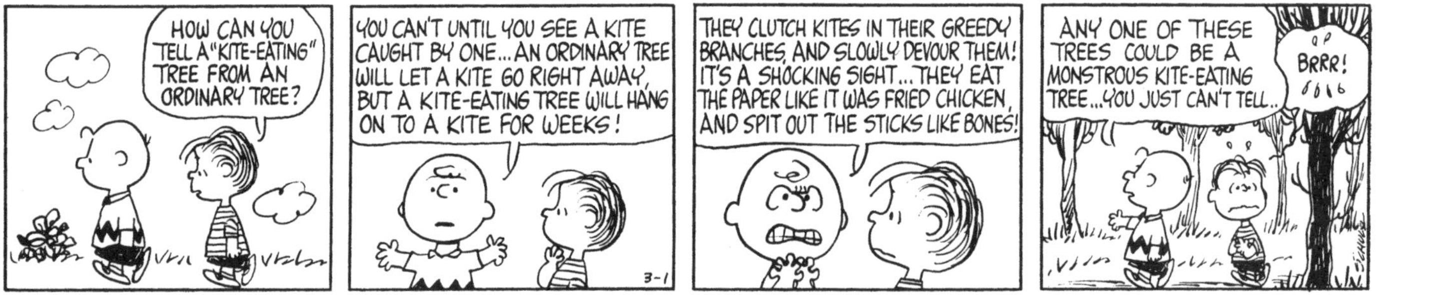
HOW CAN YOU TELL A "KITE-EATING" TREE FROM AN ORDINARY TREE?
YOU CAN'T UNTIL YOU SEE A KITE CAUGHT BY ONE... AN ORDINARY TREE WILL LET A KITE GO RIGHT AWAY, BUT A KITE-EATING TREE WILL HANG ON TO A KITE FOR WEEKS!
3-1
THEY CLUTCH KITES IN THEIR GREEDY BRANCHES, AND SLOWLY DEVOUR THEM! IT'S A SHOCKING SIGHT... THEY EAT THE PAPER LIKE IT WAS FRIED CHICKEN, AND SPIT OUT THE STICKS LIKE BONES!
ANY ONE OF THESE TREES COULD BE A MONSTROUS KITE-EATING TREE... YOU JUST CAN'T TELL..
BRRR!

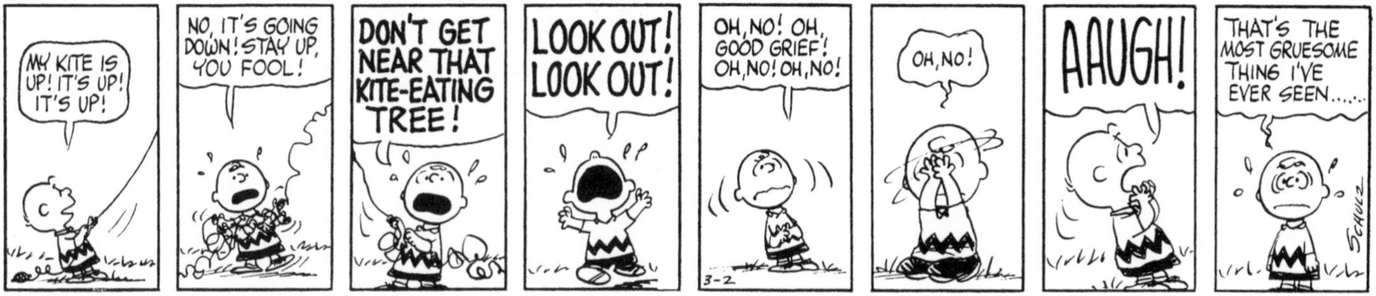
MY KITE IS UP! IT'S UP! IT'S UP!
NO, IT'S GOING DOWN! STAY UP, YOU FOOL!
DON'T GET NEAR THAT KITE-EATING TREE!
LOOK OUT! LOOK OUT!
OH, NO! OH, GOOD GRIEF! OH, NO! OH, NO!
3-2
OH, NO!
AAUGH!
THAT'S THE MOST GRUESOME THING I'VE EVER SEEN.......
SCHULZ

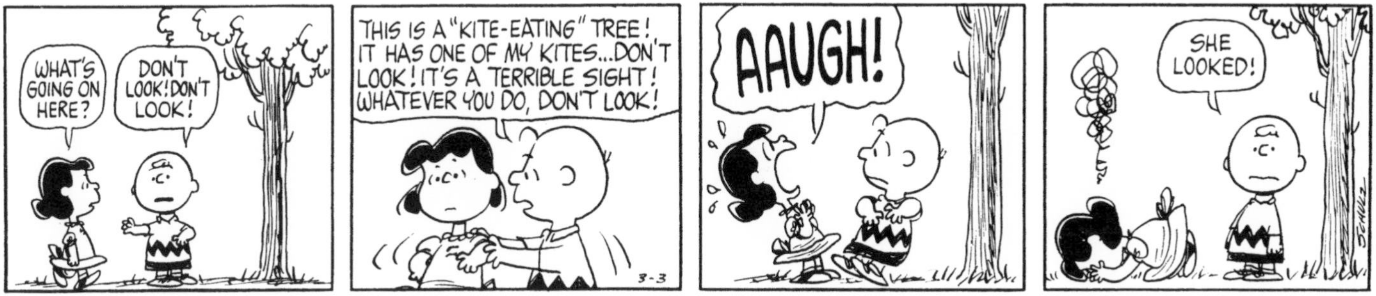
WHAT'S GOING ON HERE?
DON'T LOOK! DON'T LOOK!
THIS IS A "KITE-EATING" TREE! IT HAS ONE OF MY KITES...DON'T LOOK! IT'S A TERRIBLE SIGHT! WHATEVER YOU DO, DON'T LOOK!
3-3
AAUGH!
SHE LOOKED!
SCHULZ

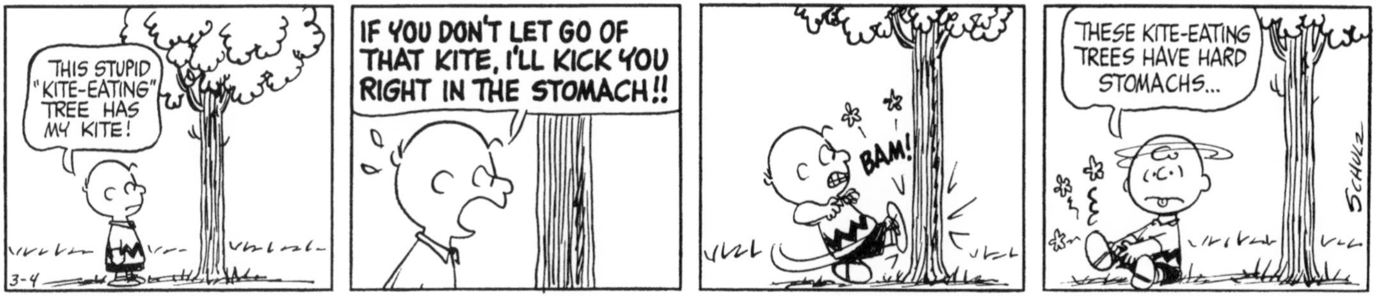
THIS STUPID "KITE-EATING" TREE HAS MY KITE!
3-4
IF YOU DON'T LET GO OF THAT KITE, I'LL KICK YOU RIGHT IN THE STOMACH!!
BAM!
THESE KITE-EATING TREES HAVE HARD STOMACHS...
SCHULZ

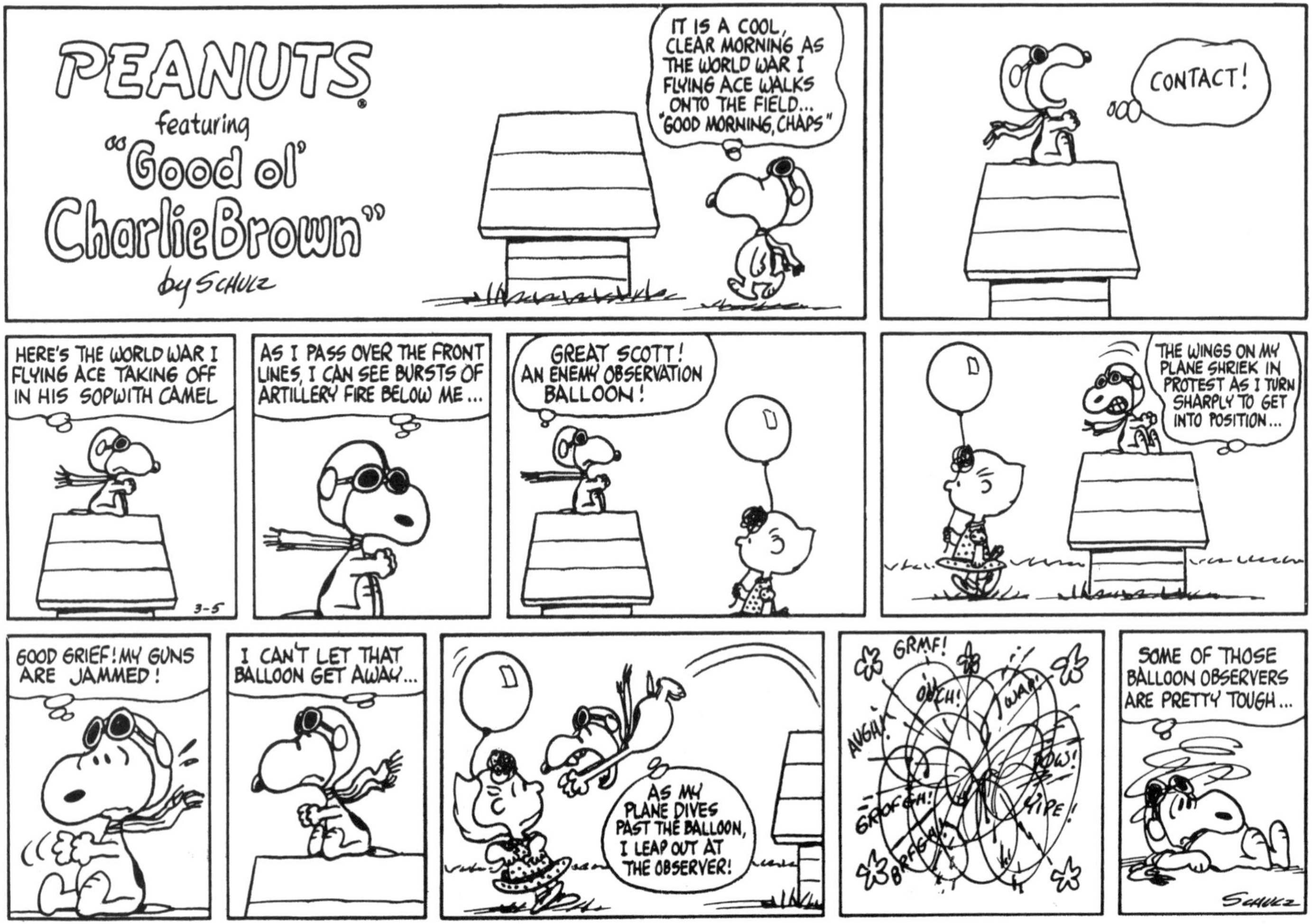
PEANUTS®
featuring "Good ol' CharlieBrown"
by SCHULZ
IT IS A COOL, CLEAR MORNING AS THE WORLD WAR I FLYING ACE WALKS ONTO THE FIELD... "GOOD MORNING, CHAPS"
CONTACT!
HERE'S THE WORLD WAR I FLYING ACE TAKING OFF IN HIS SOPWITH CAMEL
3-5
AS I PASS OVER THE FRONT LINES, I CAN SEE BURSTS OF ARTILLERY FIRE BELOW ME...
GREAT SCOTT! AN ENEMY OBSERVATION BALLOON!
THE WINGS ON MY PLANE SHRIEK IN PROTEST AS I TURN SHARPLY TO GET INTO POSITION...
GOOD GRIEF! MY GUNS ARE JAMMED!
I CAN'T LET THAT BALLOON GET AWAY...
AS MY PLANE DIVES PAST THE BALLOON, I LEAP OUT AT THE OBSERVER!
GRMF!
OUCH!
WAP!
AUGH!
POW!
GROFGH!
YIPE!
BRFGAH!
SOME OF THOSE BALLOON OBSERVERS ARE PRETTY TOUGH...
SCHULZ

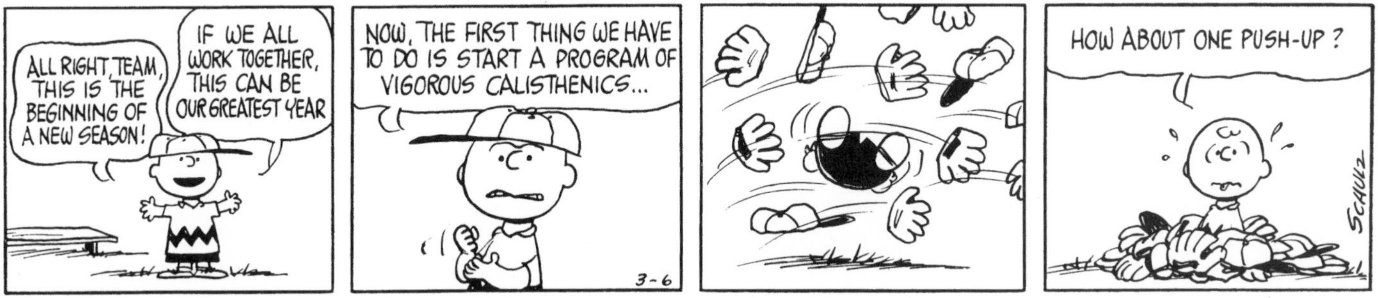
ALL RIGHT, TEAM, THIS IS THE BEGINNING OF A NEW SEASON!
IF WE ALL WORK TOGETHER, THIS CAN BE OUR GREATEST YEAR
NOW, THE FIRST THING WE HAVE TO DO IS START A PROGRAM OF VIGOROUS CALISTHENICS...
HOW ABOUT ONE PUSH-UP?

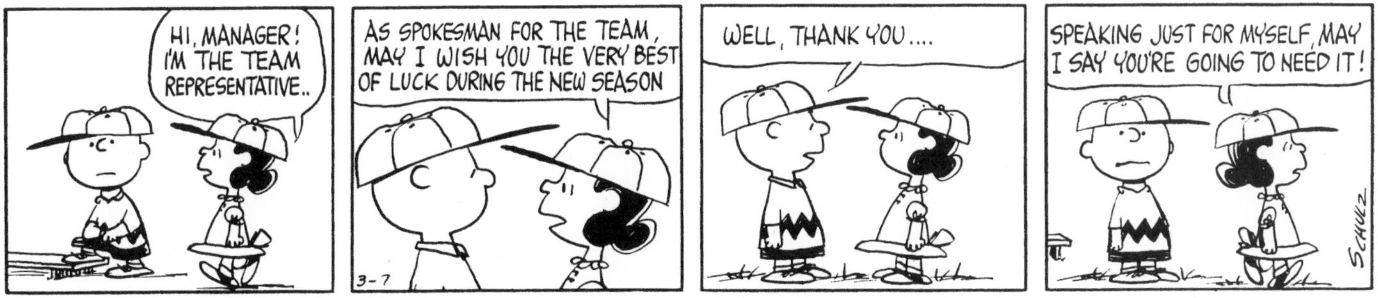
HI, MANAGER! I'M THE TEAM REPRESENTATIVE..
AS SPOKESMAN FOR THE TEAM, MAY I WISH YOU THE VERY BEST OF LUCK DURING THE NEW SEASON
WELL, THANK YOU....
SPEAKING JUST FOR MYSELF, MAY I SAY YOU'RE GOING TO NEED IT!

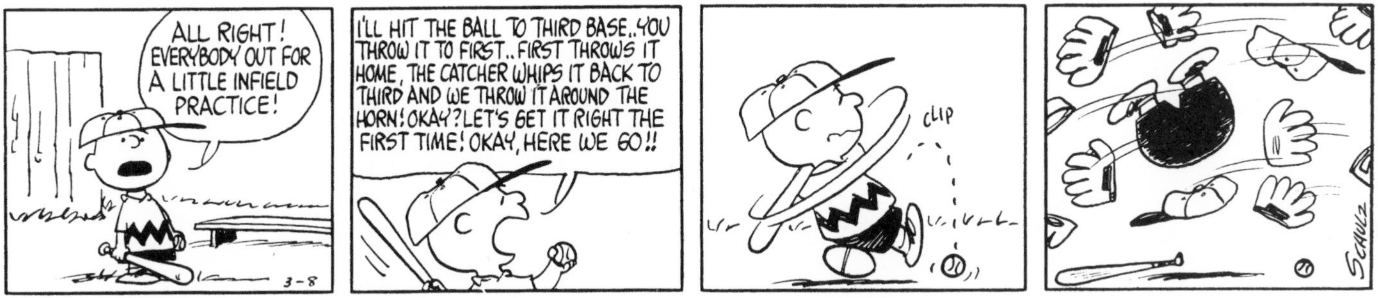
ALL RIGHT! EVERYBODY OUT FOR A LITTLE INFIELD PRACTICE!
I'LL HIT THE BALL TO THIRD BASE..YOU THROW IT TO FIRST..FIRST THROWS IT HOME, THE CATCHER WHIPS IT BACK TO THIRD AND WE THROW IT AROUND THE HORN! OKAY? LET'S GET IT RIGHT THE FIRST TIME! OKAY, HERE WE GO!!
CLIP

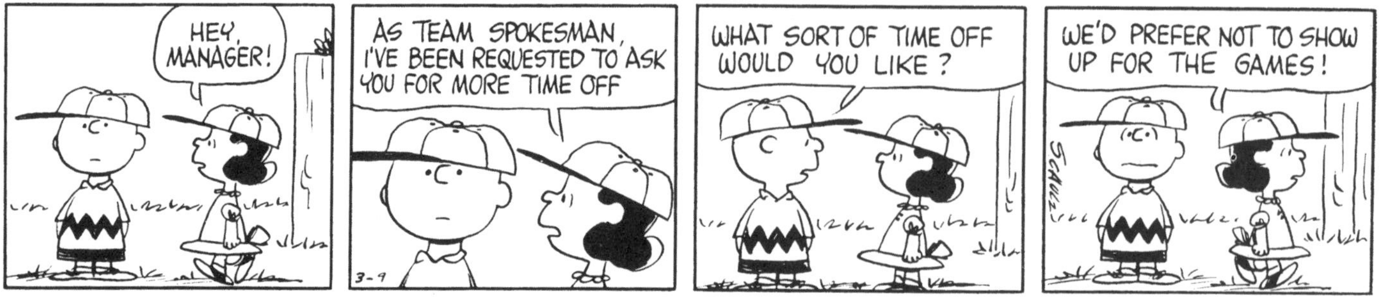
HEY, MANAGER!
AS TEAM SPOKESMAN, I'VE BEEN REQUESTED TO ASK YOU FOR MORE TIME OFF
3-9
WHAT SORT OF TIME OFF WOULD YOU LIKE ?
WE'D PREFER NOT TO SHOW UP FOR THE GAMES!
SCHULZ

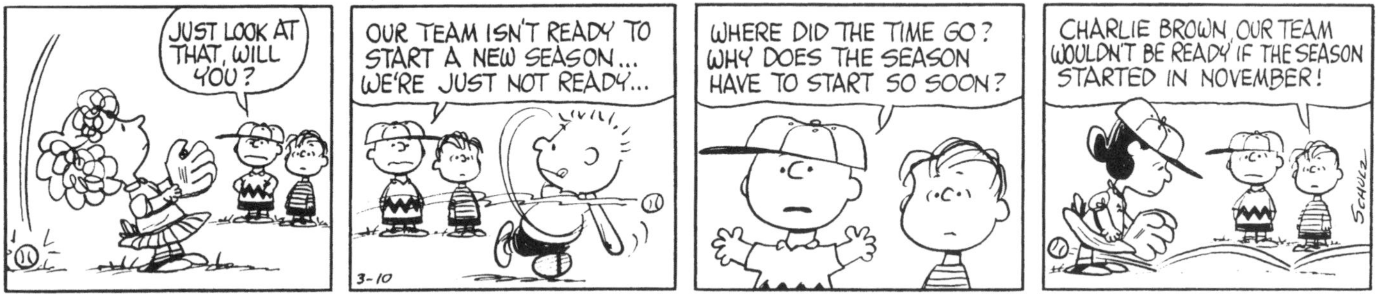
JUST LOOK AT THAT, WILL YOU?
OUR TEAM ISN'T READY TO START A NEW SEASON... WE'RE JUST NOT READY...
3-10
WHERE DID THE TIME GO? WHY DOES THE SEASON HAVE TO START SO SOON?
CHARLIE BROWN, OUR TEAM WOULDN'T BE READY IF THE SEASON STARTED IN NOVEMBER!
SCHULZ

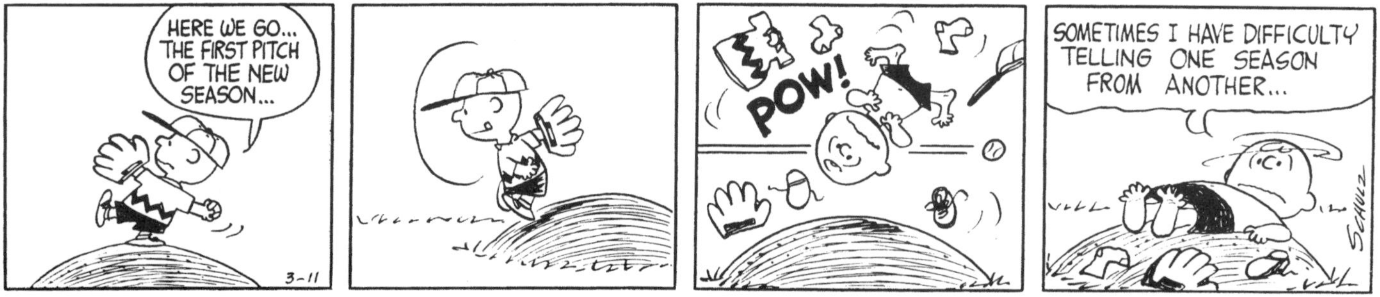
HERE WE GO... THE FIRST PITCH OF THE NEW SEASON...
3-11
POW!
SOMETIMES I HAVE DIFFICULTY TELLING ONE SEASON FROM ANOTHER...
SCHULZ

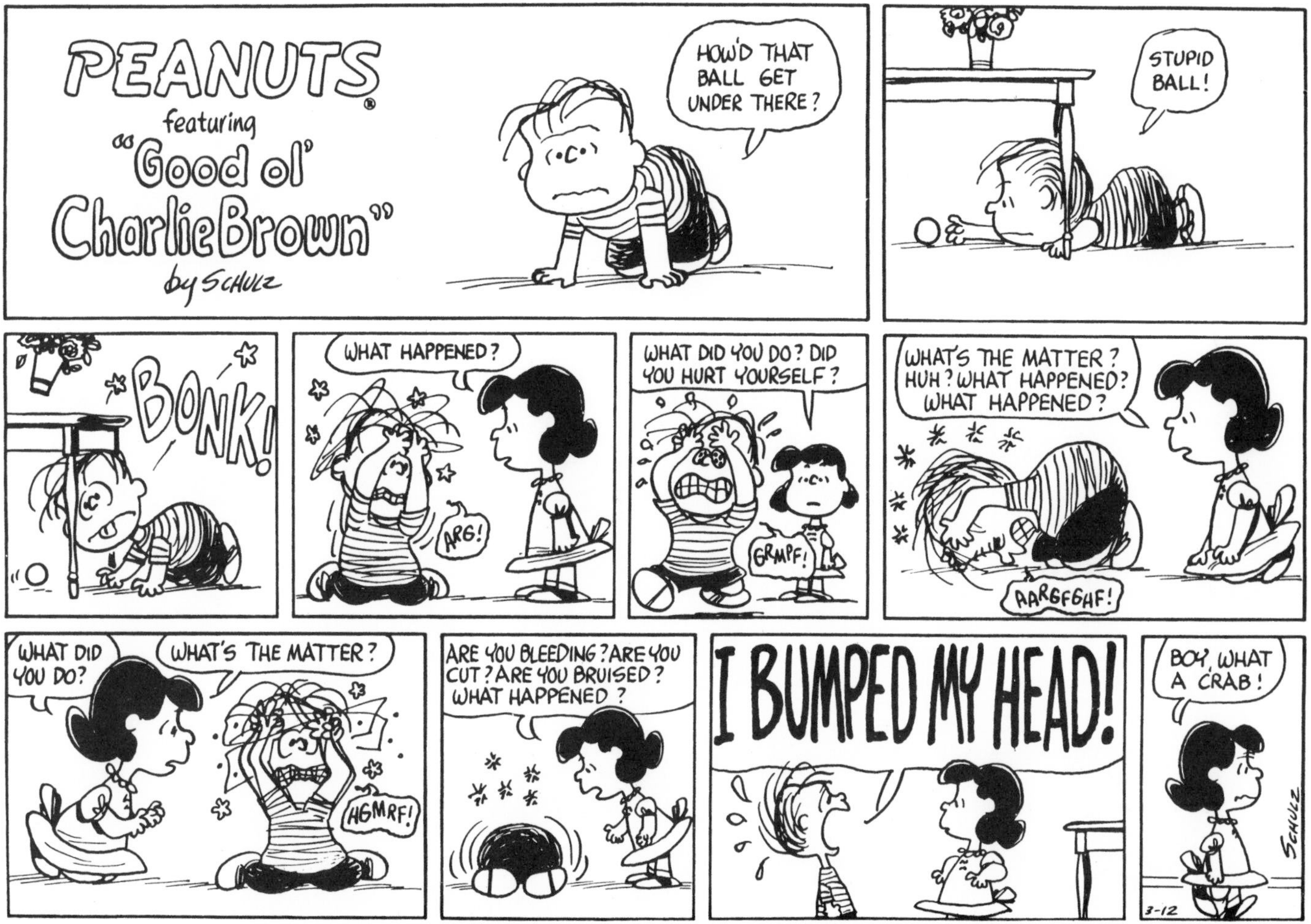
PEANUTS®
featuring
"Good ol' Charlie Brown"
by SCHULZ
HOW'D THAT BALL GET UNDER THERE?
STUPID BALL!
BONK!
WHAT HAPPENED?
ARG!
WHAT DID YOU DO? DID YOU HURT YOURSELF?
GRMPF!
WHAT'S THE MATTER? HUH? WHAT HAPPENED? WHAT HAPPENED?
AARGFGHF!
WHAT DID YOU DO?
WHAT'S THE MATTER?
HGMRF!
ARE YOU BLEEDING? ARE YOU CUT? ARE YOU BRUISED? WHAT HAPPENED?
I BUMPED MY HEAD!
BOY, WHAT A CRAB!
SCHULZ
3-12

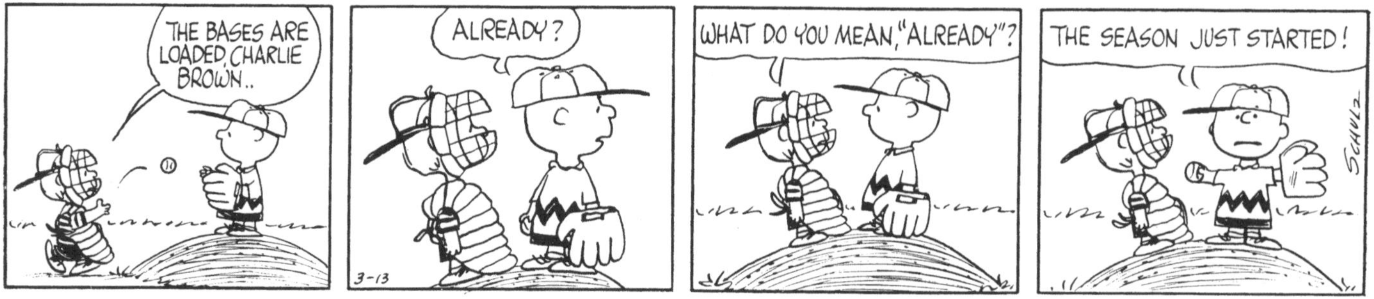
THE BASES ARE LOADED, CHARLIE BROWN..
ALREADY?
3-13
WHAT DO YOU MEAN, "ALREADY"?
THE SEASON JUST STARTED!
SCHULZ

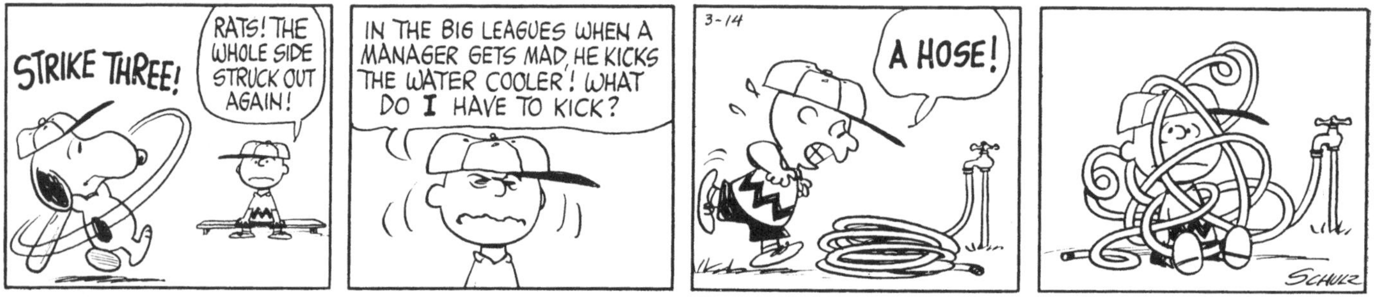
STRIKE THREE!
RATS! THE WHOLE SIDE STRUCK OUT AGAIN!
IN THE BIG LEAGUES WHEN A MANAGER GETS MAD, HE KICKS THE WATER COOLER! WHAT DO I HAVE TO KICK?
3-14
A HOSE!
SCHULZ

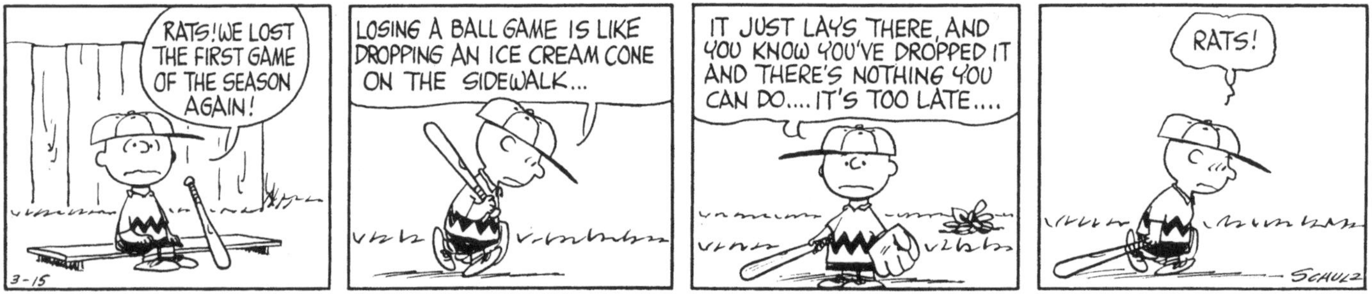
RATS! WE LOST THE FIRST GAME OF THE SEASON AGAIN!
3-15
LOSING A BALL GAME IS LIKE DROPPING AN ICE CREAM CONE ON THE SIDEWALK...
IT JUST LAYS THERE, AND YOU KNOW YOU'VE DROPPED IT AND THERE'S NOTHING YOU CAN DO.... IT'S TOO LATE....
RATS!
SCHULZ

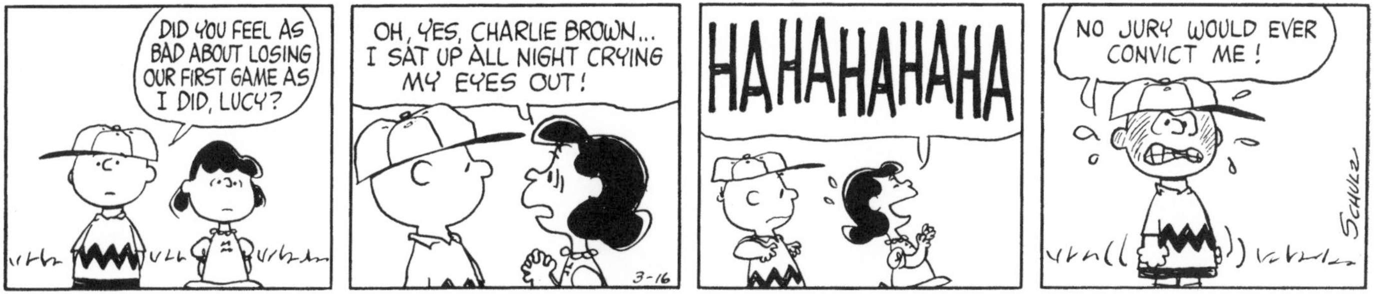
DID YOU FEEL AS BAD ABOUT LOSING OUR FIRST GAME AS I DID, LUCY?
OH, YES, CHARLIE BROWN... I SAT UP ALL NIGHT CRYING MY EYES OUT!
3-16
HAHAHAHAHA
NO JURY WOULD EVER CONVICT ME!
SCHULZ

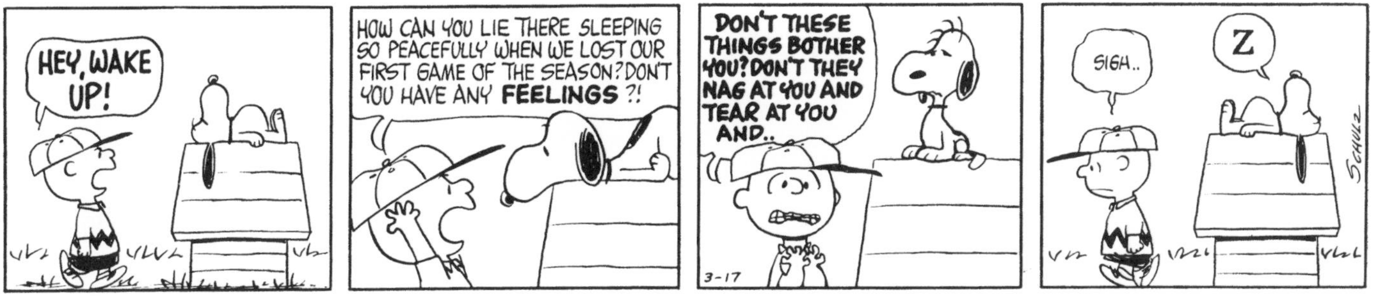
HEY, WAKE UP!
HOW CAN YOU LIE THERE SLEEPING SO PEACEFULLY WHEN WE LOST OUR FIRST GAME OF THE SEASON? DON'T YOU HAVE ANY FEELINGS ?!
DON'T THESE THINGS BOTHER YOU? DON'T THEY NAG AT YOU AND TEAR AT YOU AND..
3-17
SIGH..
Z
SCHULZ

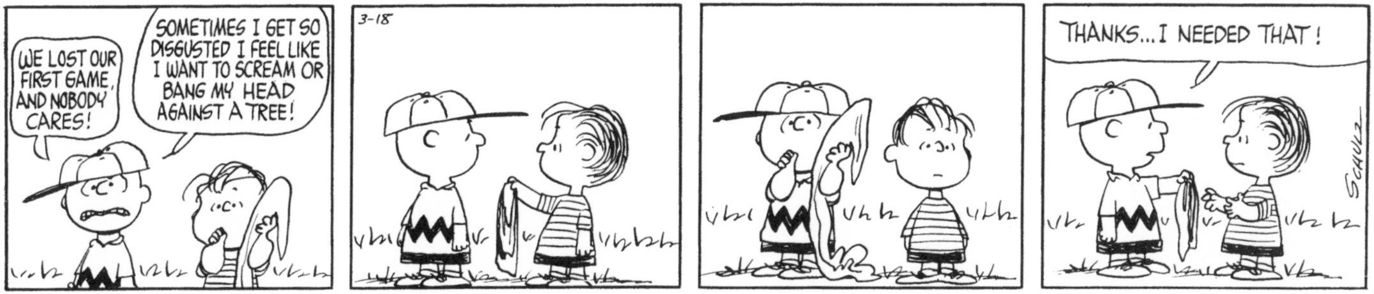
WE LOST OUR FIRST GAME, AND NOBODY CARES!
SOMETIMES I GET SO DISGUSTED I FEEL LIKE I WANT TO SCREAM OR BANG MY HEAD AGAINST A TREE!
3-18
THANKS... I NEEDED THAT!
SCHULZ

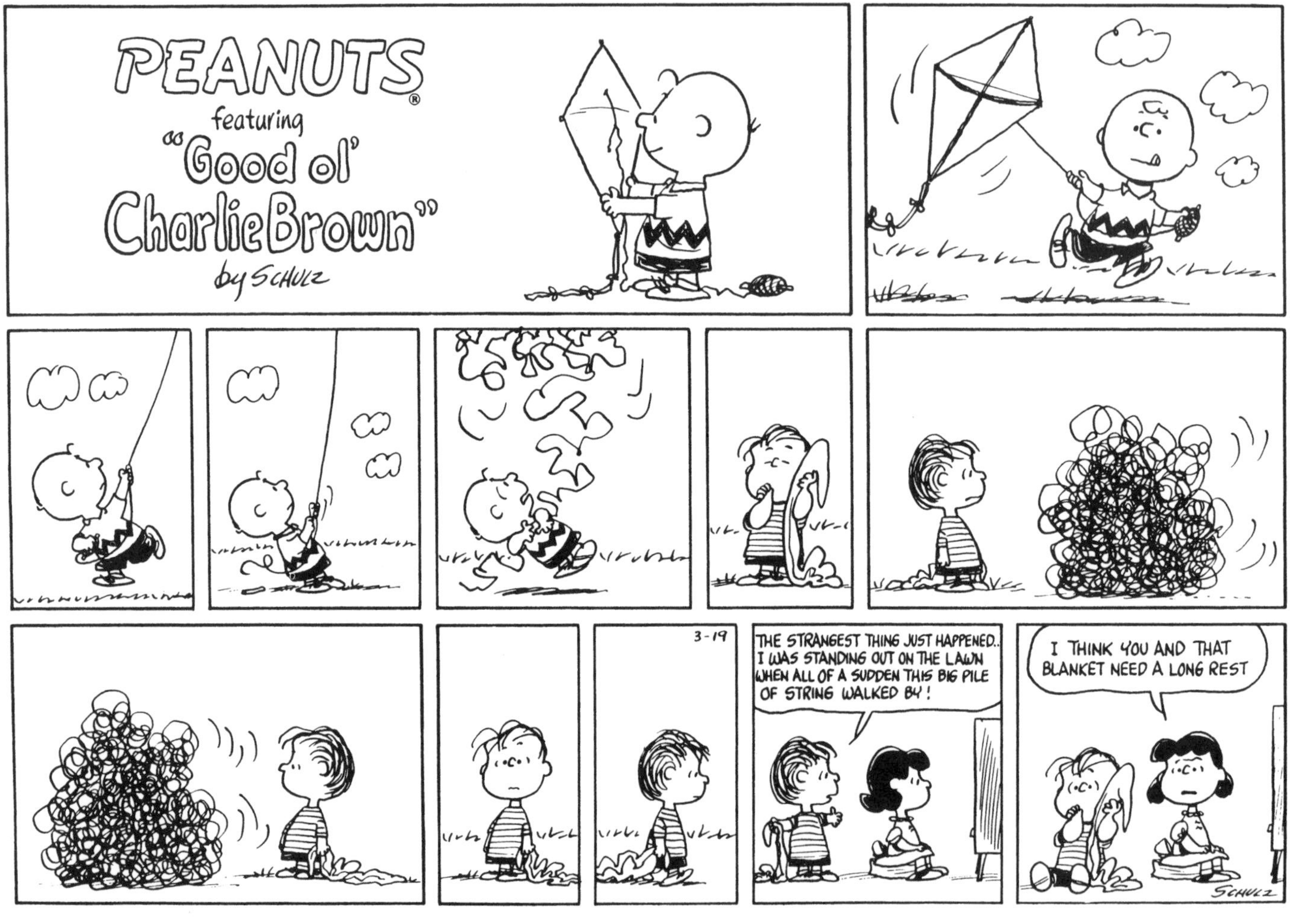
PEANUTS
featuring
"Good ol' Charlie Brown"
by SCHULZ
3-19
THE STRANGEST THING JUST HAPPENED.. I WAS STANDING OUT ON THE LAWN WHEN ALL OF A SUDDEN THIS BIG PILE OF STRING WALKED BY!
I THINK YOU AND THAT BLANKET NEED A LONG REST
SCHULZ

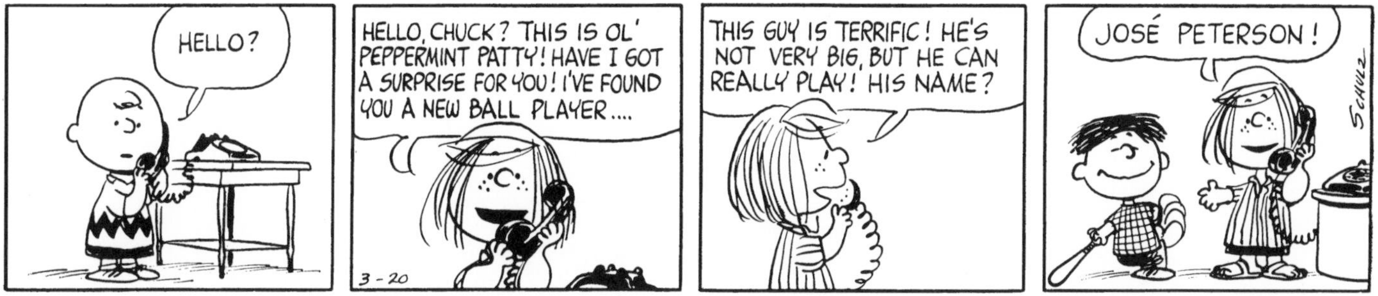
HELLO?
HELLO, CHUCK? THIS IS OL' PEPPERMINT PATTY! HAVE I GOT A SURPRISE FOR YOU! I'VE FOUND YOU A NEW BALL PLAYER....
3-20
THIS GUY IS TERRIFIC! HE'S NOT VERY BIG, BUT HE CAN REALLY PLAY! HIS NAME?
JOSÉ PETERSON!
SCHULZ

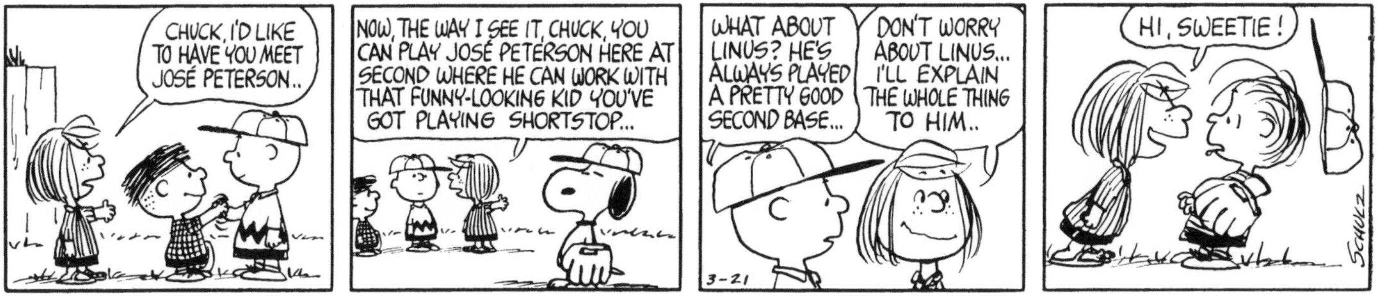
CHUCK, I'D LIKE TO HAVE YOU MEET JOSÉ PETERSON..
NOW, THE WAY I SEE IT, CHUCK, YOU CAN PLAY JOSÉ PETERSON HERE AT SECOND WHERE HE CAN WORK WITH THAT FUNNY-LOOKING KID YOU'VE GOT PLAYING SHORTSTOP...
WHAT ABOUT LINUS? HE'S ALWAYS PLAYED A PRETTY GOOD SECOND BASE...
DON'T WORRY ABOUT LINUS... I'LL EXPLAIN THE WHOLE THING TO HIM..
3-21
HI, SWEETIE!
SCHULZ

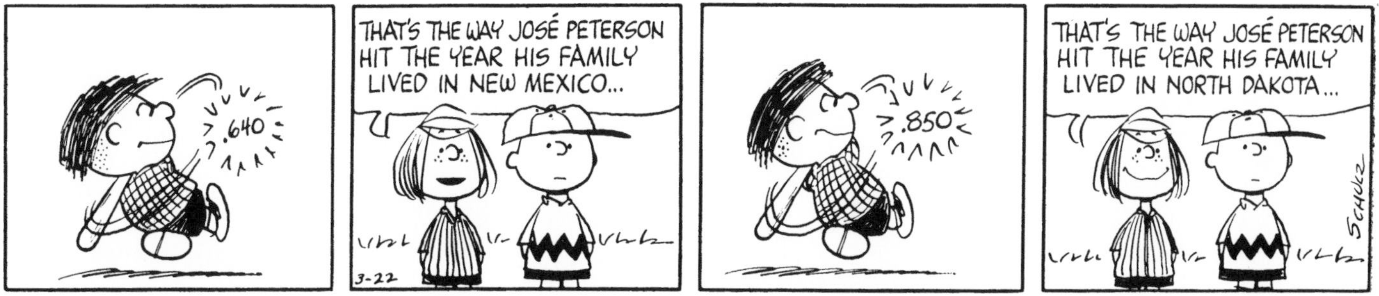
.640
THAT'S THE WAY JOSÉ PETERSON HIT THE YEAR HIS FAMILY LIVED IN NEW MEXICO...
3-22
.850
THAT'S THE WAY JOSÉ PETERSON HIT THE YEAR HIS FAMILY LIVED IN NORTH DAKOTA...
SCHULZ

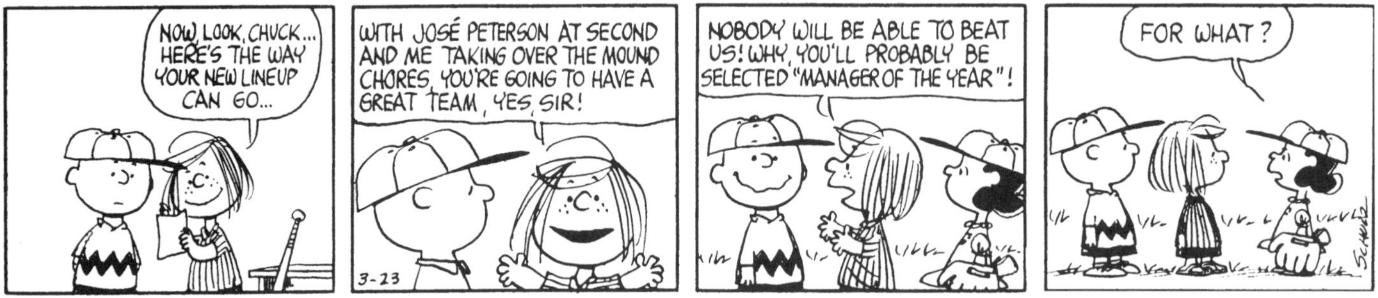
NOW, LOOK, CHUCK... HERE'S THE WAY YOUR NEW LINEUP CAN GO...
WITH JOSÉ PETERSON AT SECOND AND ME TAKING OVER THE MOUND CHORES, YOU'RE GOING TO HAVE A GREAT TEAM, YES, SIR!
3-23
NOBODY WILL BE ABLE TO BEAT US! WHY, YOU'LL PROBABLY BE SELECTED "MANAGER OF THE YEAR"!
FOR WHAT?
SCHULZ

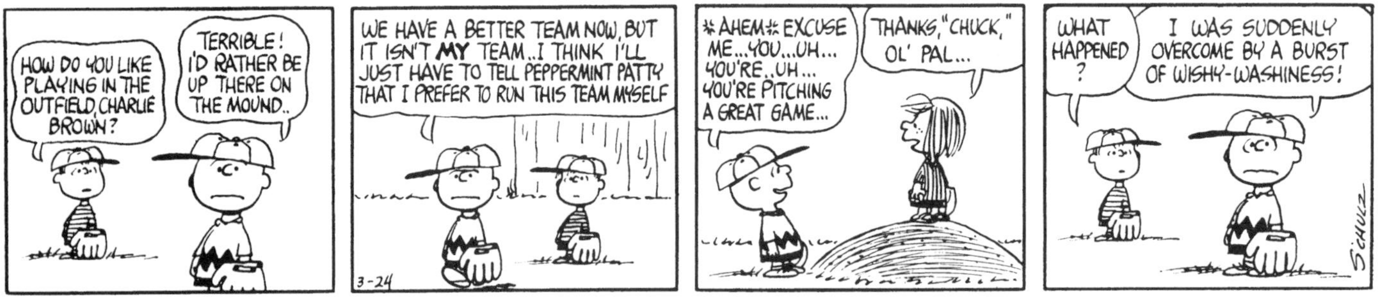
HOW DO YOU LIKE PLAYING IN THE OUTFIELD, CHARLIE BROWN?
TERRIBLE! I'D RATHER BE UP THERE ON THE MOUND..
WE HAVE A BETTER TEAM NOW, BUT IT ISN'T MY TEAM.. I THINK I'LL JUST HAVE TO TELL PEPPERMINT PATTY THAT I PREFER TO RUN THIS TEAM MYSELF
3-24
AHEM EXCUSE ME...YOU...UH... YOU'RE..UH... YOU'RE PITCHING A GREAT GAME...
THANKS, "CHUCK," OL' PAL...
WHAT HAPPENED?
I WAS SUDDENLY OVERCOME BY A BURST OF WISHY-WASHINESS!
SCHULZ

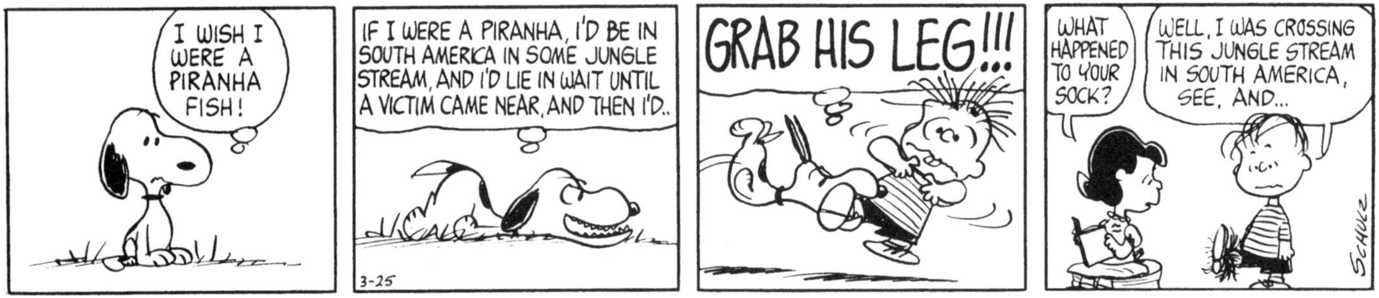
I WISH I WERE A PIRANHA FISH!
IF I WERE A PIRANHA, I'D BE IN SOUTH AMERICA IN SOME JUNGLE STREAM, AND I'D LIE IN WAIT UNTIL A VICTIM CAME NEAR, AND THEN I'D..
3-25
GRAB HIS LEG!!!
WHAT HAPPENED TO YOUR SOCK?
WELL, I WAS CROSSING THIS JUNGLE STREAM IN SOUTH AMERICA, SEE, AND...
SCHULZ

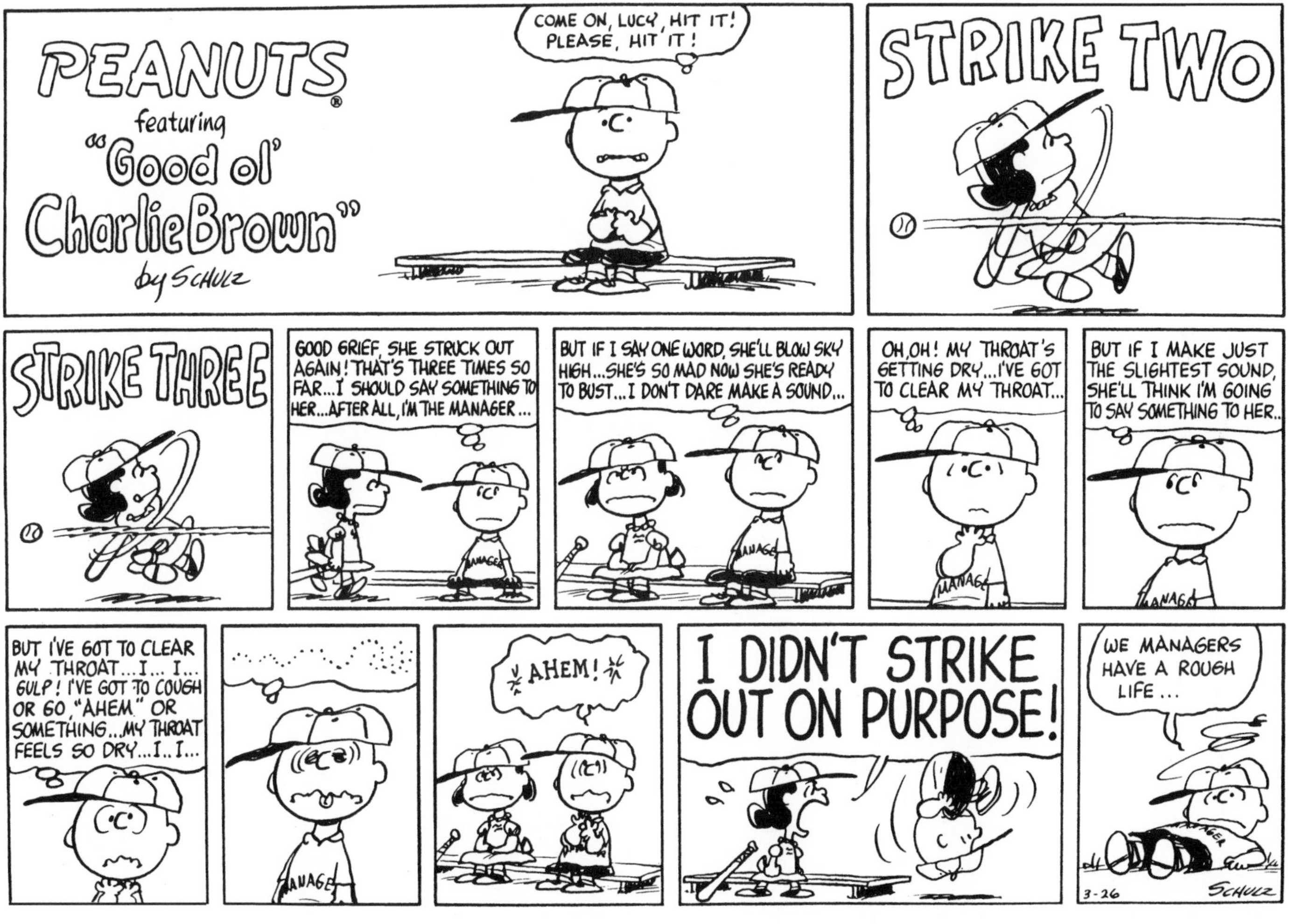
PEANUTS®
featuring
"Good ol' CharlieBrown"
by SCHULZ
COME ON, LUCY, HIT IT! PLEASE, HIT IT!
STRIKE TWO
STRIKE THREE
GOOD GRIEF, SHE STRUCK OUT AGAIN! THAT'S THREE TIMES SO FAR...I SHOULD SAY SOMETHING TO HER...AFTER ALL, I'M THE MANAGER...
BUT IF I SAY ONE WORD, SHE'LL BLOW SKY HIGH...SHE'S SO MAD NOW SHE'S READY TO BUST...I DON'T DARE MAKE A SOUND...
OH,OH! MY THROAT'S GETTING DRY...I'VE GOT TO CLEAR MY THROAT...
BUT IF I MAKE JUST THE SLIGHTEST SOUND, SHE'LL THINK I'M GOING TO SAY SOMETHING TO HER..
BUT I'VE GOT TO CLEAR MY THROAT...I... I... GULP! I'VE GOT TO COUGH OR GO, "AHEM" OR SOMETHING...MY THROAT FEELS SO DRY...I..I...
AHEM!
I DIDN'T STRIKE OUT ON PURPOSE!
WE MANAGERS HAVE A ROUGH LIFE...
3-26
SCHULZ

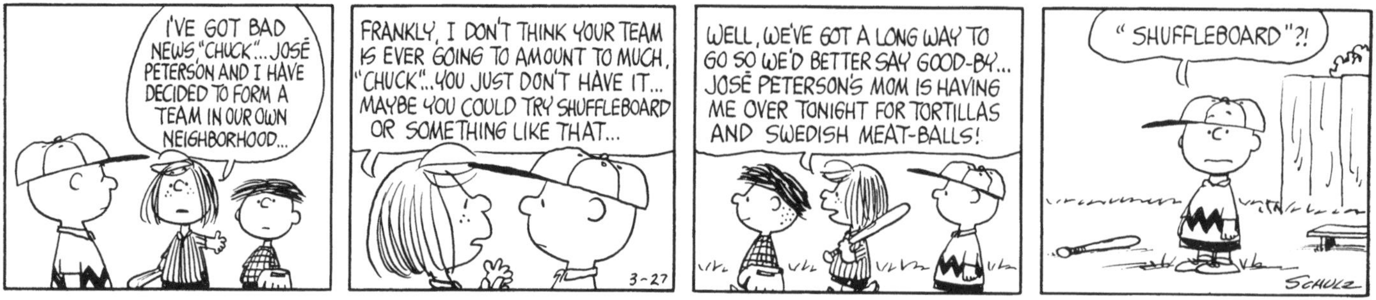
I'VE GOT BAD NEWS, "CHUCK"... JOSÉ PETERSON AND I HAVE DECIDED TO FORM A TEAM IN OUR OWN NEIGHBORHOOD...
FRANKLY, I DON'T THINK YOUR TEAM IS EVER GOING TO AMOUNT TO MUCH, "CHUCK"... YOU JUST DON'T HAVE IT... MAYBE YOU COULD TRY SHUFFLEBOARD OR SOMETHING LIKE THAT...
3-27
WELL, WE'VE GOT A LONG WAY TO GO SO WE'D BETTER SAY GOOD-BY... JOSÉ PETERSON'S MOM IS HAVING ME OVER TONIGHT FOR TORTILLAS AND SWEDISH MEAT-BALLS!
"SHUFFLEBOARD"?!
SCHULZ

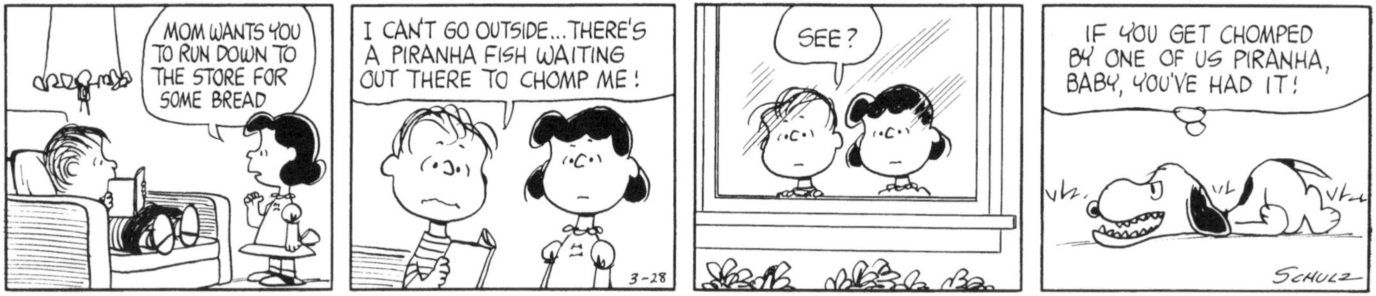
MOM WANTS YOU TO RUN DOWN TO THE STORE FOR SOME BREAD
I CAN'T GO OUTSIDE... THERE'S A PIRANHA FISH WAITING OUT THERE TO CHOMP ME!
3-28
SEE?
IF YOU GET CHOMPED BY ONE OF US PIRANHA, BABY, YOU'VE HAD IT!
SCHULZ

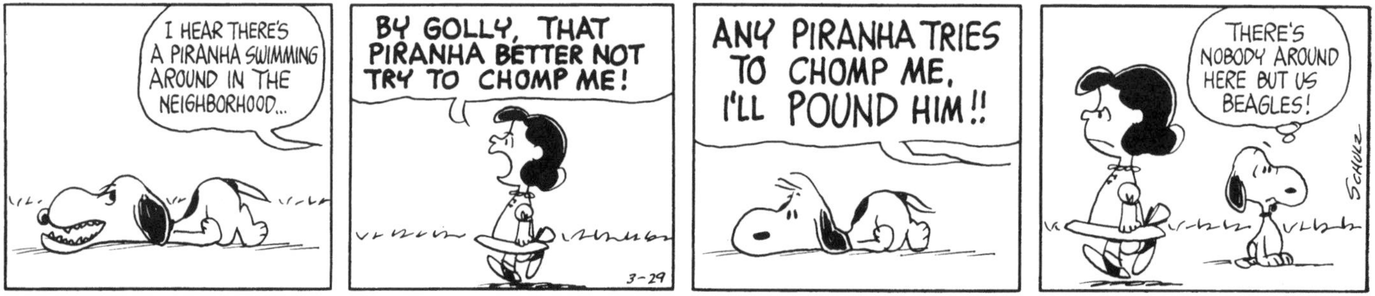
I HEAR THERE'S A PIRANHA SWIMMING AROUND IN THE NEIGHBORHOOD...
BY GOLLY, THAT PIRANHA BETTER NOT TRY TO CHOMP ME!
3-29
ANY PIRANHA TRIES TO CHOMP ME, I'LL POUND HIM!!
THERE'S NOBODY AROUND HERE BUT US BEAGLES!
SCHULZ

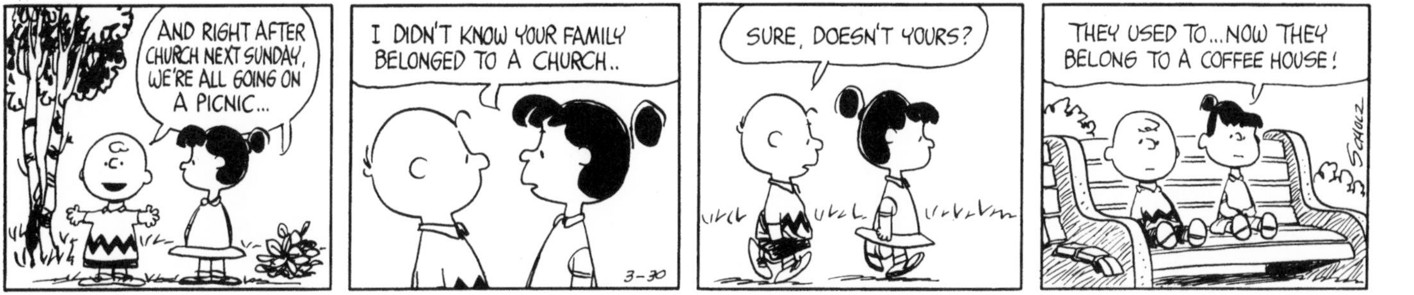
AND RIGHT AFTER CHURCH NEXT SUNDAY, WE'RE ALL GOING ON A PICNIC...
I DIDN'T KNOW YOUR FAMILY BELONGED TO A CHURCH..
3-30
SURE, DOESN'T YOURS?
THEY USED TO...NOW THEY BELONG TO A COFFEE HOUSE!
SCHULZ

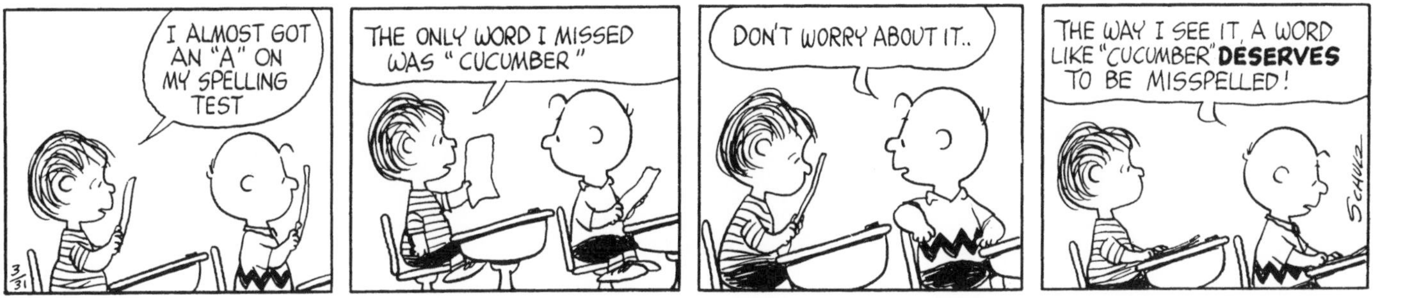
3/31
I ALMOST GOT AN "A" ON MY SPELLING TEST
THE ONLY WORD I MISSED WAS "CUCUMBER"
DON'T WORRY ABOUT IT..
THE WAY I SEE IT, A WORD LIKE "CUCUMBER" **DESERVES** TO BE MISSPELLED!
SCHULZ

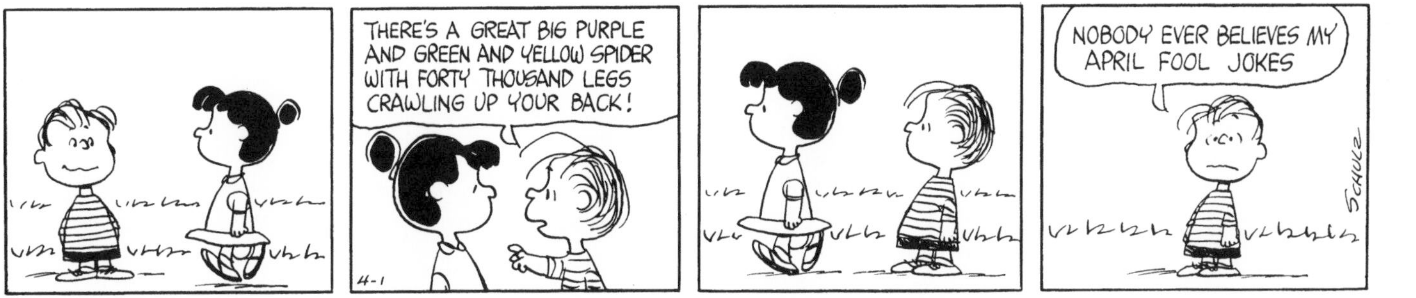
THERE'S A GREAT BIG PURPLE AND GREEN AND YELLOW SPIDER WITH FORTY THOUSAND LEGS CRAWLING UP YOUR BACK!
4-1
NOBODY EVER BELIEVES MY APRIL FOOL JOKES
SCHULZ

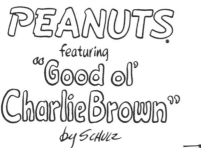

PEANUTS
featuring
"Good ol' CharlieBrown"
by SCHULZ

BONK!

I CAN'T STAND IT!

OKAY, LUCY, WHERE WERE YOU ON THAT FLY BALL? LET'S START PAYING ATTENTION!

BLEAH!

AND HOW ABOUT YOU? YOU WERE OUT OF POSITION ON THAT DOUBLE-PLAY BALL! YOU BETTER LOOK ALIVE!

BLEAH!

AND YOU SURE HAVEN'T BEEN DOING MUCH OF A JOB BEHIND THE PLATE, SCHROEDER! HOW ABOUT SHOWING SOME LIFE BACK THERE, HUH? HOW ABOUT IT?

4-2

BLEAH!

MAYBE I WAS TOO HARD ON THEM... AFTER ALL, I HAVEN'T BEEN DOING TOO WELL MYSELF... IN FACT, MY PITCHING HAS BEEN LOUSY!

BY GOLLY, CHARLIE BROWN, YOU'D BETTER START PITCHING BETTER BALL!! YOU'D BETTER BUCKLE DOWN OUT HERE!

BLEAH!

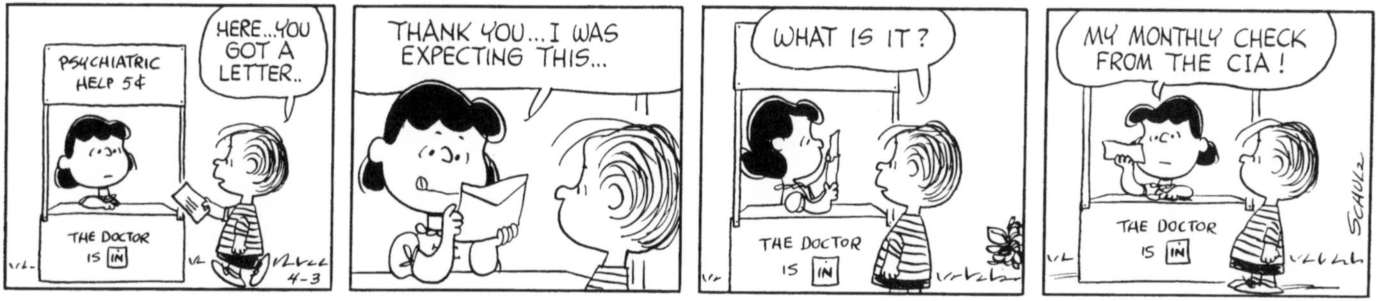
PSYCHIATRIC HELP 5¢
HERE...YOU GOT A LETTER..
THE DOCTOR IS IN
4-3
THANK YOU...I WAS EXPECTING THIS...
WHAT IS IT?
THE DOCTOR IS IN
MY MONTHLY CHECK FROM THE CIA!
THE DOCTOR IS IN
SCHULZ

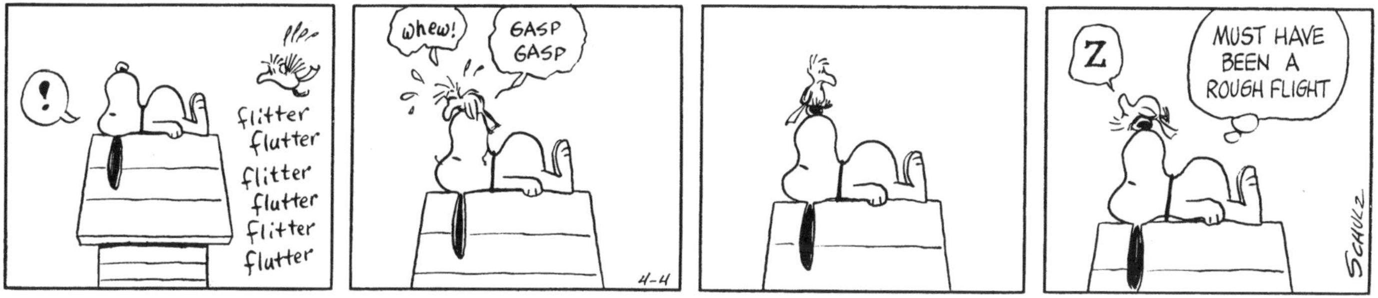
!
flitter flutter flitter flutter flitter flutter
whew!
GASP GASP
4-4
Z
MUST HAVE BEEN A ROUGH FLIGHT
SCHULZ

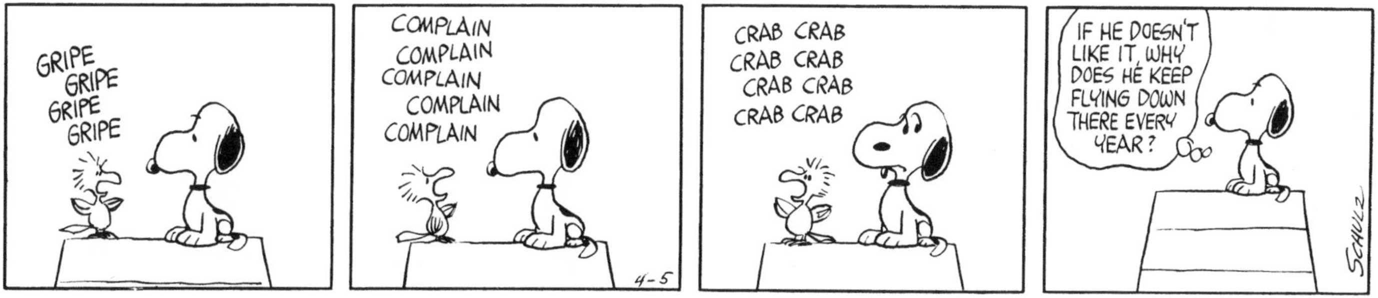
GRIPE GRIPE GRIPE GRIPE
COMPLAIN COMPLAIN COMPLAIN COMPLAIN COMPLAIN
4-5
CRAB CRAB CRAB CRAB CRAB CRAB CRAB CRAB
IF HE DOESN'T LIKE IT, WHY DOES HE KEEP FLYING DOWN THERE EVERY YEAR?
SCHULZ

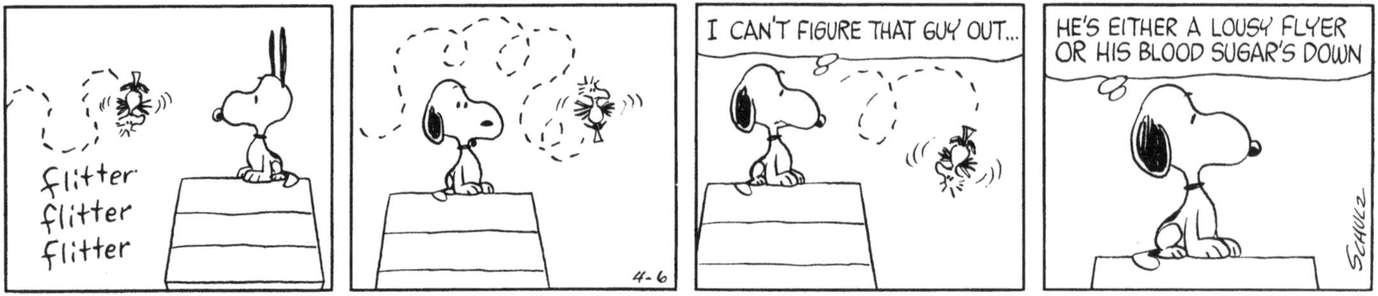
flitter flitter flitter
4-6
I CAN'T FIGURE THAT GUY OUT...
HE'S EITHER A LOUSY FLYER OR HIS BLOOD SUGAR'S DOWN
SCHULZ

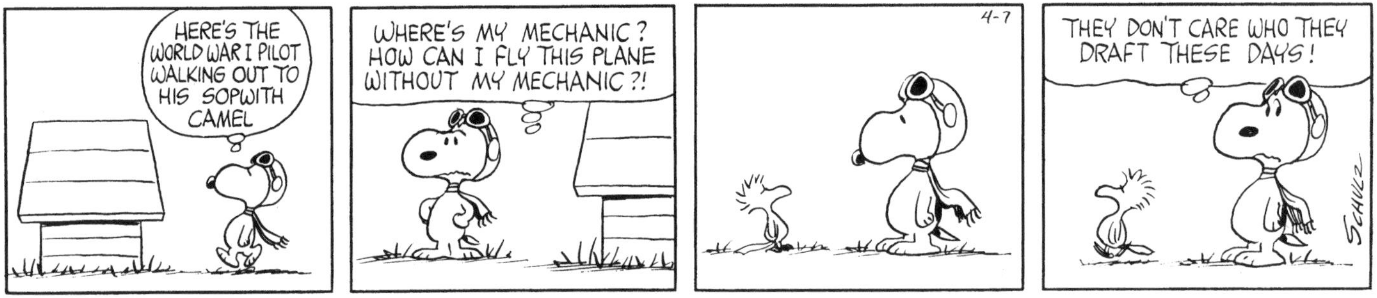
HERE'S THE WORLD WAR I PILOT WALKING OUT TO HIS SOPWITH CAMEL
WHERE'S MY MECHANIC? HOW CAN I FLY THIS PLANE WITHOUT MY MECHANIC?!
4-7
THEY DON'T CARE WHO THEY DRAFT THESE DAYS!
SCHULZ

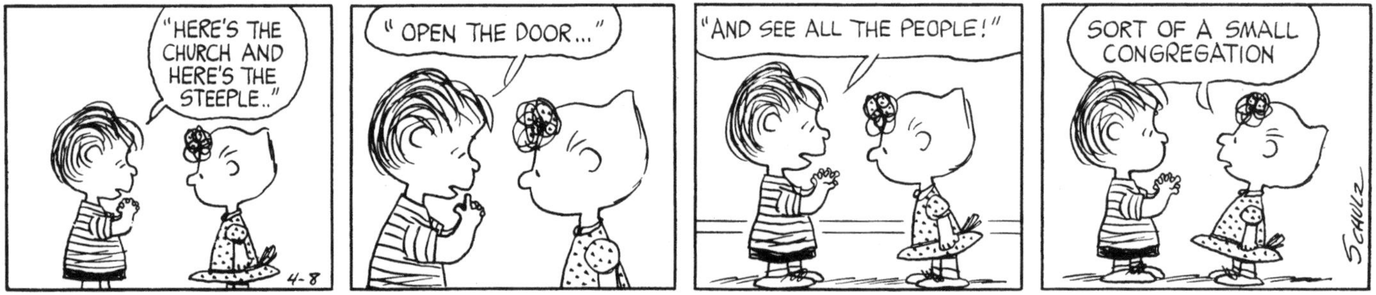
"HERE'S THE CHURCH AND HERE'S THE STEEPLE.."
4-8
" OPEN THE DOOR..."
"AND SEE ALL THE PEOPLE!"
SORT OF A SMALL CONGREGATION
SCHULZ

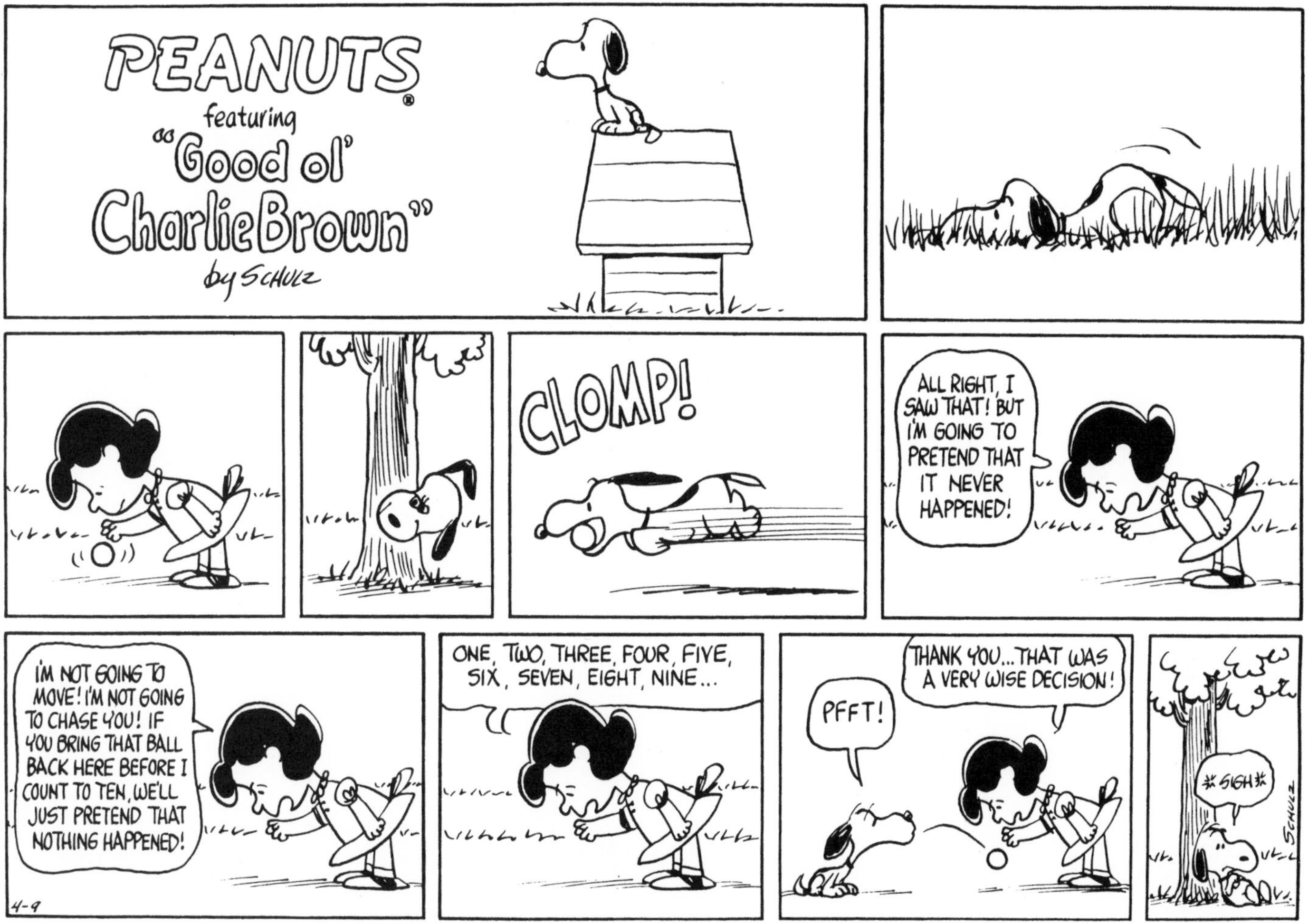
PEANUTS®
featuring
"Good ol' Charlie Brown"
by SCHULZ
CLOMP!
ALL RIGHT, I SAW THAT! BUT I'M GOING TO PRETEND THAT IT NEVER HAPPENED!
I'M NOT GOING TO MOVE! I'M NOT GOING TO CHASE YOU! IF YOU BRING THAT BALL BACK HERE BEFORE I COUNT TO TEN, WE'LL JUST PRETEND THAT NOTHING HAPPENED!
4-9
ONE, TWO, THREE, FOUR, FIVE, SIX, SEVEN, EIGHT, NINE...
PFFT!
THANK YOU...THAT WAS A VERY WISE DECISION!
SIGH
SCHULZ

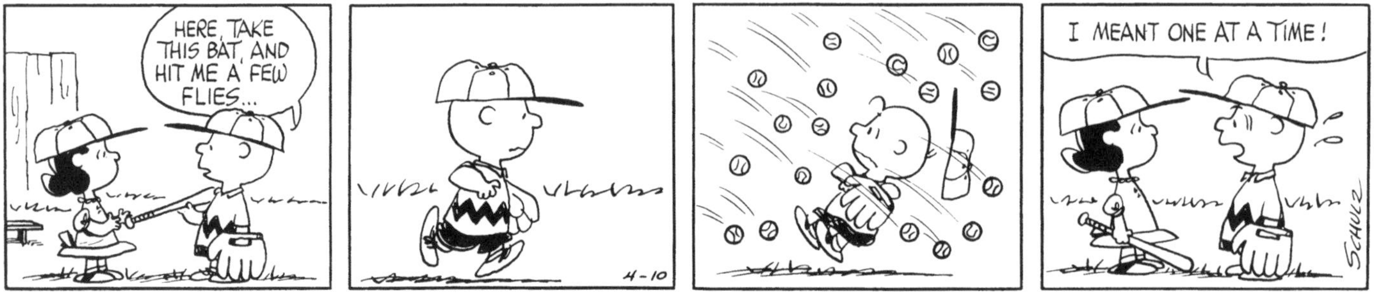
HERE, TAKE THIS BAT, AND HIT ME A FEW FLIES...
4-10
I MEANT ONE AT A TIME!
SCHULZ

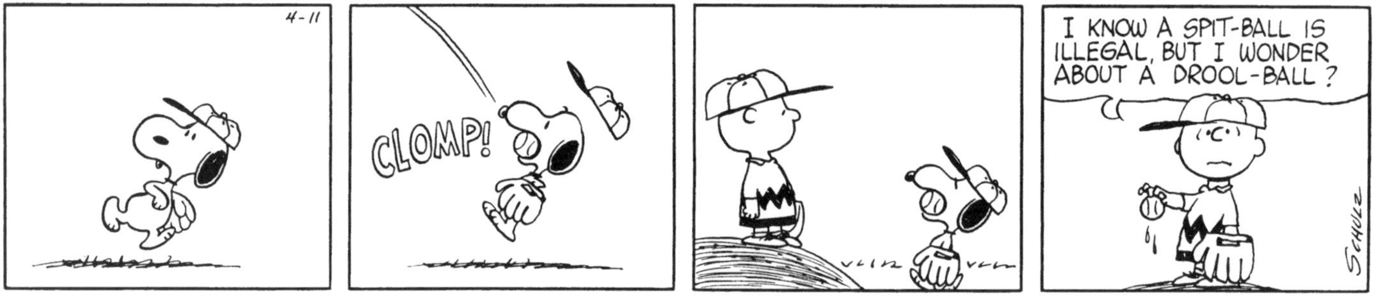
4-11
CLOMP!
I KNOW A SPIT-BALL IS ILLEGAL, BUT I WONDER ABOUT A DROOL-BALL?
SCHULZ

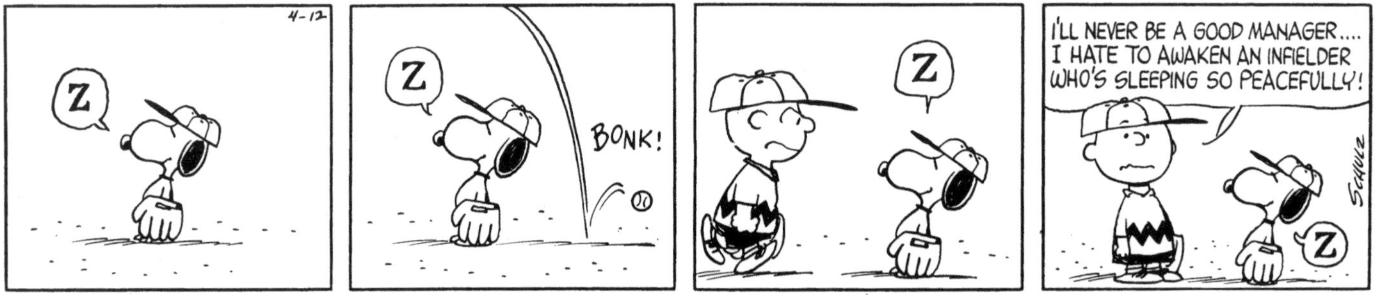
4-12
Z
Z
BONK!
Z
I'LL NEVER BE A GOOD MANAGER.... I HATE TO AWAKEN AN INFIELDER WHO'S SLEEPING SO PEACEFULLY!
Z
SCHULZ

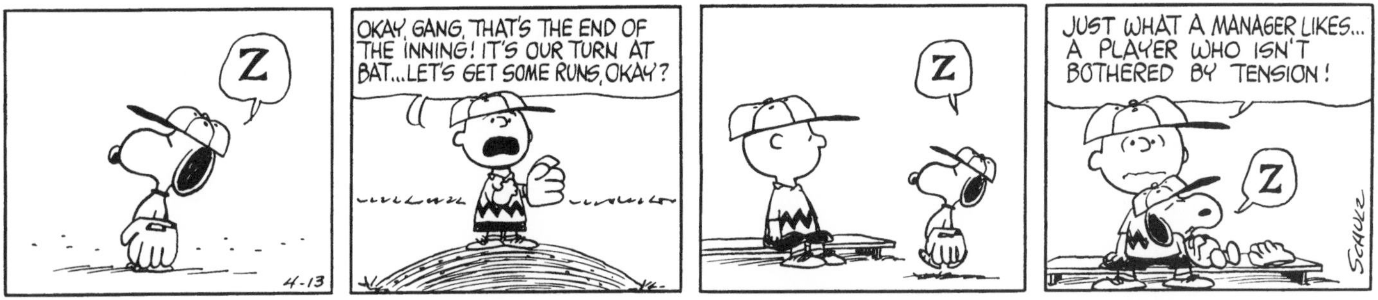
Z
4-13
OKAY, GANG, THAT'S THE END OF THE INNING! IT'S OUR TURN AT BAT...LET'S GET SOME RUNS, OKAY?
Z
JUST WHAT A MANAGER LIKES... A PLAYER WHO ISN'T BOTHERED BY TENSION!
Z
SCHULZ

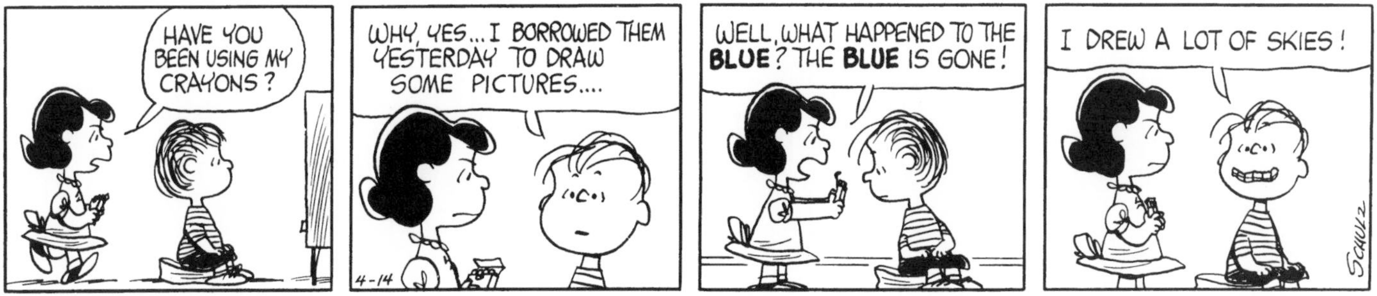
HAVE YOU BEEN USING MY CRAYONS?
WHY, YES...I BORROWED THEM YESTERDAY TO DRAW SOME PICTURES....
4-14
WELL, WHAT HAPPENED TO THE **BLUE**? THE **BLUE** IS GONE!
I DREW A LOT OF SKIES!
SCHULZ

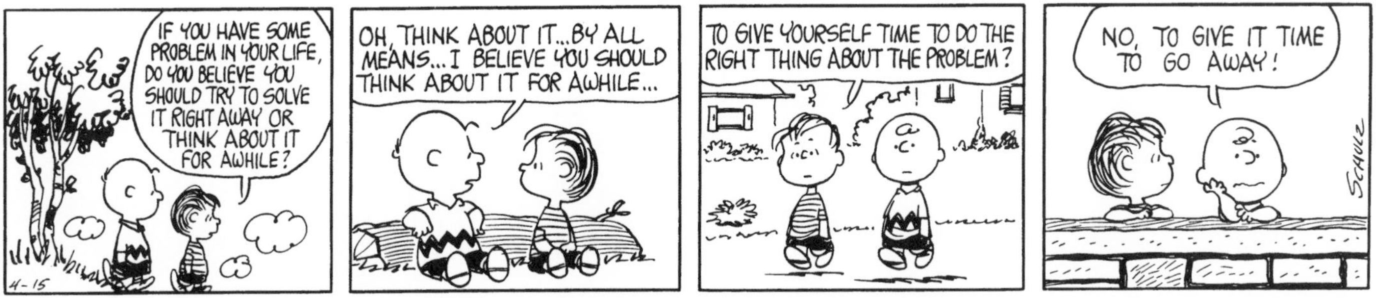
IF YOU HAVE SOME PROBLEM IN YOUR LIFE, DO YOU BELIEVE YOU SHOULD TRY TO SOLVE IT RIGHT AWAY OR THINK ABOUT IT FOR AWHILE?
4-15
OH, THINK ABOUT IT...BY ALL MEANS...I BELIEVE YOU SHOULD THINK ABOUT IT FOR AWHILE...
TO GIVE YOURSELF TIME TO DO THE RIGHT THING ABOUT THE PROBLEM?
NO, TO GIVE IT TIME TO GO AWAY!
SCHULZ

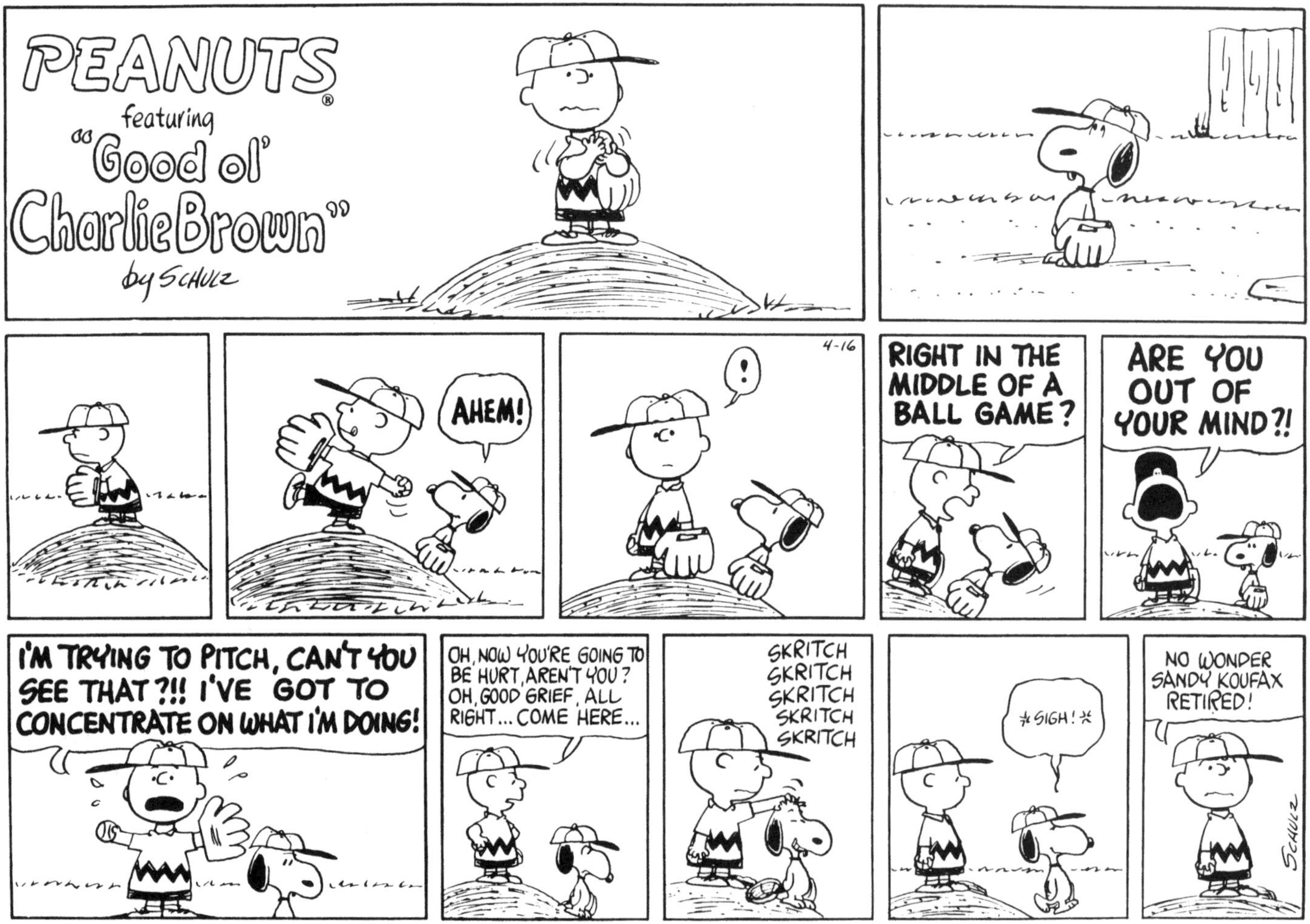
PEANUTS®
featuring "Good ol' Charlie Brown"
by SCHULZ
AHEM!
!
4-16
RIGHT IN THE MIDDLE OF A BALL GAME?
ARE YOU OUT OF YOUR MIND?!
I'M TRYING TO PITCH, CAN'T YOU SEE THAT?!! I'VE GOT TO CONCENTRATE ON WHAT I'M DOING!
OH, NOW YOU'RE GOING TO BE HURT, AREN'T YOU? OH, GOOD GRIEF, ALL RIGHT... COME HERE...
SKRITCH SKRITCH SKRITCH SKRITCH SKRITCH
SIGH!
NO WONDER SANDY KOUFAX RETIRED!
SCHULZ

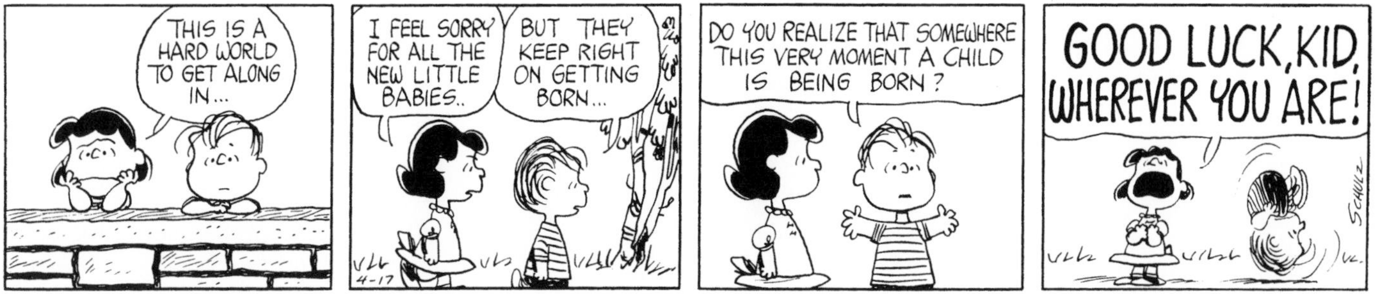
THIS IS A HARD WORLD TO GET ALONG IN...
I FEEL SORRY FOR ALL THE NEW LITTLE BABIES..
BUT THEY KEEP RIGHT ON GETTING BORN...
4-17
DO YOU REALIZE THAT SOMEWHERE THIS VERY MOMENT A CHILD IS BEING BORN?
GOOD LUCK, KID, WHEREVER YOU ARE!
SCHULZ

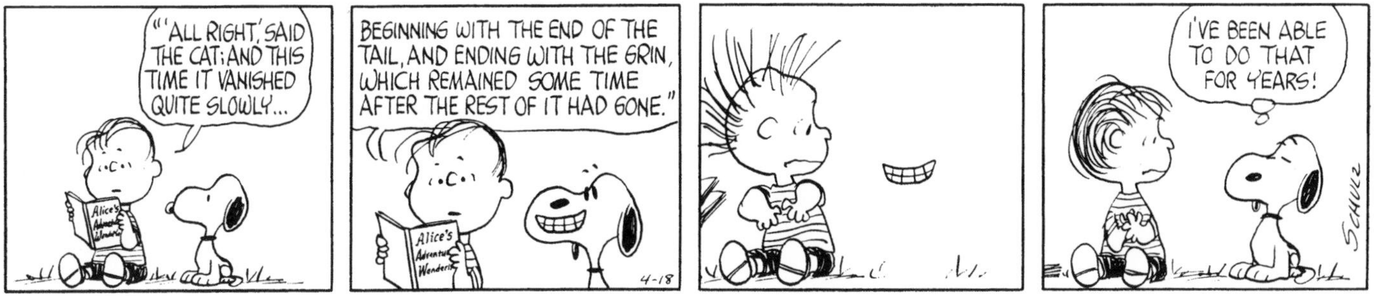
"'ALL RIGHT,' SAID THE CAT; AND THIS TIME IT VANISHED QUITE SLOWLY...
BEGINNING WITH THE END OF THE TAIL, AND ENDING WITH THE GRIN, WHICH REMAINED SOME TIME AFTER THE REST OF IT HAD GONE."
4-18
I'VE BEEN ABLE TO DO THAT FOR YEARS!
SCHULZ

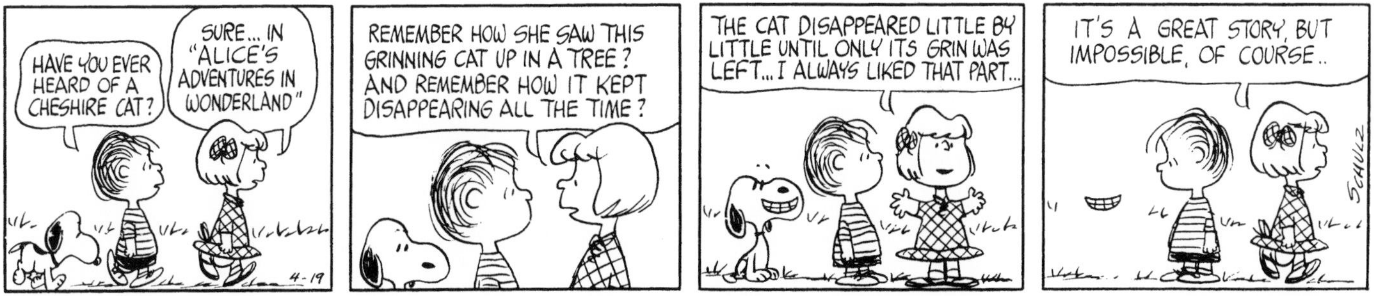
HAVE YOU EVER HEARD OF A CHESHIRE CAT?
SURE... IN "ALICE'S ADVENTURES IN WONDERLAND"
4-19
REMEMBER HOW SHE SAW THIS GRINNING CAT UP IN A TREE? AND REMEMBER HOW IT KEPT DISAPPEARING ALL THE TIME?
THE CAT DISAPPEARED LITTLE BY LITTLE UNTIL ONLY ITS GRIN WAS LEFT... I ALWAYS LIKED THAT PART...
IT'S A GREAT STORY, BUT IMPOSSIBLE, OF COURSE..
SCHULZ

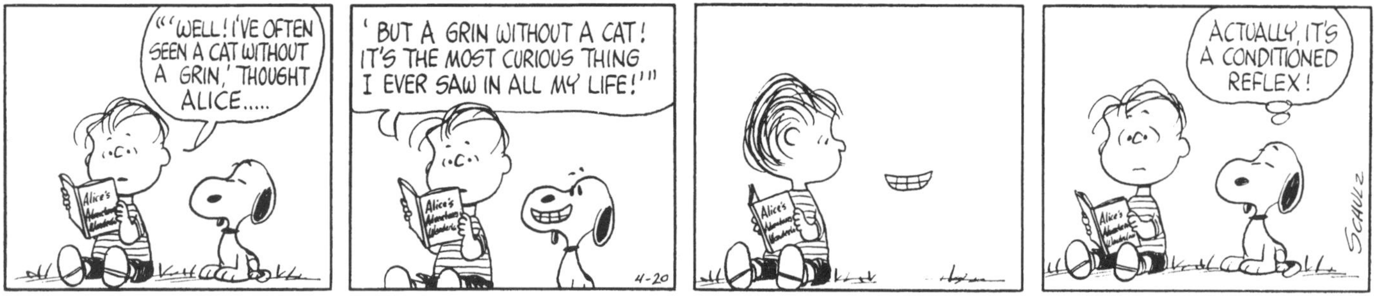
"'WELL! I'VE OFTEN SEEN A CAT WITHOUT A GRIN,' THOUGHT ALICE.....
'BUT A GRIN WITHOUT A CAT! IT'S THE MOST CURIOUS THING I EVER SAW IN ALL MY LIFE!'"
4-20
ACTUALLY, IT'S A CONDITIONED REFLEX!
SCHULZ

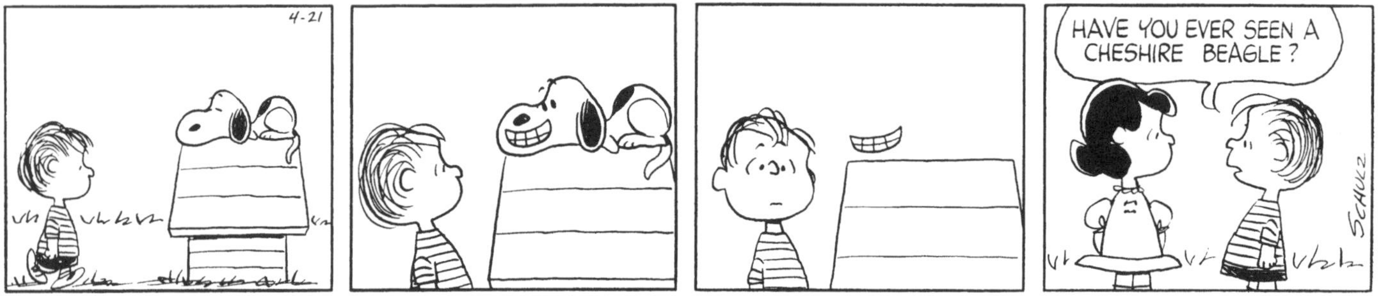
4-21
HAVE YOU EVER SEEN A CHESHIRE BEAGLE?
SCHULZ

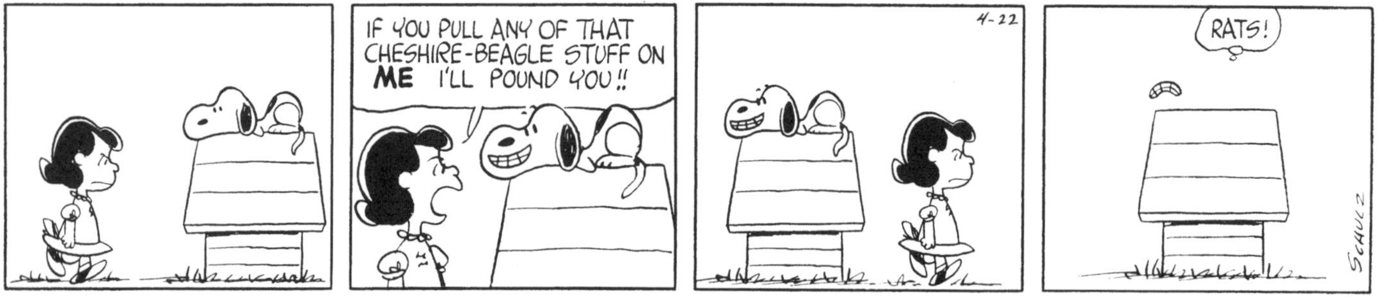
IF YOU PULL ANY OF THAT CHESHIRE-BEAGLE STUFF ON **ME** I'LL POUND YOU!!
4-22
RATS!
SCHULZ

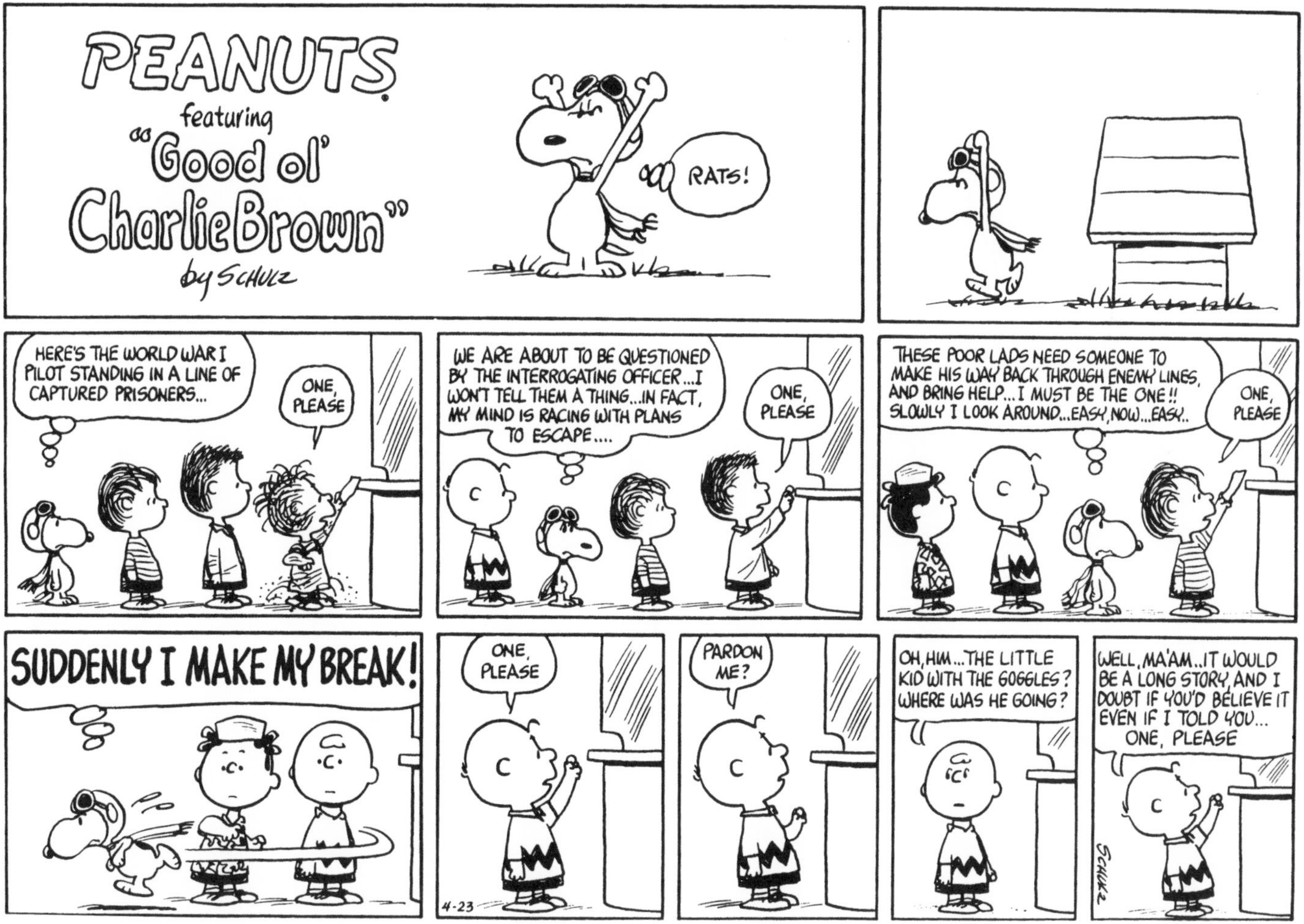
PEANUTS
featuring
"Good ol' Charlie Brown"
by SCHULZ
RATS!
HERE'S THE WORLD WAR I PILOT STANDING IN A LINE OF CAPTURED PRISONERS...
ONE, PLEASE
WE ARE ABOUT TO BE QUESTIONED BY THE INTERROGATING OFFICER...I WON'T TELL THEM A THING...IN FACT, MY MIND IS RACING WITH PLANS TO ESCAPE....
ONE, PLEASE
THESE POOR LADS NEED SOMEONE TO MAKE HIS WAY BACK THROUGH ENEMY LINES, AND BRING HELP...I MUST BE THE ONE!! SLOWLY I LOOK AROUND...EASY, NOW...EASY..
ONE, PLEASE
SUDDENLY I MAKE MY BREAK!
ONE, PLEASE
4-23
PARDON ME?
OH, HIM...THE LITTLE KID WITH THE GOGGLES? WHERE WAS HE GOING?
SCHULZ
WELL, MA'AM..IT WOULD BE A LONG STORY, AND I DOUBT IF YOU'D BELIEVE IT EVEN IF I TOLD YOU... ONE, PLEASE

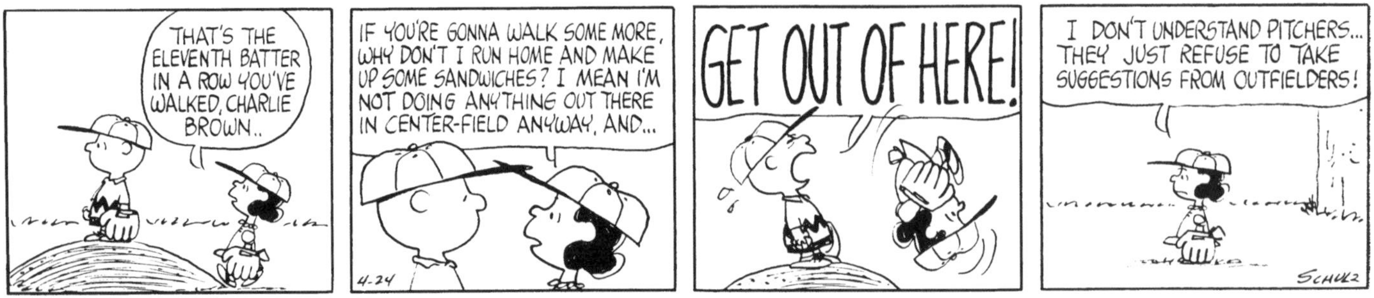
THAT'S THE ELEVENTH BATTER IN A ROW YOU'VE WALKED, CHARLIE BROWN..
IF YOU'RE GONNA WALK SOME MORE, WHY DON'T I RUN HOME AND MAKE UP SOME SANDWICHES? I MEAN I'M NOT DOING ANYTHING OUT THERE IN CENTER-FIELD ANYWAY, AND...
GET OUT OF HERE!
I DON'T UNDERSTAND PITCHERS... THEY JUST REFUSE TO TAKE SUGGESTIONS FROM OUTFIELDERS!

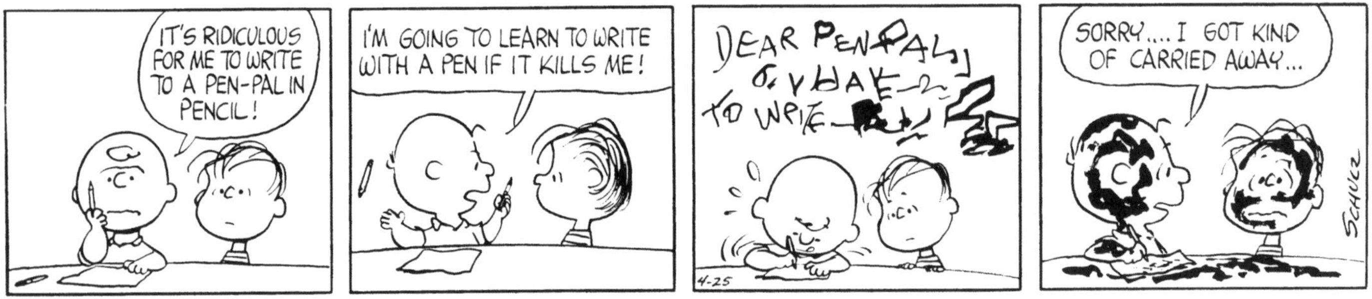
IT'S RIDICULOUS FOR ME TO WRITE TO A PEN-PAL IN PENCIL!
I'M GOING TO LEARN TO WRITE WITH A PEN IF IT KILLS ME!
SORRY.... I GOT KIND OF CARRIED AWAY...

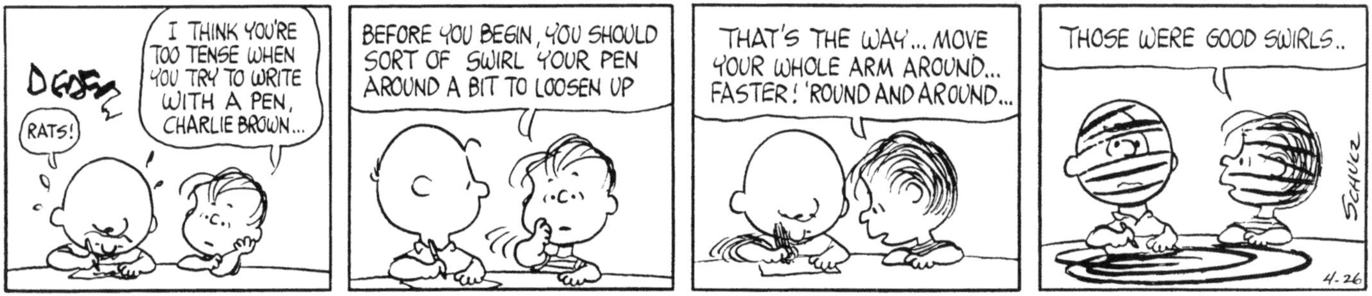
RATS!
I THINK YOU'RE TOO TENSE WHEN YOU TRY TO WRITE WITH A PEN, CHARLIE BROWN...
BEFORE YOU BEGIN, YOU SHOULD SORT OF SWIRL YOUR PEN AROUND A BIT TO LOOSEN UP
THAT'S THE WAY... MOVE YOUR WHOLE ARM AROUND... FASTER! 'ROUND AND AROUND...
THOSE WERE GOOD SWIRLS..

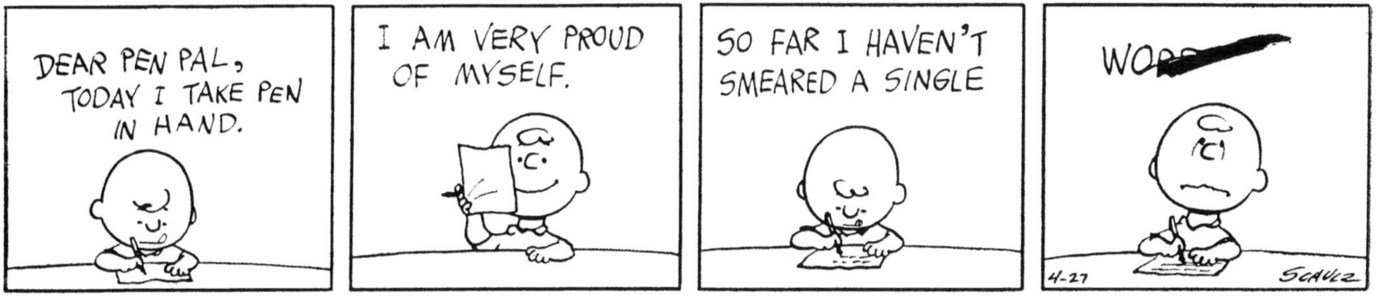
DEAR PEN PAL, TODAY I TAKE PEN IN HAND.
I AM VERY PROUD OF MYSELF.
SO FAR I HAVEN'T SMEARED A SINGLE
WO
4-27
SCHULZ

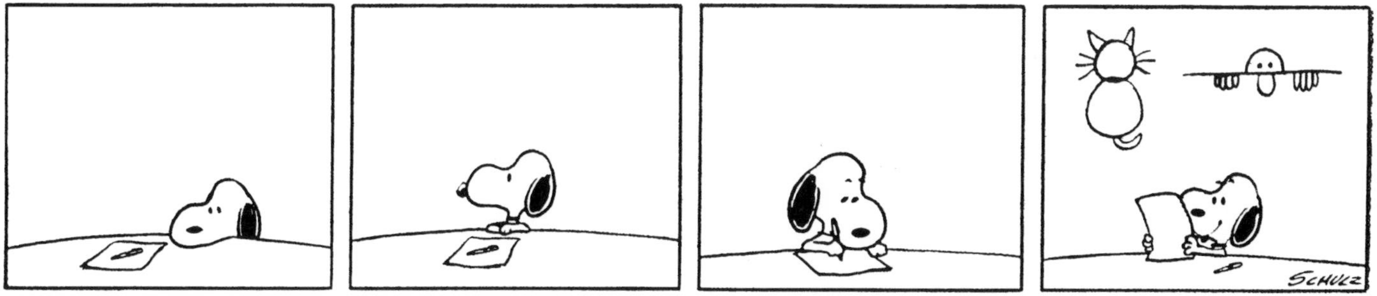
SCHULZ

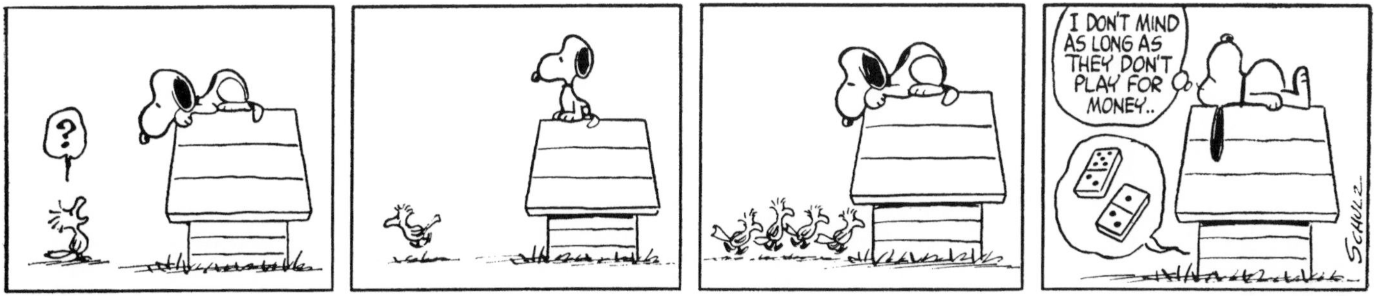
?
I DON'T MIND AS LONG AS THEY DON'T PLAY FOR MONEY..
SCHULZ

PEANUTS®
featuring
"Good ol' Charlie Brown"
by Schulz

CHOMP
CHOMP
CHOMP

HERE, HAVE A LEMON DROP...

DON'T MIND IF I DO..

(!) RATTLE RATTLE RUSTLE RUSTLE RATTLE

THANK YOU...THANK YOU VERY MUCH..

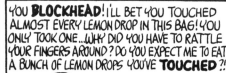

YOU **BLOCKHEAD**! I'LL BET YOU TOUCHED ALMOST EVERY LEMON DROP IN THIS BAG! YOU ONLY TOOK ONE...WHY DID YOU HAVE TO RATTLE YOUR FINGERS AROUND? DO YOU EXPECT ME TO EAT A BUNCH OF LEMON DROPS YOU'VE **TOUCHED**?!

4-30

HERE! YOU TAKE EVERY LEMON DROP OUT OF THERE THAT YOU TOUCHED! I'M NOT GOING TO EAT CANDY YOU'VE TOUCHED WITH YOUR FINGERS!

WELL, THIS ONE LOOKS LIKE I MAY HAVE TOUCHED IT, AND THIS ONE, TOO, AND MAYBE THIS ONE, AND PERHAPS THIS ONE, AND...

CARE FOR A LEMON DROP?

POW!

JUST WHAT I'VE ALWAYS WANTED...A ROOMFUL OF LEMON DROPS!

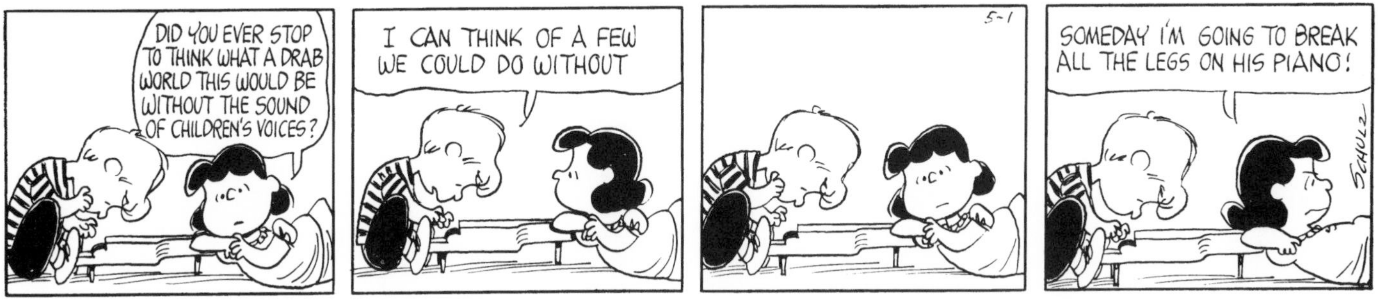
DID YOU EVER STOP TO THINK WHAT A DRAB WORLD THIS WOULD BE WITHOUT THE SOUND OF CHILDREN'S VOICES?
I CAN THINK OF A FEW WE COULD DO WITHOUT
5-1
SOMEDAY I'M GOING TO BREAK ALL THE LEGS ON HIS PIANO!
SCHULZ

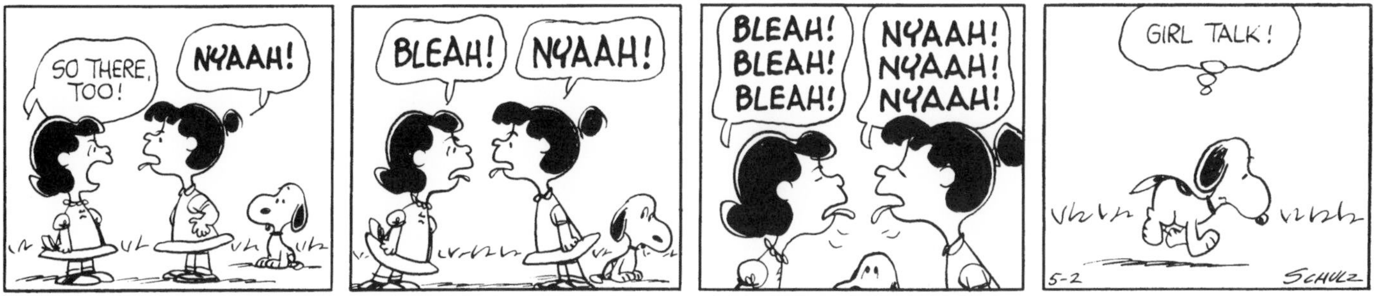
SO THERE, TOO!
NYAAH!
BLEAH!
NYAAH!
BLEAH! BLEAH! BLEAH!
NYAAH! NYAAH! NYAAH!
GIRL TALK!
5-2
SCHULZ

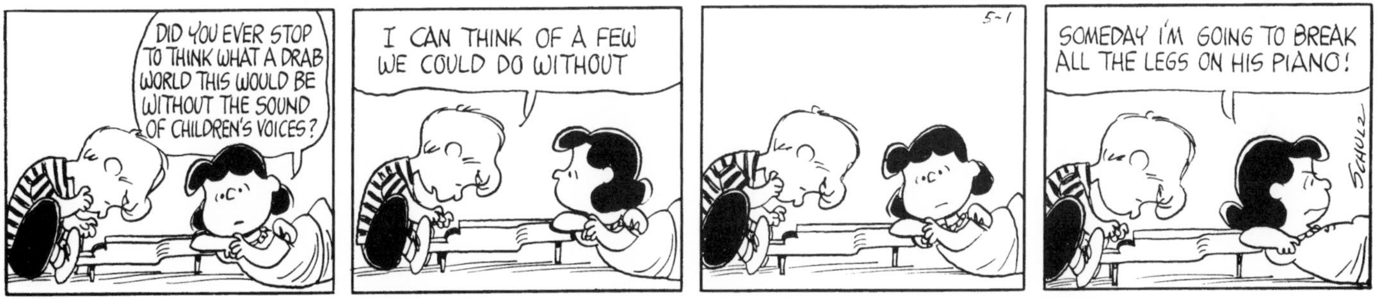
DID YOU EVER STOP TO THINK WHAT A DRAB WORLD THIS WOULD BE WITHOUT THE SOUND OF CHILDREN'S VOICES?
I CAN THINK OF A FEW WE COULD DO WITHOUT
5-1
SOMEDAY I'M GOING TO BREAK ALL THE LEGS ON HIS PIANO!
SCHULZ

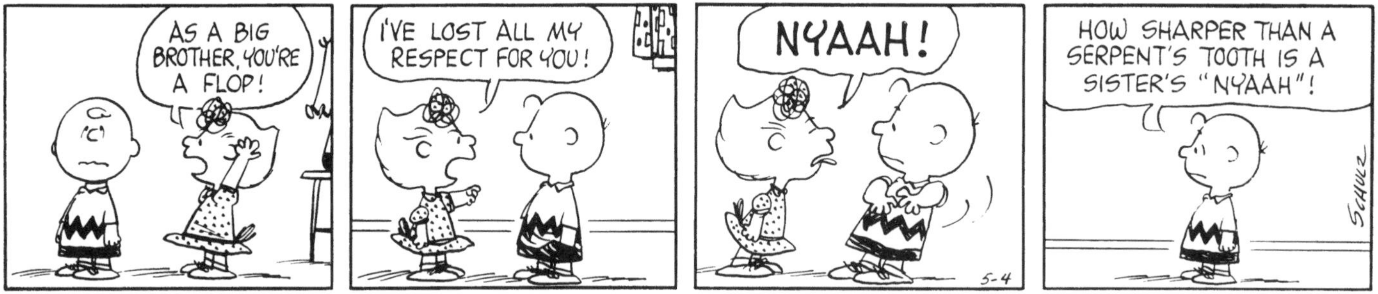
AS A BIG BROTHER, YOU'RE A FLOP!
I'VE LOST ALL MY RESPECT FOR YOU!
NYAAH!
5-4
HOW SHARPER THAN A SERPENT'S TOOTH IS A SISTER'S "NYAAH"!
SCHULZ

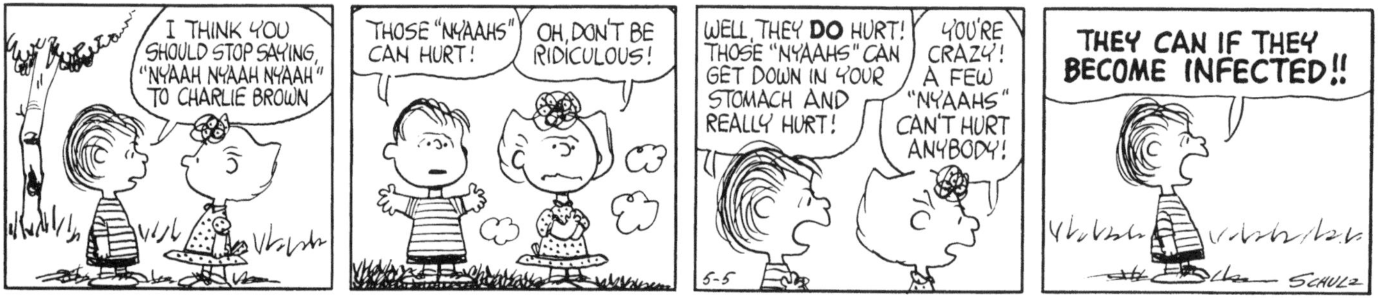
I THINK YOU SHOULD STOP SAYING, "NYAAH NYAAH NYAAH" TO CHARLIE BROWN
THOSE "NYAAHS" CAN HURT!
OH, DON'T BE RIDICULOUS!
WELL, THEY **DO** HURT! THOSE "NYAAHS" CAN GET DOWN IN YOUR STOMACH AND REALLY HURT!
YOU'RE CRAZY! A FEW "NYAAHS" CAN'T HURT ANYBODY!
5-5
THEY CAN IF THEY BECOME INFECTED!!
SCHULZ

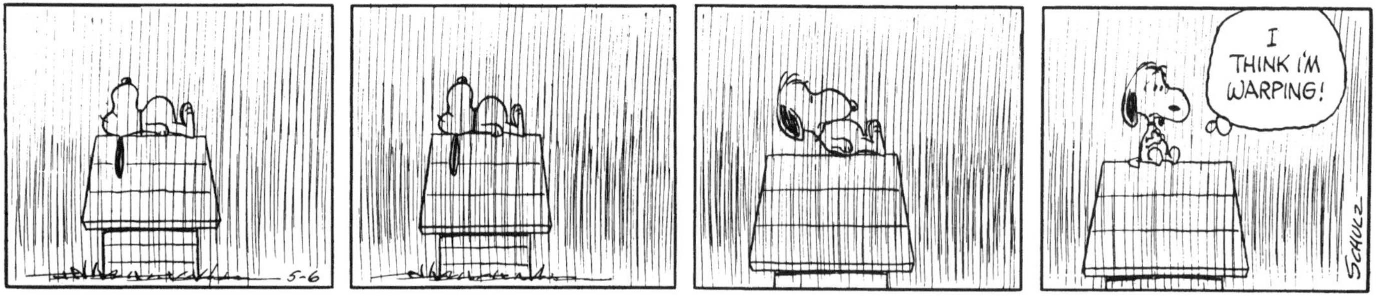
5-6
I THINK I'M WARPING!
SCHULZ

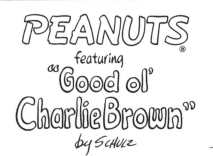

PEANUTS
featuring
"Good ol'
CharlieBrown"
by SCHULZ

I HEAR THE FLAPPING OF WINGS...

LOOK AT THAT STUPID BIRD, WILL YOU?

5-7

HE THINKS HE'S GOING TO BUILD A NEST ON TOP OF MY STOMACH...

THE NERVE OF HIM! THE UNMITIGATED GALL! HIM AND HIS TWIGS AND STRING...

BY GOLLY, I'M GOING TO FIX HIS WAGON!

THE NEXT TIME HE COMES, I'M GOING TO GIVE HIM SUCH A TUSSLE, HE WON'T KNOW WHAT HIT HIM! I'LL TWIST HIS BEAK AND TIE KNOTS IN HIS TAIL...I'LL STIR HIS FEATHERS!

GET READY, BIRD! THIS IS IT!

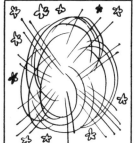

I CAN'T STAND IT!

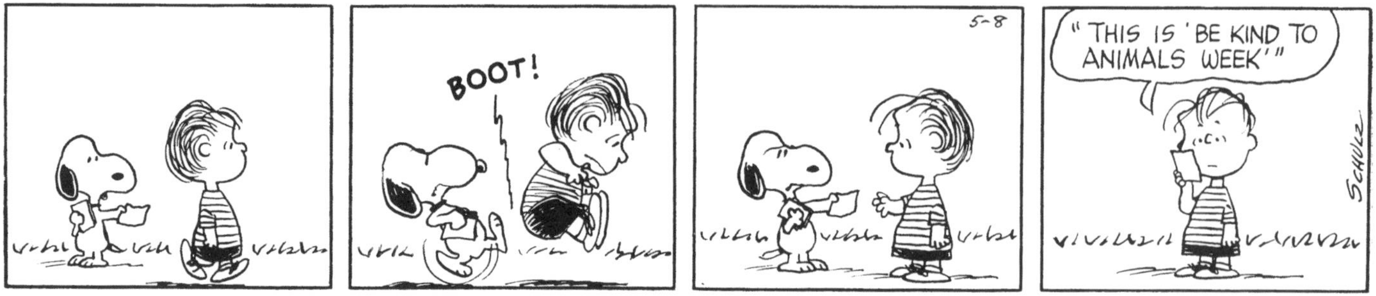
BOOT!
5-8
"THIS IS 'BE KIND TO ANIMALS WEEK'"
SCHULZ

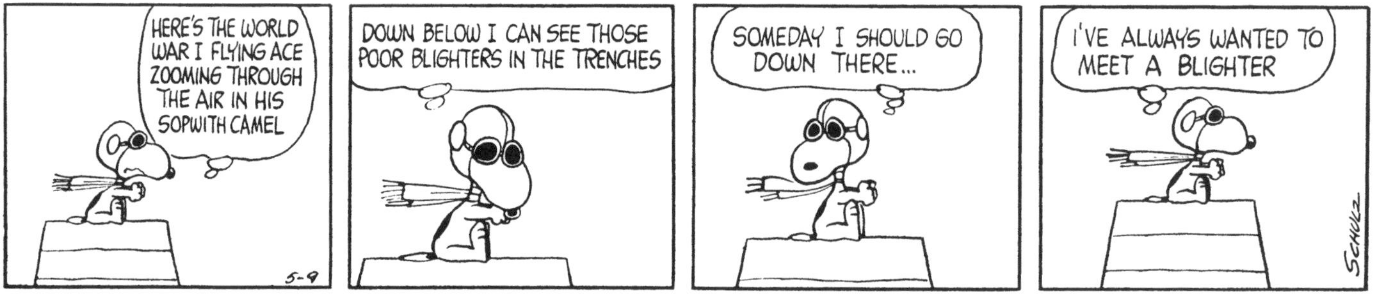
HERE'S THE WORLD WAR I FLYING ACE ZOOMING THROUGH THE AIR IN HIS SOPWITH CAMEL
5-9
DOWN BELOW I CAN SEE THOSE POOR BLIGHTERS IN THE TRENCHES
SOMEDAY I SHOULD GO DOWN THERE...
I'VE ALWAYS WANTED TO MEET A BLIGHTER
SCHULZ

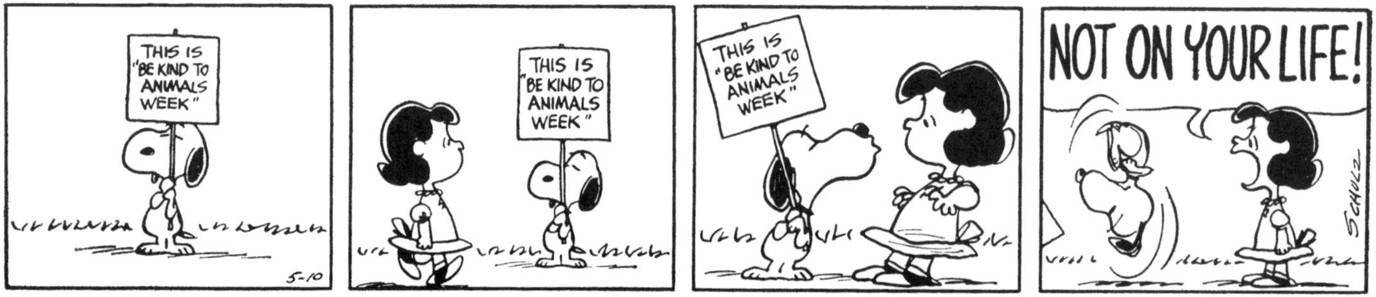
THIS IS "BE KIND TO ANIMALS WEEK"
5-10
THIS IS "BE KIND TO ANIMALS WEEK"
THIS IS "BE KIND TO ANIMALS WEEK"
NOT ON YOUR LIFE!
SCHULZ

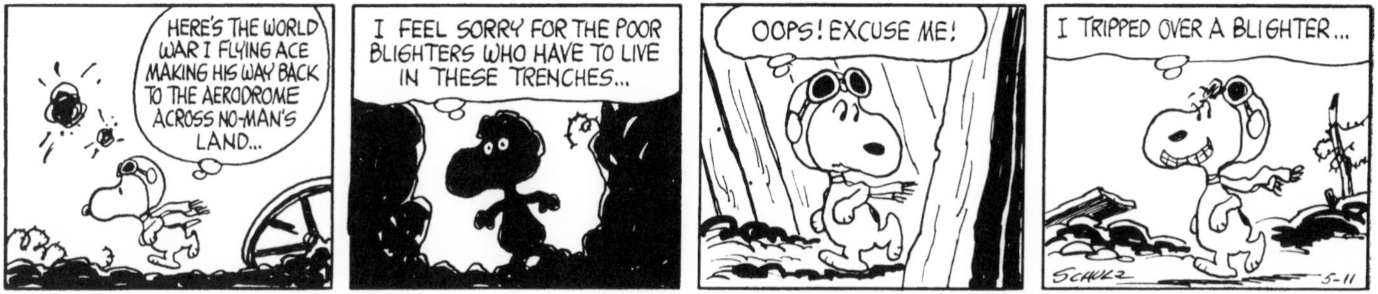
HERE'S THE WORLD WAR I FLYING ACE MAKING HIS WAY BACK TO THE AERODROME ACROSS NO-MAN'S LAND...
I FEEL SORRY FOR THE POOR BLIGHTERS WHO HAVE TO LIVE IN THESE TRENCHES...
OOPS! EXCUSE ME!
I TRIPPED OVER A BLIGHTER...
SCHULZ
5-11

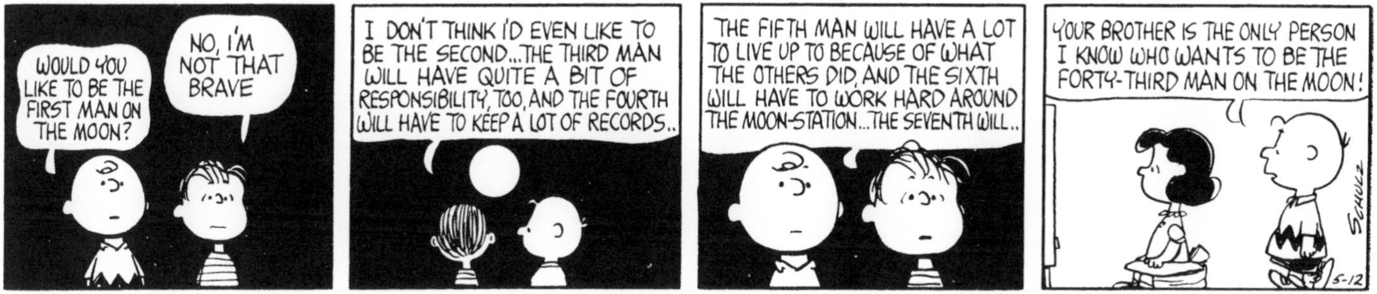
WOULD YOU LIKE TO BE THE FIRST MAN ON THE MOON?
NO, I'M NOT THAT BRAVE
I DON'T THINK I'D EVEN LIKE TO BE THE SECOND...THE THIRD MAN WILL HAVE QUITE A BIT OF RESPONSIBILITY, TOO, AND THE FOURTH WILL HAVE TO KEEP A LOT OF RECORDS..
THE FIFTH MAN WILL HAVE A LOT TO LIVE UP TO BECAUSE OF WHAT THE OTHERS DID, AND THE SIXTH WILL HAVE TO WORK HARD AROUND THE MOON-STATION...THE SEVENTH WILL..
YOUR BROTHER IS THE ONLY PERSON I KNOW WHO WANTS TO BE THE FORTY-THIRD MAN ON THE MOON!
SCHULZ
5-12

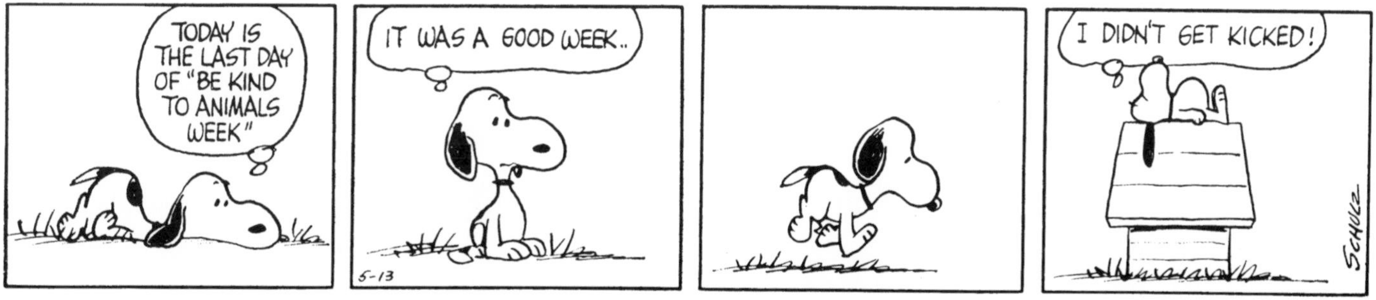
TODAY IS THE LAST DAY OF "BE KIND TO ANIMALS WEEK"
IT WAS A GOOD WEEK..
5-13
I DIDN'T GET KICKED!
SCHULZ

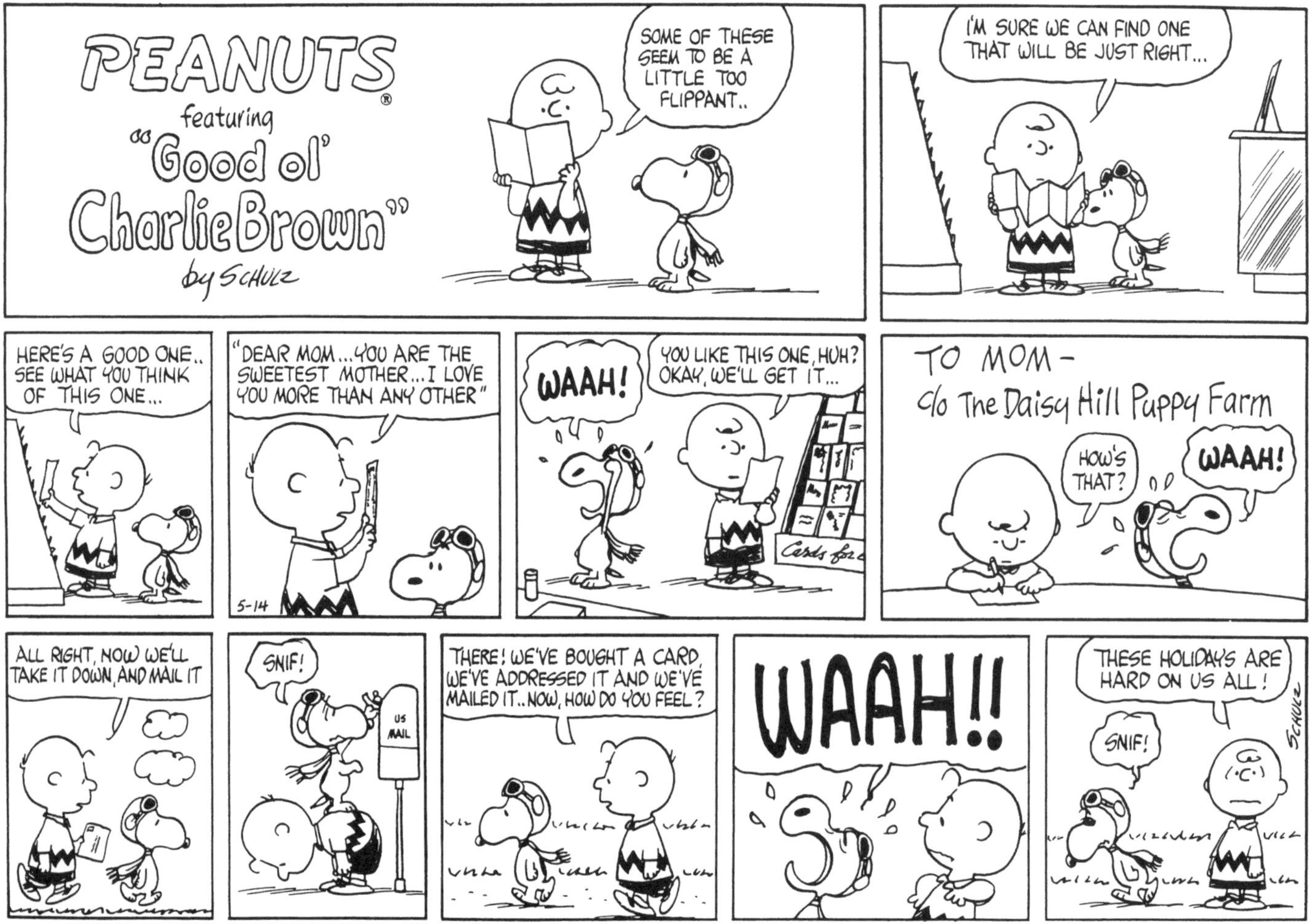
PEANUTS
featuring "Good ol' Charlie Brown"
by SCHULZ
SOME OF THESE SEEM TO BE A LITTLE TOO FLIPPANT..
I'M SURE WE CAN FIND ONE THAT WILL BE JUST RIGHT...
HERE'S A GOOD ONE.. SEE WHAT YOU THINK OF THIS ONE...
"DEAR MOM...YOU ARE THE SWEETEST MOTHER...I LOVE YOU MORE THAN ANY OTHER"
5-14
WAAH!
YOU LIKE THIS ONE, HUH? OKAY, WE'LL GET IT...
TO MOM -
c/o The Daisy Hill Puppy Farm
HOW'S THAT?
WAAH!
ALL RIGHT, NOW WE'LL TAKE IT DOWN, AND MAIL IT
SNIF!
US MAIL
THERE! WE'VE BOUGHT A CARD, WE'VE ADDRESSED IT AND WE'VE MAILED IT.. NOW, HOW DO YOU FEEL?
WAAH!!
THESE HOLIDAYS ARE HARD ON US ALL!
SNIF!
SCHULZ

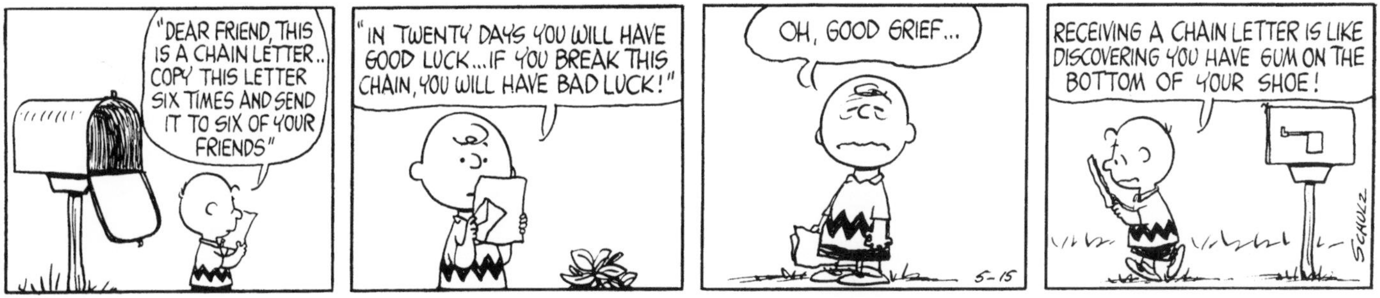
"DEAR FRIEND, THIS IS A CHAIN LETTER.. COPY THIS LETTER SIX TIMES AND SEND IT TO SIX OF YOUR FRIENDS"
"IN TWENTY DAYS YOU WILL HAVE GOOD LUCK...IF YOU BREAK THIS CHAIN, YOU WILL HAVE BAD LUCK!"
OH, GOOD GRIEF...
5-15
RECEIVING A CHAIN LETTER IS LIKE DISCOVERING YOU HAVE GUM ON THE BOTTOM OF YOUR SHOE!
SCHULZ

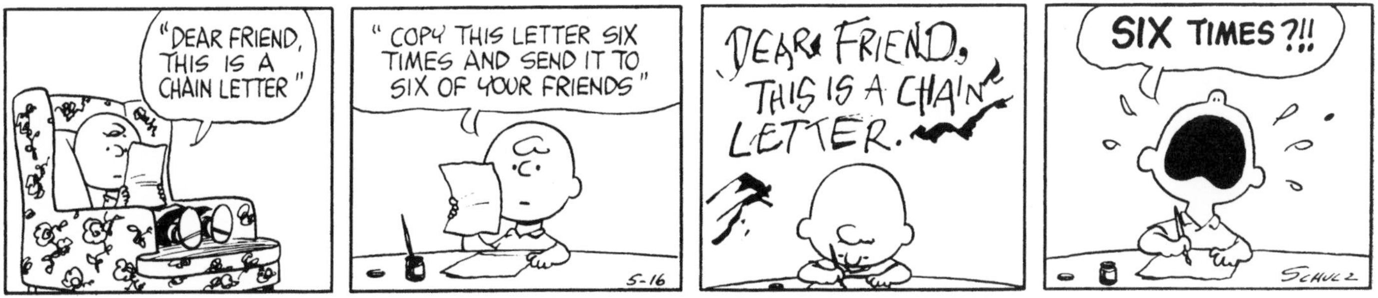
"DEAR FRIEND, THIS IS A CHAIN LETTER"
" COPY THIS LETTER SIX TIMES AND SEND IT TO SIX OF YOUR FRIENDS"
5-16
DEAR FRIEND, THIS IS A CHAIN LETTER.
SIX TIMES?!!
SCHULZ

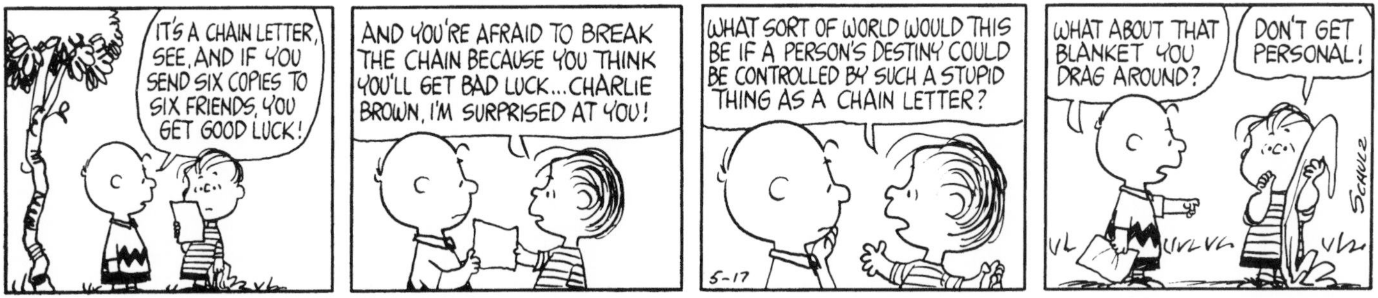
IT'S A CHAIN LETTER, SEE, AND IF YOU SEND SIX COPIES TO SIX FRIENDS, YOU GET GOOD LUCK!
AND YOU'RE AFRAID TO BREAK THE CHAIN BECAUSE YOU THINK YOU'LL GET BAD LUCK...CHARLIE BROWN, I'M SURPRISED AT YOU!
WHAT SORT OF WORLD WOULD THIS BE IF A PERSON'S DESTINY COULD BE CONTROLLED BY SUCH A STUPID THING AS A CHAIN LETTER?
5-17
WHAT ABOUT THAT BLANKET YOU DRAG AROUND?
DON'T GET PERSONAL!
SCHULZ

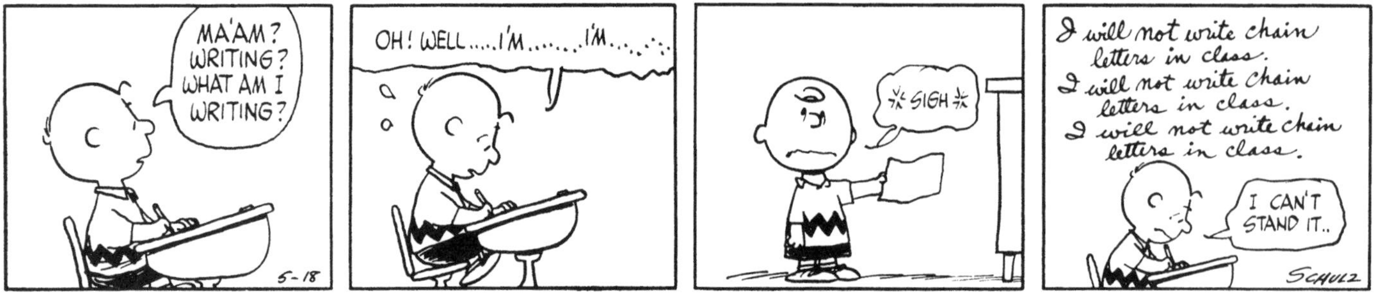
MA'AM? WRITING? WHAT AM I WRITING?
5-18
OH! WELL.....I'M.......I'M.......
SIGH
I will not write chain letters in class.
I will not write chain letters in class.
I will not write chain letters in class.
I CAN'T STAND IT..
SCHULZ

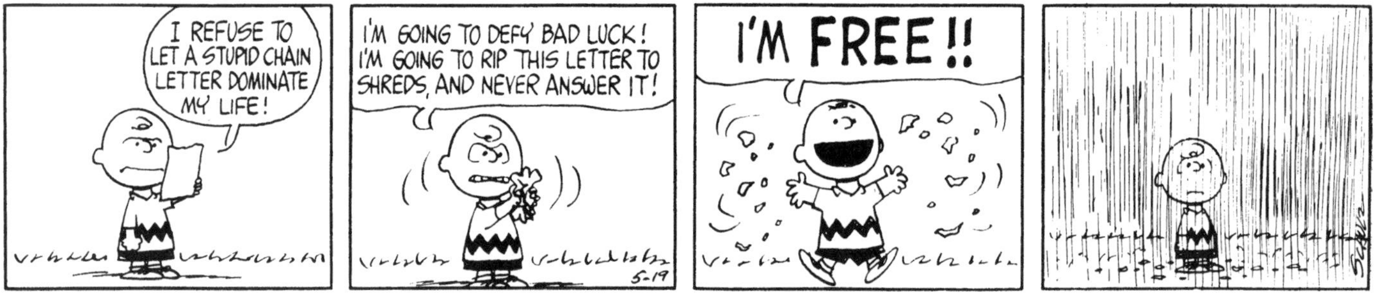
I REFUSE TO LET A STUPID CHAIN LETTER DOMINATE MY LIFE!
I'M GOING TO DEFY BAD LUCK! I'M GOING TO RIP THIS LETTER TO SHREDS, AND NEVER ANSWER IT!
5-19
I'M FREE!!
SCHULZ

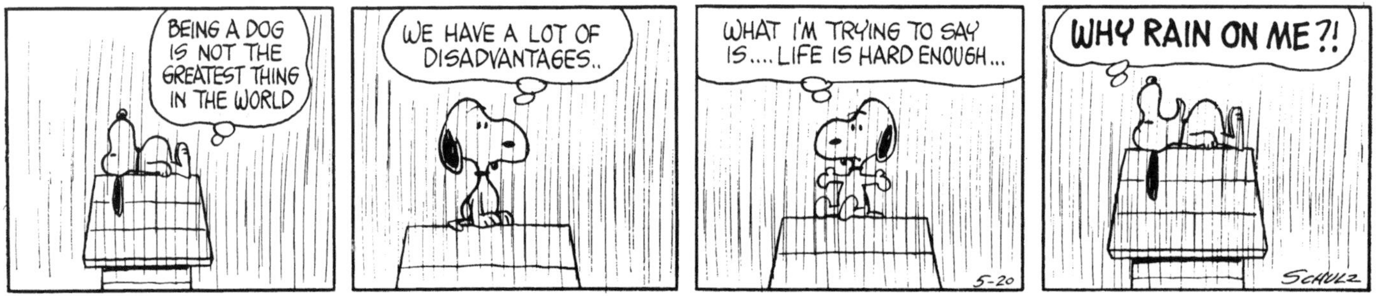
BEING A DOG IS NOT THE GREATEST THING IN THE WORLD
WE HAVE A LOT OF DISADVANTAGES..
WHAT I'M TRYING TO SAY IS.... LIFE IS HARD ENOUGH...
5-20
WHY RAIN ON ME?!
SCHULZ

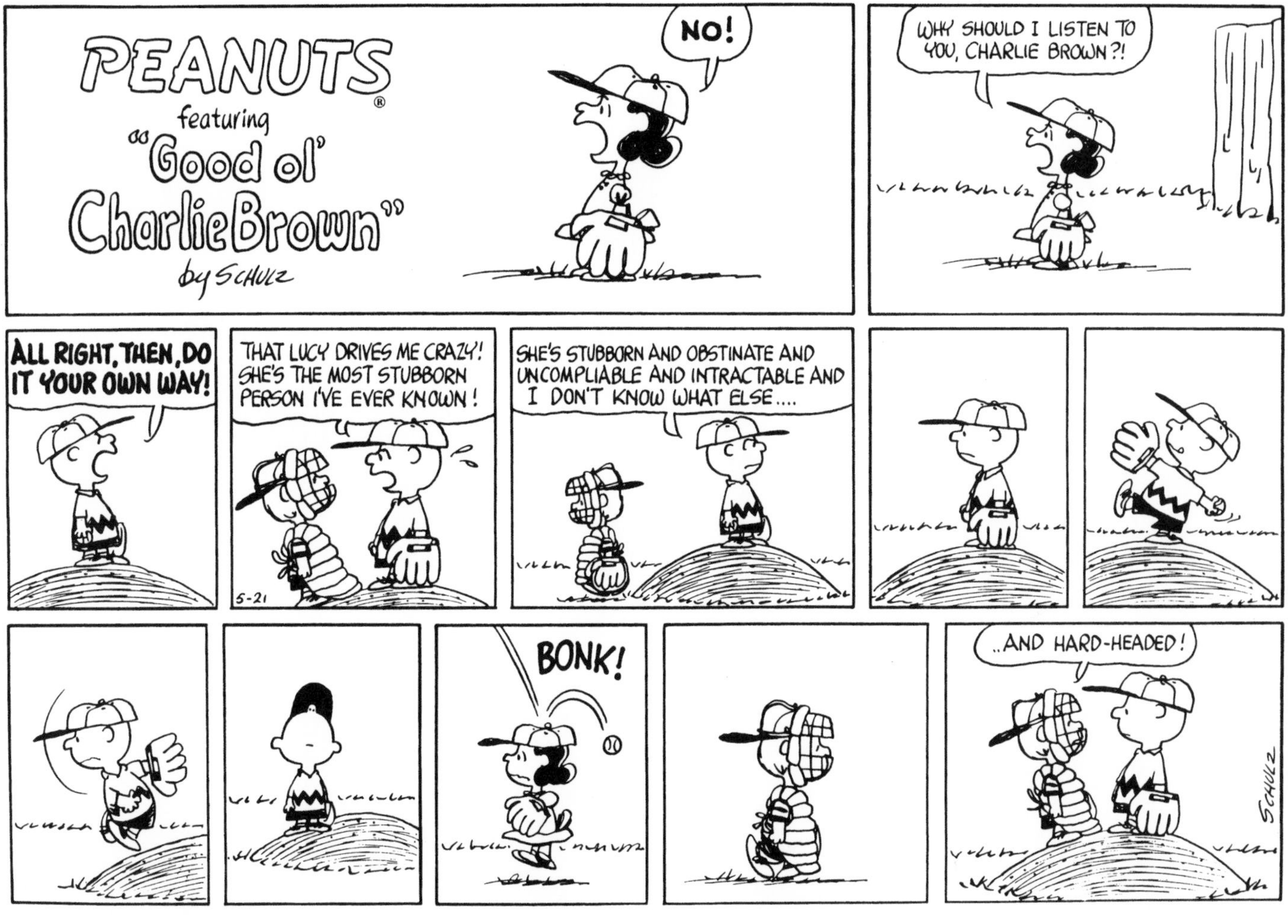
PEANUTS®
featuring "Good ol' CharlieBrown"
by SCHULZ
NO!
WHY SHOULD I LISTEN TO YOU, CHARLIE BROWN?!
ALL RIGHT, THEN, DO IT YOUR OWN WAY!
THAT LUCY DRIVES ME CRAZY! SHE'S THE MOST STUBBORN PERSON I'VE EVER KNOWN!
5-21
SHE'S STUBBORN AND OBSTINATE AND UNCOMPLIABLE AND INTRACTABLE AND I DON'T KNOW WHAT ELSE....
BONK!
..AND HARD-HEADED!
SCHULZ

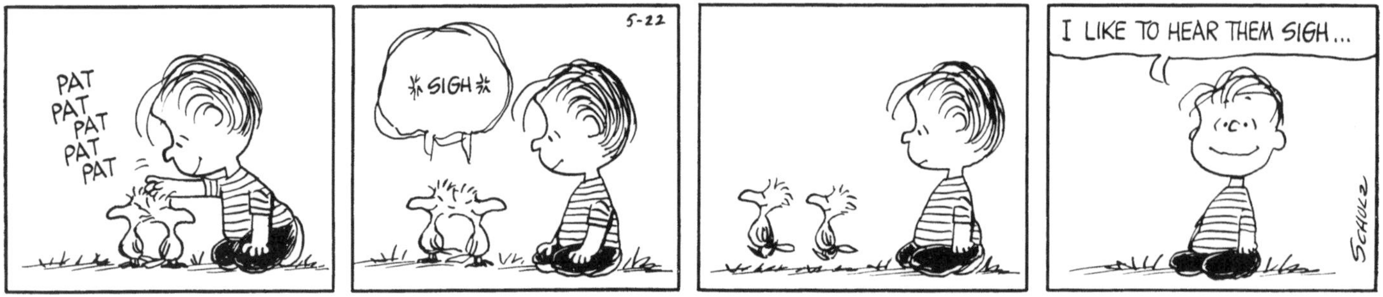
PAT
PAT
PAT
PAT
PAT
5-22
SIGH
I LIKE TO HEAR THEM SIGH...
SCHULZ

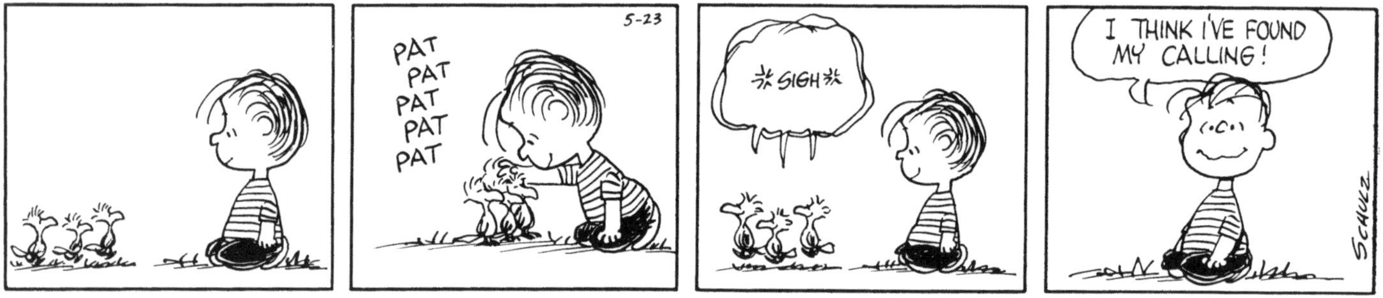
5-23
PAT
PAT
PAT
PAT
PAT
SIGH
I THINK I'VE FOUND MY CALLING!
SCHULZ

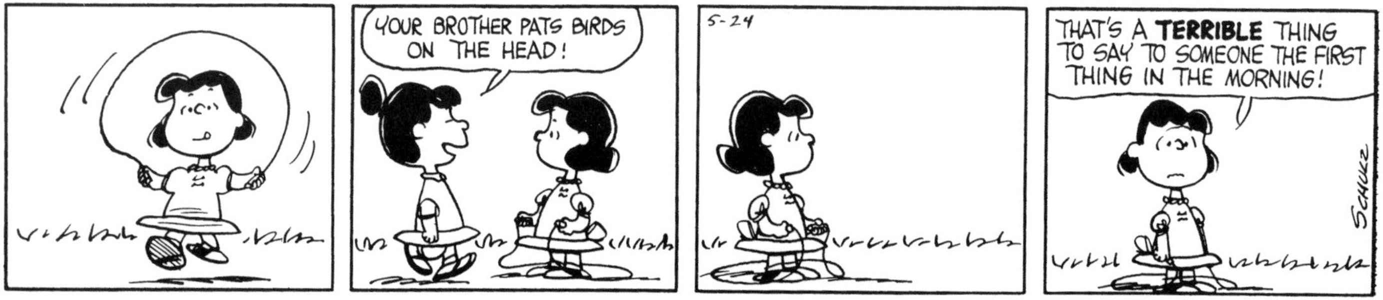
YOUR BROTHER PATS BIRDS ON THE HEAD!
5-24
THAT'S A **TERRIBLE** THING TO SAY TO SOMEONE THE FIRST THING IN THE MORNING!
SCHULZ

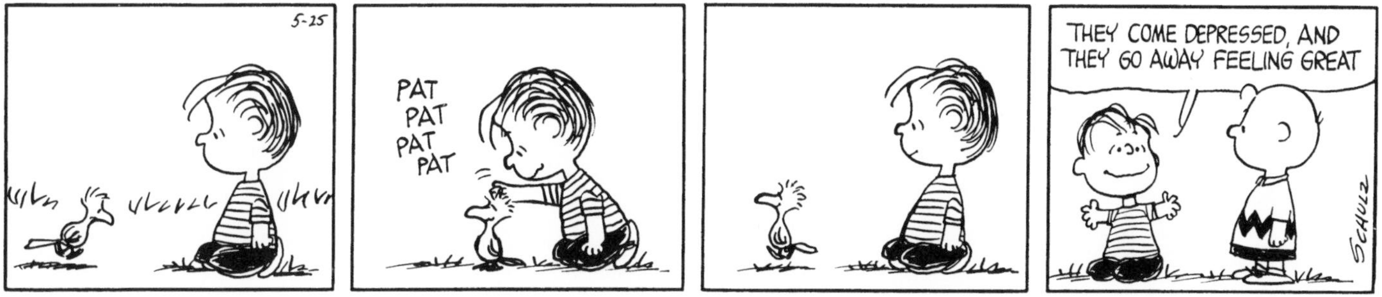
5-25
PAT
PAT
PAT
PAT
THEY COME DEPRESSED, AND THEY GO AWAY FEELING GREAT
SCHULZ

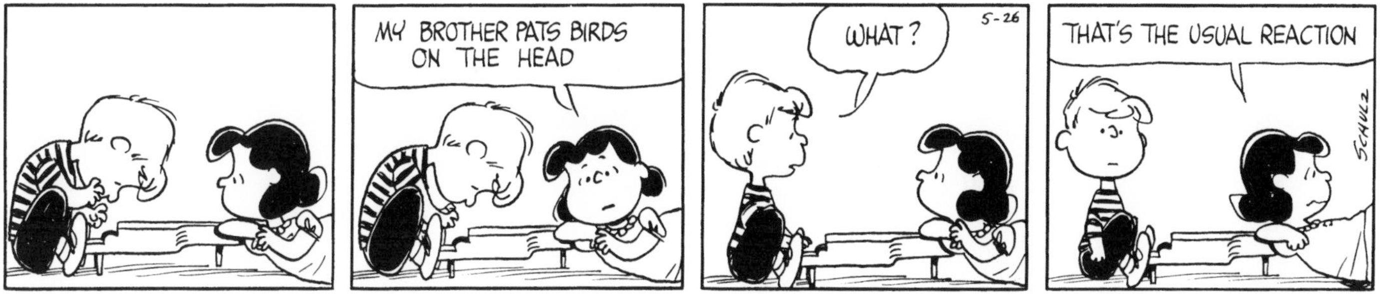
MY BROTHER PATS BIRDS ON THE HEAD
5-26
WHAT?
THAT'S THE USUAL REACTION
SCHULZ

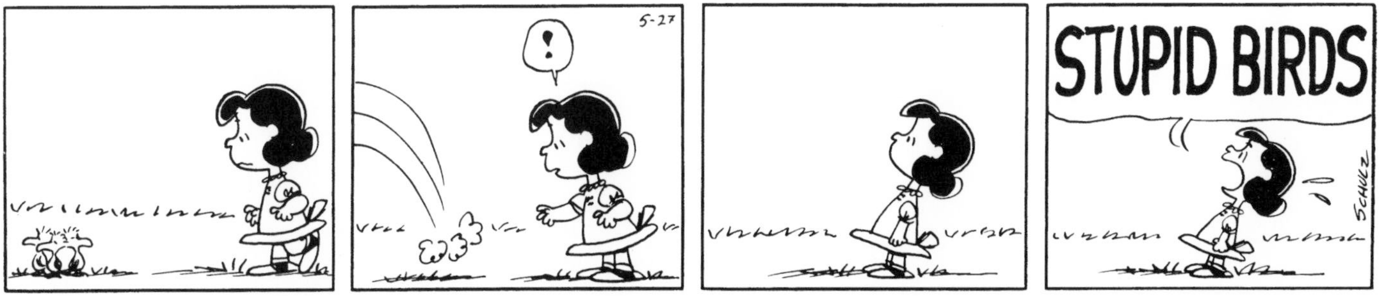
5-27
!
STUPID BIRDS
SCHULZ

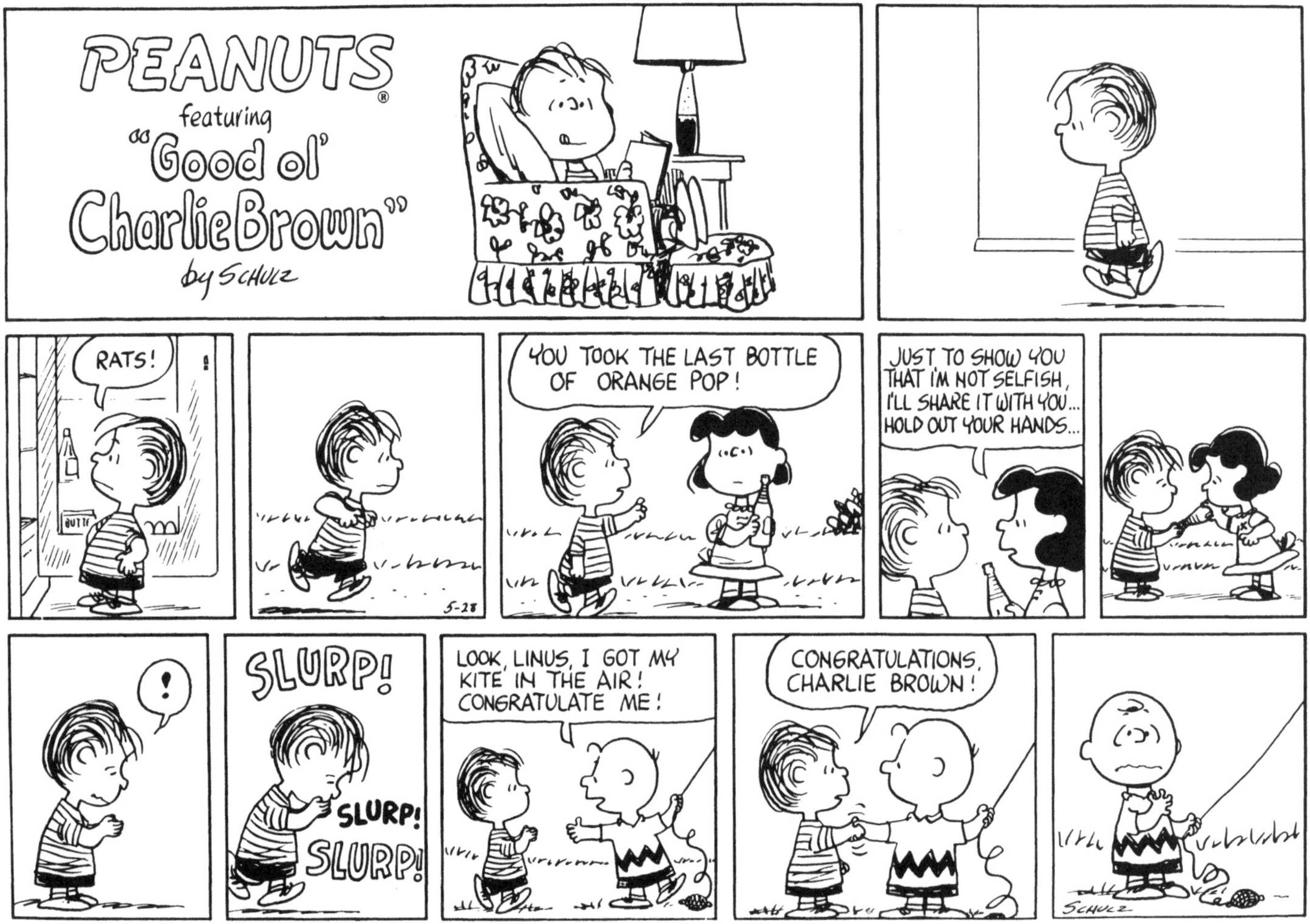
PEANUTS®
featuring
"Good ol' Charlie Brown"
by SCHULZ
RATS!
5-28
YOU TOOK THE LAST BOTTLE OF ORANGE POP!
JUST TO SHOW YOU THAT I'M NOT SELFISH, I'LL SHARE IT WITH YOU... HOLD OUT YOUR HANDS...
!
SLURP!
SLURP!
SLURP!
LOOK, LINUS, I GOT MY KITE IN THE AIR! CONGRATULATE ME!
CONGRATULATIONS, CHARLIE BROWN!
SCHULZ

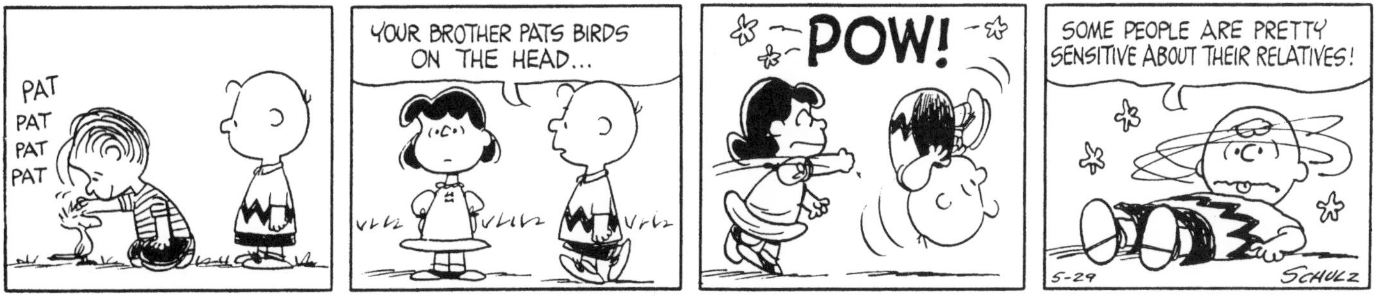
PAT
PAT
PAT
PAT
YOUR BROTHER PATS BIRDS ON THE HEAD...
POW!
SOME PEOPLE ARE PRETTY SENSITIVE ABOUT THEIR RELATIVES!
5-29
SCHULZ

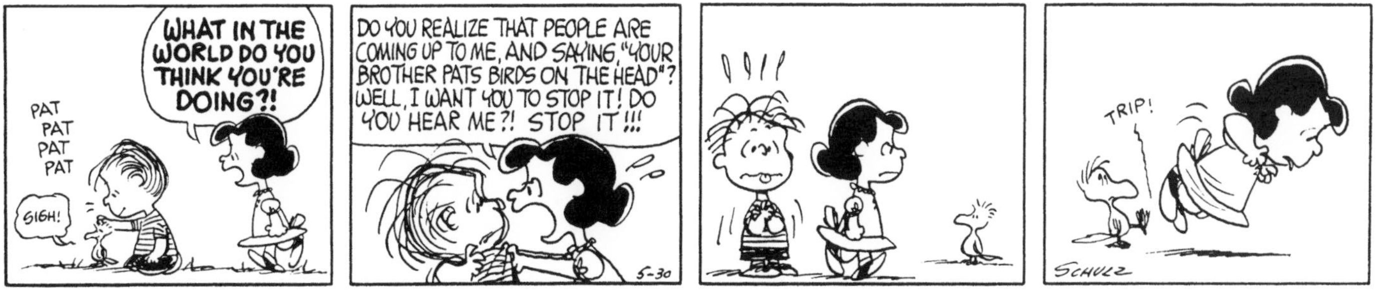
WHAT IN THE WORLD DO YOU THINK YOU'RE DOING?!
PAT
PAT
PAT
PAT
SIGH!
DO YOU REALIZE THAT PEOPLE ARE COMING UP TO ME, AND SAYING, "YOUR BROTHER PATS BIRDS ON THE HEAD"? WELL, I WANT YOU TO STOP IT! DO YOU HEAR ME?! STOP IT!!!
5-30
TRIP!
SCHULZ

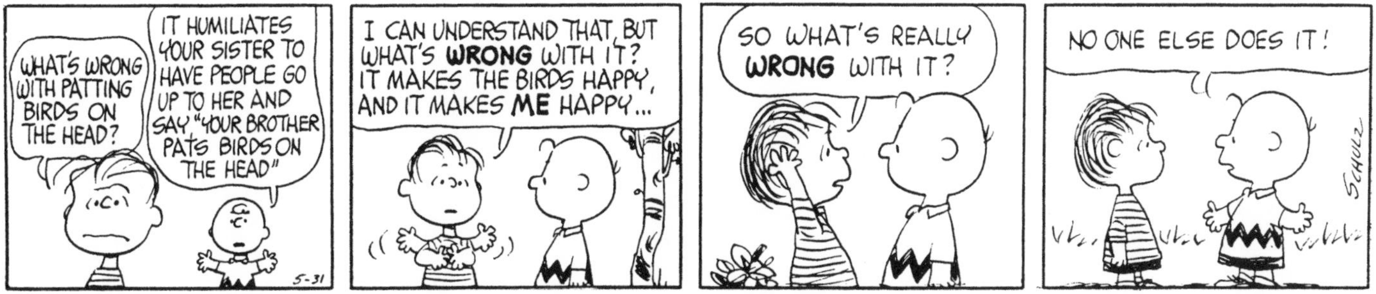
WHAT'S WRONG WITH PATTING BIRDS ON THE HEAD?
IT HUMILIATES YOUR SISTER TO HAVE PEOPLE GO UP TO HER AND SAY "YOUR BROTHER PATS BIRDS ON THE HEAD"
5-31
I CAN UNDERSTAND THAT, BUT WHAT'S WRONG WITH IT? IT MAKES THE BIRDS HAPPY, AND IT MAKES ME HAPPY...
SO WHAT'S REALLY WRONG WITH IT?
NO ONE ELSE DOES IT!
SCHULZ

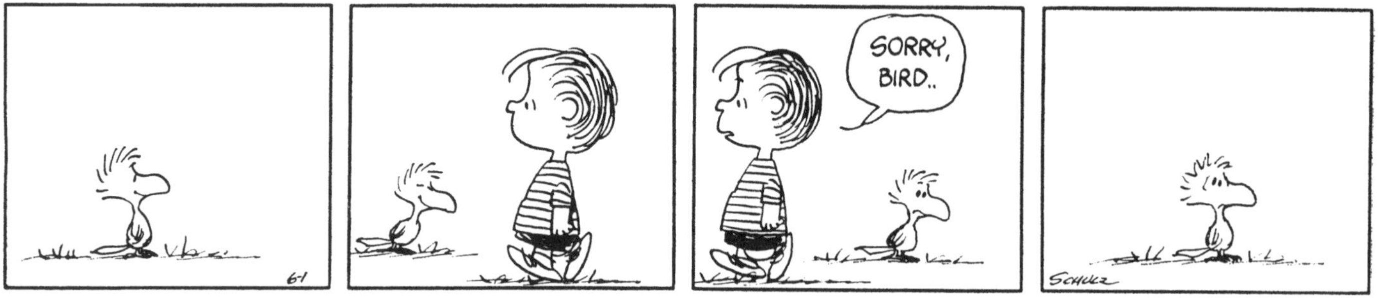
SORRY, BIRD..

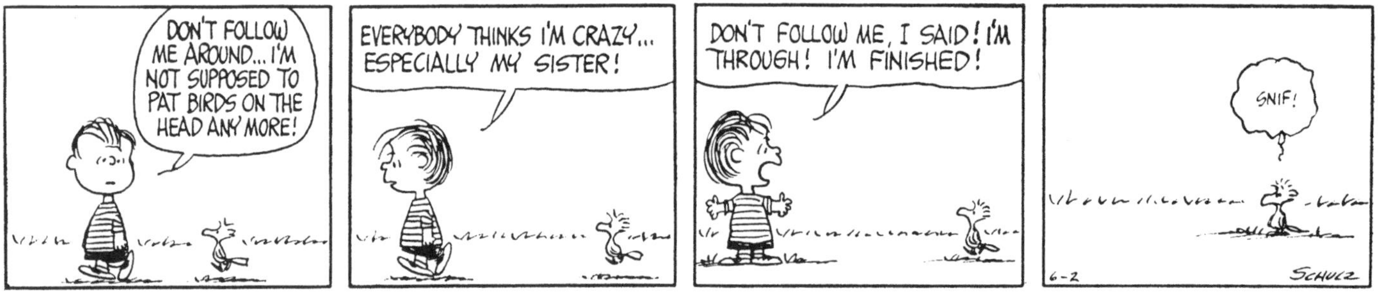
DON'T FOLLOW ME AROUND... I'M NOT SUPPOSED TO PAT BIRDS ON THE HEAD ANY MORE!
EVERYBODY THINKS I'M CRAZY... ESPECIALLY MY SISTER!
DON'T FOLLOW ME, I SAID! I'M THROUGH! I'M FINISHED!
SNIF!

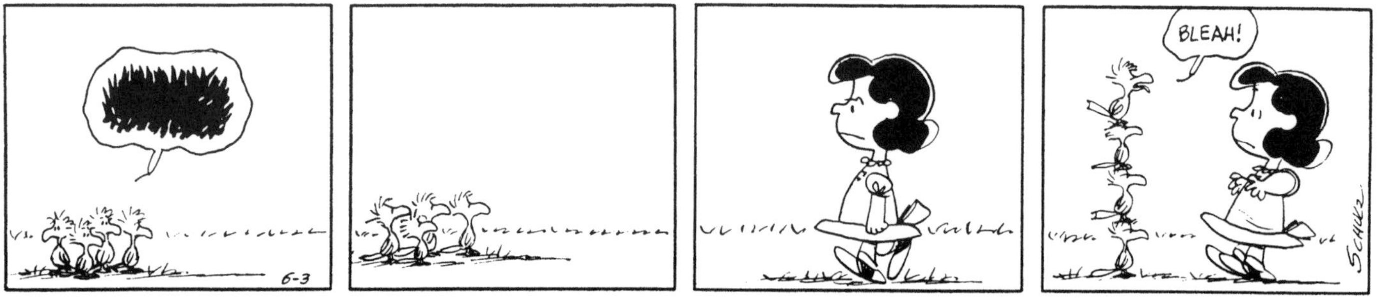
BLEAH!

PEANUTS®
featuring
"Good ol' Charlie Brown"
by SCHULZ
Z
RAP! RAP! RAP!
RAP! RAP!
NOW I'M WIDE AWAKE, AND MY WHOLE ROOM SMELLS LIKE A WET DOG!
6-4
SCHULZ

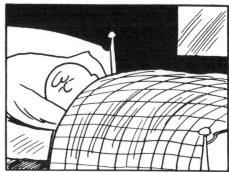

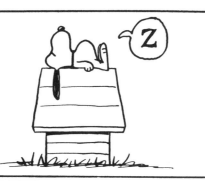

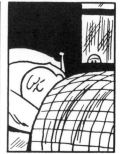

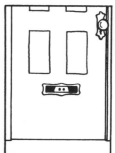

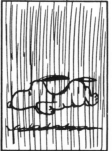

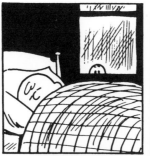

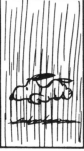

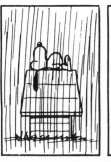

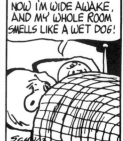

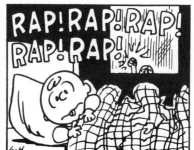

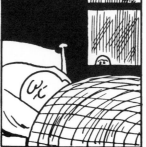

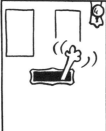

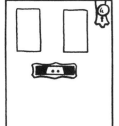

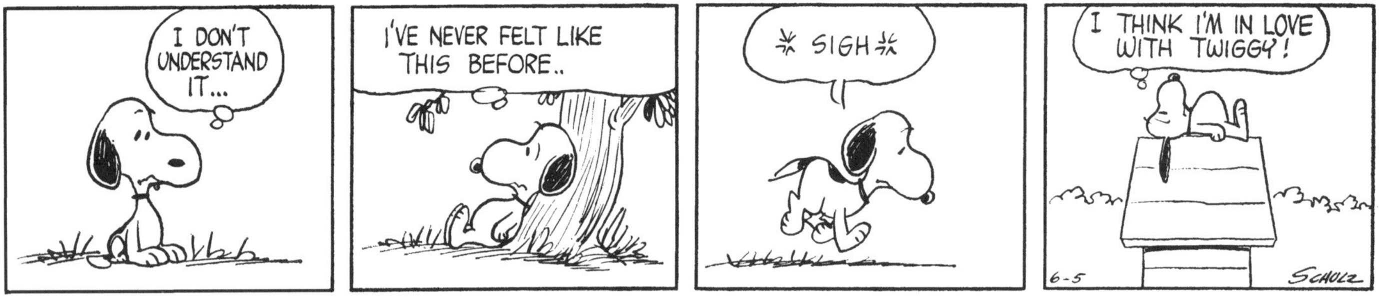
I DON'T UNDERSTAND IT...
I'VE NEVER FELT LIKE THIS BEFORE..
SIGH
I THINK I'M IN LOVE WITH TWIGGY!
6-5
SCHULZ

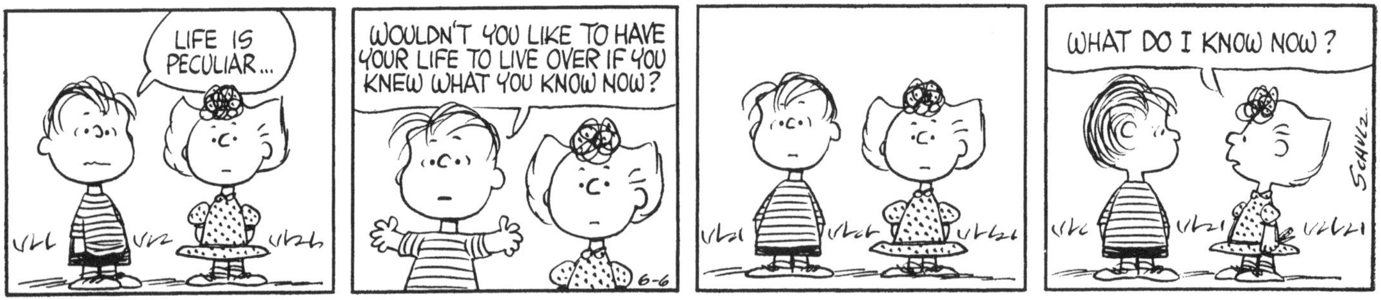
LIFE IS PECULIAR...
WOULDN'T YOU LIKE TO HAVE YOUR LIFE TO LIVE OVER IF YOU KNEW WHAT YOU KNOW NOW?
6-6
WHAT DO I KNOW NOW?
SCHULZ

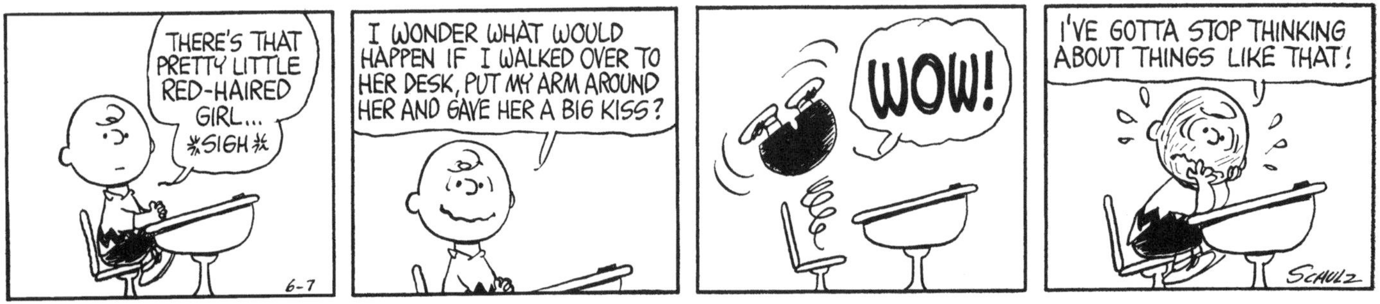
THERE'S THAT PRETTY LITTLE RED-HAIRED GIRL... *SIGH*
6-7
I WONDER WHAT WOULD HAPPEN IF I WALKED OVER TO HER DESK, PUT MY ARM AROUND HER AND GAVE HER A BIG KISS?
WOW!
I'VE GOTTA STOP THINKING ABOUT THINGS LIKE THAT!
SCHULZ

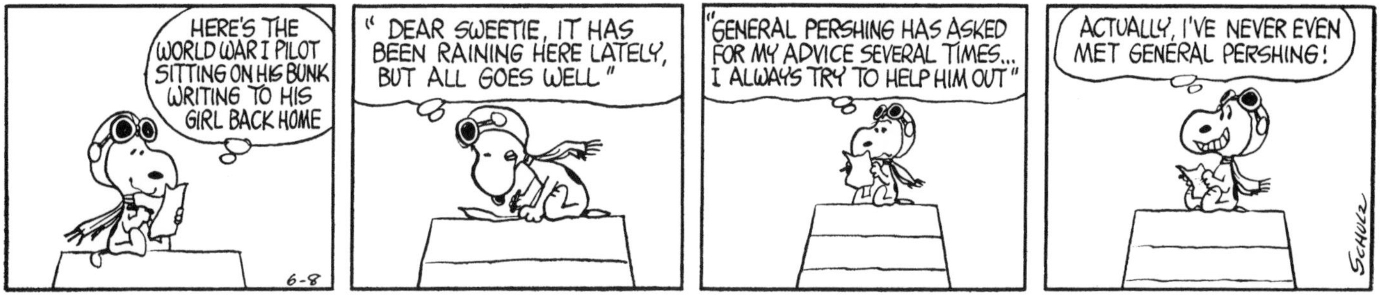
HERE'S THE WORLD WAR I PILOT SITTING ON HIS BUNK WRITING TO HIS GIRL BACK HOME
6-8
" DEAR SWEETIE, IT HAS BEEN RAINING HERE LATELY, BUT ALL GOES WELL "
"GENERAL PERSHING HAS ASKED FOR MY ADVICE SEVERAL TIMES... I ALWAYS TRY TO HELP HIM OUT"
ACTUALLY, I'VE NEVER EVEN MET GENERAL PERSHING!
SCHULZ

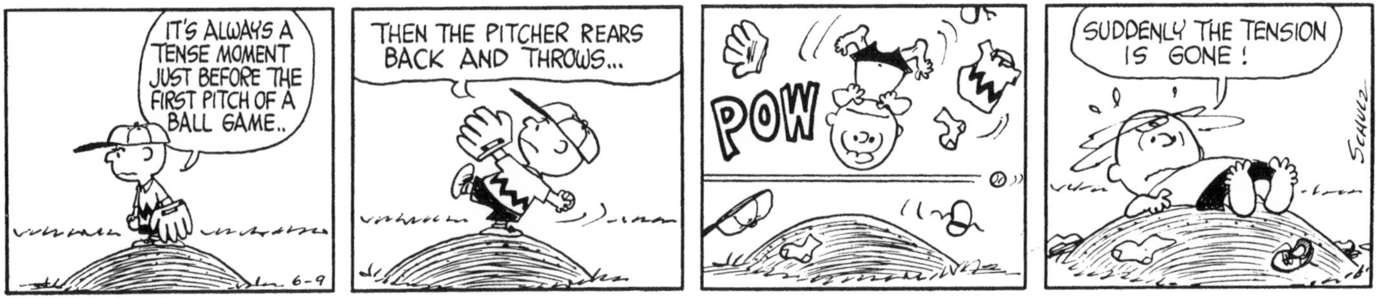
IT'S ALWAYS A TENSE MOMENT JUST BEFORE THE FIRST PITCH OF A BALL GAME..
6-9
THEN THE PITCHER REARS BACK AND THROWS...
POW
SUDDENLY THE TENSION IS GONE!
SCHULZ

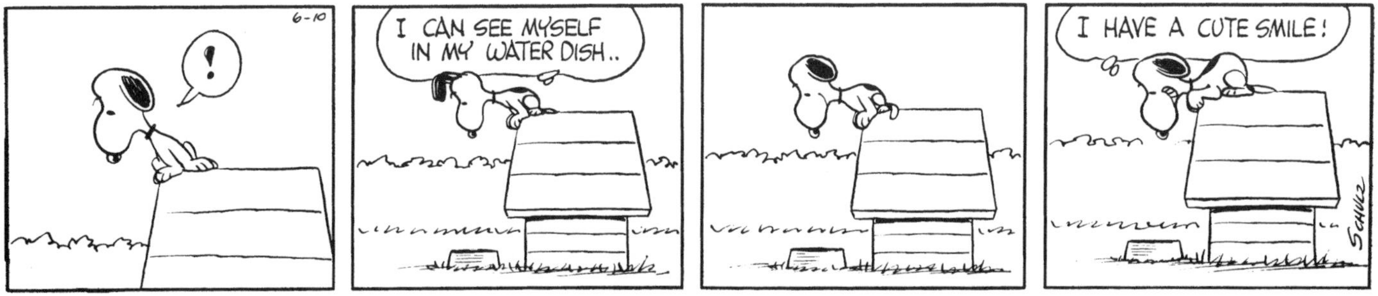
6-10
!
I CAN SEE MYSELF IN MY WATER DISH..
I HAVE A CUTE SMILE!
SCHULZ

PEANUTS featuring "Good ol' Charlie Brown" by Schulz

THANK YOU

YOU'RE WELCOME

BRING YOUR ROOT BEER IN HERE, CHARLIE BROWN..WE'LL SIT AND WATCH TV

SNIF?

YOU SNIFFED IN MY ROOT BEER!

YOUR STUPID DOG SNIFFED IN MY ROOT BEER!!

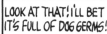

LOOK AT THAT! I'LL BET IT'S FULL OF DOG GERMS!

WHERE'S MY BINOCULARS?

BINOCULARS?

AH, HA! I THOUGHT SO!

SEE? I POURED A LITTLE ROOT BEER IN THIS SAUCER AND EXAMINED IT WITH MY BINOCULARS...IT'S FULL OF DOG GERMS!

I GUESS THAT WHOLE BUSINESS WAS MY FAULT, SNOOPY... I'VE NEVER DISCUSSED ETIQUETTE WITH YOU...

THERE'S ONE THING YOU SHOULD NEVER DO...NEVER SNIFF IN YOUR HOSTESS'S ROOT BEER!

I'LL REMEMBER THAT...

NEXT TIME I'LL BITE HER LEG!

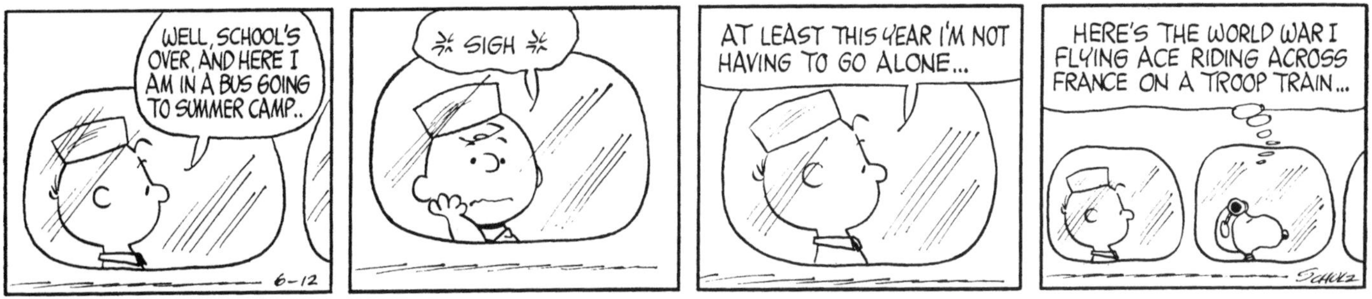
WELL, SCHOOL'S OVER, AND HERE I AM IN A BUS GOING TO SUMMER CAMP..
6-12
* SIGH *
AT LEAST THIS YEAR I'M NOT HAVING TO GO ALONE...
HERE'S THE WORLD WAR I FLYING ACE RIDING ACROSS FRANCE ON A TROOP TRAIN...
SCHULZ

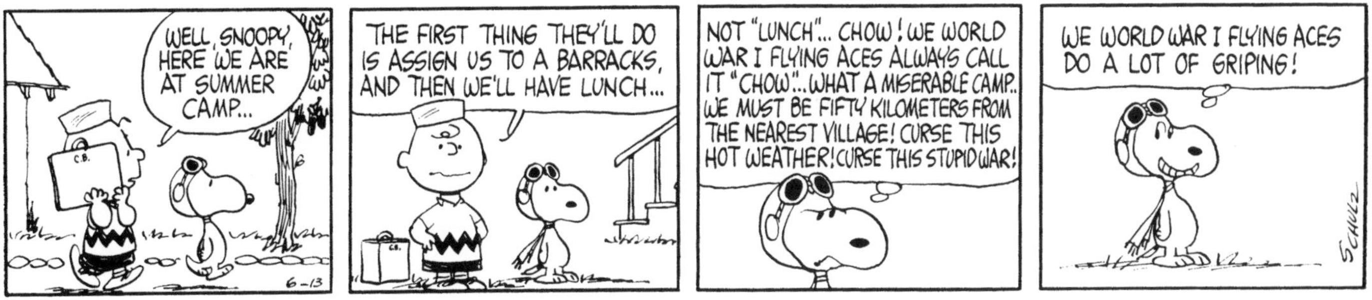
WELL, SNOOPY, HERE WE ARE AT SUMMER CAMP...
C.B.
6-13
THE FIRST THING THEY'LL DO IS ASSIGN US TO A BARRACKS, AND THEN WE'LL HAVE LUNCH...
C.B.
NOT "LUNCH"... CHOW! WE WORLD WAR I FLYING ACES ALWAYS CALL IT "CHOW"...WHAT A MISERABLE CAMP.. WE MUST BE FIFTY KILOMETERS FROM THE NEAREST VILLAGE! CURSE THIS HOT WEATHER! CURSE THIS STUPID WAR!
WE WORLD WAR I FLYING ACES DO A LOT OF GRIPING!
SCHULZ

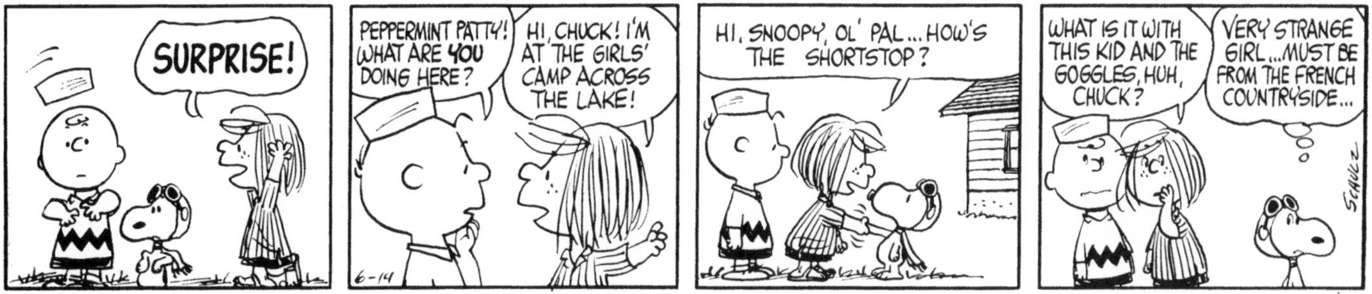
SURPRISE!
PEPPERMINT PATTY! WHAT ARE **YOU** DOING HERE?
HI, CHUCK! I'M AT THE GIRLS' CAMP ACROSS THE LAKE!
6-14
HI, SNOOPY, OL' PAL... HOW'S THE SHORTSTOP?
WHAT IS IT WITH THIS KID AND THE GOGGLES, HUH, CHUCK?
VERY STRANGE GIRL...MUST BE FROM THE FRENCH COUNTRYSIDE...
SCHULZ

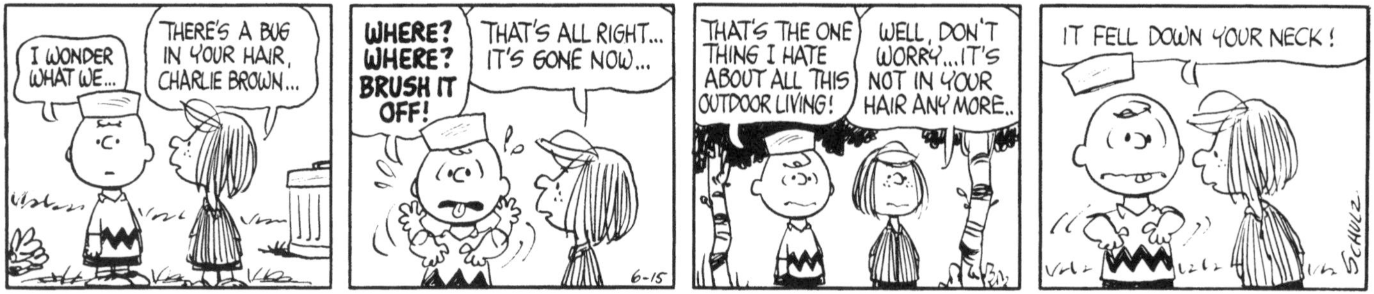
I WONDER WHAT WE...
THERE'S A BUG IN YOUR HAIR, CHARLIE BROWN...
WHERE? WHERE? BRUSH IT OFF!
THAT'S ALL RIGHT... IT'S GONE NOW...
6-15
THAT'S THE ONE THING I HATE ABOUT ALL THIS OUTDOOR LIVING!
WELL, DON'T WORRY...IT'S NOT IN YOUR HAIR ANY MORE..
IT FELL DOWN YOUR NECK!
SCHULZ

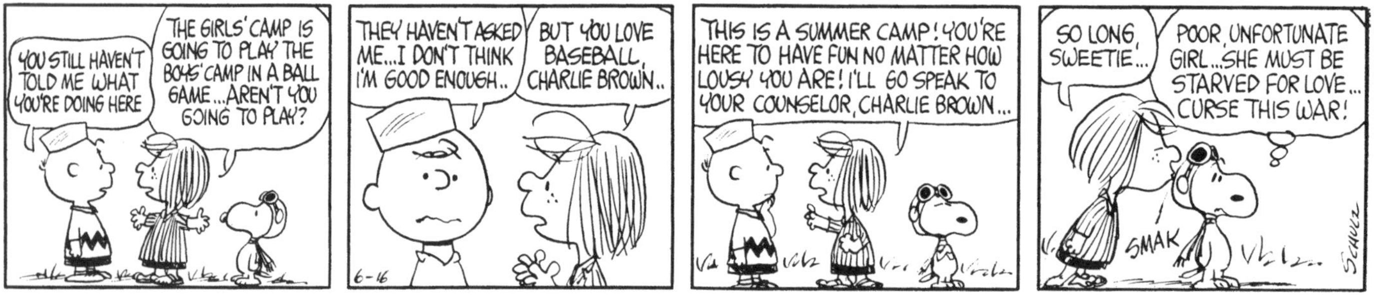
YOU STILL HAVEN'T TOLD ME WHAT YOU'RE DOING HERE
THE GIRLS' CAMP IS GOING TO PLAY THE BOYS' CAMP IN A BALL GAME...AREN'T YOU GOING TO PLAY?
THEY HAVEN'T ASKED ME...I DON'T THINK I'M GOOD ENOUGH..
BUT YOU LOVE BASEBALL, CHARLIE BROWN..
6-16
THIS IS A SUMMER CAMP! YOU'RE HERE TO HAVE FUN NO MATTER HOW LOUSY YOU ARE! I'LL GO SPEAK TO YOUR COUNSELOR, CHARLIE BROWN...
SO LONG, SWEETIE!...
POOR, UNFORTUNATE GIRL...SHE MUST BE STARVED FOR LOVE... CURSE THIS WAR!
SMAK
SCHULZ

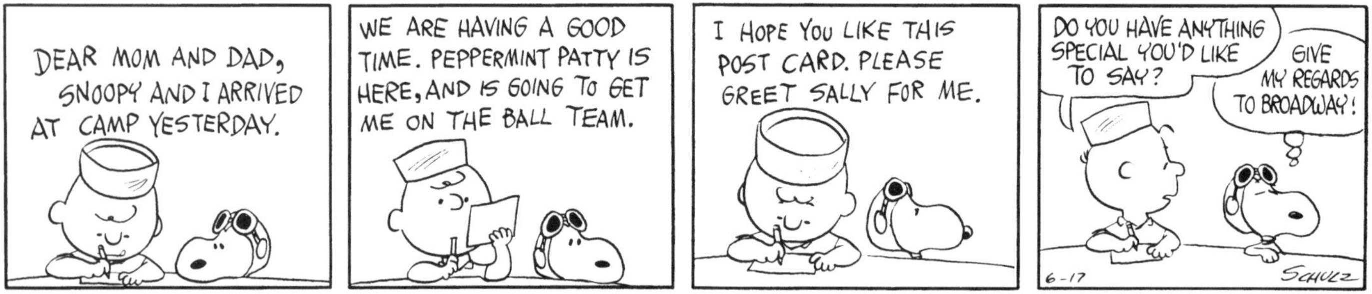
DEAR MOM AND DAD, SNOOPY AND I ARRIVED AT CAMP YESTERDAY.
WE ARE HAVING A GOOD TIME. PEPPERMINT PATTY IS HERE, AND IS GOING TO GET ME ON THE BALL TEAM.
I HOPE YOU LIKE THIS POST CARD. PLEASE GREET SALLY FOR ME.
DO YOU HAVE ANYTHING SPECIAL YOU'D LIKE TO SAY?
GIVE MY REGARDS TO BROADWAY!
6-17
SCHULZ

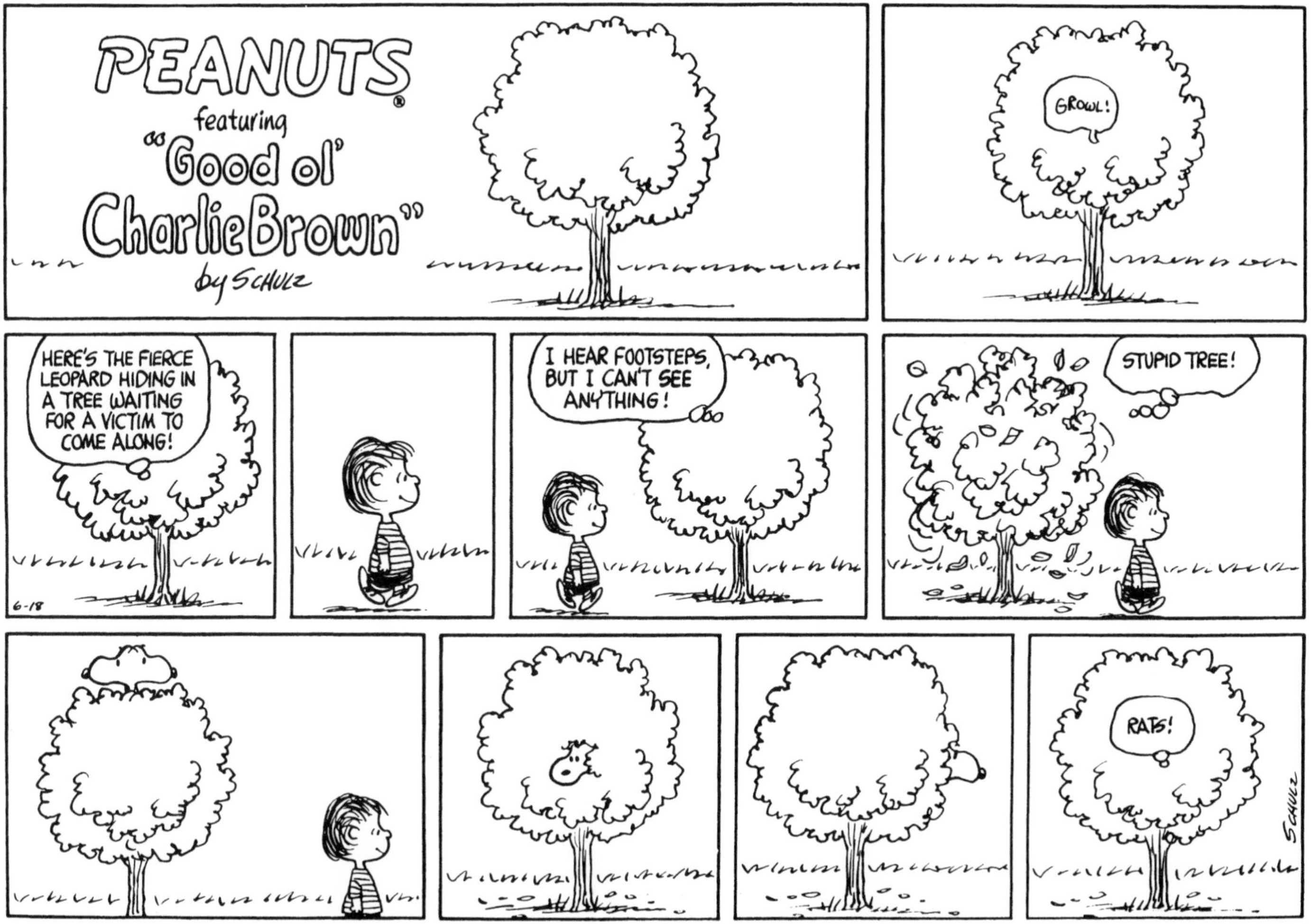
PEANUTS®
featuring
"Good ol' Charlie Brown"
by SCHULZ
GROWL!
HERE'S THE FIERCE LEOPARD HIDING IN A TREE WAITING FOR A VICTIM TO COME ALONG!
6-18
I HEAR FOOTSTEPS, BUT I CAN'T SEE ANYTHING!
STUPID TREE!
RATS!
SCHULZ

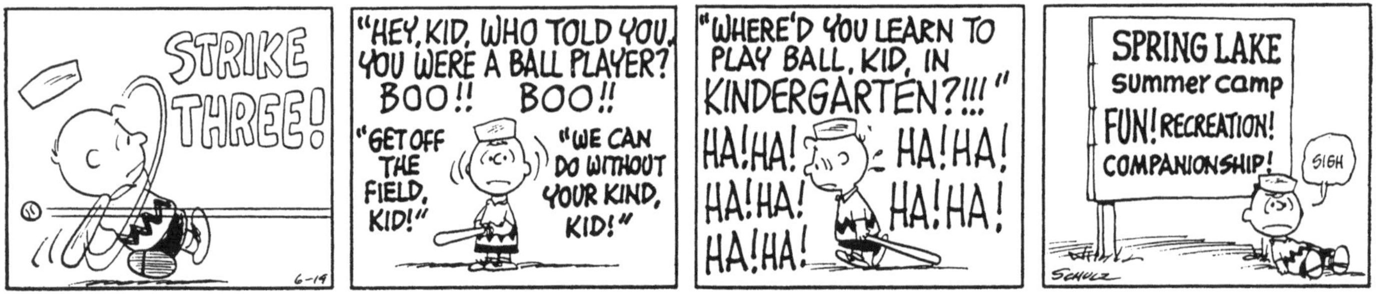
STRIKE THREE!
6-19
"HEY, KID, WHO TOLD YOU YOU WERE A BALL PLAYER? BOO!! BOO!!
"GET OFF THE FIELD, KID!"
"WE CAN DO WITHOUT YOUR KIND, KID!"
"WHERE'D YOU LEARN TO PLAY BALL, KID, IN KINDERGARTEN?!!!"
HA! HA! HA! HA! HA! HA! HA! HA! HA! HA!
SPRING LAKE summer camp FUN! RECREATION! COMPANIONSHIP!
SIGH
SCHULZ

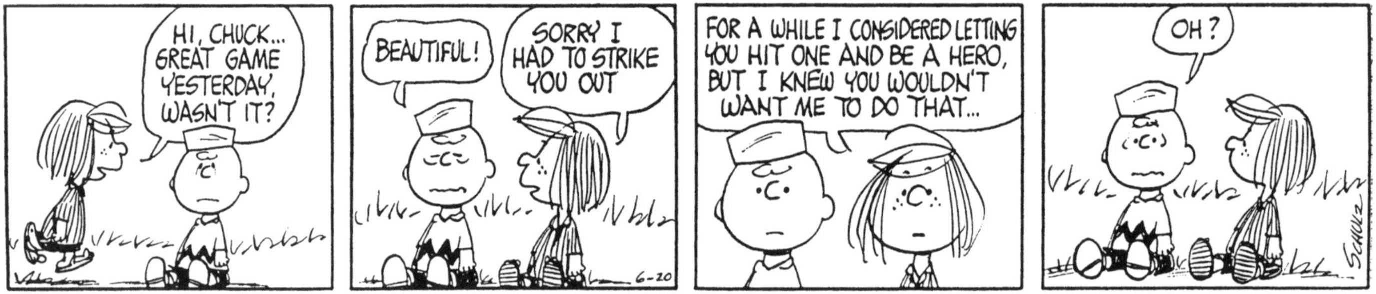
HI, CHUCK... GREAT GAME YESTERDAY, WASN'T IT?
BEAUTIFUL!
SORRY I HAD TO STRIKE YOU OUT
6-20
FOR A WHILE I CONSIDERED LETTING YOU HIT ONE AND BE A HERO, BUT I KNEW YOU WOULDN'T WANT ME TO DO THAT...
OH?
SCHULZ

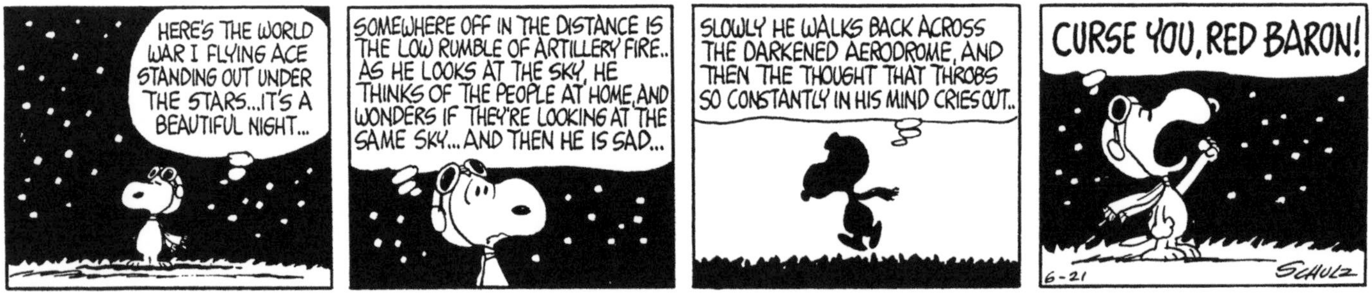
HERE'S THE WORLD WAR I FLYING ACE STANDING OUT UNDER THE STARS...IT'S A BEAUTIFUL NIGHT...
SOMEWHERE OFF IN THE DISTANCE IS THE LOW RUMBLE OF ARTILLERY FIRE.. AS HE LOOKS AT THE SKY, HE THINKS OF THE PEOPLE AT HOME, AND WONDERS IF THEY'RE LOOKING AT THE SAME SKY...AND THEN HE IS SAD...
SLOWLY HE WALKS BACK ACROSS THE DARKENED AERODROME, AND THEN THE THOUGHT THAT THROBS SO CONSTANTLY IN HIS MIND CRIES OUT..
CURSE YOU, RED BARON!
6-21
SCHULZ

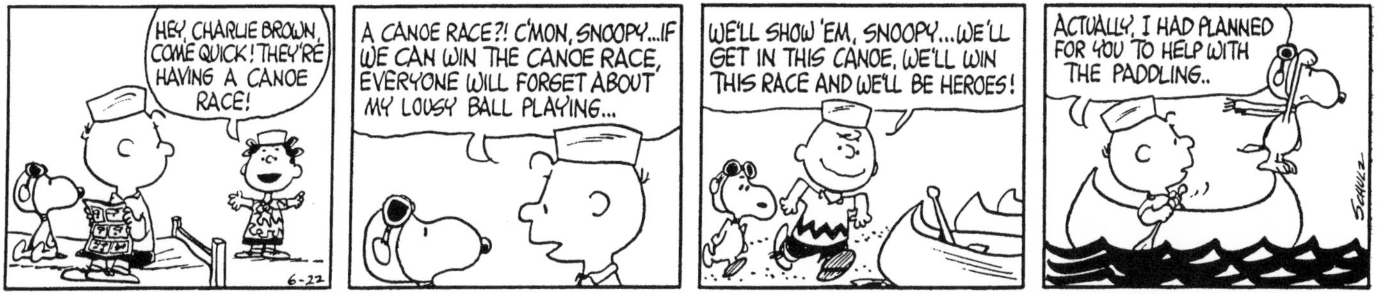
HEY, CHARLIE BROWN, COME QUICK! THEY'RE HAVING A CANOE RACE!
6-22
A CANOE RACE?! C'MON, SNOOPY...IF WE CAN WIN THE CANOE RACE, EVERYONE WILL FORGET ABOUT MY LOUSY BALL PLAYING...
WE'LL SHOW 'EM, SNOOPY...WE'LL GET IN THIS CANOE, WE'LL WIN THIS RACE AND WE'LL BE HEROES!
ACTUALLY, I HAD PLANNED FOR YOU TO HELP WITH THE PADDLING..
SCHULZ

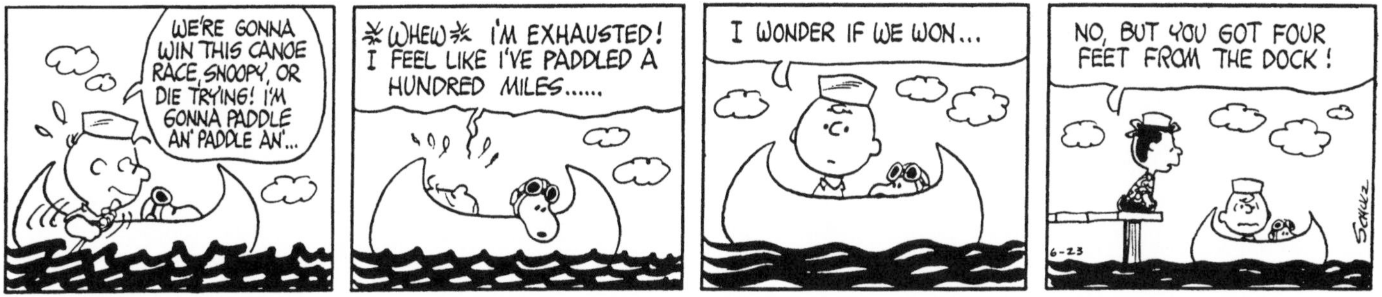
WE'RE GONNA WIN THIS CANOE RACE, SNOOPY, OR DIE TRYING! I'M GONNA PADDLE AN' PADDLE AN'...
WHEW I'M EXHAUSTED! I FEEL LIKE I'VE PADDLED A HUNDRED MILES......
I WONDER IF WE WON...
NO, BUT YOU GOT FOUR FEET FROM THE DOCK!
6-23
SCHULZ

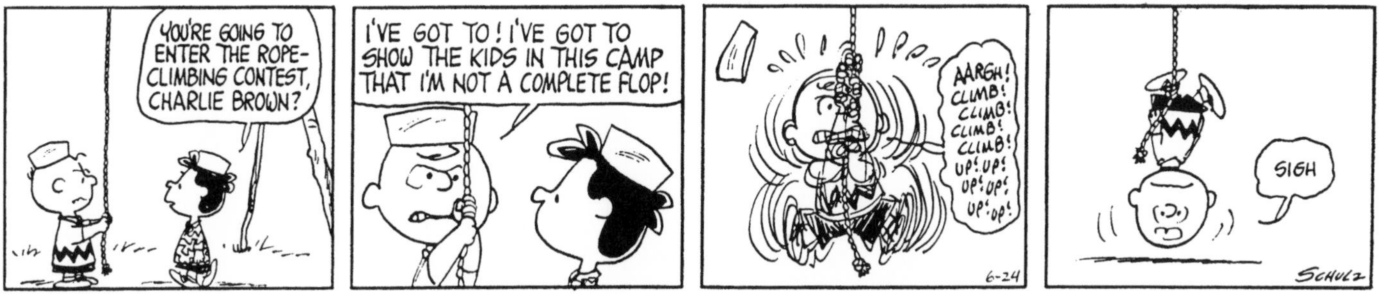
YOU'RE GOING TO ENTER THE ROPE-CLIMBING CONTEST, CHARLIE BROWN?
I'VE GOT TO! I'VE GOT TO SHOW THE KIDS IN THIS CAMP THAT I'M NOT A COMPLETE FLOP!
AARGH! CLIMB! CLIMB! CLIMB! CLIMB! UP! UP! UP! UP! UP! UP!
6-24
SIGH
SCHULZ

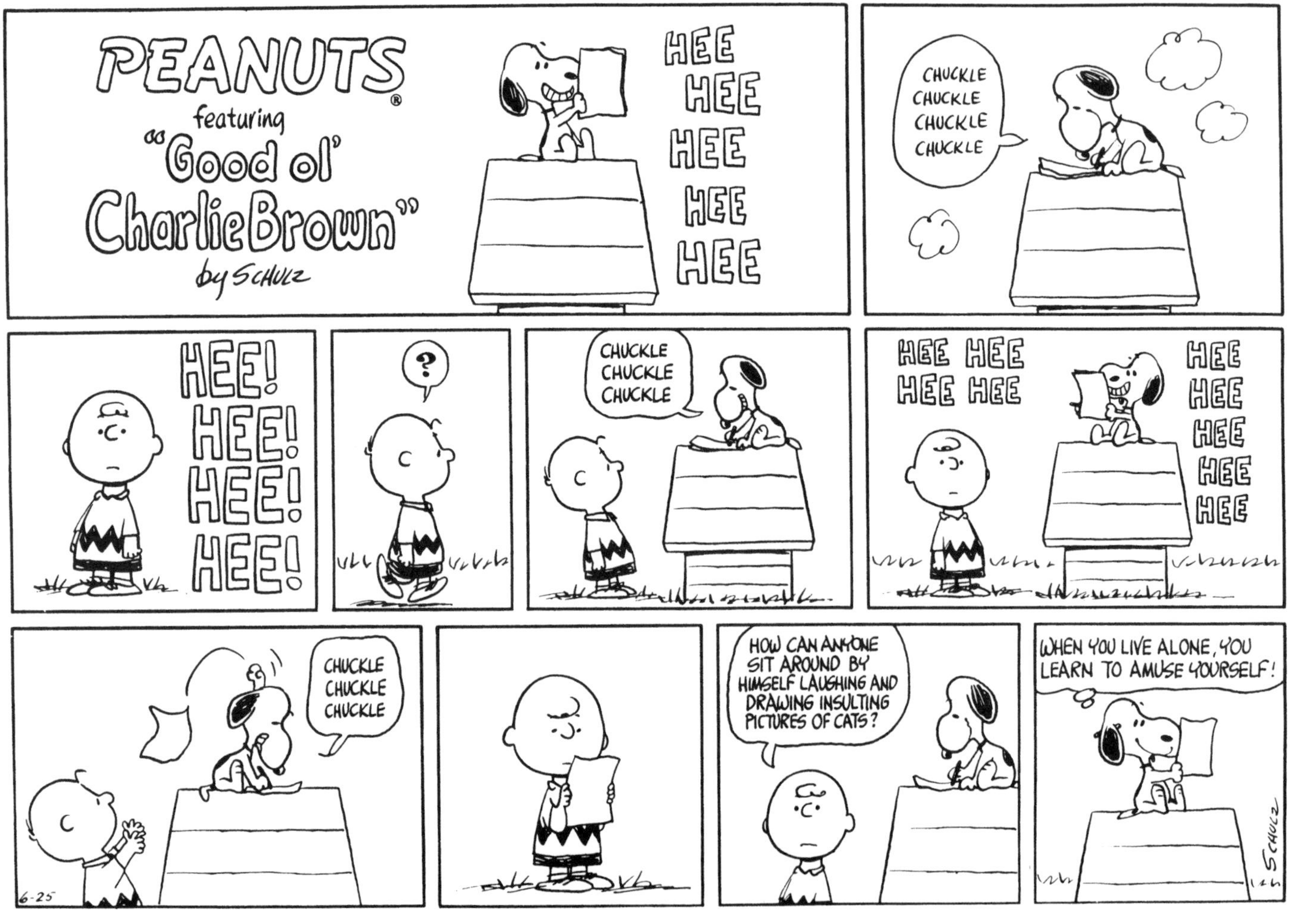
PEANUTS®
featuring
"Good ol' CharlieBrown"
by SCHULZ
HEE HEE HEE HEE HEE
CHUCKLE CHUCKLE CHUCKLE CHUCKLE
HEE! HEE! HEE! HEE!
?
CHUCKLE CHUCKLE CHUCKLE
HEE HEE HEE HEE
HEE HEE HEE HEE HEE
6-25
CHUCKLE CHUCKLE CHUCKLE
HOW CAN ANYONE SIT AROUND BY HIMSELF LAUGHING AND DRAWING INSULTING PICTURES OF CATS?
WHEN YOU LIVE ALONE, YOU LEARN TO AMUSE YOURSELF!
SCHULZ

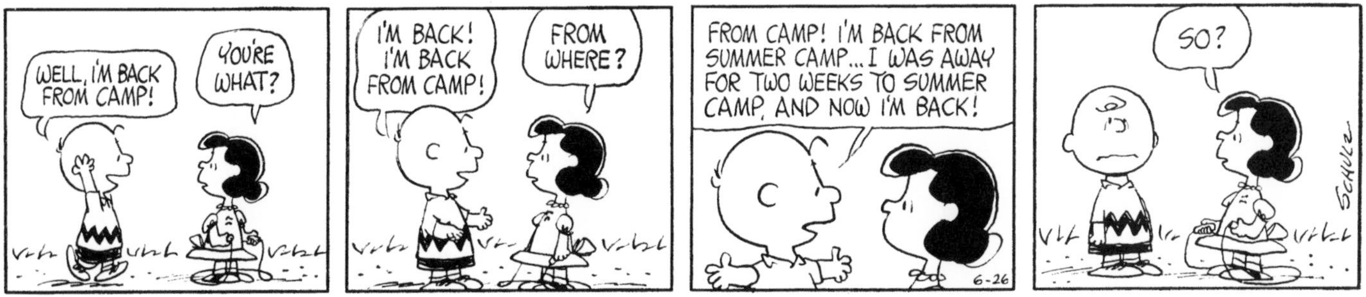
WELL, I'M BACK FROM CAMP!
YOU'RE WHAT?
I'M BACK! I'M BACK FROM CAMP!
FROM WHERE?
FROM CAMP! I'M BACK FROM SUMMER CAMP... I WAS AWAY FOR TWO WEEKS TO SUMMER CAMP, AND NOW I'M BACK!
6-26
SO?
SCHULZ

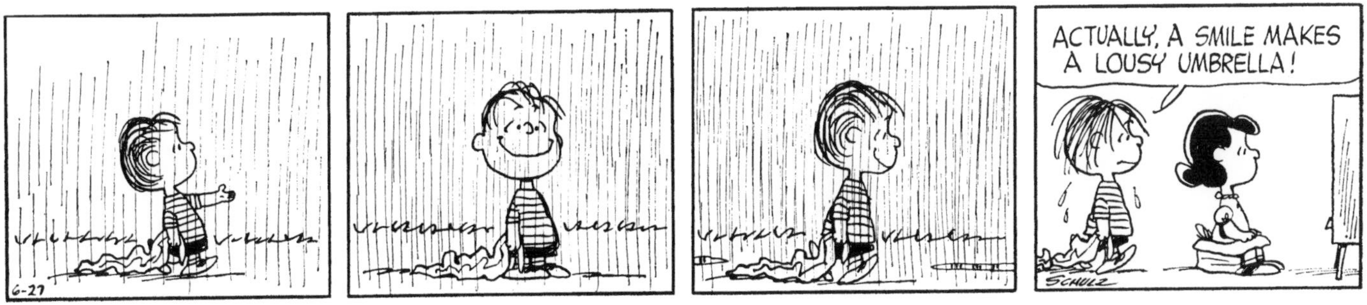
6-27
ACTUALLY, A SMILE MAKES A LOUSY UMBRELLA!
SCHULZ

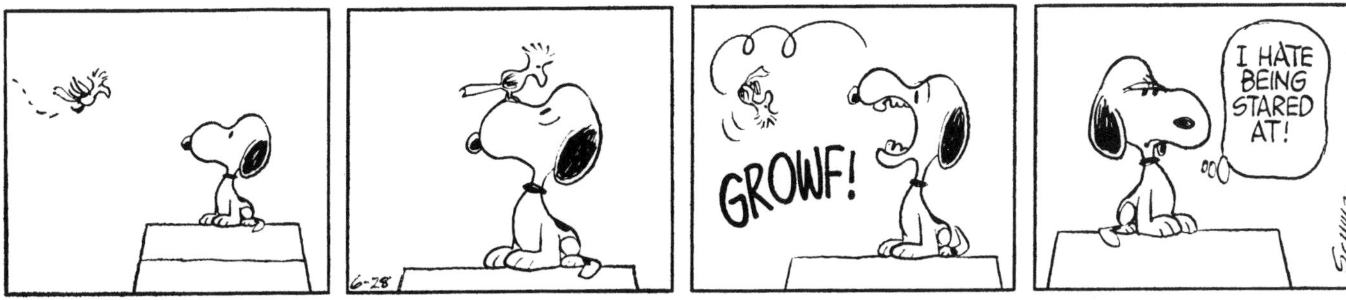
6-28
GROWF!
I HATE BEING STARED AT!
SCHULZ

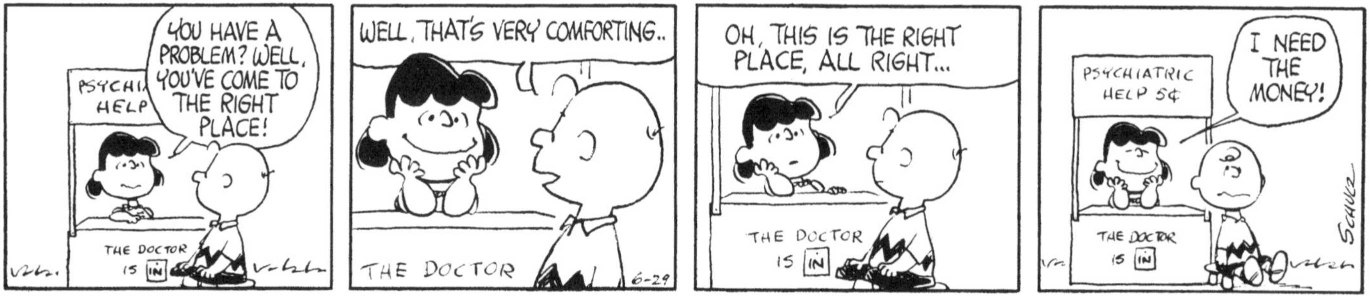
PSYCHI
HELP
THE DOCTOR IS IN
YOU HAVE A PROBLEM? WELL, YOU'VE COME TO THE RIGHT PLACE!
WELL, THAT'S VERY COMFORTING..
THE DOCTOR
6-29
OH, THIS IS THE RIGHT PLACE, ALL RIGHT...
THE DOCTOR IS IN
PSYCHIATRIC HELP 5¢
THE DOCTOR IS IN
I NEED THE MONEY!
SCHULZ

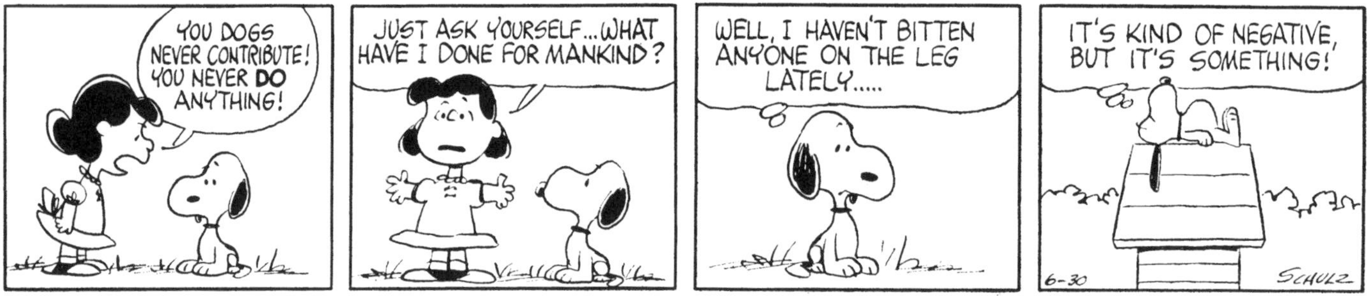
YOU DOGS NEVER CONTRIBUTE! YOU NEVER DO ANYTHING!
JUST ASK YOURSELF...WHAT HAVE I DONE FOR MANKIND?
WELL, I HAVEN'T BITTEN ANYONE ON THE LEG LATELY.....
IT'S KIND OF NEGATIVE, BUT IT'S SOMETHING!
6-30
SCHULZ

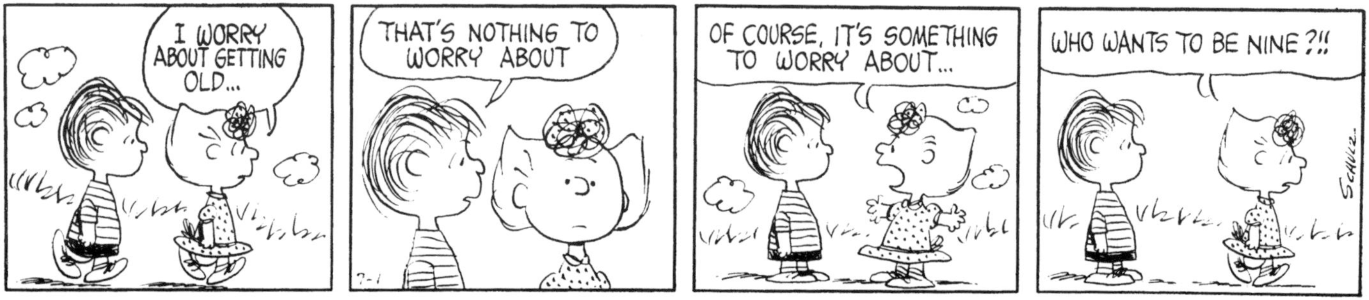
I WORRY ABOUT GETTING OLD...
THAT'S NOTHING TO WORRY ABOUT
7-1
OF COURSE, IT'S SOMETHING TO WORRY ABOUT...
WHO WANTS TO BE NINE ?!!
SCHULZ

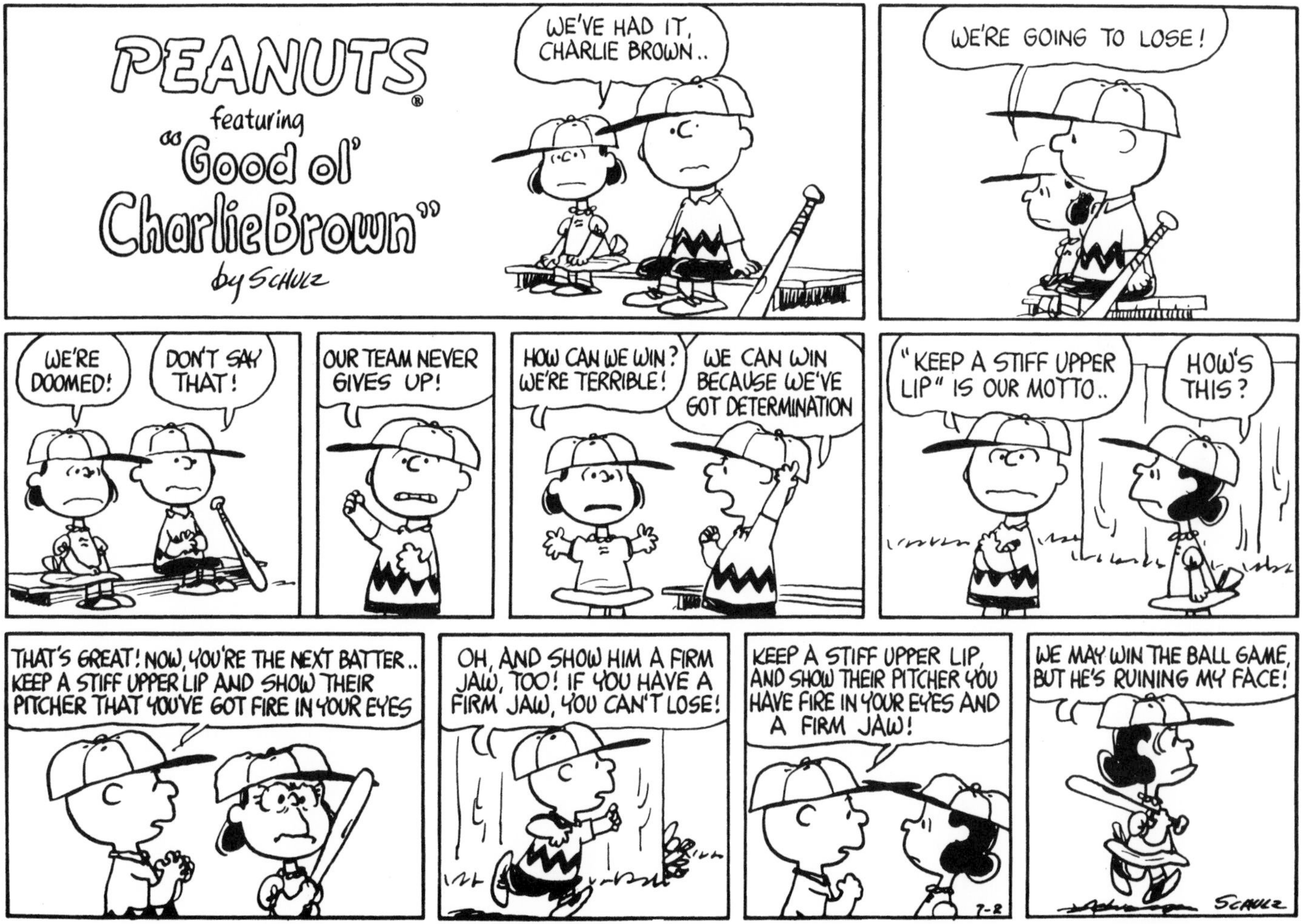
PEANUTS®
featuring "Good ol' Charlie Brown"
by SCHULZ
WE'VE HAD IT, CHARLIE BROWN..
WE'RE GOING TO LOSE!
WE'RE DOOMED!
DON'T SAY THAT!
OUR TEAM NEVER GIVES UP!
HOW CAN WE WIN? WE'RE TERRIBLE!
WE CAN WIN BECAUSE WE'VE GOT DETERMINATION
"KEEP A STIFF UPPER LIP" IS OUR MOTTO..
HOW'S THIS?
THAT'S GREAT! NOW, YOU'RE THE NEXT BATTER.. KEEP A STIFF UPPER LIP AND SHOW THEIR PITCHER THAT YOU'VE GOT FIRE IN YOUR EYES
OH, AND SHOW HIM A FIRM JAW, TOO! IF YOU HAVE A FIRM JAW, YOU CAN'T LOSE!
KEEP A STIFF UPPER LIP, AND SHOW THEIR PITCHER YOU HAVE FIRE IN YOUR EYES AND A FIRM JAW!
7-2
WE MAY WIN THE BALL GAME, BUT HE'S RUINING MY FACE!
SCHULZ

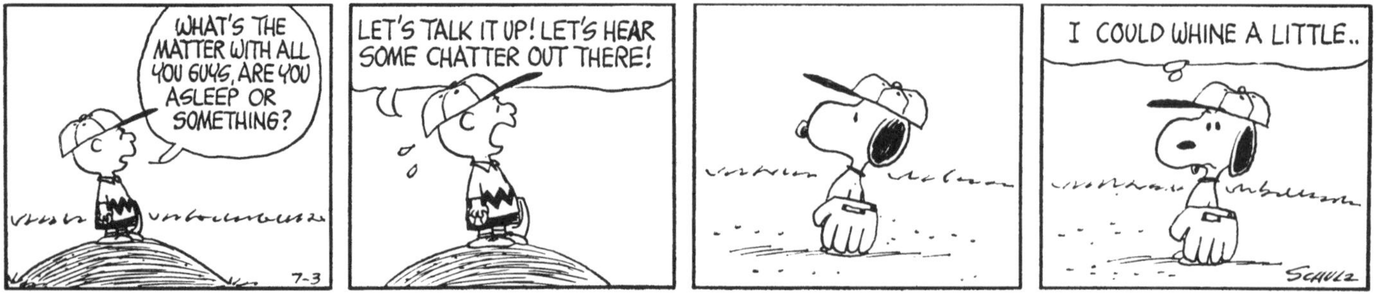
WHAT'S THE MATTER WITH ALL YOU GUYS, ARE YOU ASLEEP OR SOMETHING?
7-3
LET'S TALK IT UP! LET'S HEAR SOME CHATTER OUT THERE!
I COULD WHINE A LITTLE..
SCHULZ

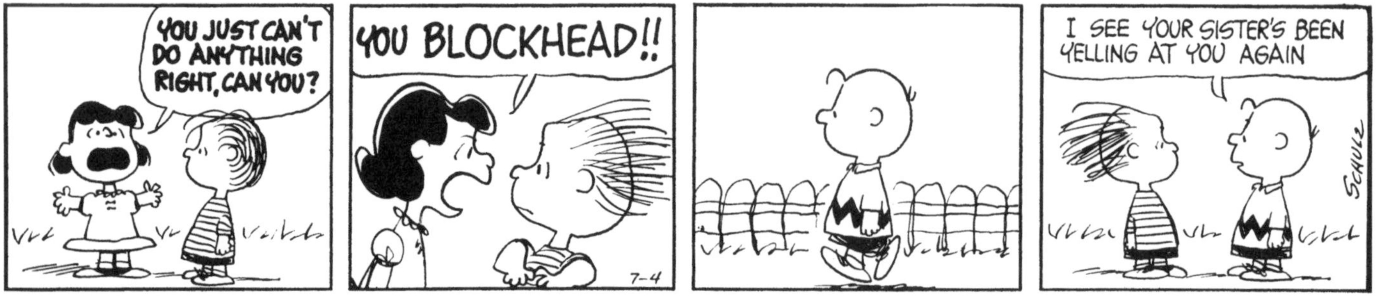
YOU JUST CAN'T DO ANYTHING RIGHT, CAN YOU?
YOU BLOCKHEAD!!
7-4
I SEE YOUR SISTER'S BEEN YELLING AT YOU AGAIN
SCHULZ

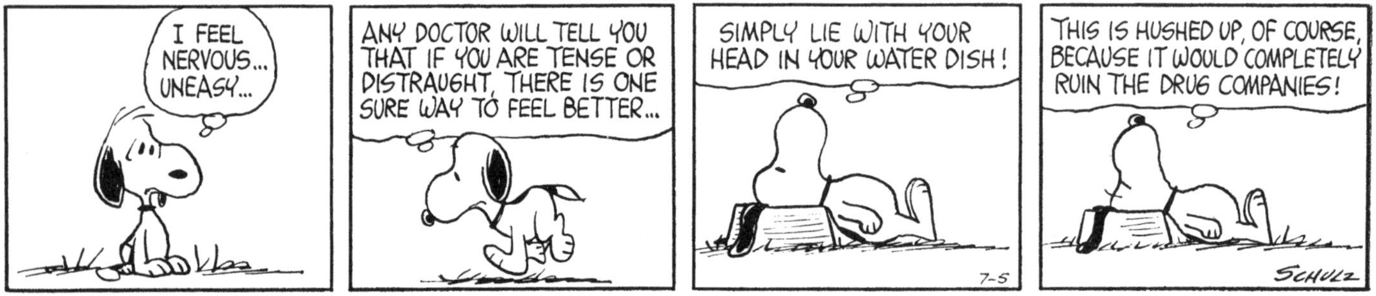
I FEEL NERVOUS... UNEASY...
ANY DOCTOR WILL TELL YOU THAT IF YOU ARE TENSE OR DISTRAUGHT, THERE IS ONE SURE WAY TO FEEL BETTER...
SIMPLY LIE WITH YOUR HEAD IN YOUR WATER DISH!
7-5
THIS IS HUSHED UP, OF COURSE, BECAUSE IT WOULD COMPLETELY RUIN THE DRUG COMPANIES!
SCHULZ

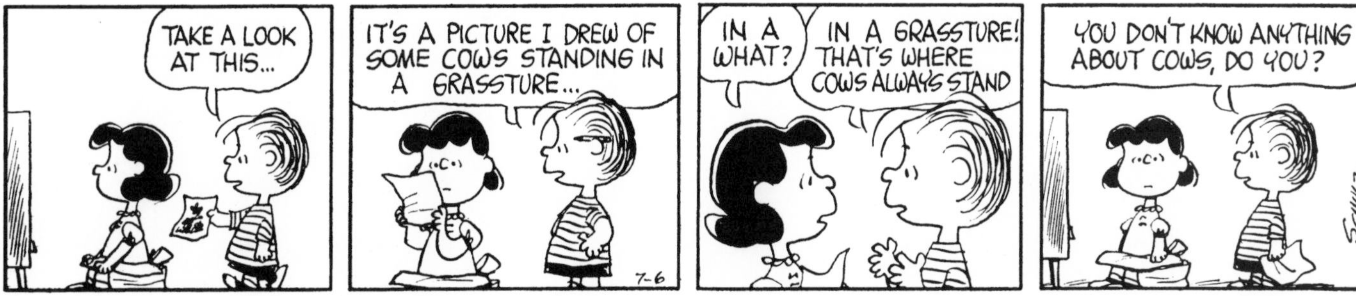
TAKE A LOOK AT THIS...
IT'S A PICTURE I DREW OF SOME COWS STANDING IN A GRASSTURE...
7-6
IN A WHAT?
IN A GRASSTURE! THAT'S WHERE COWS ALWAYS STAND
YOU DON'T KNOW ANYTHING ABOUT COWS, DO YOU?
SCHULZ

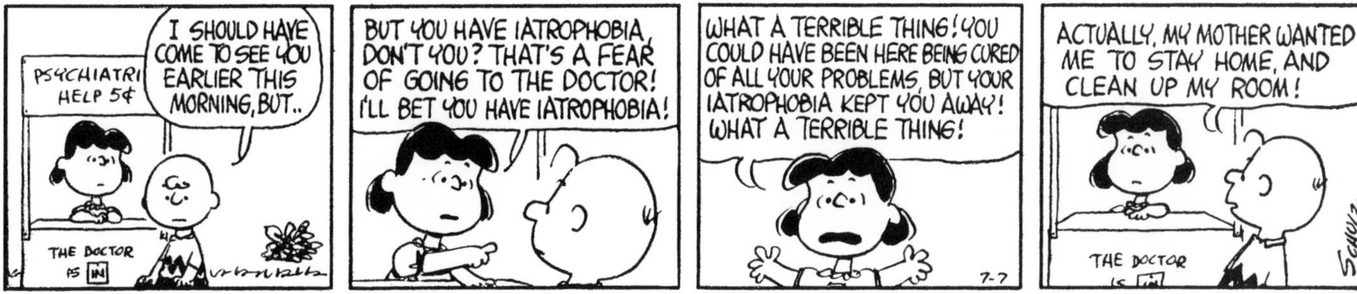
PSYCHIATRIC HELP 5¢
THE DOCTOR IS IN
I SHOULD HAVE COME TO SEE YOU EARLIER THIS MORNING, BUT..
BUT YOU HAVE IATROPHOBIA, DON'T YOU? THAT'S A FEAR OF GOING TO THE DOCTOR! I'LL BET YOU HAVE IATROPHOBIA!
WHAT A TERRIBLE THING! YOU COULD HAVE BEEN HERE BEING CURED OF ALL YOUR PROBLEMS, BUT YOUR IATROPHOBIA KEPT YOU AWAY! WHAT A TERRIBLE THING!
7-7
ACTUALLY, MY MOTHER WANTED ME TO STAY HOME, AND CLEAN UP MY ROOM!
THE DOCTOR
SCHULZ

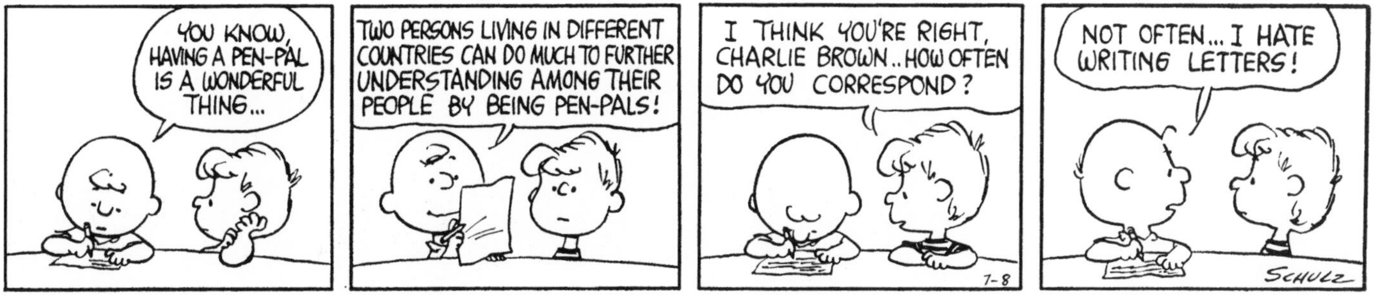
YOU KNOW, HAVING A PEN-PAL IS A WONDERFUL THING...
TWO PERSONS LIVING IN DIFFERENT COUNTRIES CAN DO MUCH TO FURTHER UNDERSTANDING AMONG THEIR PEOPLE BY BEING PEN-PALS!
I THINK YOU'RE RIGHT, CHARLIE BROWN.. HOW OFTEN DO YOU CORRESPOND?
7-8
NOT OFTEN... I HATE WRITING LETTERS!
SCHULZ

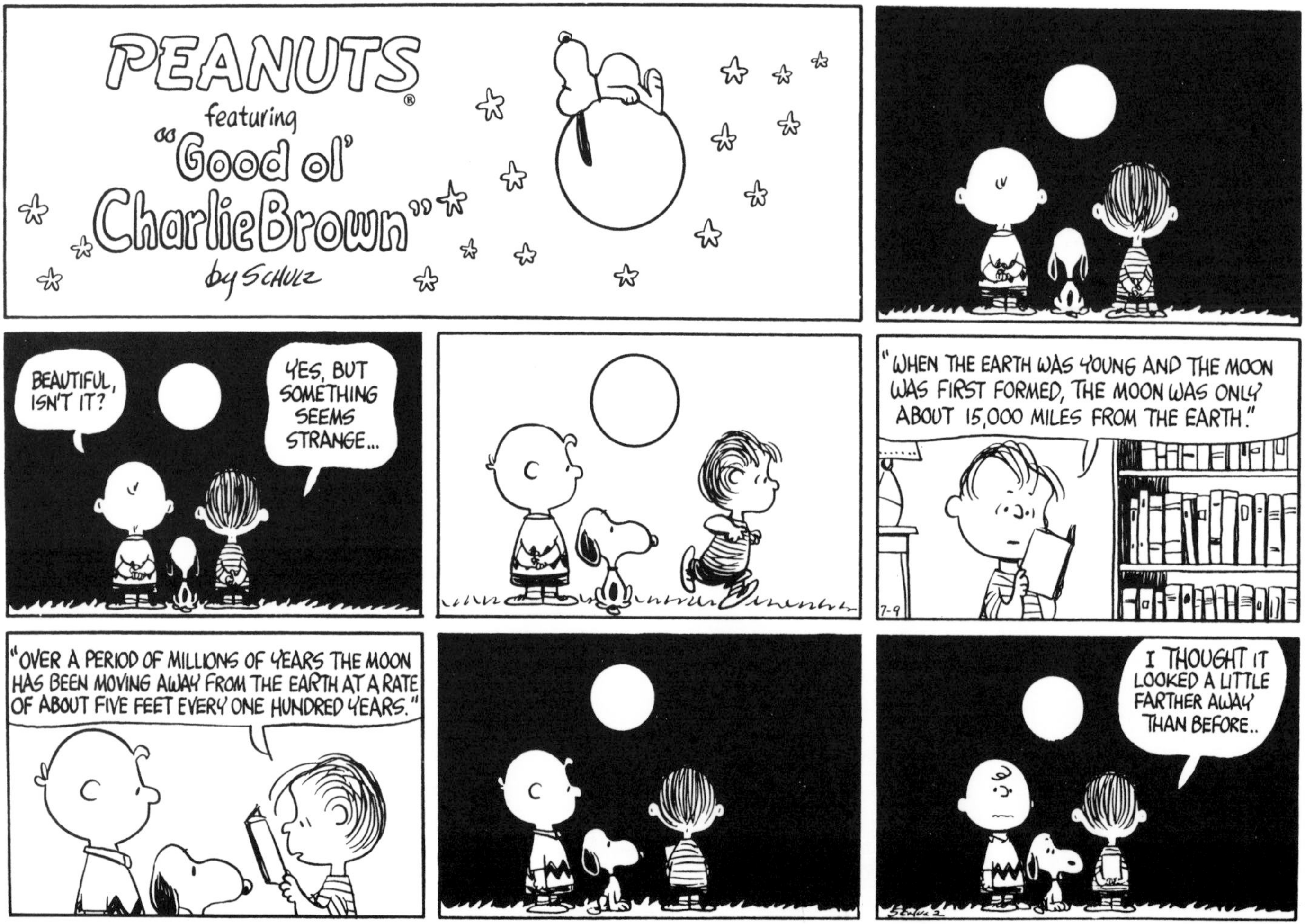
PEANUTS®
featuring
"Good ol' Charlie Brown"
by SCHULZ
BEAUTIFUL, ISN'T IT?
YES, BUT SOMETHING SEEMS STRANGE...
"WHEN THE EARTH WAS YOUNG AND THE MOON WAS FIRST FORMED, THE MOON WAS ONLY ABOUT 15,000 MILES FROM THE EARTH."
7-9
"OVER A PERIOD OF MILLIONS OF YEARS THE MOON HAS BEEN MOVING AWAY FROM THE EARTH AT A RATE OF ABOUT FIVE FEET EVERY ONE HUNDRED YEARS."
I THOUGHT IT LOOKED A LITTLE FARTHER AWAY THAN BEFORE..
SCHULZ

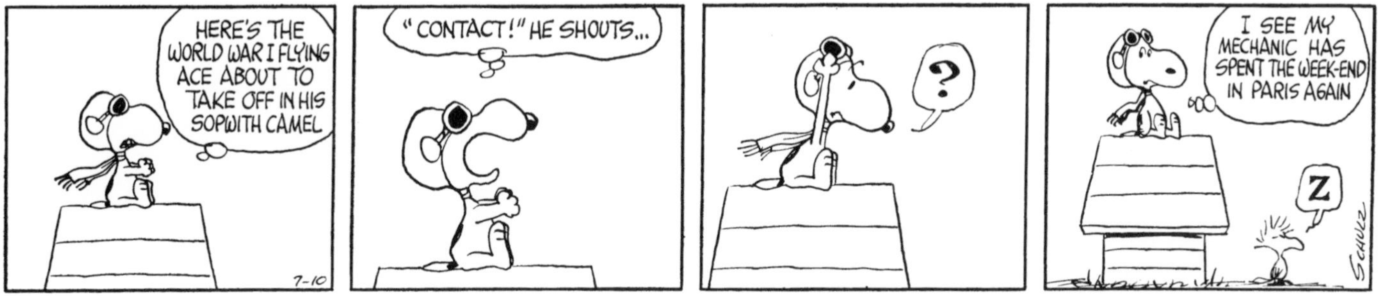
HERE'S THE WORLD WAR I FLYING ACE ABOUT TO TAKE OFF IN HIS SOPWITH CAMEL
7-10
"CONTACT!" HE SHOUTS...
?
I SEE MY MECHANIC HAS SPENT THE WEEK-END IN PARIS AGAIN
Z
SCHULZ

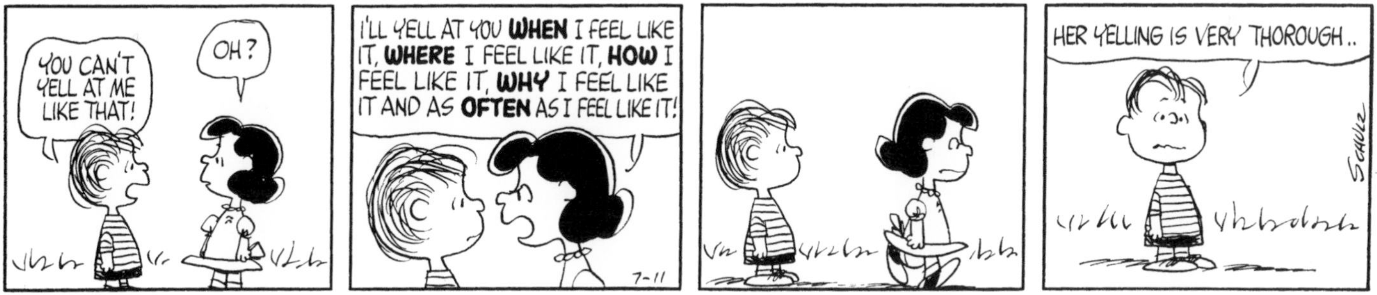
YOU CAN'T YELL AT ME LIKE THAT!
OH?
I'LL YELL AT YOU **WHEN** I FEEL LIKE IT, **WHERE** I FEEL LIKE IT, **HOW** I FEEL LIKE IT, **WHY** I FEEL LIKE IT AND AS **OFTEN** AS I FEEL LIKE IT!
7-11
HER YELLING IS VERY THOROUGH..
SCHULZ

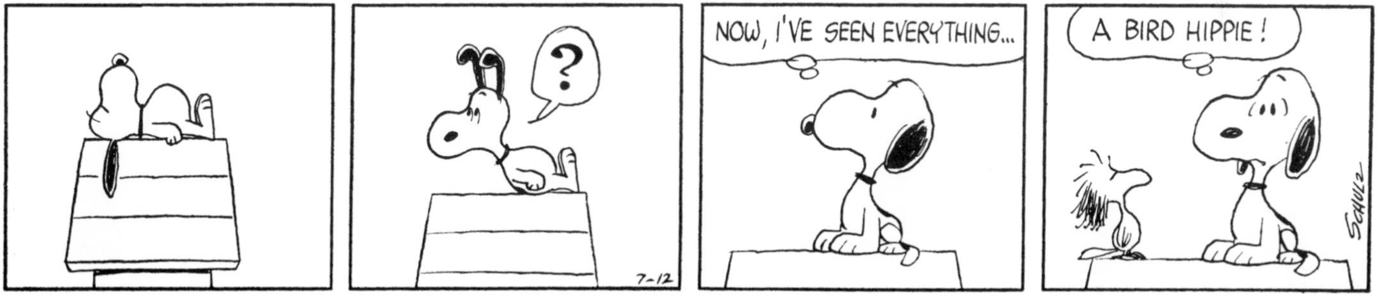
?
7-12
NOW, I'VE SEEN EVERYTHING...
A BIRD HIPPIE!
SCHULZ

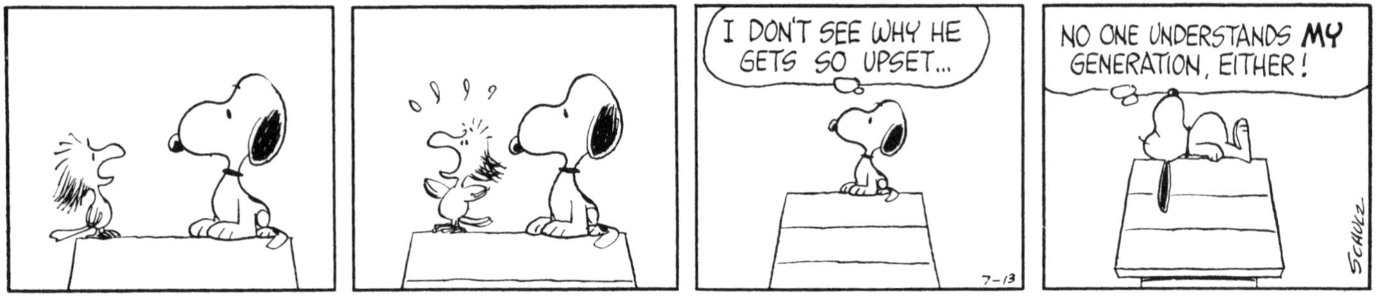
I DON'T SEE WHY HE GETS SO UPSET...
7-13
NO ONE UNDERSTANDS **MY** GENERATION, EITHER!
SCHULZ

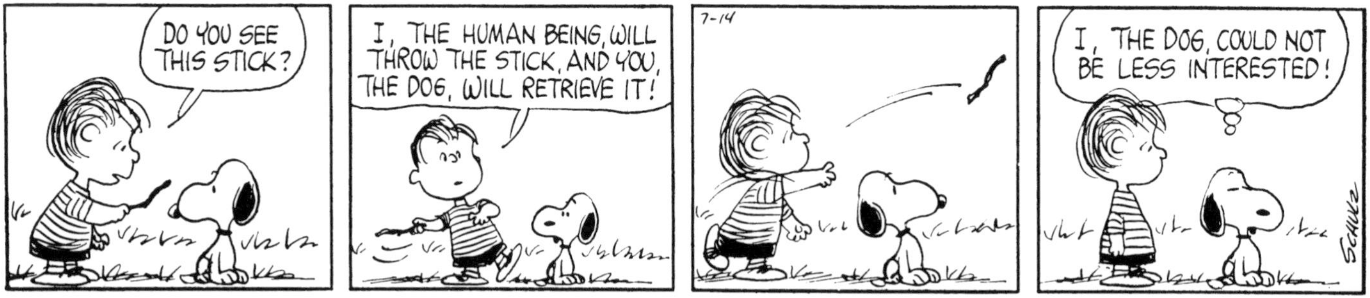
DO YOU SEE THIS STICK?
I, THE HUMAN BEING, WILL THROW THE STICK, AND YOU, THE DOG, WILL RETRIEVE IT!
7-14
I, THE DOG, COULD NOT BE LESS INTERESTED!
SCHULZ

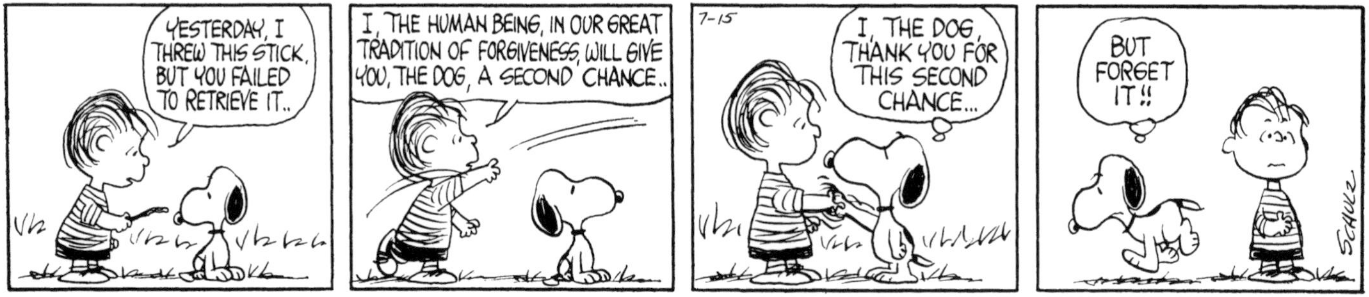
YESTERDAY, I THREW THIS STICK, BUT YOU FAILED TO RETRIEVE IT..
I, THE HUMAN BEING, IN OUR GREAT TRADITION OF FORGIVENESS, WILL GIVE YOU, THE DOG, A SECOND CHANCE..
7-15
I, THE DOG, THANK YOU FOR THIS SECOND CHANCE...
BUT FORGET IT!!
SCHULZ

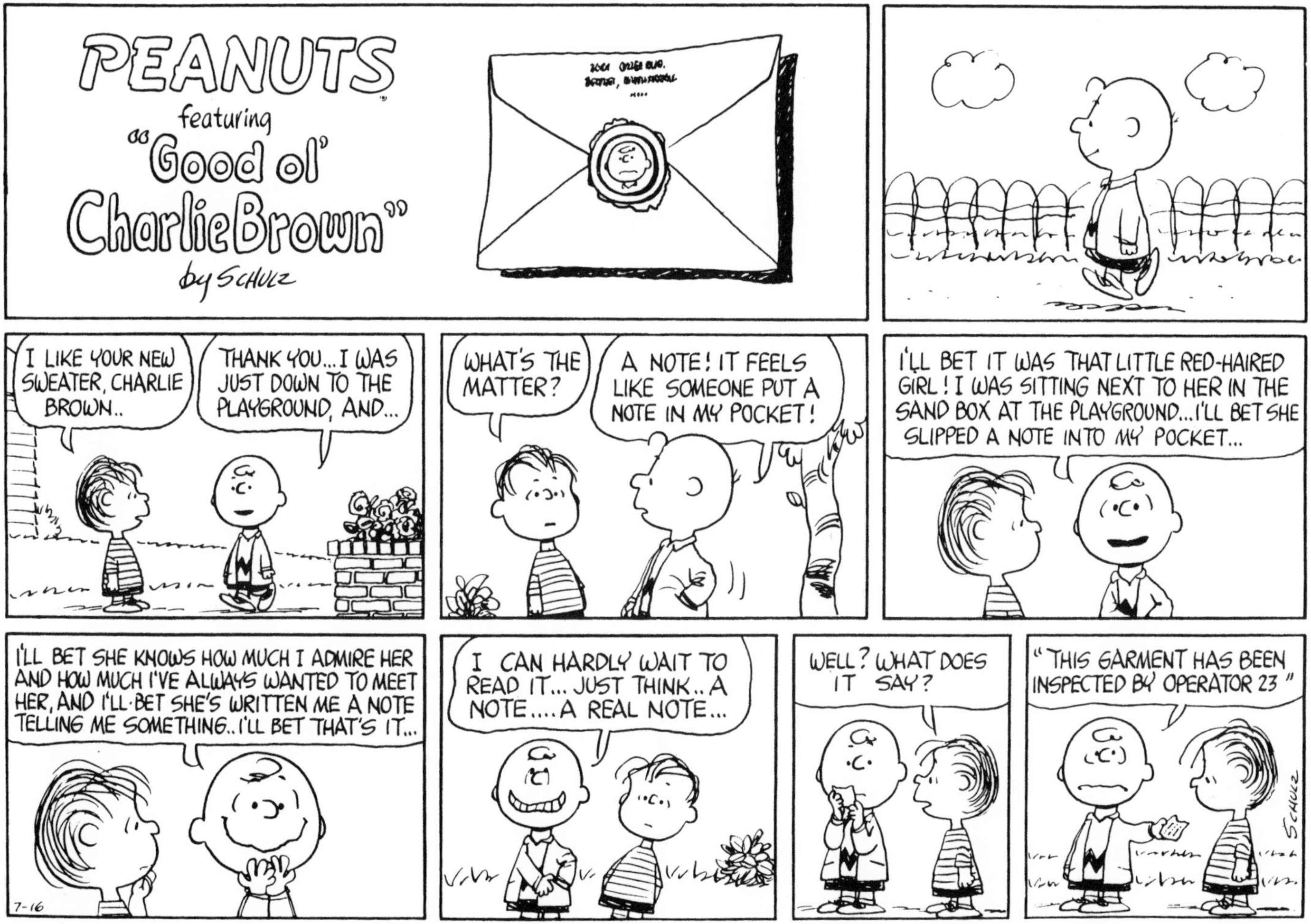
PEANUTS
featuring
"Good ol' CharlieBrown"
by SCHULZ
I LIKE YOUR NEW SWEATER, CHARLIE BROWN..
THANK YOU... I WAS JUST DOWN TO THE PLAYGROUND, AND...
WHAT'S THE MATTER?
A NOTE! IT FEELS LIKE SOMEONE PUT A NOTE IN MY POCKET!
I'LL BET IT WAS THAT LITTLE RED-HAIRED GIRL! I WAS SITTING NEXT TO HER IN THE SAND BOX AT THE PLAYGROUND... I'LL BET SHE SLIPPED A NOTE INTO MY POCKET...
I'LL BET SHE KNOWS HOW MUCH I ADMIRE HER AND HOW MUCH I'VE ALWAYS WANTED TO MEET HER, AND I'LL BET SHE'S WRITTEN ME A NOTE TELLING ME SOMETHING.. I'LL BET THAT'S IT...
7-16
I CAN HARDLY WAIT TO READ IT... JUST THINK.. A NOTE.... A REAL NOTE...
WELL? WHAT DOES IT SAY?
"THIS GARMENT HAS BEEN INSPECTED BY OPERATOR 23"
SCHULZ

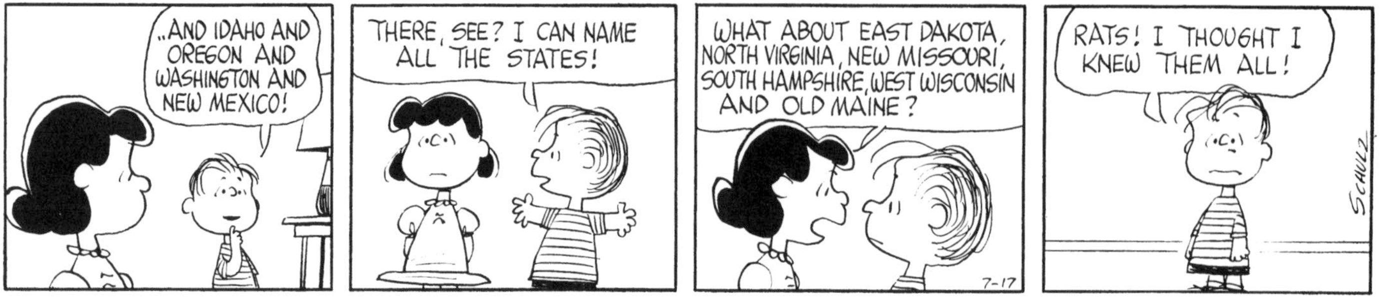
..AND IDAHO AND OREGON AND WASHINGTON AND NEW MEXICO!
THERE, SEE? I CAN NAME ALL THE STATES!
WHAT ABOUT EAST DAKOTA, NORTH VIRGINIA, NEW MISSOURI, SOUTH HAMPSHIRE, WEST WISCONSIN AND OLD MAINE?
7-17
RATS! I THOUGHT I KNEW THEM ALL!
SCHULZ

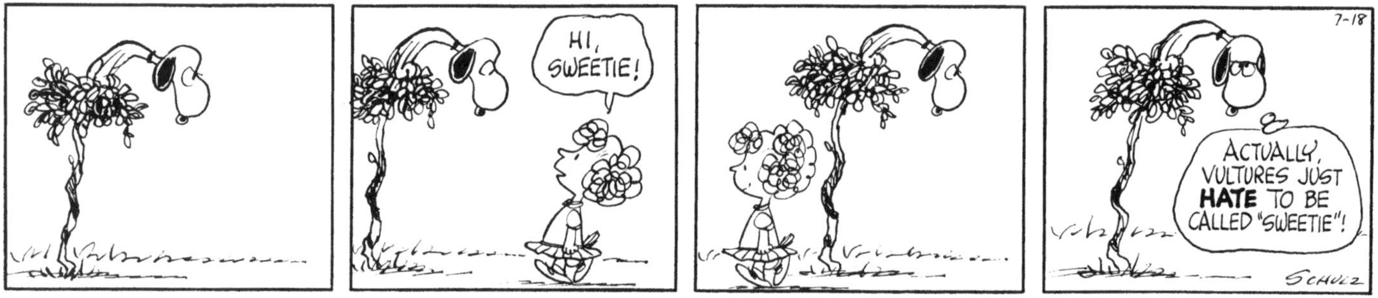
HI, SWEETIE!
7-18
ACTUALLY, VULTURES JUST **HATE** TO BE CALLED "SWEETIE"!
SCHULZ

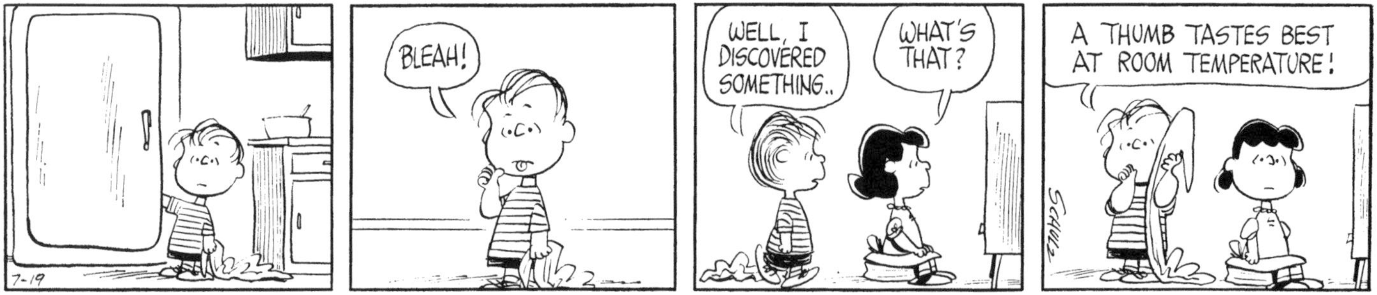
7-19
BLEAH!
WELL, I DISCOVERED SOMETHING..
WHAT'S THAT?
SCHULZ
A THUMB TASTES BEST AT ROOM TEMPERATURE!

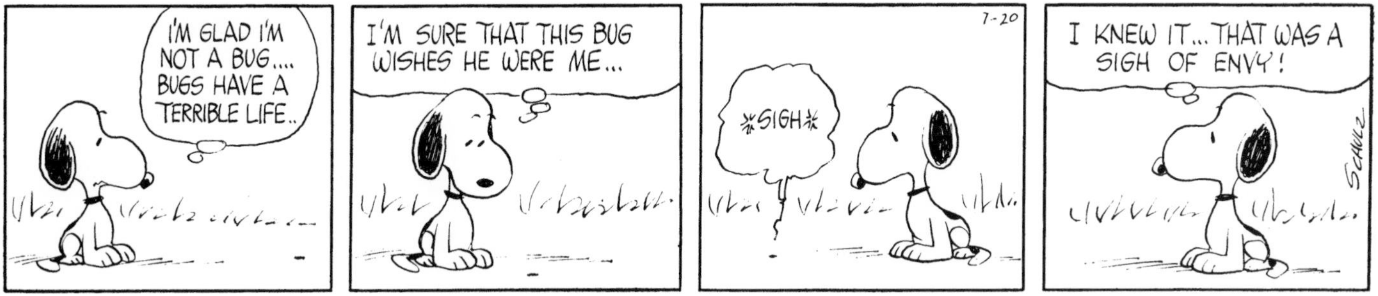
I'M GLAD I'M NOT A BUG.... BUGS HAVE A TERRIBLE LIFE..
I'M SURE THAT THIS BUG WISHES HE WERE ME...
7-20
SIGH
I KNEW IT... THAT WAS A SIGH OF ENVY!
SCHULZ

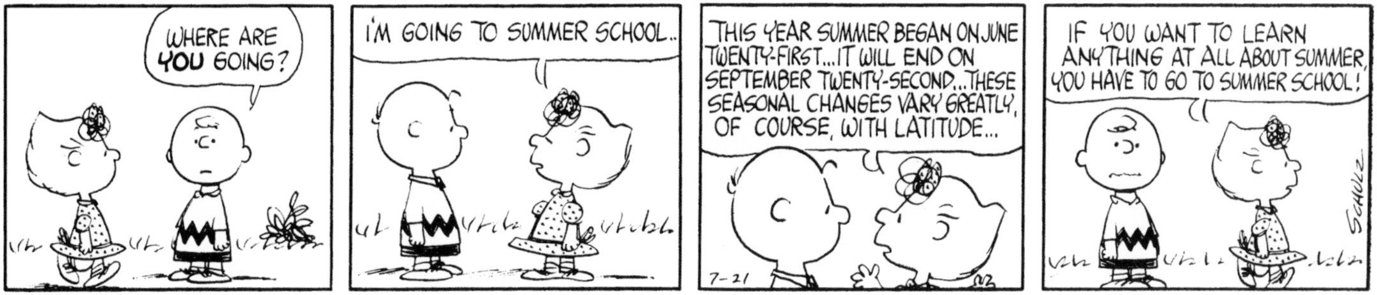
WHERE ARE **YOU** GOING?
I'M GOING TO SUMMER SCHOOL..
THIS YEAR SUMMER BEGAN ON JUNE TWENTY-FIRST...IT WILL END ON SEPTEMBER TWENTY-SECOND...THESE SEASONAL CHANGES VARY GREATLY, OF COURSE, WITH LATITUDE...
7-21
IF YOU WANT TO LEARN ANYTHING AT ALL ABOUT SUMMER, YOU HAVE TO GO TO SUMMER SCHOOL!
SCHULZ

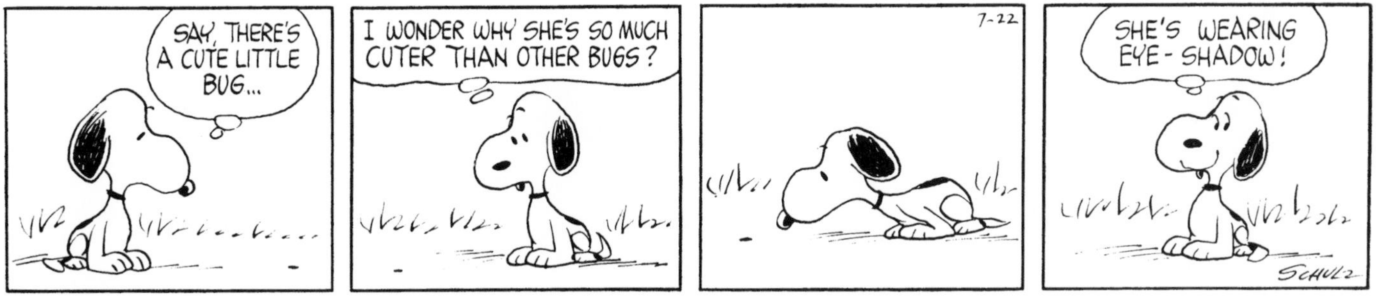
SAY, THERE'S A CUTE LITTLE BUG...
I WONDER WHY SHE'S SO MUCH CUTER THAN OTHER BUGS?
7-22
SHE'S WEARING EYE-SHADOW!
SCHULZ

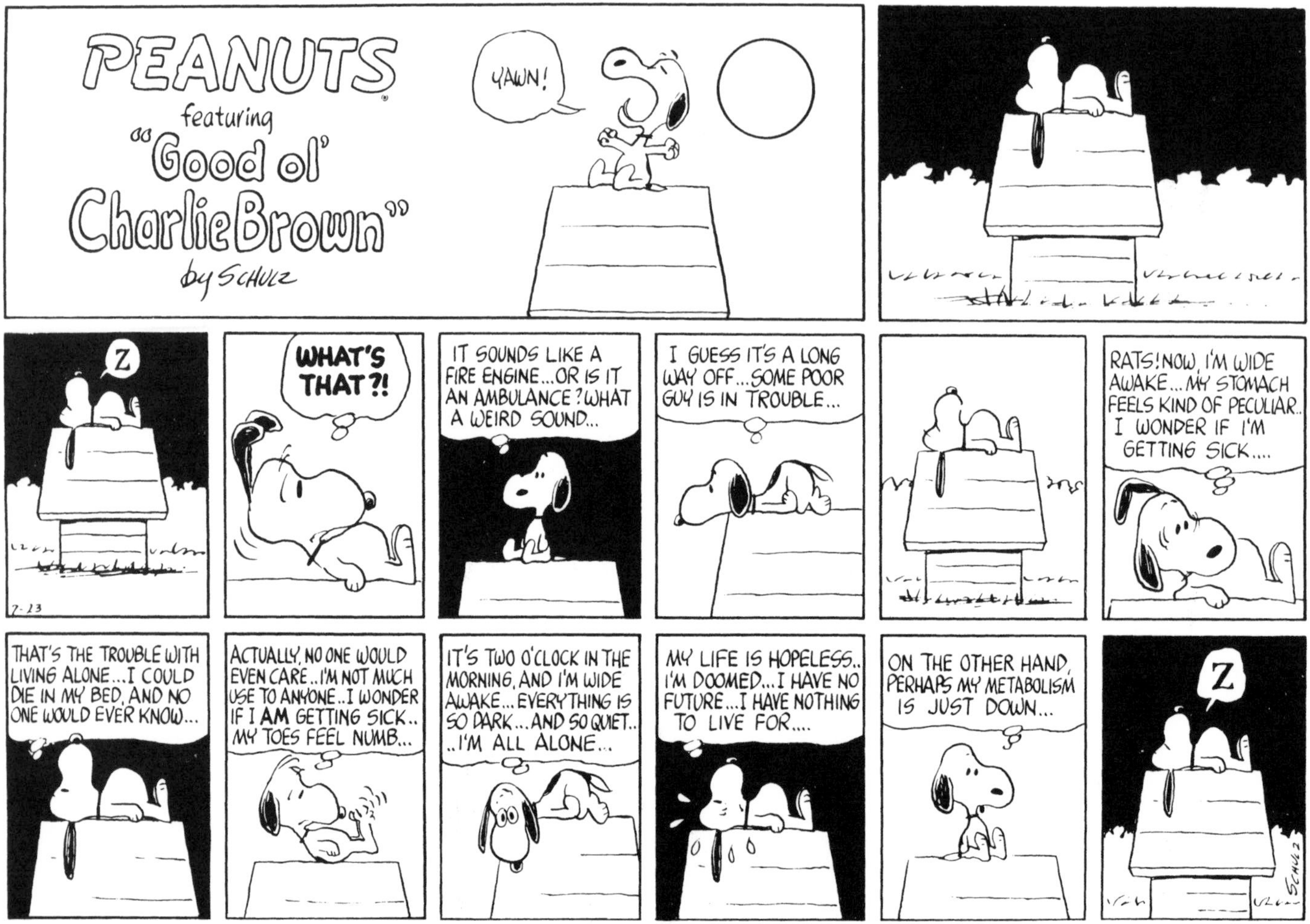
PEANUTS
featuring
"Good ol' CharlieBrown"
by SCHULZ
YAWN!
Z
7-23
WHAT'S THAT?!
IT SOUNDS LIKE A FIRE ENGINE...OR IS IT AN AMBULANCE? WHAT A WEIRD SOUND...
I GUESS IT'S A LONG WAY OFF...SOME POOR GUY IS IN TROUBLE...
RATS! NOW, I'M WIDE AWAKE... MY STOMACH FEELS KIND OF PECULIAR.. I WONDER IF I'M GETTING SICK....
THAT'S THE TROUBLE WITH LIVING ALONE...I COULD DIE IN MY BED, AND NO ONE WOULD EVER KNOW...
ACTUALLY, NO ONE WOULD EVEN CARE..I'M NOT MUCH USE TO ANYONE..I WONDER IF I AM GETTING SICK.. MY TOES FEEL NUMB...
IT'S TWO O'CLOCK IN THE MORNING, AND I'M WIDE AWAKE... EVERYTHING IS SO DARK... AND SO QUIET.. ..I'M ALL ALONE...
MY LIFE IS HOPELESS.. I'M DOOMED...I HAVE NO FUTURE...I HAVE NOTHING TO LIVE FOR....
ON THE OTHER HAND, PERHAPS MY METABOLISM IS JUST DOWN...
Z
SCHULZ

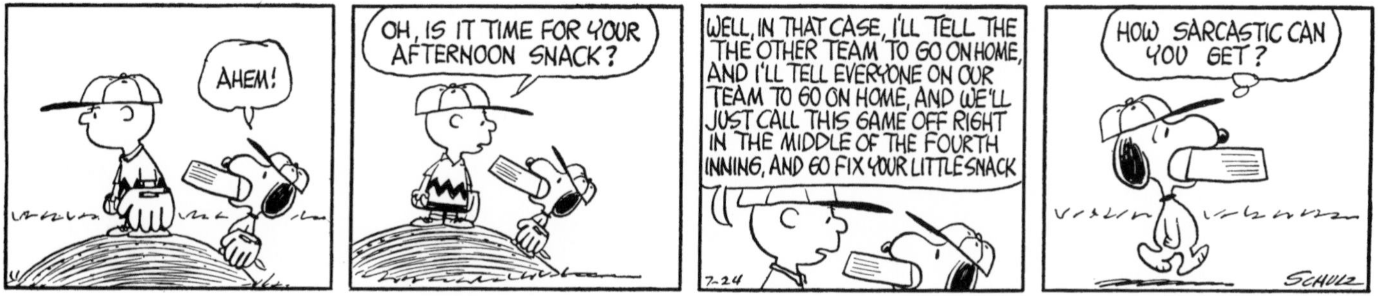

AHEM!
OH, IS IT TIME FOR YOUR AFTERNOON SNACK?
WELL, IN THAT CASE, I'LL TELL THE THE OTHER TEAM TO GO ON HOME, AND I'LL TELL EVERYONE ON OUR TEAM TO GO ON HOME, AND WE'LL JUST CALL THIS GAME OFF RIGHT IN THE MIDDLE OF THE FOURTH INNING, AND GO FIX YOUR LITTLE SNACK
7-24
HOW SARCASTIC CAN YOU GET?
SCHULZ

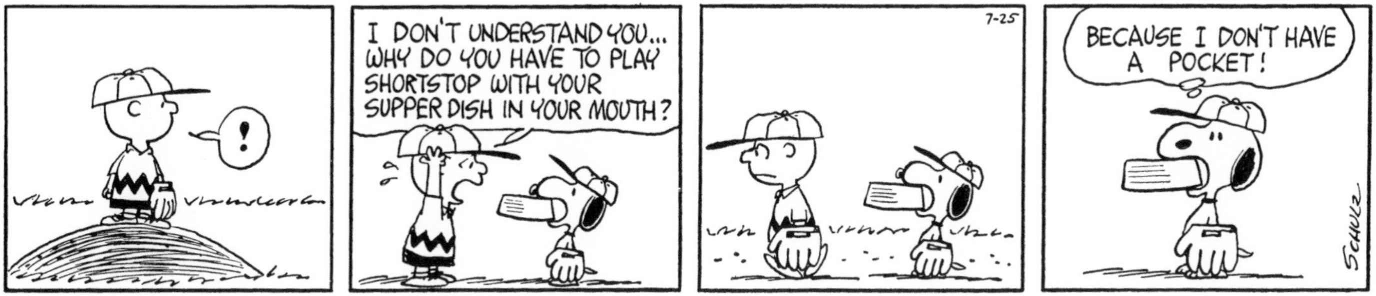

!
I DON'T UNDERSTAND YOU... WHY DO YOU HAVE TO PLAY SHORTSTOP WITH YOUR SUPPER DISH IN YOUR MOUTH?
7-25
BECAUSE I DON'T HAVE A POCKET!
SCHULZ

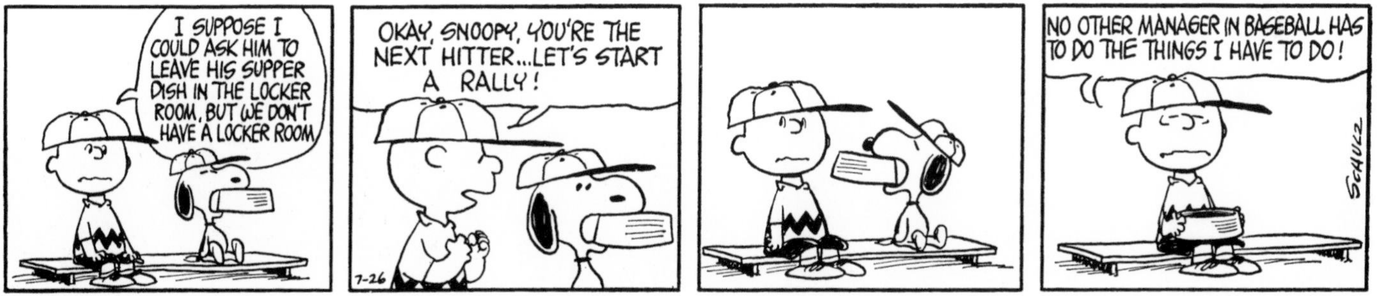

I SUPPOSE I COULD ASK HIM TO LEAVE HIS SUPPER DISH IN THE LOCKER ROOM, BUT WE DON'T HAVE A LOCKER ROOM
OKAY, SNOOPY, YOU'RE THE NEXT HITTER...LET'S START A RALLY!
7-26
NO OTHER MANAGER IN BASEBALL HAS TO DO THE THINGS I HAVE TO DO!
SCHULZ

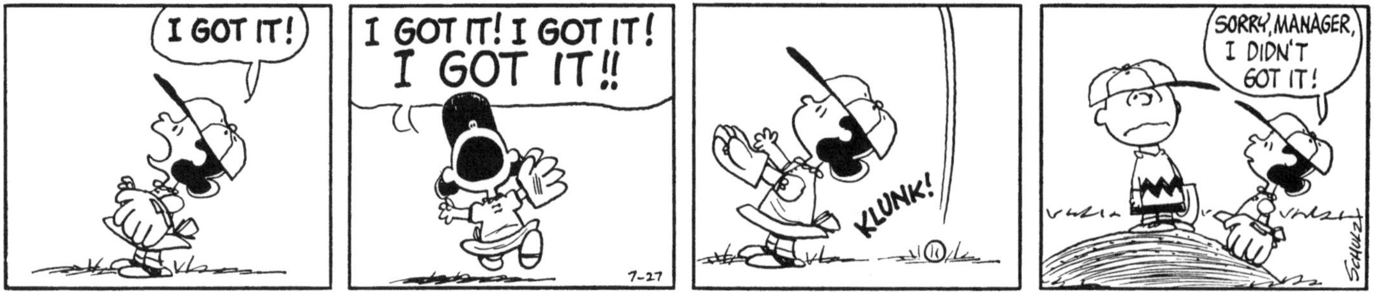
I GOT IT!
I GOT IT! I GOT IT! I GOT IT!!
7-27
KLUNK!
SORRY, MANAGER, I DIDN'T GOT IT!
SCHULZ

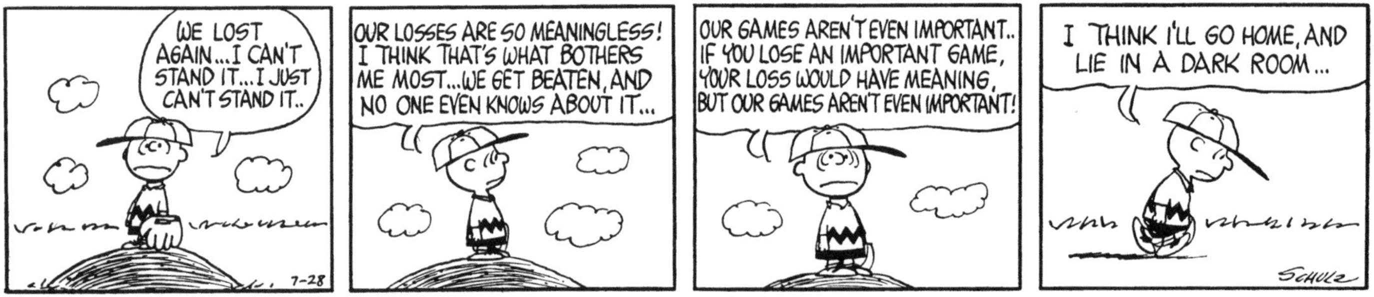
WE LOST AGAIN...I CAN'T STAND IT...I JUST CAN'T STAND IT..
7-28
OUR LOSSES ARE SO MEANINGLESS! I THINK THAT'S WHAT BOTHERS ME MOST...WE GET BEATEN, AND NO ONE EVEN KNOWS ABOUT IT...
OUR GAMES AREN'T EVEN IMPORTANT.. IF YOU LOSE AN IMPORTANT GAME, YOUR LOSS WOULD HAVE MEANING, BUT OUR GAMES AREN'T EVEN IMPORTANT!
I THINK I'LL GO HOME, AND LIE IN A DARK ROOM...
SCHULZ

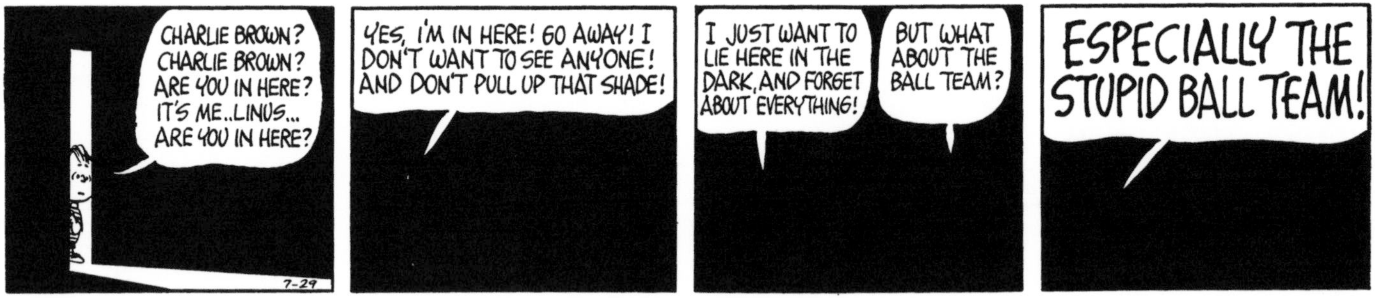
CHARLIE BROWN? CHARLIE BROWN? ARE YOU IN HERE? IT'S ME..LINUS... ARE YOU IN HERE?
7-29
YES, I'M IN HERE! GO AWAY! I DON'T WANT TO SEE ANYONE! AND DON'T PULL UP THAT SHADE!
I JUST WANT TO LIE HERE IN THE DARK, AND FORGET ABOUT EVERYTHING!
BUT WHAT ABOUT THE BALL TEAM?
ESPECIALLY THE STUPID BALL TEAM!

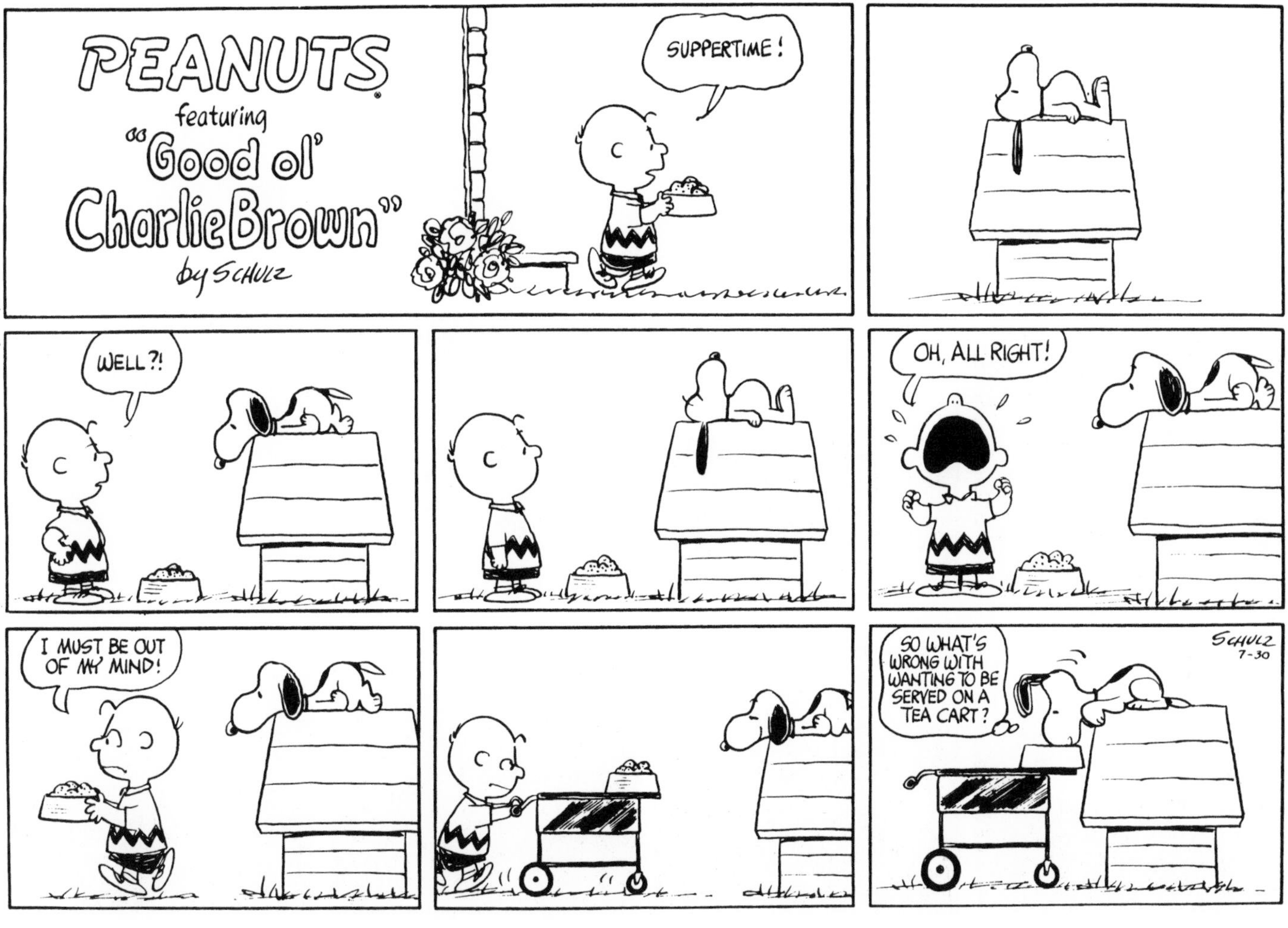
PEANUTS
featuring
"Good ol' CharlieBrown"
by SCHULZ
SUPPERTIME!
WELL?!
OH, ALL RIGHT!
I MUST BE OUT OF MY MIND!
SO WHAT'S WRONG WITH WANTING TO BE SERVED ON A TEA CART?
SCHULZ 7-30

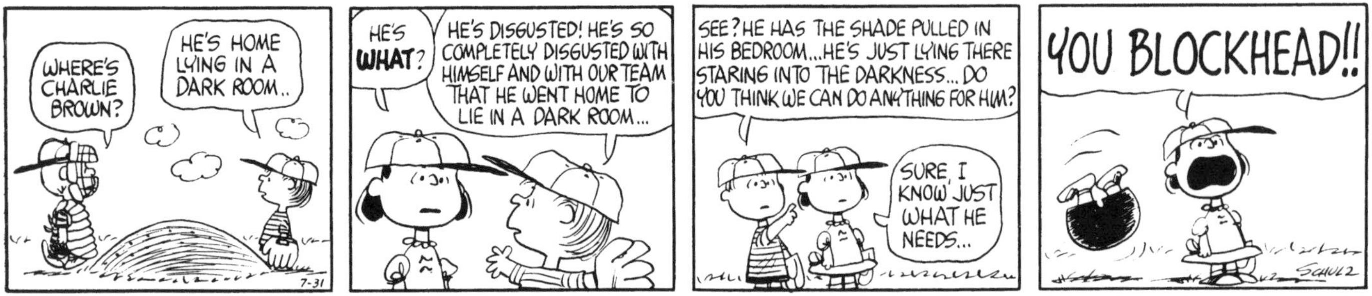
WHERE'S CHARLIE BROWN?
HE'S HOME LYING IN A DARK ROOM..
7-31
HE'S WHAT?
HE'S DISGUSTED! HE'S SO COMPLETELY DISGUSTED WITH HIMSELF AND WITH OUR TEAM THAT HE WENT HOME TO LIE IN A DARK ROOM...
SEE? HE HAS THE SHADE PULLED IN HIS BEDROOM...HE'S JUST LYING THERE STARING INTO THE DARKNESS... DO YOU THINK WE CAN DO ANYTHING FOR HIM?
SURE, I KNOW JUST WHAT HE NEEDS...
YOU BLOCKHEAD!!
SCHULZ

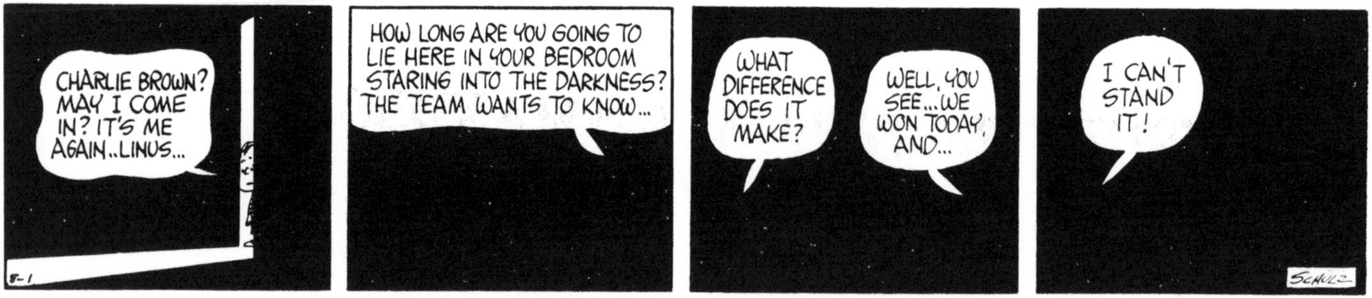
CHARLIE BROWN? MAY I COME IN? IT'S ME AGAIN..LINUS...
8-1
HOW LONG ARE YOU GOING TO LIE HERE IN YOUR BEDROOM STARING INTO THE DARKNESS? THE TEAM WANTS TO KNOW...
WHAT DIFFERENCE DOES IT MAKE?
WELL, YOU SEE...WE WON TODAY, AND...
I CAN'T STAND IT!
SCHULZ

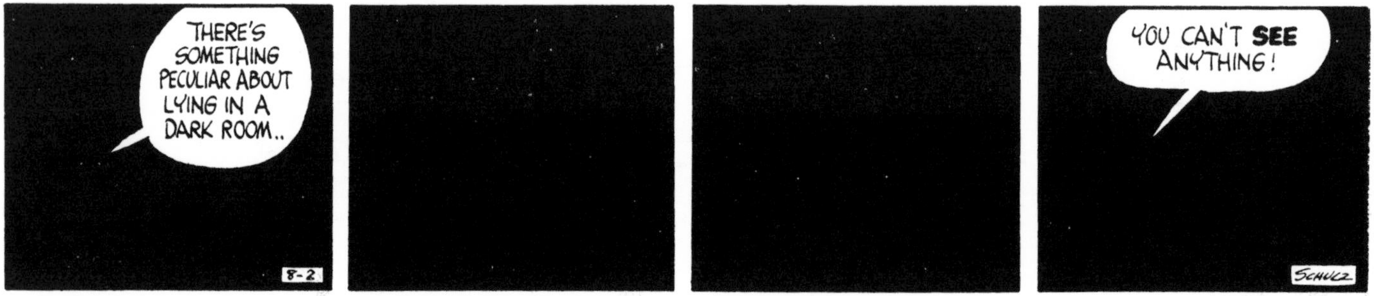
THERE'S SOMETHING PECULIAR ABOUT LYING IN A DARK ROOM..
8-2
YOU CAN'T SEE ANYTHING!
SCHULZ

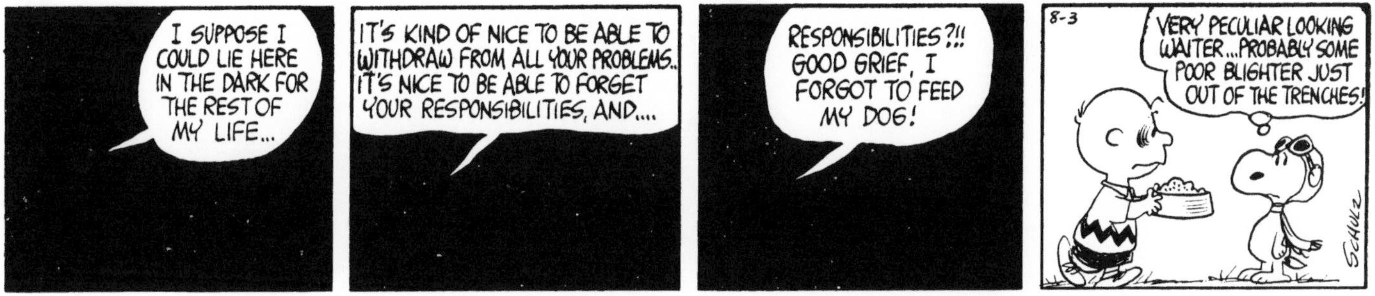
I SUPPOSE I COULD LIE HERE IN THE DARK FOR THE REST OF MY LIFE...
IT'S KIND OF NICE TO BE ABLE TO WITHDRAW FROM ALL YOUR PROBLEMS.. IT'S NICE TO BE ABLE TO FORGET YOUR RESPONSIBILITIES, AND....
RESPONSIBILITIES?!! GOOD GRIEF, I FORGOT TO FEED MY DOG!
8-3
VERY PECULIAR LOOKING WAITER...PROBABLY SOME POOR BLIGHTER JUST OUT OF THE TRENCHES!
SCHULZ
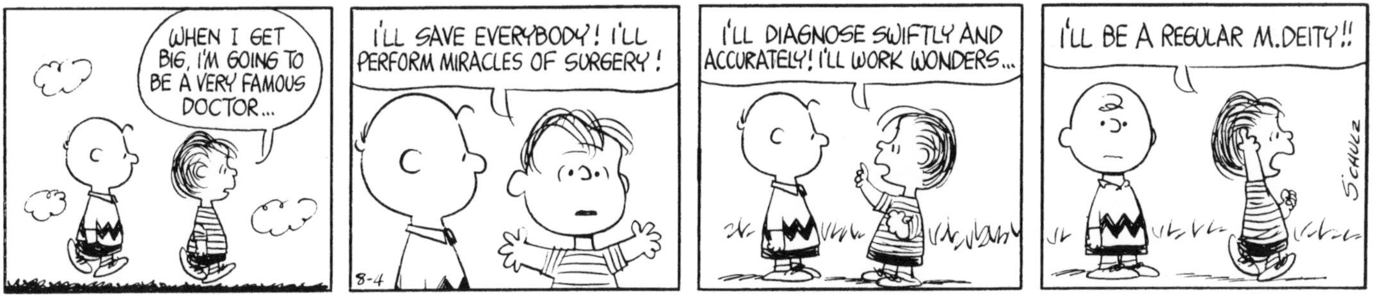
WHEN I GET BIG, I'M GOING TO BE A VERY FAMOUS DOCTOR...
I'LL SAVE EVERYBODY! I'LL PERFORM MIRACLES OF SURGERY!
8-4
I'LL DIAGNOSE SWIFTLY AND ACCURATELY! I'LL WORK WONDERS...
I'LL BE A REGULAR M.DEITY!!
SCHULZ
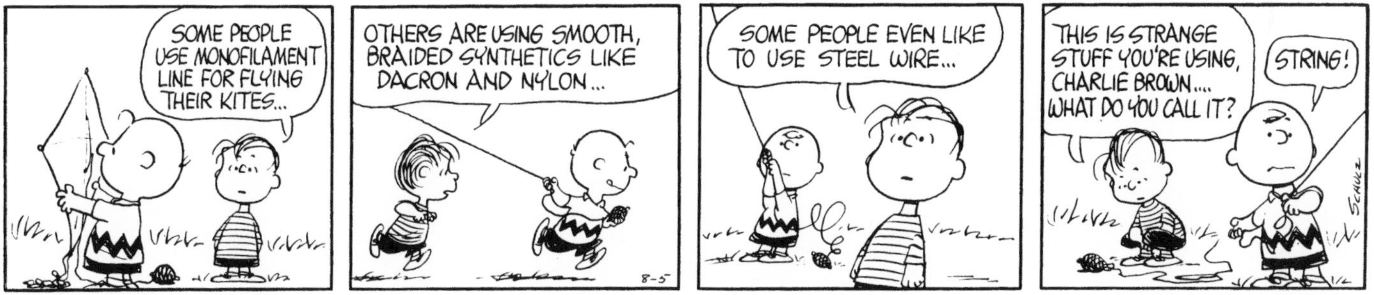
SOME PEOPLE USE MONOFILAMENT LINE FOR FLYING THEIR KITES...
OTHERS ARE USING SMOOTH, BRAIDED SYNTHETICS LIKE DACRON AND NYLON...
8-5
SOME PEOPLE EVEN LIKE TO USE STEEL WIRE...
THIS IS STRANGE STUFF YOU'RE USING, CHARLIE BROWN.... WHAT DO YOU CALL IT?
STRING!
SCHULZ

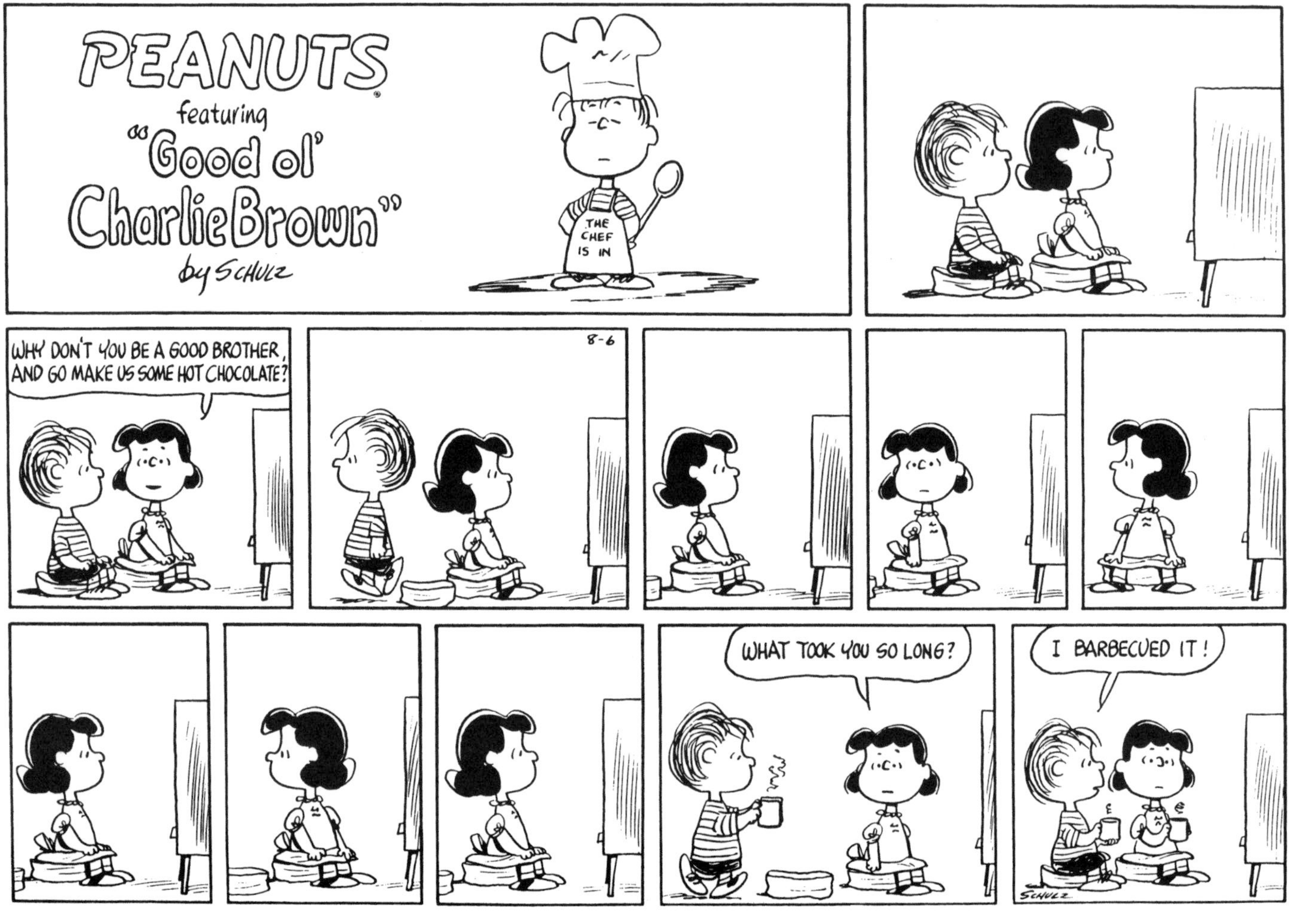
PEANUTS
featuring
"Good ol' Charlie Brown"
by SCHULZ
THE CHEF IS IN
WHY DON'T YOU BE A GOOD BROTHER, AND GO MAKE US SOME HOT CHOCOLATE?
8-6
WHAT TOOK YOU SO LONG?
I BARBECUED IT!
SCHULZ

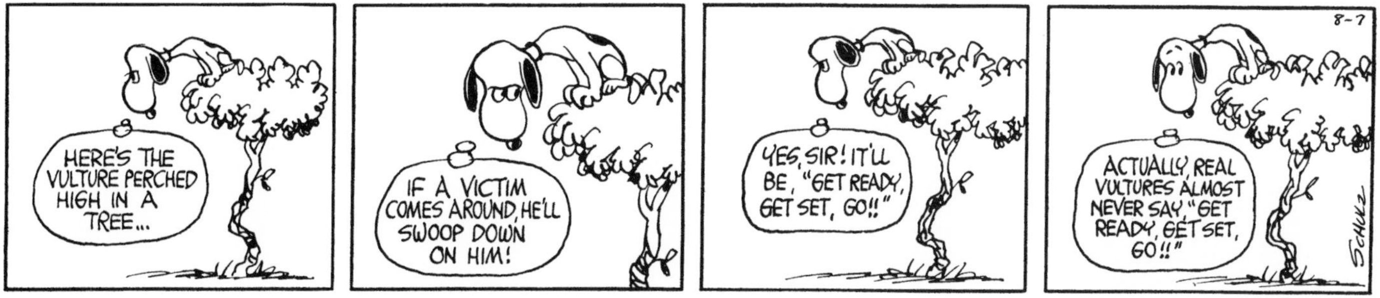
HERE'S THE VULTURE PERCHED HIGH IN A TREE...
IF A VICTIM COMES AROUND, HE'LL SWOOP DOWN ON HIM!
YES, SIR! IT'LL BE, "GET READY, GET SET, GO!!"
ACTUALLY, REAL VULTURES ALMOST NEVER SAY, "GET READY, GET SET, GO!!"

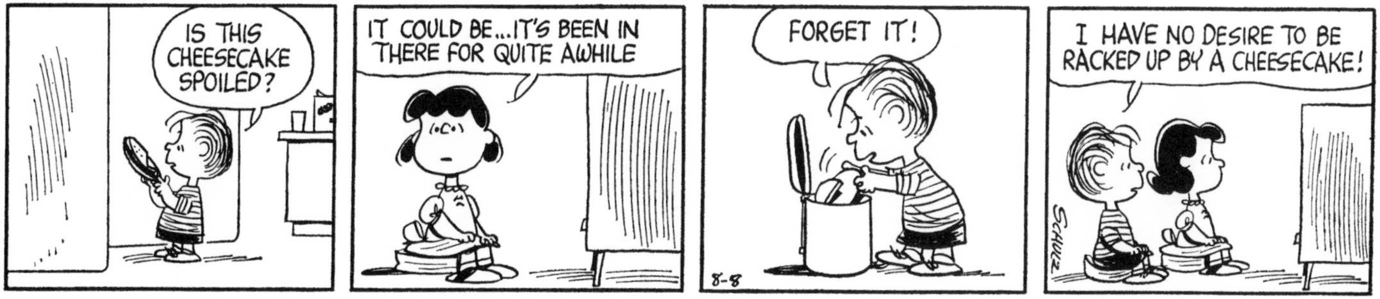
IS THIS CHEESECAKE SPOILED?
IT COULD BE...IT'S BEEN IN THERE FOR QUITE AWHILE
FORGET IT!
I HAVE NO DESIRE TO BE RACKED UP BY A CHEESECAKE!

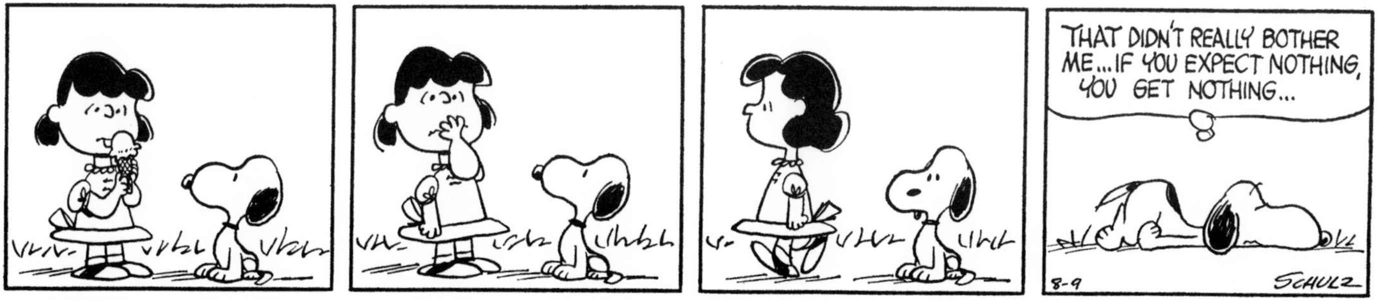
THAT DIDN'T REALLY BOTHER ME...IF YOU EXPECT NOTHING, YOU GET NOTHING...

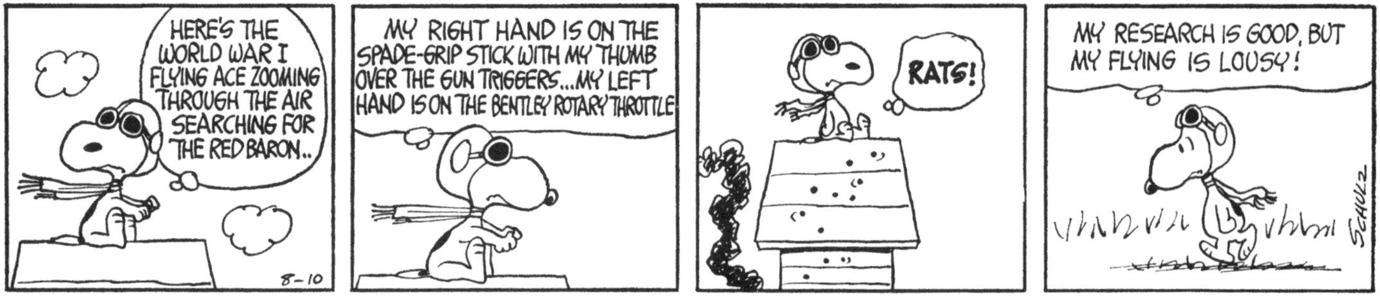
HERE'S THE WORLD WAR I FLYING ACE ZOOMING THROUGH THE AIR SEARCHING FOR THE RED BARON..
8-10
MY RIGHT HAND IS ON THE SPADE-GRIP STICK WITH MY THUMB OVER THE GUN TRIGGERS...MY LEFT HAND IS ON THE BENTLEY ROTARY THROTTLE
RATS!
MY RESEARCH IS GOOD, BUT MY FLYING IS LOUSY!
SCHULZ

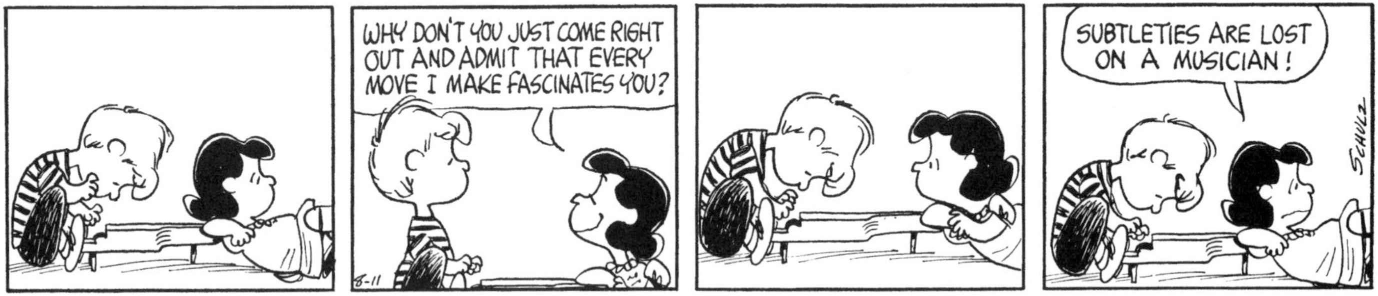
WHY DON'T YOU JUST COME RIGHT OUT AND ADMIT THAT EVERY MOVE I MAKE FASCINATES YOU?
8-11
SUBTLETIES ARE LOST ON A MUSICIAN!
SCHULZ

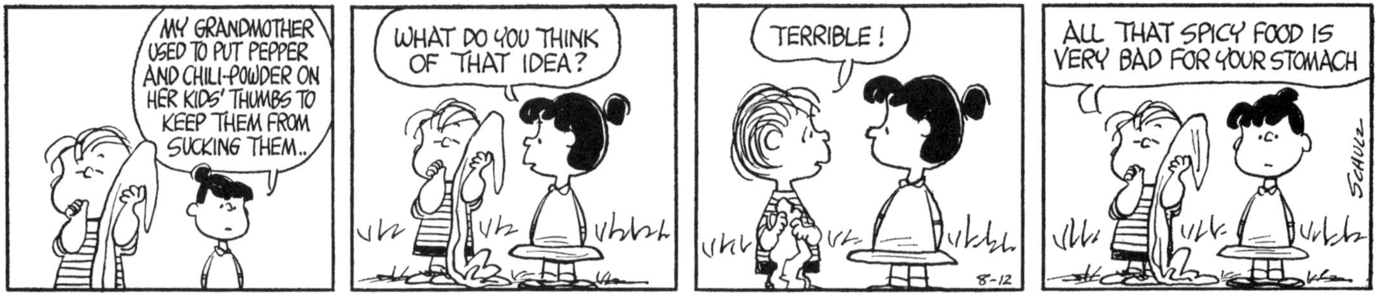
MY GRANDMOTHER USED TO PUT PEPPER AND CHILI-POWDER ON HER KIDS' THUMBS TO KEEP THEM FROM SUCKING THEM..
WHAT DO YOU THINK OF THAT IDEA?
TERRIBLE!
8-12
ALL THAT SPICY FOOD IS VERY BAD FOR YOUR STOMACH
SCHULZ

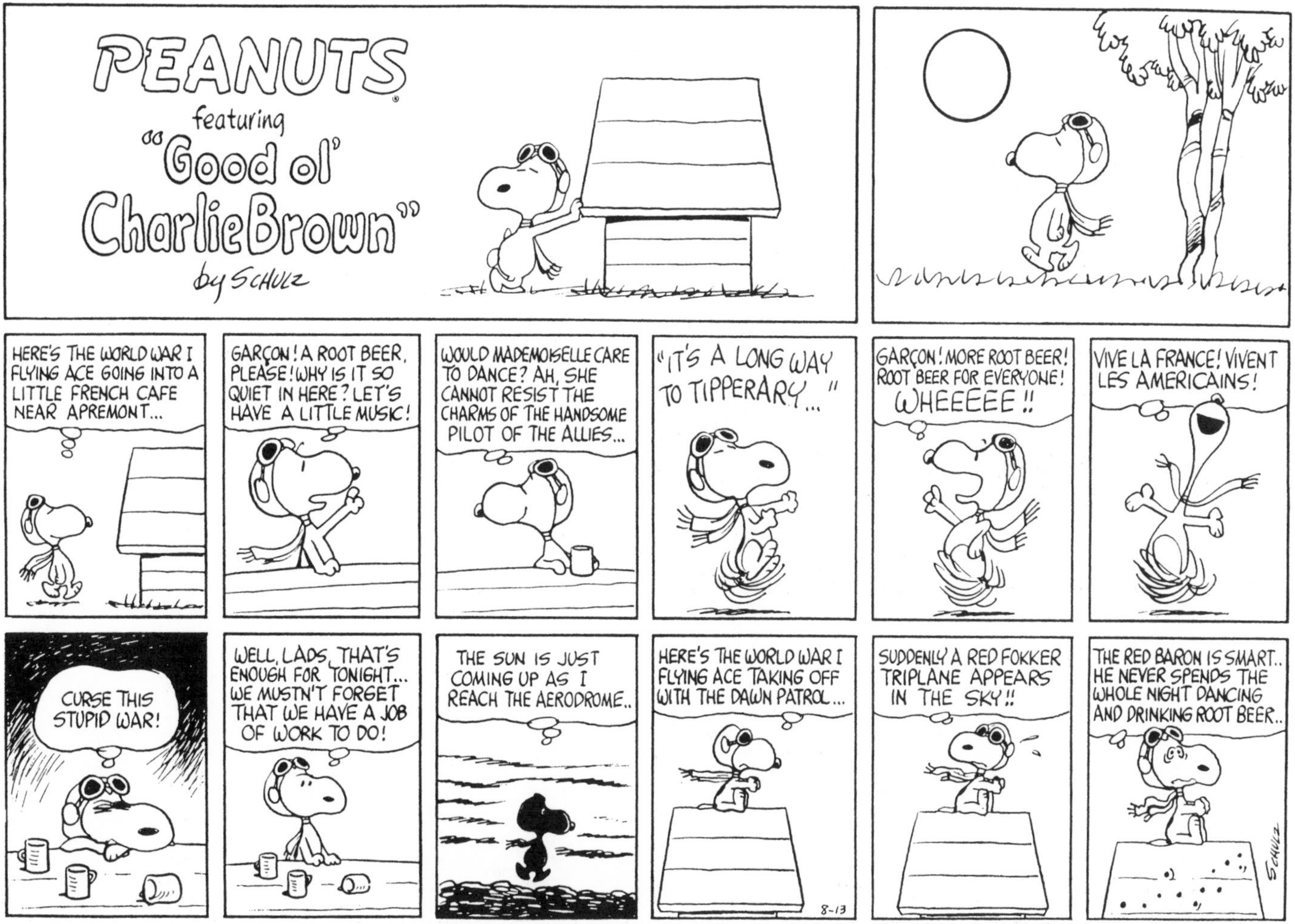
PEANUTS
featuring
"Good ol' CharlieBrown"
by SCHULZ
HERE'S THE WORLD WAR I FLYING ACE GOING INTO A LITTLE FRENCH CAFE NEAR APREMONT...
GARÇON! A ROOT BEER, PLEASE! WHY IS IT SO QUIET IN HERE? LET'S HAVE A LITTLE MUSIC!
WOULD MADEMOISELLE CARE TO DANCE? AH, SHE CANNOT RESIST THE CHARMS OF THE HANDSOME PILOT OF THE ALLIES...
"IT'S A LONG WAY TO TIPPERARY..."
GARÇON! MORE ROOT BEER! ROOT BEER FOR EVERYONE!
WHEEEEE!!
VIVE LA FRANCE! VIVENT LES AMERICAINS!
CURSE THIS STUPID WAR!
WELL, LADS, THAT'S ENOUGH FOR TONIGHT... WE MUSTN'T FORGET THAT WE HAVE A JOB OF WORK TO DO!
THE SUN IS JUST COMING UP AS I REACH THE AERODROME..
HERE'S THE WORLD WAR I FLYING ACE TAKING OFF WITH THE DAWN PATROL...
8-13
SUDDENLY A RED FOKKER TRIPLANE APPEARS IN THE SKY!!
THE RED BARON IS SMART.. HE NEVER SPENDS THE WHOLE NIGHT DANCING AND DRINKING ROOT BEER..
SCHULZ

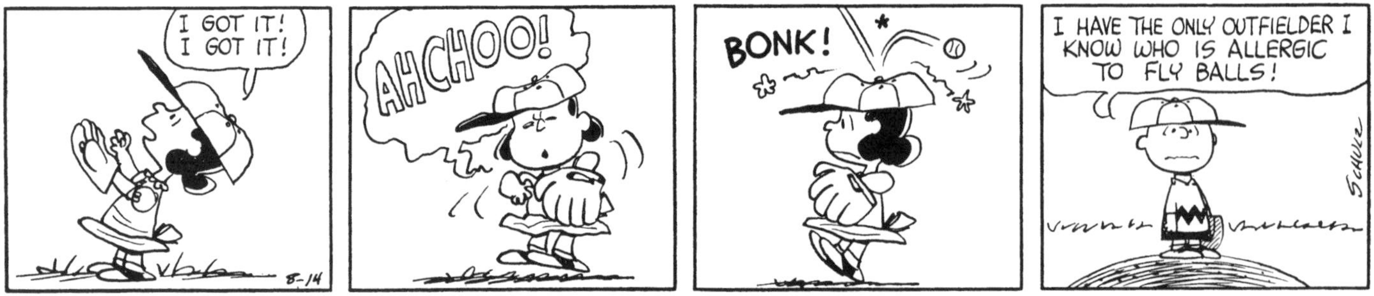
I GOT IT! I GOT IT!
8-14
AHCHOO!
BONK!
I HAVE THE ONLY OUTFIELDER I KNOW WHO IS ALLERGIC TO FLY BALLS!
SCHULZ

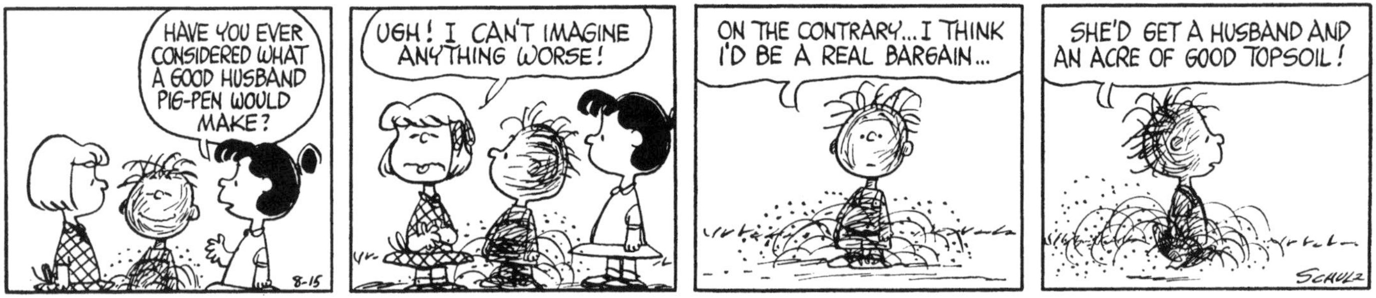
HAVE YOU EVER CONSIDERED WHAT A GOOD HUSBAND PIG-PEN WOULD MAKE?
8-15
UGH! I CAN'T IMAGINE ANYTHING WORSE!
ON THE CONTRARY...I THINK I'D BE A REAL BARGAIN...
SHE'D GET A HUSBAND AND AN ACRE OF GOOD TOPSOIL!
SCHULZ

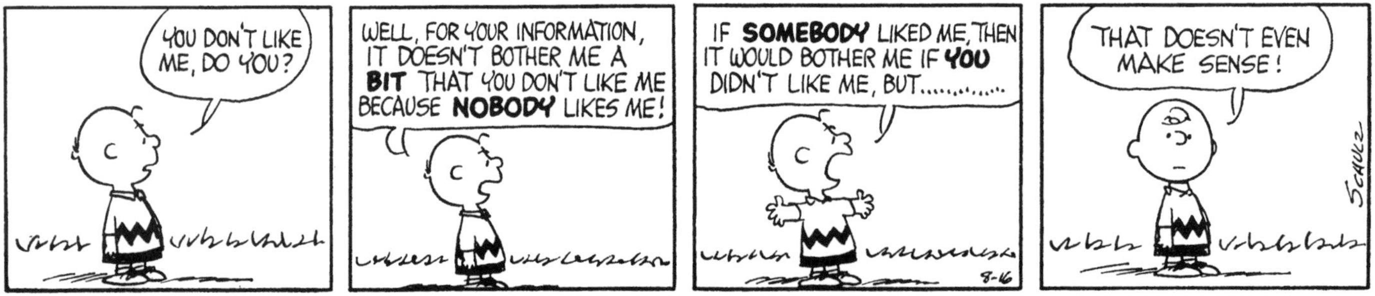
YOU DON'T LIKE ME, DO YOU?
WELL, FOR YOUR INFORMATION, IT DOESN'T BOTHER ME A **BIT** THAT YOU DON'T LIKE ME BECAUSE **NOBODY** LIKES ME!
IF **SOMEBODY** LIKED ME, THEN IT WOULD BOTHER ME IF **YOU** DIDN'T LIKE ME, BUT..........
8-16
THAT DOESN'T EVEN MAKE SENSE!
SCHULZ

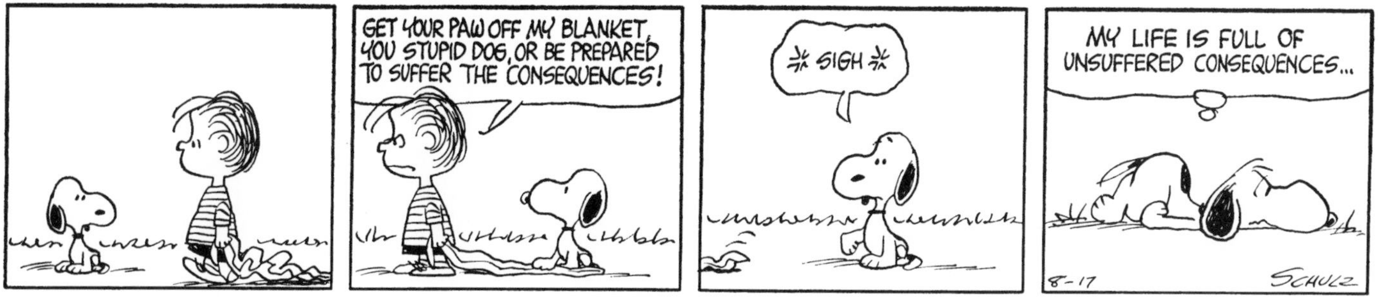
GET YOUR PAW OFF MY BLANKET, YOU STUPID DOG, OR BE PREPARED TO SUFFER THE CONSEQUENCES!
SIGH
MY LIFE IS FULL OF UNSUFFERED CONSEQUENCES...
8-17
SCHULZ

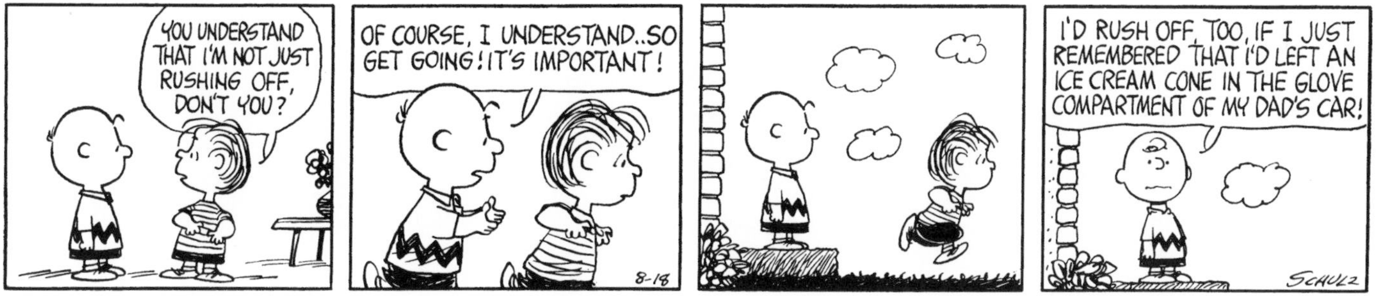
YOU UNDERSTAND THAT I'M NOT JUST RUSHING OFF, DON'T YOU?
OF COURSE, I UNDERSTAND..SO GET GOING! IT'S IMPORTANT!
8-18
I'D RUSH OFF, TOO, IF I JUST REMEMBERED THAT I'D LEFT AN ICE CREAM CONE IN THE GLOVE COMPARTMENT OF MY DAD'S CAR!
SCHULZ

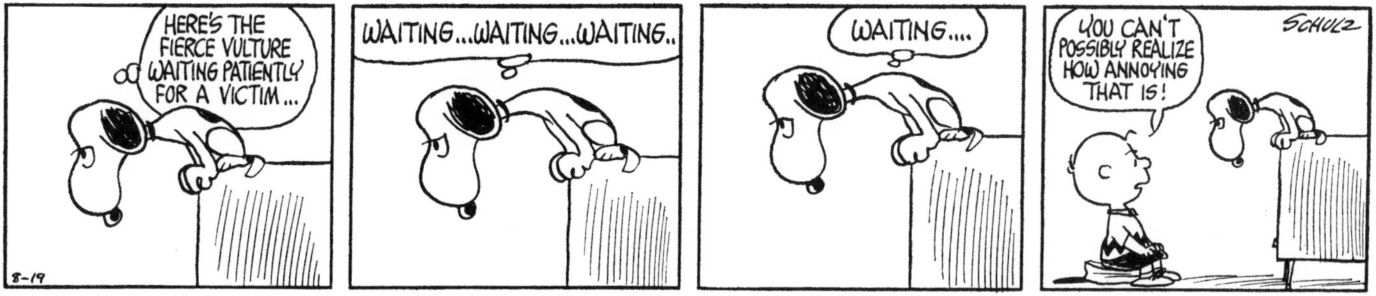
HERE'S THE FIERCE VULTURE WAITING PATIENTLY FOR A VICTIM...
8-19
WAITING...WAITING...WAITING..
WAITING....
SCHULZ
YOU CAN'T POSSIBLY REALIZE HOW ANNOYING THAT IS!

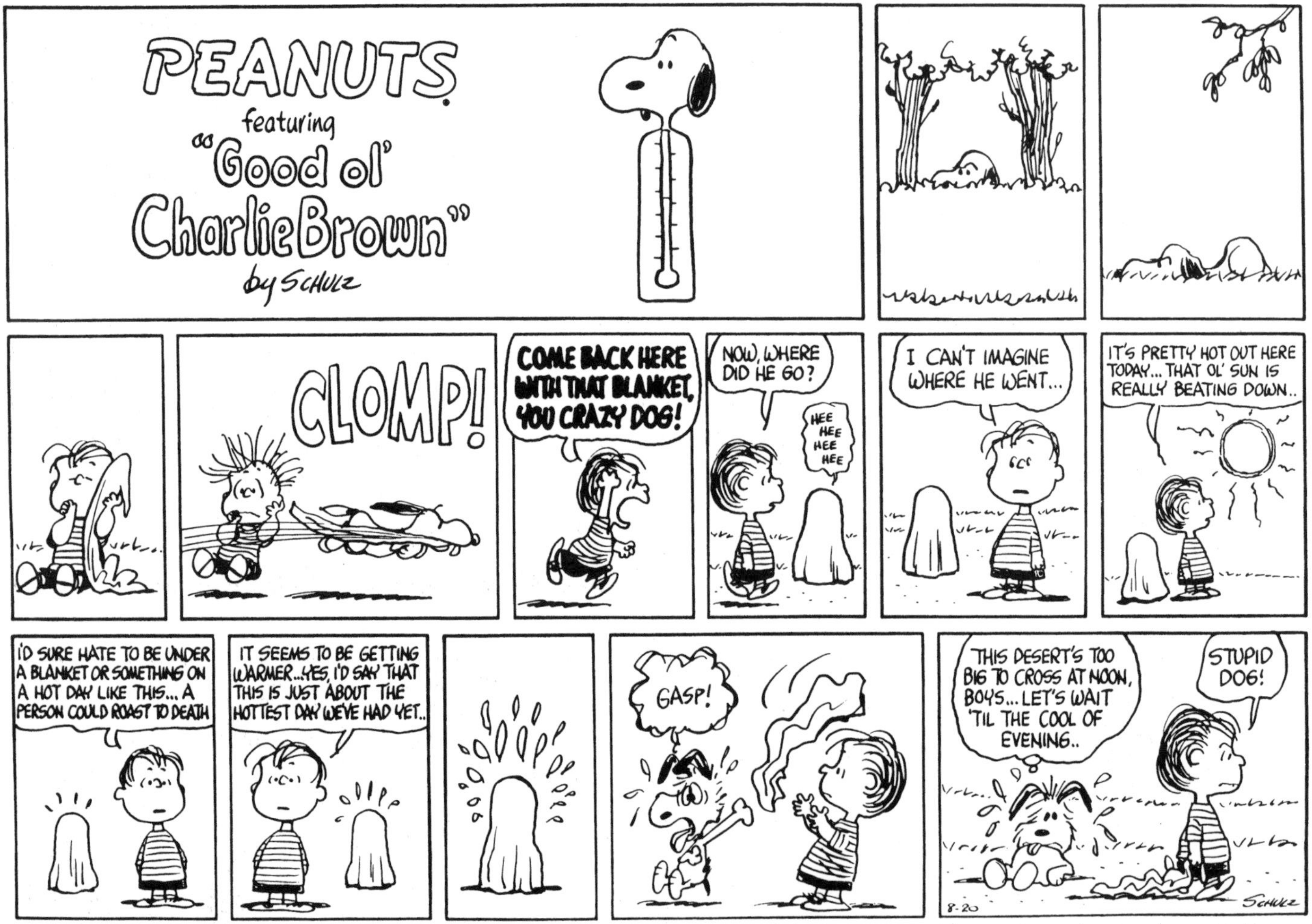
PEANUTS featuring "Good ol' Charlie Brown" by SCHULZ
CLOMP!
COME BACK HERE WITH THAT BLANKET, YOU CRAZY DOG!
NOW, WHERE DID HE GO?
HEE HEE HEE HEE
I CAN'T IMAGINE WHERE HE WENT...
IT'S PRETTY HOT OUT HERE TODAY... THAT OL' SUN IS REALLY BEATING DOWN..
I'D SURE HATE TO BE UNDER A BLANKET OR SOMETHING ON A HOT DAY LIKE THIS... A PERSON COULD ROAST TO DEATH
IT SEEMS TO BE GETTING WARMER...YES, I'D SAY THAT THIS IS JUST ABOUT THE HOTTEST DAY WE'VE HAD YET..
GASP!
THIS DESERT'S TOO BIG TO CROSS AT NOON, BOYS... LET'S WAIT 'TIL THE COOL OF EVENING..
STUPID DOG!
8-20
SCHULZ

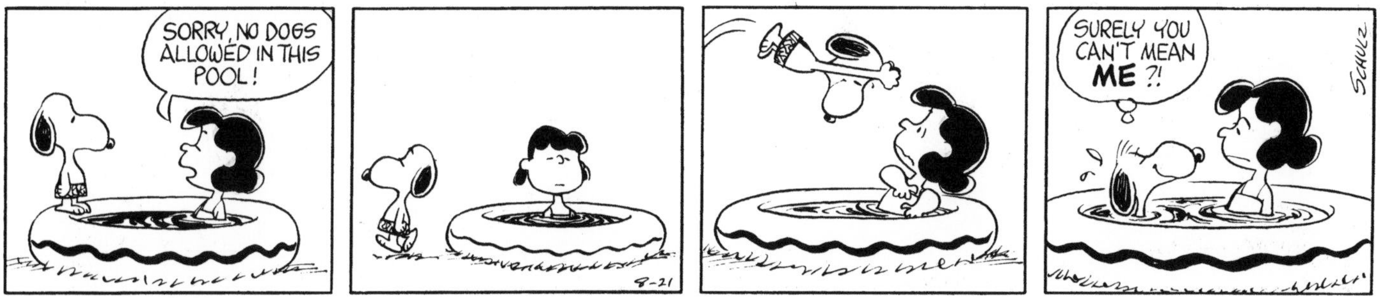
SORRY, NO DOGS ALLOWED IN THIS POOL!
8-21
SURELY YOU CAN'T MEAN **ME** ?!
SCHULZ

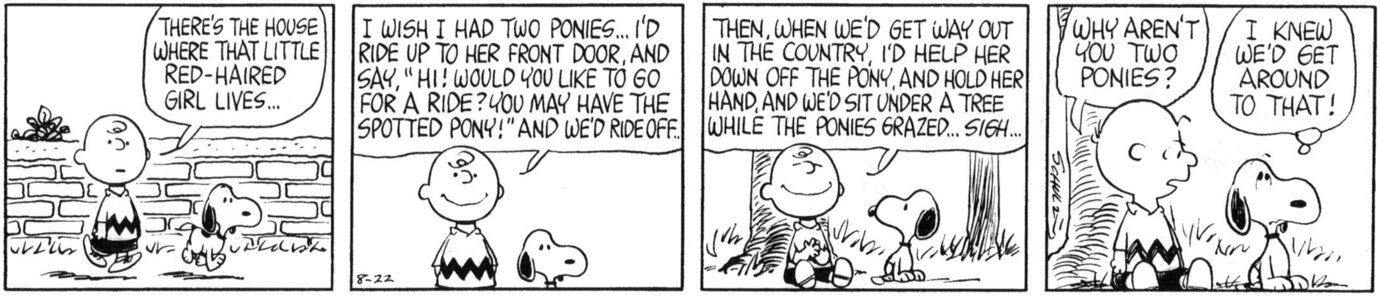
THERE'S THE HOUSE WHERE THAT LITTLE RED-HAIRED GIRL LIVES...
I WISH I HAD TWO PONIES... I'D RIDE UP TO HER FRONT DOOR, AND SAY, "HI! WOULD YOU LIKE TO GO FOR A RIDE? YOU MAY HAVE THE SPOTTED PONY!" AND WE'D RIDE OFF..
8-22
THEN, WHEN WE'D GET WAY OUT IN THE COUNTRY, I'D HELP HER DOWN OFF THE PONY, AND HOLD HER HAND, AND WE'D SIT UNDER A TREE WHILE THE PONIES GRAZED... SIGH...
WHY AREN'T YOU TWO PONIES?
I KNEW WE'D GET AROUND TO THAT!
SCHULZ

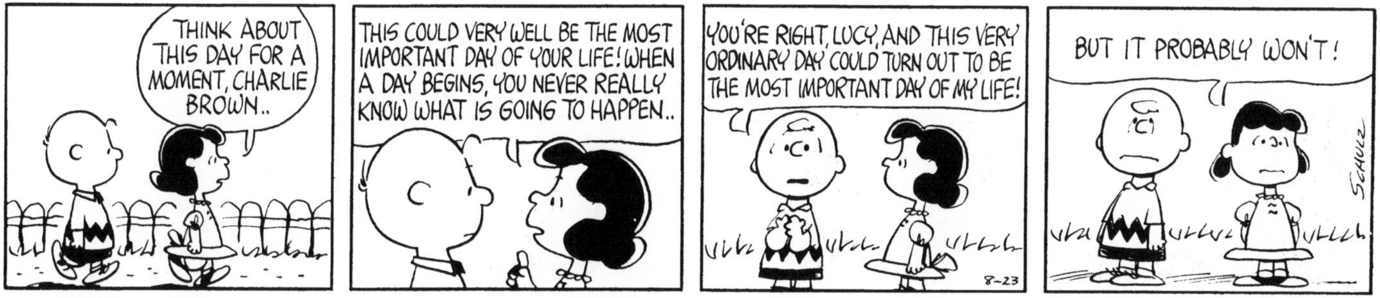
THINK ABOUT THIS DAY FOR A MOMENT, CHARLIE BROWN..
THIS COULD VERY WELL BE THE MOST IMPORTANT DAY OF YOUR LIFE! WHEN A DAY BEGINS, YOU NEVER REALLY KNOW WHAT IS GOING TO HAPPEN..
YOU'RE RIGHT, LUCY, AND THIS VERY ORDINARY DAY COULD TURN OUT TO BE THE MOST IMPORTANT DAY OF MY LIFE!
8-23
BUT IT PROBABLY WON'T!
SCHULZ

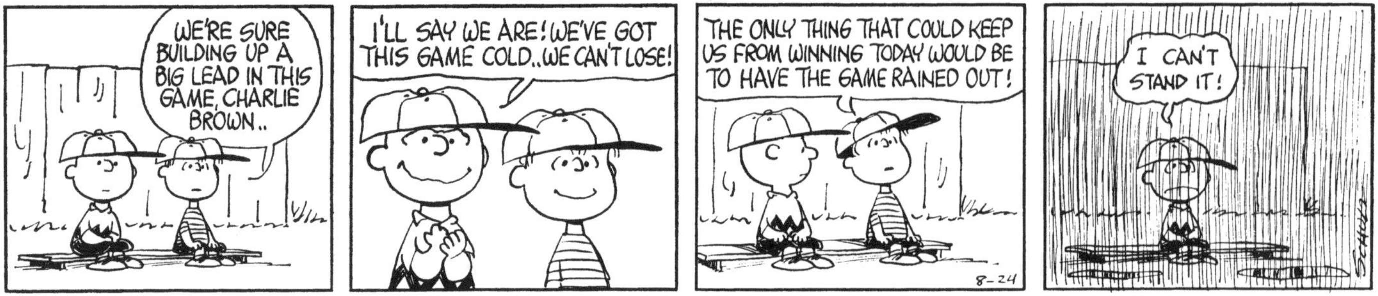
WE'RE SURE BUILDING UP A BIG LEAD IN THIS GAME, CHARLIE BROWN..
I'LL SAY WE ARE! WE'VE GOT THIS GAME COLD..WE CAN'T LOSE!
THE ONLY THING THAT COULD KEEP US FROM WINNING TODAY WOULD BE TO HAVE THE GAME RAINED OUT!
8-24
I CAN'T STAND IT!
SCHULZ

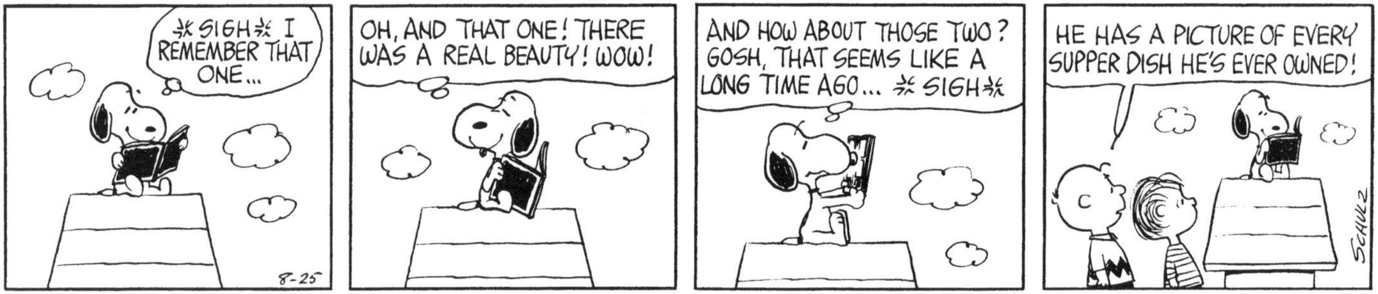
SIGH I REMEMBER THAT ONE...
8-25
OH, AND THAT ONE! THERE WAS A REAL BEAUTY! WOW!
AND HOW ABOUT THOSE TWO? GOSH, THAT SEEMS LIKE A LONG TIME AGO... *SIGH*
HE HAS A PICTURE OF EVERY SUPPER DISH HE'S EVER OWNED!
SCHULZ

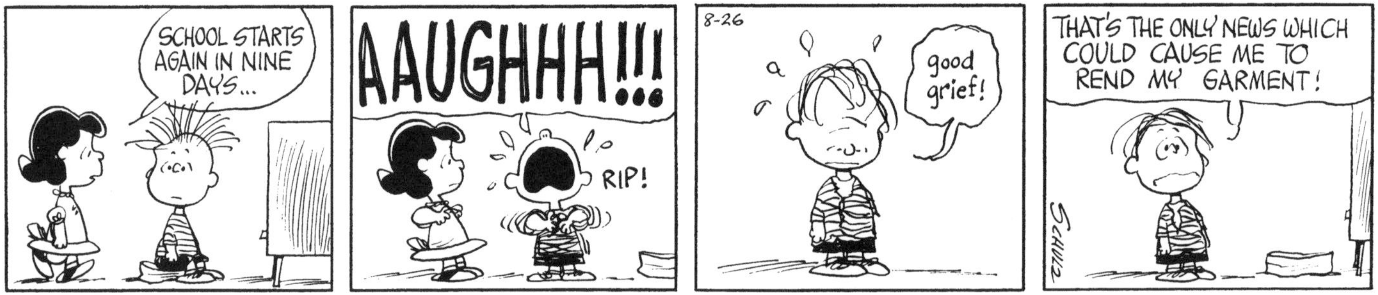
SCHOOL STARTS AGAIN IN NINE DAYS...
AAUGHHH!!!
RIP!
8-26
good grief!
SCHULZ
THAT'S THE ONLY NEWS WHICH COULD CAUSE ME TO REND MY GARMENT!

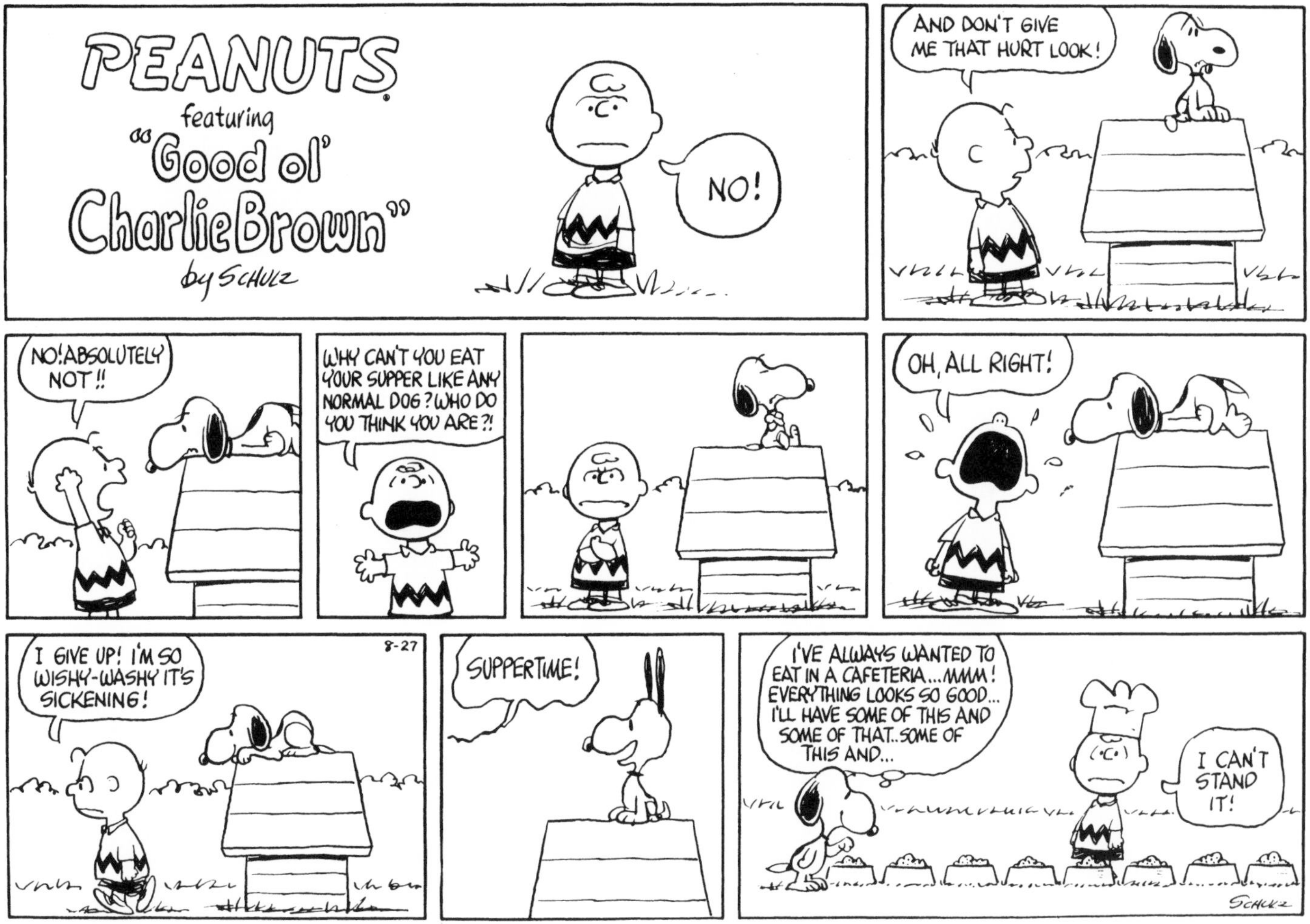

PEANUTS
featuring "Good ol' Charlie Brown"
by SCHULZ
NO!
AND DON'T GIVE ME THAT HURT LOOK!
NO! ABSOLUTELY NOT!!
WHY CAN'T YOU EAT YOUR SUPPER LIKE ANY NORMAL DOG? WHO DO YOU THINK YOU ARE?!
OH, ALL RIGHT!
I GIVE UP! I'M SO WISHY-WASHY IT'S SICKENING!
8-27
SUPPERTIME!
I'VE ALWAYS WANTED TO EAT IN A CAFETERIA...MMM! EVERYTHING LOOKS SO GOOD... I'LL HAVE SOME OF THIS AND... SOME OF THAT..SOME OF THIS AND...
I CAN'T STAND IT!
SCHULZ

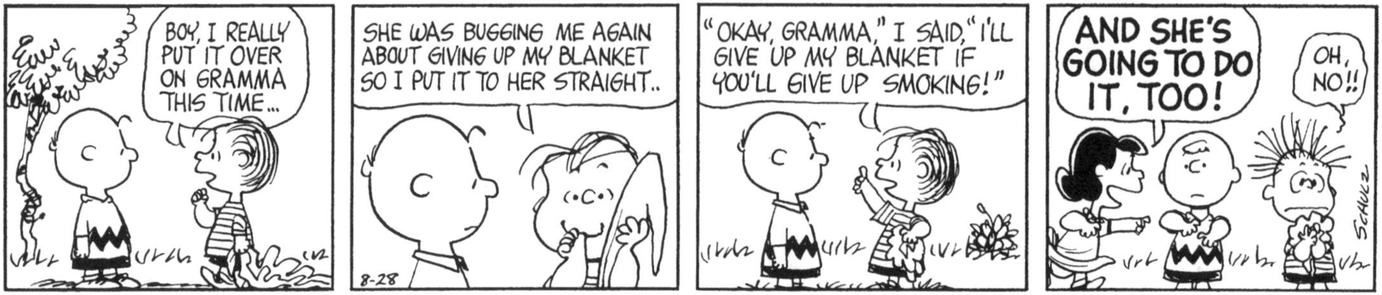
BOY, I REALLY PUT IT OVER ON GRAMMA THIS TIME...
SHE WAS BUGGING ME AGAIN ABOUT GIVING UP MY BLANKET SO I PUT IT TO HER STRAIGHT..
8-28
"OKAY, GRAMMA," I SAID, "I'LL GIVE UP MY BLANKET IF YOU'LL GIVE UP SMOKING!"
AND SHE'S GOING TO DO IT, TOO!
OH, NO!!
SCHULZ

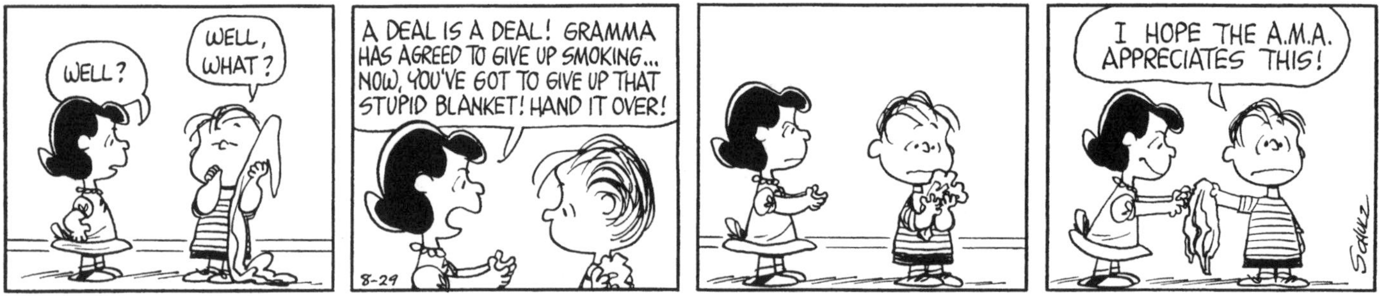
WELL?
WELL, WHAT?
A DEAL IS A DEAL! GRAMMA HAS AGREED TO GIVE UP SMOKING... NOW, YOU'VE GOT TO GIVE UP THAT STUPID BLANKET! HAND IT OVER!
8-29
I HOPE THE A.M.A. APPRECIATES THIS!
SCHULZ

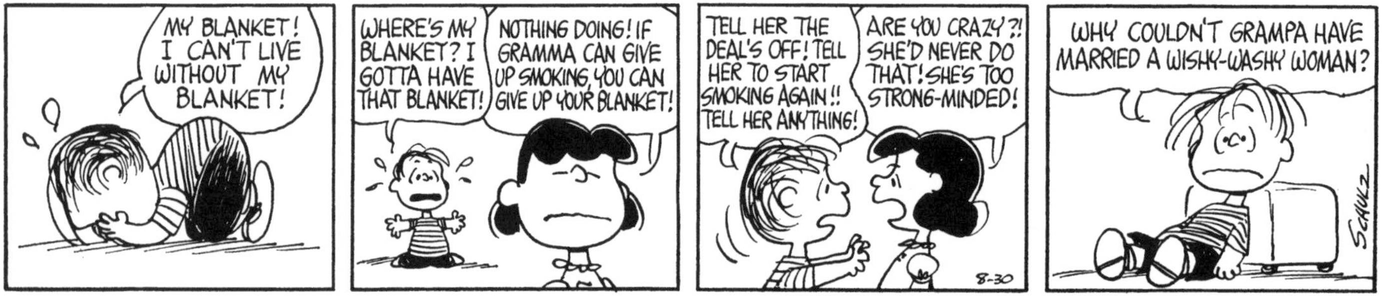
MY BLANKET! I CAN'T LIVE WITHOUT MY BLANKET!
WHERE'S MY BLANKET? I GOTTA HAVE THAT BLANKET!
NOTHING DOING! IF GRAMMA CAN GIVE UP SMOKING, YOU CAN GIVE UP YOUR BLANKET!
TELL HER THE DEAL'S OFF! TELL HER TO START SMOKING AGAIN!! TELL HER ANYTHING!
ARE YOU CRAZY?! SHE'D NEVER DO THAT! SHE'S TOO STRONG-MINDED!
8-30
WHY COULDN'T GRAMPA HAVE MARRIED A WISHY-WASHY WOMAN?
SCHULZ

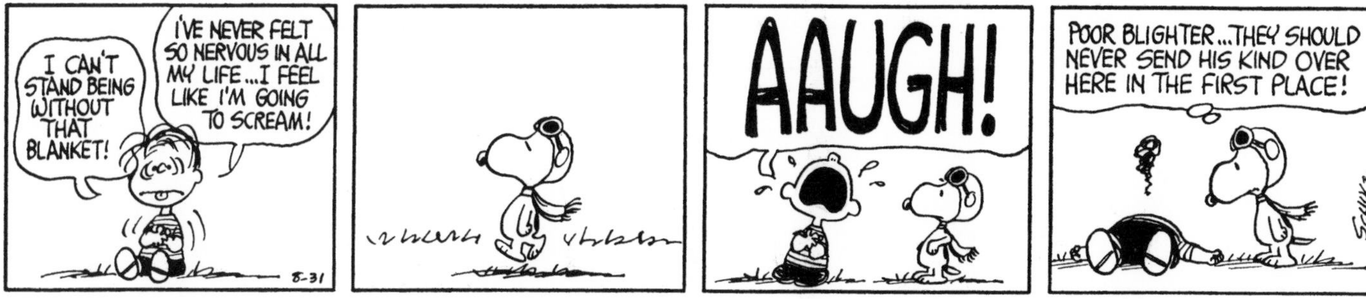
I CAN'T STAND BEING WITHOUT THAT BLANKET!
I'VE NEVER FELT SO NERVOUS IN ALL MY LIFE...I FEEL LIKE I'M GOING TO SCREAM!
8-31
AAUGH!
POOR BLIGHTER...THEY SHOULD NEVER SEND HIS KIND OVER HERE IN THE FIRST PLACE!
SCHULZ

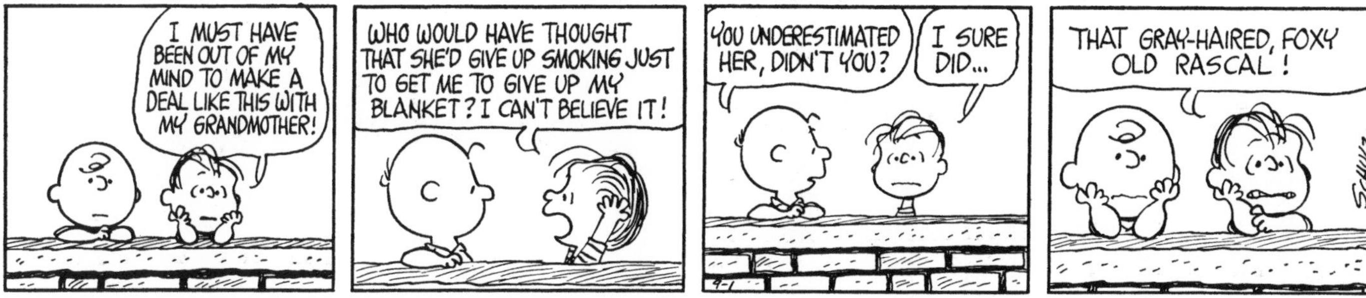
I MUST HAVE BEEN OUT OF MY MIND TO MAKE A DEAL LIKE THIS WITH MY GRANDMOTHER!
WHO WOULD HAVE THOUGHT THAT SHE'D GIVE UP SMOKING JUST TO GET ME TO GIVE UP MY BLANKET? I CAN'T BELIEVE IT!
YOU UNDERESTIMATED HER, DIDN'T YOU?
I SURE DID...
9-1
THAT GRAY-HAIRED, FOXY OLD RASCAL!
SCHULZ

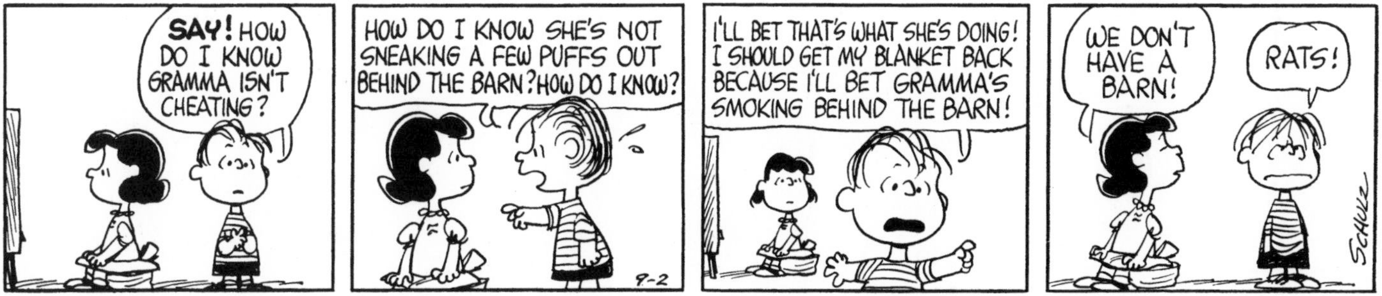
SAY! HOW DO I KNOW GRAMMA ISN'T CHEATING?
HOW DO I KNOW SHE'S NOT SNEAKING A FEW PUFFS OUT BEHIND THE BARN? HOW DO I KNOW?
9-2
I'LL BET THAT'S WHAT SHE'S DOING! I SHOULD GET MY BLANKET BACK BECAUSE I'LL BET GRAMMA'S SMOKING BEHIND THE BARN!
WE DON'T HAVE A BARN!
RATS!
SCHULZ

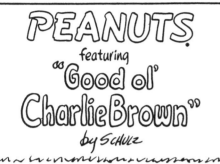

PEANUTS
featuring
"Good ol' CharlieBrown"
by SCHULZ

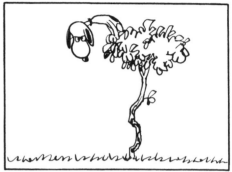

HERE'S THE FIERCE VULTURE SITTING HIGH IN A TREE WAITING FOR A VICTIM TO COME ALONG..

AH! A VICTIM APPROACHES! AS HE PASSES BY THE TREE, I SHALL SWOOP DOWN UPON HIM!

GET READY....
GET SET....

SWOOP!

KLUNK!

IF YOU'LL PARDON MY SAYING SO, YOUR "SWOOPING" LEAVES MUCH TO BE DESIRED...

MAYBE I COULD GO TO SWOOP SCHOOL...

SCHULZ   9-3

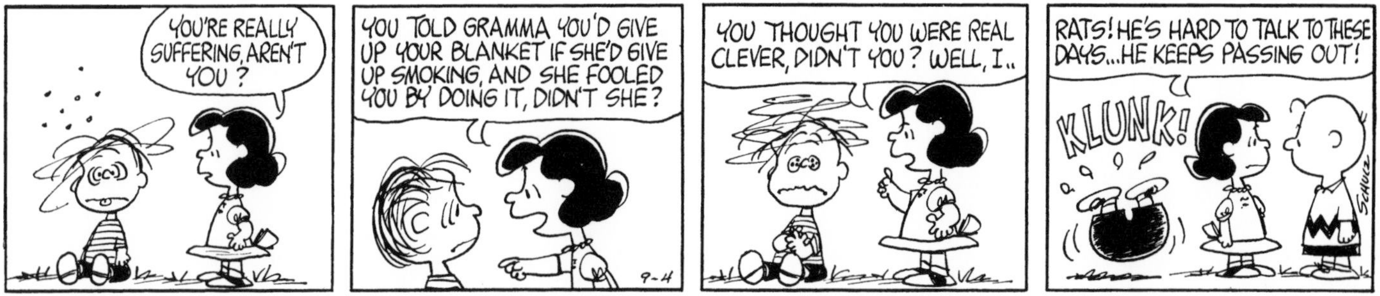
YOU'RE REALLY SUFFERING, AREN'T YOU ?
YOU TOLD GRAMMA YOU'D GIVE UP YOUR BLANKET IF SHE'D GIVE UP SMOKING, AND SHE FOOLED YOU BY DOING IT, DIDN'T SHE ?
9-4
YOU THOUGHT YOU WERE REAL CLEVER, DIDN'T YOU ? WELL, I..
RATS! HE'S HARD TO TALK TO THESE DAYS...HE KEEPS PASSING OUT!
KLUNK!
SCHULZ

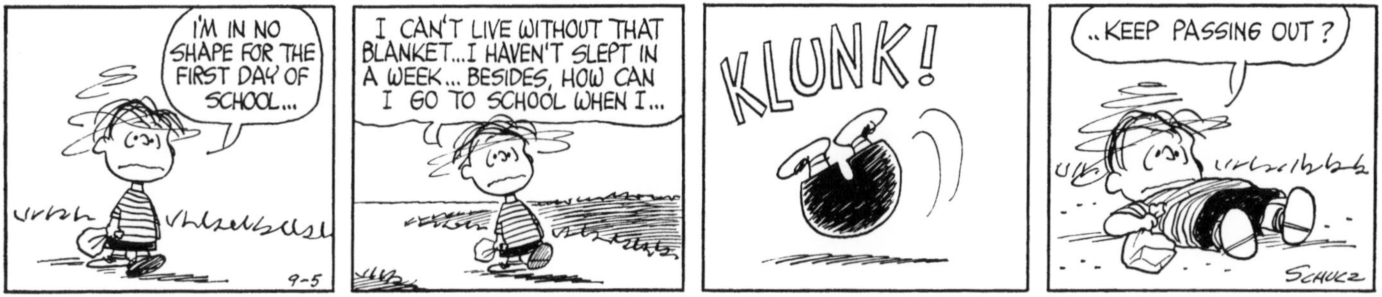
I'M IN NO SHAPE FOR THE FIRST DAY OF SCHOOL...
9-5
I CAN'T LIVE WITHOUT THAT BLANKET...I HAVEN'T SLEPT IN A WEEK... BESIDES, HOW CAN I GO TO SCHOOL WHEN I...
KLUNK!
..KEEP PASSING OUT ?
SCHULZ

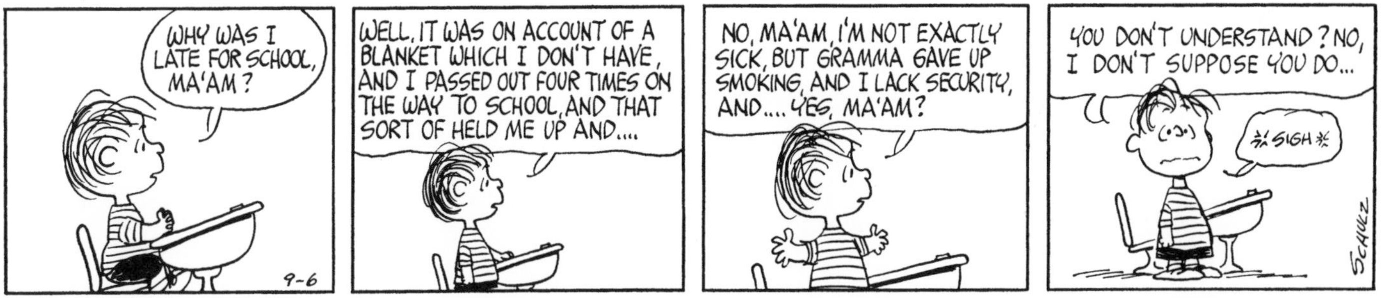
WHY WAS I LATE FOR SCHOOL, MA'AM ?
9-6
WELL, IT WAS ON ACCOUNT OF A BLANKET WHICH I DON'T HAVE, AND I PASSED OUT FOUR TIMES ON THE WAY TO SCHOOL, AND THAT SORT OF HELD ME UP AND....
NO, MA'AM, I'M NOT EXACTLY SICK, BUT GRAMMA GAVE UP SMOKING, AND I LACK SECURITY, AND.... YES, MA'AM ?
YOU DON'T UNDERSTAND ? NO, I DON'T SUPPOSE YOU DO...
SIGH
SCHULZ

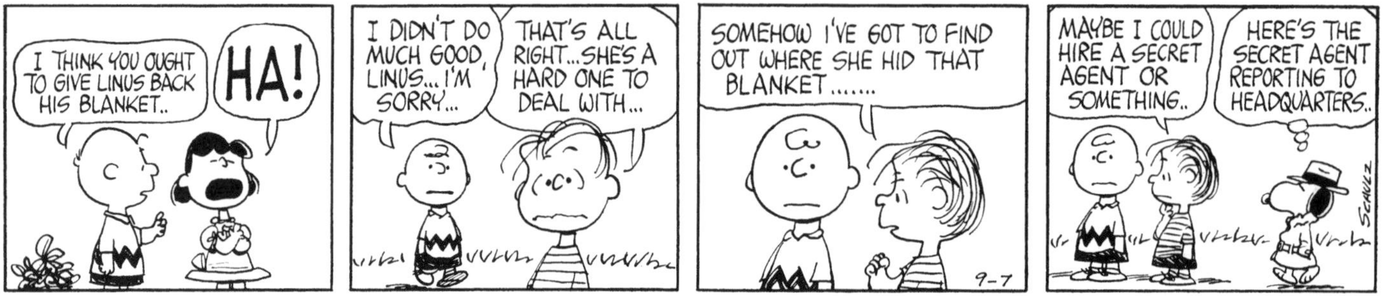
I THINK YOU OUGHT TO GIVE LINUS BACK HIS BLANKET..
HA!
I DIDN'T DO MUCH GOOD, LINUS... I'M SORRY...
THAT'S ALL RIGHT...SHE'S A HARD ONE TO DEAL WITH...
SOMEHOW I'VE GOT TO FIND OUT WHERE SHE HID THAT BLANKET.......
9-7
MAYBE I COULD HIRE A SECRET AGENT OR SOMETHING..
HERE'S THE SECRET AGENT REPORTING TO HEADQUARTERS..
SCHULZ

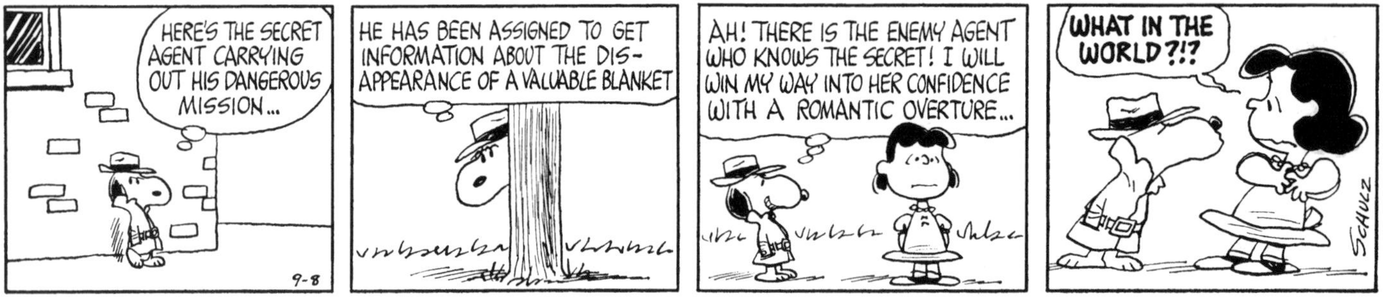
HERE'S THE SECRET AGENT CARRYING OUT HIS DANGEROUS MISSION...
9-8
HE HAS BEEN ASSIGNED TO GET INFORMATION ABOUT THE DIS-APPEARANCE OF A VALUABLE BLANKET
AH! THERE IS THE ENEMY AGENT WHO KNOWS THE SECRET! I WILL WIN MY WAY INTO HER CONFIDENCE WITH A ROMANTIC OVERTURE...
WHAT IN THE WORLD?!?
SCHULZ

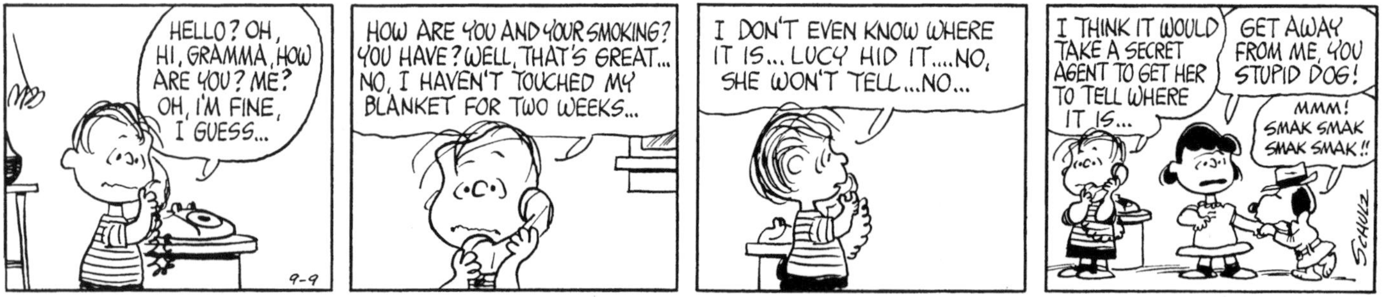
HELLO? OH, HI, GRAMMA, HOW ARE YOU? ME? OH, I'M FINE, I GUESS...
9-9
HOW ARE YOU AND YOUR SMOKING? YOU HAVE? WELL, THAT'S GREAT... NO, I HAVEN'T TOUCHED MY BLANKET FOR TWO WEEKS...
I DON'T EVEN KNOW WHERE IT IS... LUCY HID IT....NO, SHE WON'T TELL...NO...
I THINK IT WOULD TAKE A SECRET AGENT TO GET HER TO TELL WHERE IT IS...
GET AWAY FROM ME, YOU STUPID DOG!
MMM! SMAK SMAK SMAK SMAK!!
SCHULZ

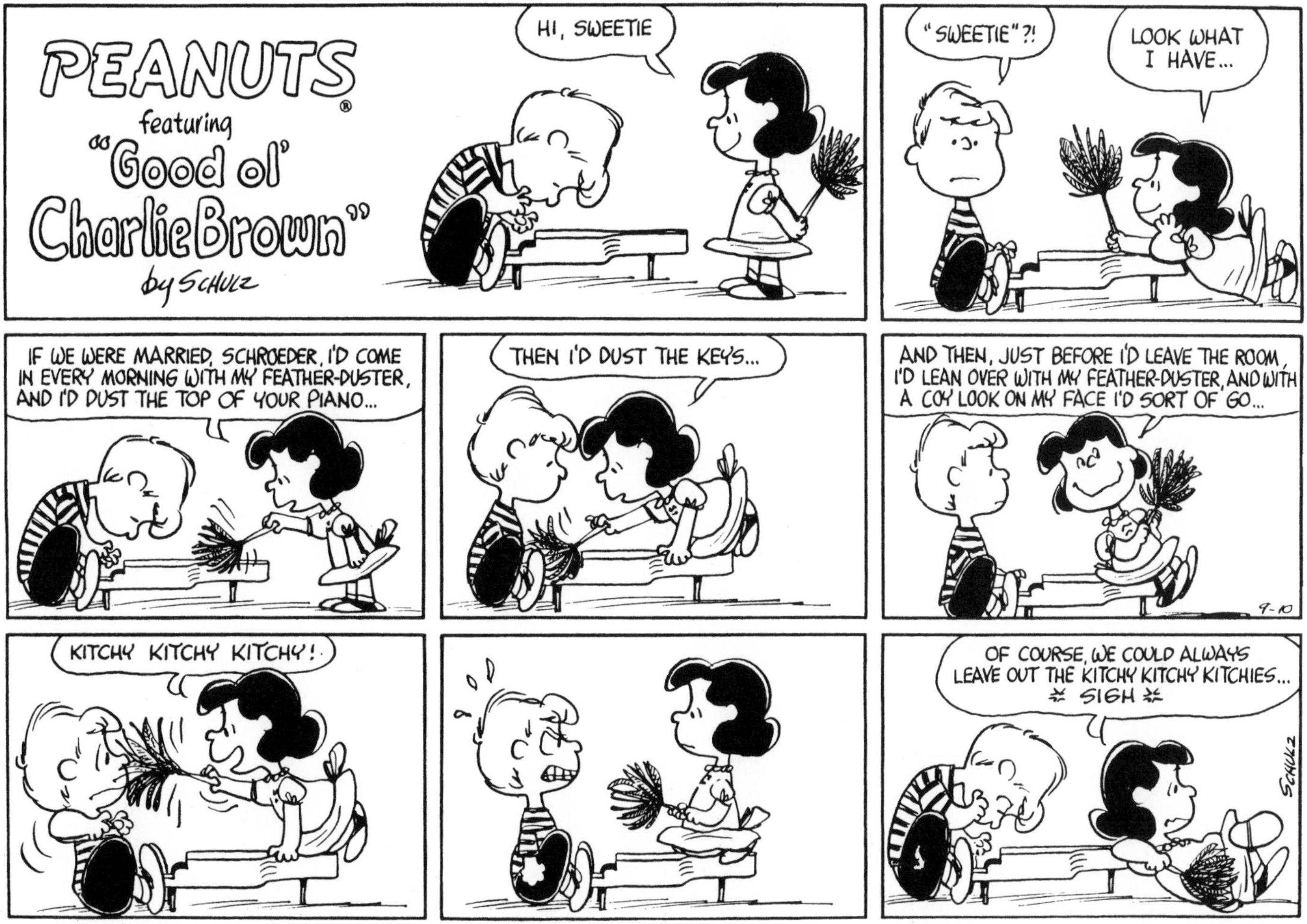
PEANUTS®
featuring "Good ol' CharlieBrown"
by SCHULZ
HI, SWEETIE
"SWEETIE"?!
LOOK WHAT I HAVE...
IF WE WERE MARRIED, SCHROEDER, I'D COME IN EVERY MORNING WITH MY FEATHER-DUSTER, AND I'D DUST THE TOP OF YOUR PIANO...
THEN I'D DUST THE KEYS...
AND THEN, JUST BEFORE I'D LEAVE THE ROOM, I'D LEAN OVER WITH MY FEATHER-DUSTER, AND WITH A COY LOOK ON MY FACE I'D SORT OF GO...
9-10
KITCHY KITCHY KITCHY!
OF COURSE, WE COULD ALWAYS LEAVE OUT THE KITCHY KITCHY KITCHIES...
SIGH
SCHULZ

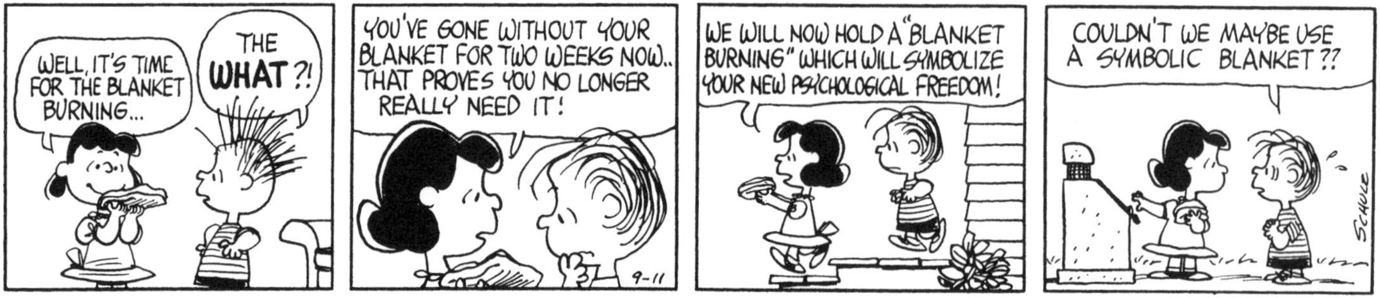
WELL, IT'S TIME FOR THE BLANKET BURNING...
THE **WHAT** ?!
YOU'VE GONE WITHOUT YOUR BLANKET FOR TWO WEEKS NOW.. THAT PROVES YOU NO LONGER REALLY NEED IT!
9-11
WE WILL NOW HOLD A "BLANKET BURNING" WHICH WILL SYMBOLIZE YOUR NEW PSYCHOLOGICAL FREEDOM!
COULDN'T WE MAYBE USE A SYMBOLIC BLANKET ??
SCHULZ

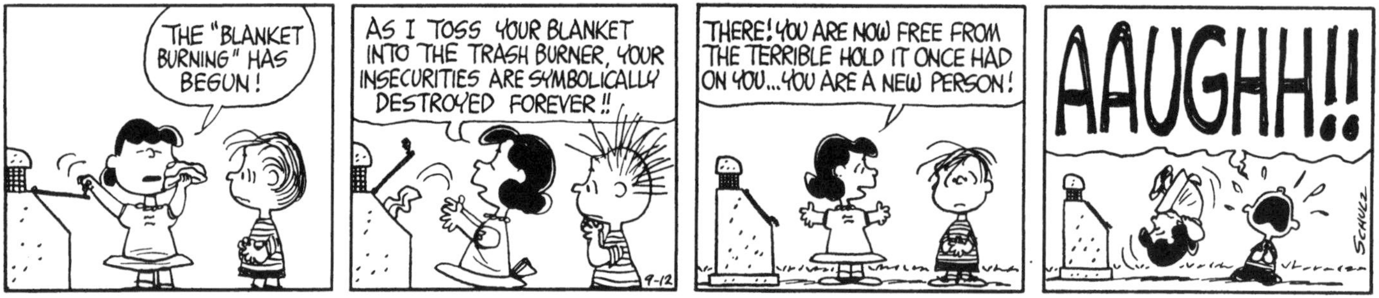
THE "BLANKET BURNING" HAS BEGUN!
AS I TOSS YOUR BLANKET INTO THE TRASH BURNER, YOUR INSECURITIES ARE SYMBOLICALLY DESTROYED FOREVER!!
9-12
THERE! YOU ARE NOW FREE FROM THE TERRIBLE HOLD IT ONCE HAD ON YOU...YOU ARE A NEW PERSON!
AAUGHH!!
SCHULZ

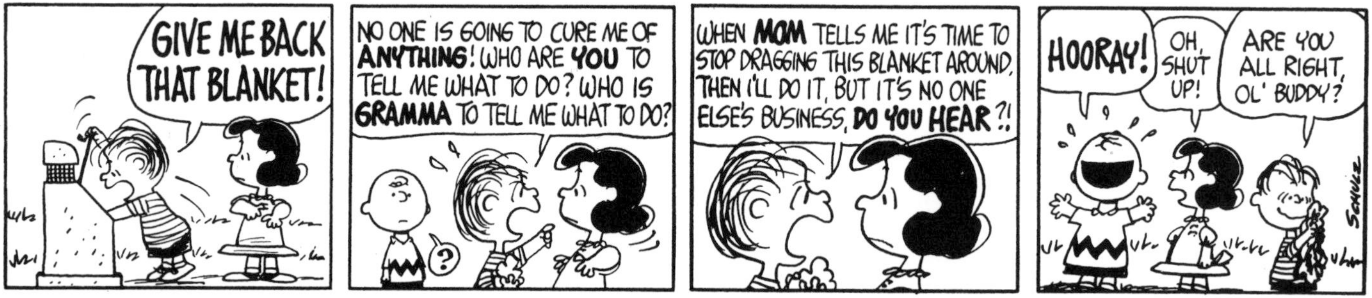
GIVE ME BACK THAT BLANKET!
NO ONE IS GOING TO CURE ME OF **ANYTHING**! WHO ARE **YOU** TO TELL ME WHAT TO DO? WHO IS **GRAMMA** TO TELL ME WHAT TO DO?
?
WHEN **MOM** TELLS ME IT'S TIME TO STOP DRAGGING THIS BLANKET AROUND, THEN I'LL DO IT, BUT IT'S NO ONE ELSE'S BUSINESS, **DO YOU HEAR** ?!
HOORAY!
OH, SHUT UP!
ARE YOU ALL RIGHT, OL' BUDDY?
SCHULZ

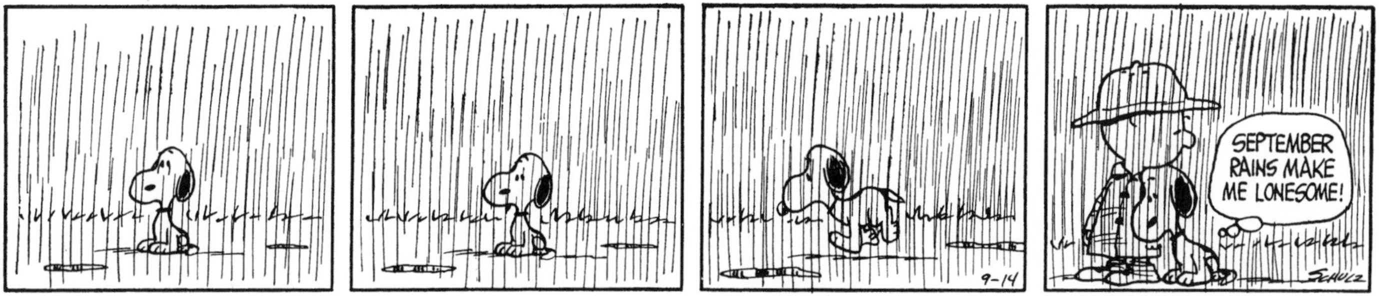
9-14
SEPTEMBER RAINS MAKE ME LONESOME!
SCHULZ

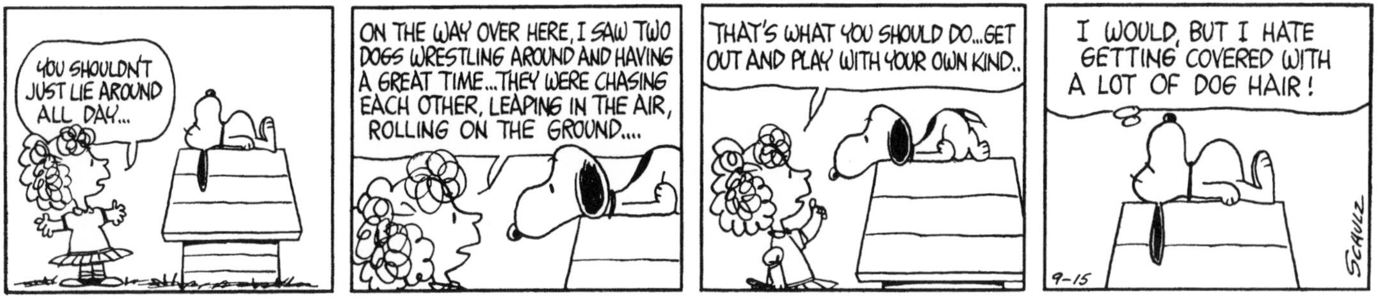
YOU SHOULDN'T JUST LIE AROUND ALL DAY...
ON THE WAY OVER HERE, I SAW TWO DOGS WRESTLING AROUND AND HAVING A GREAT TIME...THEY WERE CHASING EACH OTHER, LEAPING IN THE AIR, ROLLING ON THE GROUND....
THAT'S WHAT YOU SHOULD DO...GET OUT AND PLAY WITH YOUR OWN KIND..
I WOULD, BUT I HATE GETTING COVERED WITH A LOT OF DOG HAIR!
SCHULZ
9-15

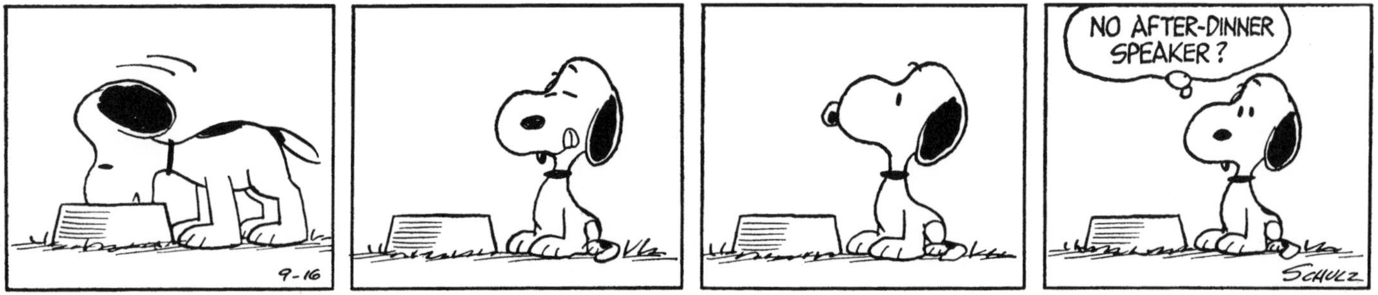
9-16
NO AFTER-DINNER SPEAKER?
SCHULZ

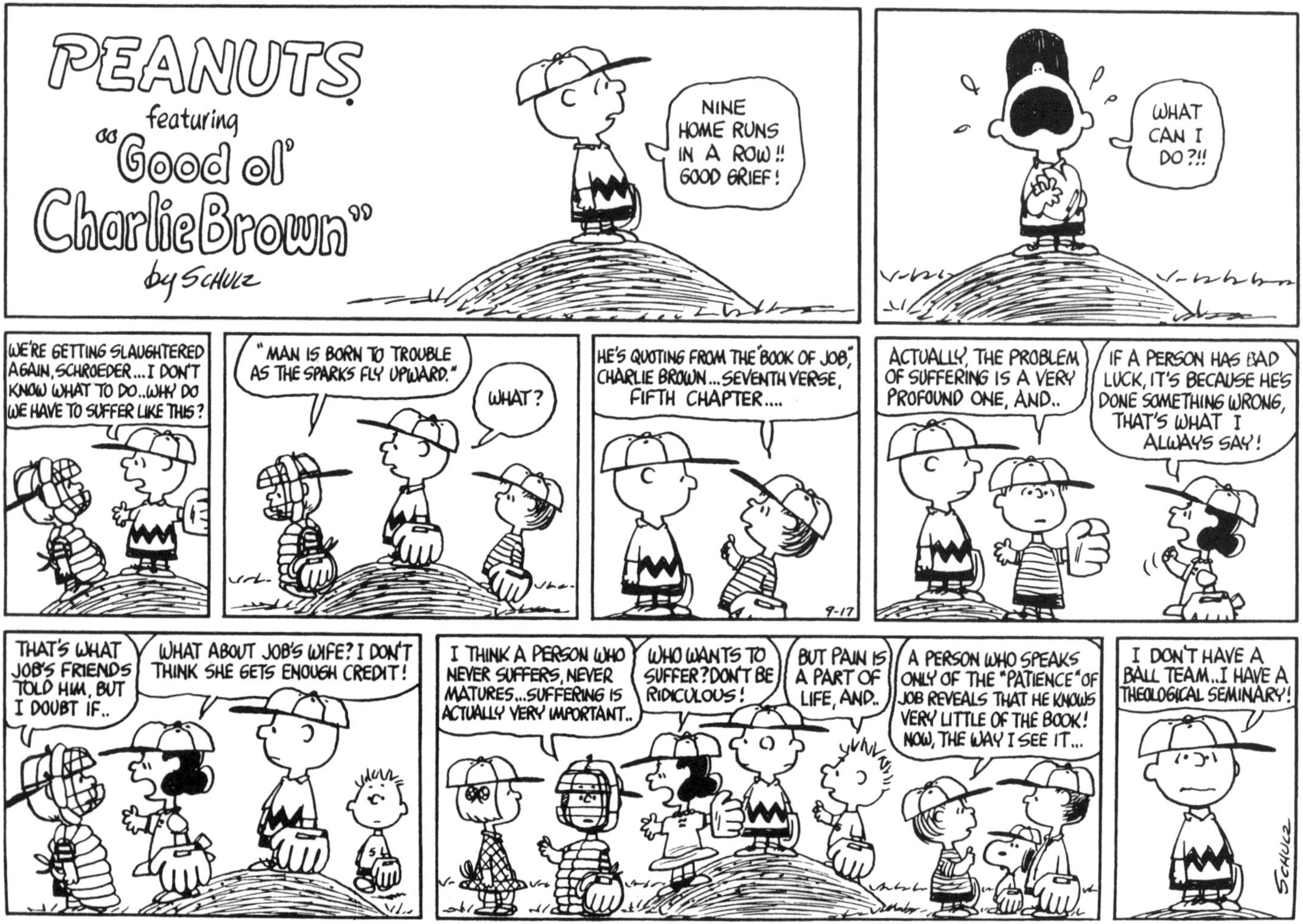
PEANUTS
featuring
"Good ol' Charlie Brown"
by SCHULZ
NINE HOME RUNS IN A ROW!! GOOD GRIEF!
WHAT CAN I DO?!!
WE'RE GETTING SLAUGHTERED AGAIN, SCHROEDER... I DON'T KNOW WHAT TO DO.. WHY DO WE HAVE TO SUFFER LIKE THIS?
"MAN IS BORN TO TROUBLE AS THE SPARKS FLY UPWARD."
WHAT?
HE'S QUOTING FROM THE "BOOK OF JOB," CHARLIE BROWN... SEVENTH VERSE, FIFTH CHAPTER....
9-17
ACTUALLY, THE PROBLEM OF SUFFERING IS A VERY PROFOUND ONE, AND..
IF A PERSON HAS BAD LUCK, IT'S BECAUSE HE'S DONE SOMETHING WRONG, THAT'S WHAT I ALWAYS SAY!
THAT'S WHAT JOB'S FRIENDS TOLD HIM, BUT I DOUBT IF..
WHAT ABOUT JOB'S WIFE? I DON'T THINK SHE GETS ENOUGH CREDIT!
I THINK A PERSON WHO NEVER SUFFERS, NEVER MATURES... SUFFERING IS ACTUALLY VERY IMPORTANT..
WHO WANTS TO SUFFER? DON'T BE RIDICULOUS!
BUT PAIN IS A PART OF LIFE, AND..
A PERSON WHO SPEAKS ONLY OF THE "PATIENCE" OF JOB REVEALS THAT HE KNOWS VERY LITTLE OF THE BOOK! NOW, THE WAY I SEE IT...
I DON'T HAVE A BALL TEAM.. I HAVE A THEOLOGICAL SEMINARY!
SCHULZ

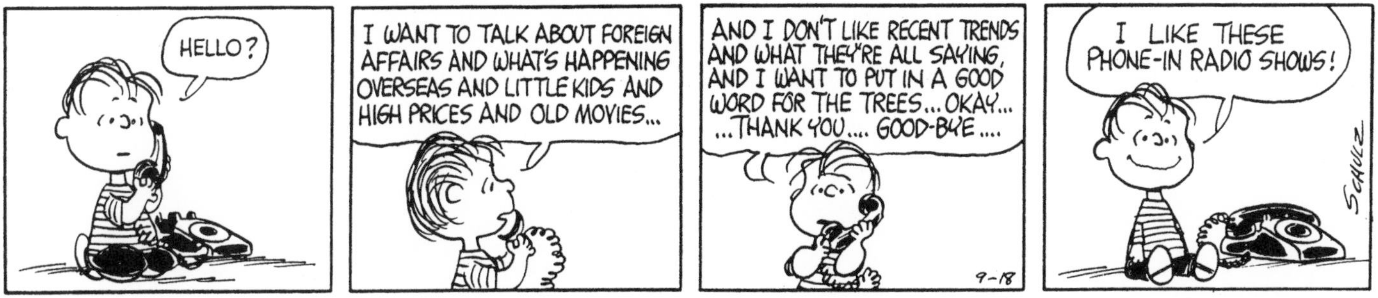
HELLO?
I WANT TO TALK ABOUT FOREIGN AFFAIRS AND WHAT'S HAPPENING OVERSEAS AND LITTLE KIDS AND HIGH PRICES AND OLD MOVIES...
AND I DON'T LIKE RECENT TRENDS AND WHAT THEY'RE ALL SAYING, AND I WANT TO PUT IN A GOOD WORD FOR THE TREES... OKAY... ...THANK YOU.... GOOD-BYE....
9-18
I LIKE THESE PHONE-IN RADIO SHOWS!
SCHULZ

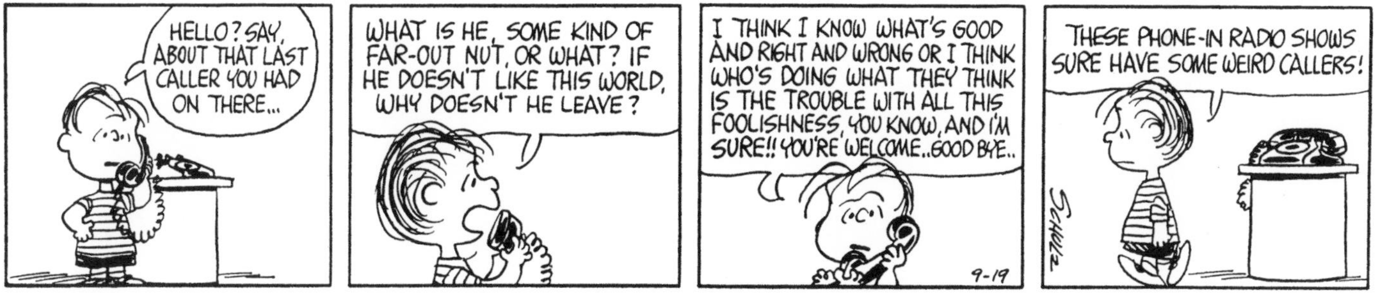
HELLO? SAY, ABOUT THAT LAST CALLER YOU HAD ON THERE...
WHAT IS HE, SOME KIND OF FAR-OUT NUT, OR WHAT? IF HE DOESN'T LIKE THIS WORLD, WHY DOESN'T HE LEAVE?
I THINK I KNOW WHAT'S GOOD AND RIGHT AND WRONG OR I THINK WHO'S DOING WHAT THEY THINK IS THE TROUBLE WITH ALL THIS FOOLISHNESS, YOU KNOW, AND I'M SURE!! YOU'RE WELCOME.. GOOD BYE..
9-19
SCHULZ
THESE PHONE-IN RADIO SHOWS SURE HAVE SOME WEIRD CALLERS!

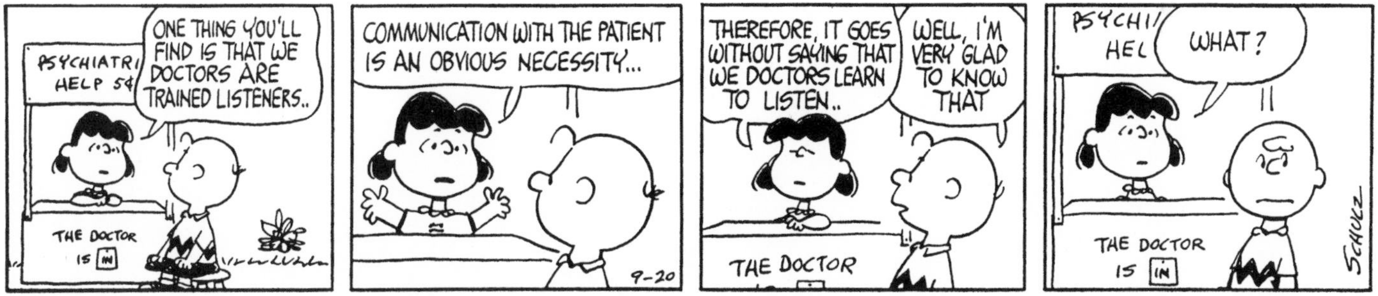
PSYCHIATRI HELP 5¢
ONE THING YOU'LL FIND IS THAT WE DOCTORS ARE TRAINED LISTENERS..
THE DOCTOR IS IN
COMMUNICATION WITH THE PATIENT IS AN OBVIOUS NECESSITY...
9-20
THEREFORE, IT GOES WITHOUT SAYING THAT WE DOCTORS LEARN TO LISTEN..
WELL, I'M VERY GLAD TO KNOW THAT
THE DOCTOR
PSYCHI HEL
WHAT?
THE DOCTOR IS IN
SCHULZ

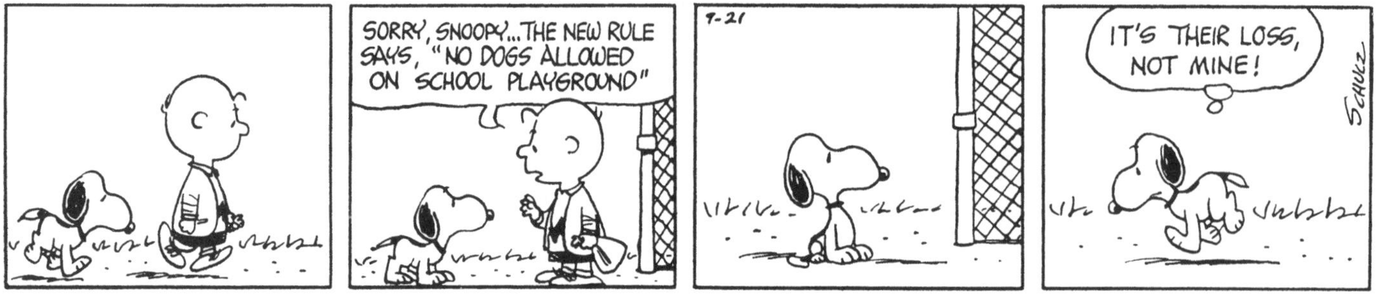
SORRY, SNOOPY...THE NEW RULE SAYS, "NO DOGS ALLOWED ON SCHOOL PLAYGROUND"
9-21
IT'S THEIR LOSS, NOT MINE!
SCHULZ

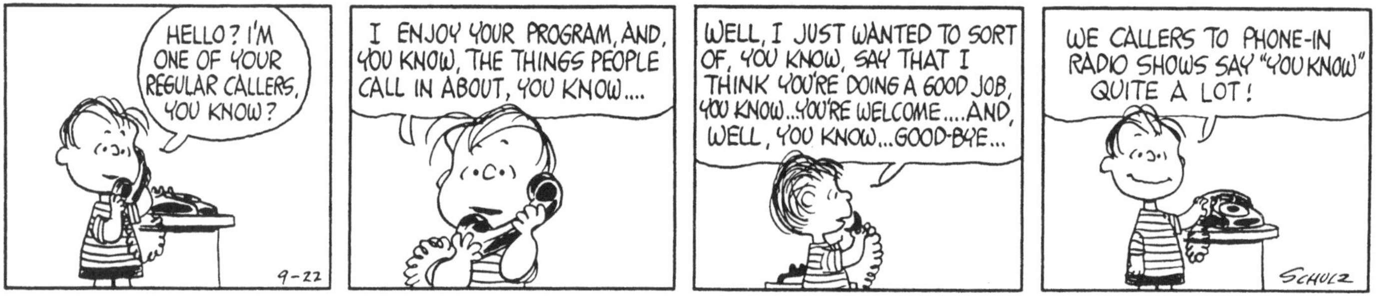
HELLO? I'M ONE OF YOUR REGULAR CALLERS, YOU KNOW?
9-22
I ENJOY YOUR PROGRAM, AND, YOU KNOW, THE THINGS PEOPLE CALL IN ABOUT, YOU KNOW....
WELL, I JUST WANTED TO SORT OF, YOU KNOW, SAY THAT I THINK YOU'RE DOING A GOOD JOB, YOU KNOW...YOU'RE WELCOME....AND, WELL, YOU KNOW...GOOD-BYE...
WE CALLERS TO PHONE-IN RADIO SHOWS SAY "YOU KNOW" QUITE A LOT!
SCHULZ

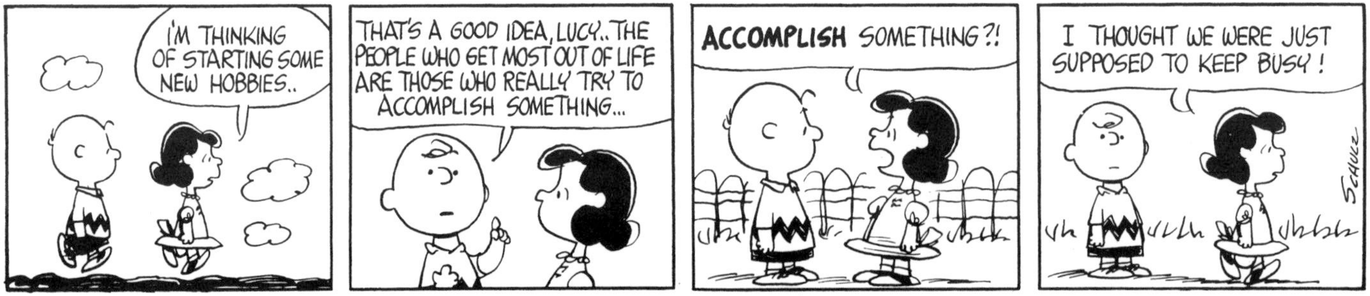
I'M THINKING OF STARTING SOME NEW HOBBIES..
THAT'S A GOOD IDEA, LUCY.. THE PEOPLE WHO GET MOST OUT OF LIFE ARE THOSE WHO REALLY TRY TO ACCOMPLISH SOMETHING...
ACCOMPLISH SOMETHING?!
I THOUGHT WE WERE JUST SUPPOSED TO KEEP BUSY!
SCHULZ

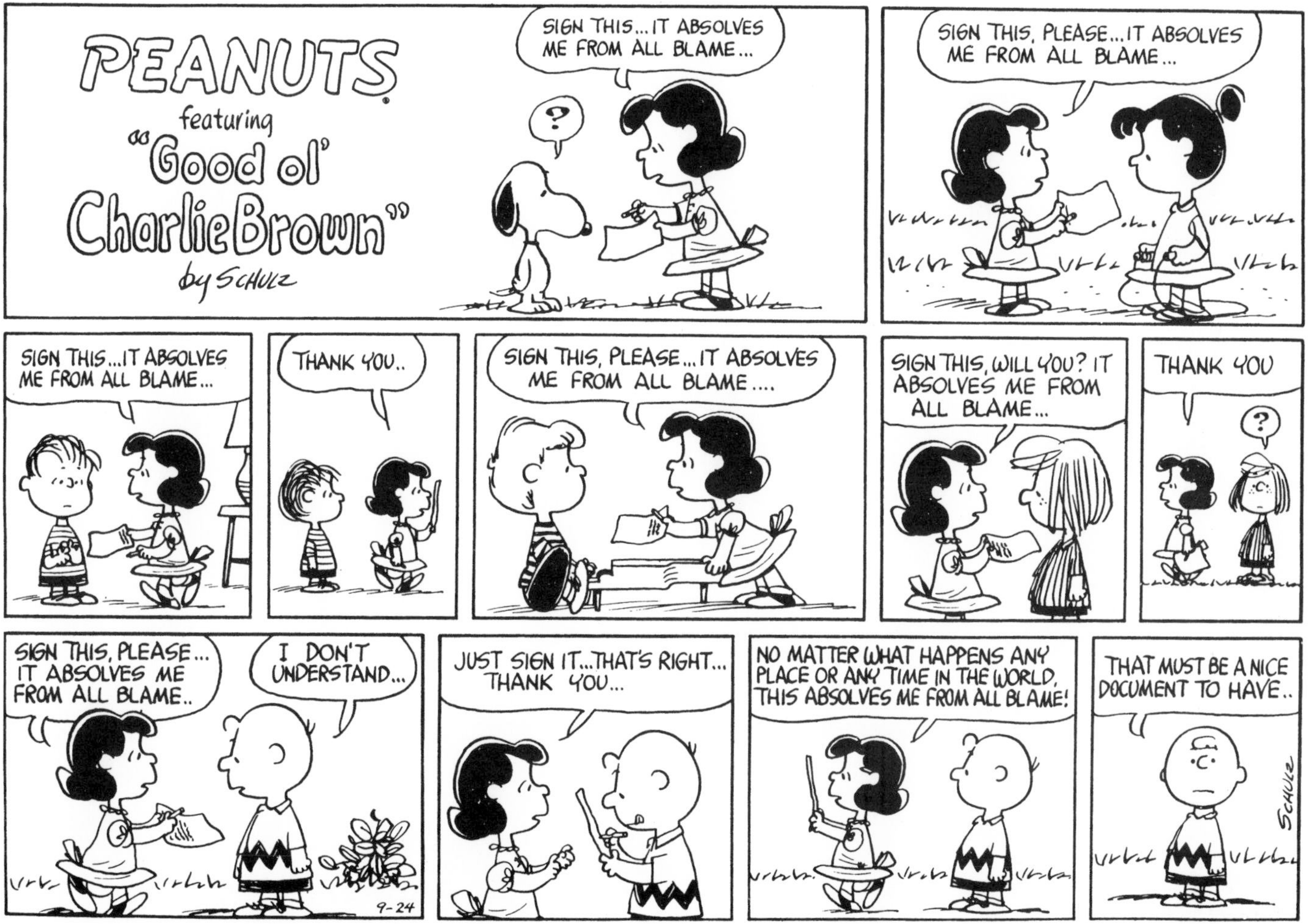
PEANUTS
featuring "Good ol' Charlie Brown"
by SCHULZ
SIGN THIS... IT ABSOLVES ME FROM ALL BLAME...
?
SIGN THIS, PLEASE... IT ABSOLVES ME FROM ALL BLAME...
SIGN THIS... IT ABSOLVES ME FROM ALL BLAME...
THANK YOU..
SIGN THIS, PLEASE... IT ABSOLVES ME FROM ALL BLAME....
SIGN THIS, WILL YOU? IT ABSOLVES ME FROM ALL BLAME...
THANK YOU
?
SIGN THIS, PLEASE... IT ABSOLVES ME FROM ALL BLAME..
I DON'T UNDERSTAND...
9-24
JUST SIGN IT... THAT'S RIGHT... THANK YOU...
NO MATTER WHAT HAPPENS ANY PLACE OR ANY TIME IN THE WORLD, THIS ABSOLVES ME FROM ALL BLAME!
THAT MUST BE A NICE DOCUMENT TO HAVE..
SCHULZ

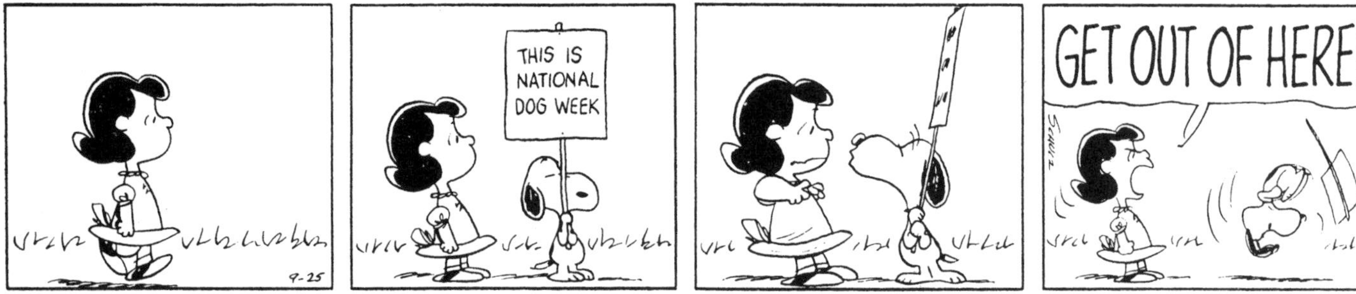
THIS IS NATIONAL DOG WEEK
GET OUT OF HERE!

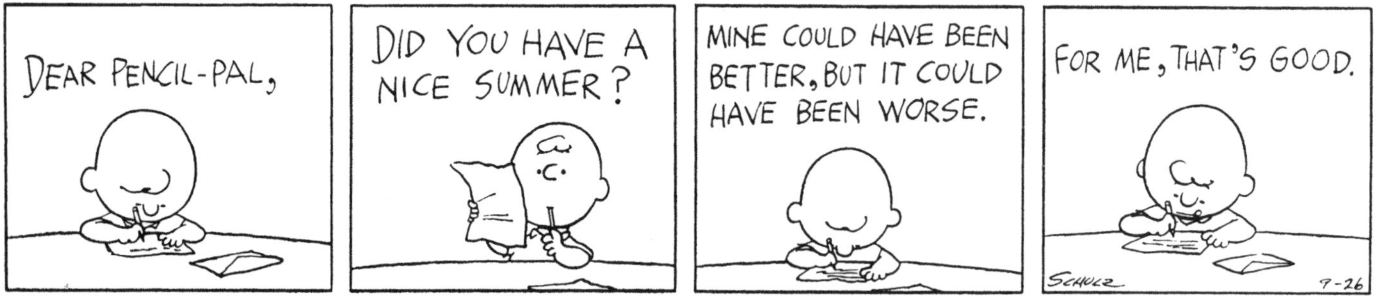
DEAR PENCIL-PAL,
DID YOU HAVE A NICE SUMMER?
MINE COULD HAVE BEEN BETTER, BUT IT COULD HAVE BEEN WORSE.
FOR ME, THAT'S GOOD.

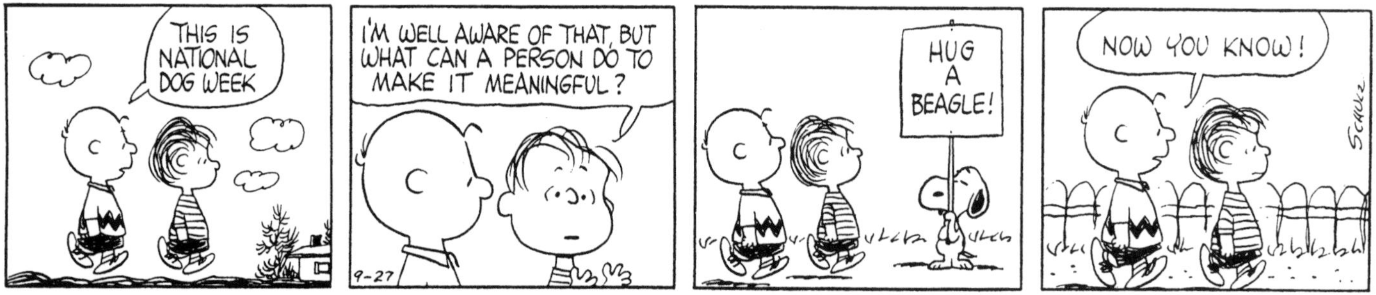
THIS IS NATIONAL DOG WEEK
I'M WELL AWARE OF THAT, BUT WHAT CAN A PERSON DO TO MAKE IT MEANINGFUL?
HUG A BEAGLE!
NOW YOU KNOW!

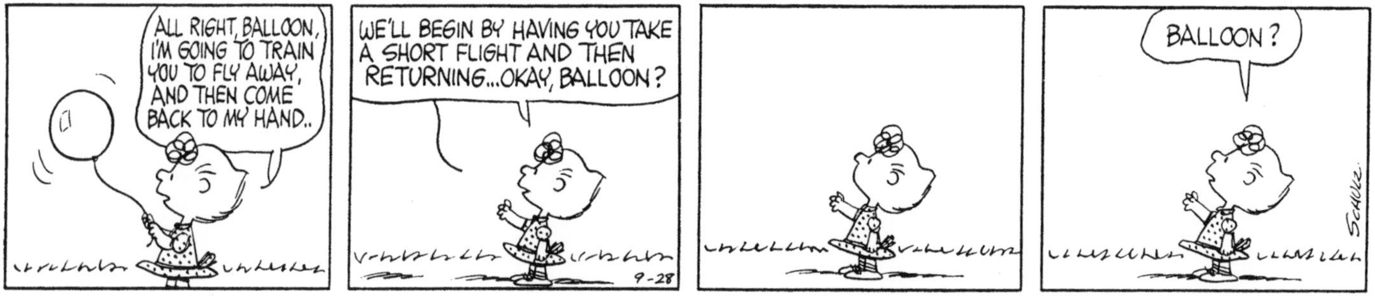
ALL RIGHT, BALLOON, I'M GOING TO TRAIN YOU TO FLY AWAY, AND THEN COME BACK TO MY HAND..
WE'LL BEGIN BY HAVING YOU TAKE A SHORT FLIGHT AND THEN RETURNING...OKAY, BALLOON?
9-28
BALLOON?
SCHULZ

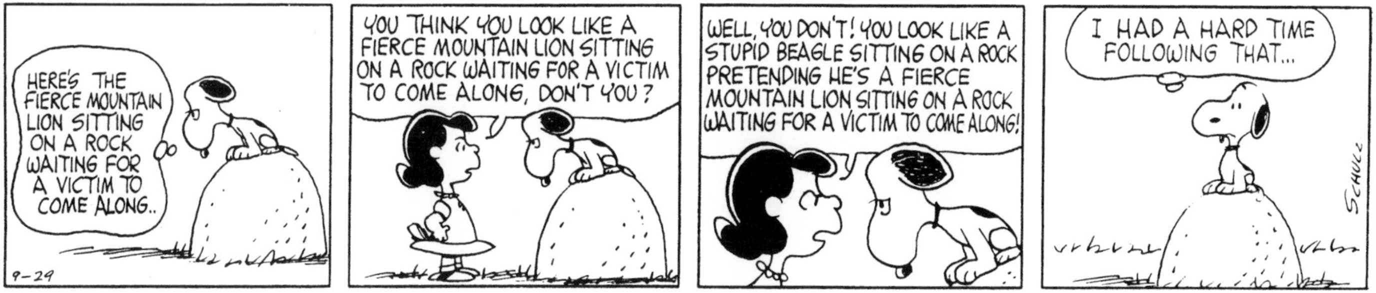
HERE'S THE FIERCE MOUNTAIN LION SITTING ON A ROCK WAITING FOR A VICTIM TO COME ALONG..
9-29
YOU THINK YOU LOOK LIKE A FIERCE MOUNTAIN LION SITTING ON A ROCK WAITING FOR A VICTIM TO COME ALONG, DON'T YOU?
WELL, YOU DON'T! YOU LOOK LIKE A STUPID BEAGLE SITTING ON A ROCK PRETENDING HE'S A FIERCE MOUNTAIN LION SITTING ON A ROCK WAITING FOR A VICTIM TO COME ALONG!
I HAD A HARD TIME FOLLOWING THAT...
SCHULZ

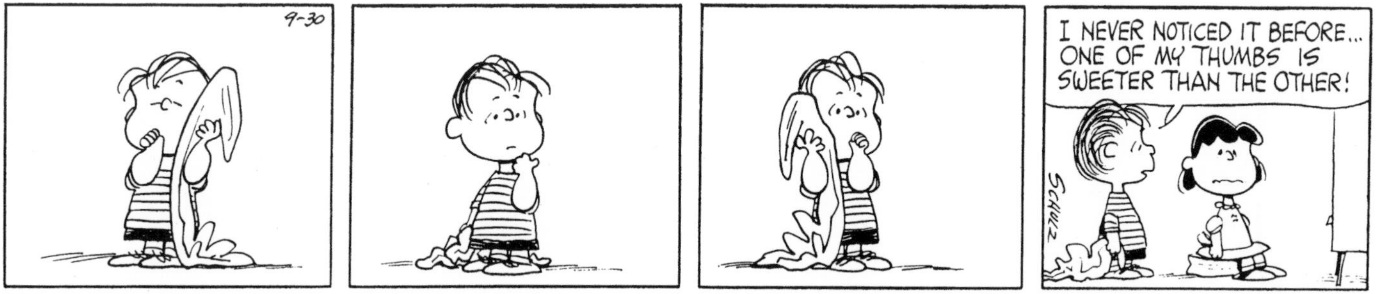
9-30
I NEVER NOTICED IT BEFORE... ONE OF MY THUMBS IS SWEETER THAN THE OTHER!
SCHULZ

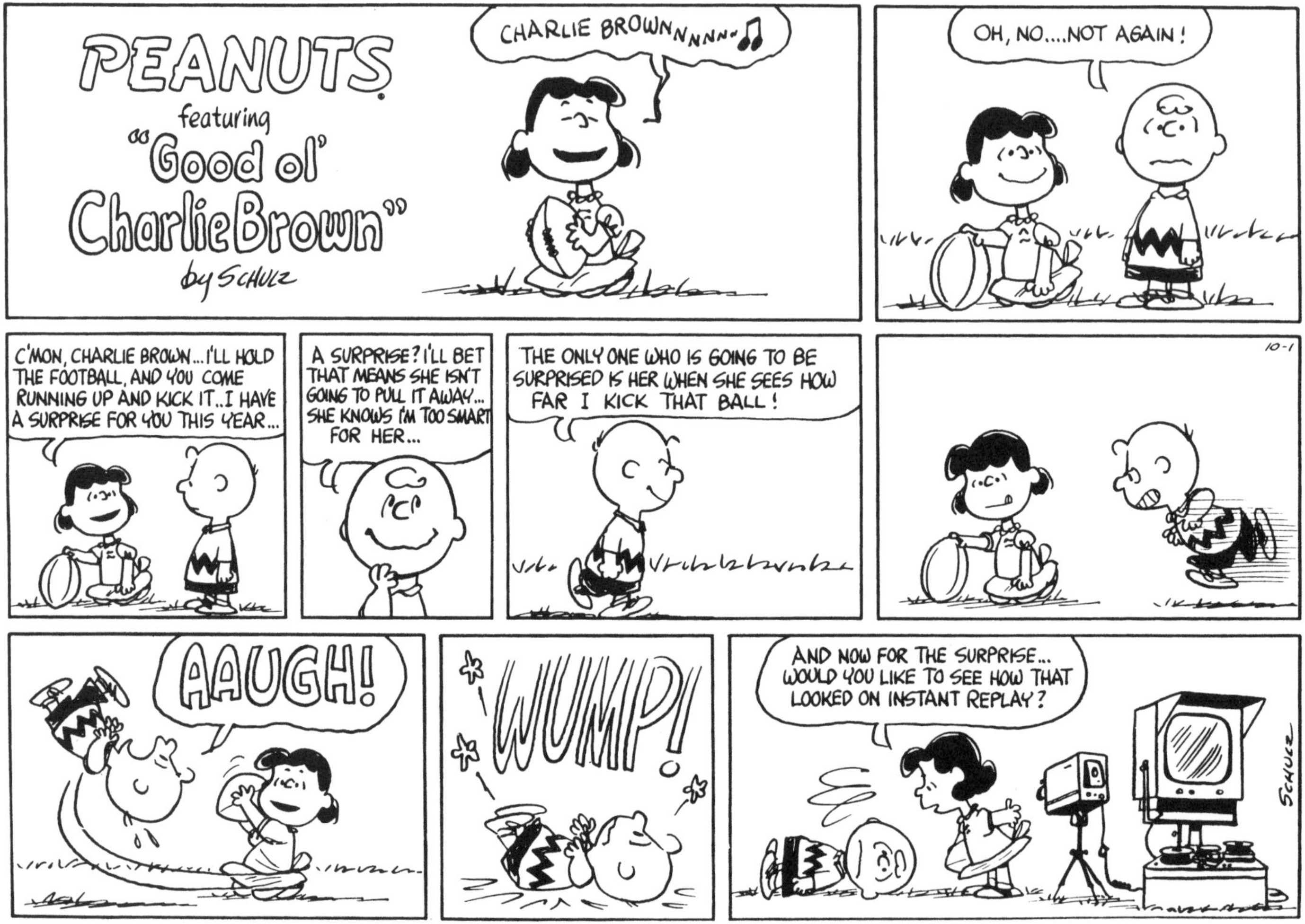
PEANUTS
featuring "Good ol' Charlie Brown"
by SCHULZ
CHARLIE BROWNNNNN
OH, NO....NOT AGAIN!
C'MON, CHARLIE BROWN...I'LL HOLD THE FOOTBALL, AND YOU COME RUNNING UP AND KICK IT..I HAVE A SURPRISE FOR YOU THIS YEAR...
A SURPRISE? I'LL BET THAT MEANS SHE ISN'T GOING TO PULL IT AWAY... SHE KNOWS I'M TOO SMART FOR HER...
THE ONLY ONE WHO IS GOING TO BE SURPRISED IS HER WHEN SHE SEES HOW FAR I KICK THAT BALL!
10-1
AAUGH!
WUMP!
AND NOW FOR THE SURPRISE... WOULD YOU LIKE TO SEE HOW THAT LOOKED ON INSTANT REPLAY?
SCHULZ

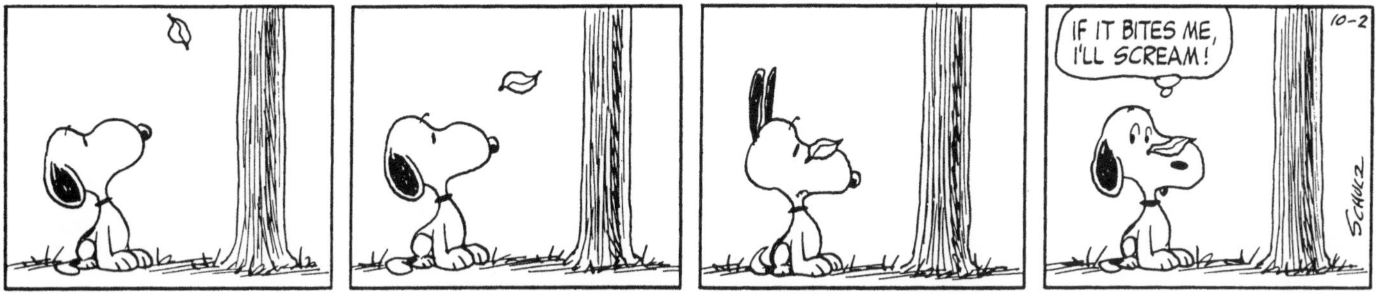
IF IT BITES ME, I'LL SCREAM!
10-2
SCHULZ

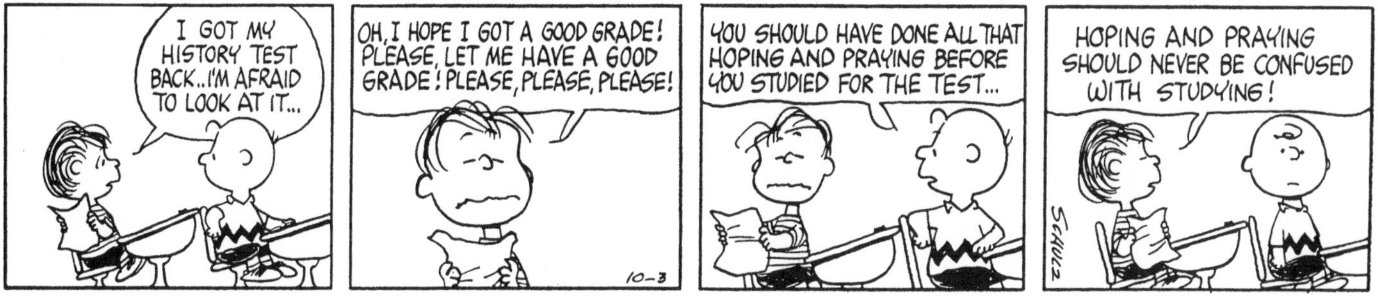
I GOT MY HISTORY TEST BACK..I'M AFRAID TO LOOK AT IT...
OH, I HOPE I GOT A GOOD GRADE! PLEASE, LET ME HAVE A GOOD GRADE! PLEASE, PLEASE, PLEASE!
10-3
YOU SHOULD HAVE DONE ALL THAT HOPING AND PRAYING BEFORE YOU STUDIED FOR THE TEST...
SCHULZ
HOPING AND PRAYING SHOULD NEVER BE CONFUSED WITH STUDYING!

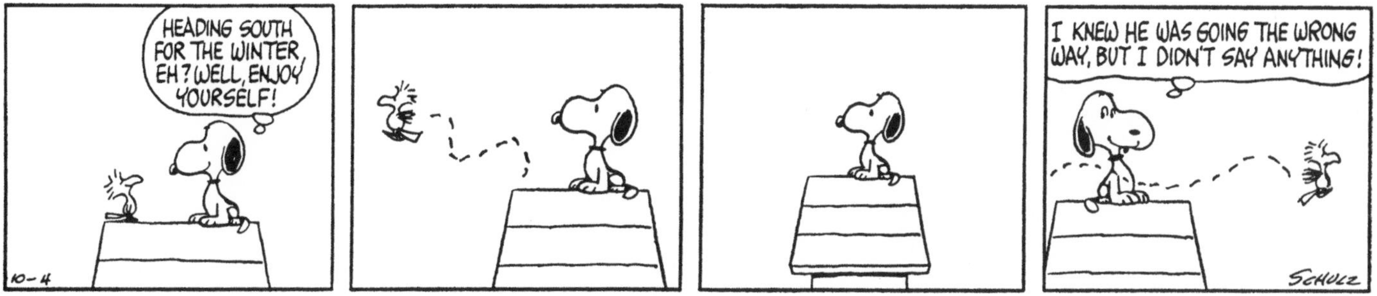
HEADING SOUTH FOR THE WINTER, EH? WELL, ENJOY YOURSELF!
10-4
I KNEW HE WAS GOING THE WRONG WAY, BUT I DIDN'T SAY ANYTHING!
SCHULZ

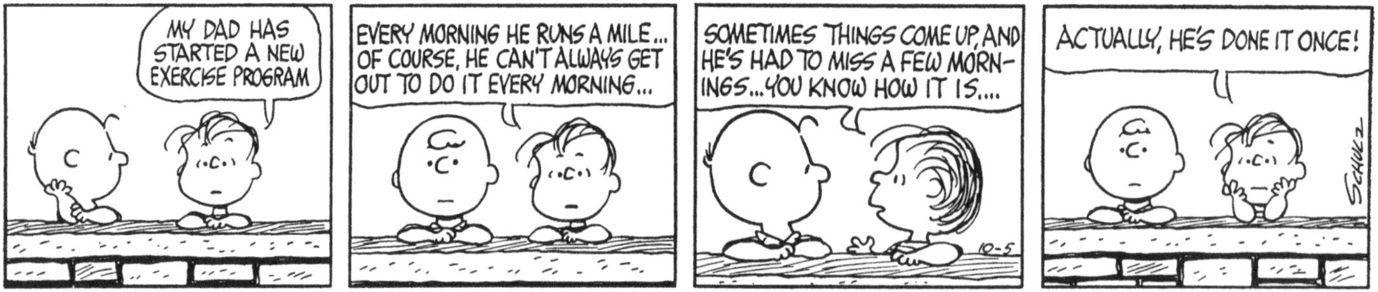
MY DAD HAS STARTED A NEW EXERCISE PROGRAM
EVERY MORNING HE RUNS A MILE... OF COURSE, HE CAN'T ALWAYS GET OUT TO DO IT EVERY MORNING...
SOMETIMES THINGS COME UP, AND HE'S HAD TO MISS A FEW MORNINGS...YOU KNOW HOW IT IS....
10-5
ACTUALLY, HE'S DONE IT ONCE!
SCHULZ

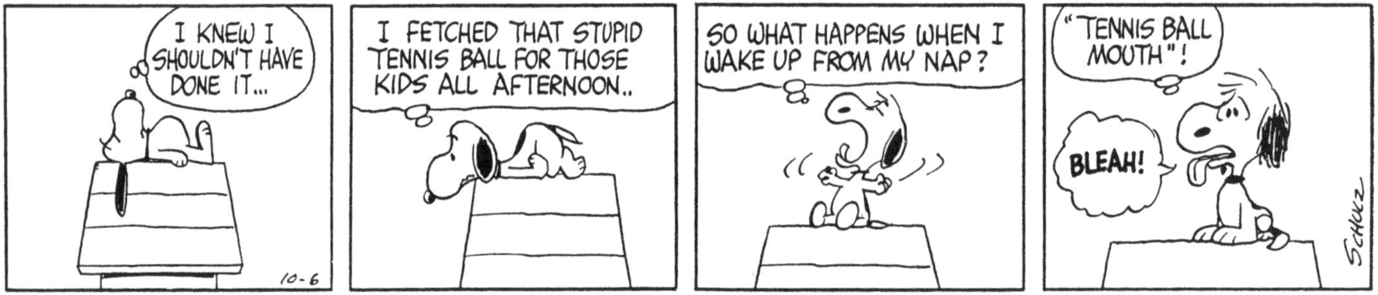
I KNEW I SHOULDN'T HAVE DONE IT...
10-6
I FETCHED THAT STUPID TENNIS BALL FOR THOSE KIDS ALL AFTERNOON..
SO WHAT HAPPENS WHEN I WAKE UP FROM MY NAP?
"TENNIS BALL MOUTH"!
BLEAH!
SCHULZ

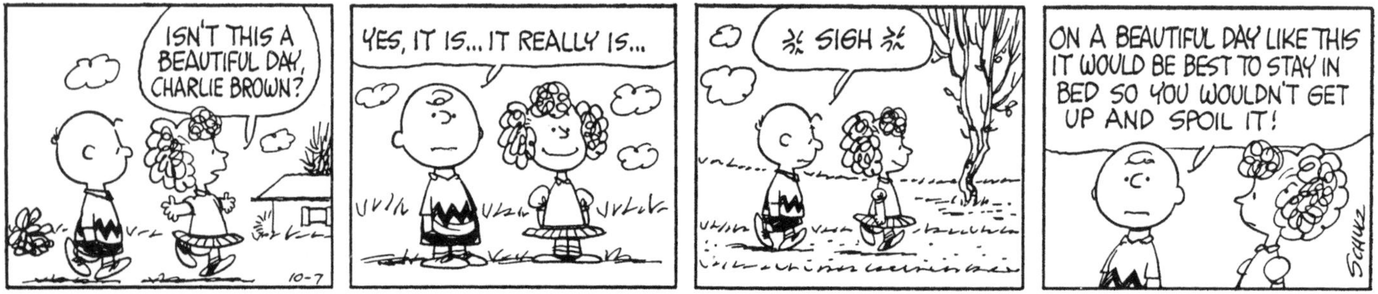
ISN'T THIS A BEAUTIFUL DAY, CHARLIE BROWN?
10-7
YES, IT IS... IT REALLY IS...
SIGH
ON A BEAUTIFUL DAY LIKE THIS IT WOULD BE BEST TO STAY IN BED SO YOU WOULDN'T GET UP AND SPOIL IT!
SCHULZ

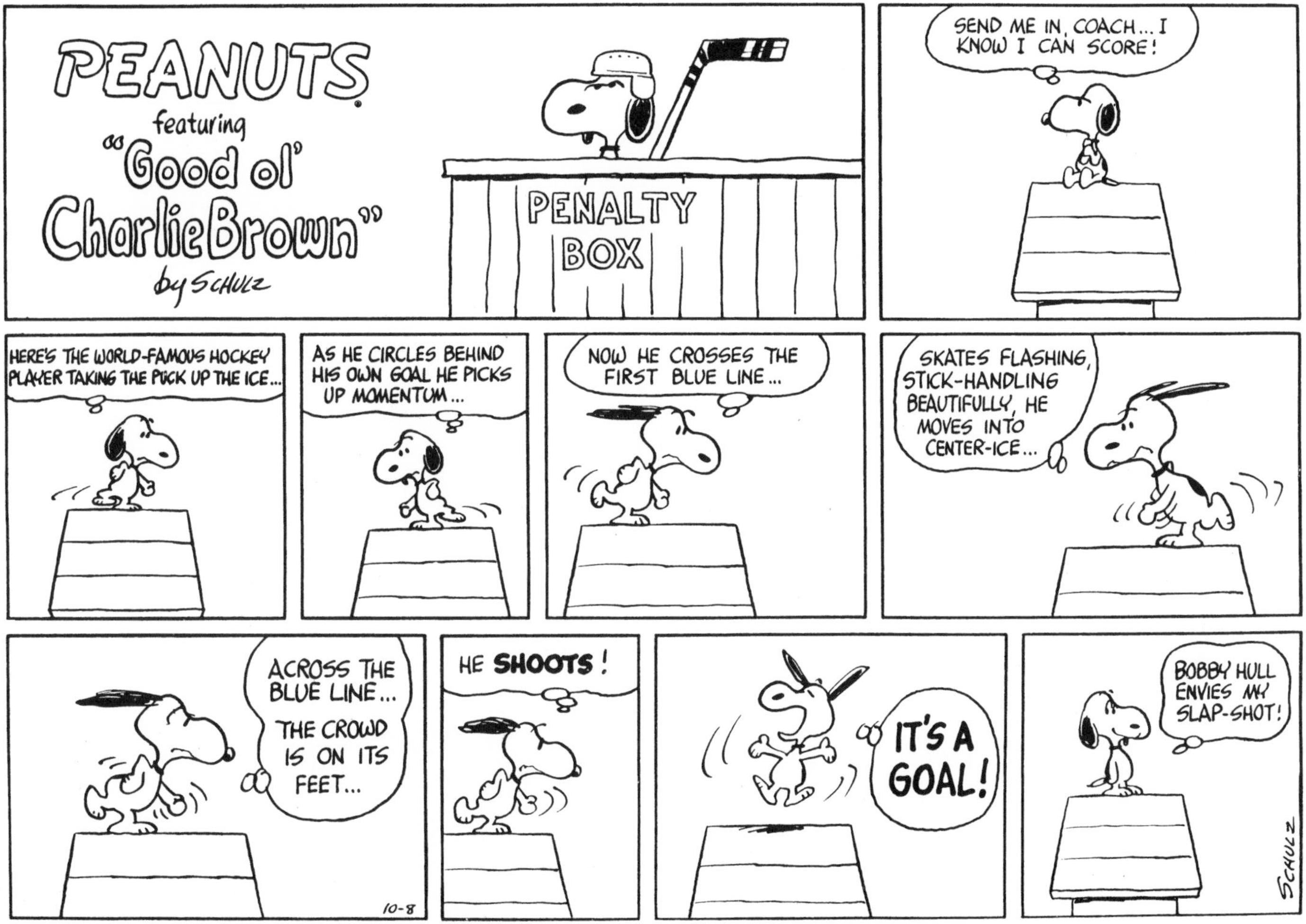
PEANUTS
featuring
"Good ol' CharlieBrown"
by SCHULZ
PENALTY BOX
SEND ME IN, COACH... I KNOW I CAN SCORE!
HERE'S THE WORLD-FAMOUS HOCKEY PLAYER TAKING THE PUCK UP THE ICE...
AS HE CIRCLES BEHIND HIS OWN GOAL HE PICKS UP MOMENTUM...
NOW HE CROSSES THE FIRST BLUE LINE...
SKATES FLASHING, STICK-HANDLING BEAUTIFULLY, HE MOVES INTO CENTER-ICE...
ACROSS THE BLUE LINE...
THE CROWD IS ON ITS FEET...
10-8
HE **SHOOTS**!
IT'S A GOAL!
BOBBY HULL ENVIES MY SLAP-SHOT!
SCHULZ

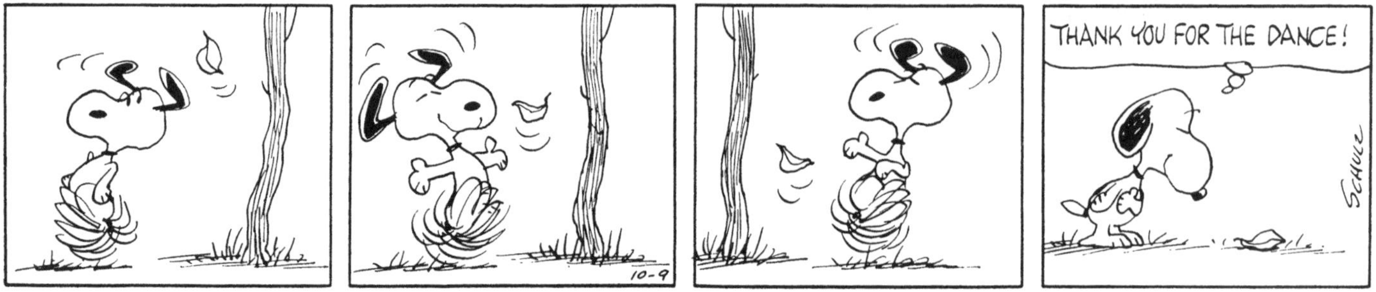
THANK YOU FOR THE DANCE!

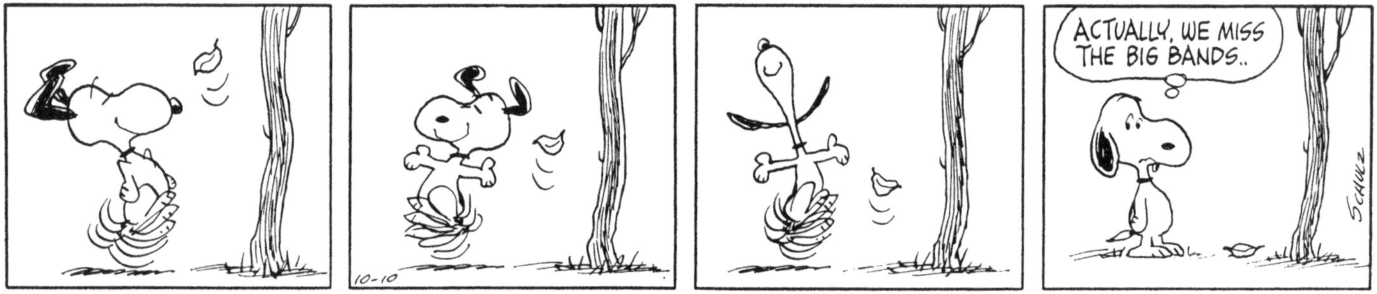
ACTUALLY, WE MISS THE BIG BANDS..

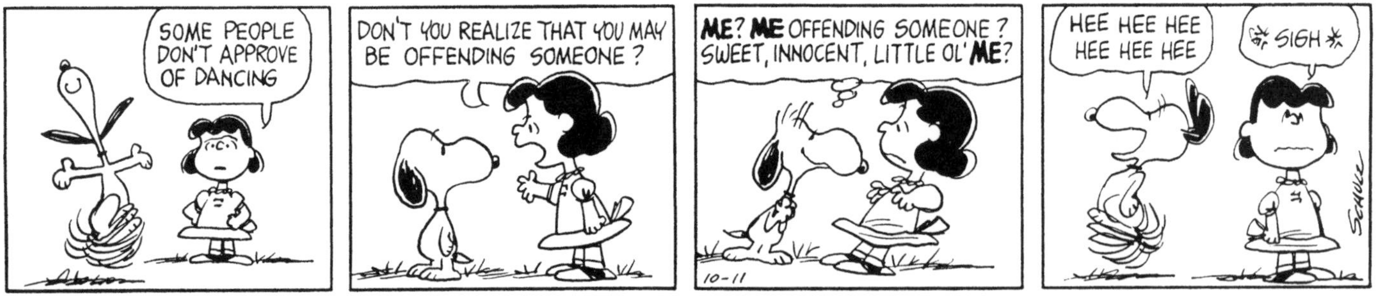
SOME PEOPLE DON'T APPROVE OF DANCING
DON'T YOU REALIZE THAT YOU MAY BE OFFENDING SOMEONE?
ME? **ME** OFFENDING SOMEONE? SWEET, INNOCENT, LITTLE OL' **ME**?
HEE HEE HEE HEE HEE HEE
SIGH

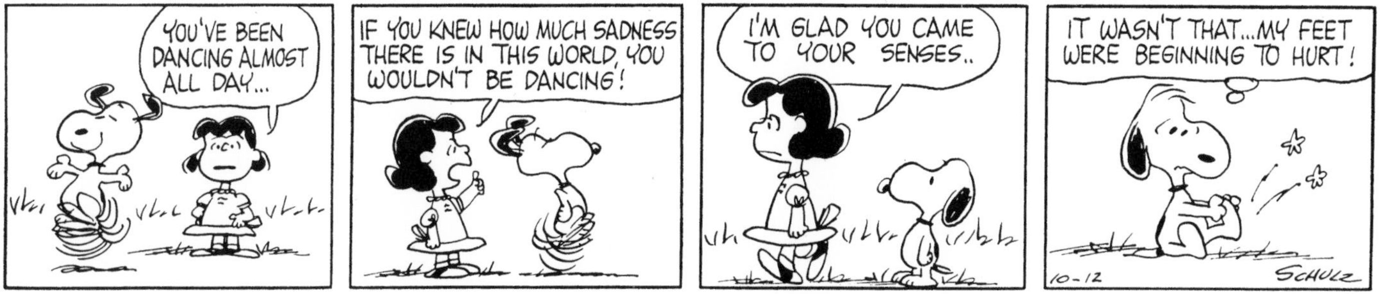

YOU'VE BEEN DANCING ALMOST ALL DAY...
IF YOU KNEW HOW MUCH SADNESS THERE IS IN THIS WORLD, YOU WOULDN'T BE DANCING!
I'M GLAD YOU CAME TO YOUR SENSES..
IT WASN'T THAT...MY FEET WERE BEGINNING TO HURT!
10-12
SCHULZ

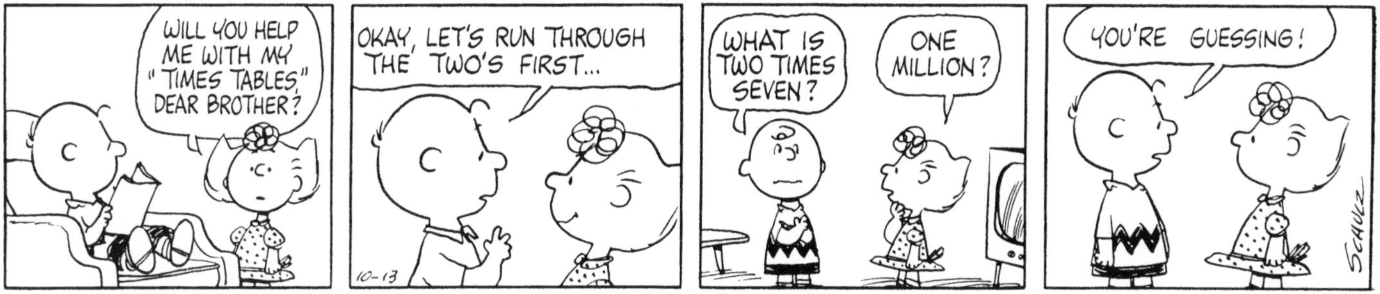

WILL YOU HELP ME WITH MY "TIMES TABLES," DEAR BROTHER?
OKAY, LET'S RUN THROUGH THE TWO'S FIRST...
10-13
WHAT IS TWO TIMES SEVEN?
ONE MILLION?
YOU'RE GUESSING!
SCHULZ

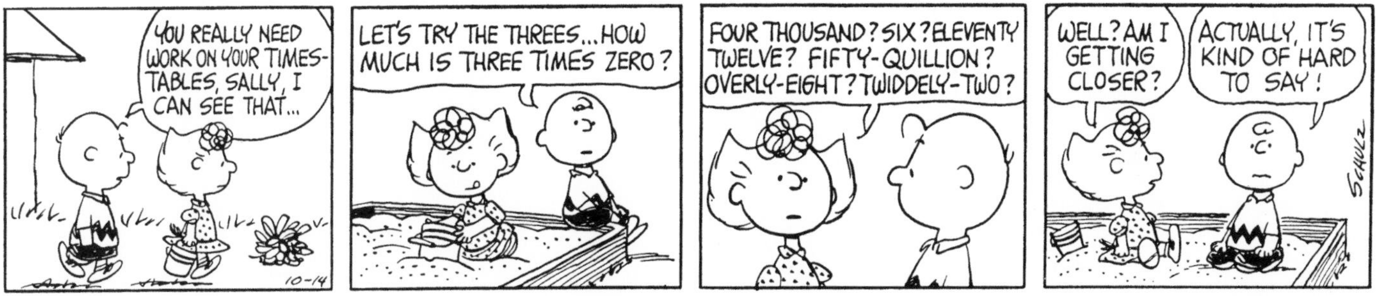

YOU REALLY NEED WORK ON YOUR TIMES-TABLES, SALLY, I CAN SEE THAT...
10-14
LET'S TRY THE THREES...HOW MUCH IS THREE TIMES ZERO?
FOUR THOUSAND? SIX? ELEVENTY TWELVE? FIFTY-QUILLION? OVERLY-EIGHT? TWIDDELY-TWO?
WELL? AM I GETTING CLOSER?
ACTUALLY, IT'S KIND OF HARD TO SAY!
SCHULZ

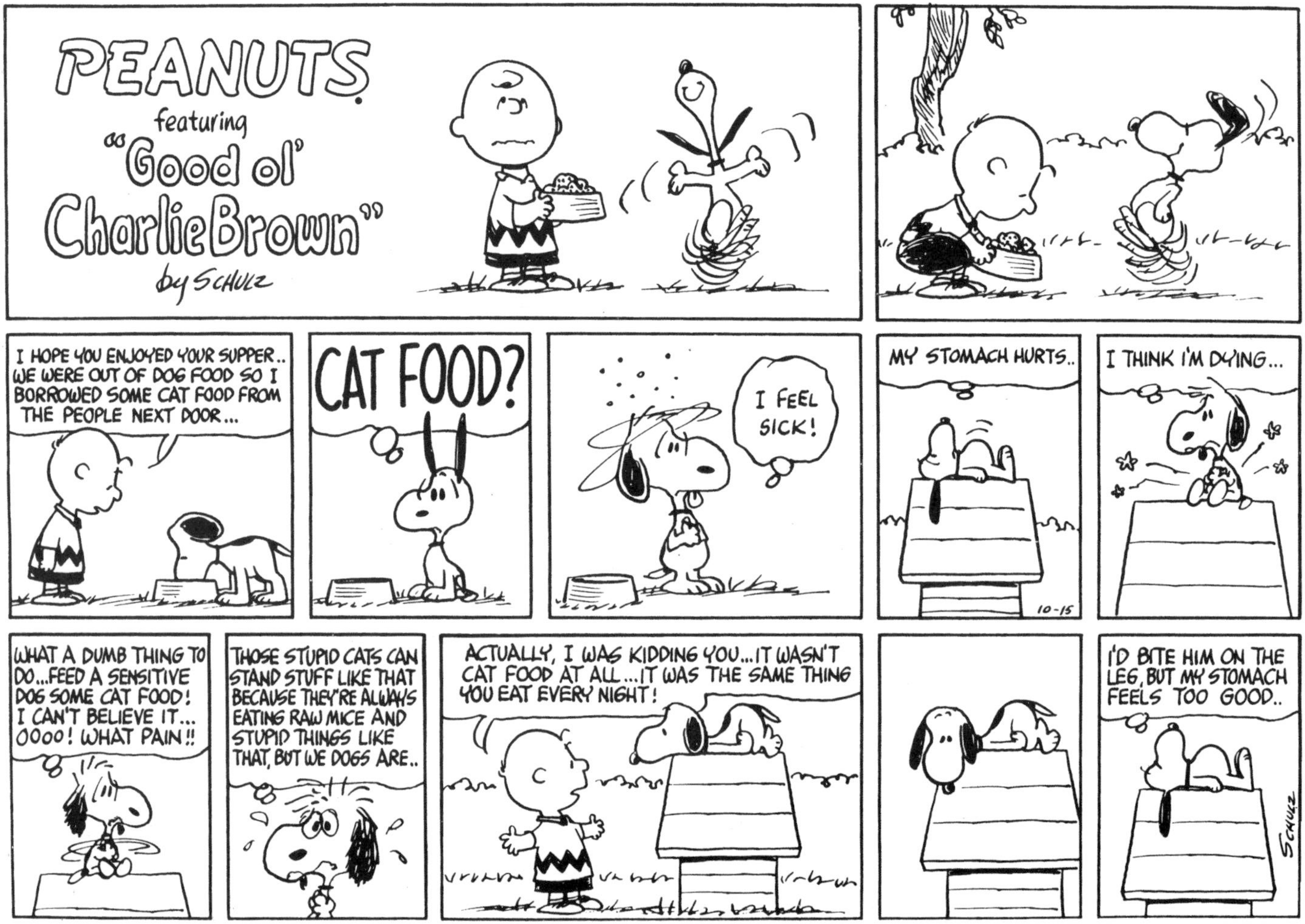
PEANUTS
featuring
"Good ol' Charlie Brown"
by SCHULZ
I HOPE YOU ENJOYED YOUR SUPPER.. WE WERE OUT OF DOG FOOD SO I BORROWED SOME CAT FOOD FROM THE PEOPLE NEXT DOOR...
CAT FOOD?
I FEEL SICK!
MY STOMACH HURTS..
10-15
I THINK I'M DYING...
WHAT A DUMB THING TO DO...FEED A SENSITIVE DOG SOME CAT FOOD! I CAN'T BELIEVE IT... OOOO! WHAT PAIN!!
THOSE STUPID CATS CAN STAND STUFF LIKE THAT BECAUSE THEY'RE ALWAYS EATING RAW MICE AND STUPID THINGS LIKE THAT, BUT WE DOGS ARE..
ACTUALLY, I WAS KIDDING YOU...IT WASN'T CAT FOOD AT ALL...IT WAS THE SAME THING YOU EAT EVERY NIGHT!
I'D BITE HIM ON THE LEG, BUT MY STOMACH FEELS TOO GOOD..
SCHULZ

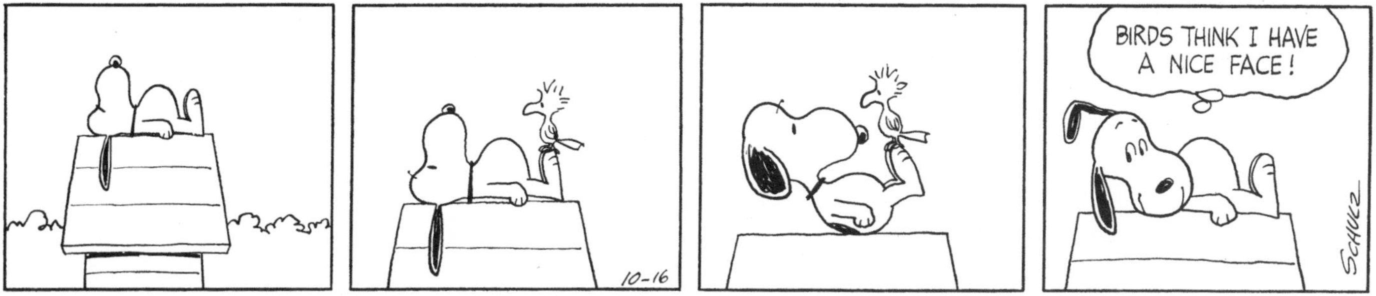
BIRDS THINK I HAVE A NICE FACE!

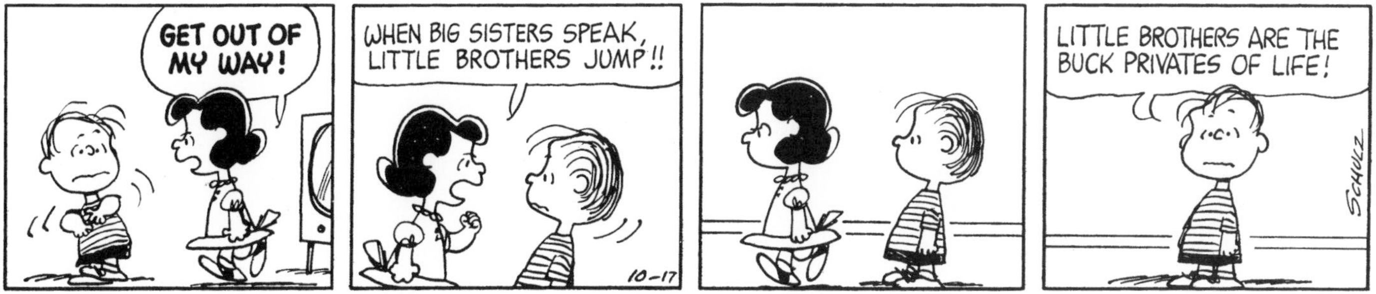
GET OUT OF MY WAY!
WHEN BIG SISTERS SPEAK, LITTLE BROTHERS JUMP!!
LITTLE BROTHERS ARE THE BUCK PRIVATES OF LIFE!

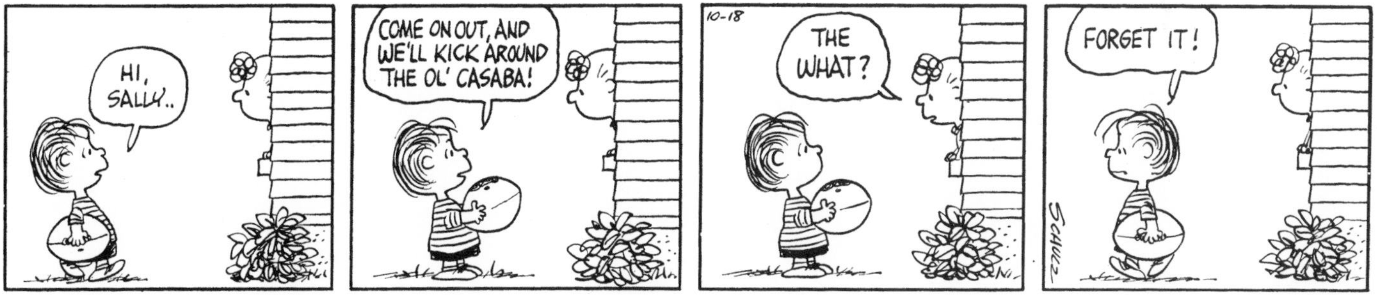
HI, SALLY..
COME ON OUT, AND WE'LL KICK AROUND THE OL' CASABA!
THE WHAT?
FORGET IT!

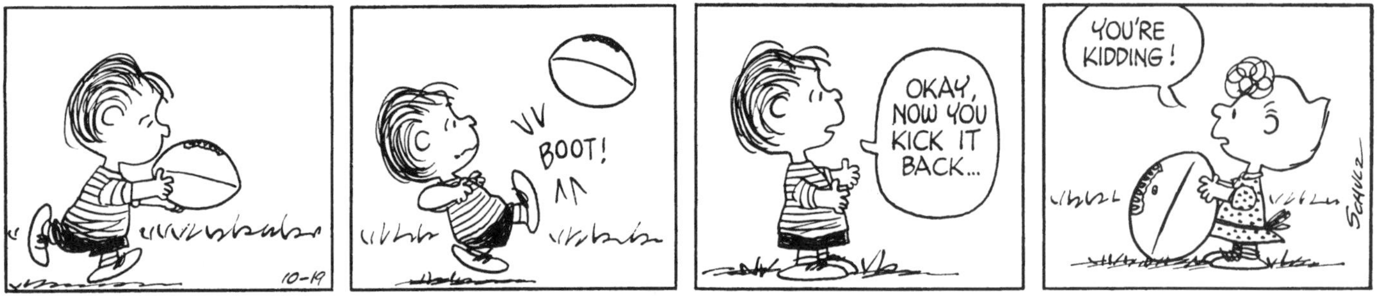
10-19
BOOT!
OKAY, NOW YOU KICK IT BACK...
YOU'RE KIDDING!
SCHULZ

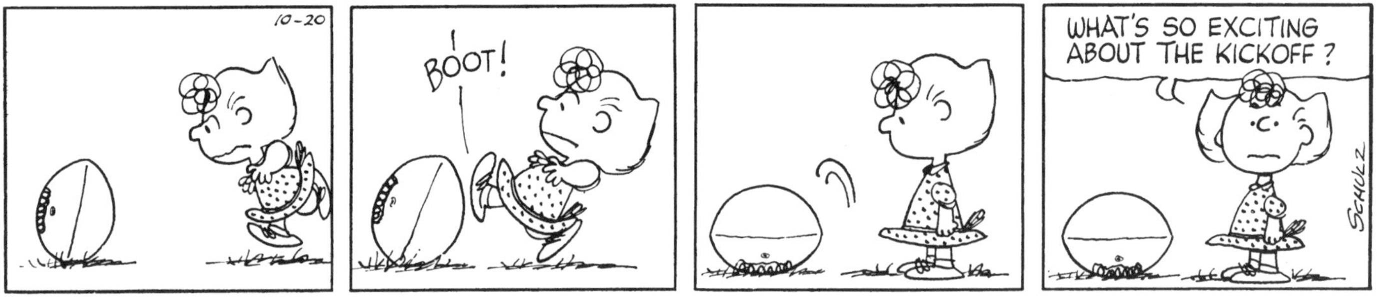
10-20
BOOT!
WHAT'S SO EXCITING ABOUT THE KICKOFF?
SCHULZ

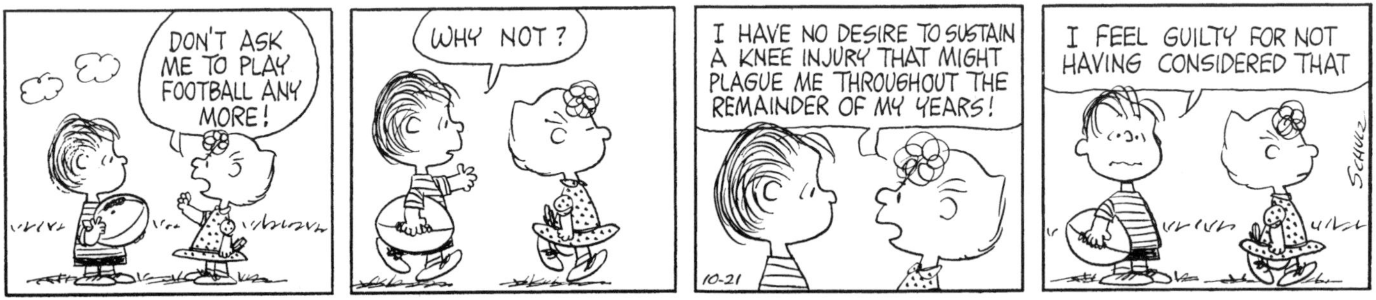
DON'T ASK ME TO PLAY FOOTBALL ANY MORE!
WHY NOT?
I HAVE NO DESIRE TO SUSTAIN A KNEE INJURY THAT MIGHT PLAGUE ME THROUGHOUT THE REMAINDER OF MY YEARS!
10-21
I FEEL GUILTY FOR NOT HAVING CONSIDERED THAT
SCHULZ

PEANUTS featuring "Good ol' Charlie Brown" *by Schulz*

I'VE TAKEN ENOUGH OF YOUR INSULTS, YOU STUPID DOG!

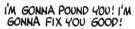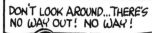

I'M GONNA POUND YOU! I'M GONNA FIX YOU GOOD!

DON'T LOOK AROUND...THERE'S NO WAY OUT! NO WAY!

YOU'VE HAD IT, DOG! PREPARE TO MEET YOUR DOOM!

10-22

SMAK!

AUGH!

WUMP!

ONE KISS IS WORTH TWO JUDO CHOPS ANY TIME!

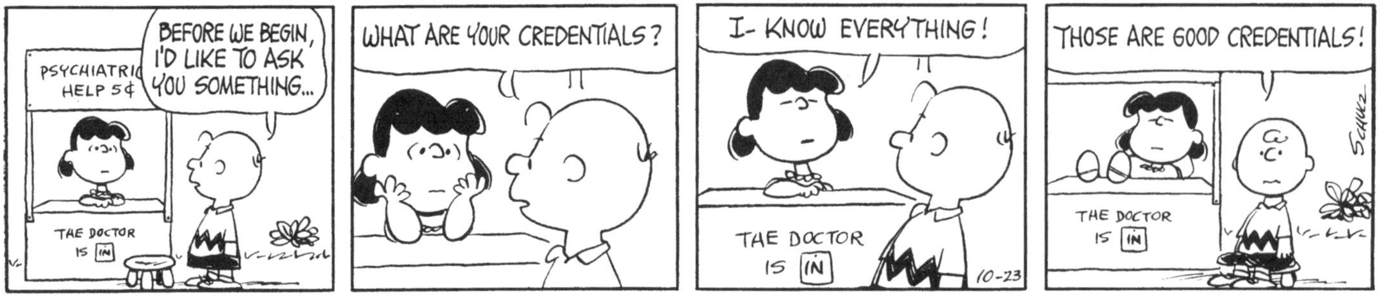
PSYCHIATRIC HELP 5¢
THE DOCTOR IS IN
BEFORE WE BEGIN, I'D LIKE TO ASK YOU SOMETHING...
WHAT ARE YOUR CREDENTIALS?
I- KNOW EVERYTHING!
THE DOCTOR IS IN
10-23
THOSE ARE GOOD CREDENTIALS!
THE DOCTOR IS IN
SCHULZ

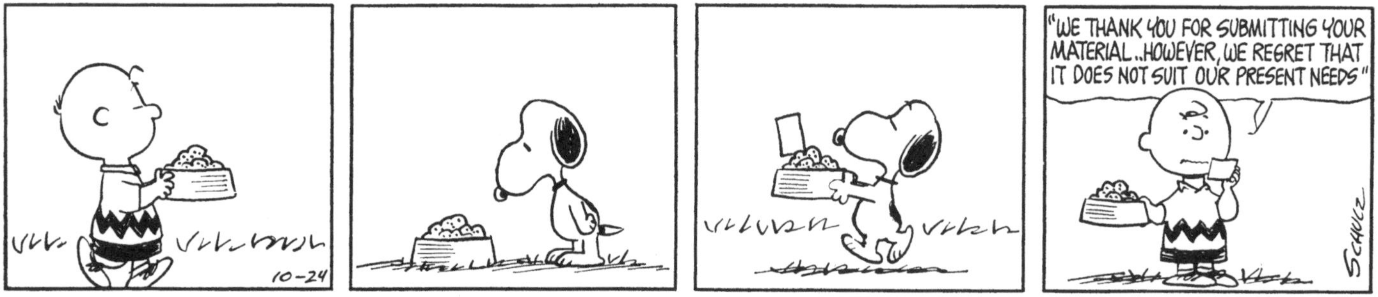
10-24
"WE THANK YOU FOR SUBMITTING YOUR MATERIAL..HOWEVER, WE REGRET THAT IT DOES NOT SUIT OUR PRESENT NEEDS"
SCHULZ

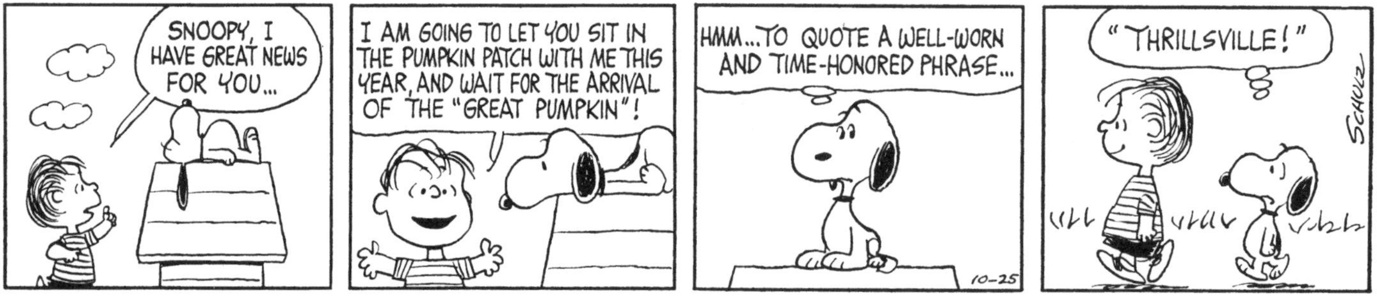
SNOOPY, I HAVE GREAT NEWS FOR YOU...
I AM GOING TO LET YOU SIT IN THE PUMPKIN PATCH WITH ME THIS YEAR, AND WAIT FOR THE ARRIVAL OF THE "GREAT PUMPKIN"!
HMM...TO QUOTE A WELL-WORN AND TIME-HONORED PHRASE...
10-25
"THRILLSVILLE!"
SCHULZ

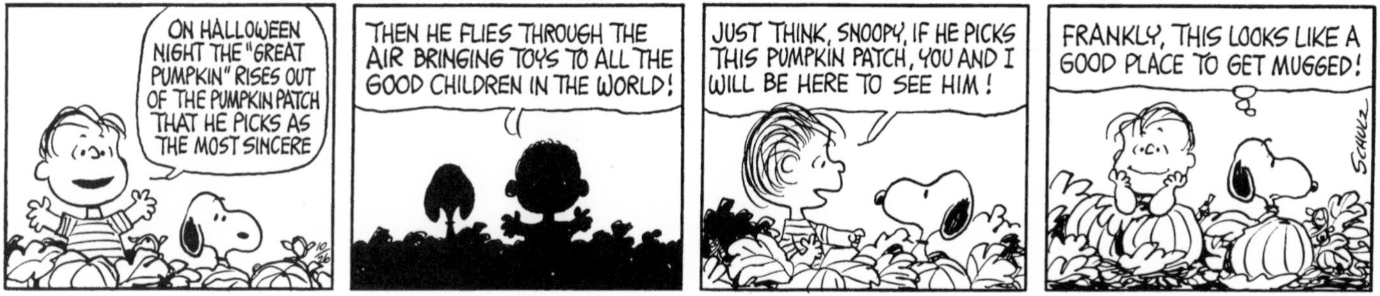
ON HALLOWEEN NIGHT THE "GREAT PUMPKIN" RISES OUT OF THE PUMPKIN PATCH THAT HE PICKS AS THE MOST SINCERE
THEN HE FLIES THROUGH THE AIR BRINGING TOYS TO ALL THE GOOD CHILDREN IN THE WORLD!
JUST THINK, SNOOPY, IF HE PICKS THIS PUMPKIN PATCH, YOU AND I WILL BE HERE TO SEE HIM!
FRANKLY, THIS LOOKS LIKE A GOOD PLACE TO GET MUGGED!

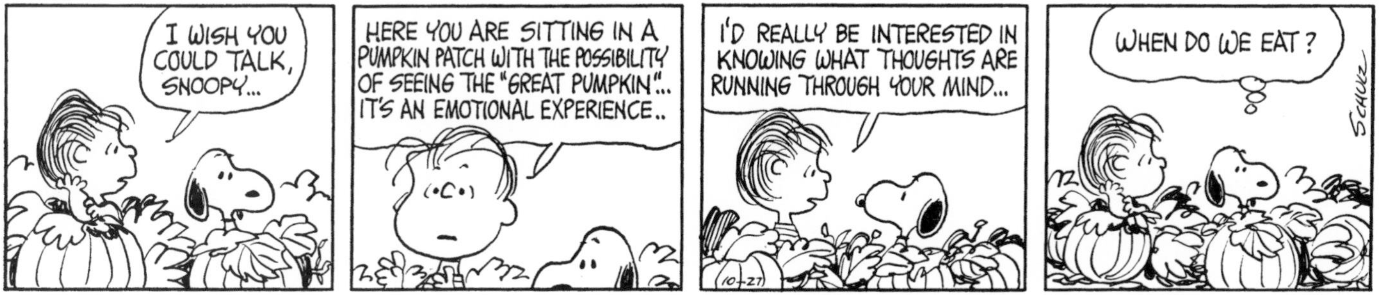
I WISH YOU COULD TALK, SNOOPY...
HERE YOU ARE SITTING IN A PUMPKIN PATCH WITH THE POSSIBILITY OF SEEING THE "GREAT PUMPKIN"... IT'S AN EMOTIONAL EXPERIENCE..
I'D REALLY BE INTERESTED IN KNOWING WHAT THOUGHTS ARE RUNNING THROUGH YOUR MIND...
WHEN DO WE EAT?

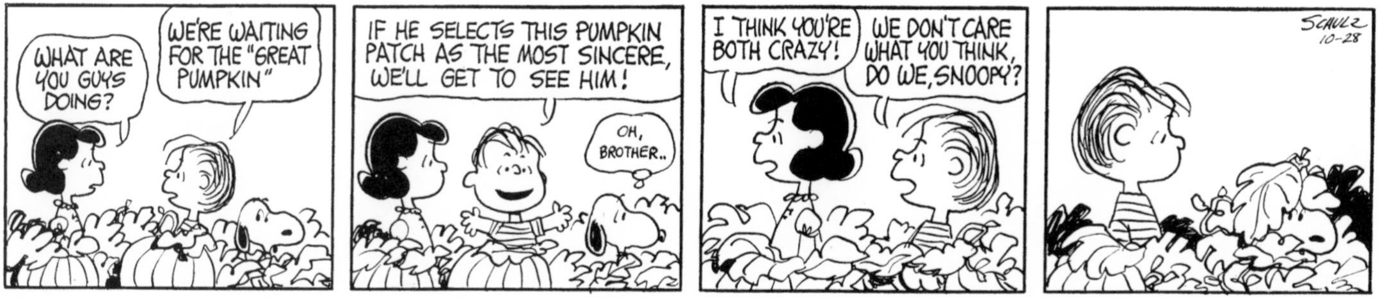
WHAT ARE YOU GUYS DOING?
WE'RE WAITING FOR THE "GREAT PUMPKIN"
IF HE SELECTS THIS PUMPKIN PATCH AS THE MOST SINCERE, WE'LL GET TO SEE HIM!
OH, BROTHER..
I THINK YOU'RE BOTH CRAZY!
WE DON'T CARE WHAT YOU THINK, DO WE, SNOOPY?

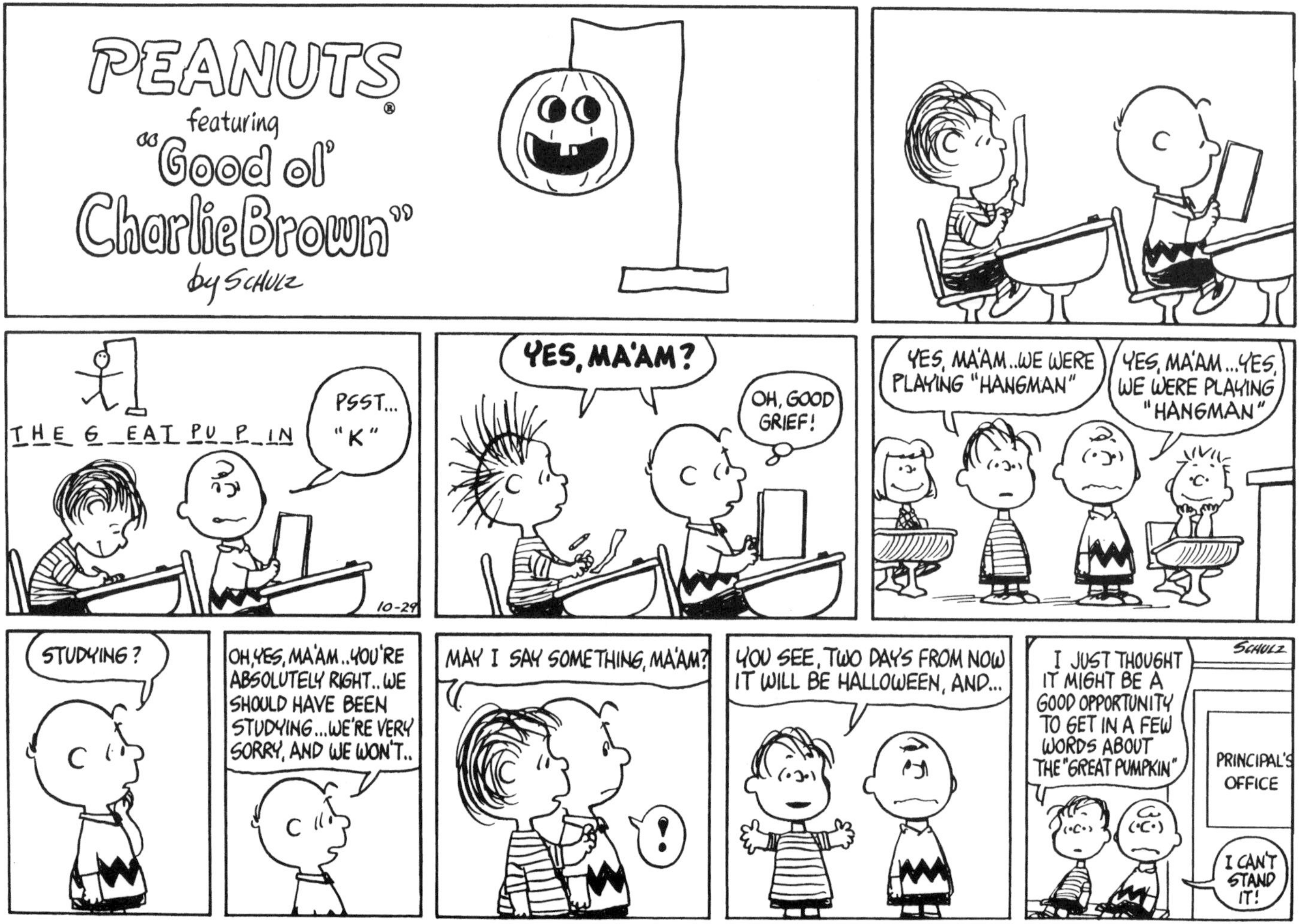
PEANUTS
featuring
"Good ol' Charlie Brown"
by SCHULZ
T H E G _ EAT PU _ P _ IN
PSST... "K"
10-29
YES, MA'AM?
OH, GOOD GRIEF!
YES, MA'AM..WE WERE PLAYING "HANGMAN"
YES, MA'AM...YES, WE WERE PLAYING "HANGMAN"
STUDYING?
OH, YES, MA'AM..YOU'RE ABSOLUTELY RIGHT..WE SHOULD HAVE BEEN STUDYING...WE'RE VERY SORRY, AND WE WON'T..
MAY I SAY SOMETHING, MA'AM?
!
YOU SEE, TWO DAYS FROM NOW IT WILL BE HALLOWEEN, AND...
SCHULZ
I JUST THOUGHT IT MIGHT BE A GOOD OPPORTUNITY TO GET IN A FEW WORDS ABOUT THE "GREAT PUMPKIN"
PRINCIPAL'S OFFICE
I CAN'T STAND IT!

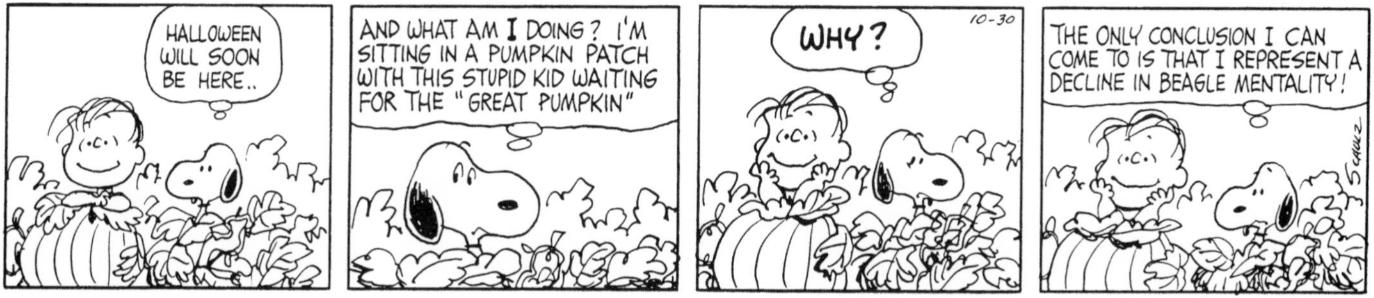
HALLOWEEN WILL SOON BE HERE..
AND WHAT AM I DOING? I'M SITTING IN A PUMPKIN PATCH WITH THIS STUPID KID WAITING FOR THE "GREAT PUMPKIN"
10-30
WHY?
THE ONLY CONCLUSION I CAN COME TO IS THAT I REPRESENT A DECLINE IN BEAGLE MENTALITY!
SCHULZ

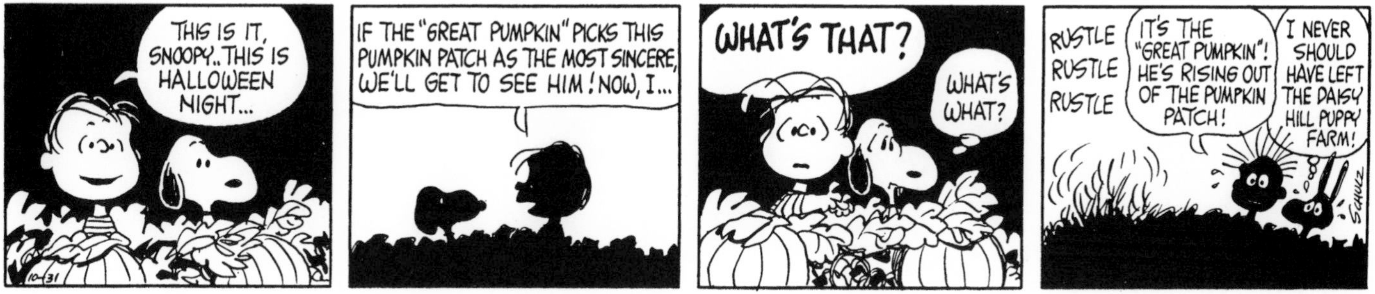
THIS IS IT, SNOOPY.. THIS IS HALLOWEEN NIGHT...
10-31
IF THE "GREAT PUMPKIN" PICKS THIS PUMPKIN PATCH AS THE MOST SINCERE, WE'LL GET TO SEE HIM! NOW, I...
WHAT'S THAT?
WHAT'S WHAT?
RUSTLE RUSTLE RUSTLE
IT'S THE "GREAT PUMPKIN"! HE'S RISING OUT OF THE PUMPKIN PATCH!
I NEVER SHOULD HAVE LEFT THE DAISY HILL PUPPY FARM!
SCHULZ

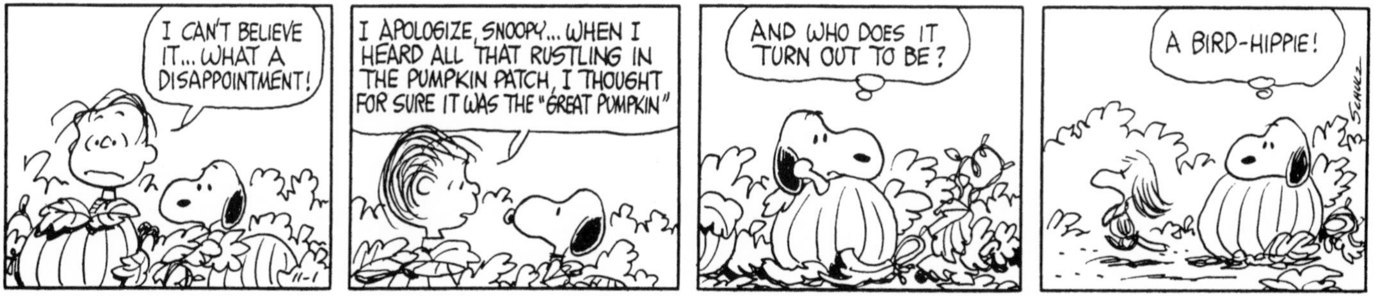
I CAN'T BELIEVE IT... WHAT A DISAPPOINTMENT!
11-1
I APOLOGIZE, SNOOPY... WHEN I HEARD ALL THAT RUSTLING IN THE PUMPKIN PATCH, I THOUGHT FOR SURE IT WAS THE "GREAT PUMPKIN"
AND WHO DOES IT TURN OUT TO BE?
A BIRD-HIPPIE!
SCHULZ

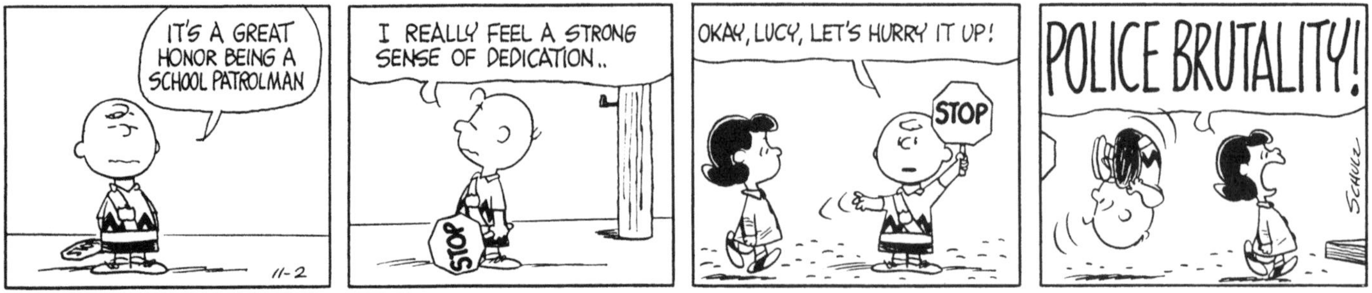
IT'S A GREAT HONOR BEING A SCHOOL PATROLMAN
11-2
I REALLY FEEL A STRONG SENSE OF DEDICATION..
STOP
OKAY, LUCY, LET'S HURRY IT UP!
STOP
POLICE BRUTALITY!
SCHULZ

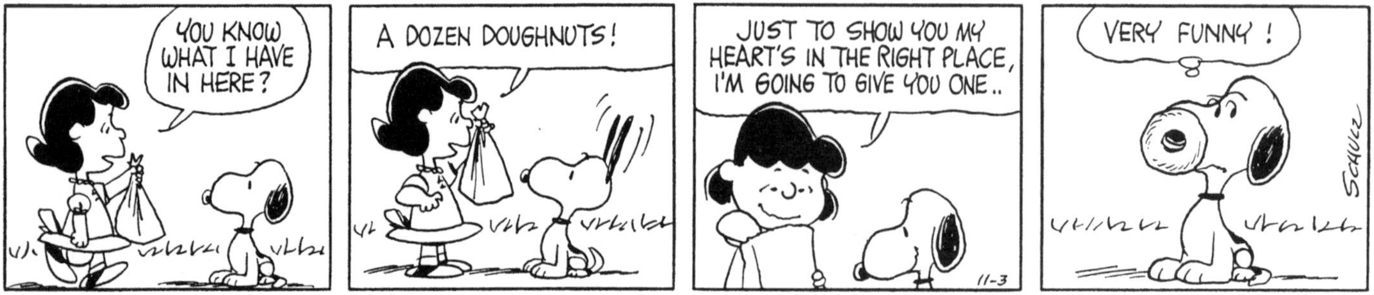
YOU KNOW WHAT I HAVE IN HERE?
A DOZEN DOUGHNUTS!
JUST TO SHOW YOU MY HEART'S IN THE RIGHT PLACE, I'M GOING TO GIVE YOU ONE..
11-3
VERY FUNNY !
SCHULZ

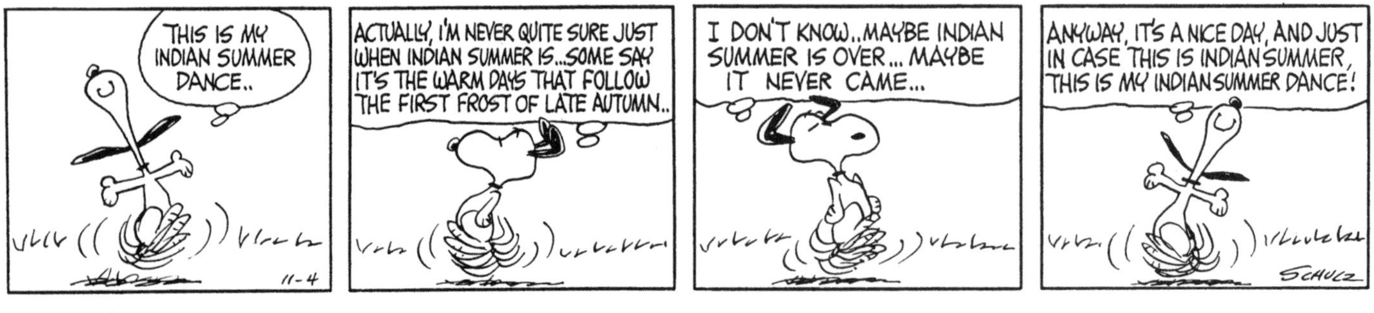
THIS IS MY INDIAN SUMMER DANCE..
11-4
ACTUALLY, I'M NEVER QUITE SURE JUST WHEN INDIAN SUMMER IS...SOME SAY IT'S THE WARM DAYS THAT FOLLOW THE FIRST FROST OF LATE AUTUMN..
I DON'T KNOW..MAYBE INDIAN SUMMER IS OVER... MAYBE IT NEVER CAME...
ANYWAY, IT'S A NICE DAY, AND JUST IN CASE THIS IS INDIAN SUMMER, THIS IS MY INDIAN SUMMER DANCE!
SCHULZ

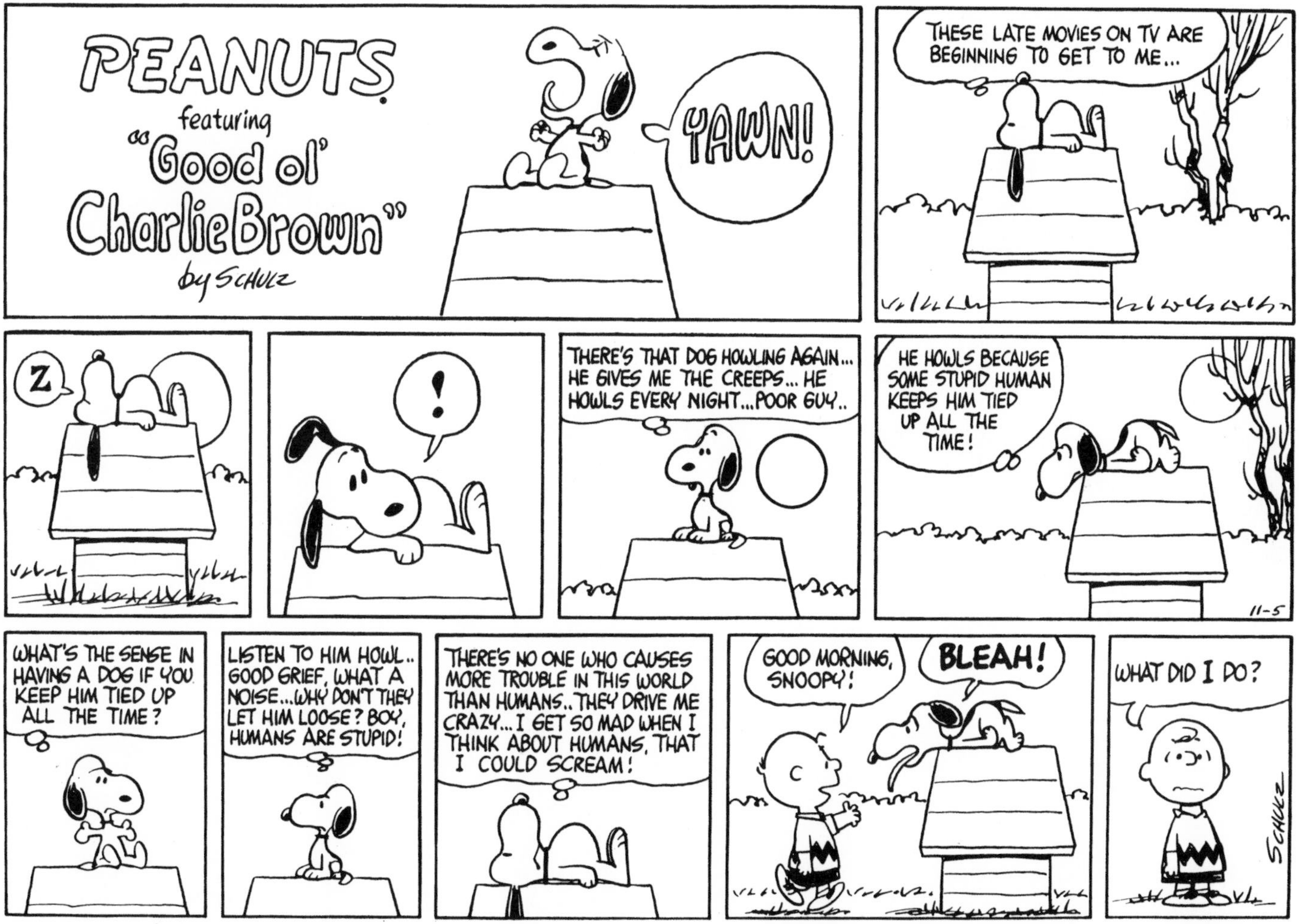
PEANUTS
featuring
"Good ol' Charlie Brown"
by SCHULZ
YAWN!
THESE LATE MOVIES ON TV ARE BEGINNING TO GET TO ME...
Z
!
THERE'S THAT DOG HOWLING AGAIN... HE GIVES ME THE CREEPS... HE HOWLS EVERY NIGHT...POOR GUY..
HE HOWLS BECAUSE SOME STUPID HUMAN KEEPS HIM TIED UP ALL THE TIME!
11-5
WHAT'S THE SENSE IN HAVING A DOG IF YOU KEEP HIM TIED UP ALL THE TIME?
LISTEN TO HIM HOWL.. GOOD GRIEF, WHAT A NOISE...WHY DON'T THEY LET HIM LOOSE? BOY, HUMANS ARE STUPID!
THERE'S NO ONE WHO CAUSES MORE TROUBLE IN THIS WORLD THAN HUMANS..THEY DRIVE ME CRAZY... I GET SO MAD WHEN I THINK ABOUT HUMANS, THAT I COULD SCREAM!
GOOD MORNING, SNOOPY!
BLEAH!
WHAT DID I DO?
SCHULZ

Panel 1: I'VE BEEN GOING OVER OUR BASEBALL STATISTICS FOR THIS PAST YEAR..

Panel 2: WHEN I THINK OF ALL THOSE GAMES WE LOST, I GET SICK..

11-6

Panel 3: WINNING ISN'T EVERYTHING, CHARLIE BROWN...

Panel 4: THAT'S TRUE, BUT LOSING ISN'T **ANYTHING**!

Panel 5: LAST YEAR WAS THE WORST BASEBALL SEASON OUR TEAM HAS HAD YET!

Panel 6: I'M REALLY WORRIED ABOUT OUR TEAM, SCHROEDER... I THINK WE'RE GETTING WORSE..

Panel 7: BEETHOVEN HAD HIS PROBLEMS, TOO!

11/7

Panel 8: THAT'S WHAT I LIKE, A NICE RELEVANT STATEMENT..

Panel 9: I'VE MADE A BIG DECISION...

Panel 10: THIS IS THE TIME OF YEAR WHEN ALL THE BIG BASEBALL TRADES ARE MADE....I'M GOING TO TRY TO IMPROVE OUR TEAM WITH A FEW SHREWD TRADES

Panel 11: THAT'S A GREAT IDEA, CHARLIE BROWN...

11-8

Panel 12: WHY DON'T YOU TRADE YOURSELF?

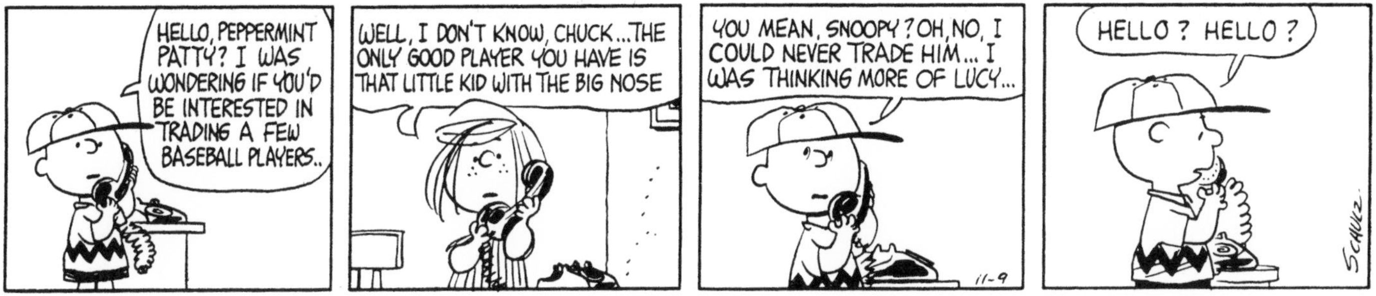
HELLO, PEPPERMINT PATTY? I WAS WONDERING IF YOU'D BE INTERESTED IN TRADING A FEW BASEBALL PLAYERS..
WELL, I DON'T KNOW, CHUCK...THE ONLY GOOD PLAYER YOU HAVE IS THAT LITTLE KID WITH THE BIG NOSE
YOU MEAN, SNOOPY? OH, NO, I COULD NEVER TRADE HIM... I WAS THINKING MORE OF LUCY...
11-9
HELLO? HELLO?
SCHULZ

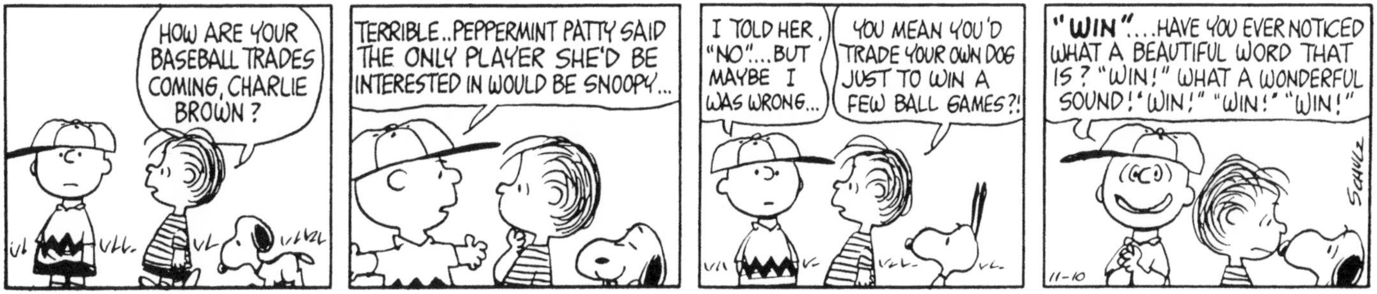
HOW ARE YOUR BASEBALL TRADES COMING, CHARLIE BROWN?
TERRIBLE..PEPPERMINT PATTY SAID THE ONLY PLAYER SHE'D BE INTERESTED IN WOULD BE SNOOPY...
I TOLD HER, "NO"....BUT MAYBE I WAS WRONG...
YOU MEAN YOU'D TRADE YOUR OWN DOG JUST TO WIN A FEW BALL GAMES?!
"WIN"....HAVE YOU EVER NOTICED WHAT A BEAUTIFUL WORD THAT IS? "WIN!" WHAT A WONDERFUL SOUND! "WIN!" "WIN!" "WIN!"
SCHULZ
11-10

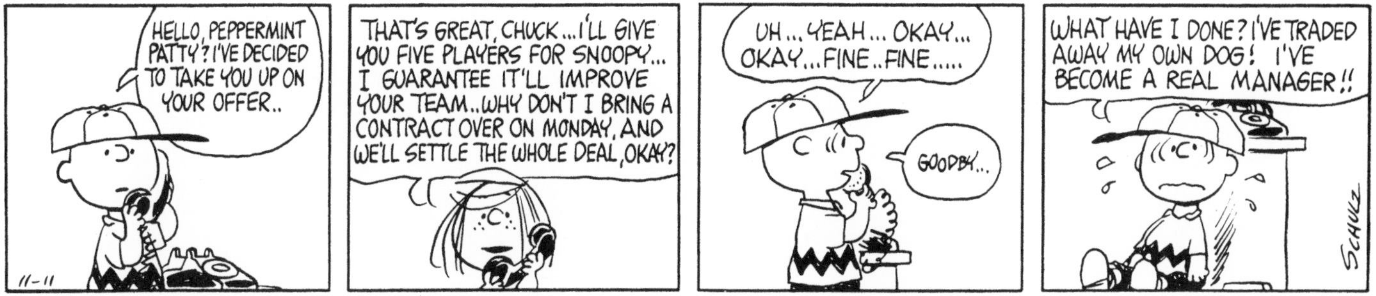
HELLO, PEPPERMINT PATTY? I'VE DECIDED TO TAKE YOU UP ON YOUR OFFER..
11-11
THAT'S GREAT, CHUCK...I'LL GIVE YOU FIVE PLAYERS FOR SNOOPY... I GUARANTEE IT'LL IMPROVE YOUR TEAM..WHY DON'T I BRING A CONTRACT OVER ON MONDAY, AND WE'LL SETTLE THE WHOLE DEAL, OKAY?
UH... YEAH... OKAY... OKAY...FINE..FINE.....
GOODBY...
WHAT HAVE I DONE? I'VE TRADED AWAY MY OWN DOG! I'VE BECOME A REAL MANAGER!!
SCHULZ

PEANUTS®

featuring "Good ol' CharlieBrown"

by Schulz

GOOD MORNING, GROUND CREW!

CURSE THESE EARLY MORNING HOURS..

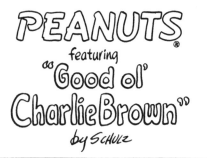

HERE'S THE WORLD WAR I FLYING ACE ZOOMING THROUGH THE AIR IN HIS SOPWITH CAMEL!

IT IS RUMORED THAT THE RED BARON IS IN THE AREA..

MY MISSION IS TO SEARCH HIM OUT, AND BRING HIM DOWN ...

HMM.. INCLEMENT WEATHER..

11-12

GENERAL PERSHING WOULD NOT BE PLEASED IF I CAUGHT COLD!

BAM! BAM! BAM!

WHAT IN THE WORLD...

HERE'S THE WORLD WAR I FLYING ACE BACK AT THE OFFICERS' CLUB THROWING DARTS

SIGH!

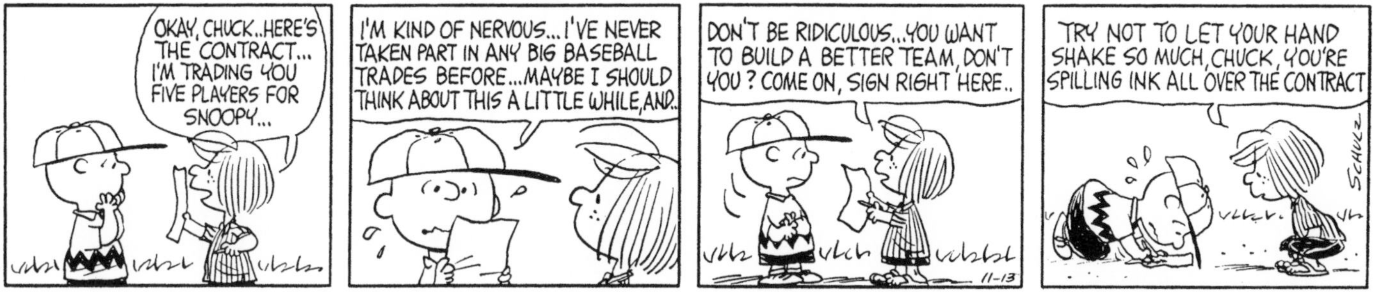
OKAY, CHUCK..HERE'S THE CONTRACT... I'M TRADING YOU FIVE PLAYERS FOR SNOOPY...
I'M KIND OF NERVOUS... I'VE NEVER TAKEN PART IN ANY BIG BASEBALL TRADES BEFORE...MAYBE I SHOULD THINK ABOUT THIS A LITTLE WHILE, AND..
DON'T BE RIDICULOUS...YOU WANT TO BUILD A BETTER TEAM, DON'T YOU ? COME ON, SIGN RIGHT HERE..
11-13
TRY NOT TO LET YOUR HAND SHAKE SO MUCH, CHUCK, YOU'RE SPILLING INK ALL OVER THE CONTRACT
SCHULZ

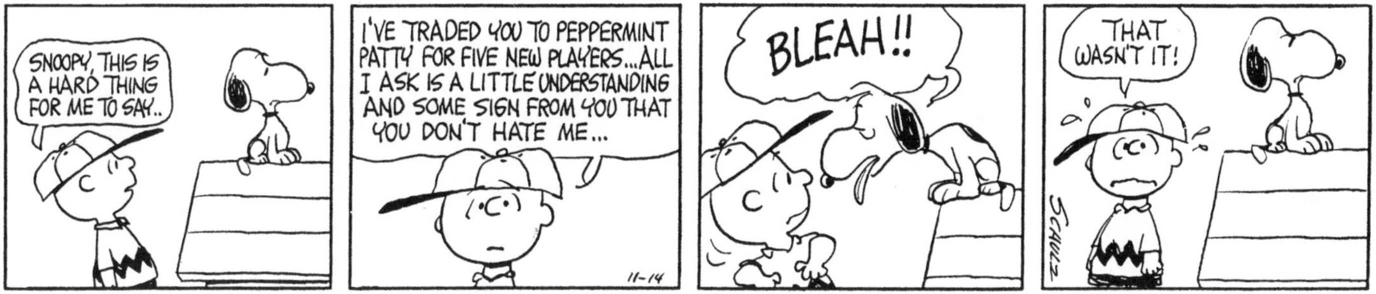
SNOOPY, THIS IS A HARD THING FOR ME TO SAY..
I'VE TRADED YOU TO PEPPERMINT PATTY FOR FIVE NEW PLAYERS...ALL I ASK IS A LITTLE UNDERSTANDING AND SOME SIGN FROM YOU THAT YOU DON'T HATE ME...
11-14
BLEAH!!
THAT WASN'T IT!
SCHULZ

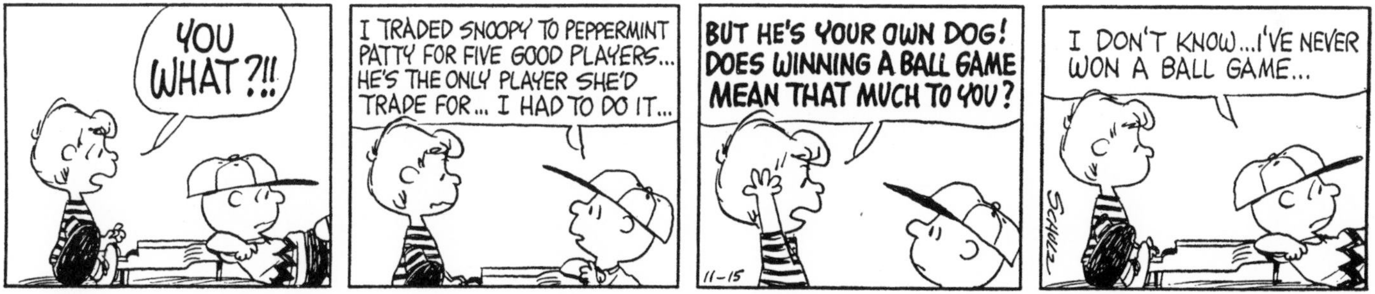
YOU WHAT ?!!
I TRADED SNOOPY TO PEPPERMINT PATTY FOR FIVE GOOD PLAYERS... HE'S THE ONLY PLAYER SHE'D TRADE FOR... I HAD TO DO IT...
BUT HE'S YOUR OWN DOG! DOES WINNING A BALL GAME MEAN THAT MUCH TO YOU ?
11-15
I DON'T KNOW...I'VE NEVER WON A BALL GAME...
SCHULZ

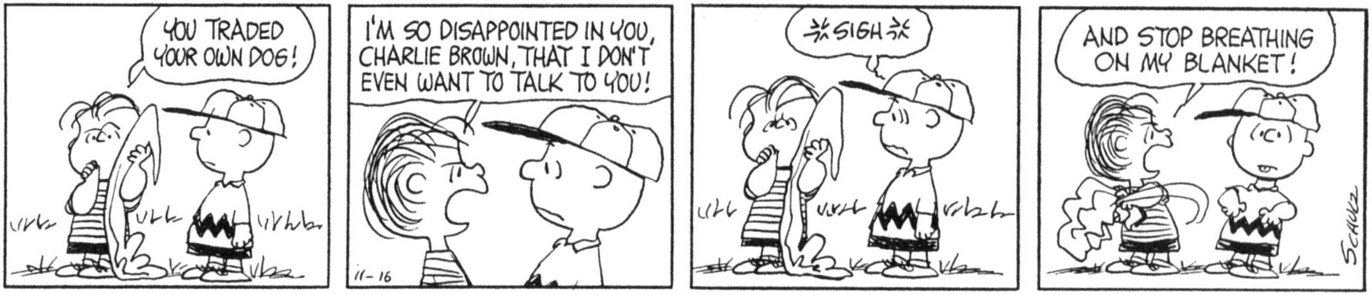
YOU TRADED YOUR OWN DOG!
I'M SO DISAPPOINTED IN YOU, CHARLIE BROWN, THAT I DON'T EVEN WANT TO TALK TO YOU!
11-16
SIGH
AND STOP BREATHING ON MY BLANKET!
SCHULZ

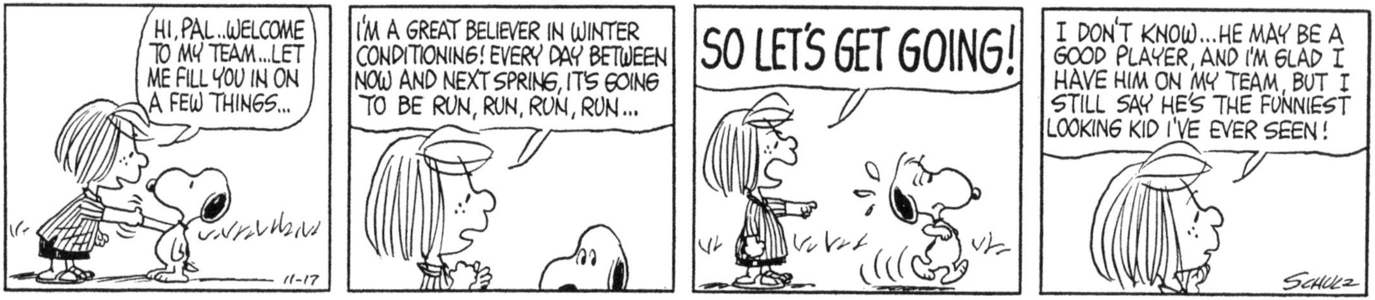
HI, PAL..WELCOME TO MY TEAM...LET ME FILL YOU IN ON A FEW THINGS...
11-17
I'M A GREAT BELIEVER IN WINTER CONDITIONING! EVERY DAY BETWEEN NOW AND NEXT SPRING, IT'S GOING TO BE RUN, RUN, RUN, RUN...
SO LET'S GET GOING!
I DON'T KNOW...HE MAY BE A GOOD PLAYER, AND I'M GLAD I HAVE HIM ON MY TEAM, BUT I STILL SAY HE'S THE FUNNIEST LOOKING KID I'VE EVER SEEN!
SCHULZ

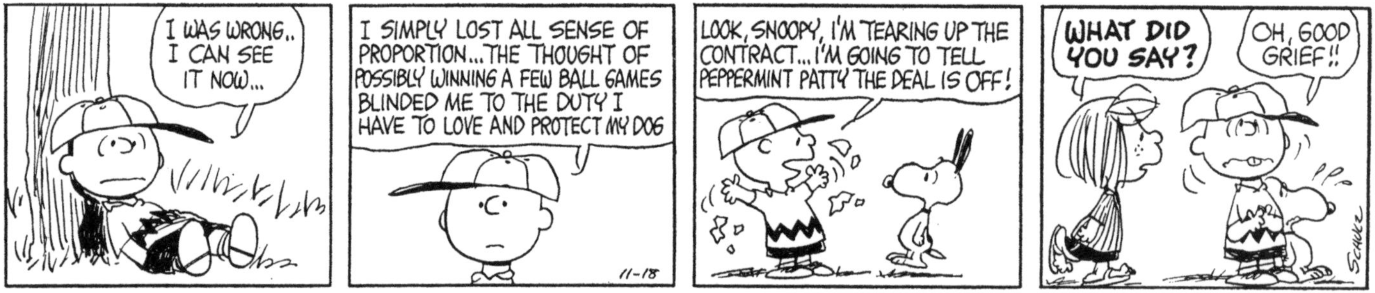
I WAS WRONG.. I CAN SEE IT NOW...
I SIMPLY LOST ALL SENSE OF PROPORTION...THE THOUGHT OF POSSIBLY WINNING A FEW BALL GAMES BLINDED ME TO THE DUTY I HAVE TO LOVE AND PROTECT MY DOG
11-18
LOOK, SNOOPY, I'M TEARING UP THE CONTRACT...I'M GOING TO TELL PEPPERMINT PATTY THE DEAL IS OFF!
WHAT DID YOU SAY?
OH, GOOD GRIEF!!
SCHULZ

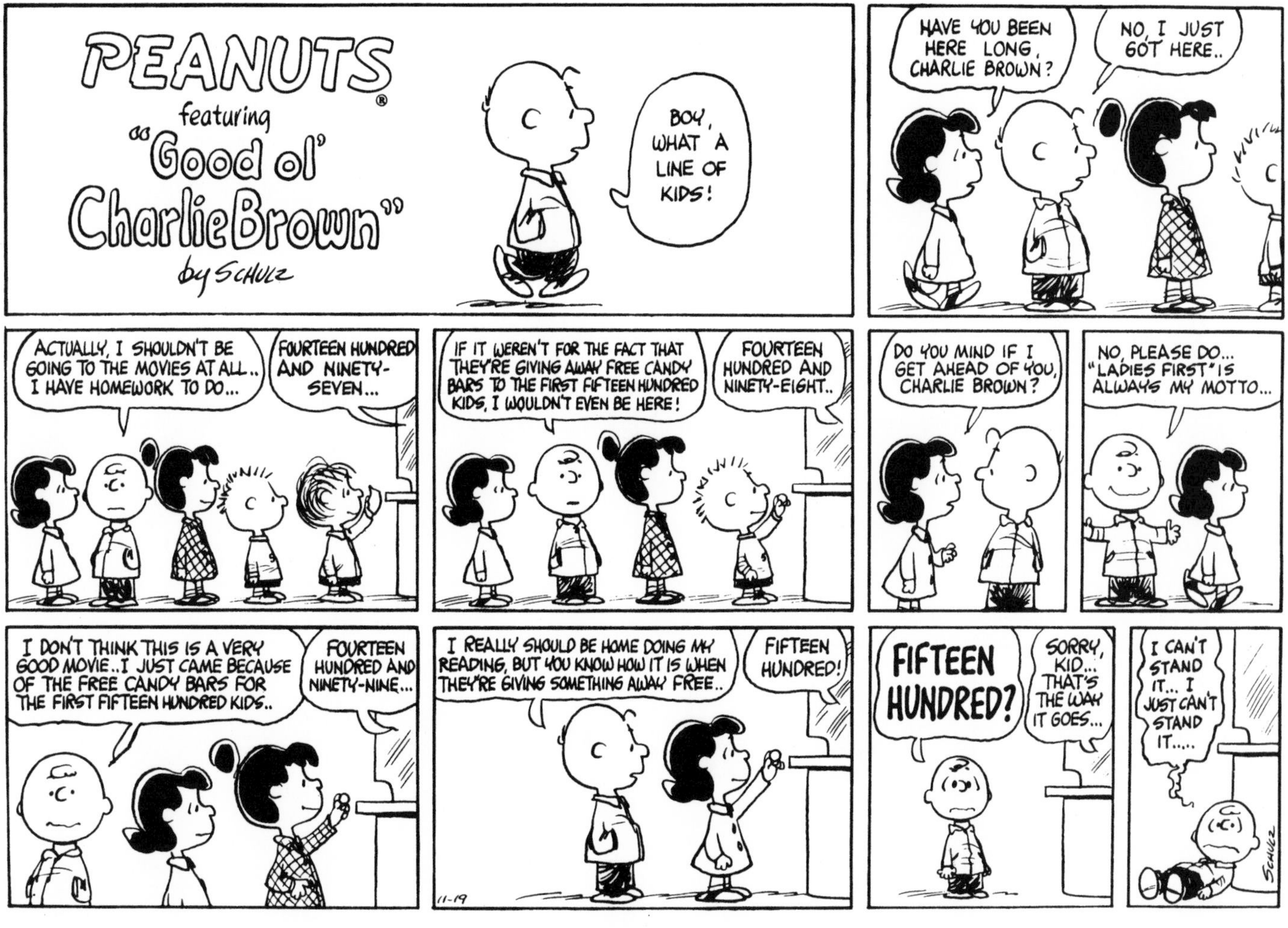
PEANUTS
featuring "Good ol' CharlieBrown"
by SCHULZ
BOY, WHAT A LINE OF KIDS!
HAVE YOU BEEN HERE LONG, CHARLIE BROWN?
NO, I JUST GOT HERE..
ACTUALLY, I SHOULDN'T BE GOING TO THE MOVIES AT ALL.. I HAVE HOMEWORK TO DO...
FOURTEEN HUNDRED AND NINETY-SEVEN...
IF IT WEREN'T FOR THE FACT THAT THEY'RE GIVING AWAY FREE CANDY BARS TO THE FIRST FIFTEEN HUNDRED KIDS, I WOULDN'T EVEN BE HERE!
FOURTEEN HUNDRED AND NINETY-EIGHT..
DO YOU MIND IF I GET AHEAD OF YOU, CHARLIE BROWN?
NO, PLEASE DO... "LADIES FIRST" IS ALWAYS MY MOTTO...
I DON'T THINK THIS IS A VERY GOOD MOVIE..I JUST CAME BECAUSE OF THE FREE CANDY BARS FOR THE FIRST FIFTEEN HUNDRED KIDS..
FOURTEEN HUNDRED AND NINETY-NINE...
I REALLY SHOULD BE HOME DOING MY READING, BUT YOU KNOW HOW IT IS WHEN THEY'RE GIVING SOMETHING AWAY FREE..
FIFTEEN HUNDRED!
11-19
FIFTEEN HUNDRED?
SORRY, KID... THAT'S THE WAY IT GOES...
I CAN'T STAND IT... I JUST CAN'T STAND IT.....
SCHULZ

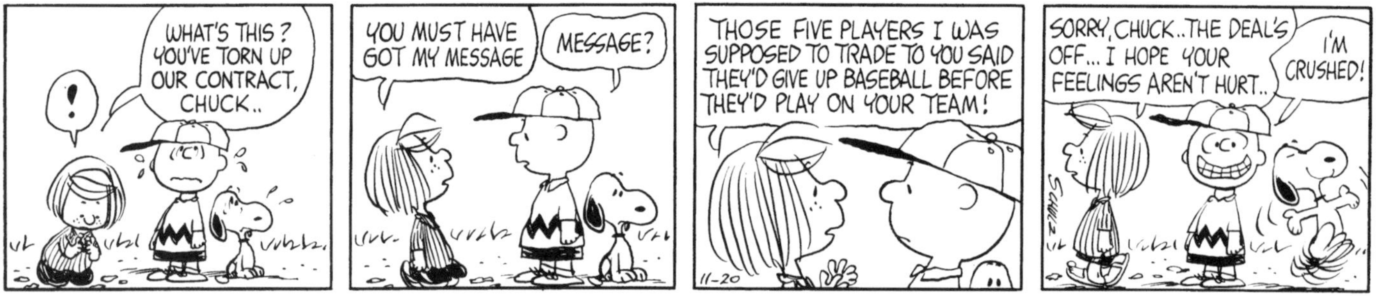
!
WHAT'S THIS? YOU'VE TORN UP OUR CONTRACT, CHUCK..
YOU MUST HAVE GOT MY MESSAGE
MESSAGE?
THOSE FIVE PLAYERS I WAS SUPPOSED TO TRADE TO YOU SAID THEY'D GIVE UP BASEBALL BEFORE THEY'D PLAY ON YOUR TEAM!
11-20
SORRY, CHUCK..THE DEAL'S OFF... I HOPE YOUR FEELINGS AREN'T HURT..
I'M CRUSHED!
SCHULZ

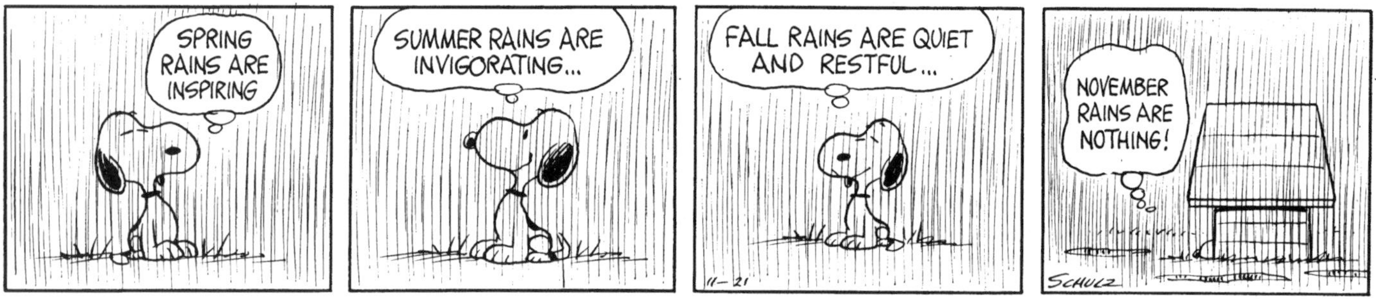
SPRING RAINS ARE INSPIRING
SUMMER RAINS ARE INVIGORATING...
FALL RAINS ARE QUIET AND RESTFUL...
11-21
NOVEMBER RAINS ARE NOTHING!
SCHULZ

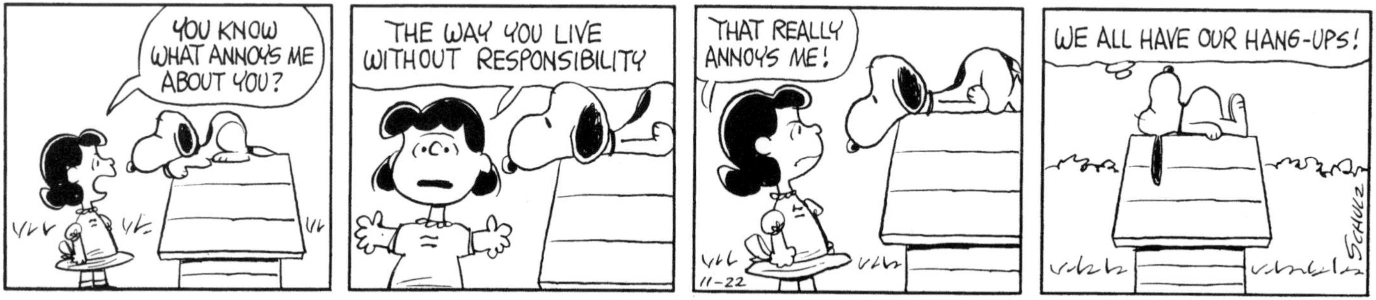
YOU KNOW WHAT ANNOYS ME ABOUT YOU?
THE WAY YOU LIVE WITHOUT RESPONSIBILITY
THAT REALLY ANNOYS ME!
11-22
WE ALL HAVE OUR HANG-UPS!
SCHULZ

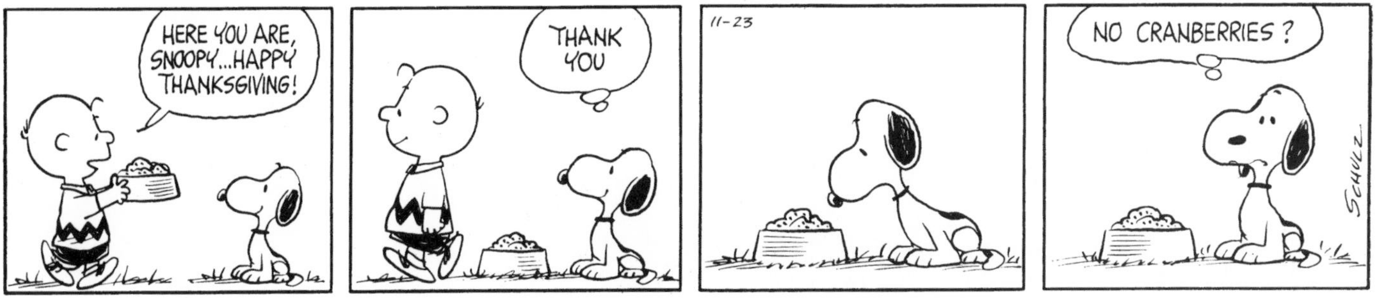
HERE YOU ARE, SNOOPY...HAPPY THANKSGIVING!
THANK YOU
11-23
NO CRANBERRIES ?
SCHULZ

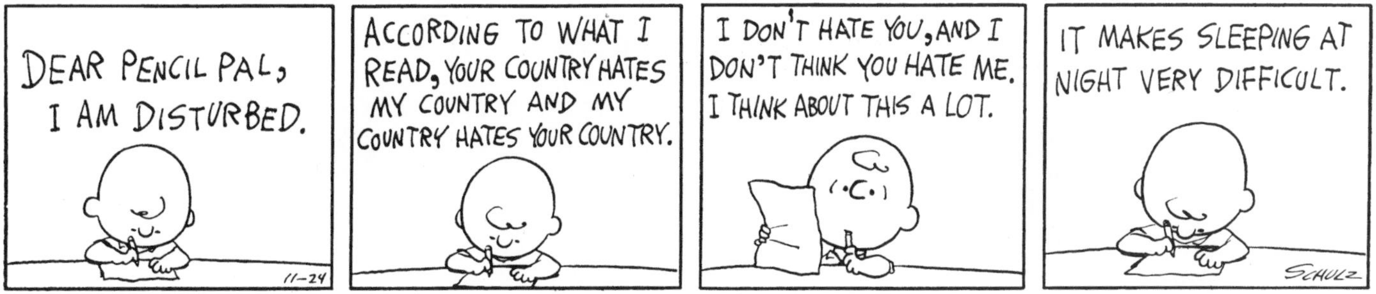
DEAR PENCIL PAL,
I AM DISTURBED.
11-24
ACCORDING TO WHAT I READ, YOUR COUNTRY HATES MY COUNTRY AND MY COUNTRY HATES YOUR COUNTRY.
I DON'T HATE YOU, AND I DON'T THINK YOU HATE ME. I THINK ABOUT THIS A LOT.
IT MAKES SLEEPING AT NIGHT VERY DIFFICULT.
SCHULZ

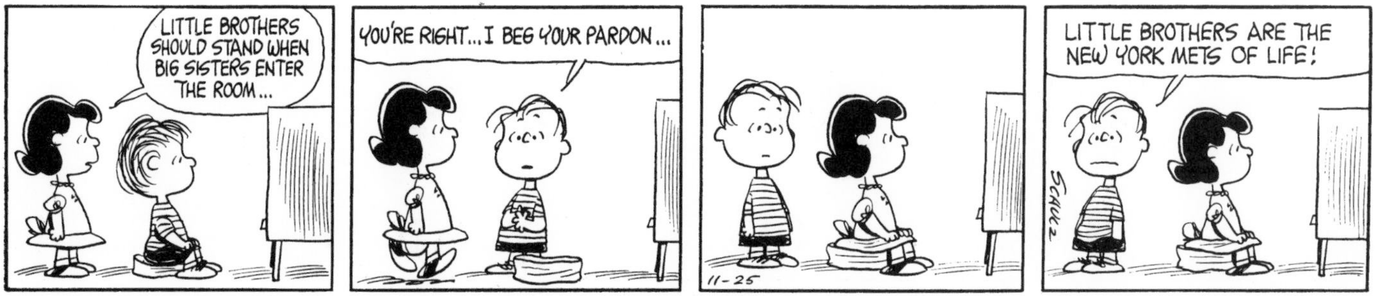
LITTLE BROTHERS SHOULD STAND WHEN BIG SISTERS ENTER THE ROOM...
YOU'RE RIGHT...I BEG YOUR PARDON...
11-25
LITTLE BROTHERS ARE THE NEW YORK METS OF LIFE!
SCHULZ

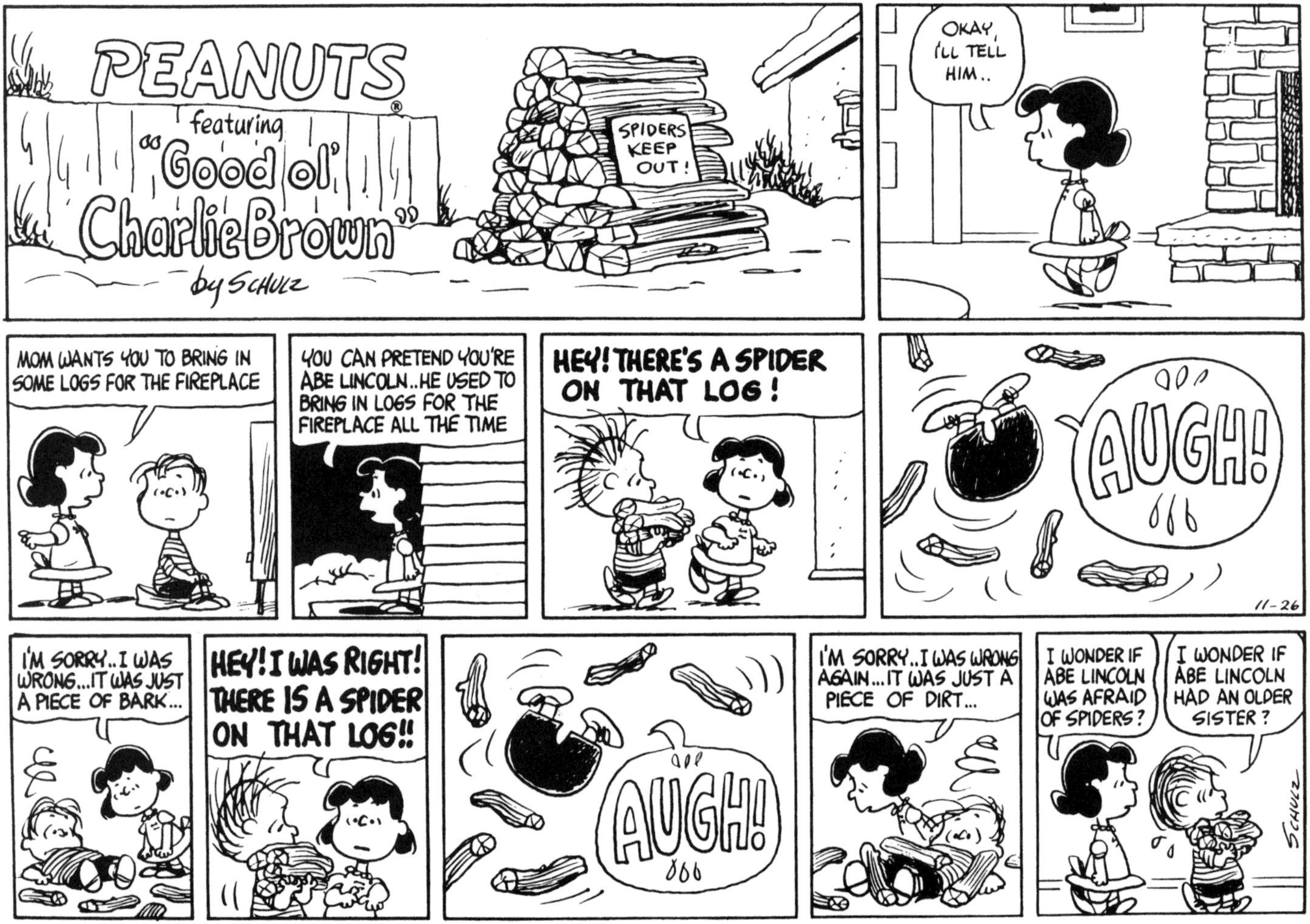
PEANUTS
featuring "Good ol' Charlie Brown"
by SCHULZ
SPIDERS KEEP OUT!
OKAY, I'LL TELL HIM..
MOM WANTS YOU TO BRING IN SOME LOGS FOR THE FIREPLACE
YOU CAN PRETEND YOU'RE ABE LINCOLN..HE USED TO BRING IN LOGS FOR THE FIREPLACE ALL THE TIME
HEY! THERE'S A SPIDER ON THAT LOG!
AUGH!
11-26
I'M SORRY..I WAS WRONG...IT WAS JUST A PIECE OF BARK...
HEY! I WAS RIGHT! THERE IS A SPIDER ON THAT LOG!!
AUGH!
I'M SORRY..I WAS WRONG AGAIN...IT WAS JUST A PIECE OF DIRT...
I WONDER IF ABE LINCOLN WAS AFRAID OF SPIDERS?
I WONDER IF ABE LINCOLN HAD AN OLDER SISTER?
SCHULZ

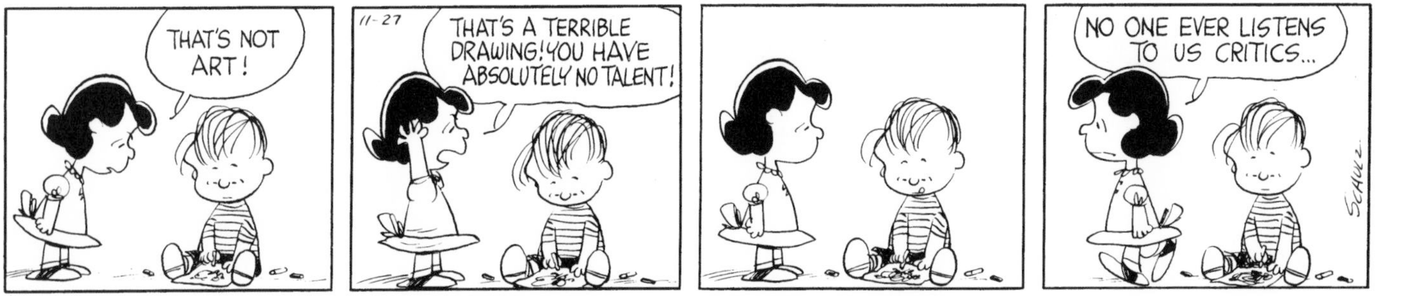
THAT'S NOT ART!
11-27
THAT'S A TERRIBLE DRAWING! YOU HAVE ABSOLUTELY NO TALENT!
NO ONE EVER LISTENS TO US CRITICS...
SCHULZ

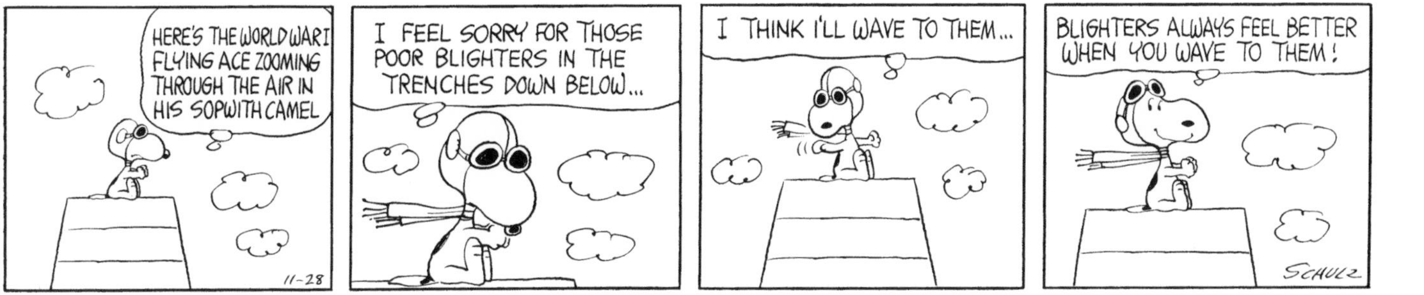
HERE'S THE WORLD WAR I FLYING ACE ZOOMING THROUGH THE AIR IN HIS SOPWITH CAMEL
11-28
I FEEL SORRY FOR THOSE POOR BLIGHTERS IN THE TRENCHES DOWN BELOW...
I THINK I'LL WAVE TO THEM...
BLIGHTERS ALWAYS FEEL BETTER WHEN YOU WAVE TO THEM!
SCHULZ

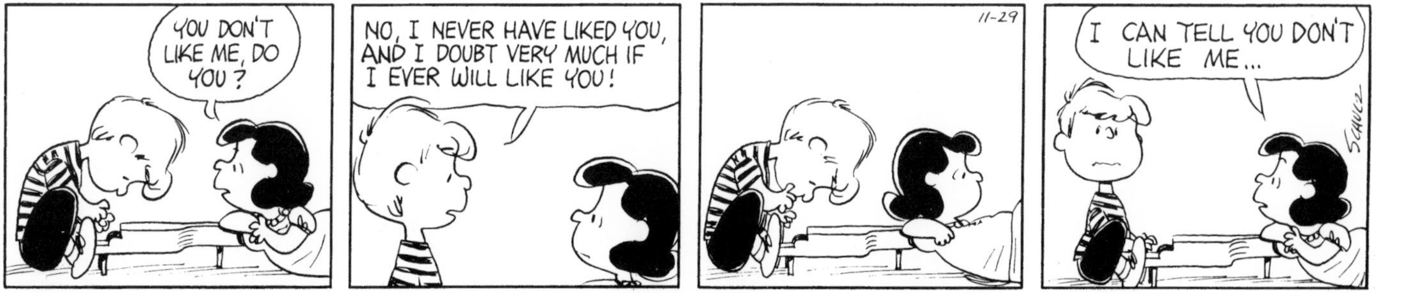
YOU DON'T LIKE ME, DO YOU?
NO, I NEVER HAVE LIKED YOU, AND I DOUBT VERY MUCH IF I EVER WILL LIKE YOU!
11-29
I CAN TELL YOU DON'T LIKE ME...
SCHULZ

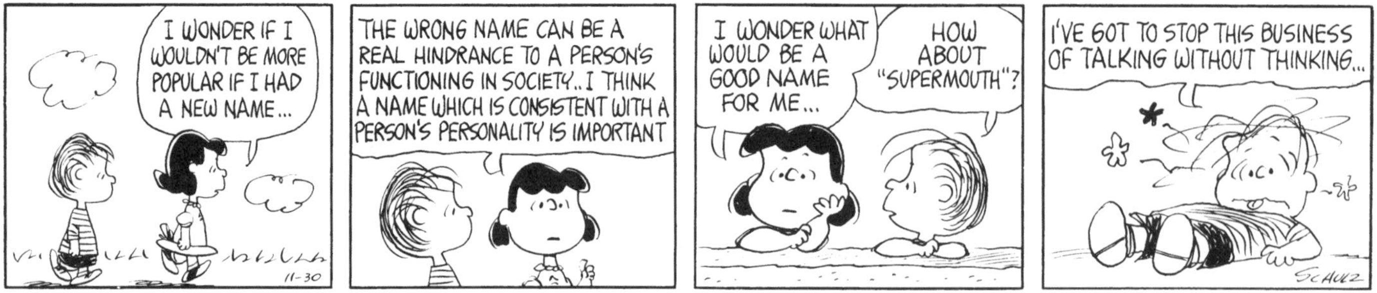
I WONDER IF I WOULDN'T BE MORE POPULAR IF I HAD A NEW NAME...
11-30
THE WRONG NAME CAN BE A REAL HINDRANCE TO A PERSON'S FUNCTIONING IN SOCIETY.. I THINK A NAME WHICH IS CONSISTENT WITH A PERSON'S PERSONALITY IS IMPORTANT
I WONDER WHAT WOULD BE A GOOD NAME FOR ME...
HOW ABOUT "SUPERMOUTH"?
I'VE GOT TO STOP THIS BUSINESS OF TALKING WITHOUT THINKING...
SCHULZ

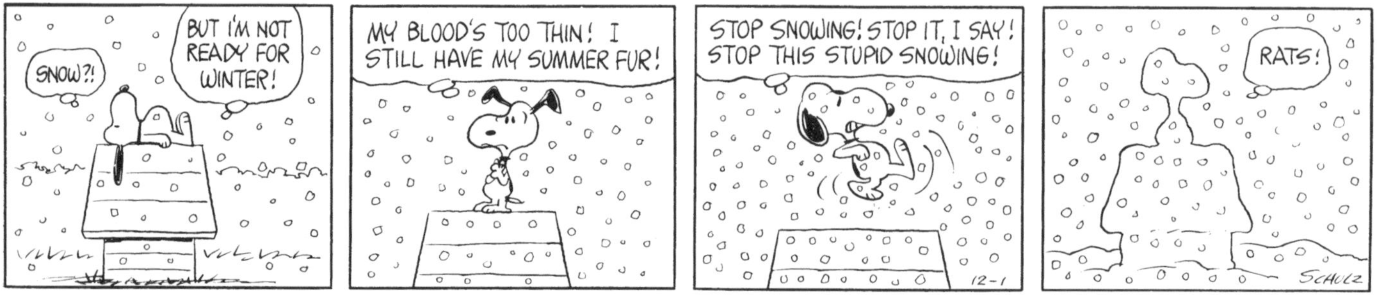
SNOW?!
BUT I'M NOT READY FOR WINTER!
MY BLOOD'S TOO THIN! I STILL HAVE MY SUMMER FUR!
STOP SNOWING! STOP IT, I SAY! STOP THIS STUPID SNOWING!
12-1
RATS!
SCHULZ

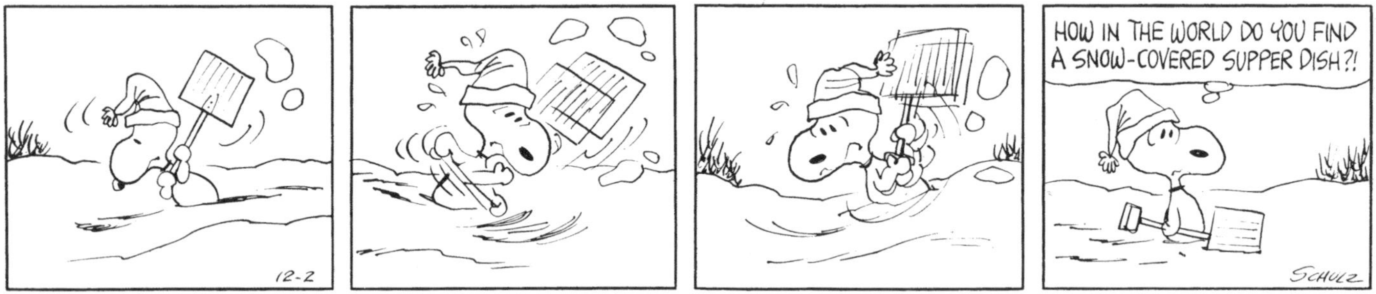
12-2
HOW IN THE WORLD DO YOU FIND A SNOW-COVERED SUPPER DISH?!
SCHULZ

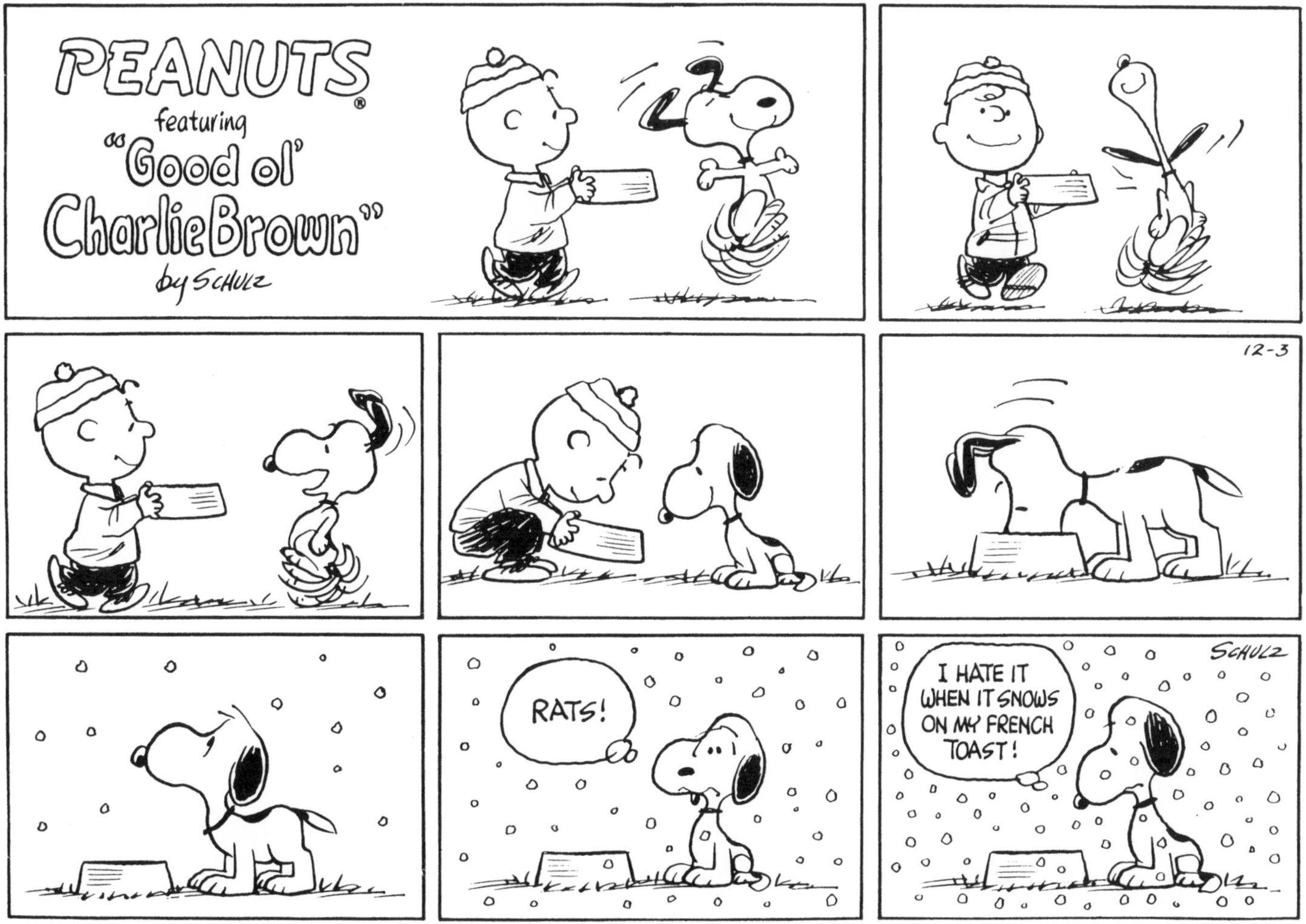
PEANUTS®
featuring
"Good ol' CharlieBrown"
by SCHULZ
12-3
RATS!
I HATE IT WHEN IT SNOWS ON MY FRENCH TOAST!
SCHULZ

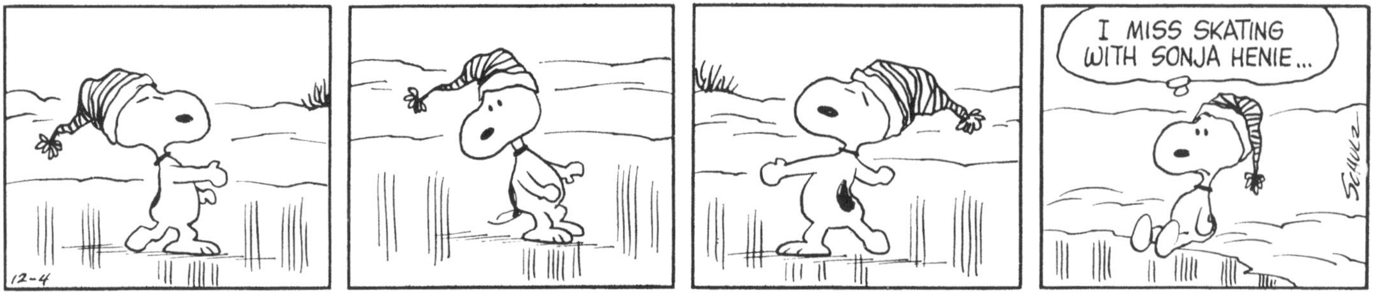
I MISS SKATING WITH SONJA HENIE...

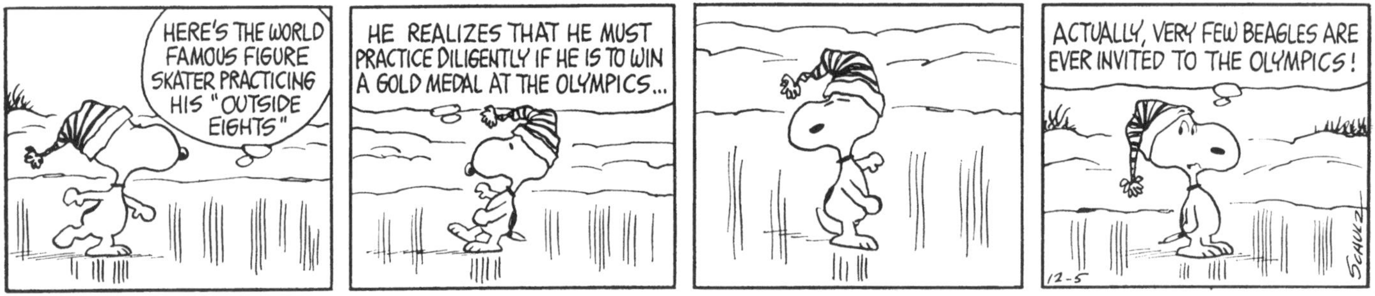
HERE'S THE WORLD FAMOUS FIGURE SKATER PRACTICING HIS "OUTSIDE EIGHTS"
HE REALIZES THAT HE MUST PRACTICE DILIGENTLY IF HE IS TO WIN A GOLD MEDAL AT THE OLYMPICS...
ACTUALLY, VERY FEW BEAGLES ARE EVER INVITED TO THE OLYMPICS!

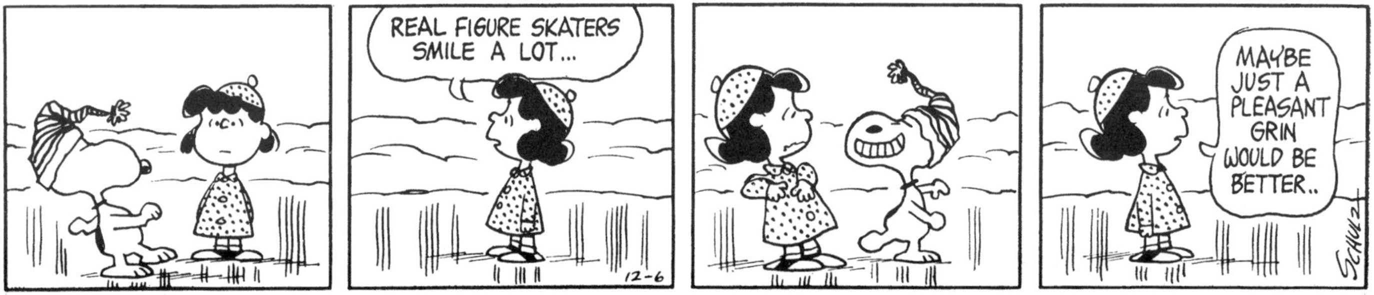
REAL FIGURE SKATERS SMILE A LOT...
MAYBE JUST A PLEASANT GRIN WOULD BE BETTER..

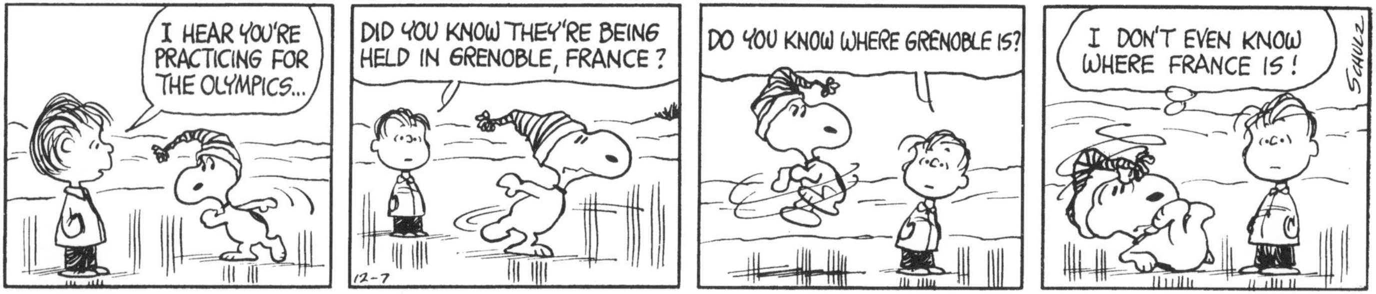
I HEAR YOU'RE PRACTICING FOR THE OLYMPICS...
DID YOU KNOW THEY'RE BEING HELD IN GRENOBLE, FRANCE ?
12-7
DO YOU KNOW WHERE GRENOBLE IS?
I DON'T EVEN KNOW WHERE FRANCE IS !
SCHULZ

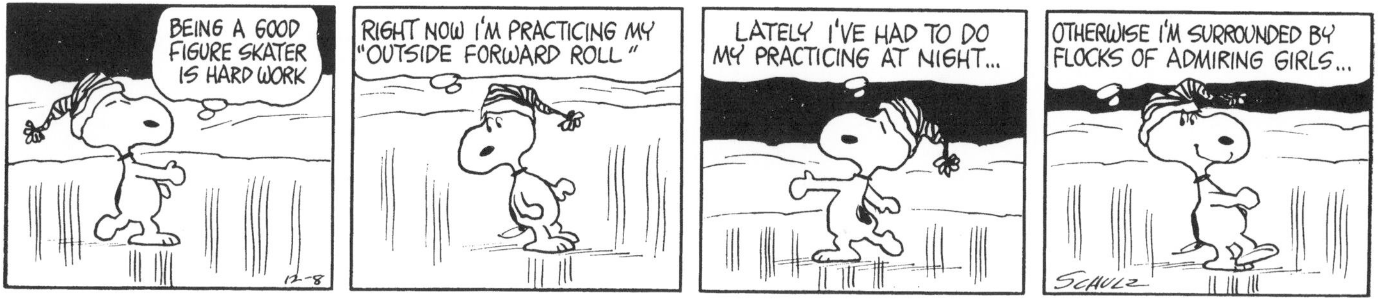
BEING A GOOD FIGURE SKATER IS HARD WORK
12-8
RIGHT NOW I'M PRACTICING MY "OUTSIDE FORWARD ROLL"
LATELY I'VE HAD TO DO MY PRACTICING AT NIGHT...
OTHERWISE I'M SURROUNDED BY FLOCKS OF ADMIRING GIRLS...
SCHULZ

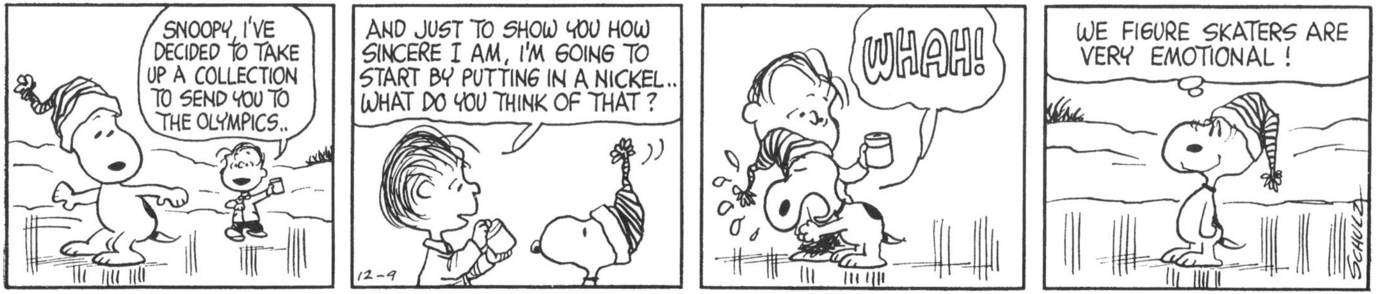
SNOOPY, I'VE DECIDED TO TAKE UP A COLLECTION TO SEND YOU TO THE OLYMPICS..
AND JUST TO SHOW YOU HOW SINCERE I AM, I'M GOING TO START BY PUTTING IN A NICKEL.. WHAT DO YOU THINK OF THAT ?
12-9
WHAH!
WE FIGURE SKATERS ARE VERY EMOTIONAL !
SCHULZ

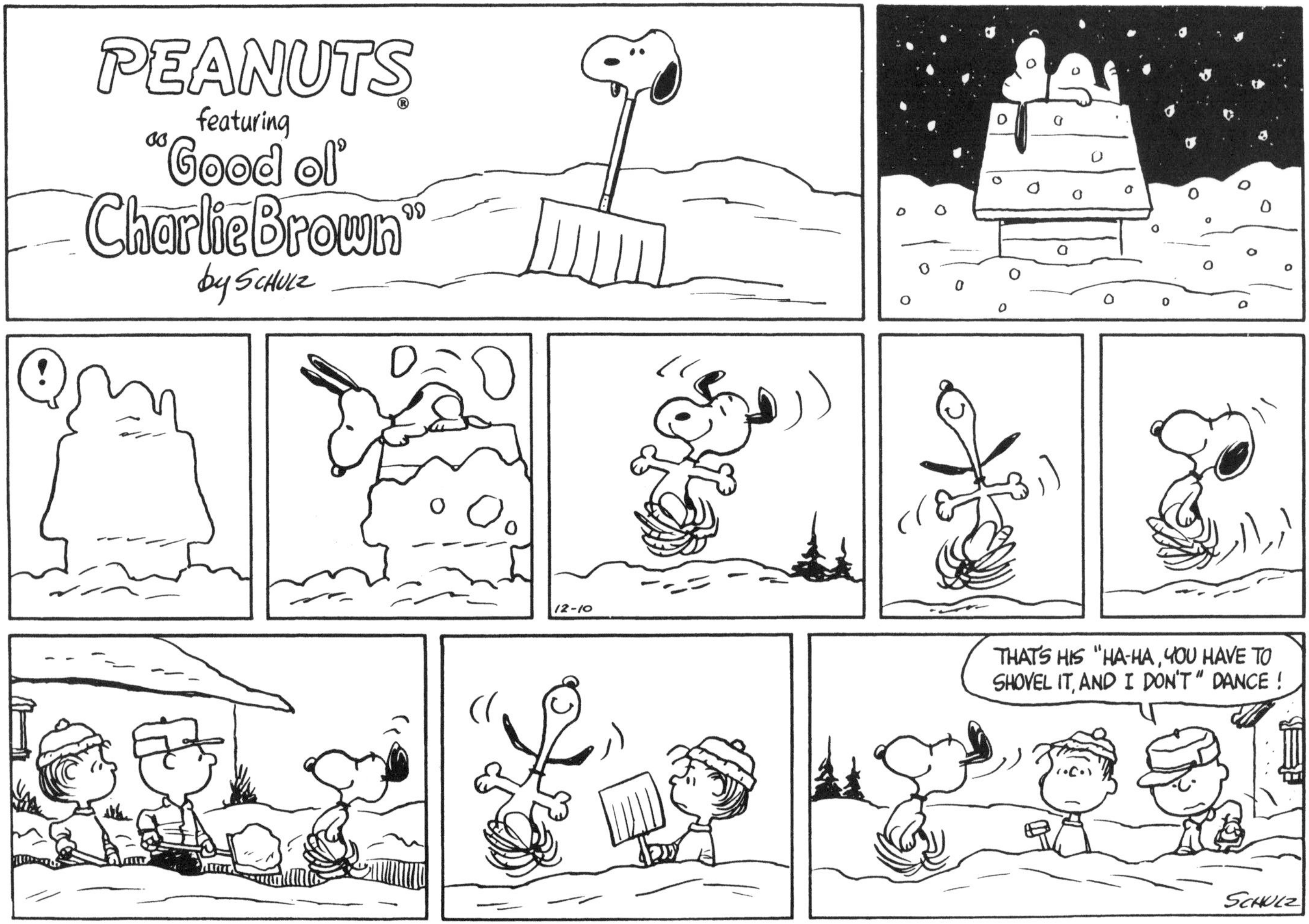
PEANUTS®
featuring
"Good ol' Charlie Brown"
by SCHULZ
!
12-10
THAT'S HIS "HA-HA, YOU HAVE TO SHOVEL IT, AND I DON'T" DANCE!
SCHULZ

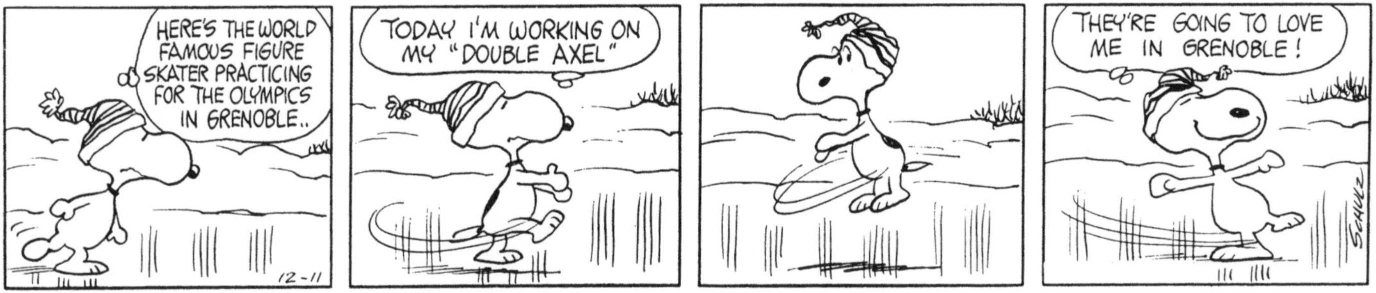
HERE'S THE WORLD FAMOUS FIGURE SKATER PRACTICING FOR THE OLYMPICS IN GRENOBLE..
TODAY I'M WORKING ON MY "DOUBLE AXEL"
THEY'RE GOING TO LOVE ME IN GRENOBLE!

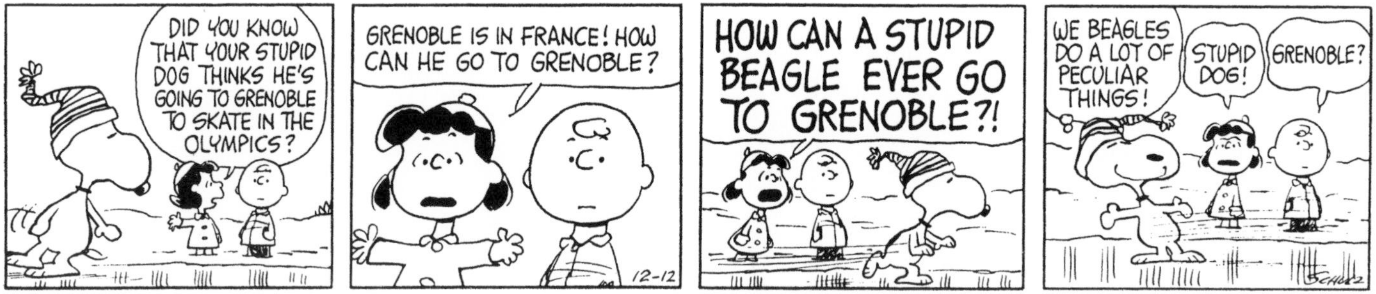
DID YOU KNOW THAT YOUR STUPID DOG THINKS HE'S GOING TO GRENOBLE TO SKATE IN THE OLYMPICS?
GRENOBLE IS IN FRANCE! HOW CAN HE GO TO GRENOBLE?
HOW CAN A STUPID BEAGLE EVER GO TO GRENOBLE?!
WE BEAGLES DO A LOT OF PECULIAR THINGS!
STUPID DOG!
GRENOBLE?

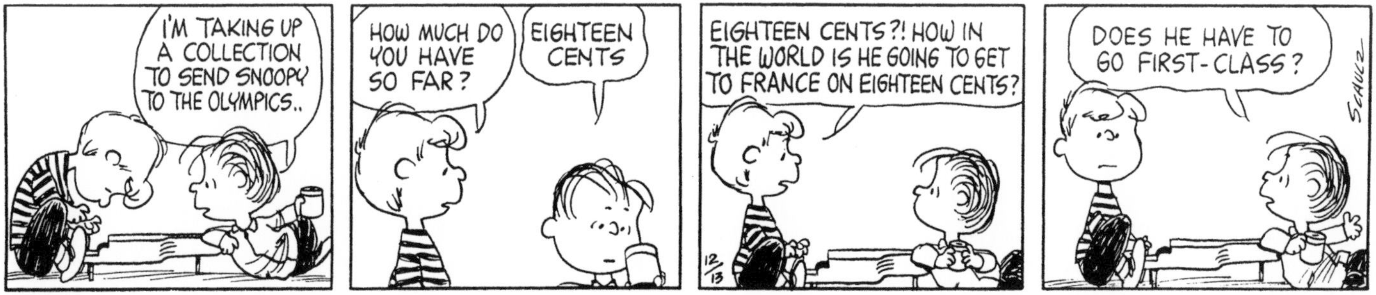
I'M TAKING UP A COLLECTION TO SEND SNOOPY TO THE OLYMPICS..
HOW MUCH DO YOU HAVE SO FAR?
EIGHTEEN CENTS
EIGHTEEN CENTS?! HOW IN THE WORLD IS HE GOING TO GET TO FRANCE ON EIGHTEEN CENTS?
DOES HE HAVE TO GO FIRST-CLASS?

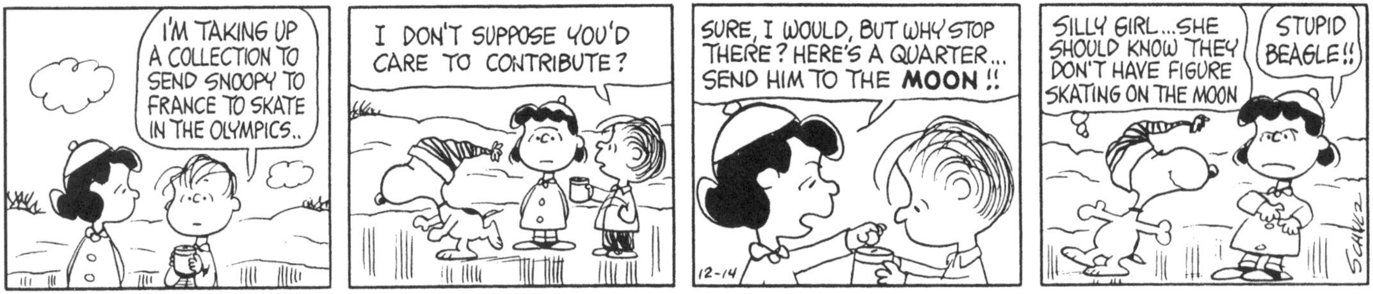
I'M TAKING UP A COLLECTION TO SEND SNOOPY TO FRANCE TO SKATE IN THE OLYMPICS..
I DON'T SUPPOSE YOU'D CARE TO CONTRIBUTE?
SURE, I WOULD, BUT WHY STOP THERE? HERE'S A QUARTER... SEND HIM TO THE **MOON**!!
12-14
SILLY GIRL...SHE SHOULD KNOW THEY DON'T HAVE FIGURE SKATING ON THE MOON
STUPID BEAGLE!!
SCHULZ

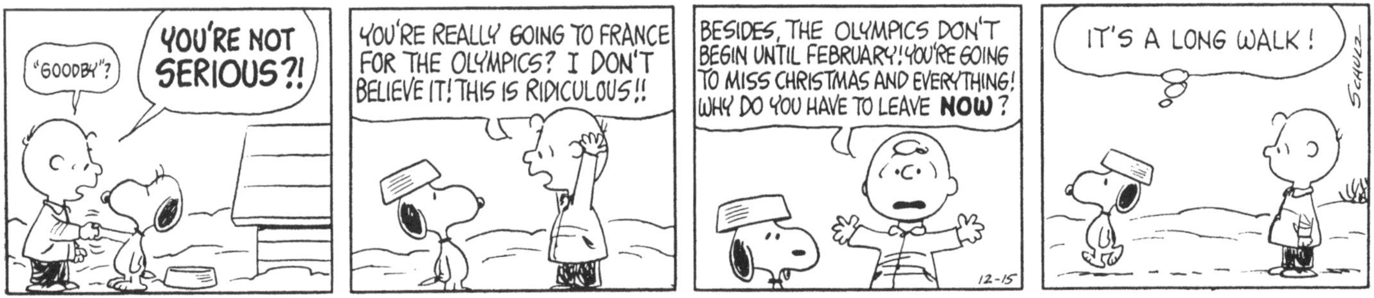
"GOODBY"?
YOU'RE NOT SERIOUS?!
YOU'RE REALLY GOING TO FRANCE FOR THE OLYMPICS? I DON'T BELIEVE IT! THIS IS RIDICULOUS!!
BESIDES, THE OLYMPICS DON'T BEGIN UNTIL FEBRUARY! YOU'RE GOING TO MISS CHRISTMAS AND EVERYTHING! WHY DO YOU HAVE TO LEAVE **NOW**?
12-15
IT'S A LONG WALK!
SCHULZ

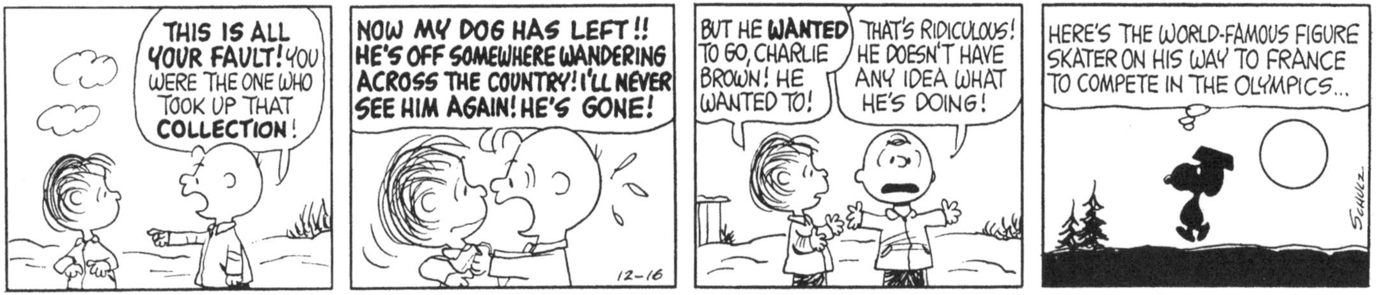
THIS IS ALL YOUR FAULT! YOU WERE THE ONE WHO TOOK UP THAT **COLLECTION**!
NOW MY DOG HAS LEFT!! HE'S OFF SOMEWHERE WANDERING ACROSS THE COUNTRY! I'LL NEVER SEE HIM AGAIN! HE'S GONE!
12-16
BUT HE **WANTED** TO GO, CHARLIE BROWN! HE WANTED TO!
THAT'S RIDICULOUS! HE DOESN'T HAVE ANY IDEA WHAT HE'S DOING!
HERE'S THE WORLD-FAMOUS FIGURE SKATER ON HIS WAY TO FRANCE TO COMPETE IN THE OLYMPICS...
SCHULZ

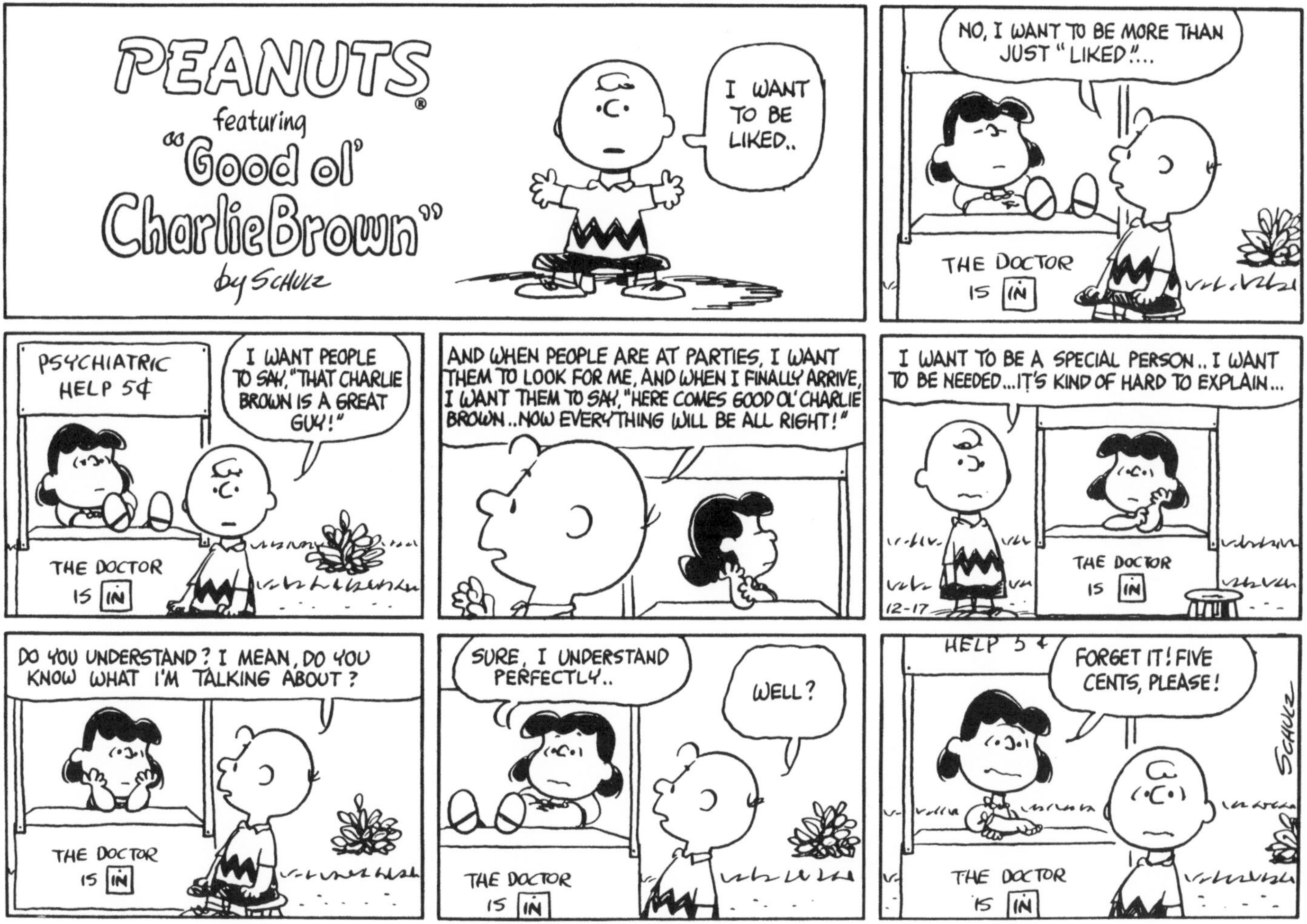
PEANUTS
featuring
"Good ol' CharlieBrown"
by SCHULZ
I WANT TO BE LIKED..
NO, I WANT TO BE MORE THAN JUST "LIKED"!...
THE DOCTOR IS IN
PSYCHIATRIC HELP 5¢
I WANT PEOPLE TO SAY, "THAT CHARLIE BROWN IS A GREAT GUY!"
THE DOCTOR IS IN
AND WHEN PEOPLE ARE AT PARTIES, I WANT THEM TO LOOK FOR ME, AND WHEN I FINALLY ARRIVE, I WANT THEM TO SAY, "HERE COMES GOOD OL' CHARLIE BROWN..NOW EVERYTHING WILL BE ALL RIGHT!"
I WANT TO BE A SPECIAL PERSON.. I WANT TO BE NEEDED...IT'S KIND OF HARD TO EXPLAIN...
THE DOCTOR IS IN
12-17
DO YOU UNDERSTAND? I MEAN, DO YOU KNOW WHAT I'M TALKING ABOUT?
THE DOCTOR IS IN
SURE, I UNDERSTAND PERFECTLY..
WELL?
THE DOCTOR IS IN
HELP 5¢
FORGET IT! FIVE CENTS, PLEASE!
SCHULZ
THE DOCTOR IS IN

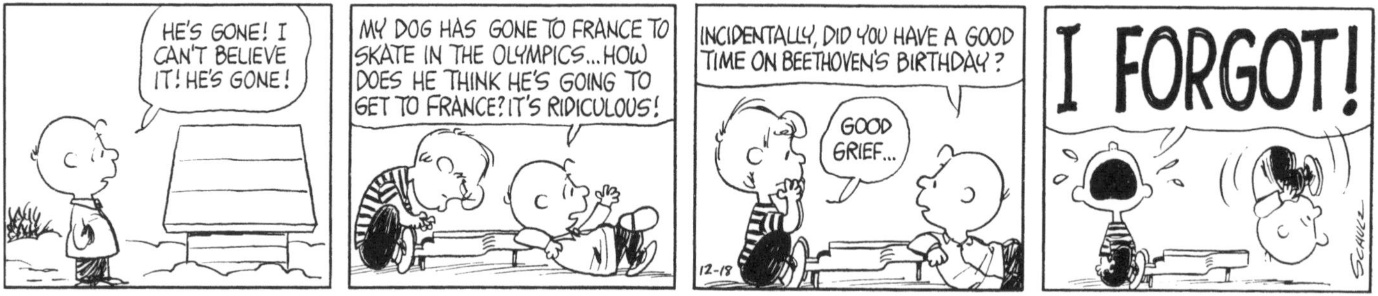
HE'S GONE! I CAN'T BELIEVE IT! HE'S GONE!
MY DOG HAS GONE TO FRANCE TO SKATE IN THE OLYMPICS...HOW DOES HE THINK HE'S GOING TO GET TO FRANCE? IT'S RIDICULOUS!
INCIDENTALLY, DID YOU HAVE A GOOD TIME ON BEETHOVEN'S BIRTHDAY?
GOOD GRIEF...
12-18
I FORGOT!
SCHULZ

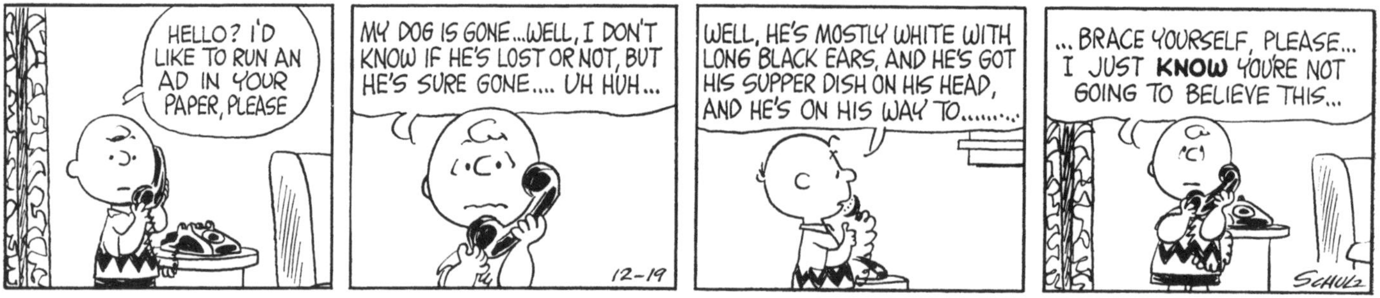
HELLO? I'D LIKE TO RUN AN AD IN YOUR PAPER, PLEASE
MY DOG IS GONE...WELL, I DON'T KNOW IF HE'S LOST OR NOT, BUT HE'S SURE GONE.... UH HUH...
12-19
WELL, HE'S MOSTLY WHITE WITH LONG BLACK EARS, AND HE'S GOT HIS SUPPER DISH ON HIS HEAD, AND HE'S ON HIS WAY TO.........
...BRACE YOURSELF, PLEASE... I JUST KNOW YOU'RE NOT GOING TO BELIEVE THIS...
SCHULZ

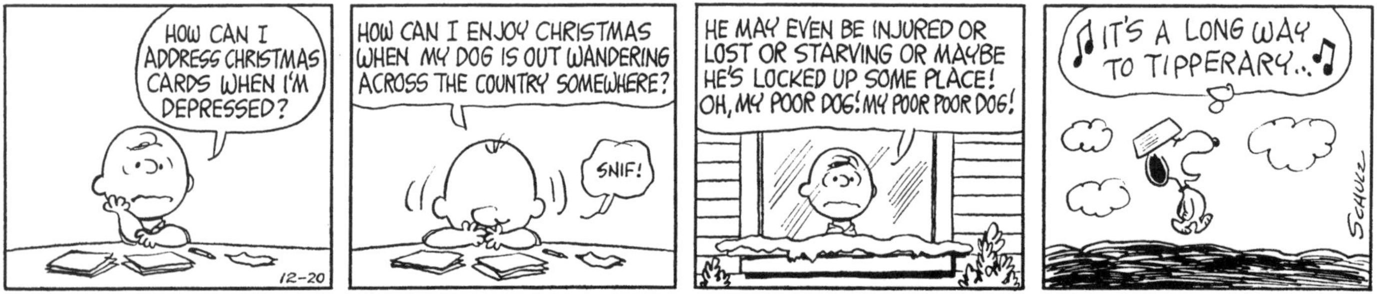
HOW CAN I ADDRESS CHRISTMAS CARDS WHEN I'M DEPRESSED?
12-20
HOW CAN I ENJOY CHRISTMAS WHEN MY DOG IS OUT WANDERING ACROSS THE COUNTRY SOMEWHERE?
SNIF!
HE MAY EVEN BE INJURED OR LOST OR STARVING OR MAYBE HE'S LOCKED UP SOME PLACE! OH, MY POOR DOG! MY POOR POOR DOG!
♪ IT'S A LONG WAY TO TIPPERARY... ♪
SCHULZ

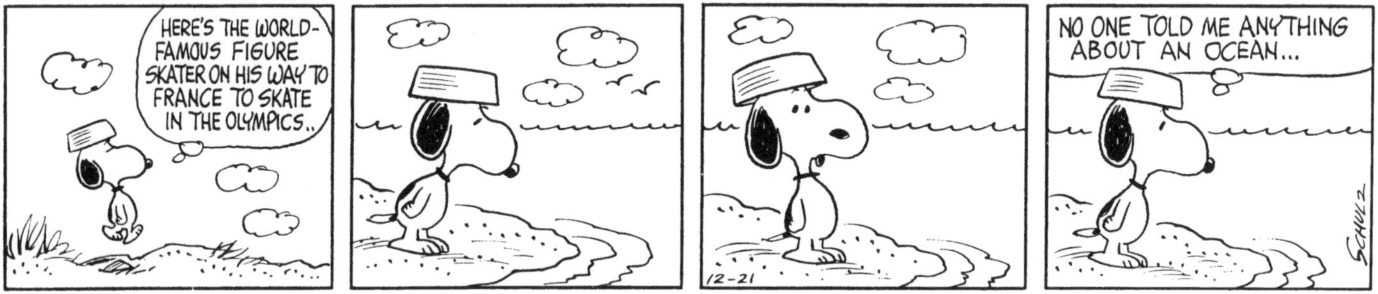
HERE'S THE WORLD-FAMOUS FIGURE SKATER ON HIS WAY TO FRANCE TO SKATE IN THE OLYMPICS..
12-21
NO ONE TOLD ME ANYTHING ABOUT AN OCEAN...
SCHULZ

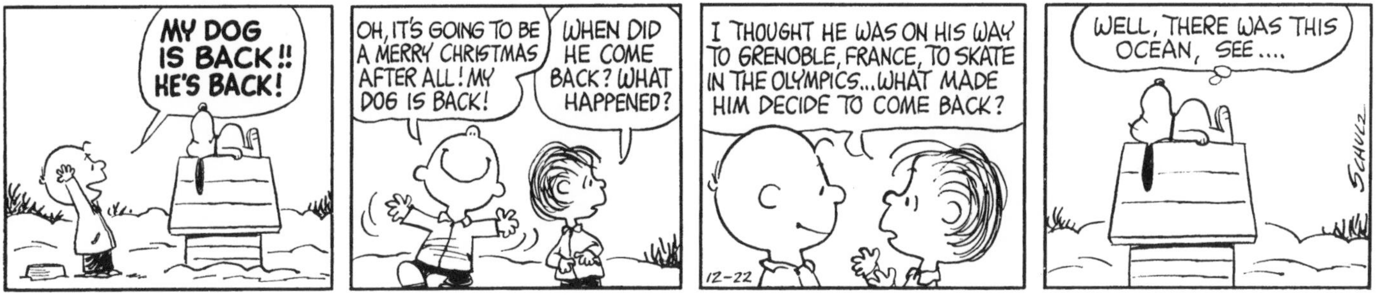
MY DOG IS BACK!! HE'S BACK!
OH, IT'S GOING TO BE A MERRY CHRISTMAS AFTER ALL! MY DOG IS BACK!
WHEN DID HE COME BACK? WHAT HAPPENED?
I THOUGHT HE WAS ON HIS WAY TO GRENOBLE, FRANCE, TO SKATE IN THE OLYMPICS...WHAT MADE HIM DECIDE TO COME BACK?
12-22
WELL, THERE WAS THIS OCEAN, SEE....
SCHULZ

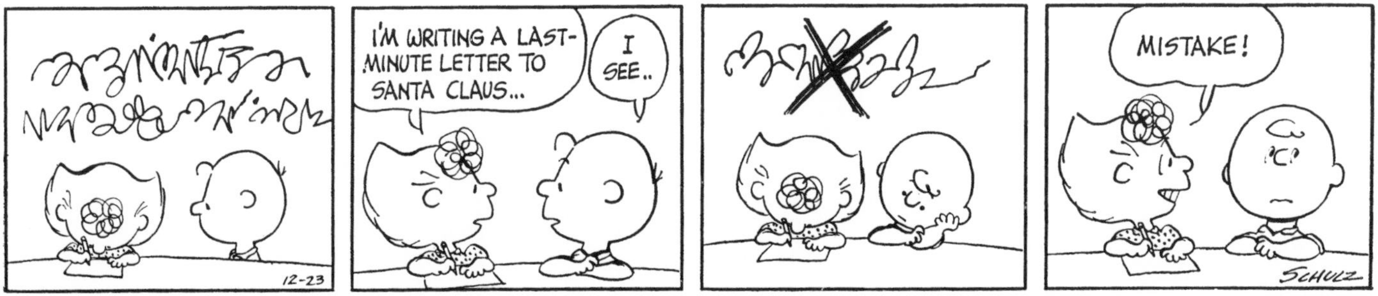
12-23
I'M WRITING A LAST-MINUTE LETTER TO SANTA CLAUS...
I SEE..
MISTAKE!
SCHULZ

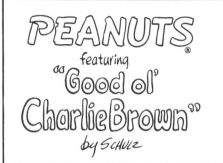

PEANUTS
featuring
"Good ol' Charlie Brown"
by Schulz

HERE'S THE WORLD WAR I FLYING ACE IN HIS SOPWITH CAMEL ZOOMING OVER ENEMY LINES..

PRESIDENT WILSON SAID WE'D BE HOME BY CHRISTMAS... HA!

HERE'S THE WORLD WAR I FLYING ACE SITTING IN A LITTLE FRENCH CAFE DRINKING ROOT BEER..HE IS DISGUSTED..

ACTUALLY, WORLD WAR I FLYING ACES VERY SELDOM DRANK ROOT BEER..

WE'LL NEVER GET HOME BY CHRISTMAS! THIS STUPID WAR WILL GO ON FOREVER!

I THINK I'LL TAKE A BOTTLE OF ROOT BEER OVER TO THE ENLISTED MEN... POOR CHAPS, THEY PROBABLY NEED A LITTLE CHEERING UP...

HMM...IT'S BEGINNING TO SNOW...

WHAT'S THAT? THE ENLISTED MEN ARE SINGING CHRISTMAS CAROLS!

THOSE POOR BLIGHTERS ARE CHEERING THEMSELVES UP! THEY DON'T NEED ME!

SUDDENLY THE LONELINESS OF HIS DAYS BECOMES TOO MUCH FOR THE FLYING ACE TO BEAR..HE CRIES OUT IN TERRIBLE ANGUISH...

AAUGH!!

WHAT IN THE WORLD WAS THAT?

LET'S NOT SING ANY MORE CHRISTMAS CAROLS..

IF YOU'RE A LONG WAY FROM HOME, THEY CAN BE VERY DEPRESSING..

SOMETIMES I HAVE NO IDEA WHAT HE'S TALKING ABOUT ???

12-24

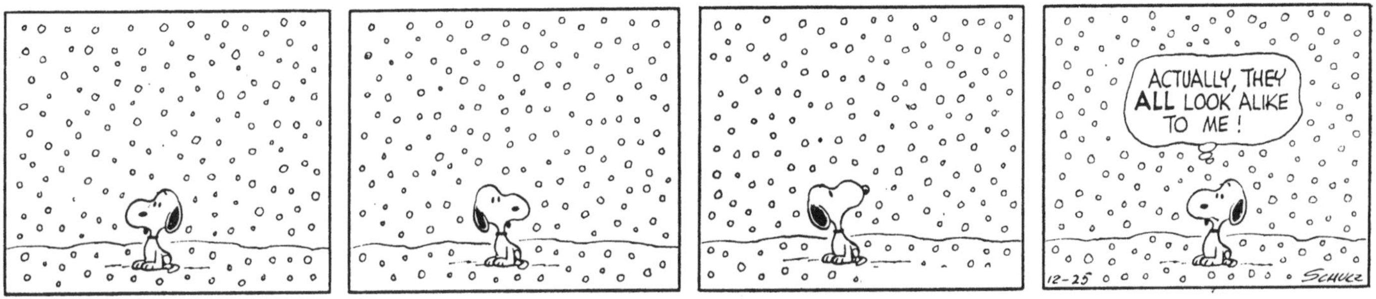
ACTUALLY, THEY **ALL** LOOK ALIKE TO ME!
12-25
SCHULZ

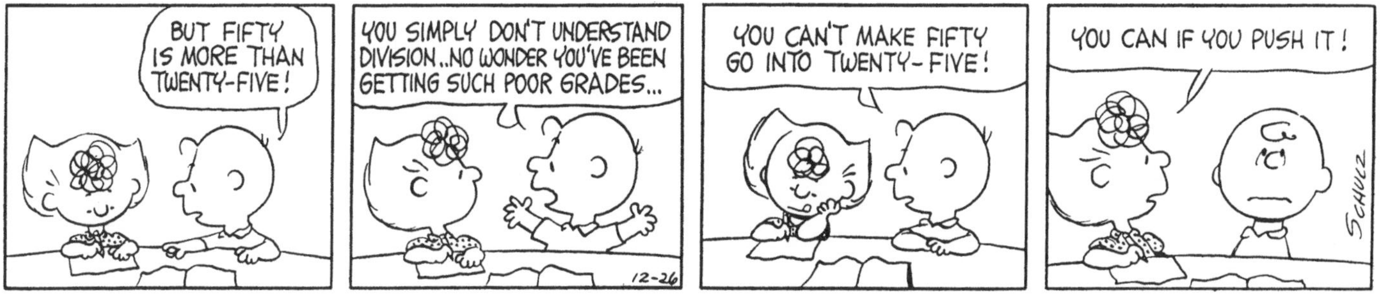
BUT FIFTY IS MORE THAN TWENTY-FIVE!
YOU SIMPLY DON'T UNDERSTAND DIVISION..NO WONDER YOU'VE BEEN GETTING SUCH POOR GRADES...
12-26
YOU CAN'T MAKE FIFTY GO INTO TWENTY-FIVE!
YOU CAN IF YOU PUSH IT!
SCHULZ

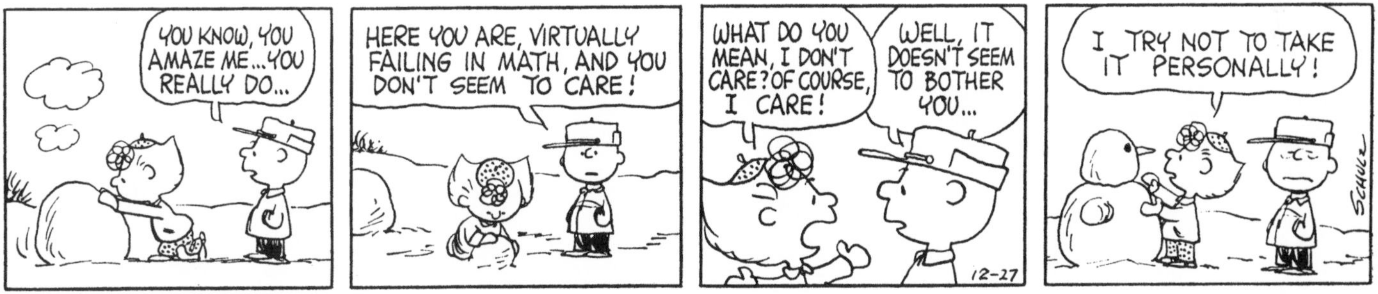
YOU KNOW, YOU AMAZE ME...YOU REALLY DO...
HERE YOU ARE, VIRTUALLY FAILING IN MATH, AND YOU DON'T SEEM TO CARE!
WHAT DO YOU MEAN, I DON'T CARE? OF COURSE, I CARE!
WELL, IT DOESN'T SEEM TO BOTHER YOU...
12-27
I TRY NOT TO TAKE IT PERSONALLY!
SCHULZ

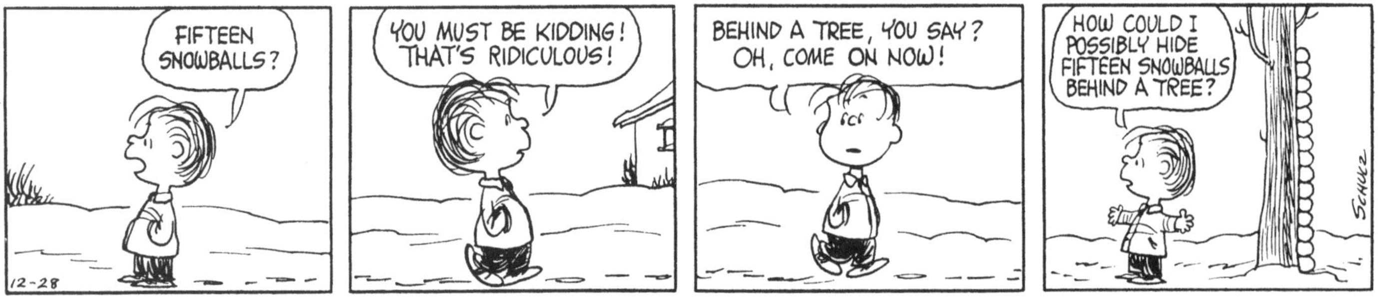
FIFTEEN SNOWBALLS?
12-28
YOU MUST BE KIDDING! THAT'S RIDICULOUS!
BEHIND A TREE, YOU SAY? OH, COME ON NOW!
HOW COULD I POSSIBLY HIDE FIFTEEN SNOWBALLS BEHIND A TREE?
SCHULZ

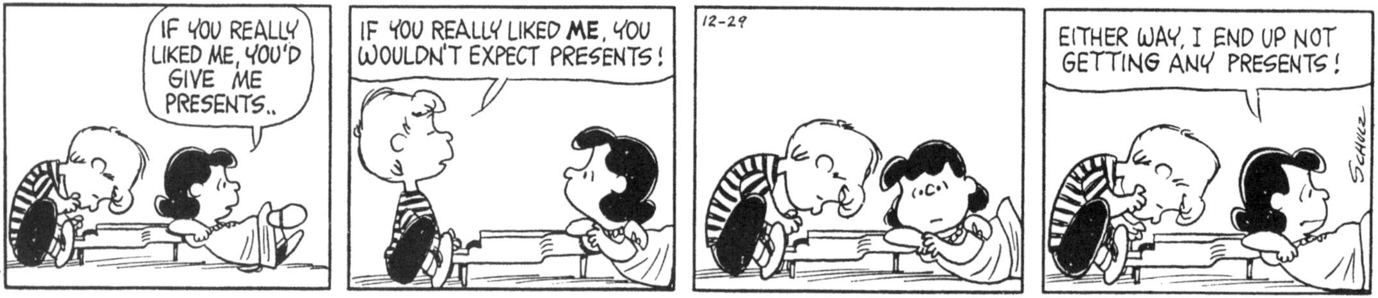
IF YOU REALLY LIKED ME, YOU'D GIVE ME PRESENTS..
IF YOU REALLY LIKED **ME**, YOU WOULDN'T EXPECT PRESENTS!
12-29
EITHER WAY, I END UP NOT GETTING ANY PRESENTS!
SCHULZ

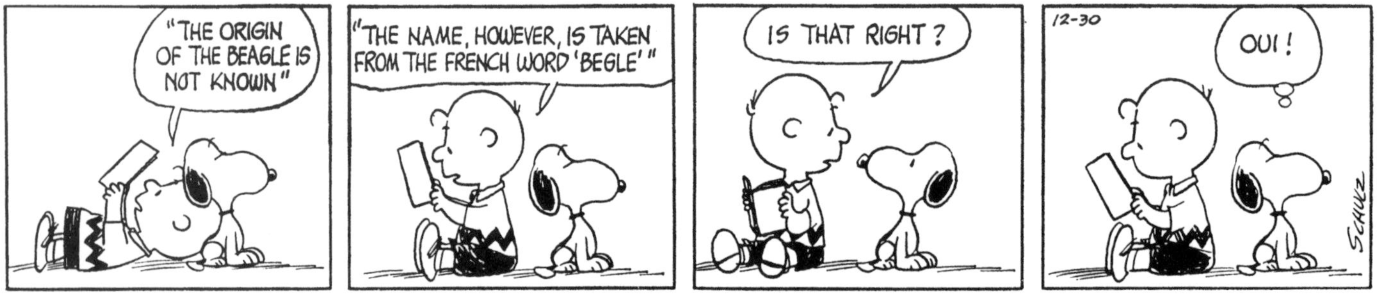
"THE ORIGIN OF THE BEAGLE IS NOT KNOWN"
"THE NAME, HOWEVER, IS TAKEN FROM THE FRENCH WORD 'BEGLE' "
IS THAT RIGHT?
12-30
OUI!
SCHULZ

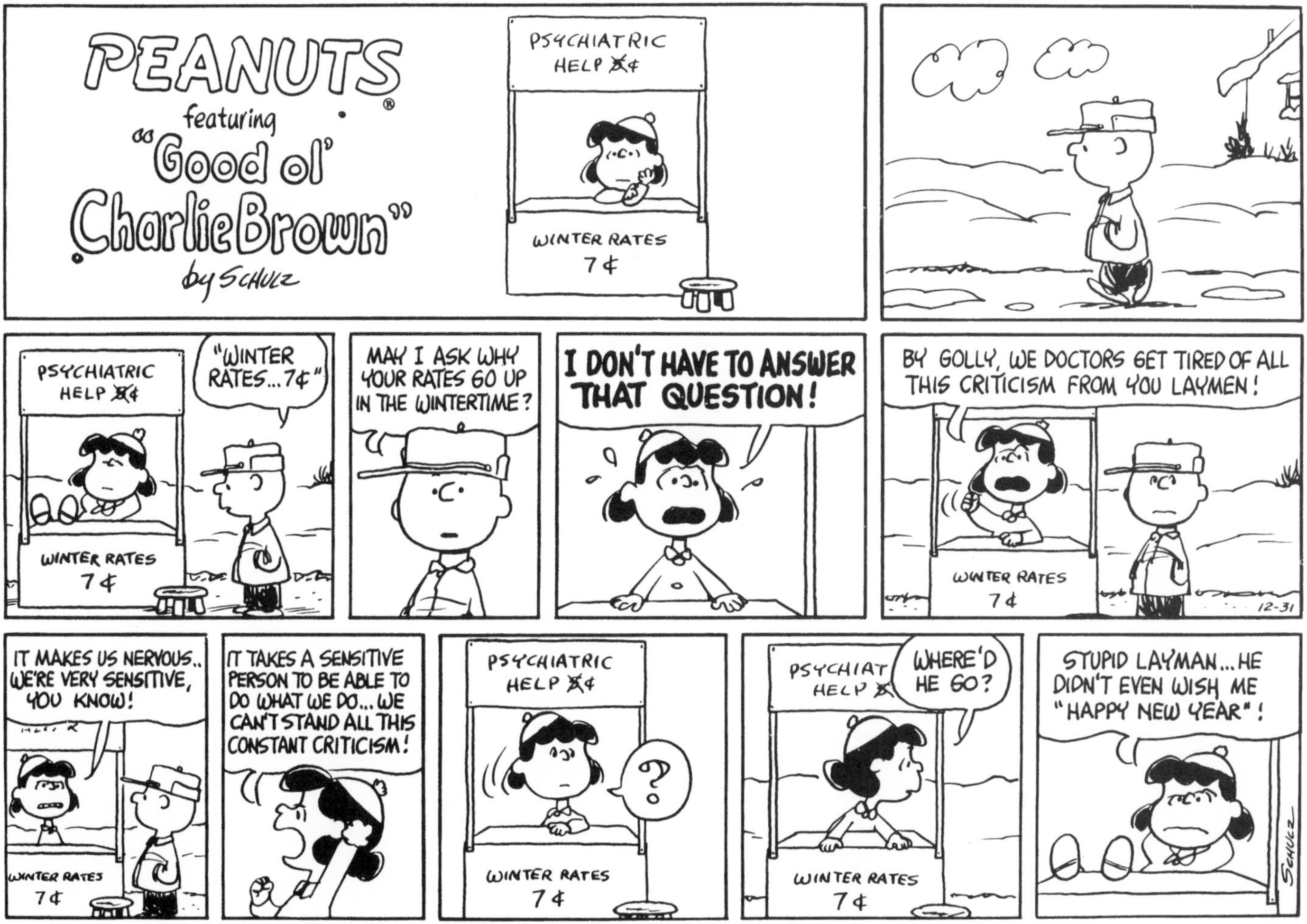
PEANUTS
featuring
"Good ol' Charlie Brown"
by SCHULZ
PSYCHIATRIC HELP 5¢
WINTER RATES 7¢
PSYCHIATRIC HELP 5¢
WINTER RATES 7¢
"WINTER RATES...7¢"
MAY I ASK WHY YOUR RATES GO UP IN THE WINTERTIME?
I DON'T HAVE TO ANSWER THAT QUESTION!
BY GOLLY, WE DOCTORS GET TIRED OF ALL THIS CRITICISM FROM YOU LAYMEN!
WINTER RATES 7¢
12-31
IT MAKES US NERVOUS.. WE'RE VERY SENSITIVE, YOU KNOW!
WINTER RATES 7¢
IT TAKES A SENSITIVE PERSON TO BE ABLE TO DO WHAT WE DO... WE CAN'T STAND ALL THIS CONSTANT CRITICISM!
PSYCHIATRIC HELP 5¢
?
WINTER RATES 7¢
PSYCHIAT HELP 5
WHERE'D HE GO?
WINTER RATES 7¢
STUPID LAYMAN... HE DIDN'T EVEN WISH ME "HAPPY NEW YEAR"!
SCHULZ

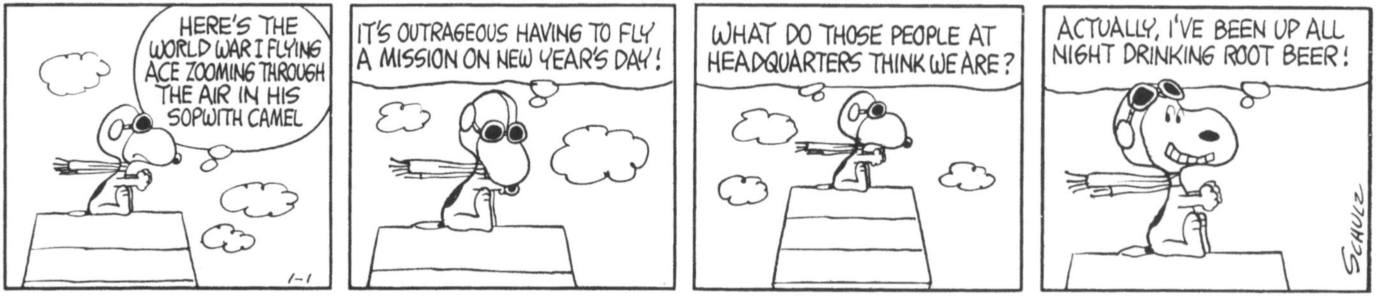
HERE'S THE WORLD WAR I FLYING ACE ZOOMING THROUGH THE AIR IN HIS SOPWITH CAMEL
IT'S OUTRAGEOUS HAVING TO FLY A MISSION ON NEW YEAR'S DAY!
WHAT DO THOSE PEOPLE AT HEADQUARTERS THINK WE ARE?
ACTUALLY, I'VE BEEN UP ALL NIGHT DRINKING ROOT BEER!
SCHULZ

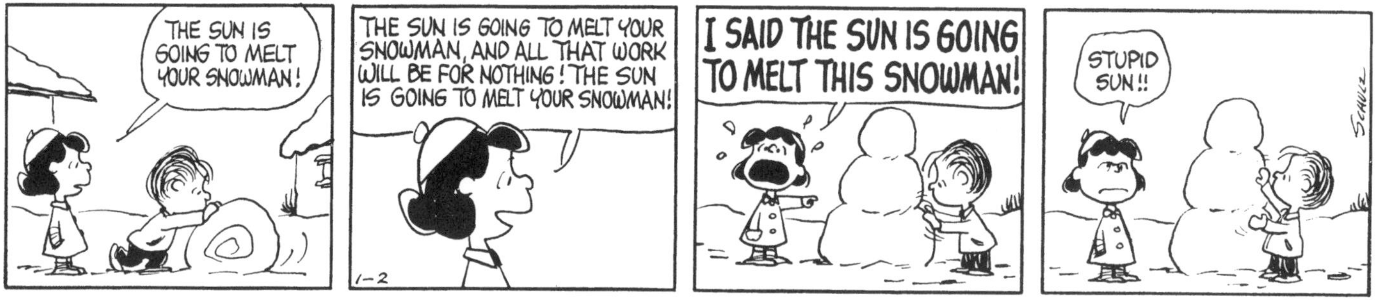
THE SUN IS GOING TO MELT YOUR SNOWMAN!
THE SUN IS GOING TO MELT YOUR SNOWMAN, AND ALL THAT WORK WILL BE FOR NOTHING! THE SUN IS GOING TO MELT YOUR SNOWMAN!
I SAID THE SUN IS GOING TO MELT THIS SNOWMAN!
STUPID SUN!!
SCHULZ

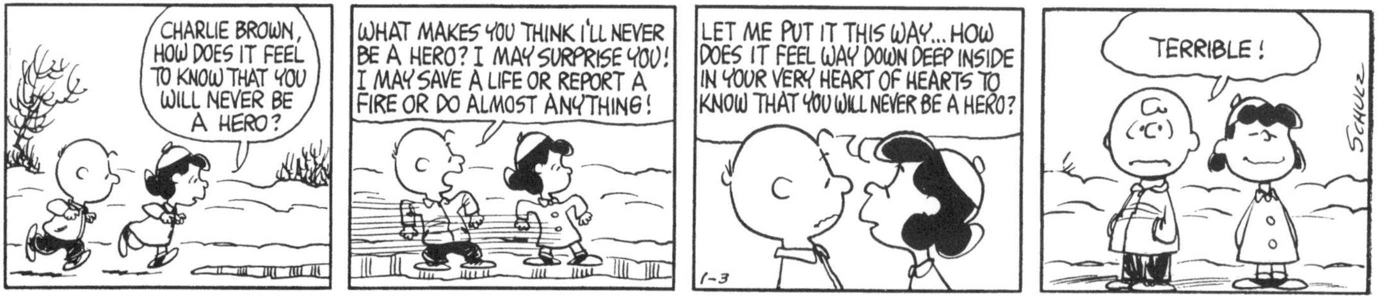
CHARLIE BROWN, HOW DOES IT FEEL TO KNOW THAT YOU WILL NEVER BE A HERO?
WHAT MAKES YOU THINK I'LL NEVER BE A HERO? I MAY SURPRISE YOU! I MAY SAVE A LIFE OR REPORT A FIRE OR DO ALMOST ANYTHING!
LET ME PUT IT THIS WAY... HOW DOES IT FEEL WAY DOWN DEEP INSIDE IN YOUR VERY HEART OF HEARTS TO KNOW THAT YOU WILL NEVER BE A HERO?
TERRIBLE!
SCHULZ

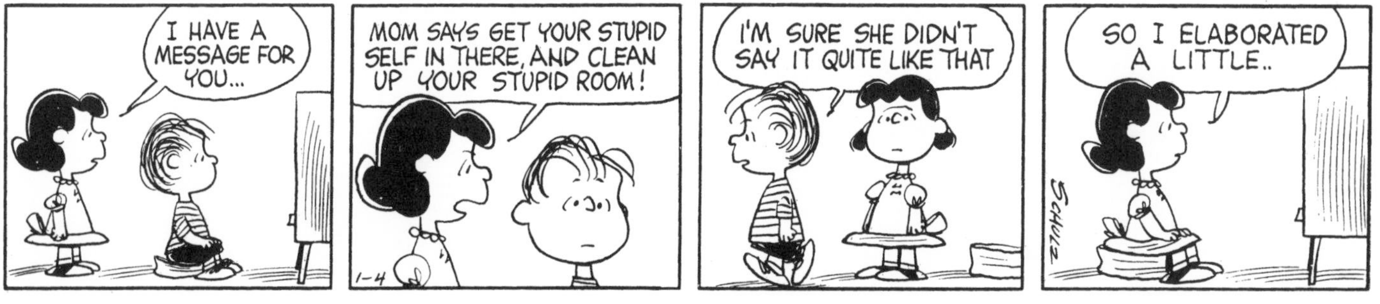
I HAVE A MESSAGE FOR YOU...
MOM SAYS GET YOUR STUPID SELF IN THERE, AND CLEAN UP YOUR STUPID ROOM!
I'M SURE SHE DIDN'T SAY IT QUITE LIKE THAT
SO I ELABORATED A LITTLE..

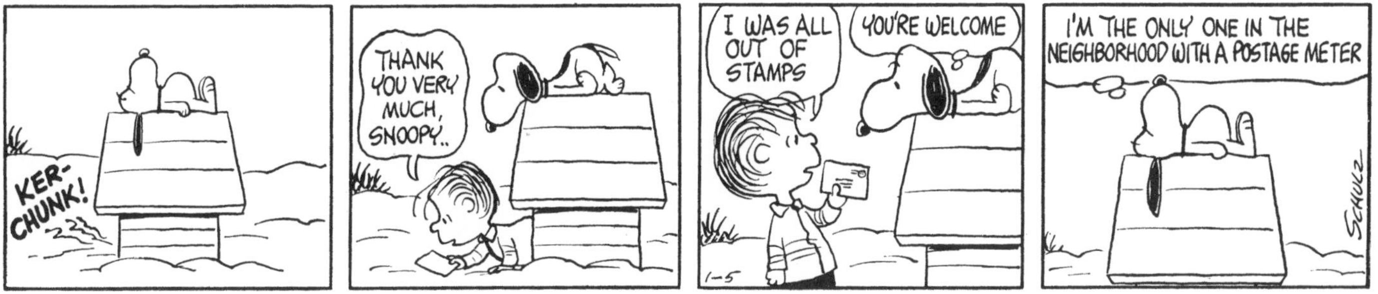
KER-CHUNK!
THANK YOU VERY MUCH, SNOOPY..
I WAS ALL OUT OF STAMPS
YOU'RE WELCOME
I'M THE ONLY ONE IN THE NEIGHBORHOOD WITH A POSTAGE METER

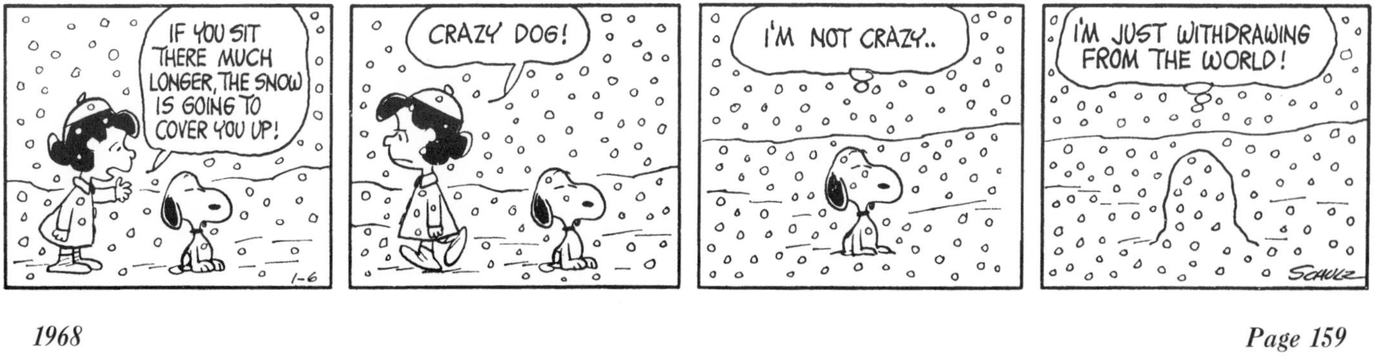
IF YOU SIT THERE MUCH LONGER, THE SNOW IS GOING TO COVER YOU UP!
CRAZY DOG!
I'M NOT CRAZY..
I'M JUST WITHDRAWING FROM THE WORLD!

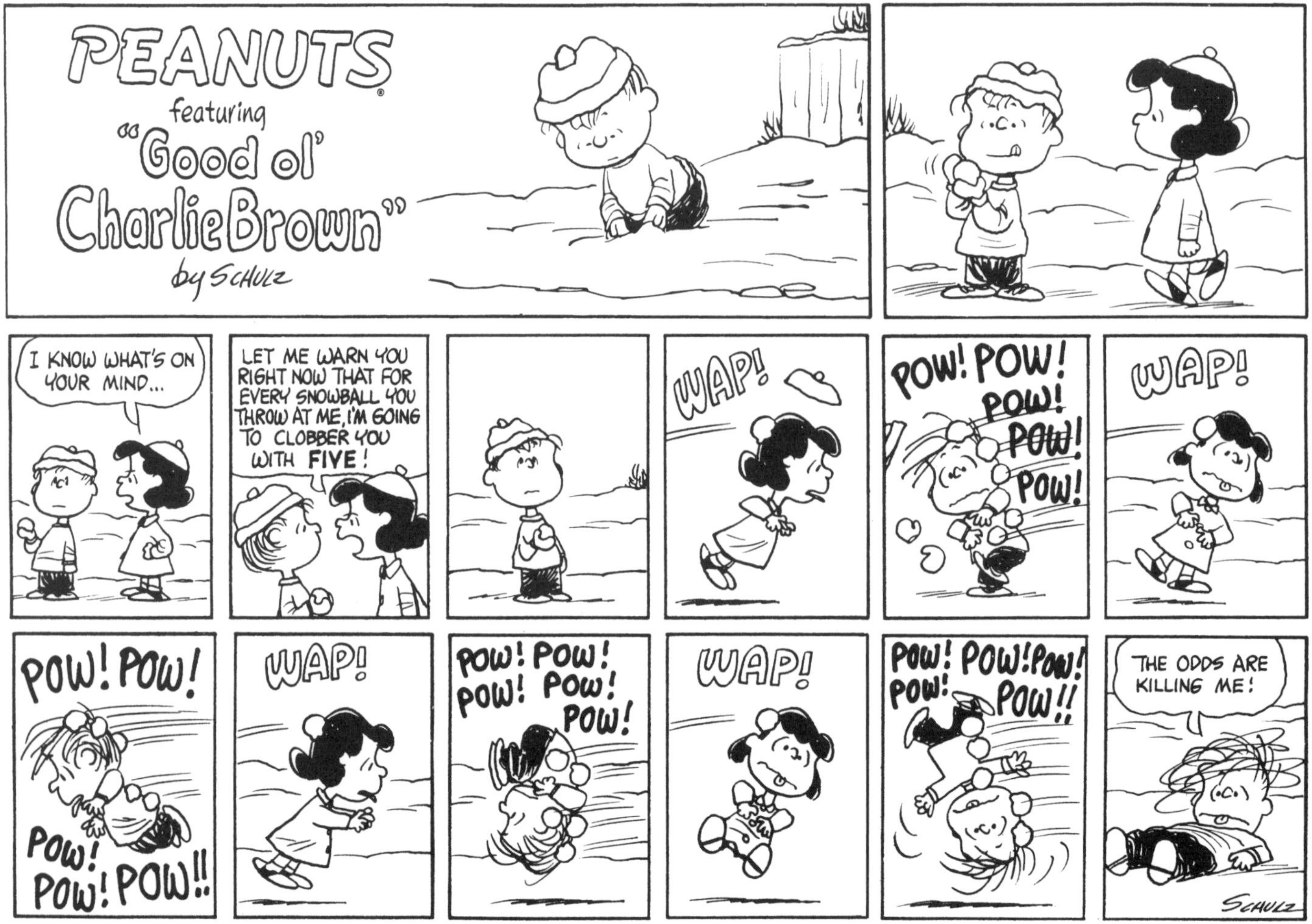
PEANUTS
featuring
"Good ol' CharlieBrown"
by SCHULZ
I KNOW WHAT'S ON YOUR MIND...
LET ME WARN YOU RIGHT NOW THAT FOR EVERY SNOWBALL YOU THROW AT ME, I'M GOING TO CLOBBER YOU WITH FIVE!
WAP!
POW! POW! POW! POW! POW!
WAP!
POW! POW!
POW! POW! POW!!
WAP!
POW! POW! POW! POW! POW!
WAP!
POW! POW! POW! POW! POW!!
THE ODDS ARE KILLING ME!
SCHULZ

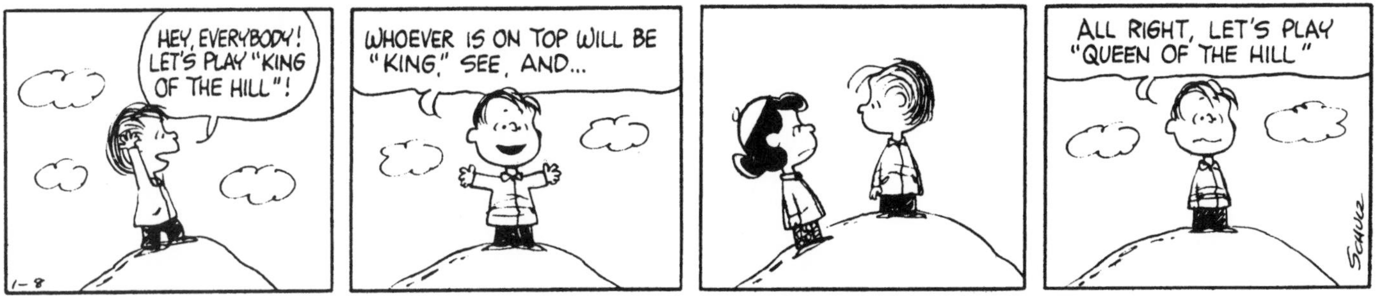
HEY, EVERYBODY! LET'S PLAY "KING OF THE HILL"!
WHOEVER IS ON TOP WILL BE "KING," SEE, AND...
ALL RIGHT, LET'S PLAY "QUEEN OF THE HILL"

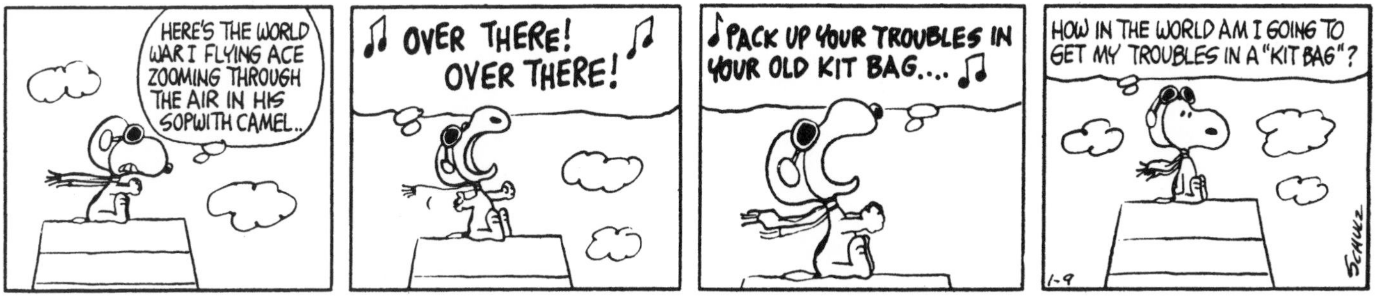
HERE'S THE WORLD WAR I FLYING ACE ZOOMING THROUGH THE AIR IN HIS SOPWITH CAMEL..
♫ OVER THERE! OVER THERE! ♫
♪ PACK UP YOUR TROUBLES IN YOUR OLD KIT BAG.... ♫
HOW IN THE WORLD AM I GOING TO GET MY TROUBLES IN A "KIT BAG"?

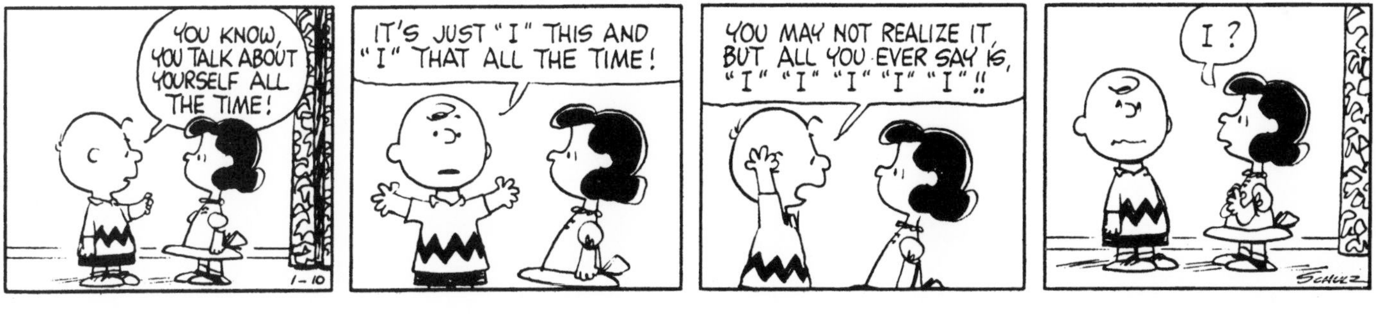
YOU KNOW, YOU TALK ABOUT YOURSELF ALL THE TIME!
IT'S JUST "I" THIS AND "I" THAT ALL THE TIME!
YOU MAY NOT REALIZE IT, BUT ALL YOU EVER SAY IS, "I" "I" "I" "I" "I"!!
I ?

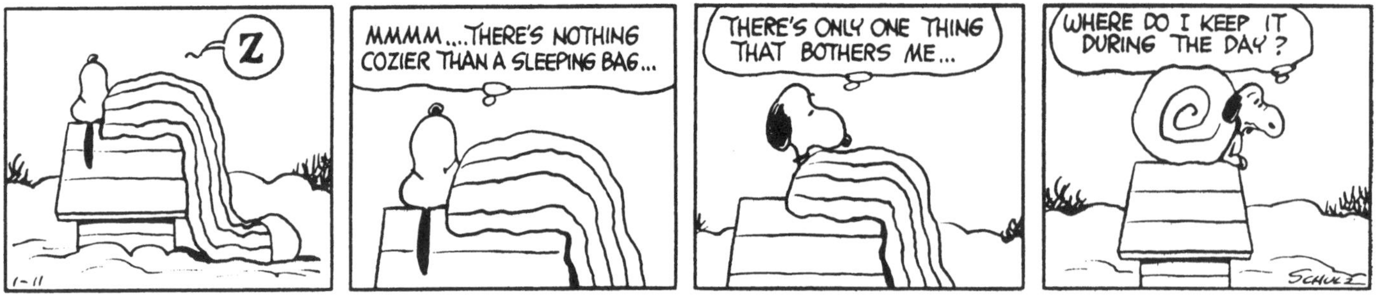
Z
MMMM....THERE'S NOTHING COZIER THAN A SLEEPING BAG...
THERE'S ONLY ONE THING THAT BOTHERS ME...
WHERE DO I KEEP IT DURING THE DAY ?

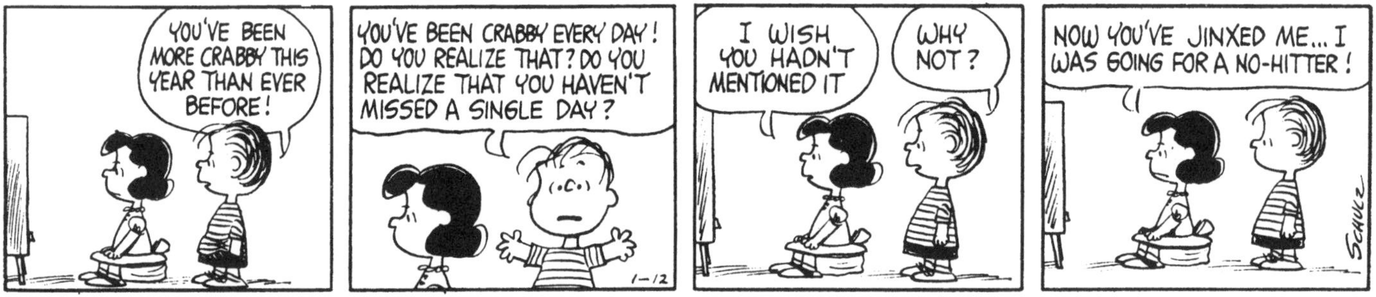
YOU'VE BEEN MORE CRABBY THIS YEAR THAN EVER BEFORE!
YOU'VE BEEN CRABBY EVERY DAY! DO YOU REALIZE THAT? DO YOU REALIZE THAT YOU HAVEN'T MISSED A SINGLE DAY?
I WISH YOU HADN'T MENTIONED IT
WHY NOT?
NOW YOU'VE JINXED ME... I WAS GOING FOR A NO-HITTER!

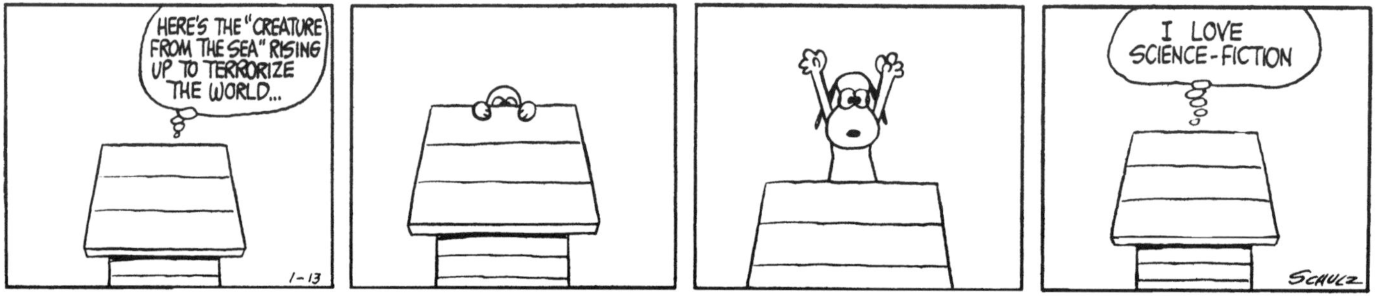
HERE'S THE "CREATURE FROM THE SEA" RISING UP TO TERRORIZE THE WORLD...
I LOVE SCIENCE-FICTION

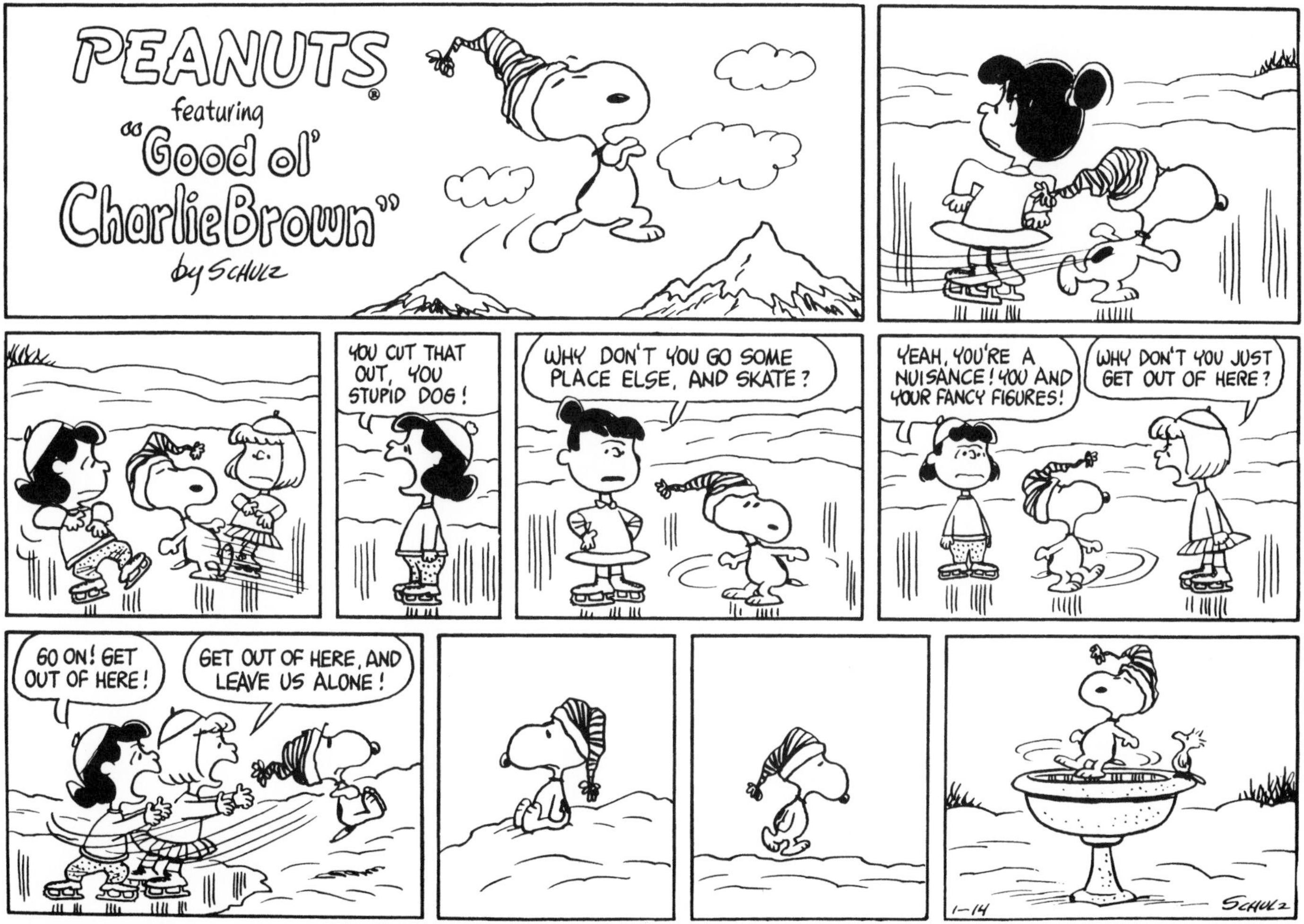
PEANUTS
featuring
"Good ol' Charlie Brown"
by SCHULZ
YOU CUT THAT OUT, YOU STUPID DOG!
WHY DON'T YOU GO SOME PLACE ELSE, AND SKATE?
YEAH, YOU'RE A NUISANCE! YOU AND YOUR FANCY FIGURES!
WHY DON'T YOU JUST GET OUT OF HERE?
GO ON! GET OUT OF HERE!
GET OUT OF HERE, AND LEAVE US ALONE!
1-14
SCHULZ

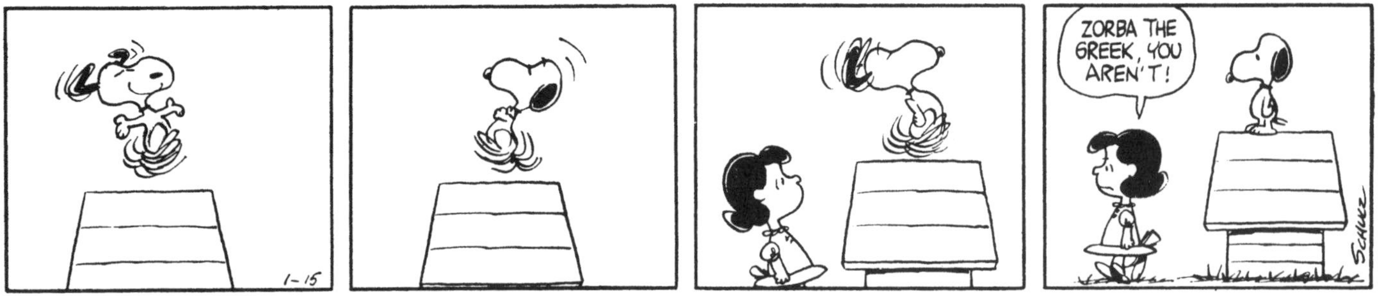
ZORBA THE GREEK, YOU AREN'T!

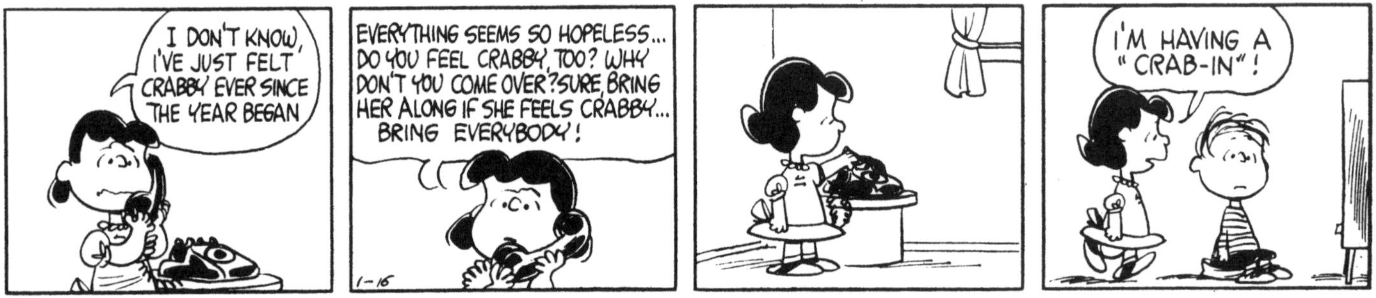
I DON'T KNOW, I'VE JUST FELT CRABBY EVER SINCE THE YEAR BEGAN
EVERYTHING SEEMS SO HOPELESS... DO YOU FEEL CRABBY, TOO? WHY DON'T YOU COME OVER? SURE, BRING HER ALONG IF SHE FEELS CRABBY... BRING EVERYBODY!
I'M HAVING A "CRAB-IN"!

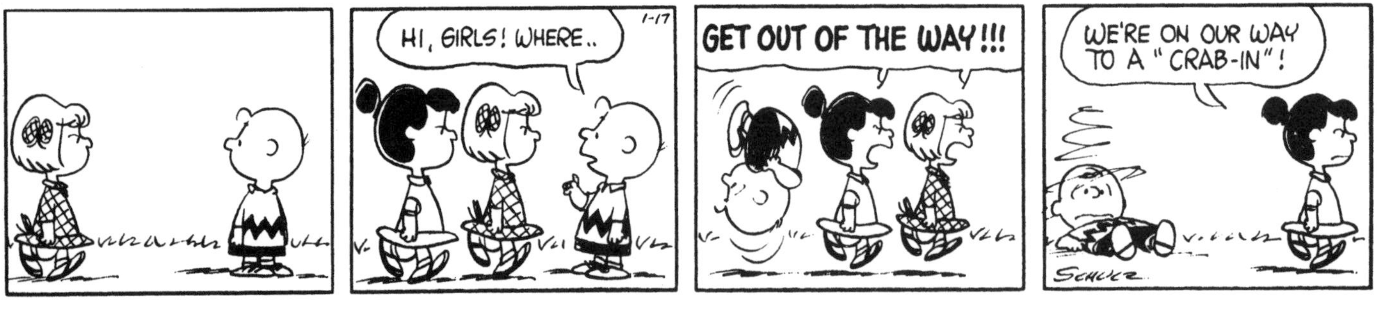
HI, GIRLS! WHERE..
GET OUT OF THE WAY!!!
WE'RE ON OUR WAY TO A "CRAB-IN"!

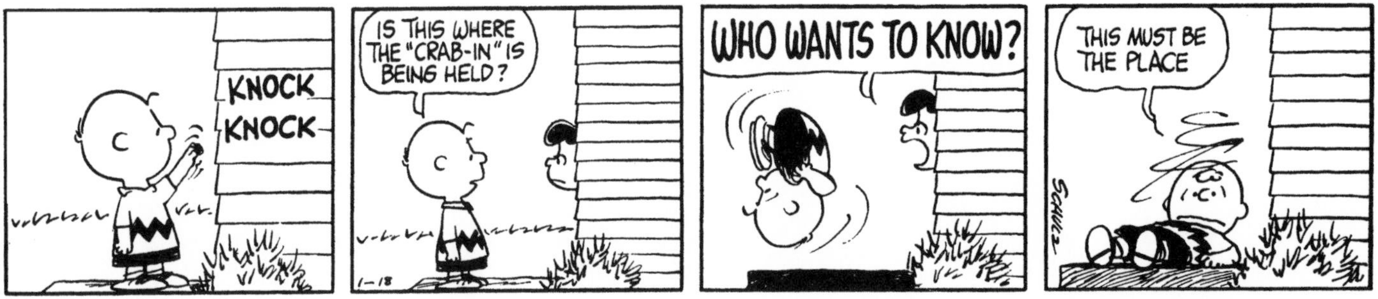
KNOCK KNOCK
IS THIS WHERE THE "CRAB-IN" IS BEING HELD?
WHO WANTS TO KNOW?
THIS MUST BE THE PLACE

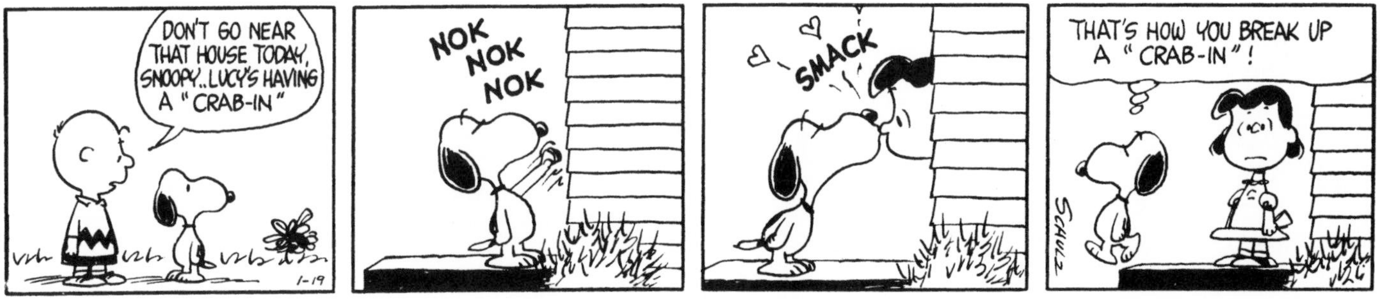
DON'T GO NEAR THAT HOUSE TODAY, SNOOPY..LUCY'S HAVING A "CRAB-IN"
NOK NOK NOK
SMACK
THAT'S HOW YOU BREAK UP A "CRAB-IN"!

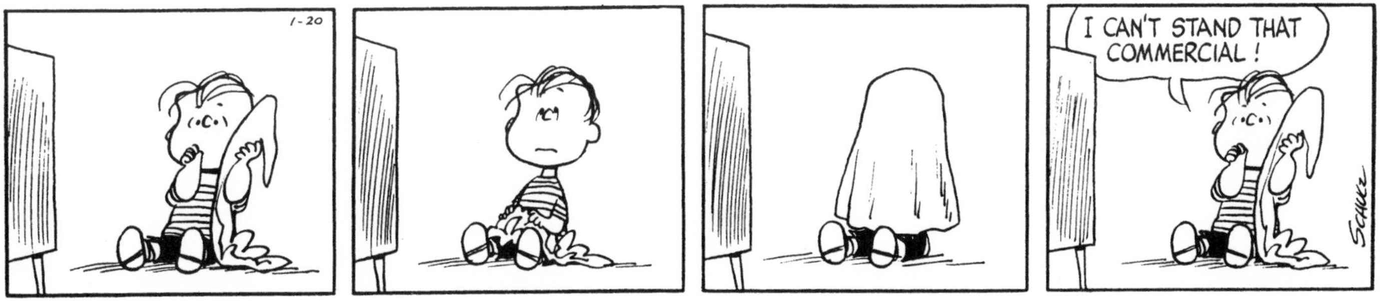
I CAN'T STAND THAT COMMERCIAL!

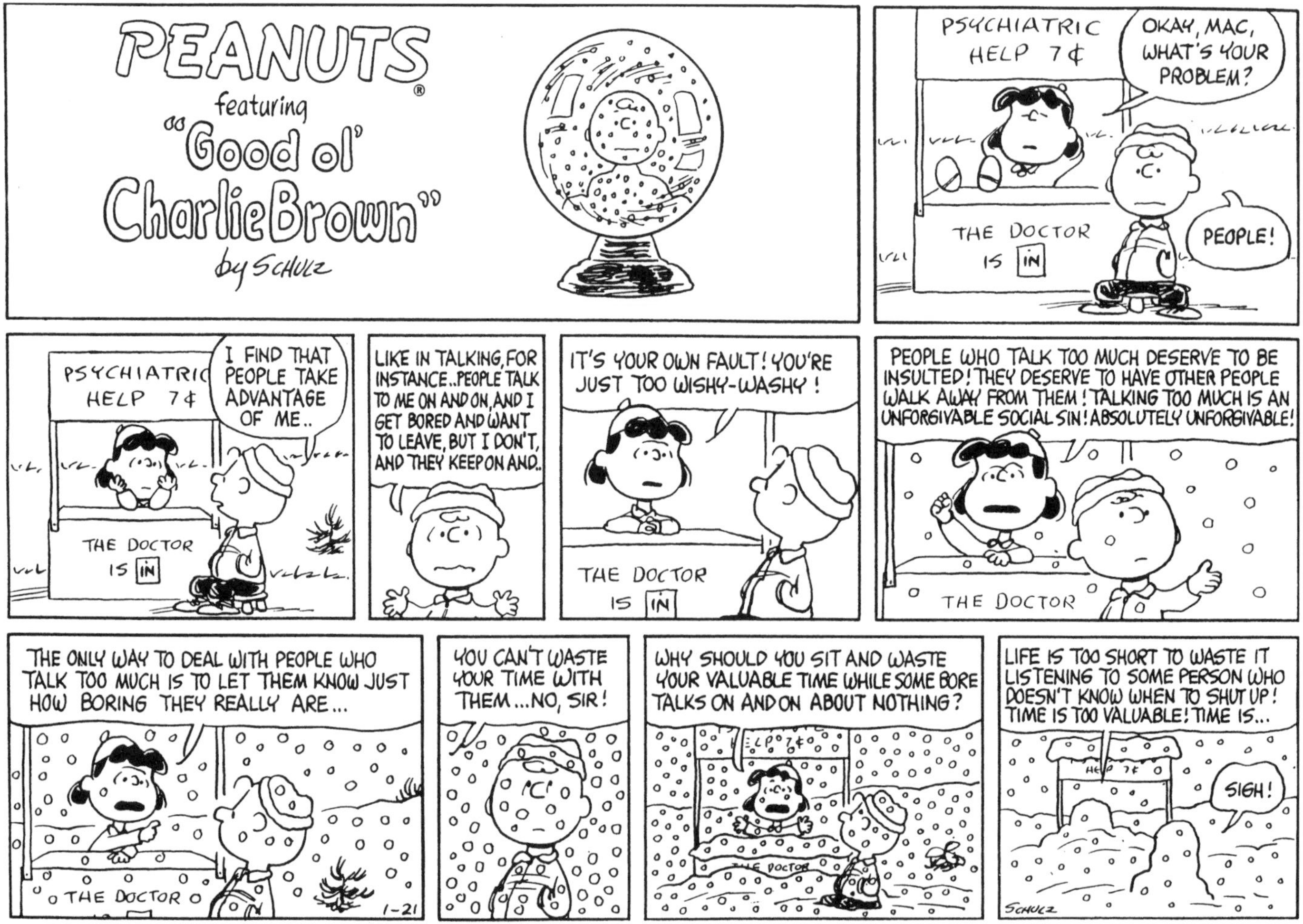
PEANUTS®
featuring
"Good ol' Charlie Brown"
by SCHULZ
PSYCHIATRIC HELP 7¢
OKAY, MAC, WHAT'S YOUR PROBLEM?
THE DOCTOR IS IN
PEOPLE!
PSYCHIATRIC HELP 7¢
I FIND THAT PEOPLE TAKE ADVANTAGE OF ME..
THE DOCTOR IS IN
LIKE IN TALKING, FOR INSTANCE..PEOPLE TALK TO ME ON AND ON, AND I GET BORED AND WANT TO LEAVE, BUT I DON'T, AND THEY KEEP ON AND..
IT'S YOUR OWN FAULT! YOU'RE JUST TOO WISHY-WASHY!
THE DOCTOR IS IN
PEOPLE WHO TALK TOO MUCH DESERVE TO BE INSULTED! THEY DESERVE TO HAVE OTHER PEOPLE WALK AWAY FROM THEM! TALKING TOO MUCH IS AN UNFORGIVABLE SOCIAL SIN! ABSOLUTELY UNFORGIVABLE!
THE DOCTOR
THE ONLY WAY TO DEAL WITH PEOPLE WHO TALK TOO MUCH IS TO LET THEM KNOW JUST HOW BORING THEY REALLY ARE...
THE DOCTOR
1-21
YOU CAN'T WASTE YOUR TIME WITH THEM...NO, SIR!
WHY SHOULD YOU SIT AND WASTE YOUR VALUABLE TIME WHILE SOME BORE TALKS ON AND ON ABOUT NOTHING?
LIFE IS TOO SHORT TO WASTE IT LISTENING TO SOME PERSON WHO DOESN'T KNOW WHEN TO SHUT UP! TIME IS TOO VALUABLE! TIME IS...
SIGH!
SCHULZ

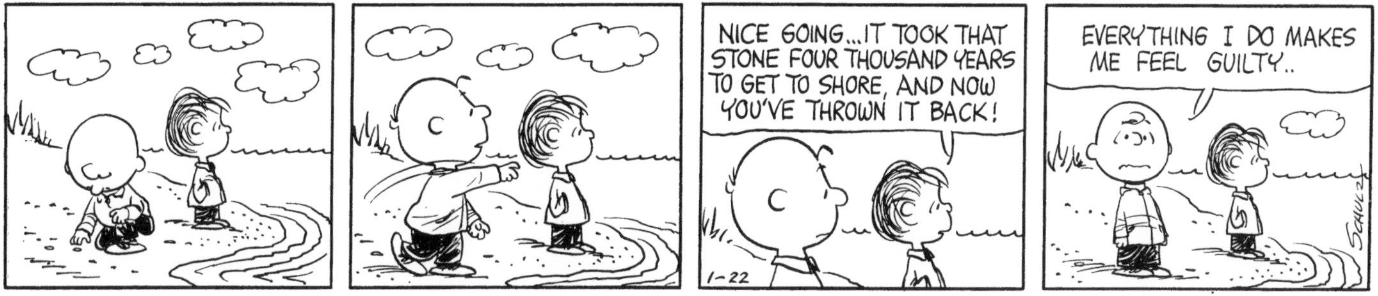
NICE GOING...IT TOOK THAT STONE FOUR THOUSAND YEARS TO GET TO SHORE, AND NOW YOU'VE THROWN IT BACK!
1-22
EVERYTHING I DO MAKES ME FEEL GUILTY..
SCHULZ

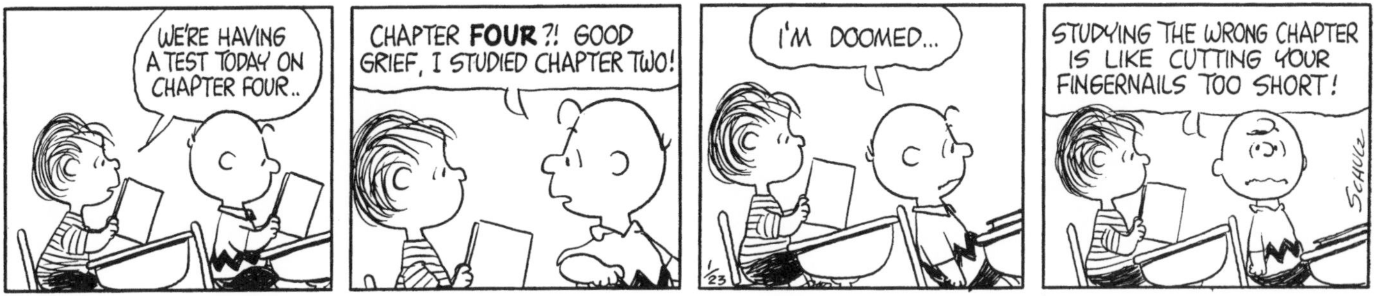
WE'RE HAVING A TEST TODAY ON CHAPTER FOUR..
CHAPTER **FOUR**?! GOOD GRIEF, I STUDIED CHAPTER TWO!
I'M DOOMED...
1/23
STUDYING THE WRONG CHAPTER IS LIKE CUTTING YOUR FINGERNAILS TOO SHORT!
SCHULZ

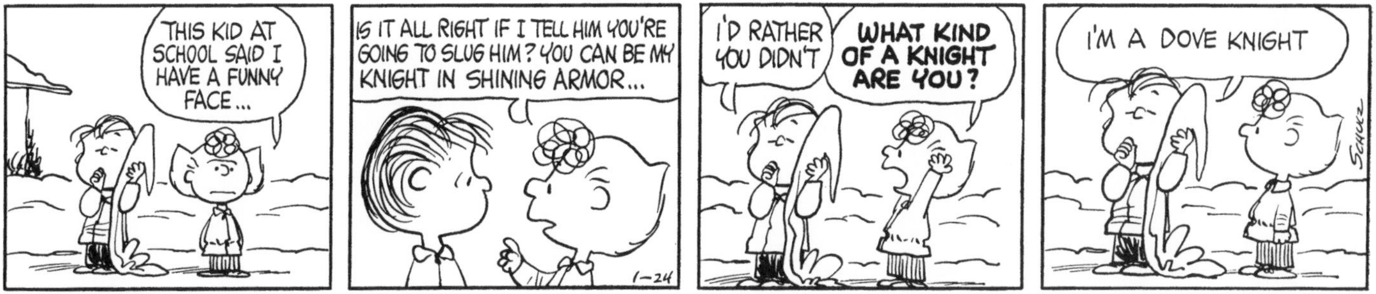
THIS KID AT SCHOOL SAID I HAVE A FUNNY FACE...
IS IT ALL RIGHT IF I TELL HIM YOU'RE GOING TO SLUG HIM? YOU CAN BE MY KNIGHT IN SHINING ARMOR...
1-24
I'D RATHER YOU DIDN'T
WHAT KIND OF A KNIGHT ARE YOU?
I'M A DOVE KNIGHT
SCHULZ

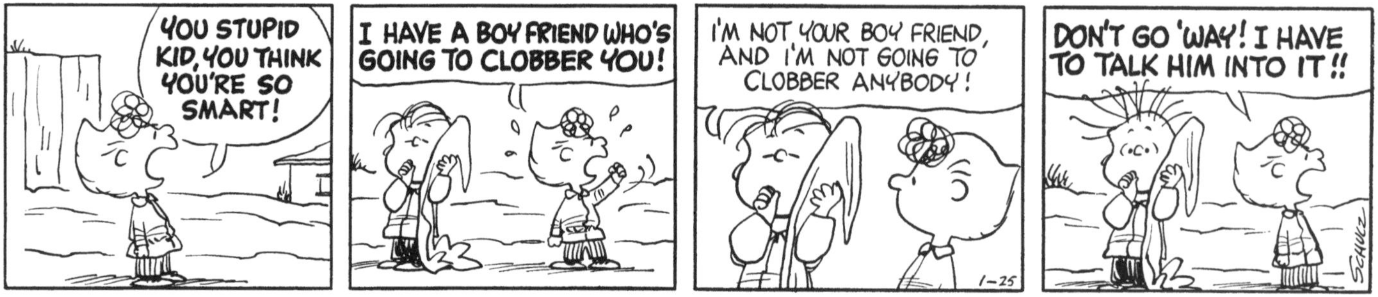
YOU STUPID KID, YOU THINK YOU'RE SO SMART!
I HAVE A BOY FRIEND WHO'S GOING TO CLOBBER YOU!
I'M NOT YOUR BOY FRIEND, AND I'M NOT GOING TO CLOBBER ANYBODY!
1-25
DON'T GO 'WAY! I HAVE TO TALK HIM INTO IT!!
SCHULZ

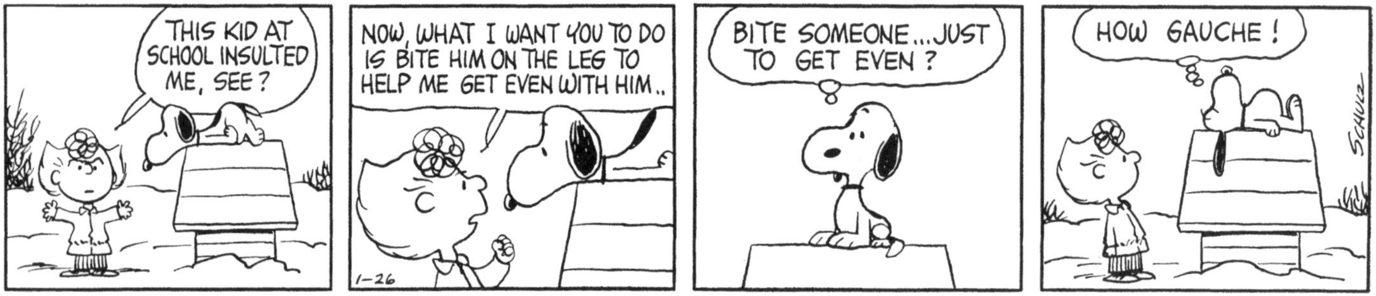
THIS KID AT SCHOOL INSULTED ME, SEE?
NOW, WHAT I WANT YOU TO DO IS BITE HIM ON THE LEG TO HELP ME GET EVEN WITH HIM..
1-26
BITE SOMEONE...JUST TO GET EVEN?
HOW GAUCHE!
SCHULZ

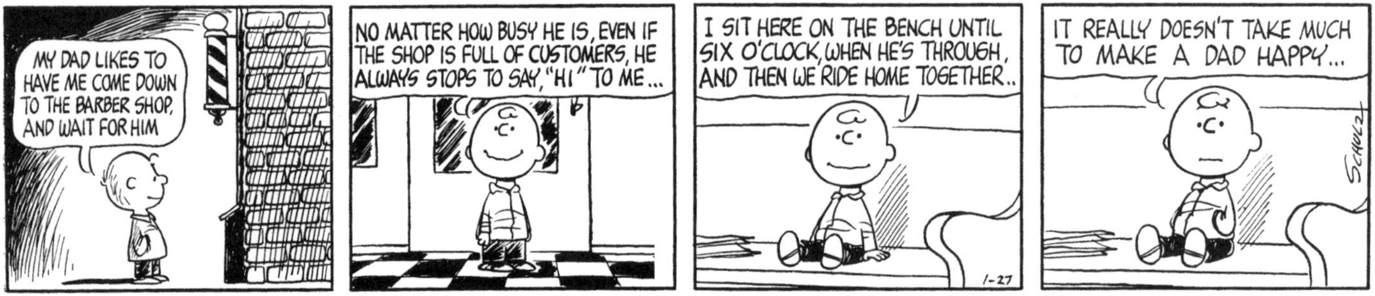
MY DAD LIKES TO HAVE ME COME DOWN TO THE BARBER SHOP, AND WAIT FOR HIM
NO MATTER HOW BUSY HE IS, EVEN IF THE SHOP IS FULL OF CUSTOMERS, HE ALWAYS STOPS TO SAY, "HI" TO ME...
I SIT HERE ON THE BENCH UNTIL SIX O'CLOCK, WHEN HE'S THROUGH, AND THEN WE RIDE HOME TOGETHER..
1-27
IT REALLY DOESN'T TAKE MUCH TO MAKE A DAD HAPPY...
SCHULZ

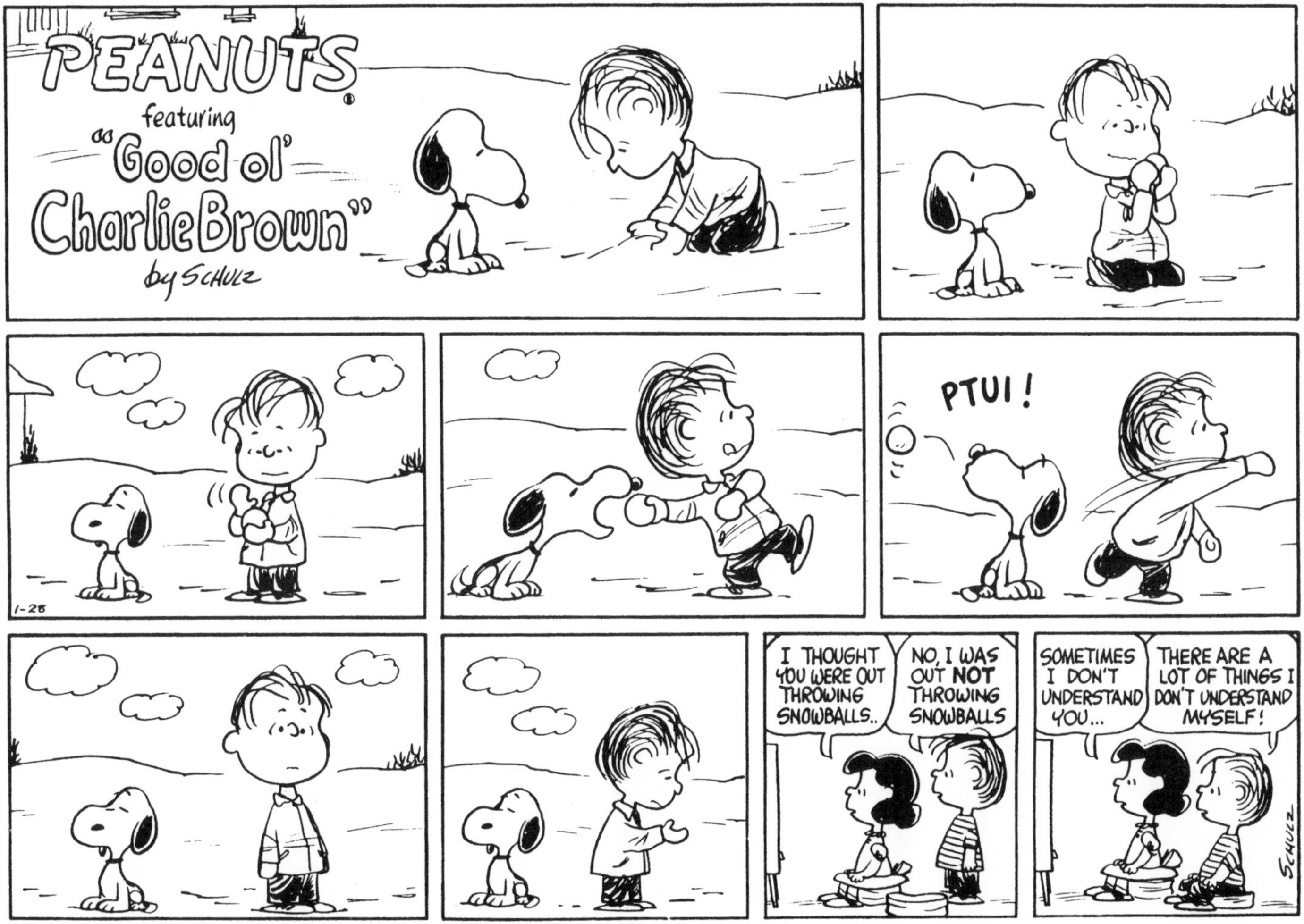
PEANUTS
featuring
"Good ol' Charlie Brown"
by SCHULZ
1-28
PTUI!
I THOUGHT YOU WERE OUT THROWING SNOWBALLS..
NO, I WAS OUT **NOT** THROWING SNOWBALLS
SOMETIMES I DON'T UNDERSTAND YOU...
THERE ARE A LOT OF THINGS I DON'T UNDERSTAND MYSELF!
SCHULZ

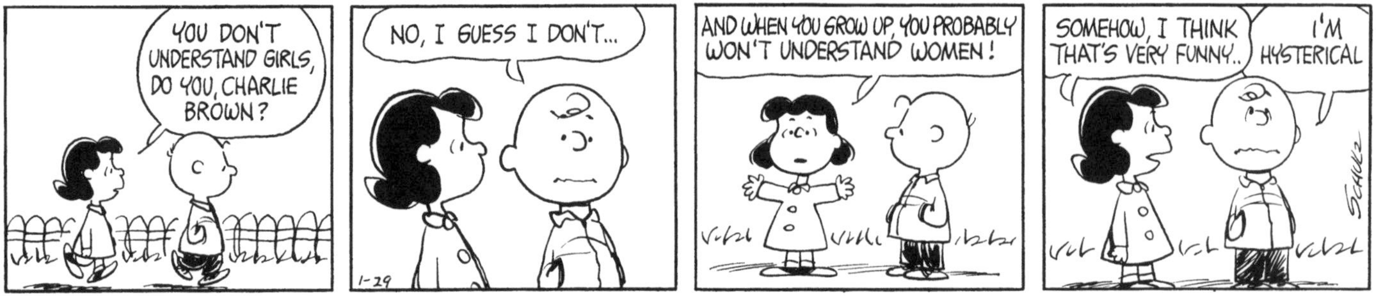
YOU DON'T UNDERSTAND GIRLS, DO YOU, CHARLIE BROWN?
NO, I GUESS I DON'T...
1-29
AND WHEN YOU GROW UP, YOU PROBABLY WON'T UNDERSTAND WOMEN!
SOMEHOW, I THINK THAT'S VERY FUNNY..
I'M HYSTERICAL
SCHULZ

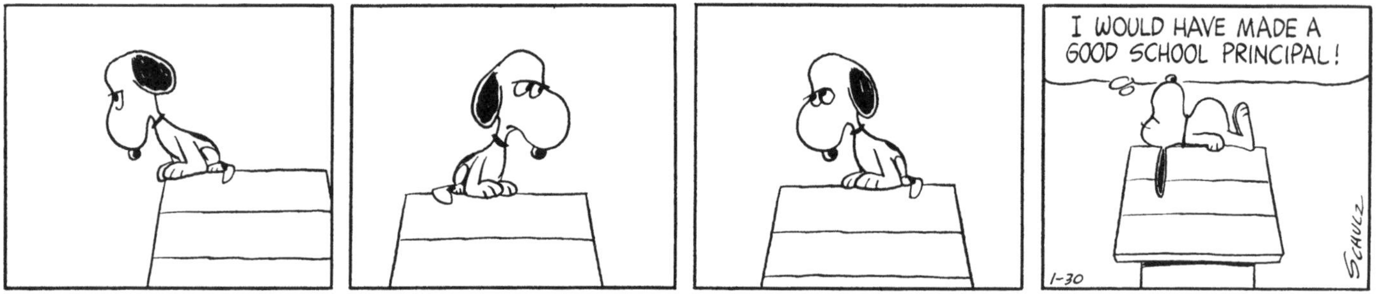
I WOULD HAVE MADE A GOOD SCHOOL PRINCIPAL!
1-30
SCHULZ

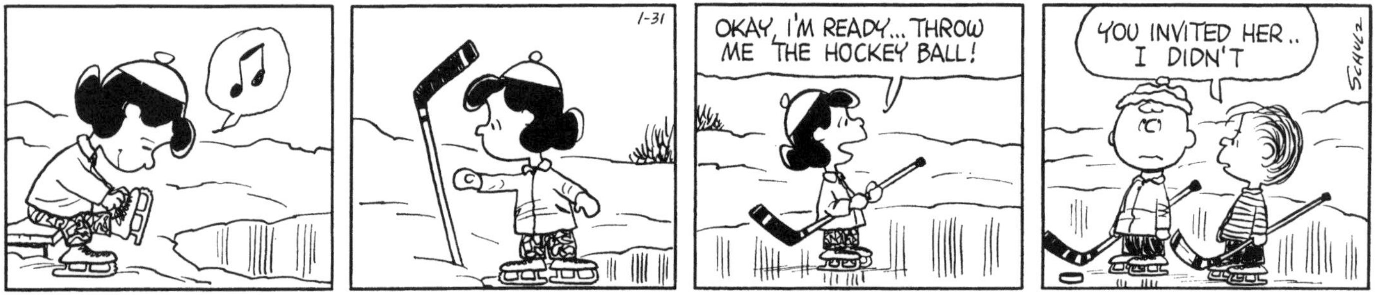
1-31
OKAY, I'M READY... THROW ME THE HOCKEY BALL!
YOU INVITED HER.. I DIDN'T
SCHULZ

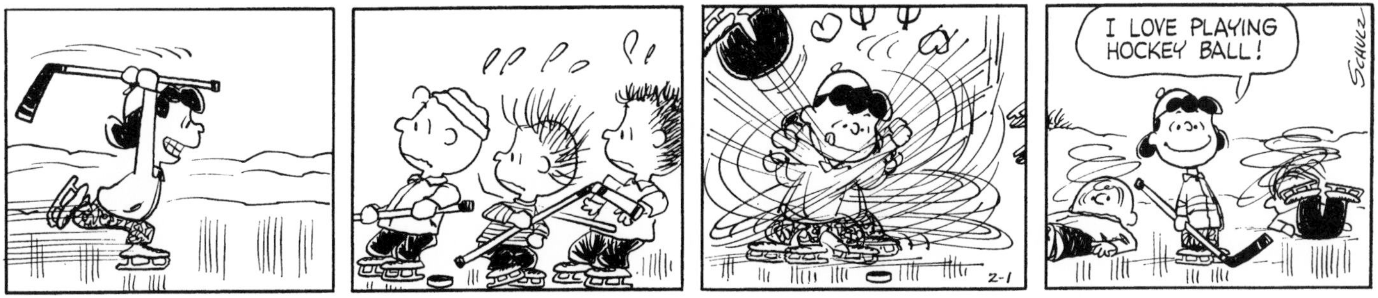
2-1
I LOVE PLAYING HOCKEY BALL!
SCHULZ

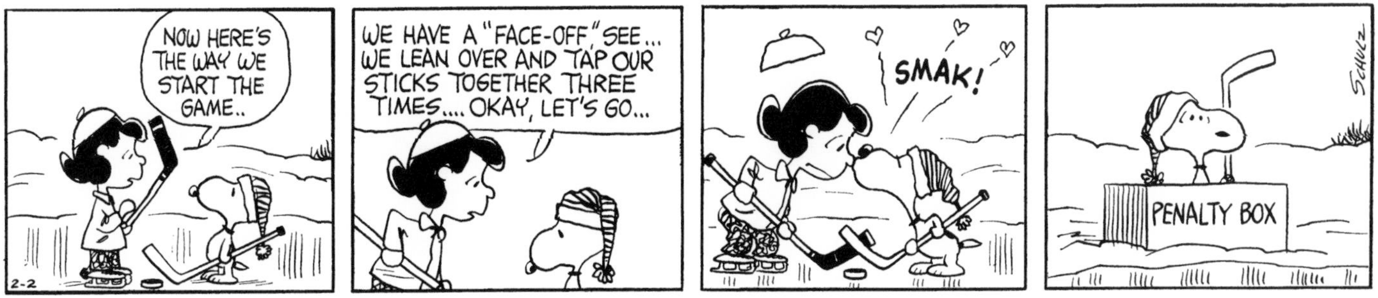
NOW HERE'S THE WAY WE START THE GAME..
2-2
WE HAVE A "FACE-OFF," SEE... WE LEAN OVER AND TAP OUR STICKS TOGETHER THREE TIMES.... OKAY, LET'S GO...
SMAK!
PENALTY BOX
SCHULZ

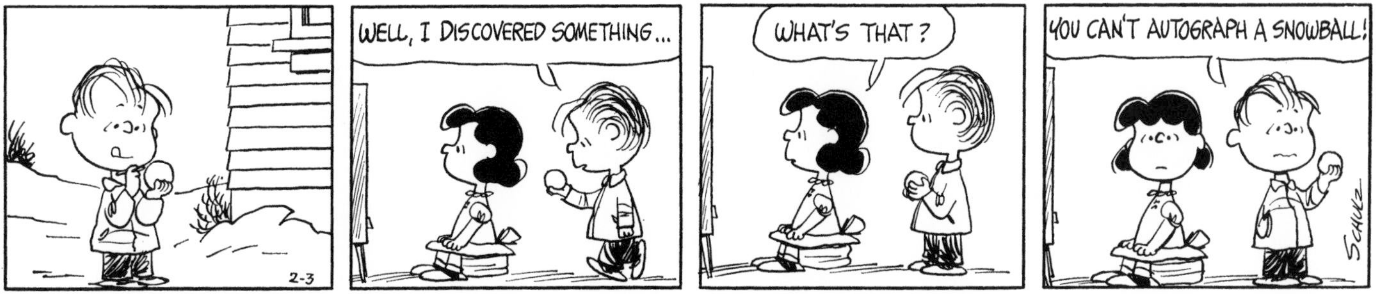
2-3
WELL, I DISCOVERED SOMETHING...
WHAT'S THAT?
YOU CAN'T AUTOGRAPH A SNOWBALL!
SCHULZ

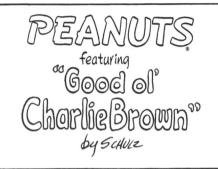

PEANUTS
featuring
"Good ol' Charlie Brown"
by Schulz

WHAT ARE YOU HANGING AROUND THE HOUSE FOR?

I'M AFRAID

AFRAID?!

I'M AFRAID TO GO OUTSIDE.. THERE'S A VULTURE SITTING ON MY SNOWMAN!

SEE?

WELL, HE WON'T BE SITTING THERE VERY LONG THE WAY THE SUN IS SHINING...

STUPID BEAGLE!

WE VULTURES HAVE A HARD LIFE...

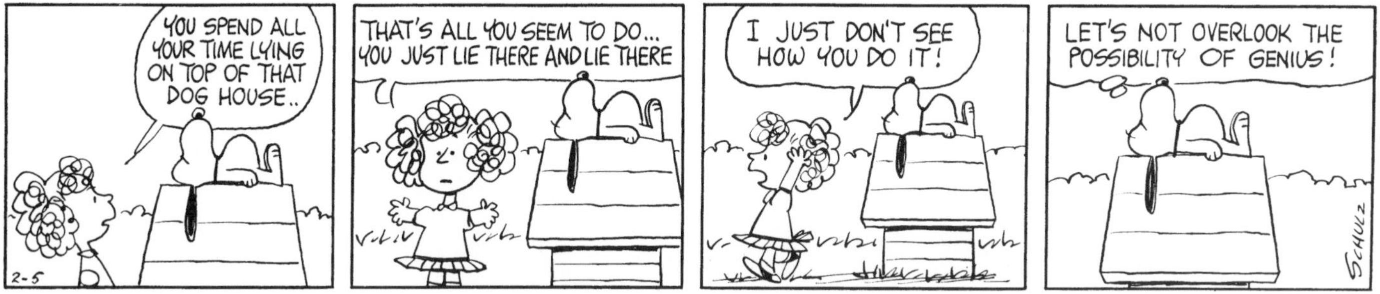
YOU SPEND ALL YOUR TIME LYING ON TOP OF THAT DOG HOUSE..
THAT'S ALL YOU SEEM TO DO... YOU JUST LIE THERE AND LIE THERE
I JUST DON'T SEE HOW YOU DO IT!
LET'S NOT OVERLOOK THE POSSIBILITY OF GENIUS!

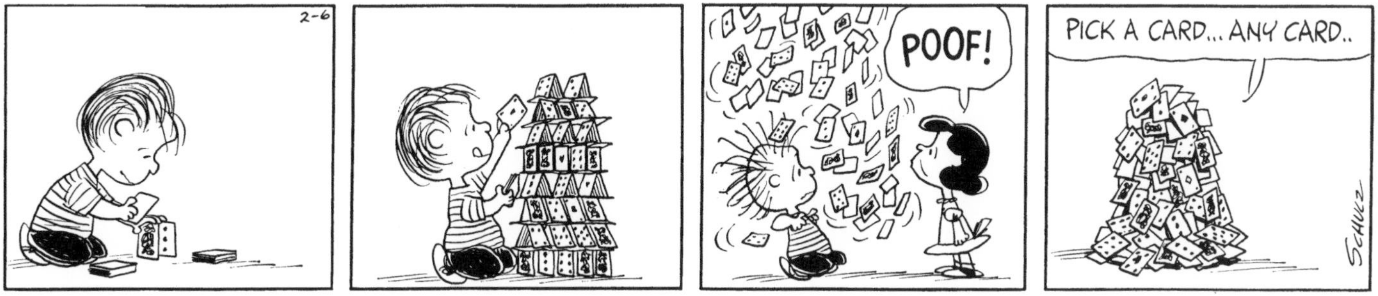
POOF!
PICK A CARD... ANY CARD..

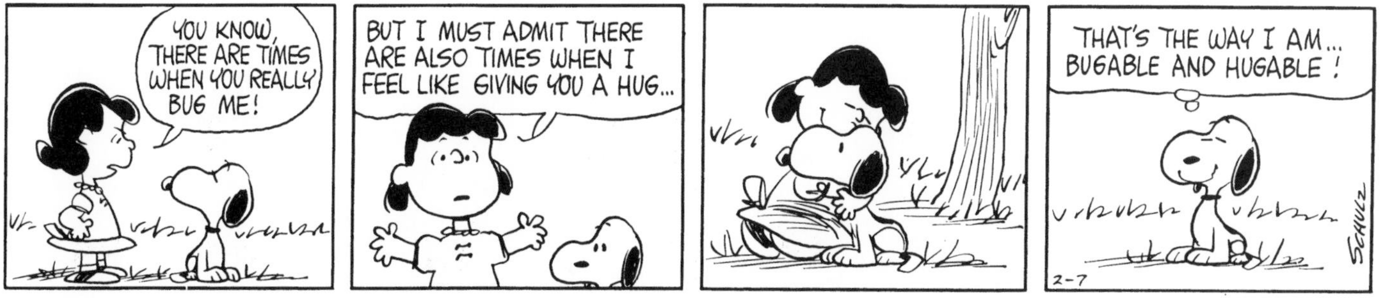
YOU KNOW, THERE ARE TIMES WHEN YOU REALLY BUG ME!
BUT I MUST ADMIT THERE ARE ALSO TIMES WHEN I FEEL LIKE GIVING YOU A HUG...
THAT'S THE WAY I AM... BUGABLE AND HUGABLE!

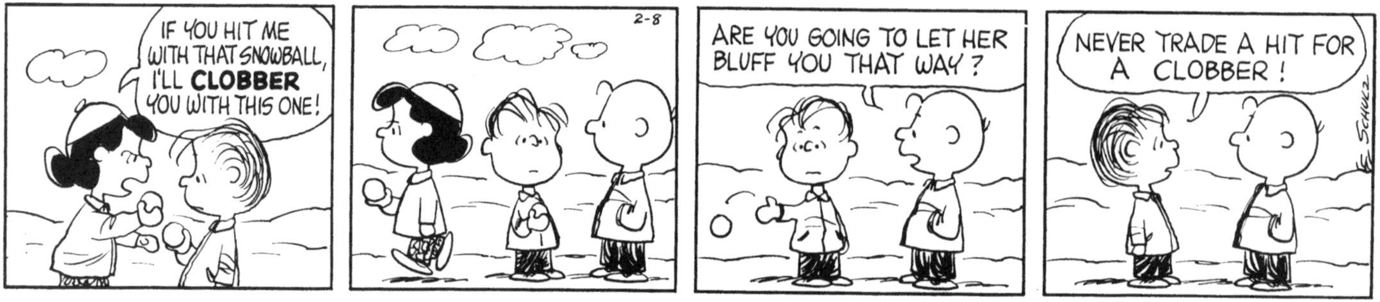
IF YOU HIT ME WITH THAT SNOWBALL, I'LL **CLOBBER** YOU WITH THIS ONE!
2-8
ARE YOU GOING TO LET HER BLUFF YOU THAT WAY?
NEVER TRADE A HIT FOR A CLOBBER!
SCHULZ

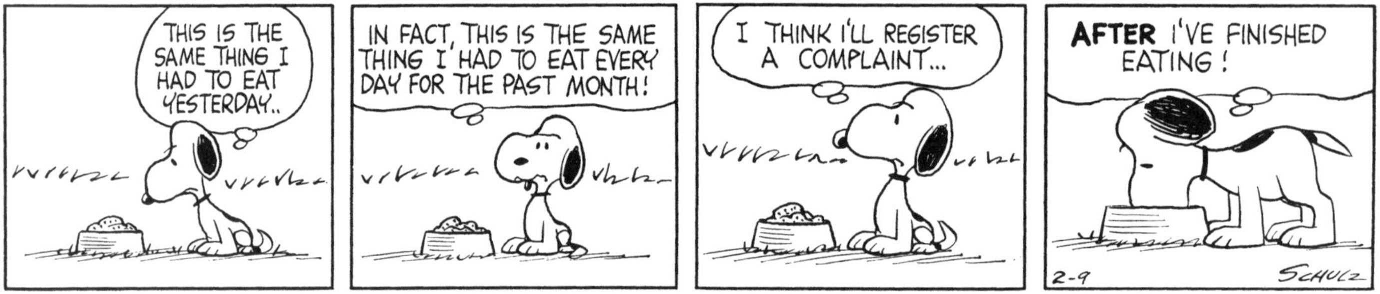
THIS IS THE SAME THING I HAD TO EAT YESTERDAY..
IN FACT, THIS IS THE SAME THING I HAD TO EAT EVERY DAY FOR THE PAST MONTH!
I THINK I'LL REGISTER A COMPLAINT...
AFTER I'VE FINISHED EATING!
2-9
SCHULZ

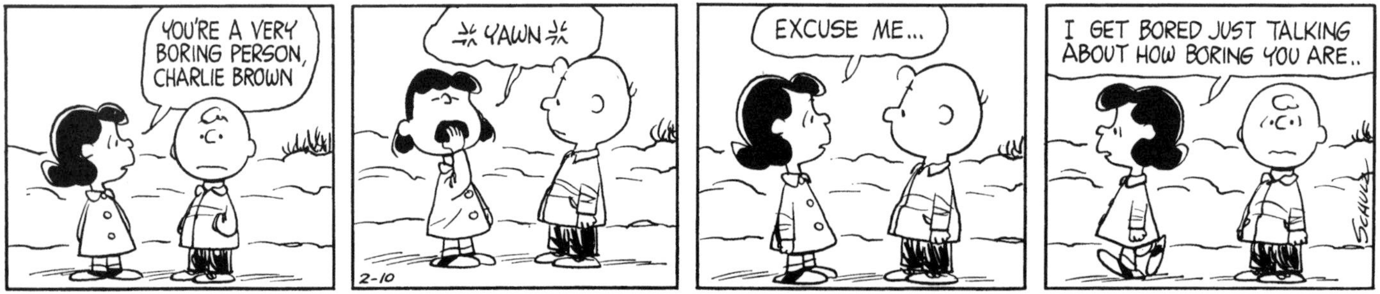
YOU'RE A VERY BORING PERSON, CHARLIE BROWN
YAWN
2-10
EXCUSE ME...
I GET BORED JUST TALKING ABOUT HOW BORING YOU ARE..
SCHULZ

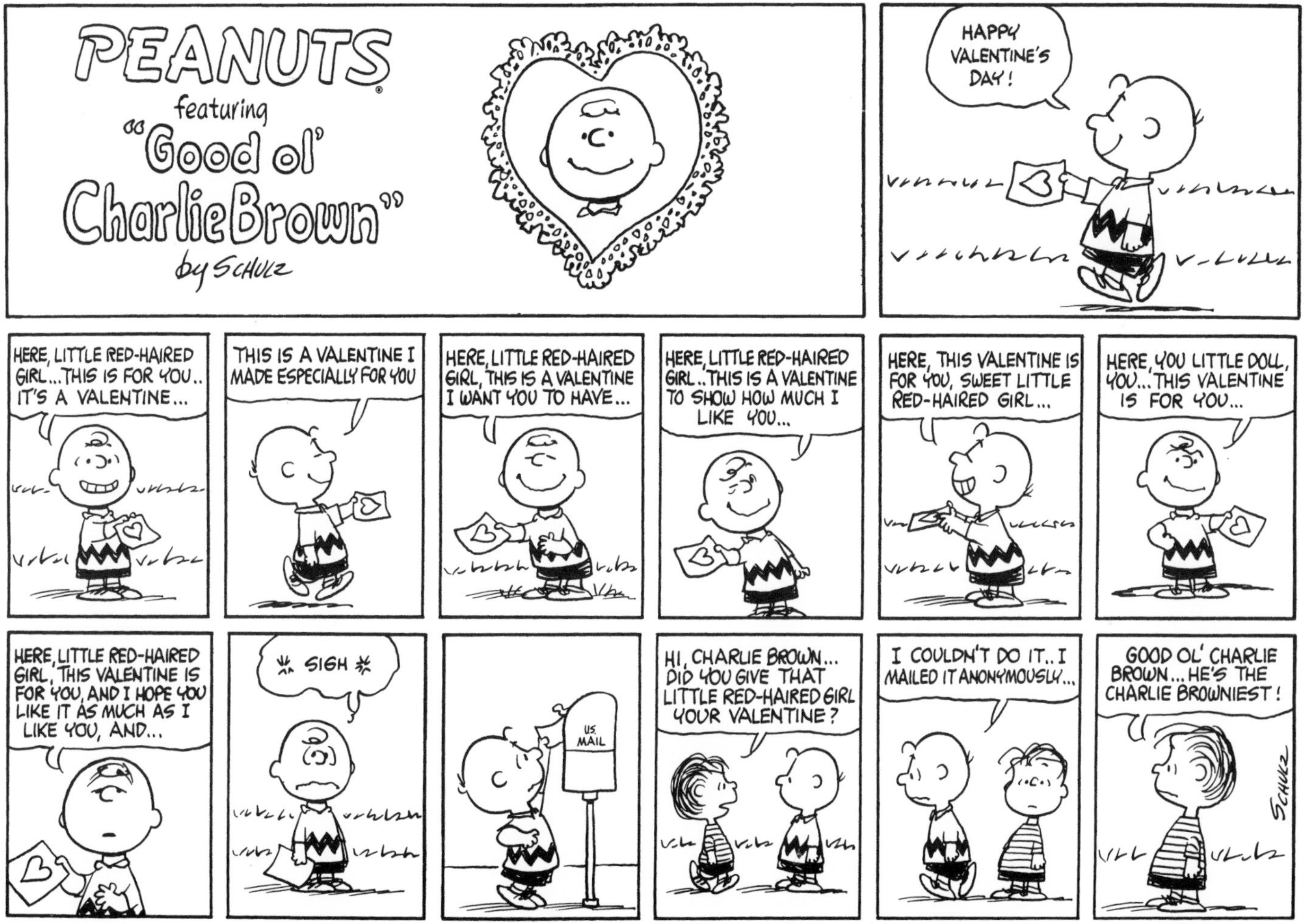
PEANUTS
featuring
"Good ol' Charlie Brown"
by SCHULZ
HAPPY VALENTINE'S DAY!
HERE, LITTLE RED-HAIRED GIRL...THIS IS FOR YOU.. IT'S A VALENTINE...
THIS IS A VALENTINE I MADE ESPECIALLY FOR YOU
HERE, LITTLE RED-HAIRED GIRL, THIS IS A VALENTINE I WANT YOU TO HAVE...
HERE, LITTLE RED-HAIRED GIRL..THIS IS A VALENTINE TO SHOW HOW MUCH I LIKE YOU...
HERE, THIS VALENTINE IS FOR YOU, SWEET LITTLE RED-HAIRED GIRL...
HERE, YOU LITTLE DOLL, YOU...THIS VALENTINE IS FOR YOU...
HERE, LITTLE RED-HAIRED GIRL, THIS VALENTINE IS FOR YOU, AND I HOPE YOU LIKE IT AS MUCH AS I LIKE YOU, AND...
SIGH
U.S. MAIL
HI, CHARLIE BROWN... DID YOU GIVE THAT LITTLE RED-HAIRED GIRL YOUR VALENTINE?
I COULDN'T DO IT.. I MAILED IT ANONYMOUSLY...
GOOD OL' CHARLIE BROWN... HE'S THE CHARLIE BROWNIEST!
SCHULZ

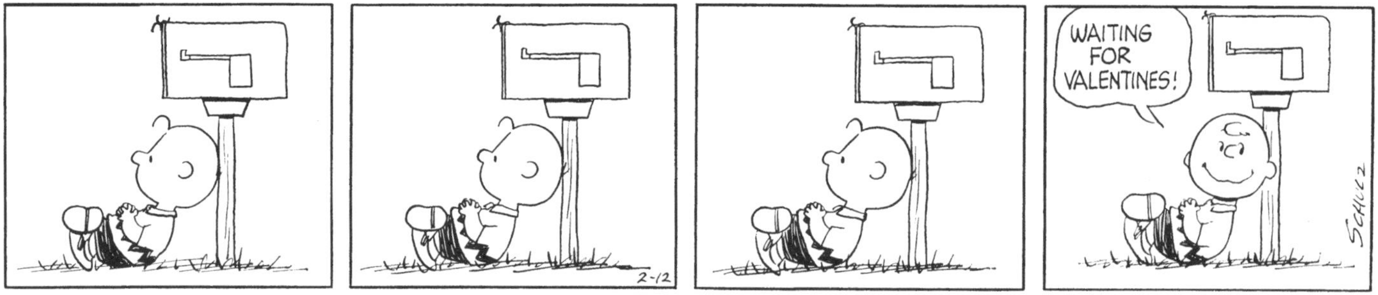
2-12
WAITING FOR VALENTINES!
SCHULZ

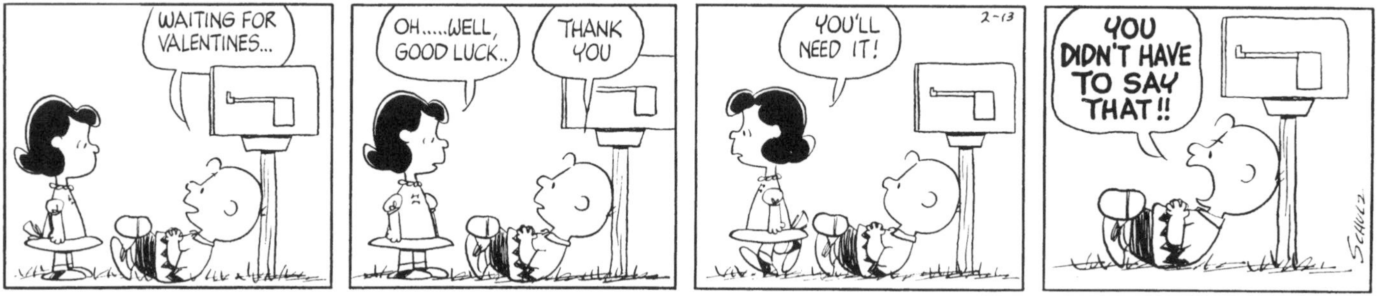
WAITING FOR VALENTINES...
OH.....WELL, GOOD LUCK..
THANK YOU
2-13
YOU'LL NEED IT!
YOU DIDN'T HAVE TO SAY THAT!!
SCHULZ

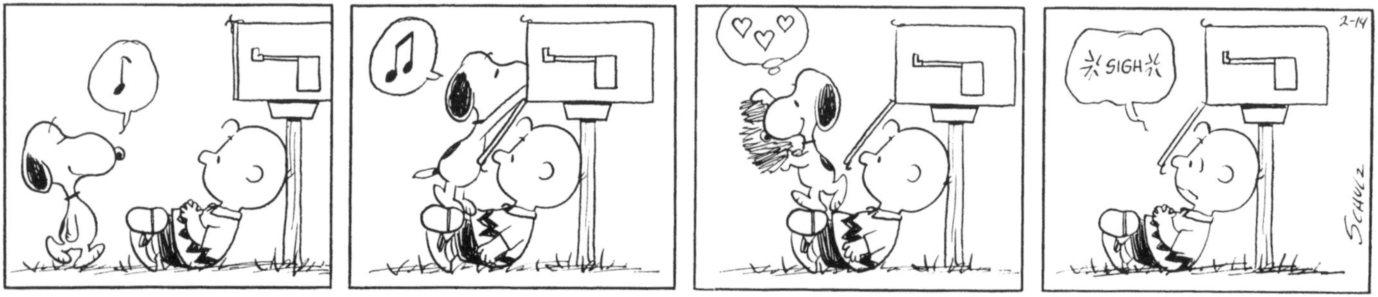
2-14
SIGH
SCHULZ

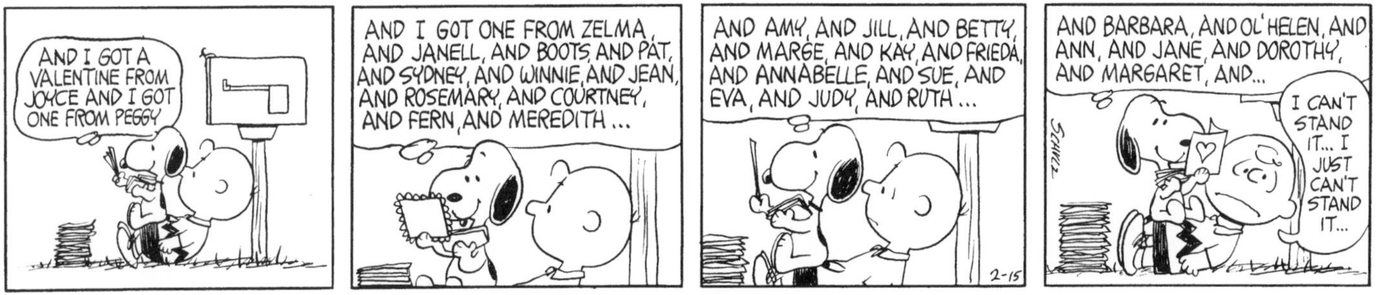
AND I GOT A VALENTINE FROM JOYCE AND I GOT ONE FROM PEGGY
AND I GOT ONE FROM ZELMA, AND JANELL, AND BOOTS, AND PAT, AND SYDNEY, AND WINNIE, AND JEAN, AND ROSEMARY, AND COURTNEY, AND FERN, AND MEREDITH...
AND AMY, AND JILL, AND BETTY, AND MARGE, AND KAY, AND FRIEDA, AND ANNABELLE, AND SUE, AND EVA, AND JUDY, AND RUTH...
2-15
AND BARBARA, AND OL' HELEN, AND ANN, AND JANE, AND DOROTHY, AND MARGARET, AND...
I CAN'T STAND IT... I JUST CAN'T STAND IT...
SCHULZ

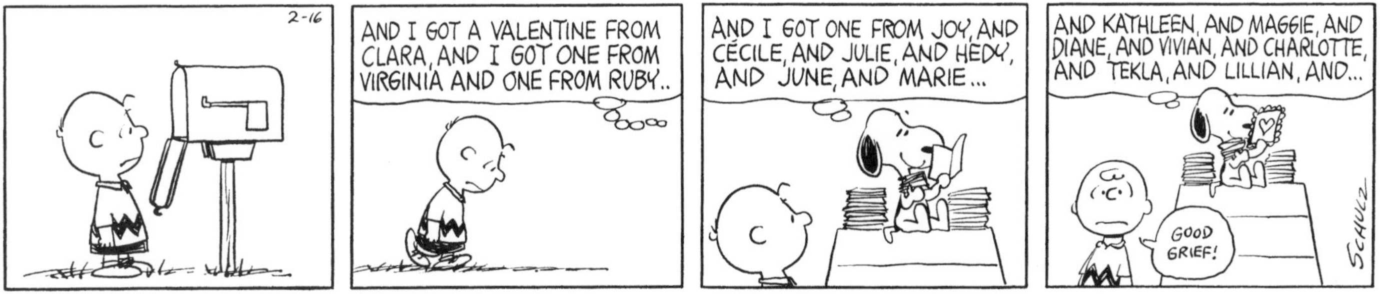
2-16
AND I GOT A VALENTINE FROM CLARA, AND I GOT ONE FROM VIRGINIA AND ONE FROM RUBY..
AND I GOT ONE FROM JOY, AND CÉCILE, AND JULIE, AND HEDY, AND JUNE, AND MARIE...
AND KATHLEEN, AND MAGGIE, AND DIANE, AND VIVIAN, AND CHARLOTTE, AND TEKLA, AND LILLIAN, AND...
GOOD GRIEF!
SCHULZ

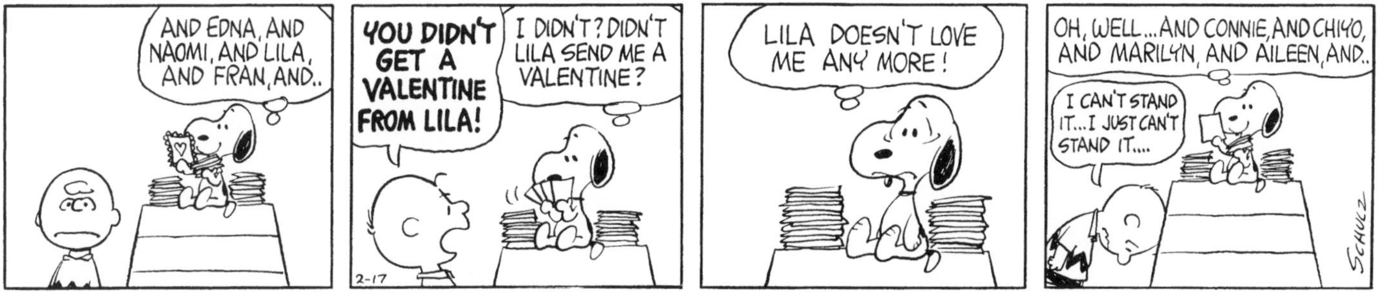
AND EDNA, AND NAOMI, AND LILA, AND FRAN, AND..
YOU DIDN'T GET A VALENTINE FROM LILA!
I DIDN'T? DIDN'T LILA SEND ME A VALENTINE?
2-17
LILA DOESN'T LOVE ME ANY MORE!
OH, WELL... AND CONNIE, AND CHIYO, AND MARILYN, AND AILEEN, AND..
I CAN'T STAND IT... I JUST CAN'T STAND IT....
SCHULZ

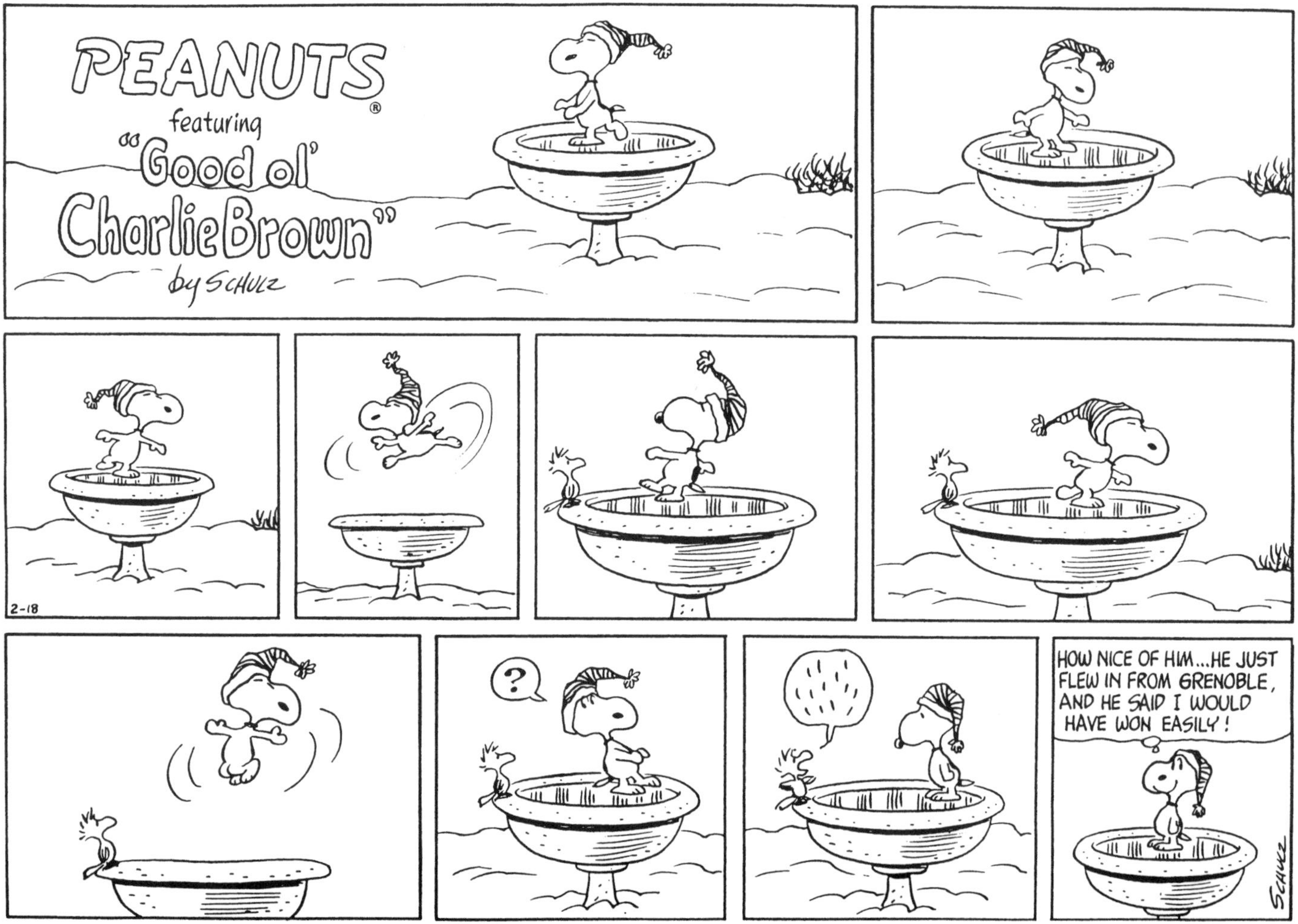
PEANUTS
featuring
"Good ol' CharlieBrown"
by SCHULZ
2-18
?
HOW NICE OF HIM...HE JUST FLEW IN FROM GRENOBLE, AND HE SAID I WOULD HAVE WON EASILY!
SCHULZ

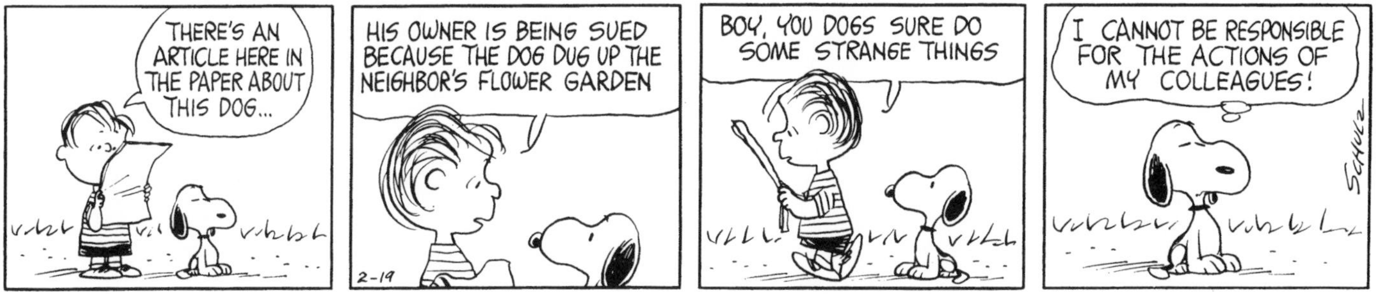
THERE'S AN ARTICLE HERE IN THE PAPER ABOUT THIS DOG...
HIS OWNER IS BEING SUED BECAUSE THE DOG DUG UP THE NEIGHBOR'S FLOWER GARDEN
2-19
BOY, YOU DOGS SURE DO SOME STRANGE THINGS
I CANNOT BE RESPONSIBLE FOR THE ACTIONS OF MY COLLEAGUES!
SCHULZ

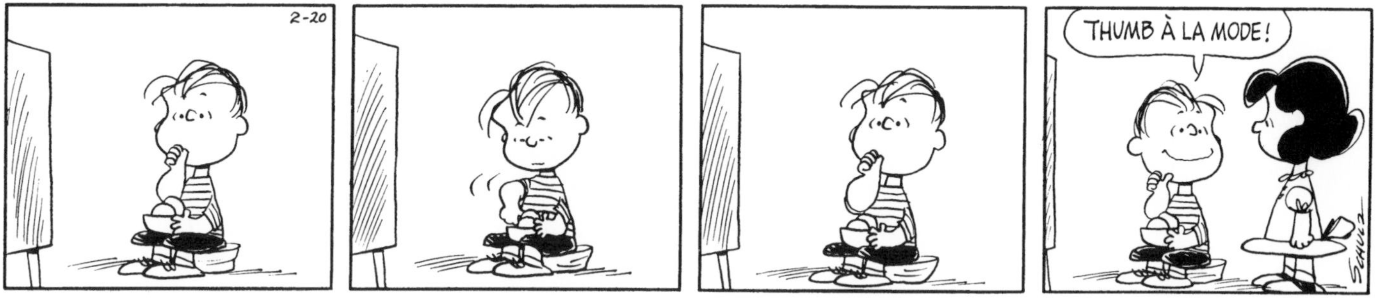
2-20
THUMB À LA MODE!
SCHULZ

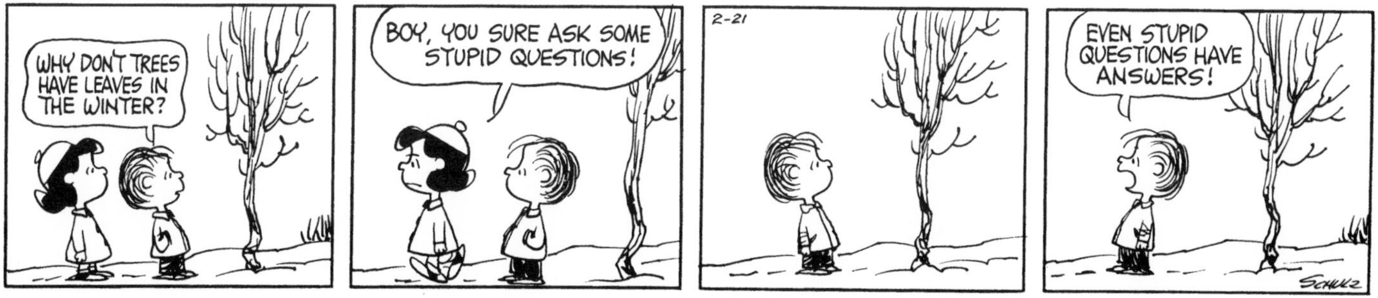
WHY DON'T TREES HAVE LEAVES IN THE WINTER?
BOY, YOU SURE ASK SOME STUPID QUESTIONS!
2-21
EVEN STUPID QUESTIONS HAVE ANSWERS!
SCHULZ

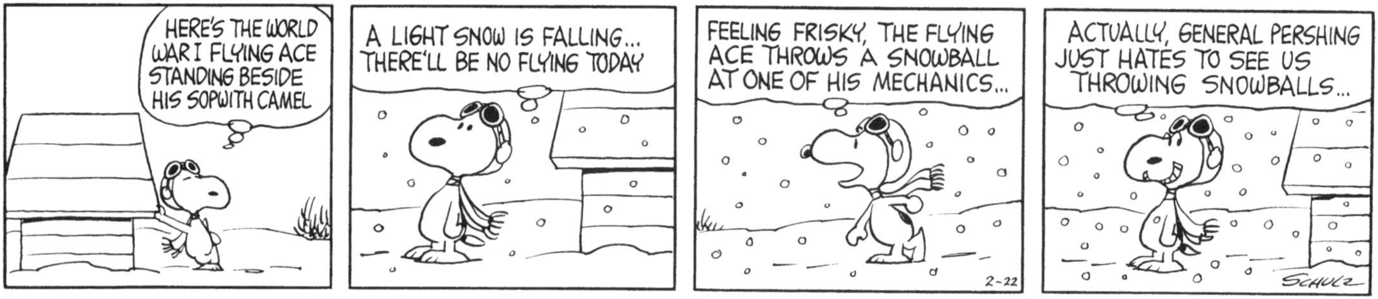
HERE'S THE WORLD WAR I FLYING ACE STANDING BESIDE HIS SOPWITH CAMEL
A LIGHT SNOW IS FALLING... THERE'LL BE NO FLYING TODAY
FEELING FRISKY, THE FLYING ACE THROWS A SNOWBALL AT ONE OF HIS MECHANICS...
2-22
ACTUALLY, GENERAL PERSHING JUST HATES TO SEE US THROWING SNOWBALLS...
SCHULZ

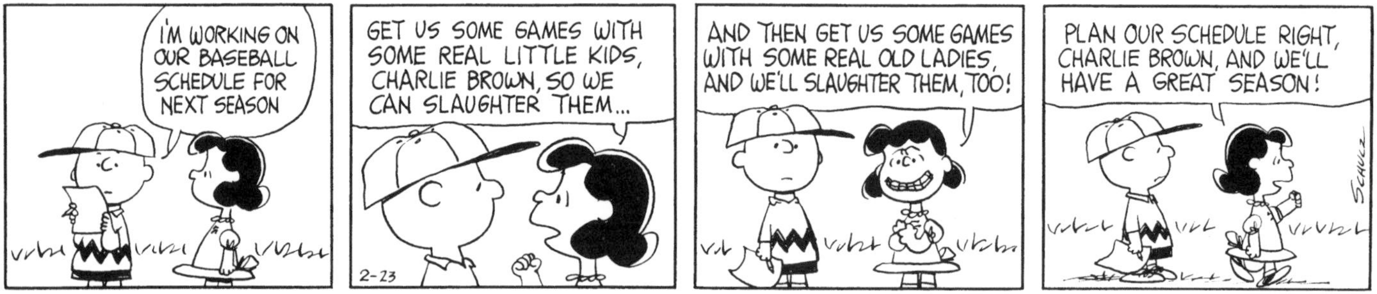
I'M WORKING ON OUR BASEBALL SCHEDULE FOR NEXT SEASON
GET US SOME GAMES WITH SOME REAL LITTLE KIDS, CHARLIE BROWN, SO WE CAN SLAUGHTER THEM...
2-23
AND THEN GET US SOME GAMES WITH SOME REAL OLD LADIES, AND WE'LL SLAUGHTER THEM, TOO!
PLAN OUR SCHEDULE RIGHT, CHARLIE BROWN, AND WE'LL HAVE A GREAT SEASON!
SCHULZ

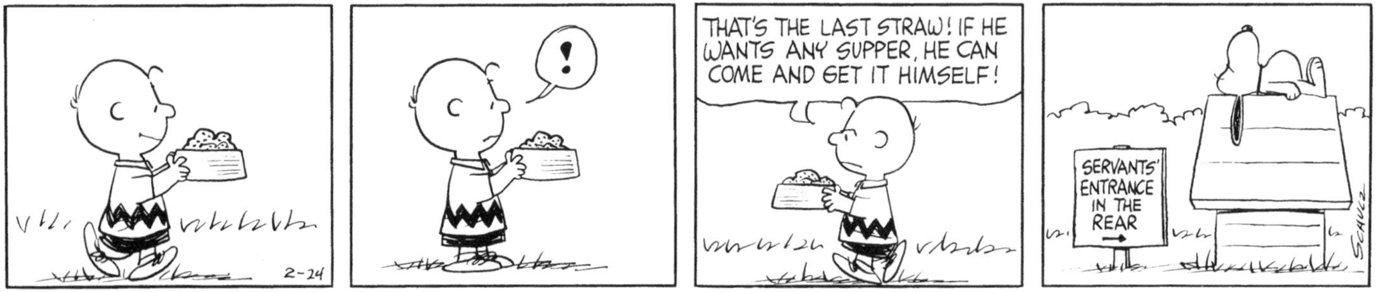
2-24
!
THAT'S THE LAST STRAW! IF HE WANTS ANY SUPPER, HE CAN COME AND GET IT HIMSELF!
SERVANTS' ENTRANCE IN THE REAR →
SCHULZ

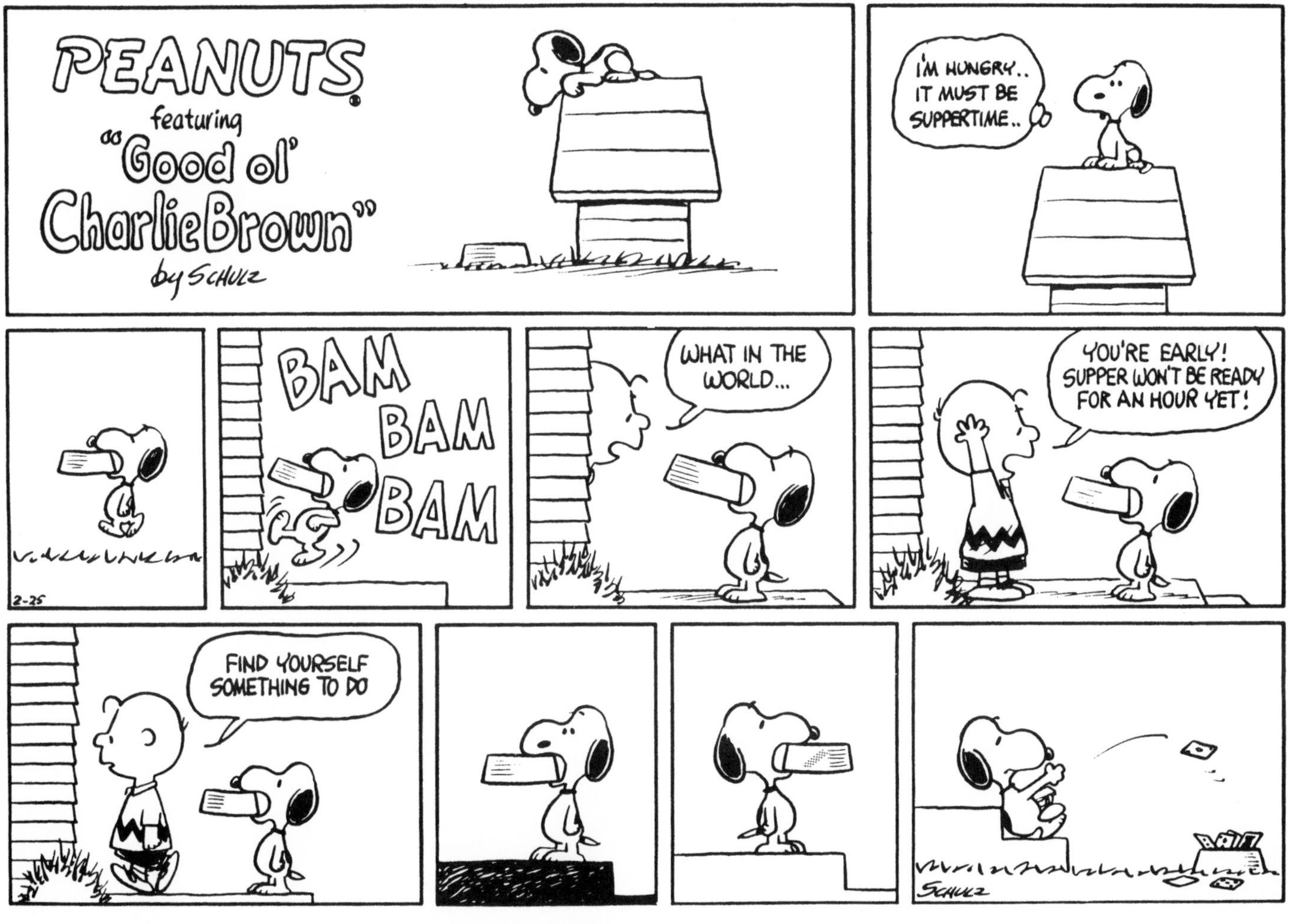
PEANUTS
featuring
"Good ol' Charlie Brown"
by SCHULZ
I'M HUNGRY.. IT MUST BE SUPPERTIME..
2-25
BAM
BAM
BAM
WHAT IN THE WORLD...
YOU'RE EARLY! SUPPER WON'T BE READY FOR AN HOUR YET!
FIND YOURSELF SOMETHING TO DO
SCHULZ

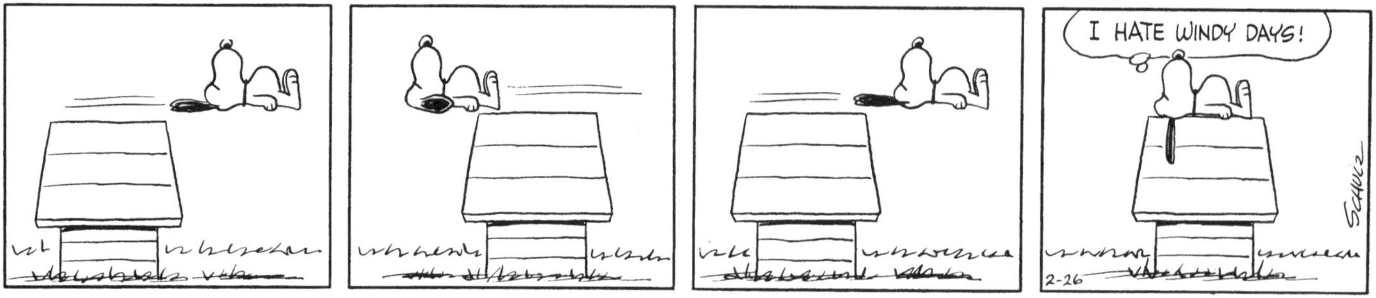
I HATE WINDY DAYS!
SCHULZ
2-26

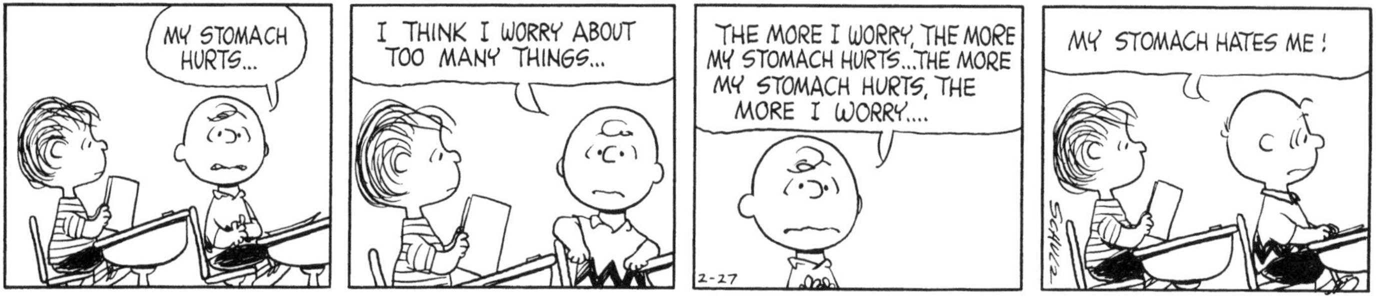
MY STOMACH HURTS...
I THINK I WORRY ABOUT TOO MANY THINGS...
THE MORE I WORRY, THE MORE MY STOMACH HURTS...THE MORE MY STOMACH HURTS, THE MORE I WORRY....
2-27
MY STOMACH HATES ME!
SCHULZ

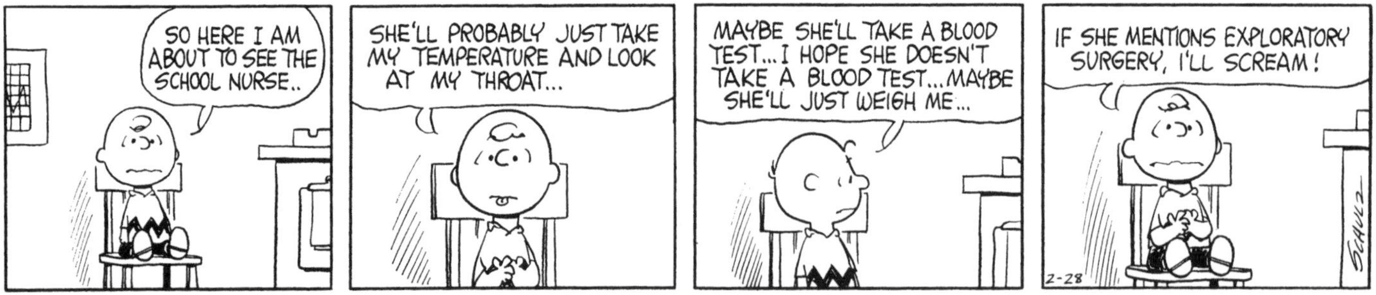
SO HERE I AM ABOUT TO SEE THE SCHOOL NURSE..
SHE'LL PROBABLY JUST TAKE MY TEMPERATURE AND LOOK AT MY THROAT...
MAYBE SHE'LL TAKE A BLOOD TEST...I HOPE SHE DOESN'T TAKE A BLOOD TEST...MAYBE SHE'LL JUST WEIGH ME...
IF SHE MENTIONS EXPLORATORY SURGERY, I'LL SCREAM!
SCHULZ
2-28

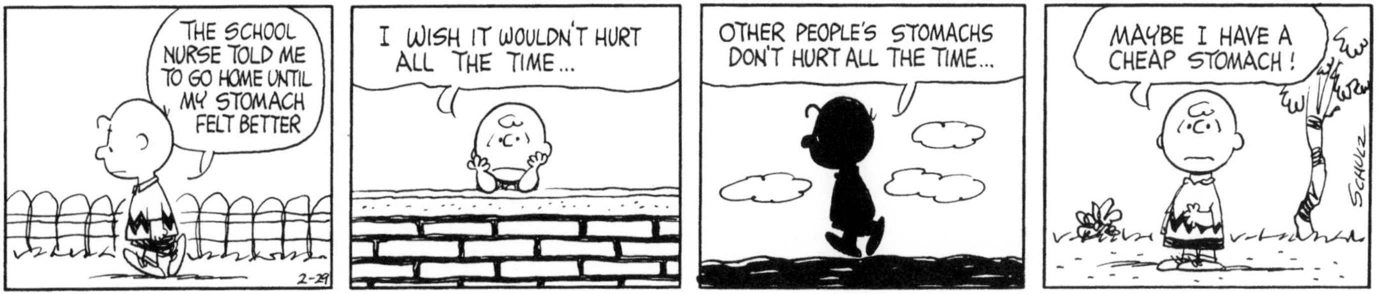
THE SCHOOL NURSE TOLD ME TO GO HOME UNTIL MY STOMACH FELT BETTER
2-29
I WISH IT WOULDN'T HURT ALL THE TIME...
OTHER PEOPLE'S STOMACHS DON'T HURT ALL THE TIME...
MAYBE I HAVE A CHEAP STOMACH!
SCHULZ

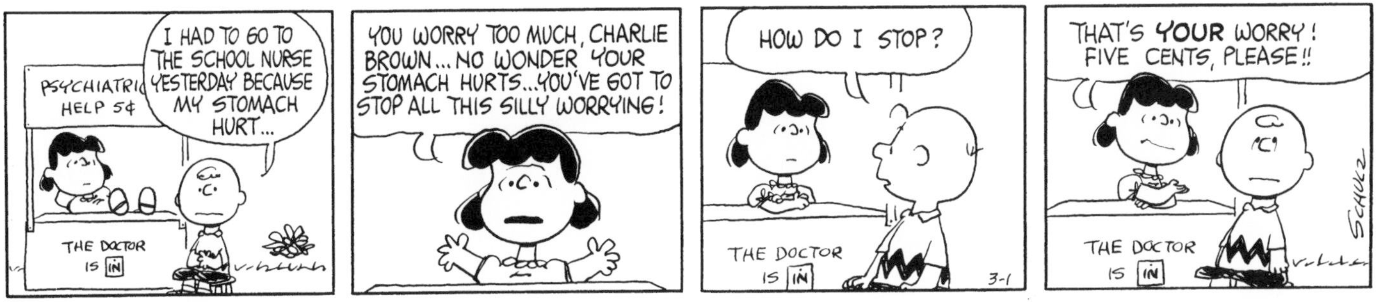
PSYCHIATRIC HELP 5¢
THE DOCTOR IS IN
I HAD TO GO TO THE SCHOOL NURSE YESTERDAY BECAUSE MY STOMACH HURT...
YOU WORRY TOO MUCH, CHARLIE BROWN... NO WONDER YOUR STOMACH HURTS...YOU'VE GOT TO STOP ALL THIS SILLY WORRYING!
HOW DO I STOP?
THE DOCTOR IS IN
3-1
THAT'S **YOUR** WORRY! FIVE CENTS, PLEASE!!
THE DOCTOR IS IN
SCHULZ

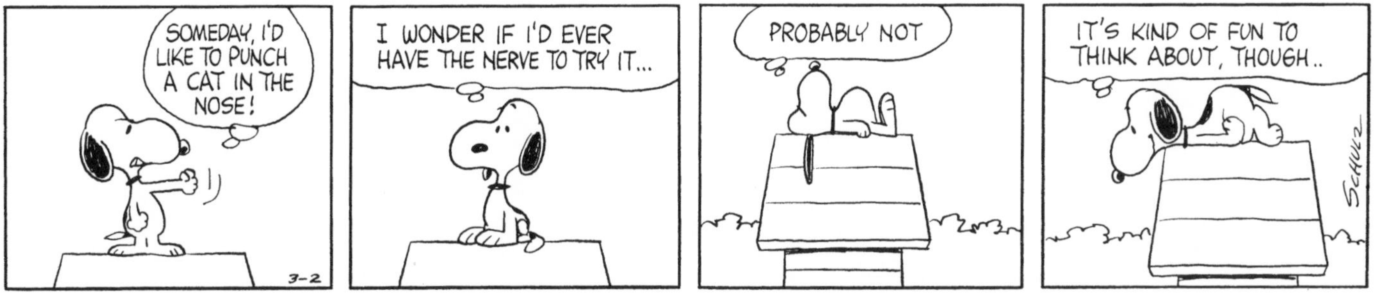
SOMEDAY, I'D LIKE TO PUNCH A CAT IN THE NOSE!
3-2
I WONDER IF I'D EVER HAVE THE NERVE TO TRY IT...
PROBABLY NOT
IT'S KIND OF FUN TO THINK ABOUT, THOUGH..
SCHULZ

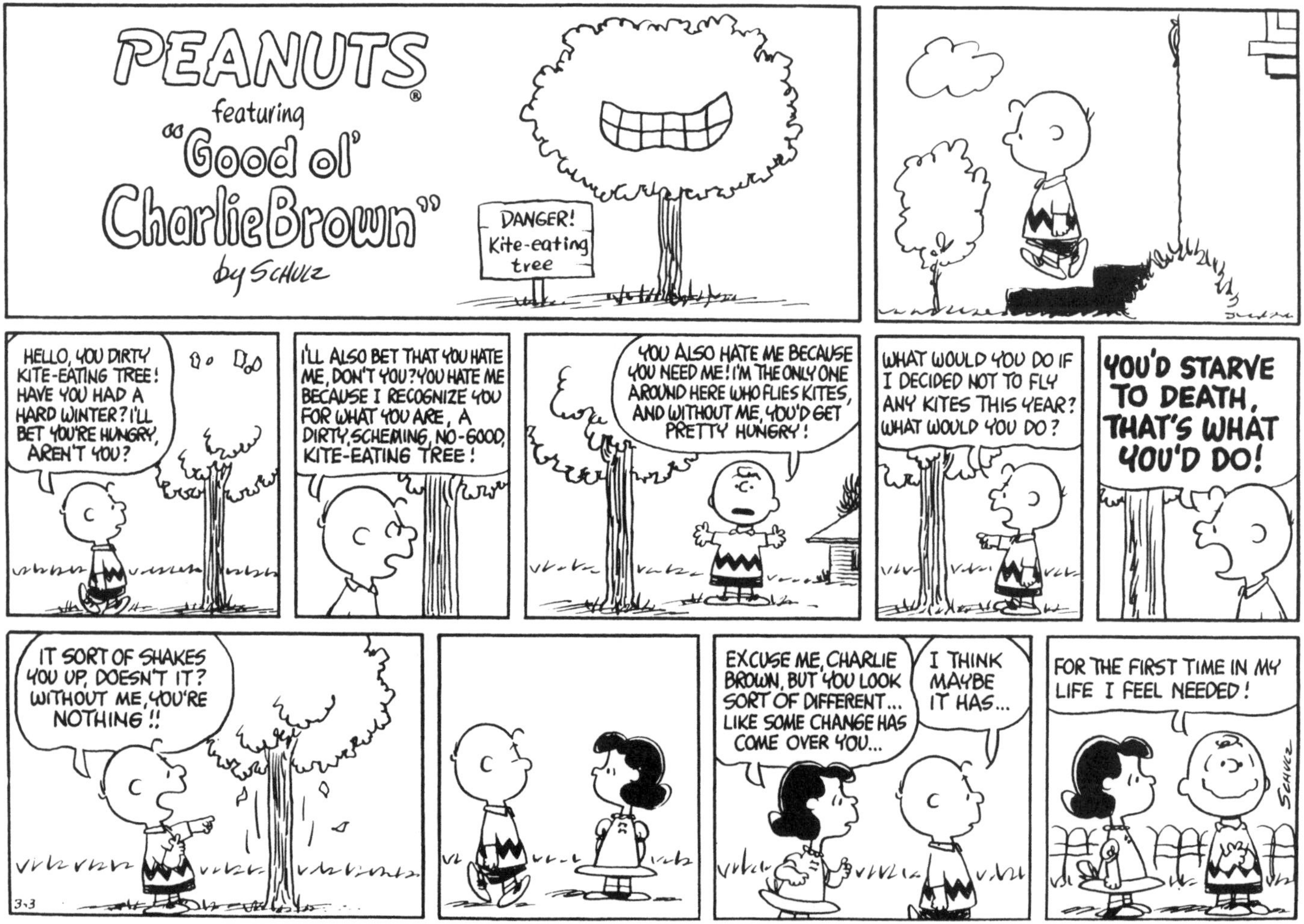
PEANUTS®
featuring
"Good ol' Charlie Brown"
by SCHULZ
DANGER! Kite-eating tree
HELLO, YOU DIRTY KITE-EATING TREE! HAVE YOU HAD A HARD WINTER? I'LL BET YOU'RE HUNGRY, AREN'T YOU?
I'LL ALSO BET THAT YOU HATE ME, DON'T YOU? YOU HATE ME BECAUSE I RECOGNIZE YOU FOR WHAT YOU ARE, A DIRTY, SCHEMING, NO-GOOD, KITE-EATING TREE!
YOU ALSO HATE ME BECAUSE YOU NEED ME! I'M THE ONLY ONE AROUND HERE WHO FLIES KITES, AND WITHOUT ME, YOU'D GET PRETTY HUNGRY!
WHAT WOULD YOU DO IF I DECIDED NOT TO FLY ANY KITES THIS YEAR? WHAT WOULD YOU DO?
YOU'D STARVE TO DEATH, THAT'S WHAT YOU'D DO!
IT SORT OF SHAKES YOU UP, DOESN'T IT? WITHOUT ME, YOU'RE NOTHING!!
3-3
EXCUSE ME, CHARLIE BROWN, BUT YOU LOOK SORT OF DIFFERENT... LIKE SOME CHANGE HAS COME OVER YOU...
I THINK MAYBE IT HAS...
FOR THE FIRST TIME IN MY LIFE I FEEL NEEDED!
SCHULZ

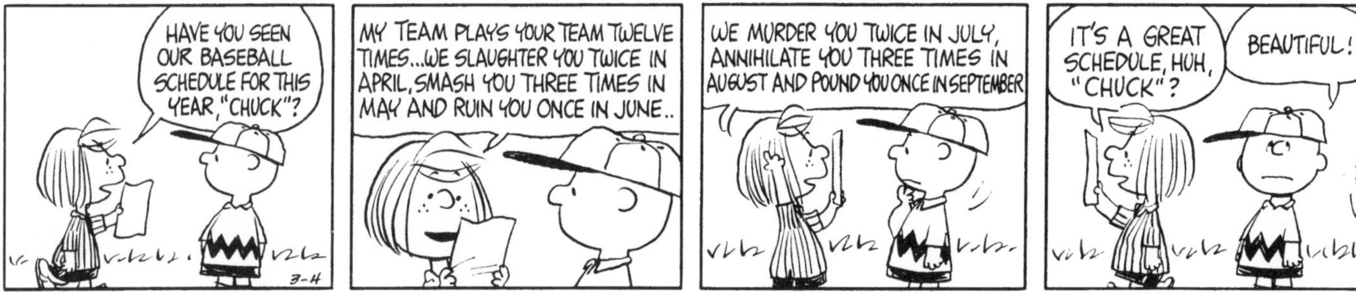
HAVE YOU SEEN OUR BASEBALL SCHEDULE FOR THIS YEAR, "CHUCK"?
MY TEAM PLAYS YOUR TEAM TWELVE TIMES...WE SLAUGHTER YOU TWICE IN APRIL, SMASH YOU THREE TIMES IN MAY AND RUIN YOU ONCE IN JUNE..
WE MURDER YOU TWICE IN JULY, ANNIHILATE YOU THREE TIMES IN AUGUST AND POUND YOU ONCE IN SEPTEMBER
IT'S A GREAT SCHEDULE, HUH, "CHUCK"?
BEAUTIFUL!
SCHULZ
3-4

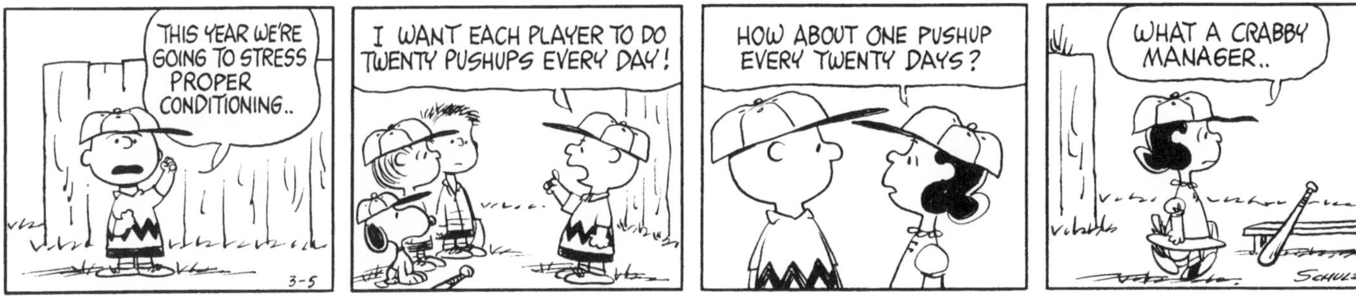
THIS YEAR WE'RE GOING TO STRESS PROPER CONDITIONING..
3-5
I WANT EACH PLAYER TO DO TWENTY PUSHUPS EVERY DAY!
HOW ABOUT ONE PUSHUP EVERY TWENTY DAYS?
WHAT A CRABBY MANAGER..
SCHULZ

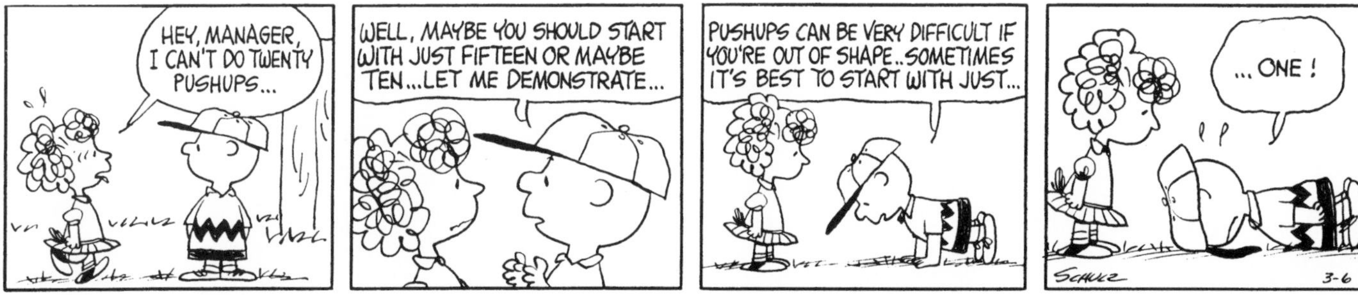
HEY, MANAGER, I CAN'T DO TWENTY PUSHUPS...
WELL, MAYBE YOU SHOULD START WITH JUST FIFTEEN OR MAYBE TEN...LET ME DEMONSTRATE...
PUSHUPS CAN BE VERY DIFFICULT IF YOU'RE OUT OF SHAPE..SOMETIMES IT'S BEST TO START WITH JUST...
...ONE!
SCHULZ
3-6

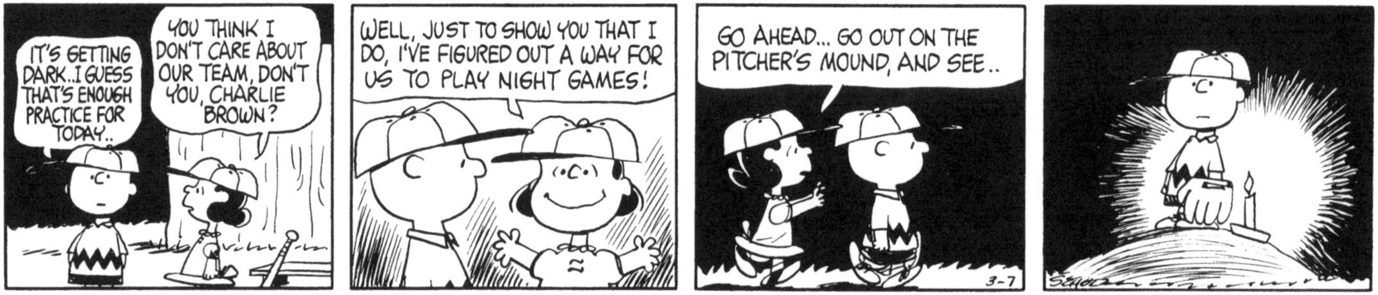
IT'S GETTING DARK..I GUESS THAT'S ENOUGH PRACTICE FOR TODAY..
YOU THINK I DON'T CARE ABOUT OUR TEAM, DON'T YOU, CHARLIE BROWN?
WELL, JUST TO SHOW YOU THAT I DO, I'VE FIGURED OUT A WAY FOR US TO PLAY NIGHT GAMES!
GO AHEAD... GO OUT ON THE PITCHER'S MOUND, AND SEE..
3-7
SCHULZ

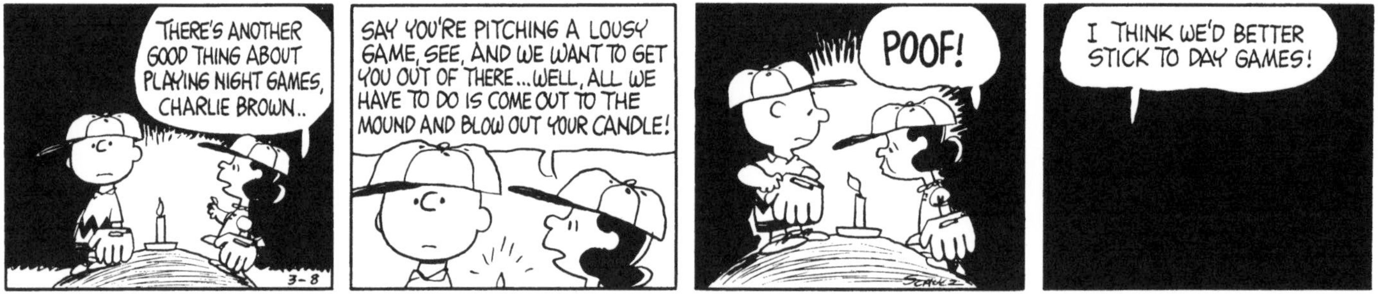
THERE'S ANOTHER GOOD THING ABOUT PLAYING NIGHT GAMES, CHARLIE BROWN..
3-8
SAY YOU'RE PITCHING A LOUSY GAME, SEE, AND WE WANT TO GET YOU OUT OF THERE...WELL, ALL WE HAVE TO DO IS COME OUT TO THE MOUND AND BLOW OUT YOUR CANDLE!
POOF!
SCHULZ
I THINK WE'D BETTER STICK TO DAY GAMES!

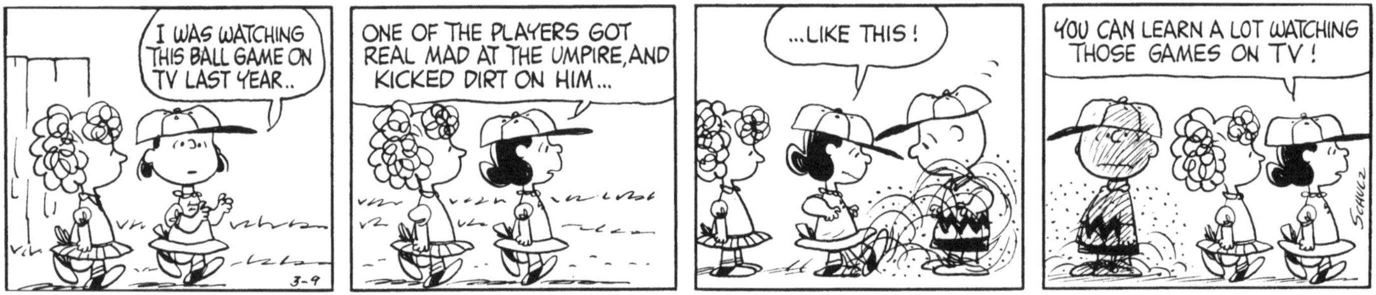
I WAS WATCHING THIS BALL GAME ON TV LAST YEAR..
3-9
ONE OF THE PLAYERS GOT REAL MAD AT THE UMPIRE, AND KICKED DIRT ON HIM...
...LIKE THIS!
YOU CAN LEARN A LOT WATCHING THOSE GAMES ON TV!
SCHULZ

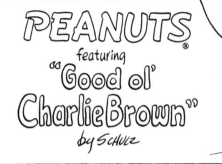

PEANUTS featuring "Good ol' CharlieBrown" by SCHULZ

Z

CLUMP!

!

EVENTUALLY, I MAY HAVE TO GIVE UP KITE FLYING...

3-10

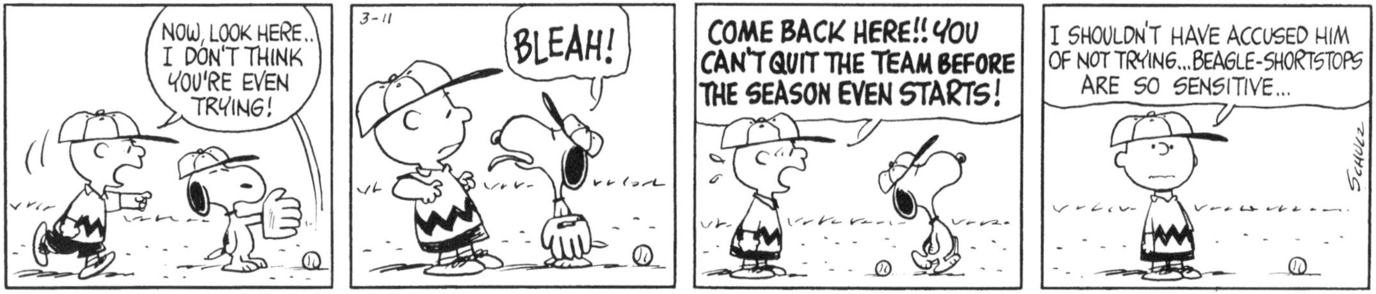
NOW, LOOK HERE.. I DON'T THINK YOU'RE EVEN TRYING!
3-11
BLEAH!
COME BACK HERE!! YOU CAN'T QUIT THE TEAM BEFORE THE SEASON EVEN STARTS!
I SHOULDN'T HAVE ACCUSED HIM OF NOT TRYING...BEAGLE-SHORTSTOPS ARE SO SENSITIVE...
SCHULZ

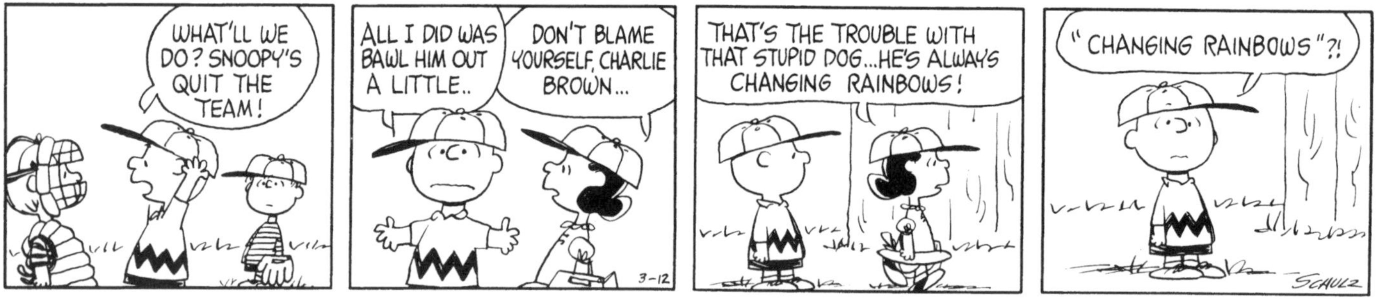
WHAT'LL WE DO? SNOOPY'S QUIT THE TEAM!
ALL I DID WAS BAWL HIM OUT A LITTLE..
DON'T BLAME YOURSELF, CHARLIE BROWN...
3-12
THAT'S THE TROUBLE WITH THAT STUPID DOG...HE'S ALWAYS CHANGING RAINBOWS!
"CHANGING RAINBOWS"?!
SCHULZ

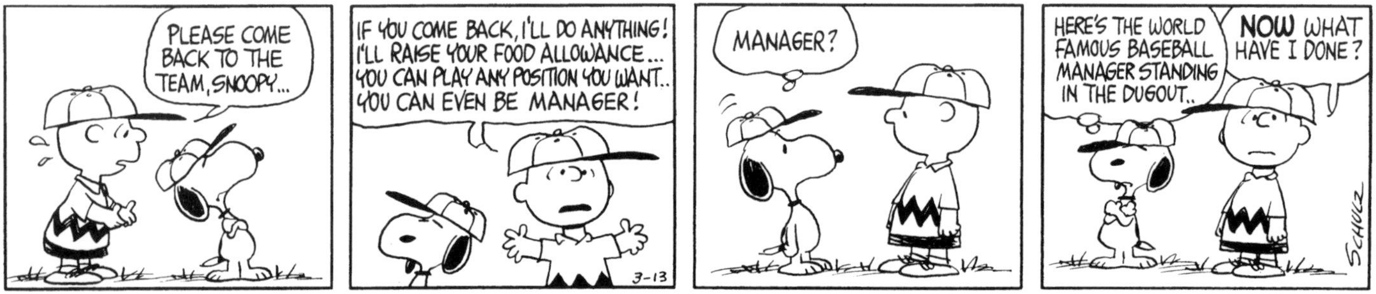
PLEASE COME BACK TO THE TEAM, SNOOPY...
IF YOU COME BACK, I'LL DO ANYTHING! I'LL RAISE YOUR FOOD ALLOWANCE... YOU CAN PLAY ANY POSITION YOU WANT.. YOU CAN EVEN BE MANAGER!
3-13
MANAGER?
HERE'S THE WORLD FAMOUS BASEBALL MANAGER STANDING IN THE DUGOUT..
NOW WHAT HAVE I DONE?
SCHULZ

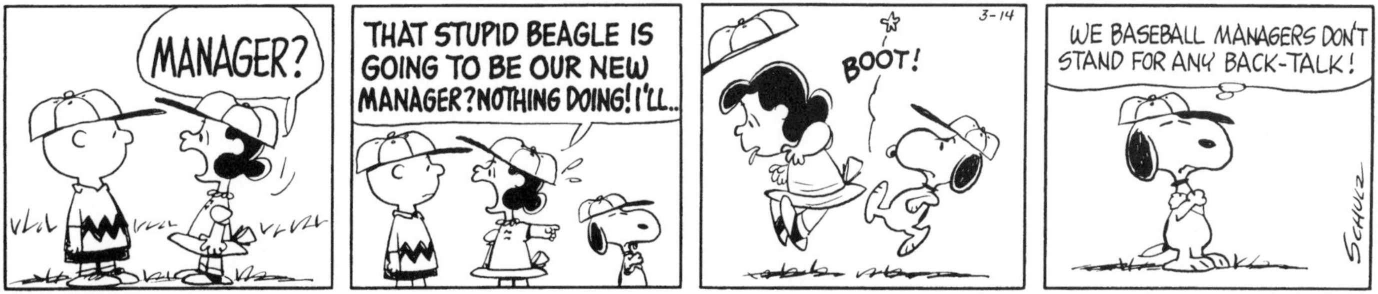
MANAGER?
THAT STUPID BEAGLE IS GOING TO BE OUR NEW MANAGER? NOTHING DOING! I'LL..
3-14
BOOT!
WE BASEBALL MANAGERS DON'T STAND FOR ANY BACK-TALK!
SCHULZ

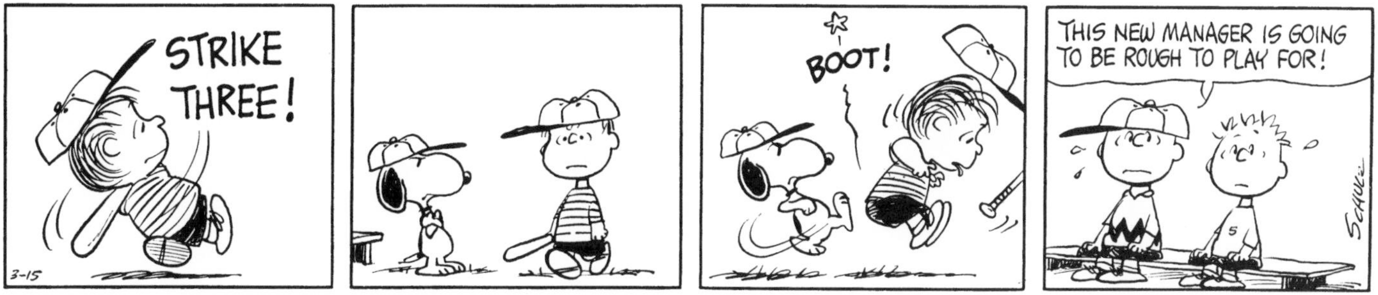
STRIKE THREE!
3-15
BOOT!
THIS NEW MANAGER IS GOING TO BE ROUGH TO PLAY FOR!
5
SCHULZ

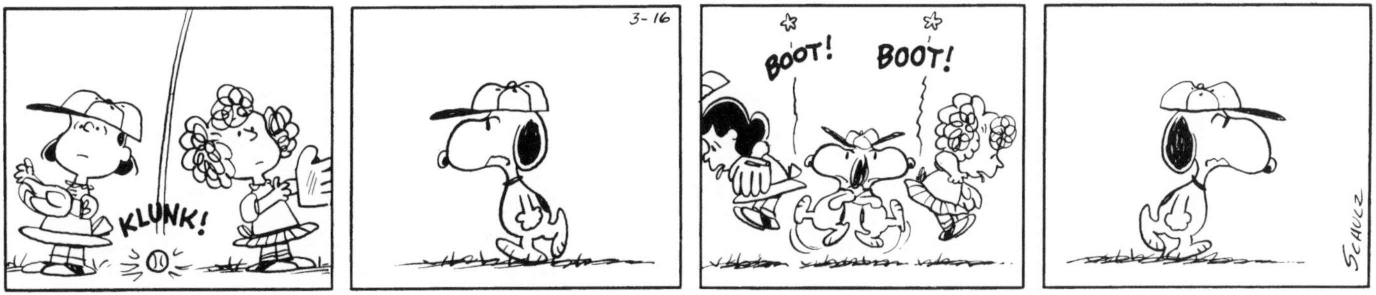
KLUNK!
3-16
BOOT!
BOOT!
SCHULZ

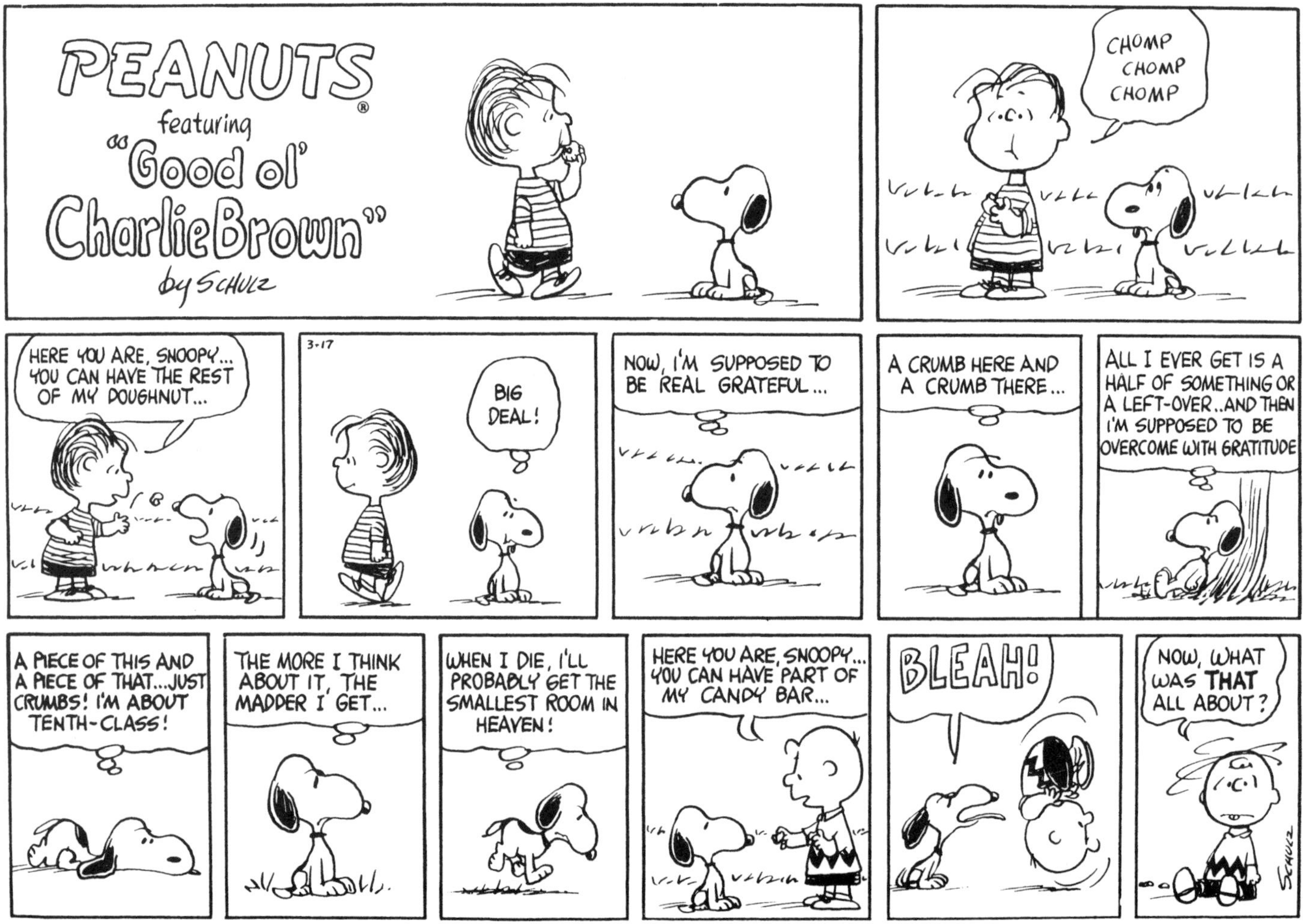
PEANUTS®
featuring "Good ol' CharlieBrown"
by SCHULZ
CHOMP CHOMP CHOMP
HERE YOU ARE, SNOOPY... YOU CAN HAVE THE REST OF MY DOUGHNUT...
3-17
BIG DEAL!
NOW, I'M SUPPOSED TO BE REAL GRATEFUL...
A CRUMB HERE AND A CRUMB THERE...
ALL I EVER GET IS A HALF OF SOMETHING OR A LEFT-OVER..AND THEN I'M SUPPOSED TO BE OVERCOME WITH GRATITUDE
A PIECE OF THIS AND A PIECE OF THAT...JUST CRUMBS! I'M ABOUT TENTH-CLASS!
THE MORE I THINK ABOUT IT, THE MADDER I GET...
WHEN I DIE, I'LL PROBABLY GET THE SMALLEST ROOM IN HEAVEN!
HERE YOU ARE, SNOOPY... YOU CAN HAVE PART OF MY CANDY BAR...
BLEAH!
NOW, WHAT WAS THAT ALL ABOUT?
SCHULZ

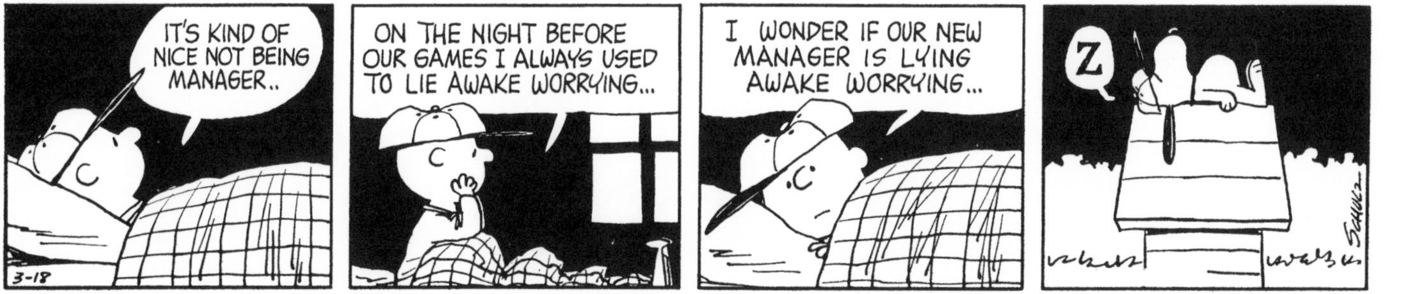
IT'S KIND OF NICE NOT BEING MANAGER..
3-18
ON THE NIGHT BEFORE OUR GAMES I ALWAYS USED TO LIE AWAKE WORRYING...
I WONDER IF OUR NEW MANAGER IS LYING AWAKE WORRYING...
Z
SCHULZ

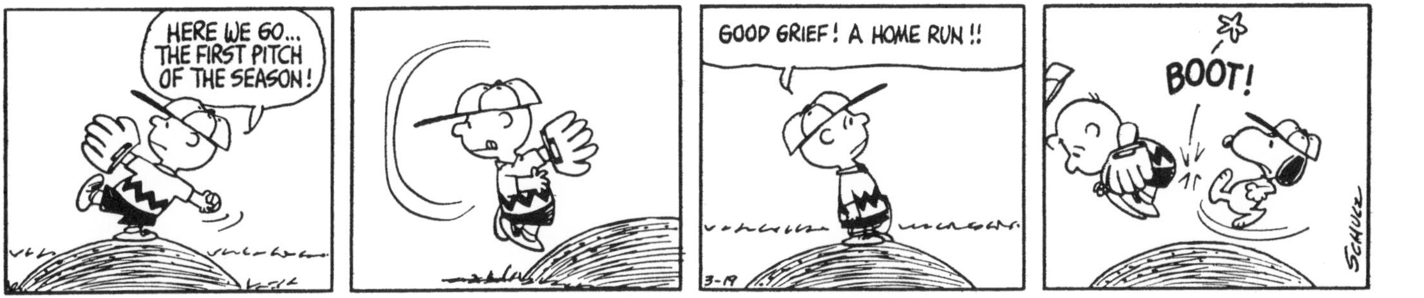
HERE WE GO... THE FIRST PITCH OF THE SEASON!
GOOD GRIEF! A HOME RUN!!
3-19
BOOT!
SCHULZ

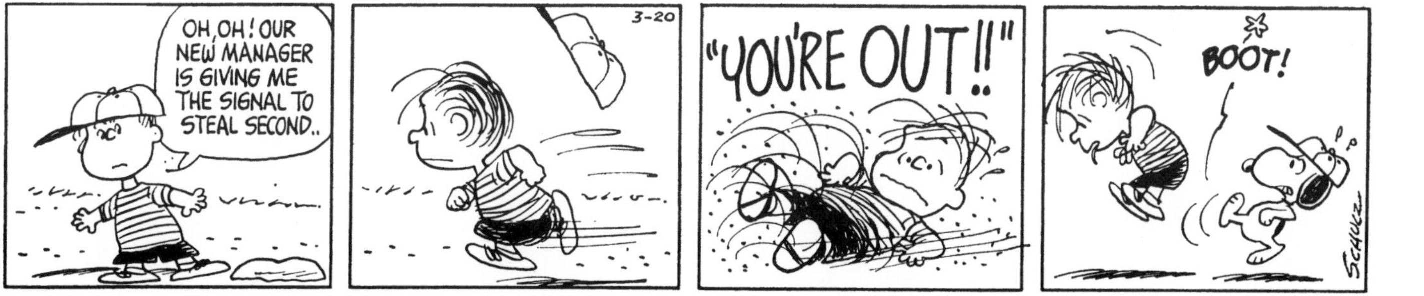
OH, OH! OUR NEW MANAGER IS GIVING ME THE SIGNAL TO STEAL SECOND..
3-20
"YOU'RE OUT!!"
BOOT!
SCHULZ

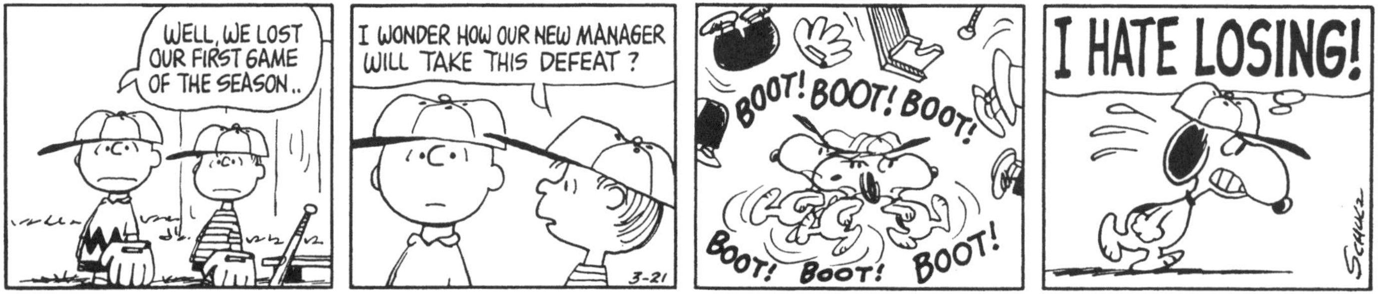
WELL, WE LOST OUR FIRST GAME OF THE SEASON..
I WONDER HOW OUR NEW MANAGER WILL TAKE THIS DEFEAT ?
3-21
BOOT! BOOT! BOOT!
BOOT! BOOT! BOOT!
I HATE LOSING!
SCHULZ

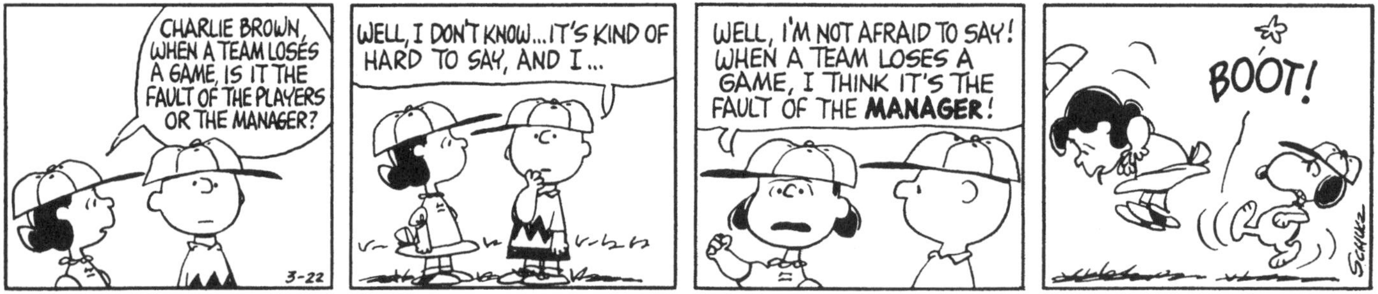
CHARLIE BROWN, WHEN A TEAM LOSES A GAME, IS IT THE FAULT OF THE PLAYERS OR THE MANAGER?
3-22
WELL, I DON'T KNOW...IT'S KIND OF HARD TO SAY, AND I...
WELL, I'M NOT AFRAID TO SAY! WHEN A TEAM LOSES A GAME, I THINK IT'S THE FAULT OF THE **MANAGER**!
BOOT!
SCHULZ

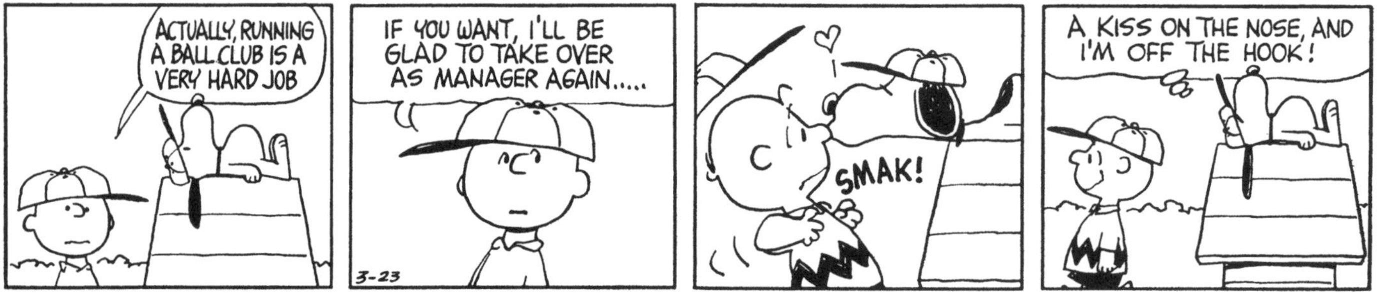
ACTUALLY, RUNNING A BALL CLUB IS A VERY HARD JOB
IF YOU WANT, I'LL BE GLAD TO TAKE OVER AS MANAGER AGAIN.....
3-23
SMAK!
A KISS ON THE NOSE, AND I'M OFF THE HOOK!

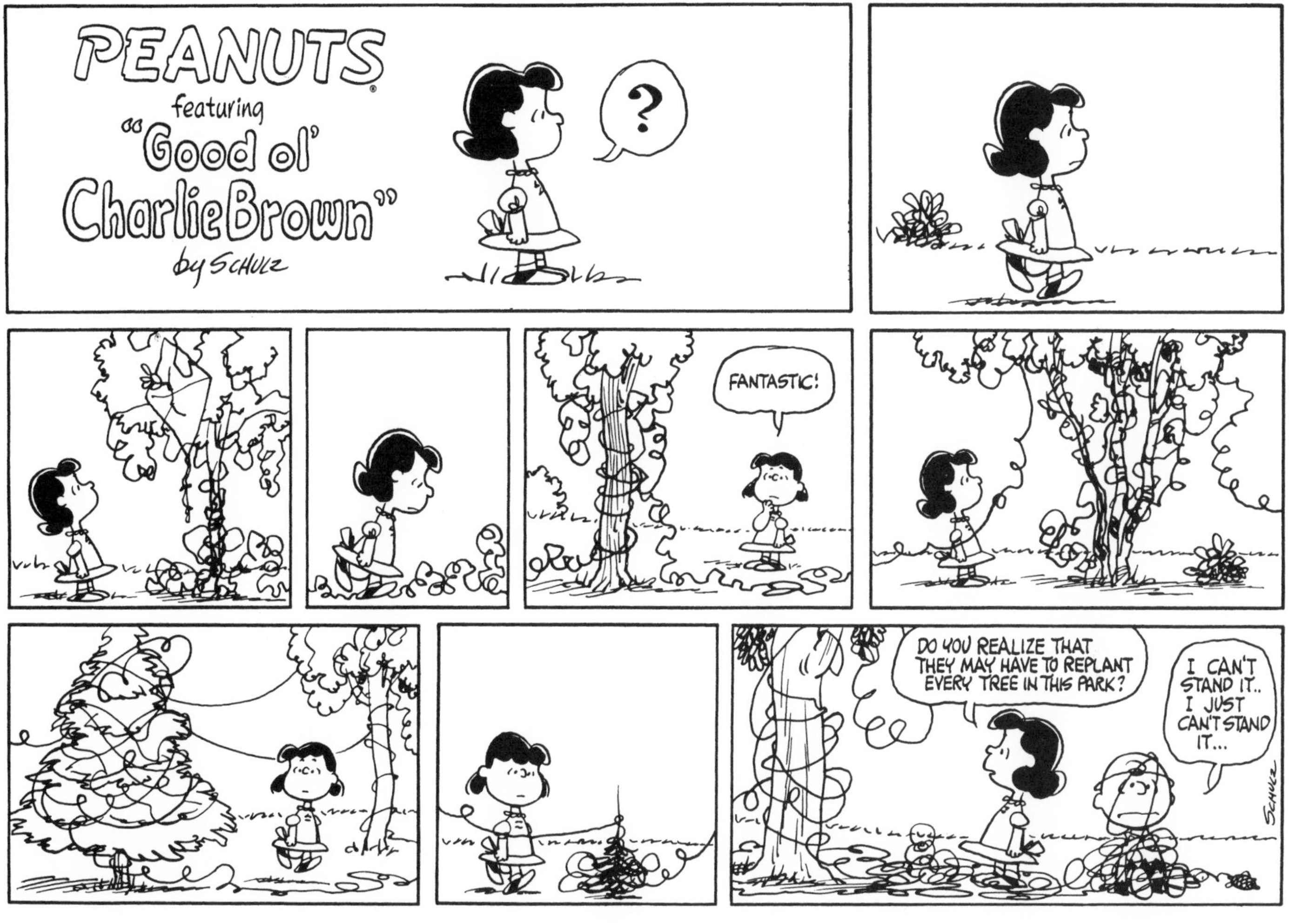
PEANUTS
featuring
"Good ol' Charlie Brown"
by SCHULZ
?
FANTASTIC!
DO YOU REALIZE THAT THEY MAY HAVE TO REPLANT EVERY TREE IN THIS PARK?
I CAN'T STAND IT.. I JUST CAN'T STAND IT...
SCHULZ

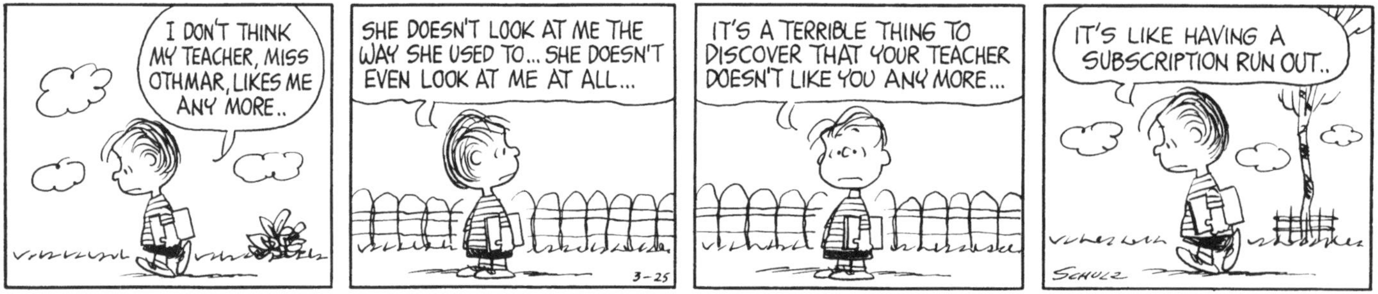
I DON'T THINK MY TEACHER, MISS OTHMAR, LIKES ME ANY MORE..
SHE DOESN'T LOOK AT ME THE WAY SHE USED TO... SHE DOESN'T EVEN LOOK AT ME AT ALL...
3-25
IT'S A TERRIBLE THING TO DISCOVER THAT YOUR TEACHER DOESN'T LIKE YOU ANY MORE...
IT'S LIKE HAVING A SUBSCRIPTION RUN OUT..
SCHULZ

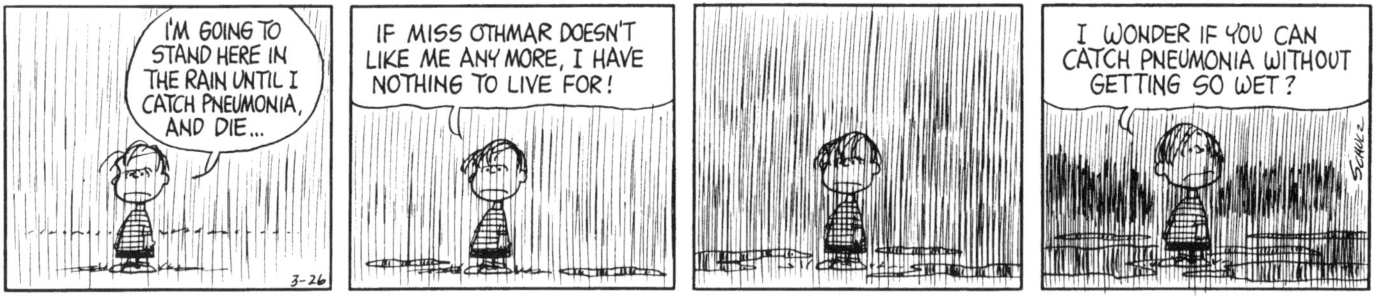
I'M GOING TO STAND HERE IN THE RAIN UNTIL I CATCH PNEUMONIA, AND DIE...
3-26
IF MISS OTHMAR DOESN'T LIKE ME ANY MORE, I HAVE NOTHING TO LIVE FOR!
I WONDER IF YOU CAN CATCH PNEUMONIA WITHOUT GETTING SO WET?
SCHULZ

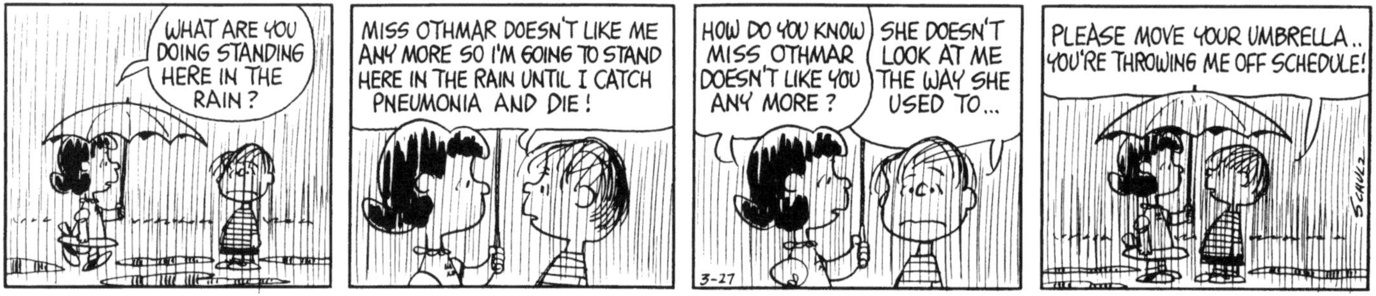
WHAT ARE YOU DOING STANDING HERE IN THE RAIN?
MISS OTHMAR DOESN'T LIKE ME ANY MORE SO I'M GOING TO STAND HERE IN THE RAIN UNTIL I CATCH PNEUMONIA AND DIE!
HOW DO YOU KNOW MISS OTHMAR DOESN'T LIKE YOU ANY MORE?
SHE DOESN'T LOOK AT ME THE WAY SHE USED TO...
3-27
PLEASE MOVE YOUR UMBRELLA.. YOU'RE THROWING ME OFF SCHEDULE!
SCHULZ

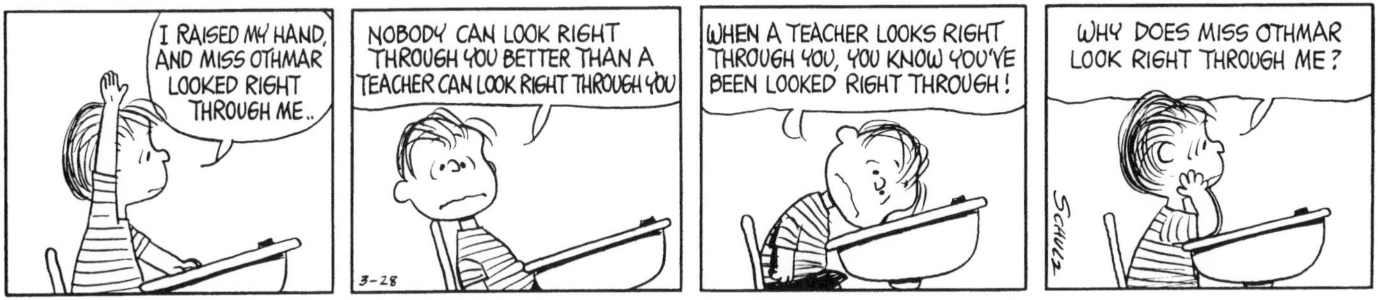
I RAISED MY HAND, AND MISS OTHMAR LOOKED RIGHT THROUGH ME..
NOBODY CAN LOOK RIGHT THROUGH YOU BETTER THAN A TEACHER CAN LOOK RIGHT THROUGH YOU
3-28
WHEN A TEACHER LOOKS RIGHT THROUGH YOU, YOU KNOW YOU'VE BEEN LOOKED RIGHT THROUGH!
WHY DOES MISS OTHMAR LOOK RIGHT THROUGH ME?
SCHULZ

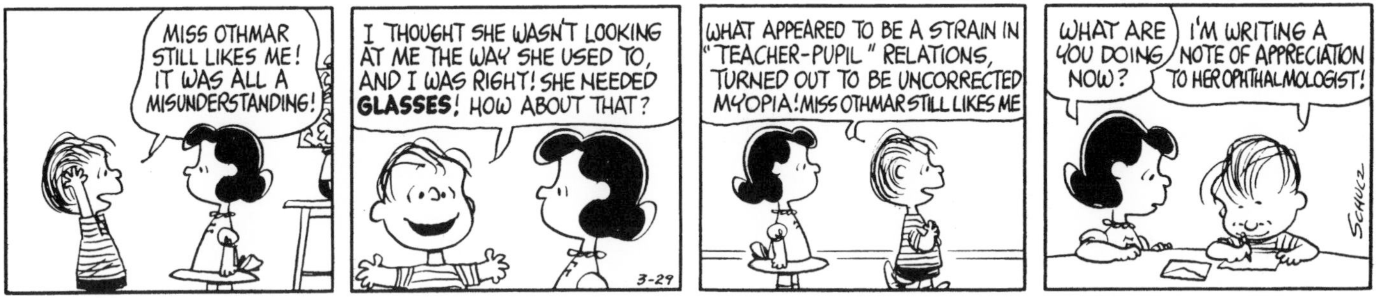
MISS OTHMAR STILL LIKES ME! IT WAS ALL A MISUNDERSTANDING!
I THOUGHT SHE WASN'T LOOKING AT ME THE WAY SHE USED TO, AND I WAS RIGHT! SHE NEEDED **GLASSES**! HOW ABOUT THAT?
3-29
WHAT APPEARED TO BE A STRAIN IN "TEACHER-PUPIL" RELATIONS, TURNED OUT TO BE UNCORRECTED MYOPIA! MISS OTHMAR STILL LIKES ME
WHAT ARE YOU DOING NOW?
I'M WRITING A NOTE OF APPRECIATION TO HER OPHTHALMOLOGIST!
SCHULZ

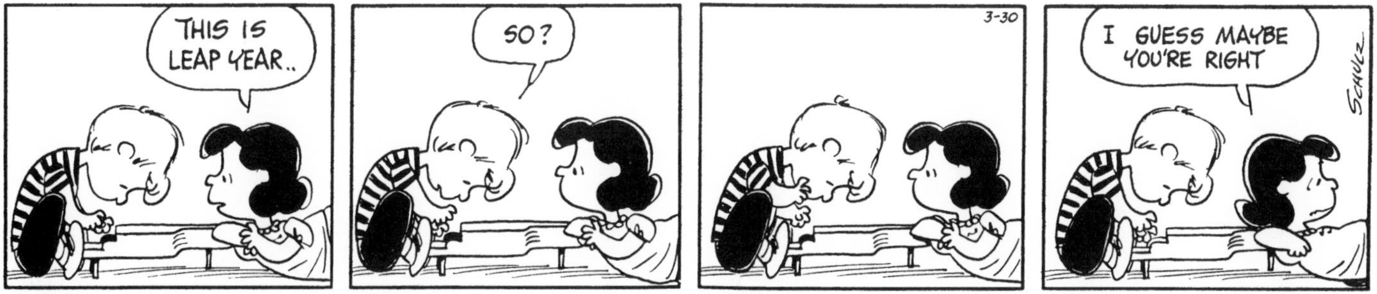
THIS IS LEAP YEAR..
SO?
3-30
I GUESS MAYBE YOU'RE RIGHT
SCHULZ

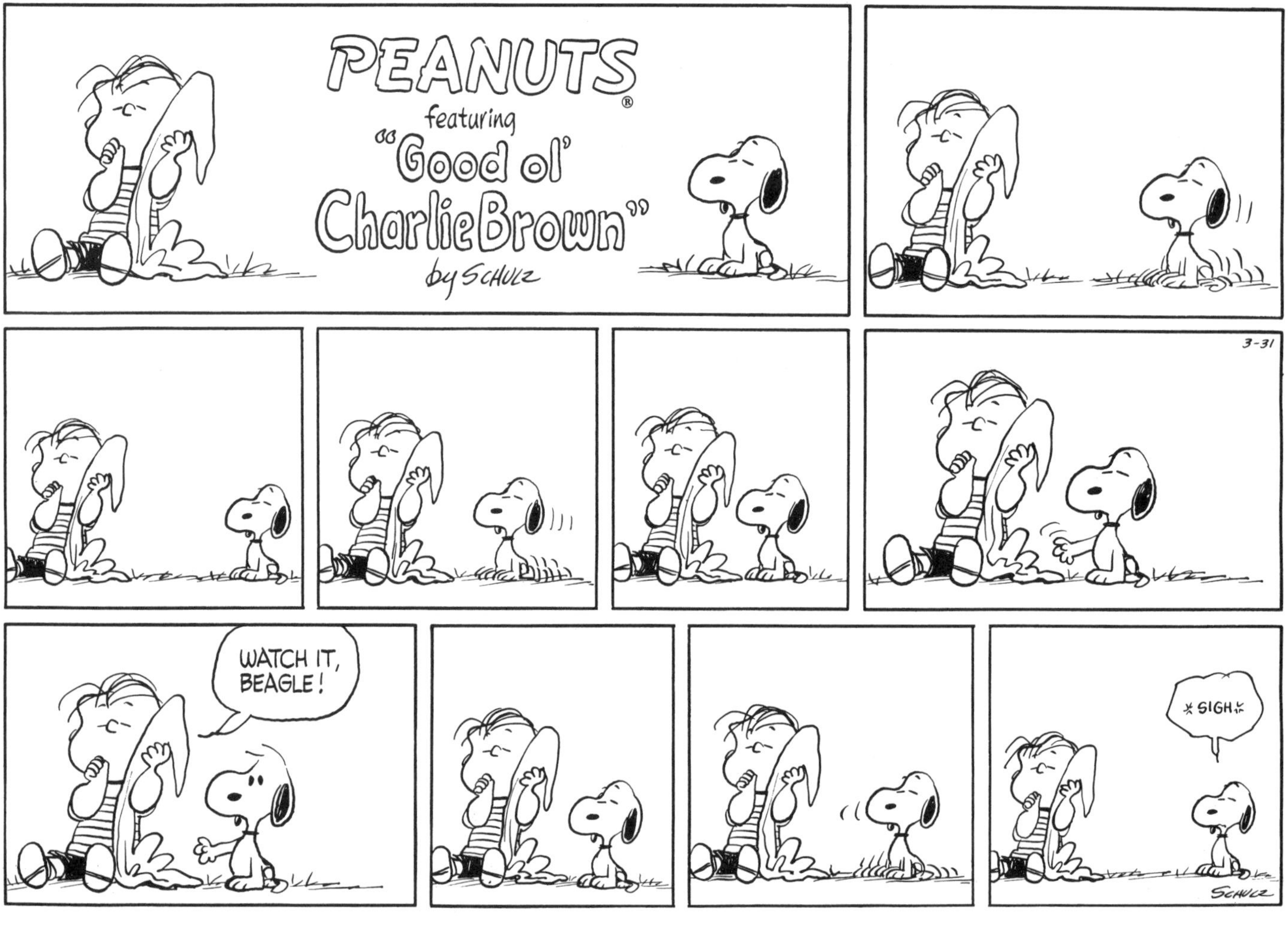
PEANUTS®
featuring
"Good ol' Charlie Brown"
by SCHULZ
3-31
WATCH IT, BEAGLE!
SIGH
SCHULZ

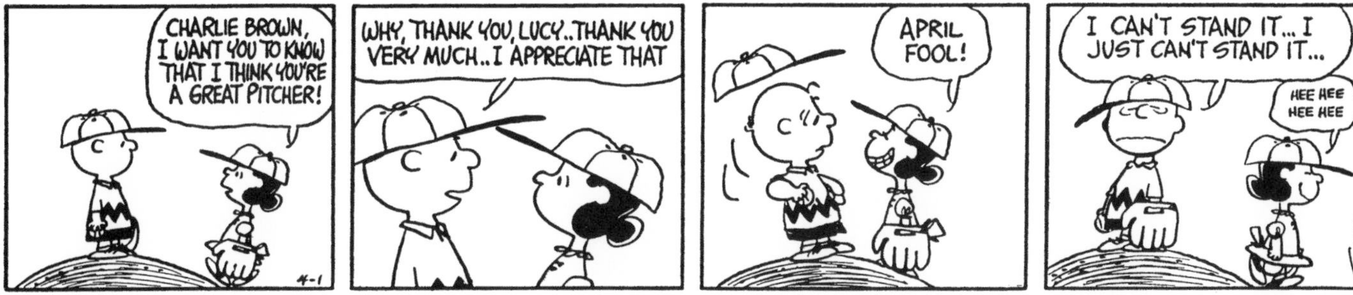
CHARLIE BROWN, I WANT YOU TO KNOW THAT I THINK YOU'RE A GREAT PITCHER!
WHY, THANK YOU, LUCY..THANK YOU VERY MUCH..I APPRECIATE THAT
APRIL FOOL!
I CAN'T STAND IT... I JUST CAN'T STAND IT...
HEE HEE HEE HEE

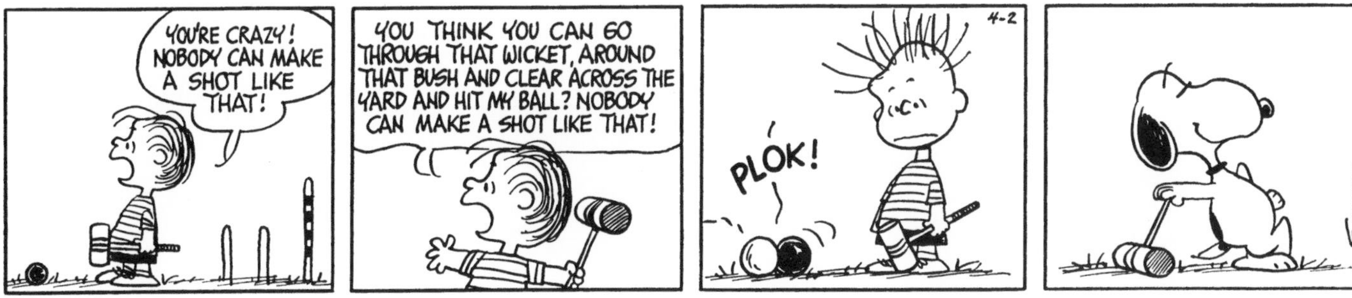
YOU'RE CRAZY! NOBODY CAN MAKE A SHOT LIKE THAT!
YOU THINK YOU CAN GO THROUGH THAT WICKET, AROUND THAT BUSH AND CLEAR ACROSS THE YARD AND HIT MY BALL? NOBODY CAN MAKE A SHOT LIKE THAT!
PLOK!

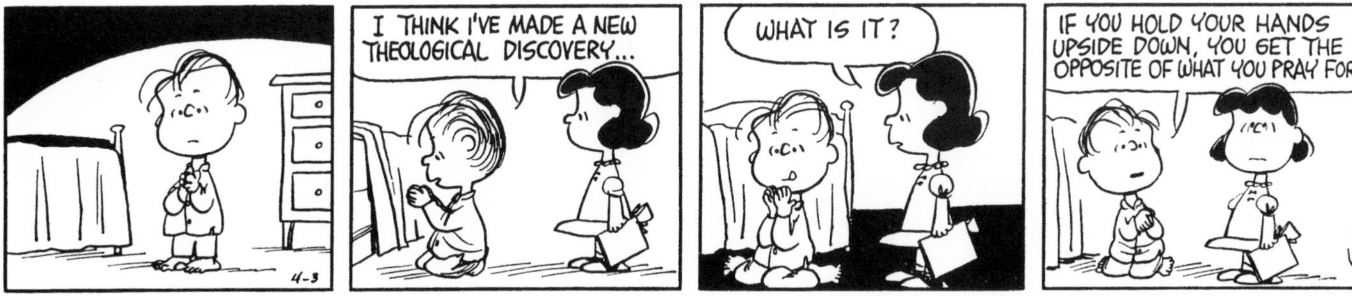
I THINK I'VE MADE A NEW THEOLOGICAL DISCOVERY...
WHAT IS IT?
IF YOU HOLD YOUR HANDS UPSIDE DOWN, YOU GET THE OPPOSITE OF WHAT YOU PRAY FOR!

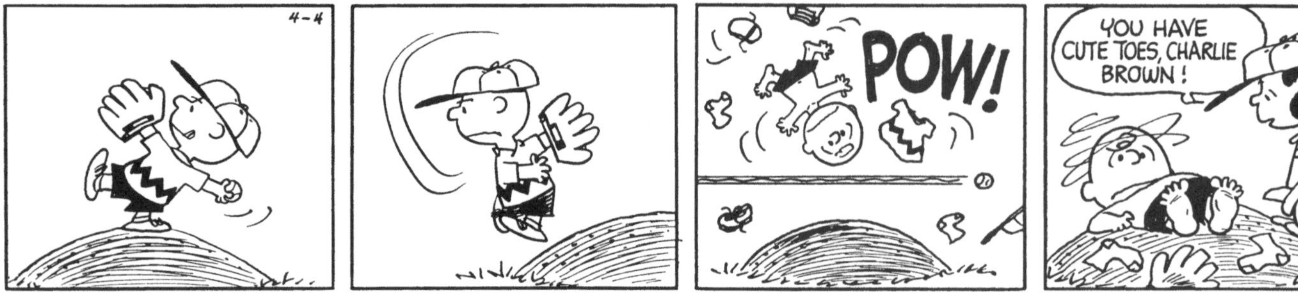
4-4
POW!
YOU HAVE CUTE TOES, CHARLIE BROWN!
SCHULZ

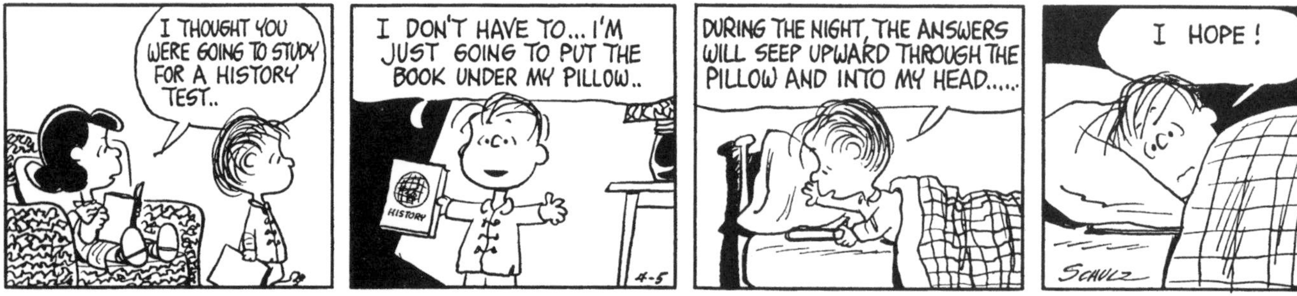
I THOUGHT YOU WERE GOING TO STUDY FOR A HISTORY TEST..
I DON'T HAVE TO... I'M JUST GOING TO PUT THE BOOK UNDER MY PILLOW..
HISTORY
4-5
DURING THE NIGHT, THE ANSWERS WILL SEEP UPWARD THROUGH THE PILLOW AND INTO MY HEAD.....
I HOPE!
SCHULZ

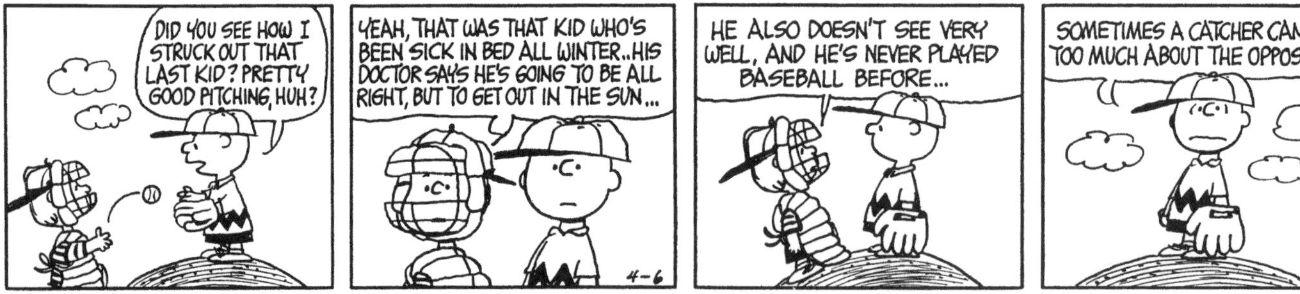
DID YOU SEE HOW I STRUCK OUT THAT LAST KID? PRETTY GOOD PITCHING, HUH?
YEAH, THAT WAS THAT KID WHO'S BEEN SICK IN BED ALL WINTER..HIS DOCTOR SAYS HE'S GOING TO BE ALL RIGHT, BUT TO GET OUT IN THE SUN...
4-6
HE ALSO DOESN'T SEE VERY WELL, AND HE'S NEVER PLAYED BASEBALL BEFORE...
SOMETIMES A CATCHER CAN KNOW TOO MUCH ABOUT THE OPPOSITION...
SCHULZ

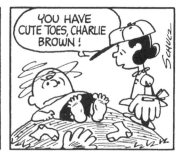

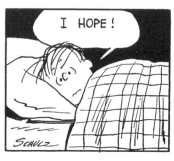

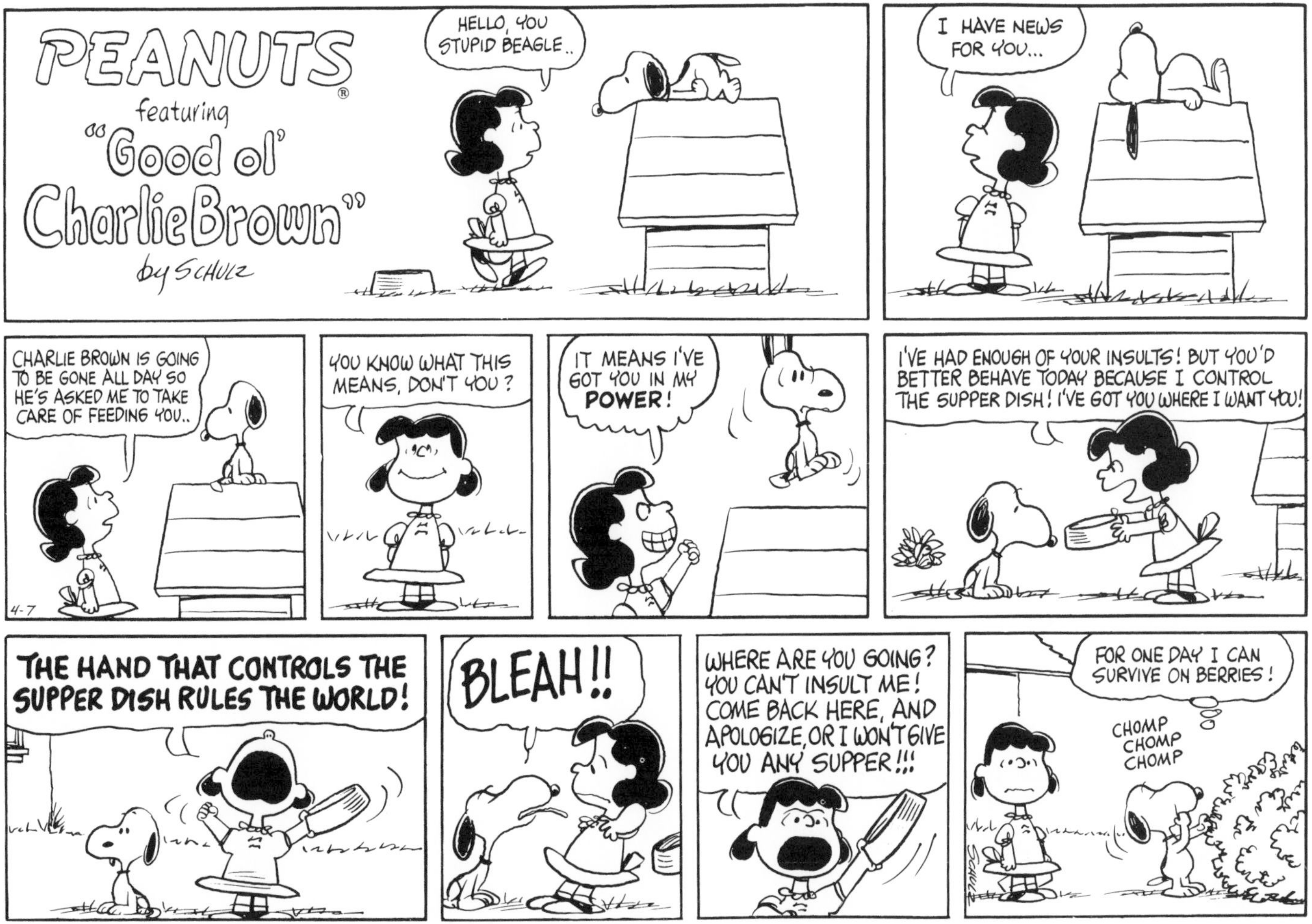
PEANUTS
featuring
"Good ol' CharlieBrown"
by SCHULZ
HELLO, YOU STUPID BEAGLE..
I HAVE NEWS FOR YOU...
CHARLIE BROWN IS GOING TO BE GONE ALL DAY SO HE'S ASKED ME TO TAKE CARE OF FEEDING YOU..
4-7
YOU KNOW WHAT THIS MEANS, DON'T YOU ?
IT MEANS I'VE GOT YOU IN MY POWER!
I'VE HAD ENOUGH OF YOUR INSULTS! BUT YOU'D BETTER BEHAVE TODAY BECAUSE I CONTROL THE SUPPER DISH! I'VE GOT YOU WHERE I WANT YOU!
THE HAND THAT CONTROLS THE SUPPER DISH RULES THE WORLD!
BLEAH!!
WHERE ARE YOU GOING? YOU CAN'T INSULT ME! COME BACK HERE, AND APOLOGIZE, OR I WON'T GIVE YOU ANY SUPPER!!!
SCHULZ
FOR ONE DAY I CAN SURVIVE ON BERRIES!
CHOMP CHOMP CHOMP

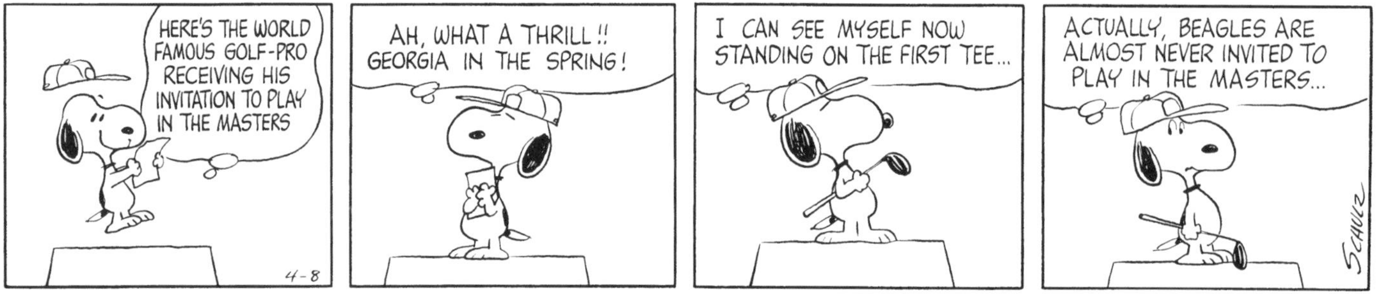
HERE'S THE WORLD FAMOUS GOLF-PRO RECEIVING HIS INVITATION TO PLAY IN THE MASTERS
4-8
AH, WHAT A THRILL!! GEORGIA IN THE SPRING!
I CAN SEE MYSELF NOW STANDING ON THE FIRST TEE...
ACTUALLY, BEAGLES ARE ALMOST NEVER INVITED TO PLAY IN THE MASTERS...
SCHULZ

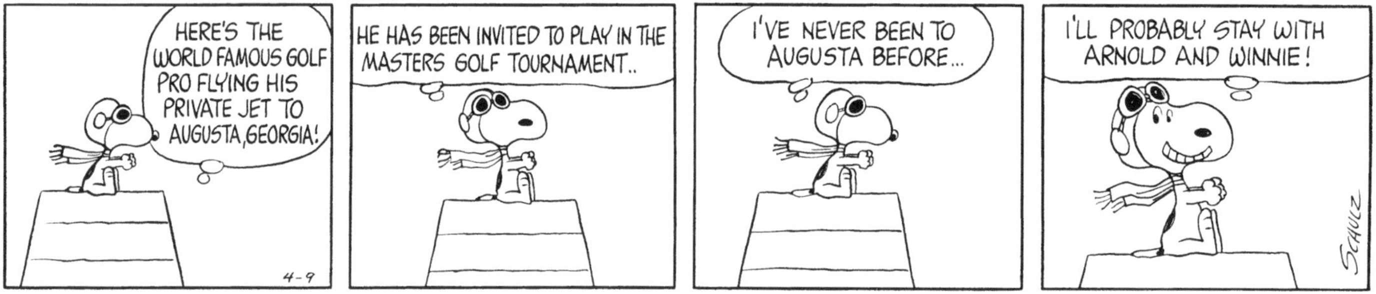
HERE'S THE WORLD FAMOUS GOLF PRO FLYING HIS PRIVATE JET TO AUGUSTA, GEORGIA!
4-9
HE HAS BEEN INVITED TO PLAY IN THE MASTERS GOLF TOURNAMENT..
I'VE NEVER BEEN TO AUGUSTA BEFORE...
I'LL PROBABLY STAY WITH ARNOLD AND WINNIE!
SCHULZ

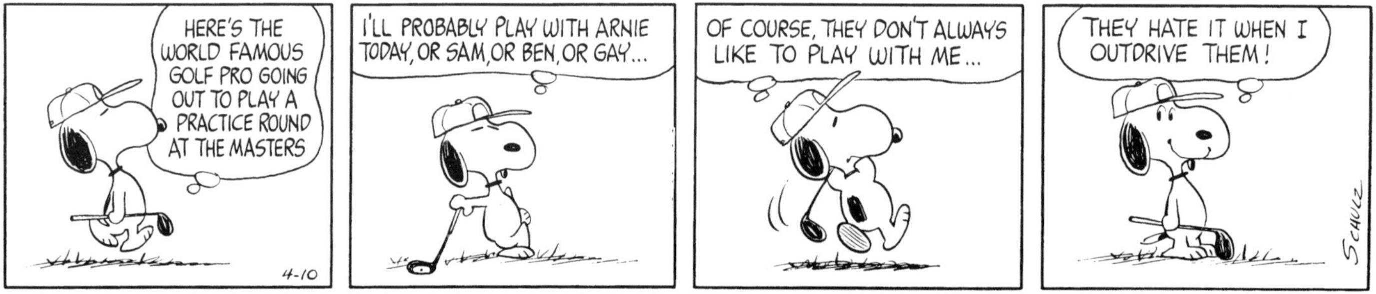
HERE'S THE WORLD FAMOUS GOLF PRO GOING OUT TO PLAY A PRACTICE ROUND AT THE MASTERS
4-10
I'LL PROBABLY PLAY WITH ARNIE TODAY, OR SAM, OR BEN, OR GAY...
OF COURSE, THEY DON'T ALWAYS LIKE TO PLAY WITH ME...
THEY HATE IT WHEN I OUTDRIVE THEM!
SCHULZ

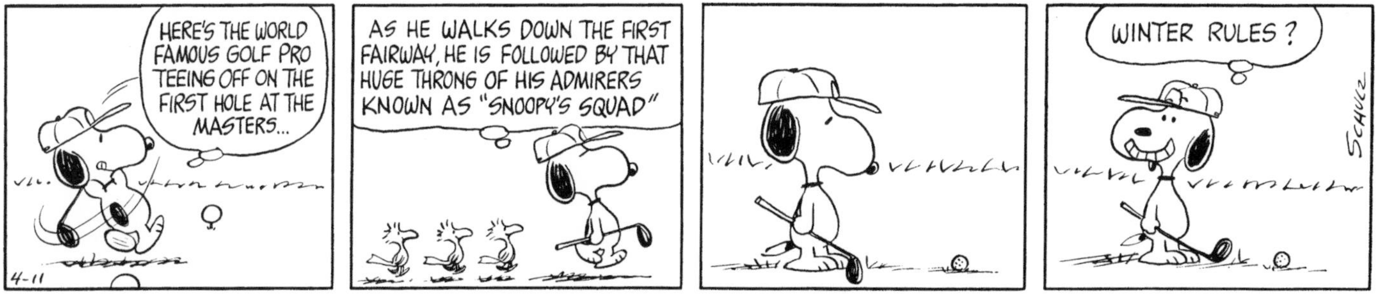
HERE'S THE WORLD FAMOUS GOLF PRO TEEING OFF ON THE FIRST HOLE AT THE MASTERS...
4-11
AS HE WALKS DOWN THE FIRST FAIRWAY, HE IS FOLLOWED BY THAT HUGE THRONG OF HIS ADMIRERS KNOWN AS "SNOOPY'S SQUAD"
WINTER RULES?
SCHULZ

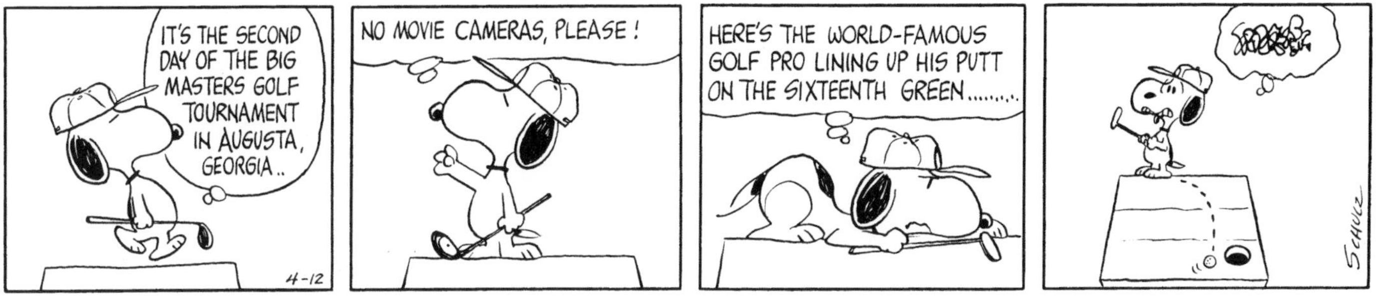
IT'S THE SECOND DAY OF THE BIG MASTERS GOLF TOURNAMENT IN AUGUSTA, GEORGIA..
4-12
NO MOVIE CAMERAS, PLEASE!
HERE'S THE WORLD-FAMOUS GOLF PRO LINING UP HIS PUTT ON THE SIXTEENTH GREEN........
SCHULZ

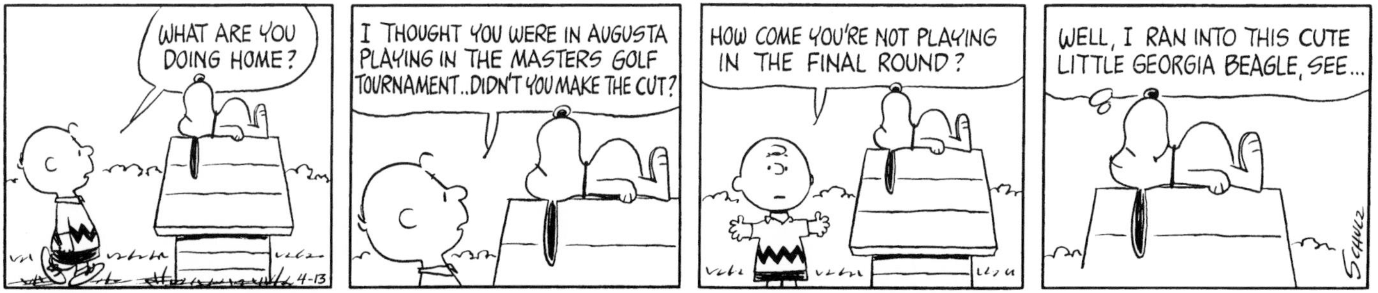
WHAT ARE YOU DOING HOME?
4-13
I THOUGHT YOU WERE IN AUGUSTA PLAYING IN THE MASTERS GOLF TOURNAMENT..DIDN'T YOU MAKE THE CUT?
HOW COME YOU'RE NOT PLAYING IN THE FINAL ROUND?
WELL, I RAN INTO THIS CUTE LITTLE GEORGIA BEAGLE, SEE...
SCHULZ

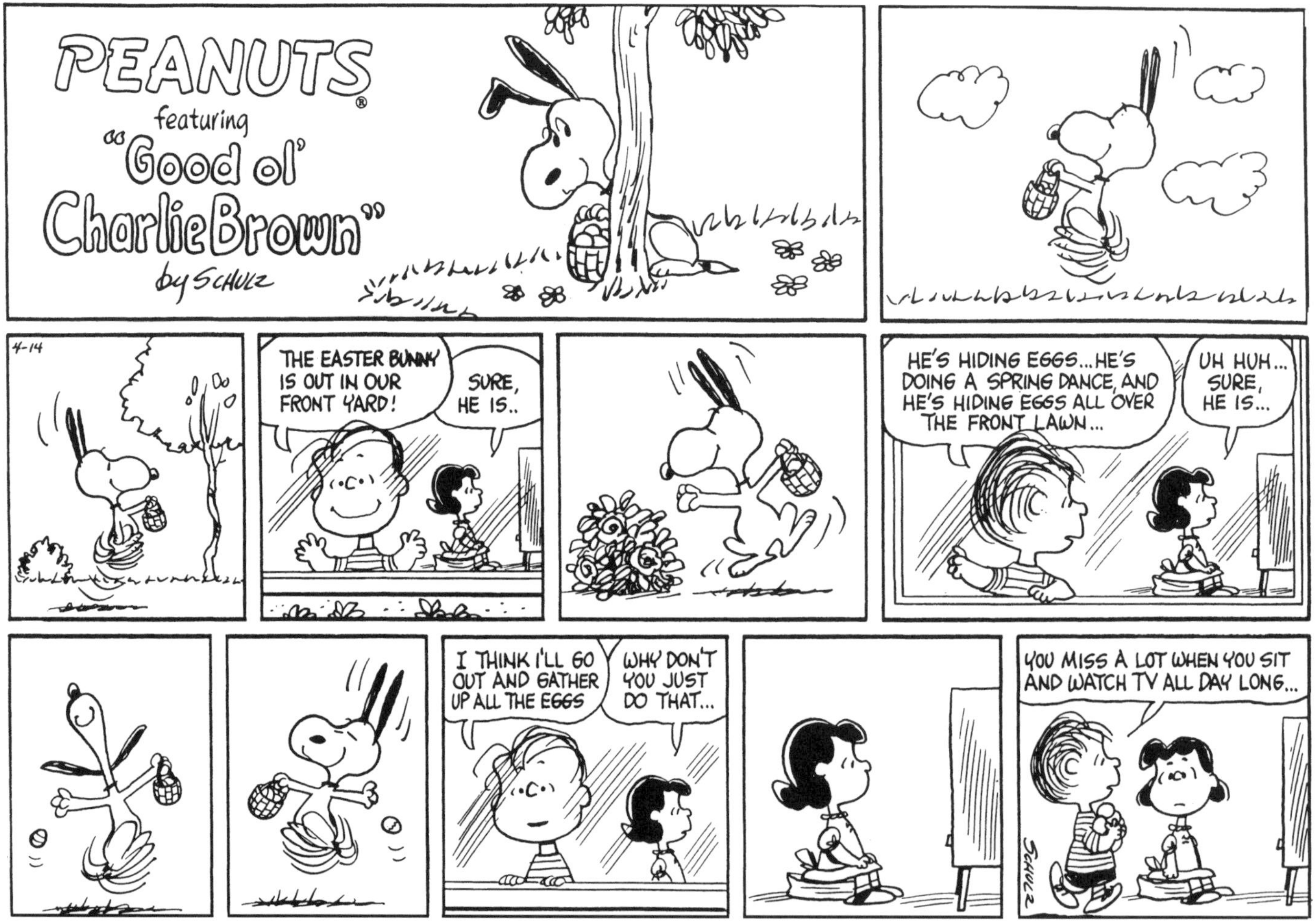
PEANUTS®
featuring "Good ol' Charlie Brown"
by SCHULZ
4-14
THE EASTER BUNNY IS OUT IN OUR FRONT YARD!
SURE, HE IS..
HE'S HIDING EGGS...HE'S DOING A SPRING DANCE, AND HE'S HIDING EGGS ALL OVER THE FRONT LAWN...
UH HUH... SURE, HE IS...
I THINK I'LL GO OUT AND GATHER UP ALL THE EGGS
WHY DON'T YOU JUST DO THAT...
YOU MISS A LOT WHEN YOU SIT AND WATCH TV ALL DAY LONG...
SCHULZ

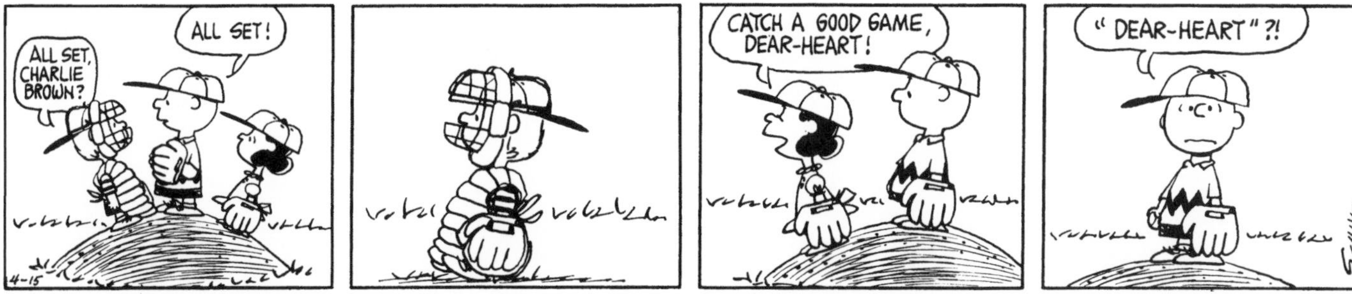
ALL SET, CHARLIE BROWN?
ALL SET!
4-15
CATCH A GOOD GAME, DEAR-HEART!
" DEAR-HEART " ?!
SCHULZ

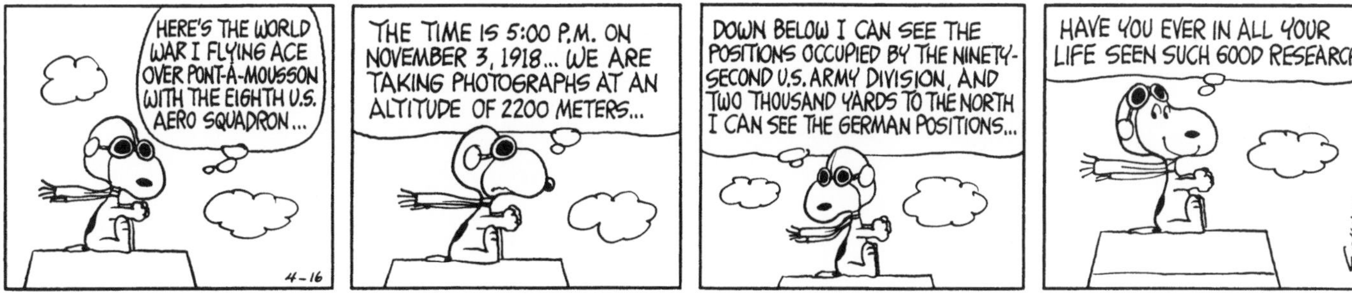
HERE'S THE WORLD WAR I FLYING ACE OVER PONT-A-MOUSSON WITH THE EIGHTH U.S. AERO SQUADRON...
4-16
THE TIME IS 5:00 P.M. ON NOVEMBER 3, 1918... WE ARE TAKING PHOTOGRAPHS AT AN ALTITUDE OF 2200 METERS...
DOWN BELOW I CAN SEE THE POSITIONS OCCUPIED BY THE NINETY-SECOND U.S. ARMY DIVISION, AND TWO THOUSAND YARDS TO THE NORTH I CAN SEE THE GERMAN POSITIONS...
HAVE YOU EVER IN ALL YOUR LIFE SEEN SUCH GOOD RESEARCH?
SCHULZ

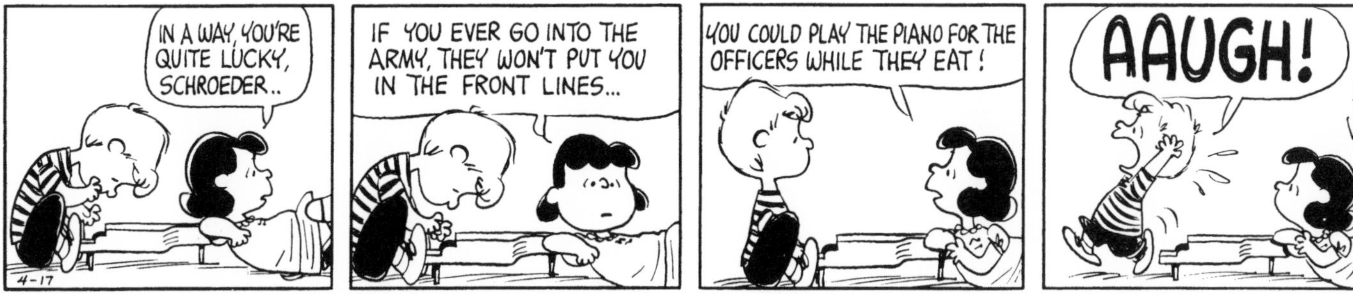
IN A WAY, YOU'RE QUITE LUCKY, SCHROEDER..
4-17
IF YOU EVER GO INTO THE ARMY, THEY WON'T PUT YOU IN THE FRONT LINES...
YOU COULD PLAY THE PIANO FOR THE OFFICERS WHILE THEY EAT!
AAUGH!
SCHULZ

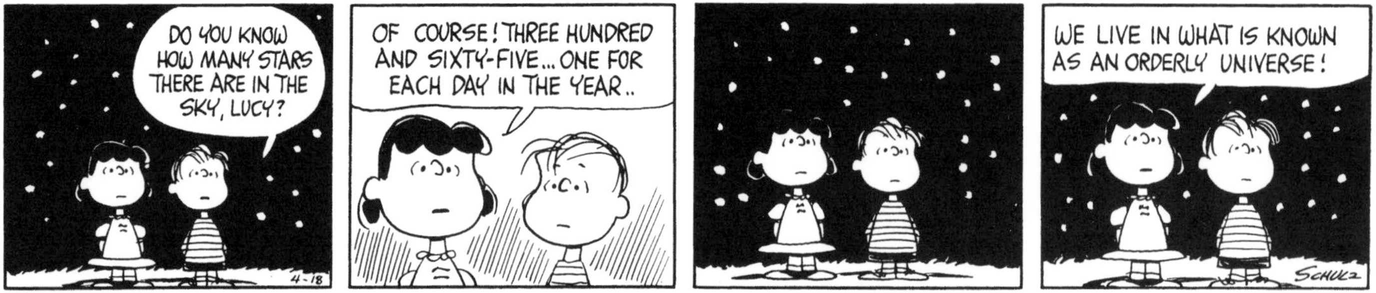
DO YOU KNOW HOW MANY STARS THERE ARE IN THE SKY, LUCY?
4-18
OF COURSE! THREE HUNDRED AND SIXTY-FIVE... ONE FOR EACH DAY IN THE YEAR..
WE LIVE IN WHAT IS KNOWN AS AN ORDERLY UNIVERSE!
SCHULZ

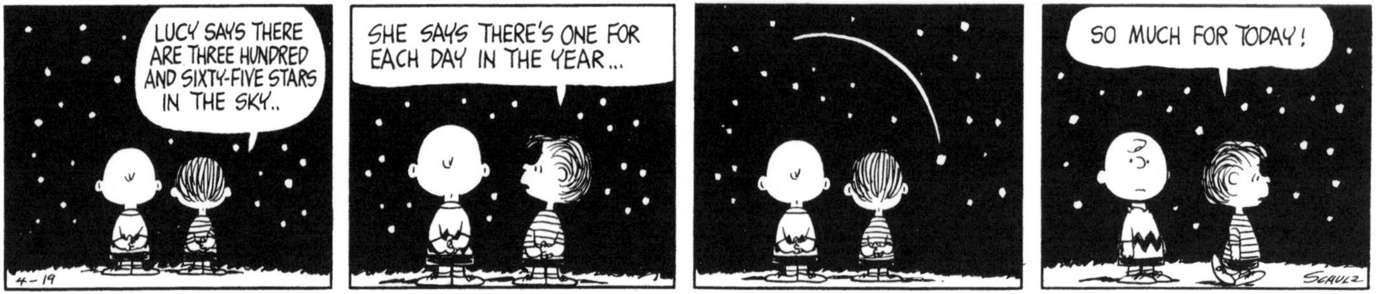
LUCY SAYS THERE ARE THREE HUNDRED AND SIXTY-FIVE STARS IN THE SKY..
4-19
SHE SAYS THERE'S ONE FOR EACH DAY IN THE YEAR...
SO MUCH FOR TODAY!
SCHULZ

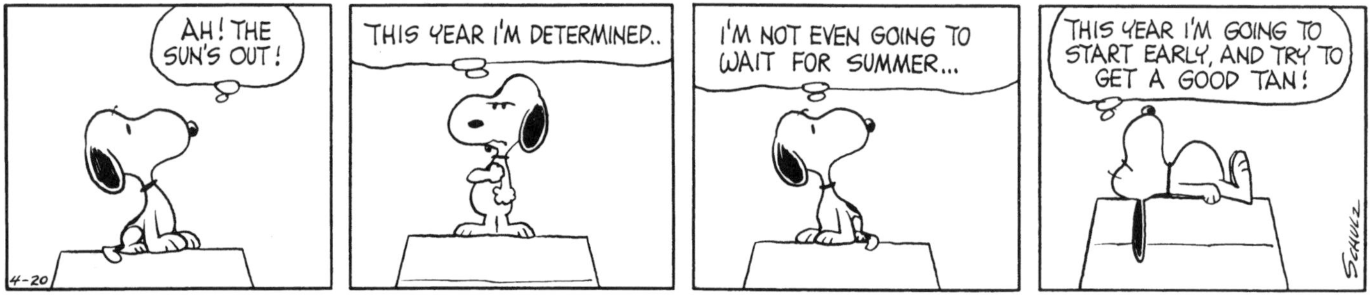
AH! THE SUN'S OUT!
4-20
THIS YEAR I'M DETERMINED..
I'M NOT EVEN GOING TO WAIT FOR SUMMER...
THIS YEAR I'M GOING TO START EARLY, AND TRY TO GET A GOOD TAN!
SCHULZ

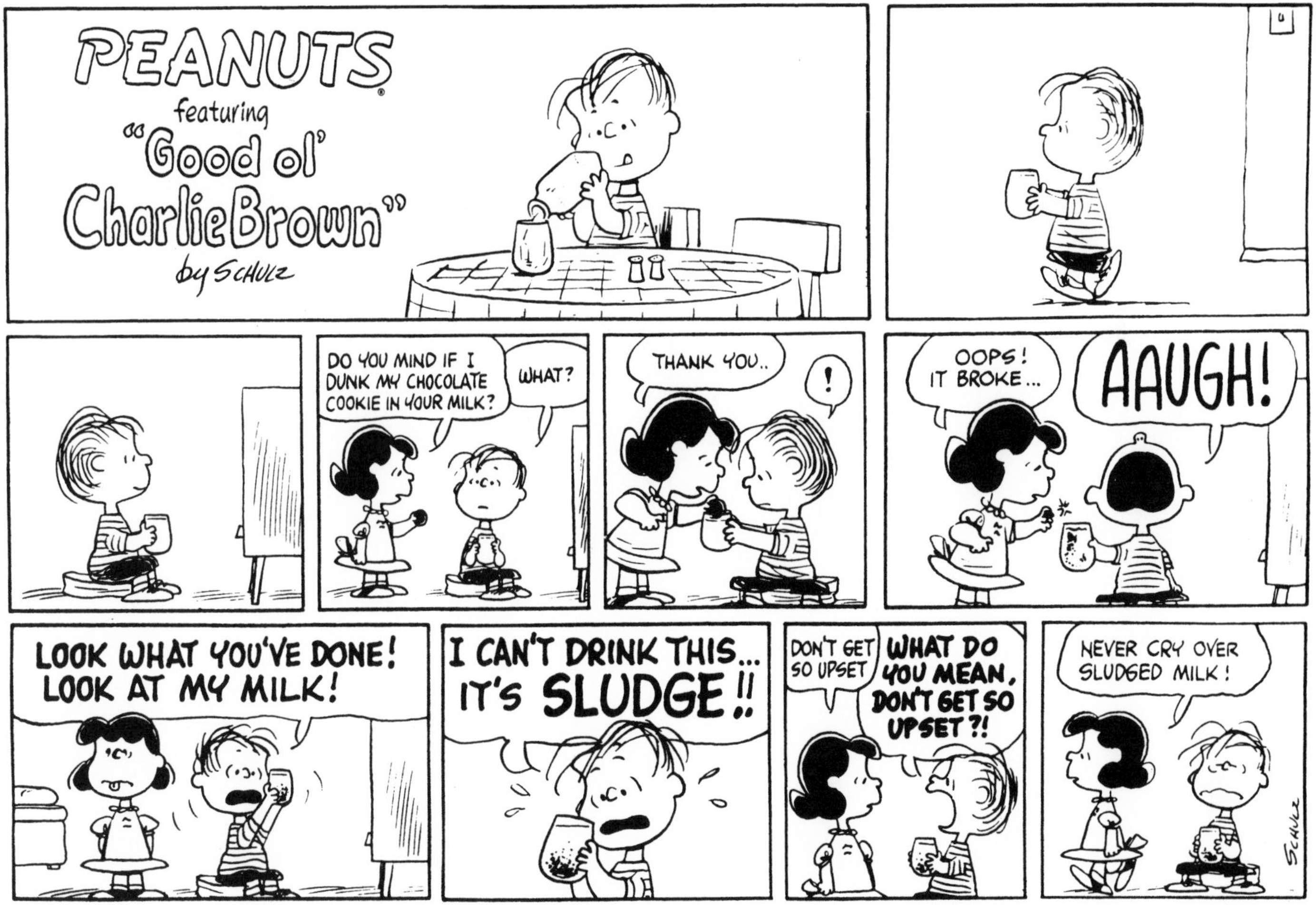
PEANUTS
featuring
"Good ol' Charlie Brown"
by SCHULZ
DO YOU MIND IF I DUNK MY CHOCOLATE COOKIE IN YOUR MILK?
WHAT?
THANK YOU..
!
OOPS! IT BROKE...
AAUGH!
LOOK WHAT YOU'VE DONE! LOOK AT MY MILK!
I CAN'T DRINK THIS... IT'S SLUDGE!!
DON'T GET SO UPSET
WHAT DO YOU MEAN, DON'T GET SO UPSET?!
NEVER CRY OVER SLUDGED MILK!
SCHULZ

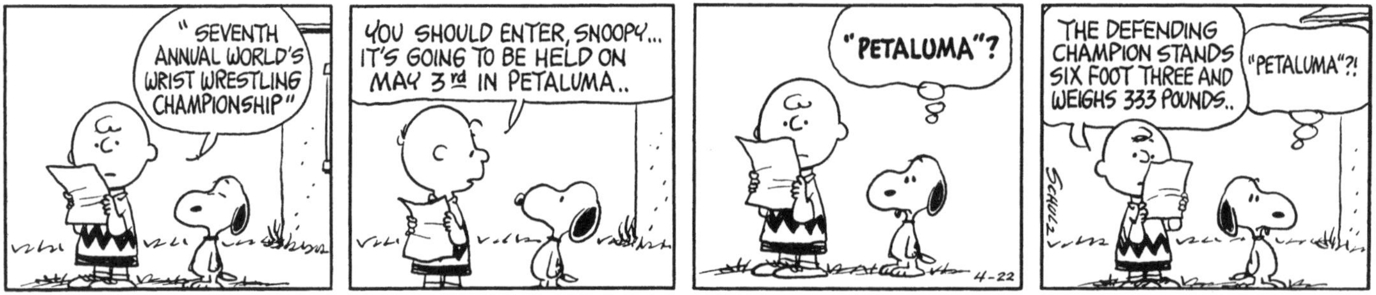
" SEVENTH ANNUAL WORLD'S WRIST WRESTLING CHAMPIONSHIP"
YOU SHOULD ENTER, SNOOPY... IT'S GOING TO BE HELD ON MAY 3rd IN PETALUMA..
"PETALUMA"?
4-22
THE DEFENDING CHAMPION STANDS SIX FOOT THREE AND WEIGHS 333 POUNDS..
"PETALUMA"?!
SCHULZ

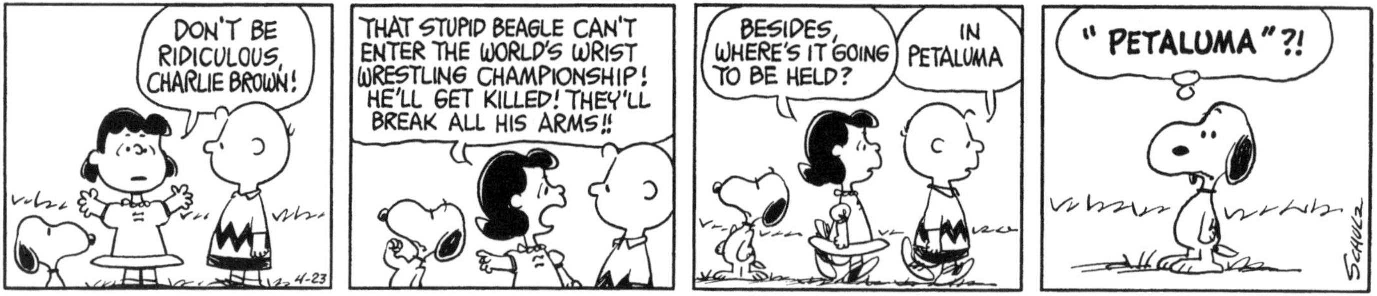
DON'T BE RIDICULOUS, CHARLIE BROWN!
4-23
THAT STUPID BEAGLE CAN'T ENTER THE WORLD'S WRIST WRESTLING CHAMPIONSHIP! HE'LL GET KILLED! THEY'LL BREAK ALL HIS ARMS!!
BESIDES, WHERE'S IT GOING TO BE HELD?
IN PETALUMA
" PETALUMA "?!
SCHULZ

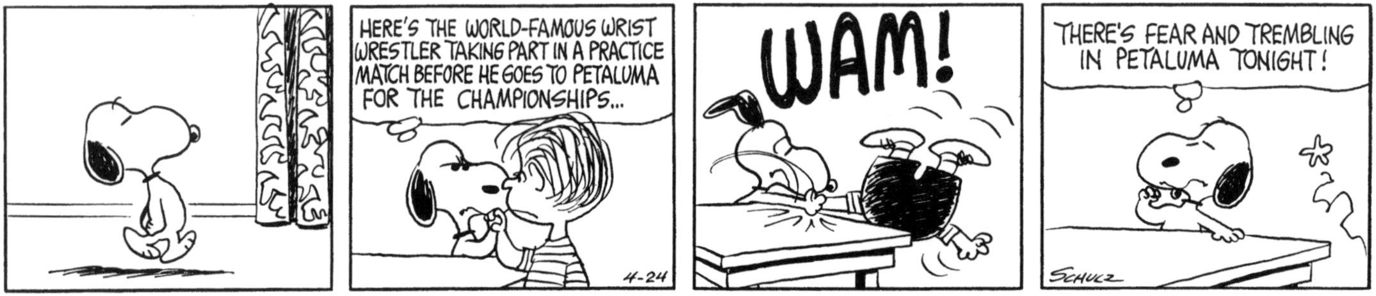
HERE'S THE WORLD-FAMOUS WRIST WRESTLER TAKING PART IN A PRACTICE MATCH BEFORE HE GOES TO PETALUMA FOR THE CHAMPIONSHIPS...
4-24
WAM!
THERE'S FEAR AND TREMBLING IN PETALUMA TONIGHT!
SCHULZ

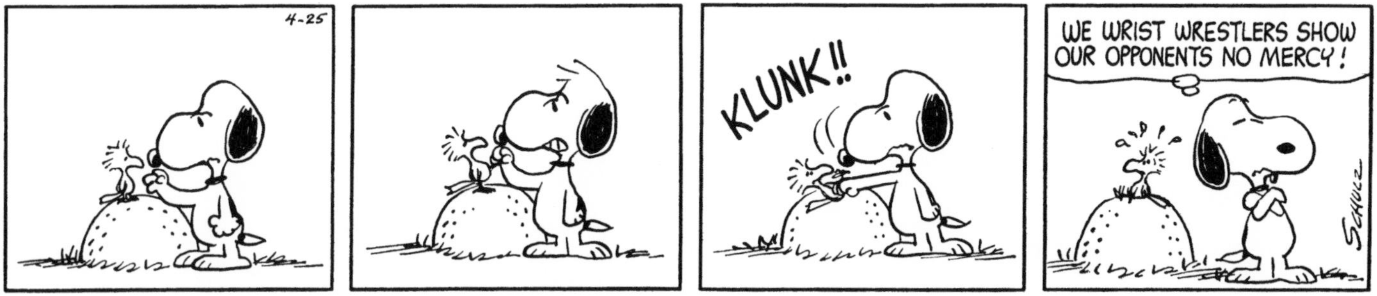
4-25
KLUNK!!
WE WRIST WRESTLERS SHOW OUR OPPONENTS NO MERCY!
SCHULZ

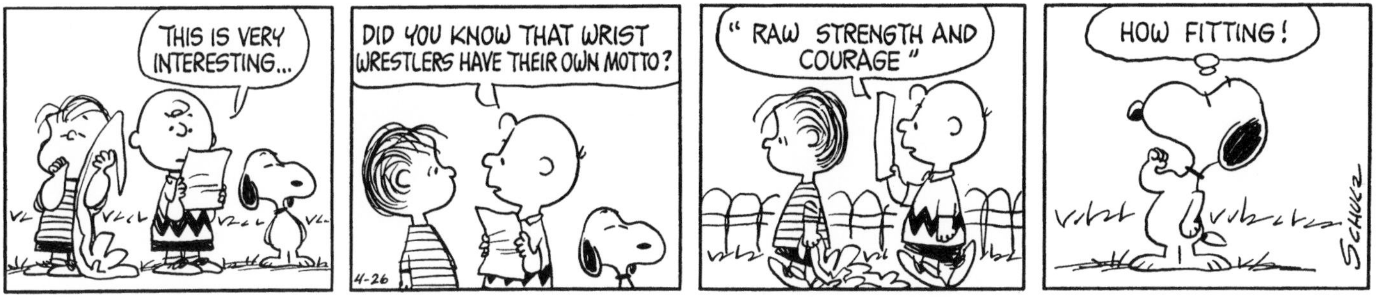
THIS IS VERY INTERESTING...
DID YOU KNOW THAT WRIST WRESTLERS HAVE THEIR OWN MOTTO?
4-26
" RAW STRENGTH AND COURAGE "
HOW FITTING!
SCHULZ

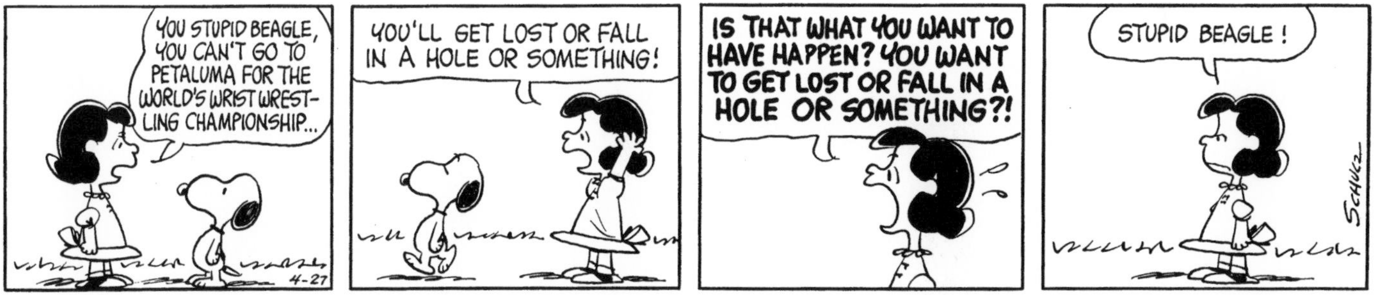
YOU STUPID BEAGLE, YOU CAN'T GO TO PETALUMA FOR THE WORLD'S WRIST WRESTLING CHAMPIONSHIP...
4-27
YOU'LL GET LOST OR FALL IN A HOLE OR SOMETHING!
IS THAT WHAT YOU WANT TO HAVE HAPPEN? YOU WANT TO GET LOST OR FALL IN A HOLE OR SOMETHING?!
STUPID BEAGLE!
SCHULZ

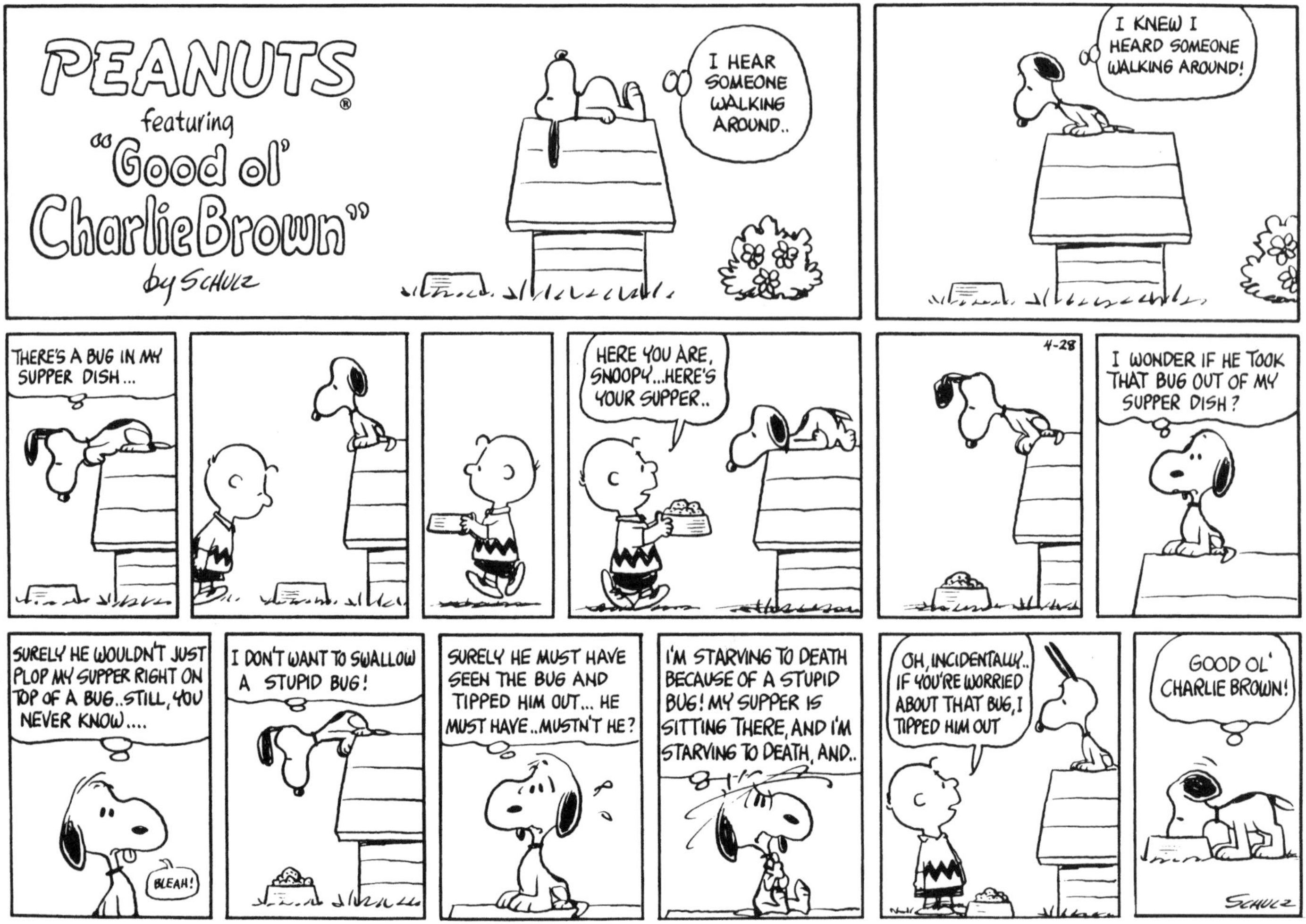
PEANUTS®
featuring "Good ol' Charlie Brown"
by SCHULZ
I HEAR SOMEONE WALKING AROUND..
I KNEW I HEARD SOMEONE WALKING AROUND!
THERE'S A BUG IN MY SUPPER DISH...
HERE YOU ARE, SNOOPY...HERE'S YOUR SUPPER..
4-28
I WONDER IF HE TOOK THAT BUG OUT OF MY SUPPER DISH?
SURELY HE WOULDN'T JUST PLOP MY SUPPER RIGHT ON TOP OF A BUG..STILL, YOU NEVER KNOW....
BLEAH!
I DON'T WANT TO SWALLOW A STUPID BUG!
SURELY HE MUST HAVE SEEN THE BUG AND TIPPED HIM OUT... HE MUST HAVE..MUSTN'T HE?
I'M STARVING TO DEATH BECAUSE OF A STUPID BUG! MY SUPPER IS SITTING THERE, AND I'M STARVING TO DEATH, AND..
OH, INCIDENTALLY.. IF YOU'RE WORRIED ABOUT THAT BUG, I TIPPED HIM OUT
GOOD OL' CHARLIE BROWN!
SCHULZ

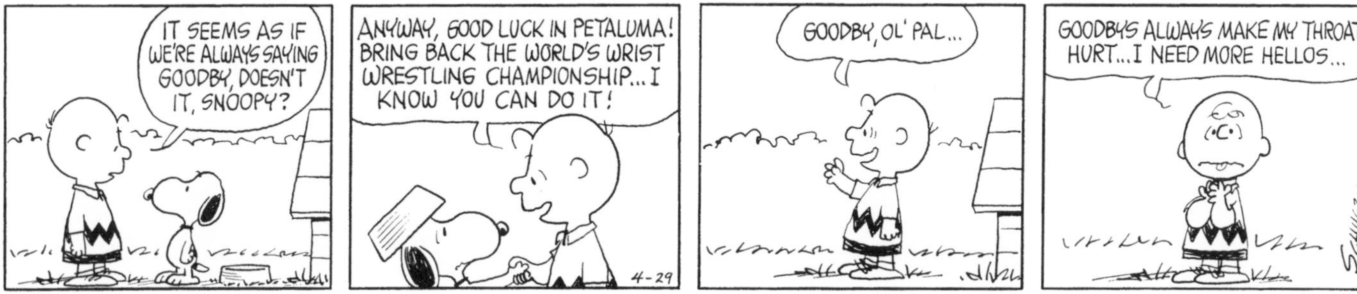
IT SEEMS AS IF WE'RE ALWAYS SAYING GOODBY, DOESN'T IT, SNOOPY?
ANYWAY, GOOD LUCK IN PETALUMA! BRING BACK THE WORLD'S WRIST WRESTLING CHAMPIONSHIP... I KNOW YOU CAN DO IT!
4-29
GOODBY, OL' PAL...
GOODBYS ALWAYS MAKE MY THROAT HURT... I NEED MORE HELLOS...
SCHULZ

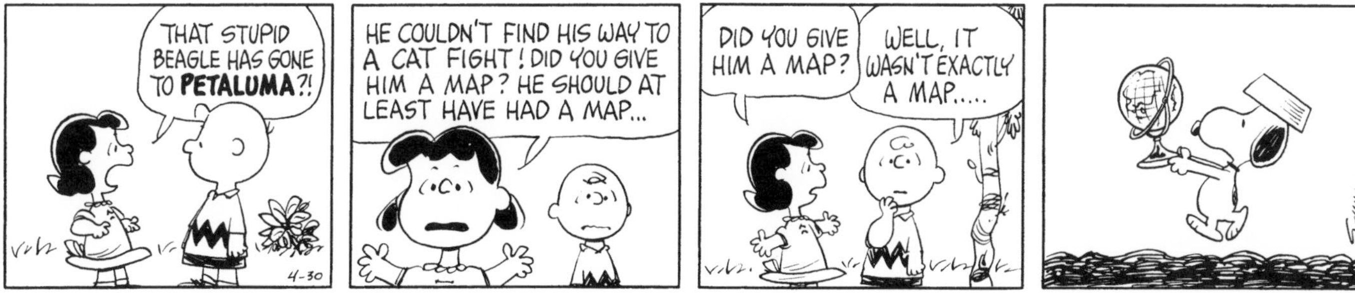
THAT STUPID BEAGLE HAS GONE TO **PETALUMA**?!
4-30
HE COULDN'T FIND HIS WAY TO A CAT FIGHT! DID YOU GIVE HIM A MAP? HE SHOULD AT LEAST HAVE HAD A MAP...
DID YOU GIVE HIM A MAP?
WELL, IT WASN'T EXACTLY A MAP.....
SCHULZ

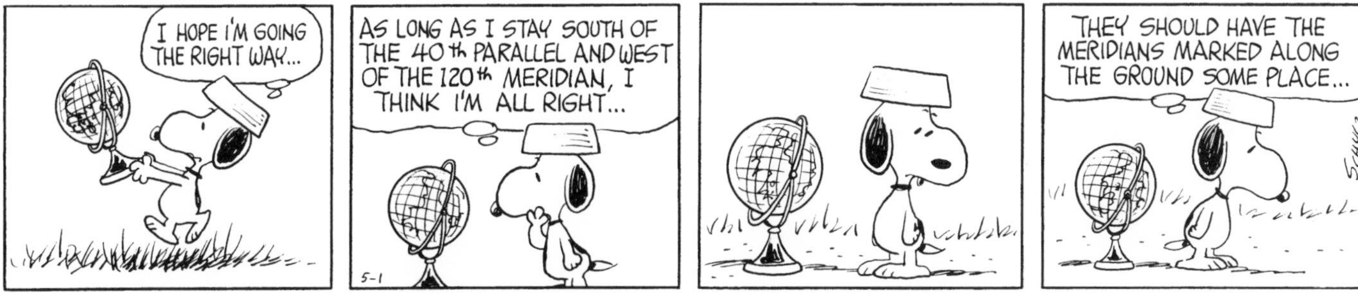
I HOPE I'M GOING THE RIGHT WAY...
AS LONG AS I STAY SOUTH OF THE 40th PARALLEL AND WEST OF THE 120th MERIDIAN, I THINK I'M ALL RIGHT...
5-1
THEY SHOULD HAVE THE MERIDIANS MARKED ALONG THE GROUND SOME PLACE...
SCHULZ

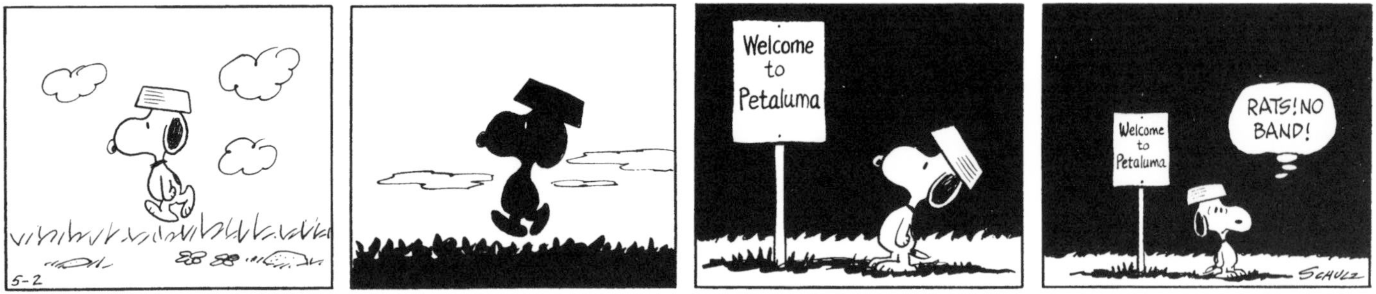
5-2
Welcome to Petaluma
Welcome to Petaluma
RATS! NO BAND!
SCHULZ

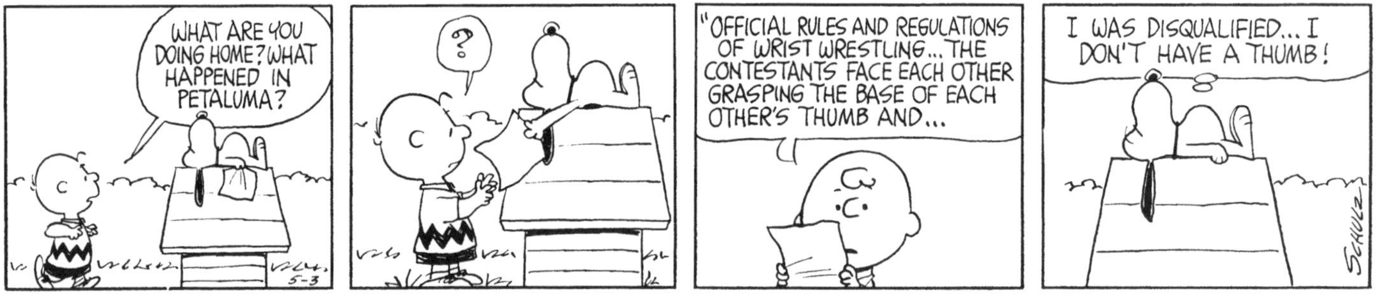
WHAT ARE YOU DOING HOME? WHAT HAPPENED IN PETALUMA?
5-3
?
"OFFICIAL RULES AND REGULATIONS OF WRIST WRESTLING... THE CONTESTANTS FACE EACH OTHER GRASPING THE BASE OF EACH OTHER'S THUMB AND...
I WAS DISQUALIFIED... I DON'T HAVE A THUMB!
SCHULZ

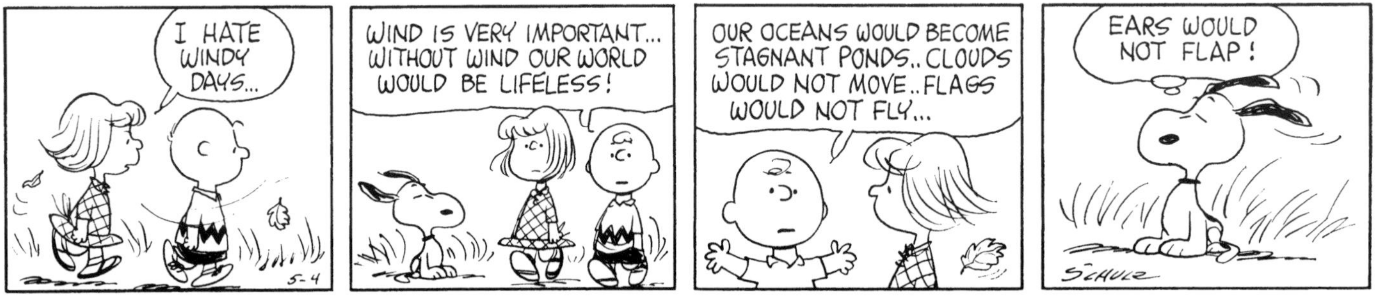
I HATE WINDY DAYS...
5-4
WIND IS VERY IMPORTANT... WITHOUT WIND OUR WORLD WOULD BE LIFELESS!
OUR OCEANS WOULD BECOME STAGNANT PONDS.. CLOUDS WOULD NOT MOVE.. FLAGS WOULD NOT FLY...
EARS WOULD NOT FLAP!
SCHULZ

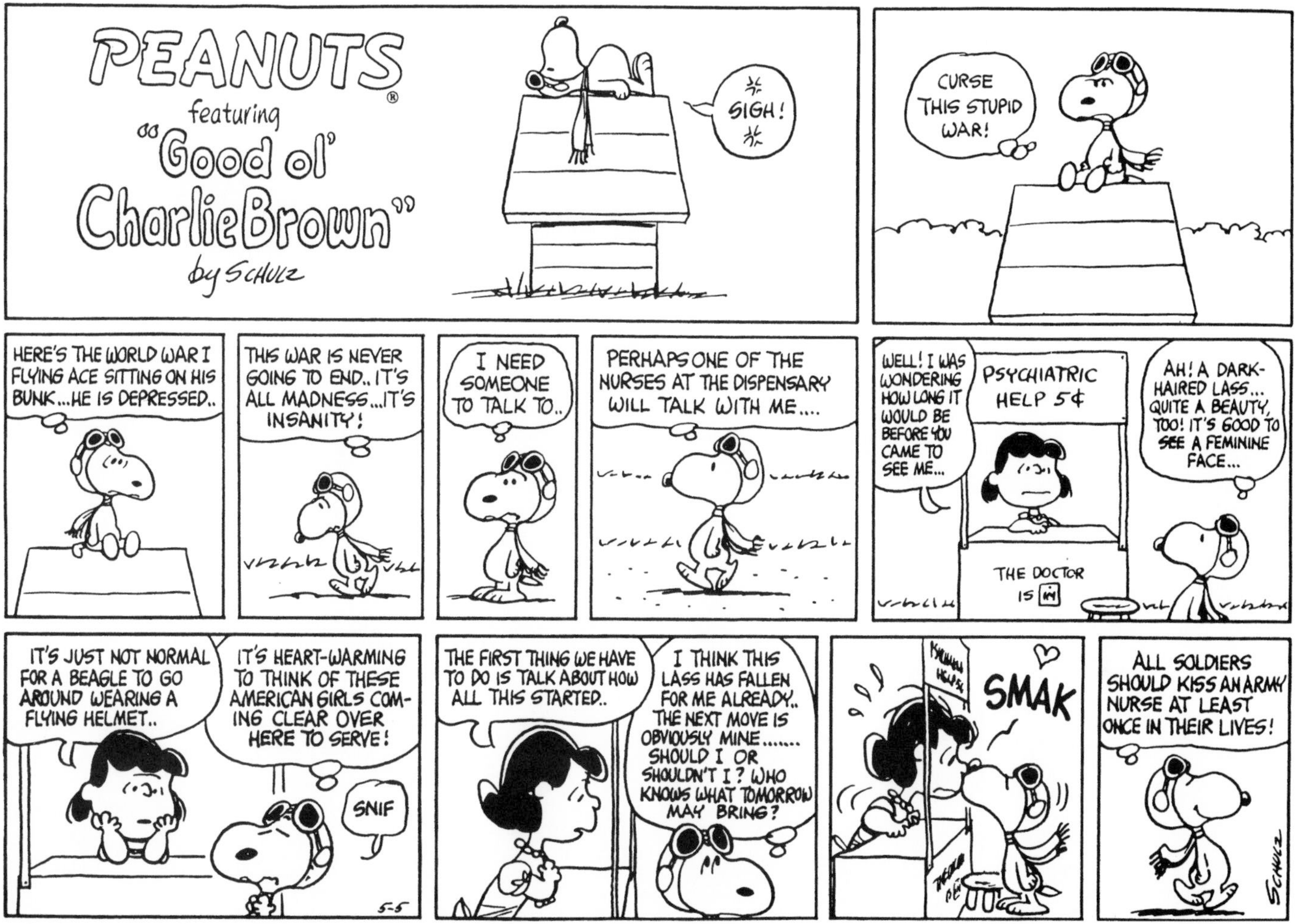
PEANUTS®
featuring "Good ol' Charlie Brown"
by SCHULZ
SIGH!
CURSE THIS STUPID WAR!
HERE'S THE WORLD WAR I FLYING ACE SITTING ON HIS BUNK...HE IS DEPRESSED..
THIS WAR IS NEVER GOING TO END.. IT'S ALL MADNESS...IT'S INSANITY!
I NEED SOMEONE TO TALK TO..
PERHAPS ONE OF THE NURSES AT THE DISPENSARY WILL TALK WITH ME....
WELL! I WAS WONDERING HOW LONG IT WOULD BE BEFORE YOU CAME TO SEE ME...
PSYCHIATRIC HELP 5¢
THE DOCTOR IS IN
AH! A DARK-HAIRED LASS... QUITE A BEAUTY, TOO! IT'S GOOD TO SEE A FEMININE FACE...
IT'S JUST NOT NORMAL FOR A BEAGLE TO GO AROUND WEARING A FLYING HELMET..
IT'S HEART-WARMING TO THINK OF THESE AMERICAN GIRLS COMING CLEAR OVER HERE TO SERVE!
SNIF
5-5
THE FIRST THING WE HAVE TO DO IS TALK ABOUT HOW ALL THIS STARTED..
I THINK THIS LASS HAS FALLEN FOR ME ALREADY.. THE NEXT MOVE IS OBVIOUSLY MINE....... SHOULD I OR SHOULDN'T I? WHO KNOWS WHAT TOMORROW MAY BRING?
SMAK
ALL SOLDIERS SHOULD KISS AN ARMY NURSE AT LEAST ONCE IN THEIR LIVES!
SCHULZ

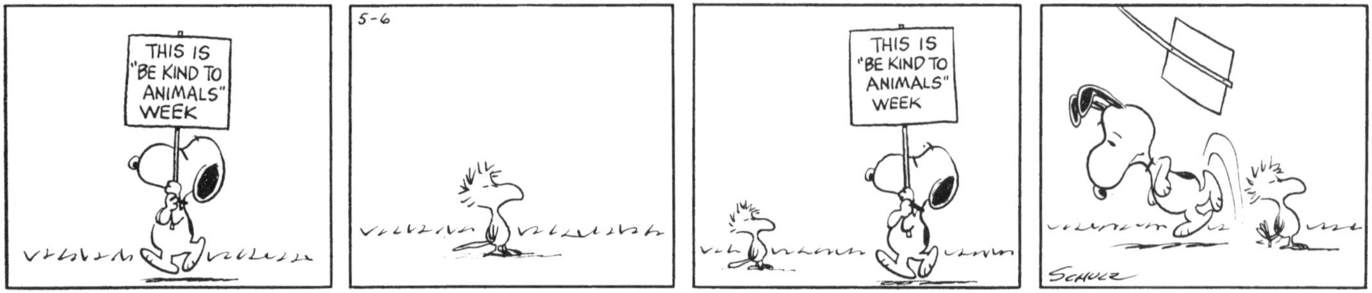
THIS IS "BE KIND TO ANIMALS" WEEK
5-6
THIS IS "BE KIND TO ANIMALS" WEEK
SCHULZ

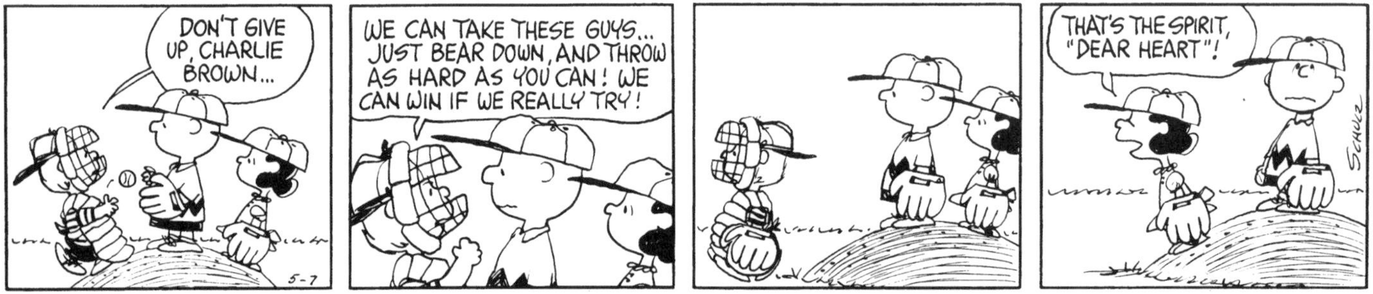
DON'T GIVE UP, CHARLIE BROWN...
5-7
WE CAN TAKE THESE GUYS... JUST BEAR DOWN, AND THROW AS HARD AS YOU CAN! WE CAN WIN IF WE REALLY TRY!
THAT'S THE SPIRIT, "DEAR HEART"!
SCHULZ

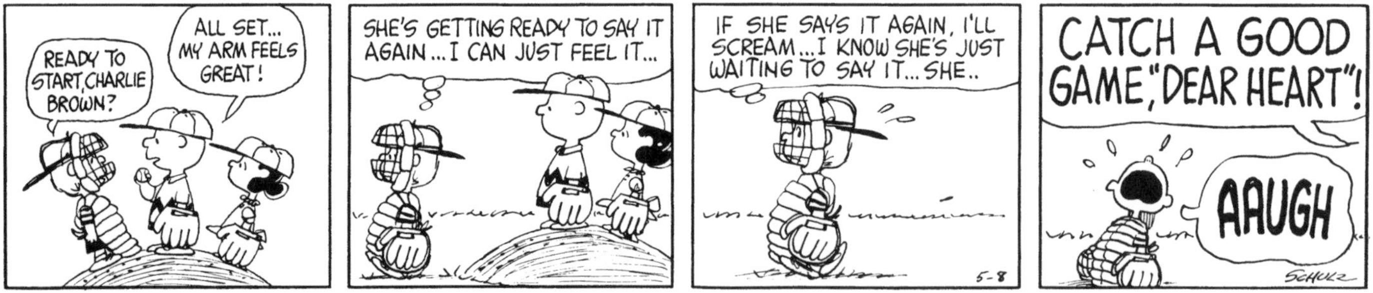
READY TO START, CHARLIE BROWN?
ALL SET... MY ARM FEELS GREAT!
SHE'S GETTING READY TO SAY IT AGAIN... I CAN JUST FEEL IT...
IF SHE SAYS IT AGAIN, I'LL SCREAM... I KNOW SHE'S JUST WAITING TO SAY IT... SHE..
5-8
CATCH A GOOD GAME, "DEAR HEART"!
AAUGH
SCHULZ

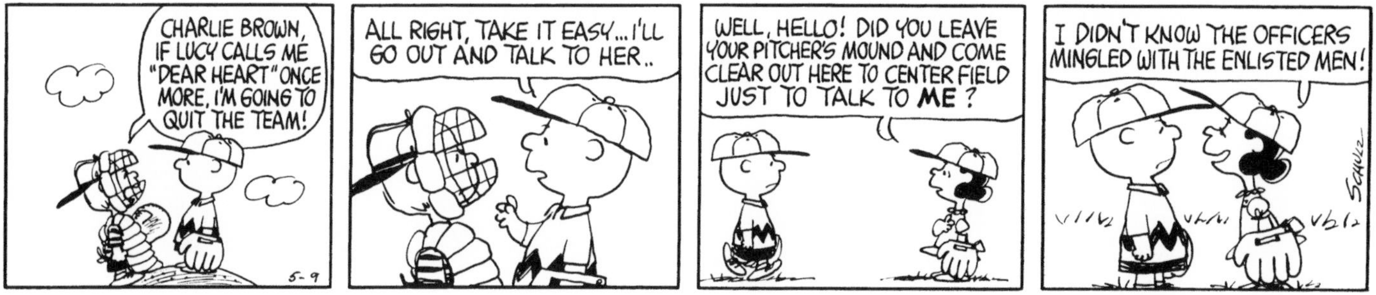
CHARLIE BROWN, IF LUCY CALLS ME "DEAR HEART" ONCE MORE, I'M GOING TO QUIT THE TEAM!
ALL RIGHT, TAKE IT EASY... I'LL GO OUT AND TALK TO HER..
WELL, HELLO! DID YOU LEAVE YOUR PITCHER'S MOUND AND COME CLEAR OUT HERE TO CENTER FIELD JUST TO TALK TO ME ?
I DIDN'T KNOW THE OFFICERS MINGLED WITH THE ENLISTED MEN!

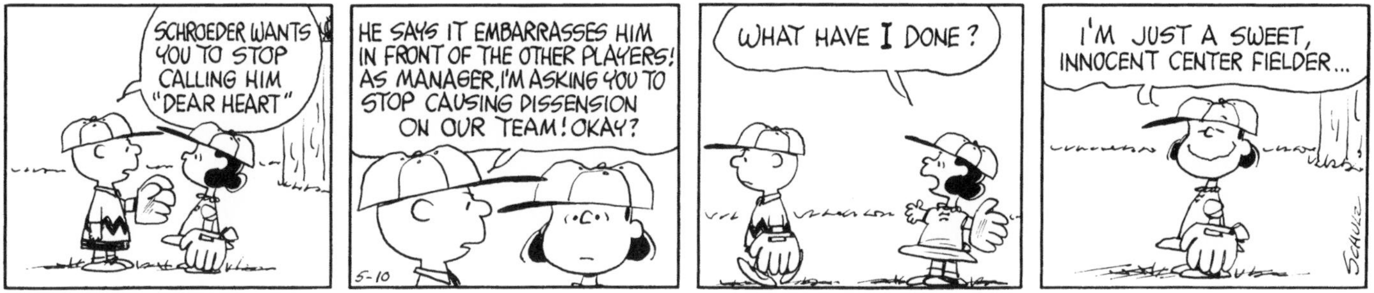
SCHROEDER WANTS YOU TO STOP CALLING HIM "DEAR HEART"
HE SAYS IT EMBARRASSES HIM IN FRONT OF THE OTHER PLAYERS! AS MANAGER, I'M ASKING YOU TO STOP CAUSING DISSENSION ON OUR TEAM! OKAY?
WHAT HAVE I DONE ?
I'M JUST A SWEET, INNOCENT CENTER FIELDER...

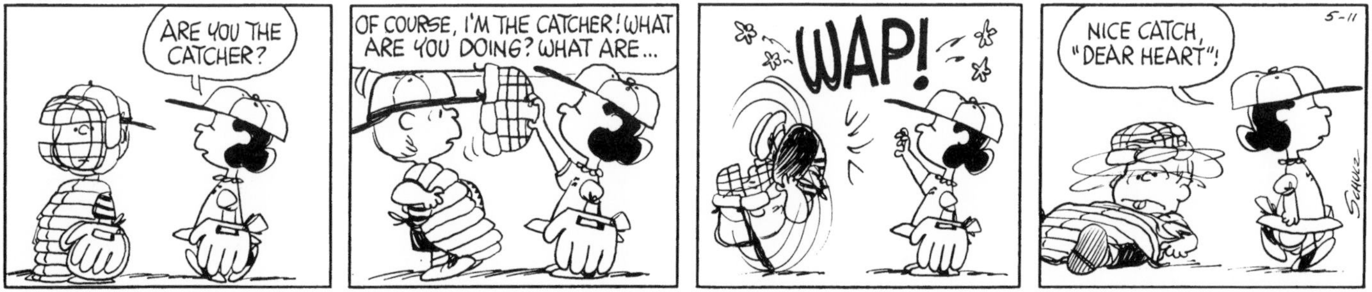
ARE YOU THE CATCHER?
OF COURSE, I'M THE CATCHER! WHAT ARE YOU DOING? WHAT ARE...
WAP!
NICE CATCH, "DEAR HEART"!

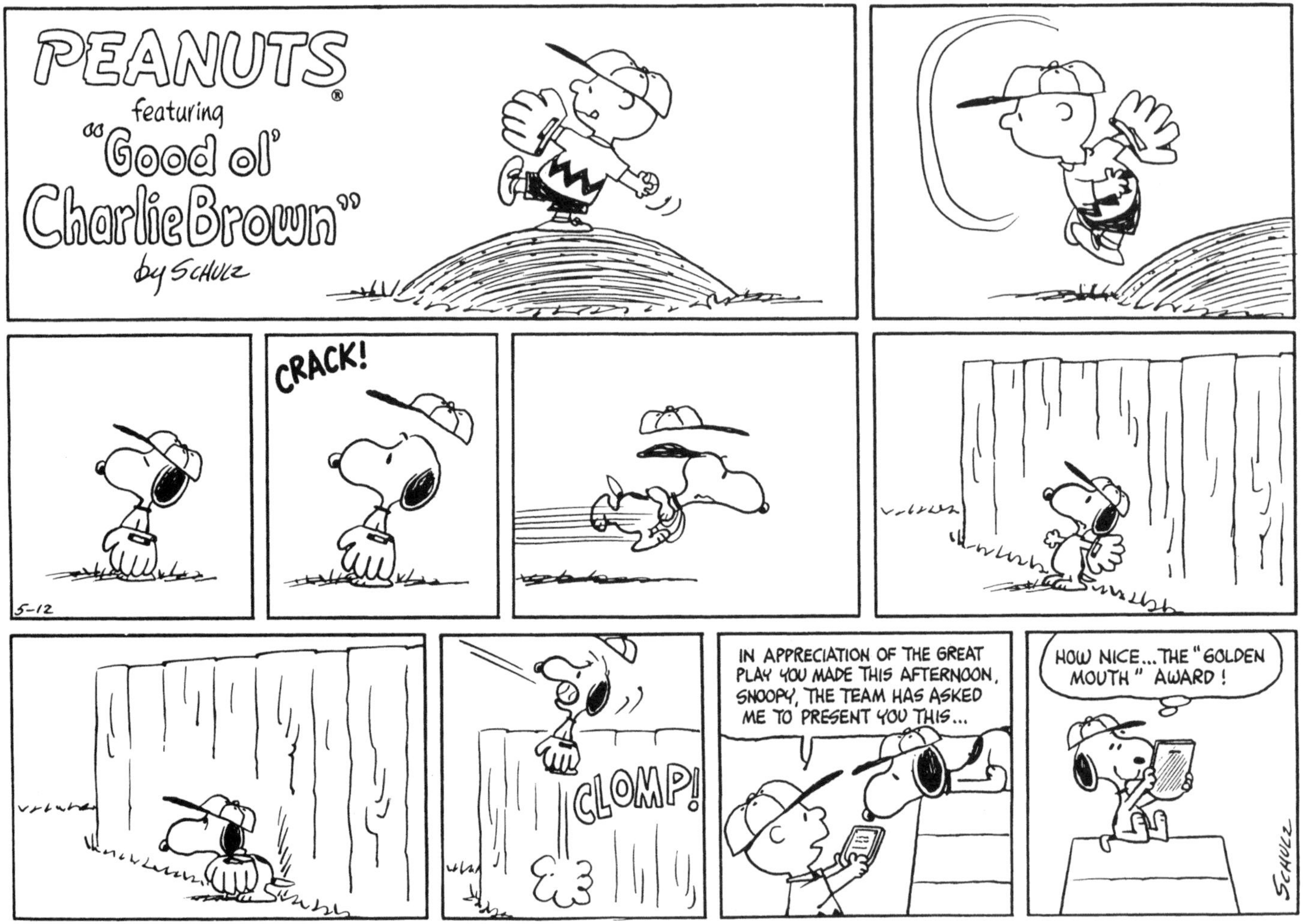
PEANUTS®
featuring
"Good ol' Charlie Brown"
by SCHULZ
5-12
CRACK!
CLOMP!
IN APPRECIATION OF THE GREAT PLAY YOU MADE THIS AFTERNOON, SNOOPY, THE TEAM HAS ASKED ME TO PRESENT YOU THIS...
HOW NICE...THE "GOLDEN MOUTH" AWARD!
SCHULZ

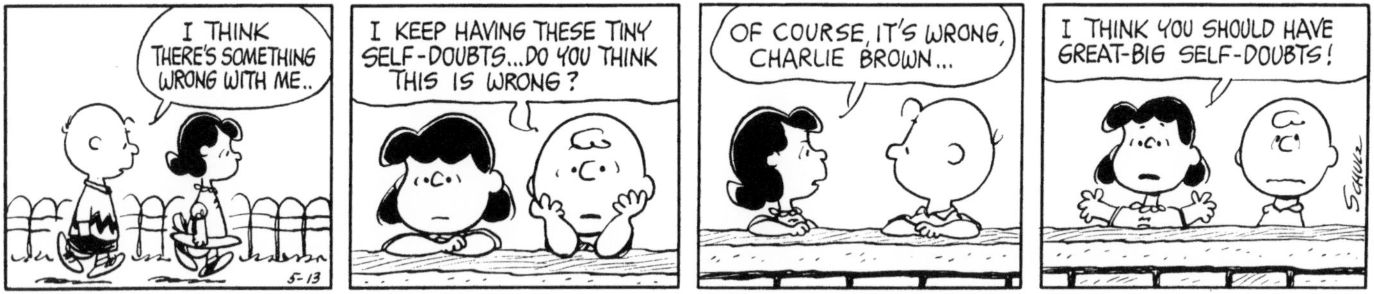
I THINK THERE'S SOMETHING WRONG WITH ME..
5-13
I KEEP HAVING THESE TINY SELF-DOUBTS...DO YOU THINK THIS IS WRONG?
OF COURSE, IT'S WRONG, CHARLIE BROWN...
I THINK YOU SHOULD HAVE GREAT-BIG SELF-DOUBTS!
SCHULZ

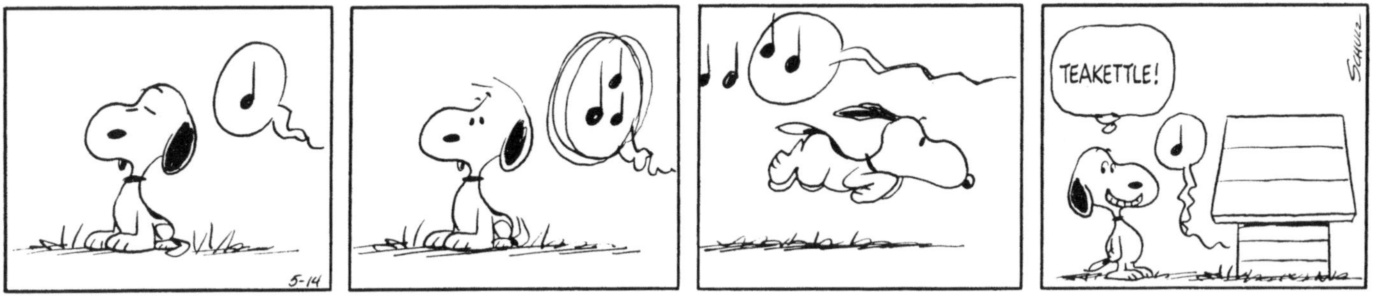
5-14
TEAKETTLE!
SCHULZ

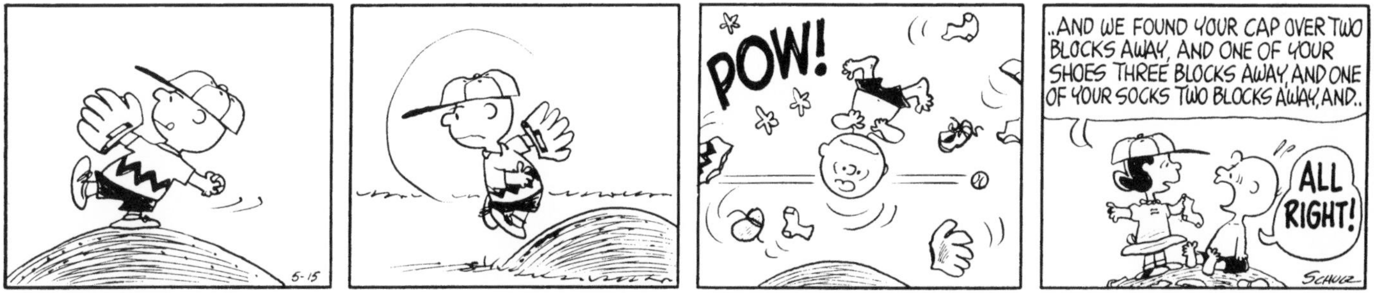
5-15
POW!
..AND WE FOUND YOUR CAP OVER TWO BLOCKS AWAY, AND ONE OF YOUR SHOES THREE BLOCKS AWAY, AND ONE OF YOUR SOCKS TWO BLOCKS AWAY, AND..
ALL RIGHT!
SCHULZ

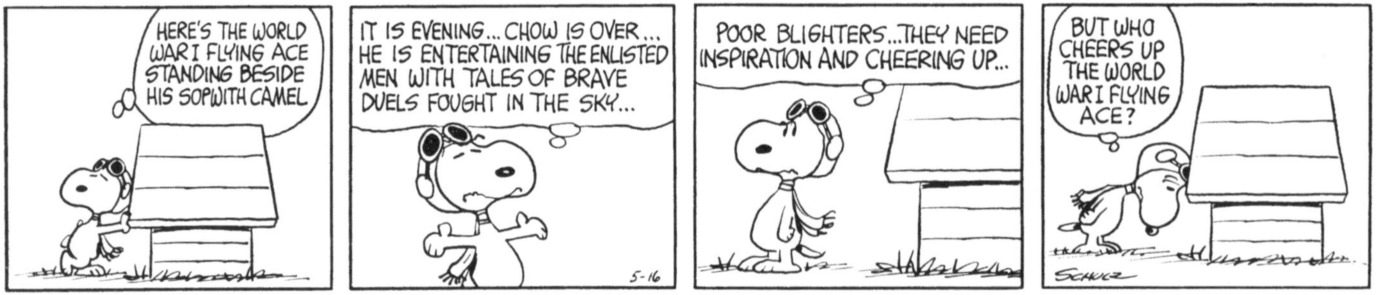
HERE'S THE WORLD WAR I FLYING ACE STANDING BESIDE HIS SOPWITH CAMEL
IT IS EVENING... CHOW IS OVER... HE IS ENTERTAINING THE ENLISTED MEN WITH TALES OF BRAVE DUELS FOUGHT IN THE SKY...
5-16
POOR BLIGHTERS...THEY NEED INSPIRATION AND CHEERING UP...
BUT WHO CHEERS UP THE WORLD WAR I FLYING ACE?
SCHULZ

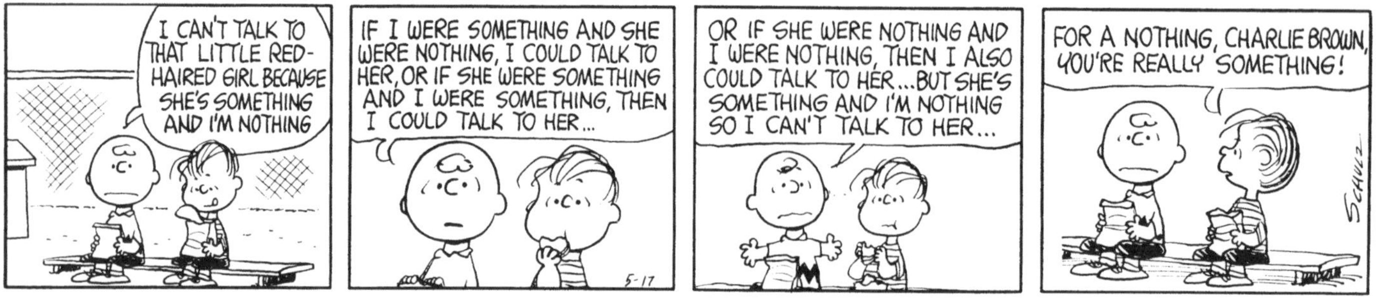
I CAN'T TALK TO THAT LITTLE RED-HAIRED GIRL BECAUSE SHE'S SOMETHING AND I'M NOTHING
IF I WERE SOMETHING AND SHE WERE NOTHING, I COULD TALK TO HER, OR IF SHE WERE SOMETHING AND I WERE SOMETHING, THEN I COULD TALK TO HER...
5-17
OR IF SHE WERE NOTHING AND I WERE NOTHING, THEN I ALSO COULD TALK TO HER...BUT SHE'S SOMETHING AND I'M NOTHING SO I CAN'T TALK TO HER...
FOR A NOTHING, CHARLIE BROWN, YOU'RE REALLY SOMETHING!
SCHULZ

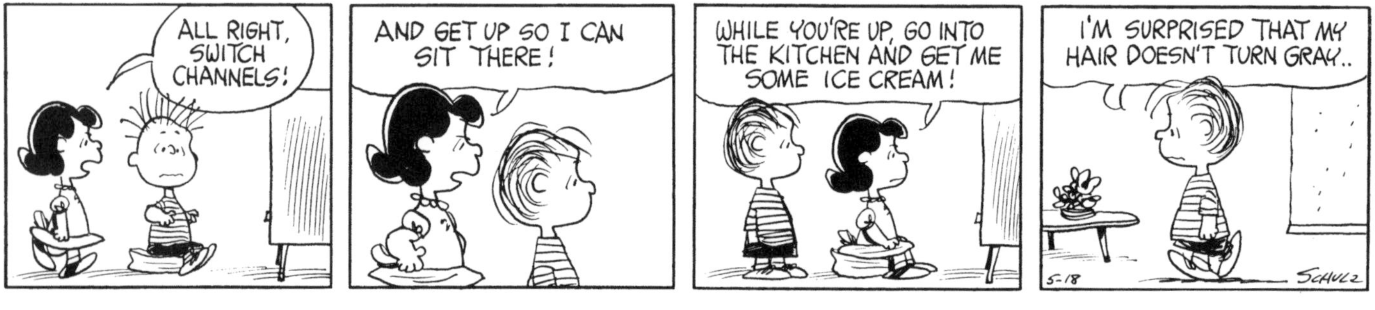
ALL RIGHT, SWITCH CHANNELS!
AND GET UP SO I CAN SIT THERE!
WHILE YOU'RE UP, GO INTO THE KITCHEN AND GET ME SOME ICE CREAM!
I'M SURPRISED THAT MY HAIR DOESN'T TURN GRAY..
5-18
SCHULZ

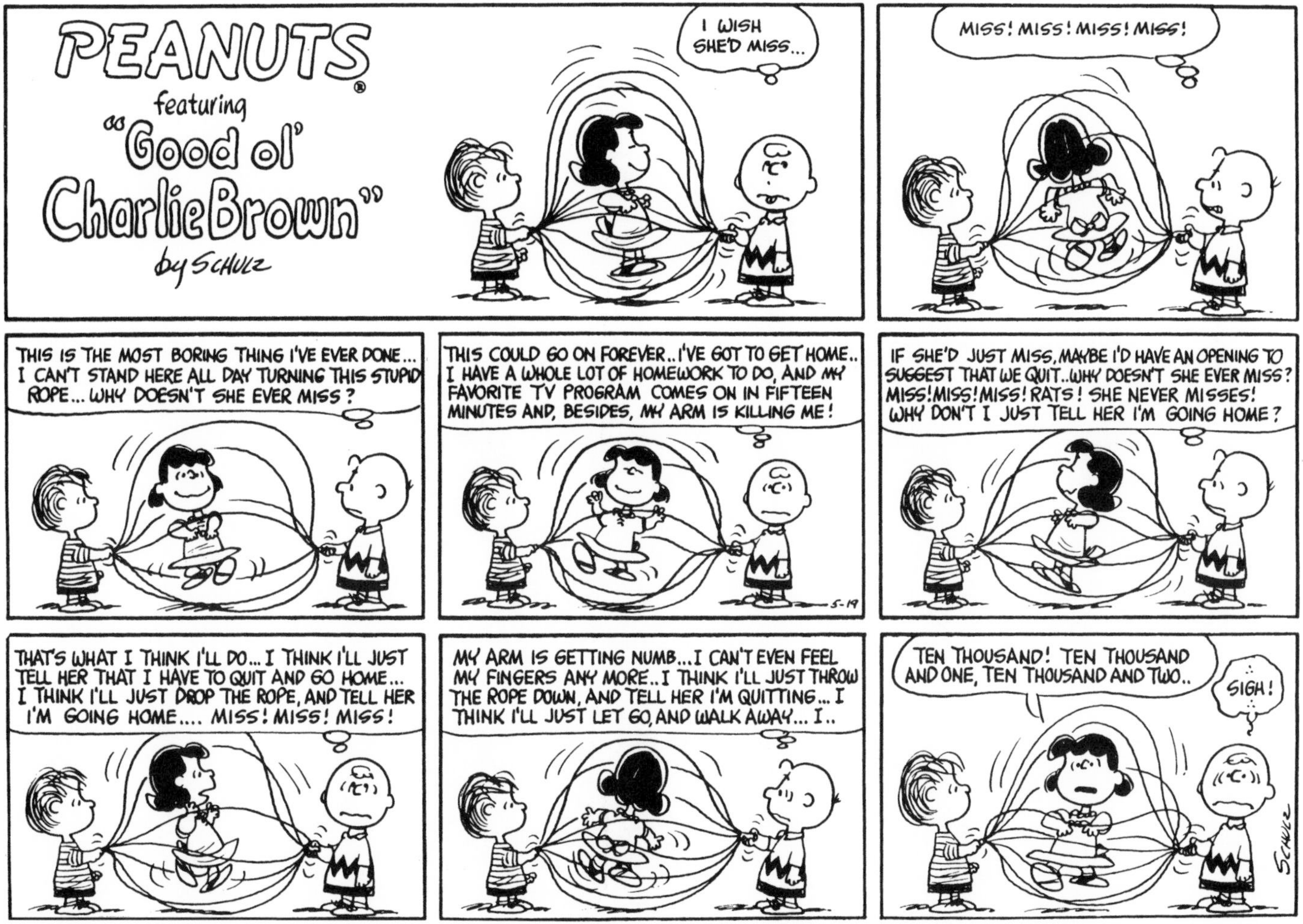
PEANUTS®
featuring
"Good ol' CharlieBrown"
by SCHULZ
I WISH SHE'D MISS...
MISS! MISS! MISS! MISS!
THIS IS THE MOST BORING THING I'VE EVER DONE... I CAN'T STAND HERE ALL DAY TURNING THIS STUPID ROPE... WHY DOESN'T SHE EVER MISS?
THIS COULD GO ON FOREVER.. I'VE GOT TO GET HOME.. I HAVE A WHOLE LOT OF HOMEWORK TO DO, AND MY FAVORITE TV PROGRAM COMES ON IN FIFTEEN MINUTES AND, BESIDES, MY ARM IS KILLING ME!
5-19
IF SHE'D JUST MISS, MAYBE I'D HAVE AN OPENING TO SUGGEST THAT WE QUIT..WHY DOESN'T SHE EVER MISS? MISS! MISS! MISS! RATS! SHE NEVER MISSES! WHY DON'T I JUST TELL HER I'M GOING HOME?
THAT'S WHAT I THINK I'LL DO... I THINK I'LL JUST TELL HER THAT I HAVE TO QUIT AND GO HOME... I THINK I'LL JUST DROP THE ROPE, AND TELL HER I'M GOING HOME.... MISS! MISS! MISS!
MY ARM IS GETTING NUMB... I CAN'T EVEN FEEL MY FINGERS ANY MORE.. I THINK I'LL JUST THROW THE ROPE DOWN, AND TELL HER I'M QUITTING... I THINK I'LL JUST LET GO, AND WALK AWAY... I..
TEN THOUSAND! TEN THOUSAND AND ONE, TEN THOUSAND AND TWO..
SIGH!
SCHULZ

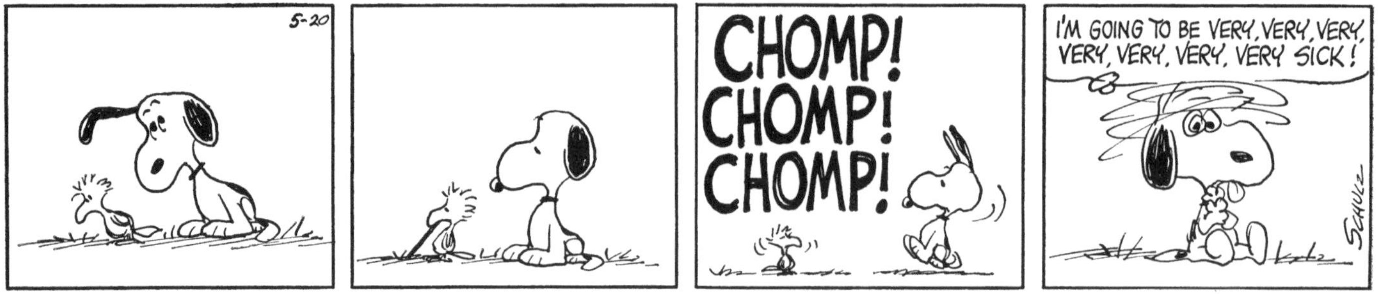
5-20
CHOMP! CHOMP! CHOMP!
I'M GOING TO BE VERY, VERY, VERY, VERY, VERY, VERY, VERY, VERY SICK!

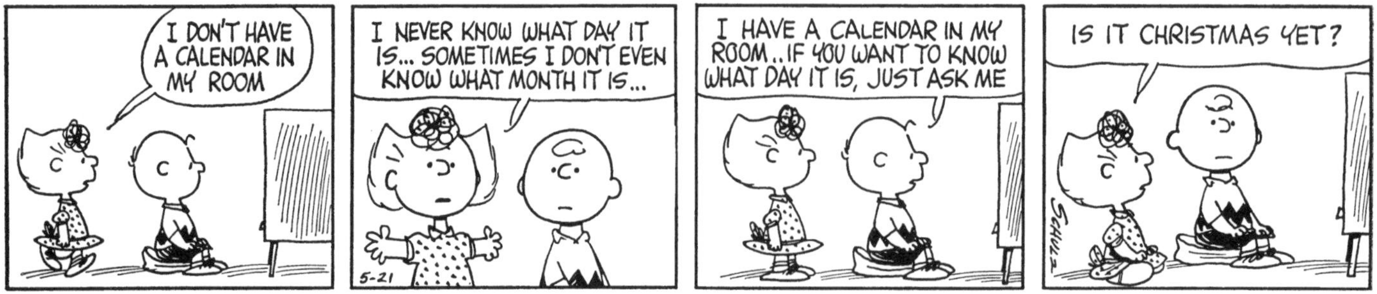
I DON'T HAVE A CALENDAR IN MY ROOM
I NEVER KNOW WHAT DAY IT IS... SOMETIMES I DON'T EVEN KNOW WHAT MONTH IT IS...
5-21
I HAVE A CALENDAR IN MY ROOM..IF YOU WANT TO KNOW WHAT DAY IT IS, JUST ASK ME
IS IT CHRISTMAS YET?

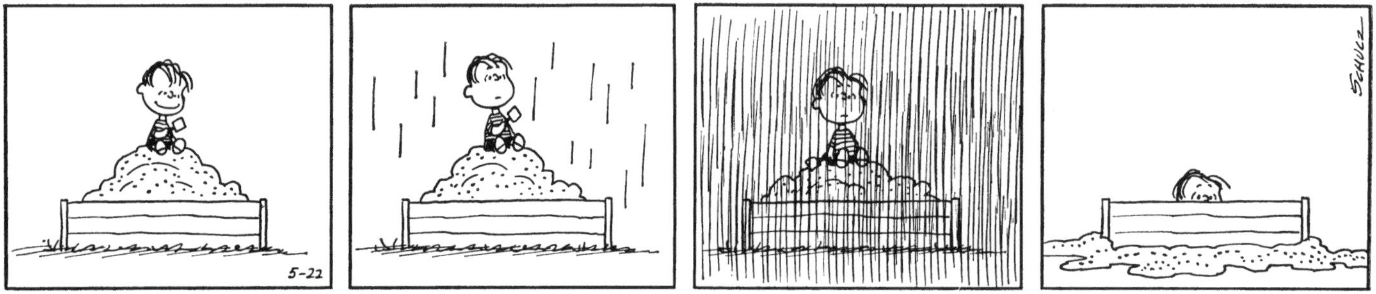
5-22

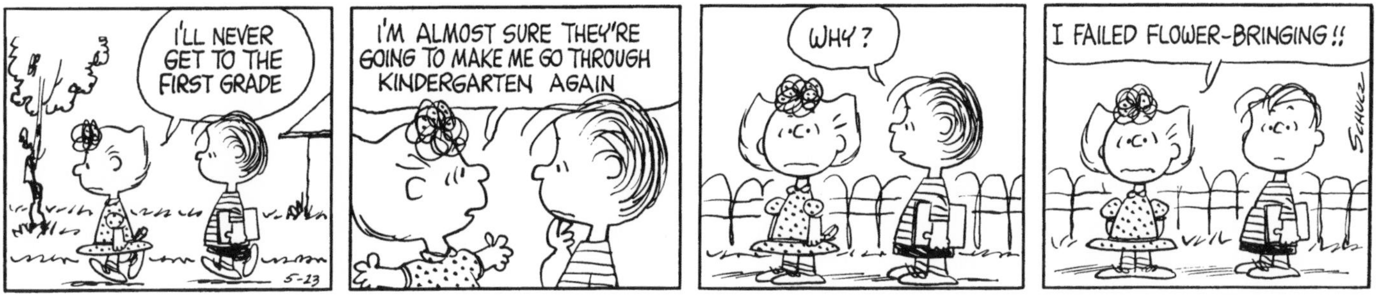
I'LL NEVER GET TO THE FIRST GRADE
I'M ALMOST SURE THEY'RE GOING TO MAKE ME GO THROUGH KINDERGARTEN AGAIN
WHY?
I FAILED FLOWER-BRINGING!!

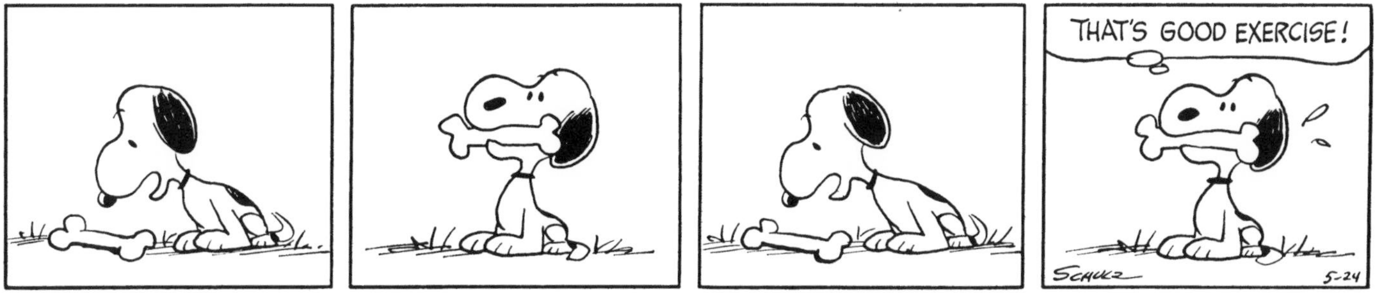
THAT'S GOOD EXERCISE!

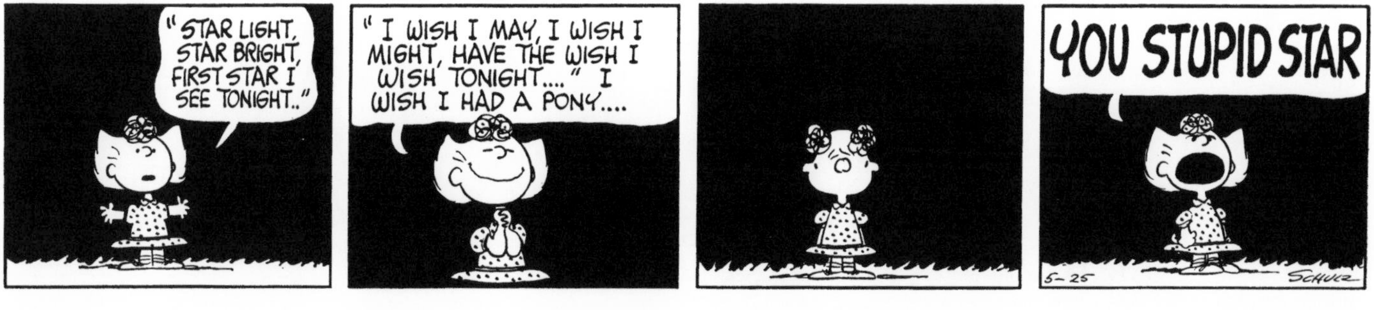
"STAR LIGHT, STAR BRIGHT, FIRST STAR I SEE TONIGHT.."
"I WISH I MAY, I WISH I MIGHT, HAVE THE WISH I WISH TONIGHT...." I WISH I HAD A PONY....
YOU STUPID STAR

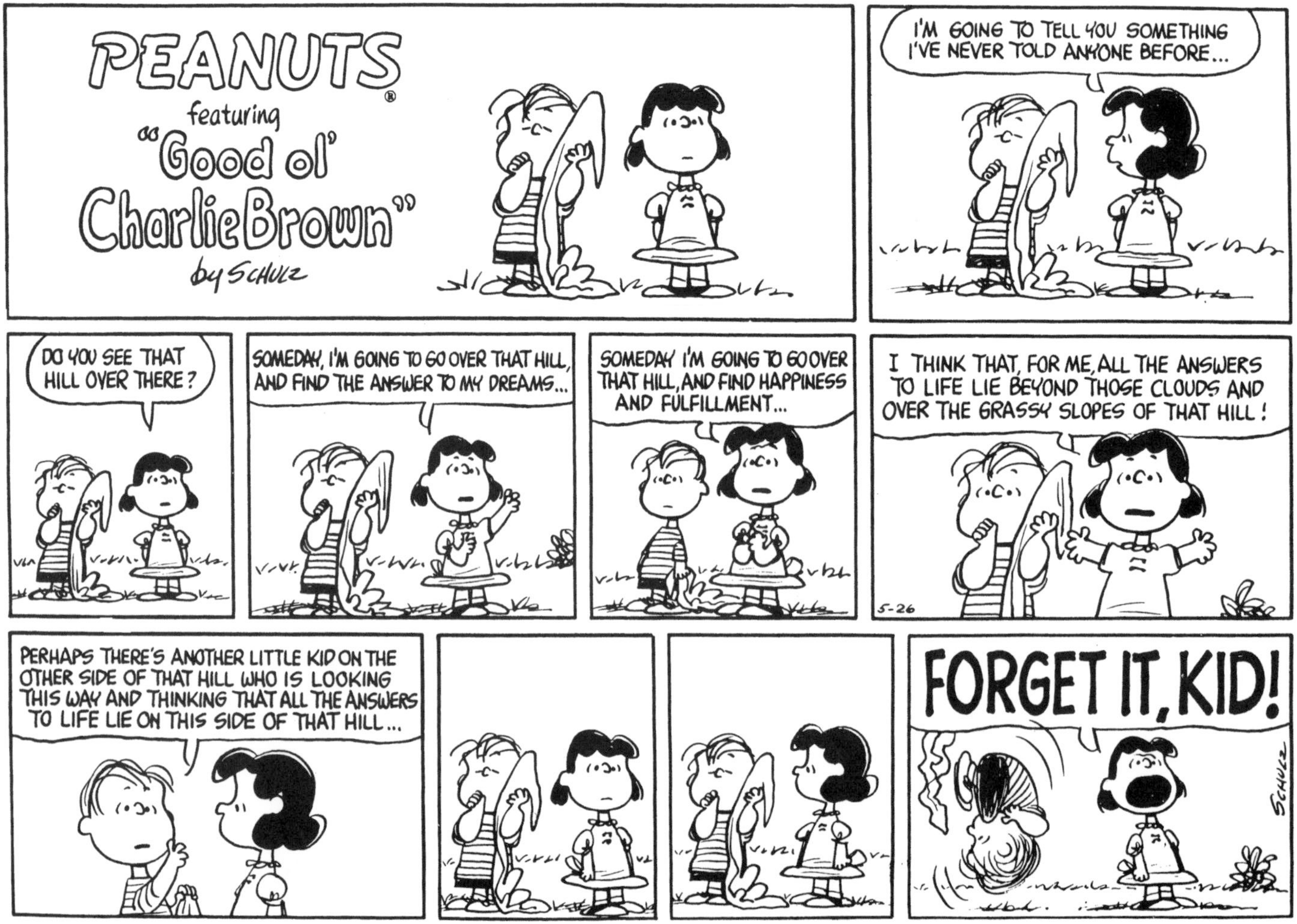
PEANUTS®
featuring
"Good ol' CharlieBrown"
by SCHULZ
I'M GOING TO TELL YOU SOMETHING I'VE NEVER TOLD ANYONE BEFORE...
DO YOU SEE THAT HILL OVER THERE?
SOMEDAY, I'M GOING TO GO OVER THAT HILL, AND FIND THE ANSWER TO MY DREAMS...
SOMEDAY I'M GOING TO GO OVER THAT HILL, AND FIND HAPPINESS AND FULFILLMENT...
I THINK THAT, FOR ME, ALL THE ANSWERS TO LIFE LIE BEYOND THOSE CLOUDS AND OVER THE GRASSY SLOPES OF THAT HILL!
5-26
PERHAPS THERE'S ANOTHER LITTLE KID ON THE OTHER SIDE OF THAT HILL WHO IS LOOKING THIS WAY AND THINKING THAT ALL THE ANSWERS TO LIFE LIE ON THIS SIDE OF THAT HILL...
FORGET IT, KID!
SCHULZ

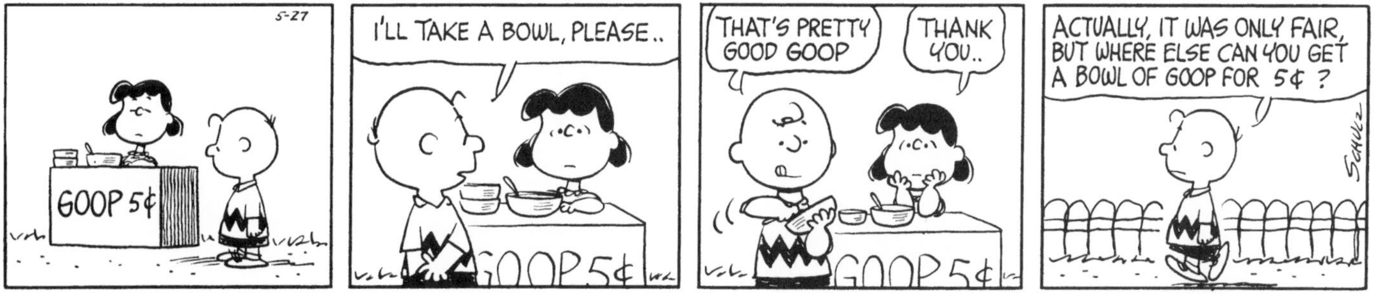
5-27
GOOP 5¢
I'LL TAKE A BOWL, PLEASE..
GOOP 5¢
THAT'S PRETTY GOOD GOOP
THANK YOU..
GOOP 5¢
ACTUALLY, IT WAS ONLY FAIR, BUT WHERE ELSE CAN YOU GET A BOWL OF GOOP FOR 5¢ ?
SCHULZ

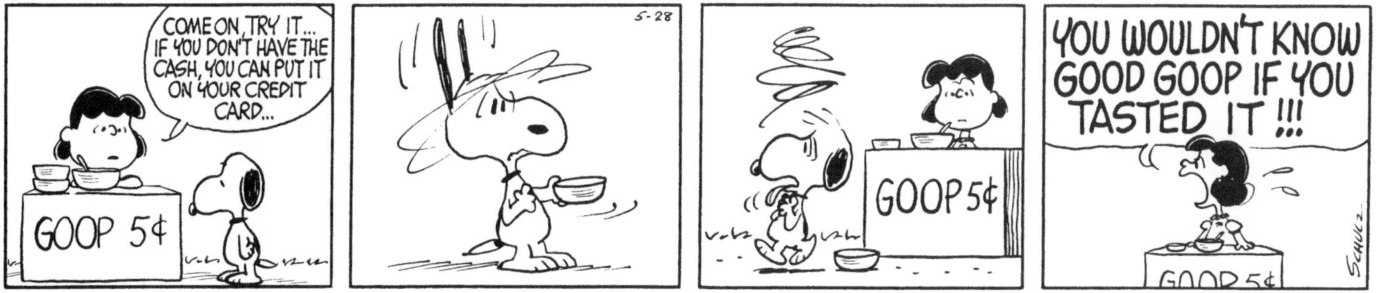
COME ON, TRY IT... IF YOU DON'T HAVE THE CASH, YOU CAN PUT IT ON YOUR CREDIT CARD...
GOOP 5¢
5-28
GOOP 5¢
YOU WOULDN'T KNOW GOOD GOOP IF YOU TASTED IT !!!
SCHULZ

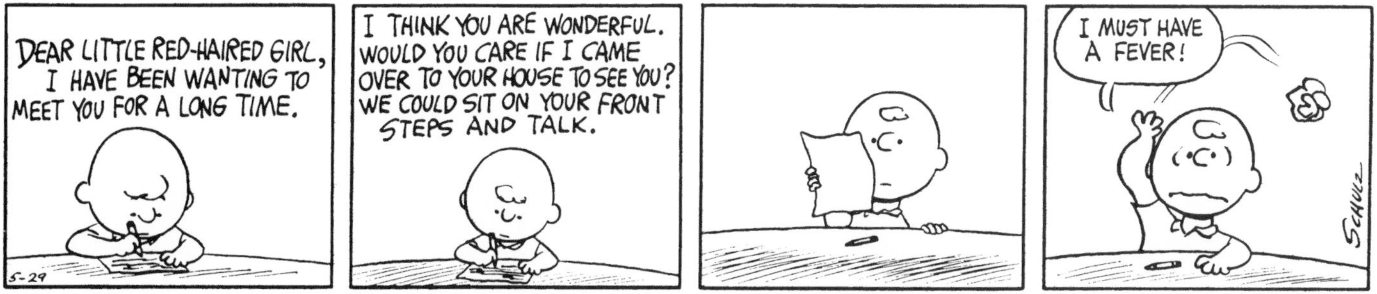
DEAR LITTLE RED-HAIRED GIRL, I HAVE BEEN WANTING TO MEET YOU FOR A LONG TIME.
5-29
I THINK YOU ARE WONDERFUL. WOULD YOU CARE IF I CAME OVER TO YOUR HOUSE TO SEE YOU? WE COULD SIT ON YOUR FRONT STEPS AND TALK.
I MUST HAVE A FEVER!
SCHULZ

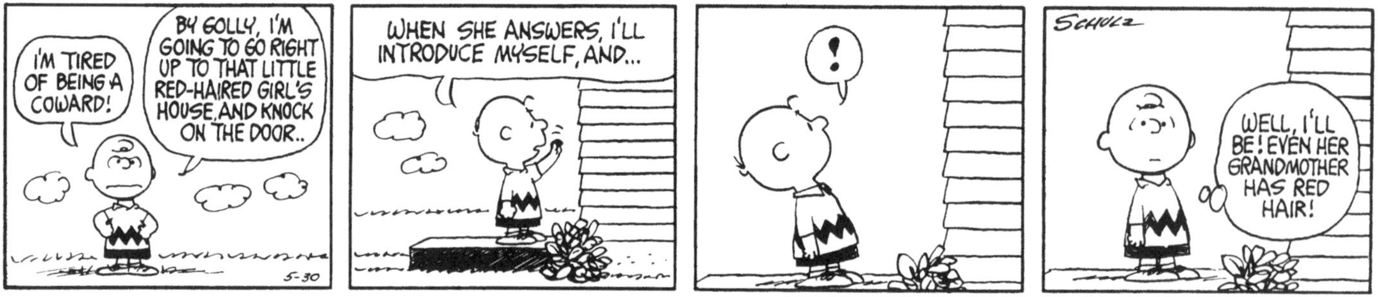
I'M TIRED OF BEING A COWARD!
BY GOLLY, I'M GOING TO GO RIGHT UP TO THAT LITTLE RED-HAIRED GIRL'S HOUSE, AND KNOCK ON THE DOOR..
5-30
WHEN SHE ANSWERS, I'LL INTRODUCE MYSELF, AND...
!
SCHULZ
WELL, I'LL BE! EVEN HER GRANDMOTHER HAS RED HAIR!

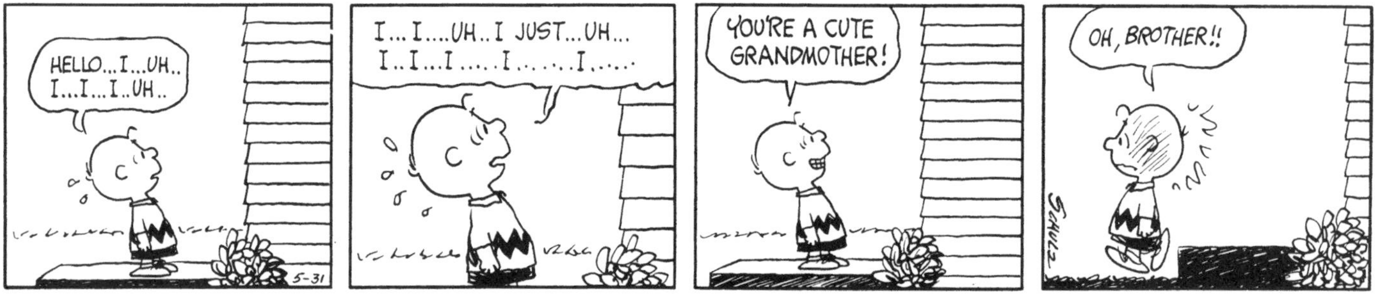
HELLO...I...UH.. I...I...I..UH..
5-31
I...I....UH..I JUST...UH... I..I...I .....I.......I......
YOU'RE A CUTE GRANDMOTHER!
OH, BROTHER!!
SCHULZ

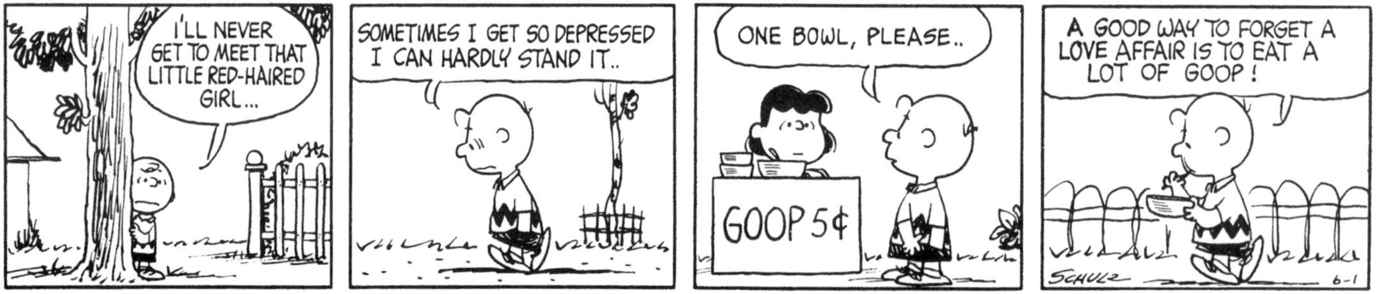
I'LL NEVER GET TO MEET THAT LITTLE RED-HAIRED GIRL...
SOMETIMES I GET SO DEPRESSED I CAN HARDLY STAND IT..
ONE BOWL, PLEASE..
GOOP 5¢
A GOOD WAY TO FORGET A LOVE AFFAIR IS TO EAT A LOT OF GOOP!
SCHULZ
6-1

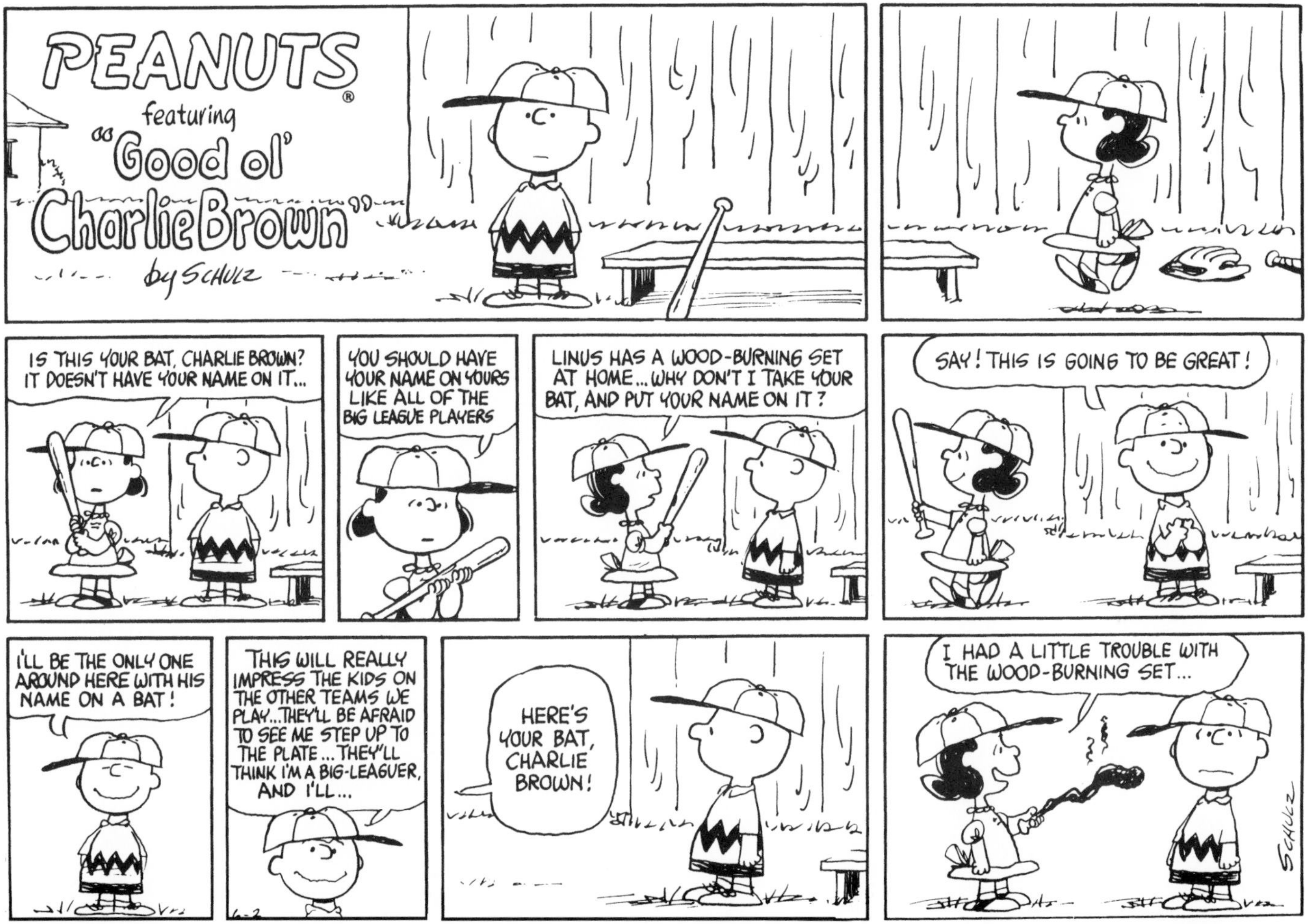
PEANUTS®
featuring "Good ol' Charlie Brown"
by SCHULZ
IS THIS YOUR BAT, CHARLIE BROWN? IT DOESN'T HAVE YOUR NAME ON IT...
YOU SHOULD HAVE YOUR NAME ON YOURS LIKE ALL OF THE BIG LEAGUE PLAYERS
LINUS HAS A WOOD-BURNING SET AT HOME... WHY DON'T I TAKE YOUR BAT, AND PUT YOUR NAME ON IT?
SAY! THIS IS GOING TO BE GREAT!
I'LL BE THE ONLY ONE AROUND HERE WITH HIS NAME ON A BAT!
THIS WILL REALLY IMPRESS THE KIDS ON THE OTHER TEAMS WE PLAY...THEY'LL BE AFRAID TO SEE ME STEP UP TO THE PLATE... THEY'LL THINK I'M A BIG-LEAGUER, AND I'LL...
HERE'S YOUR BAT, CHARLIE BROWN!
I HAD A LITTLE TROUBLE WITH THE WOOD-BURNING SET...
SCHULZ

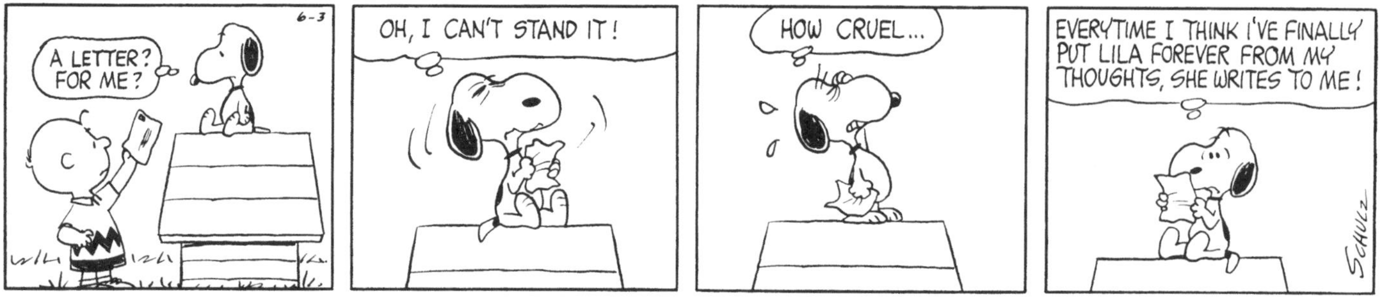
6-3
A LETTER? FOR ME?
OH, I CAN'T STAND IT!
HOW CRUEL...
EVERYTIME I THINK I'VE FINALLY PUT LILA FOREVER FROM MY THOUGHTS, SHE WRITES TO ME!
SCHULZ

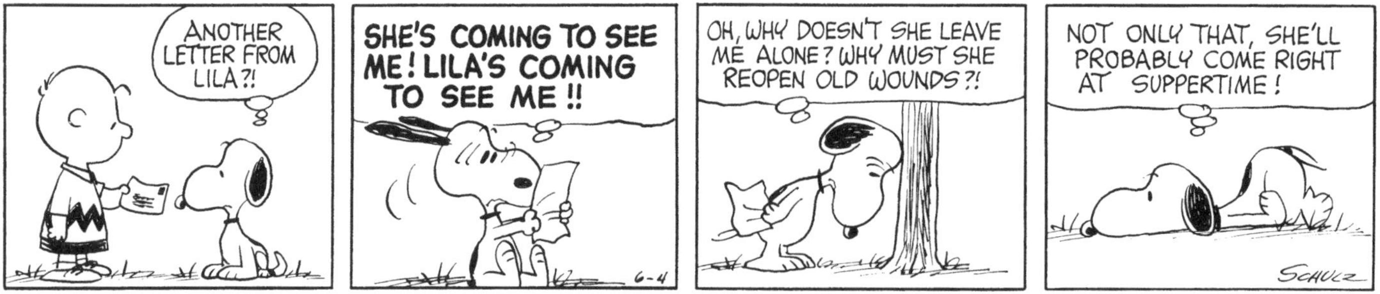
ANOTHER LETTER FROM LILA?!
SHE'S COMING TO SEE ME! LILA'S COMING TO SEE ME!!
6-4
OH, WHY DOESN'T SHE LEAVE ME ALONE? WHY MUST SHE REOPEN OLD WOUNDS?!
NOT ONLY THAT, SHE'LL PROBABLY COME RIGHT AT SUPPERTIME!
SCHULZ

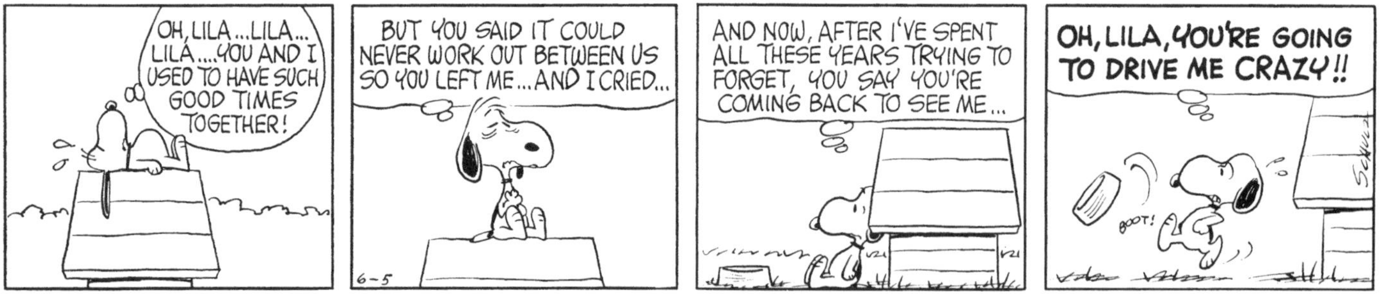
OH, LILA...LILA... LILA....YOU AND I USED TO HAVE SUCH GOOD TIMES TOGETHER!
BUT YOU SAID IT COULD NEVER WORK OUT BETWEEN US SO YOU LEFT ME...AND I CRIED...
6-5
AND NOW, AFTER I'VE SPENT ALL THESE YEARS TRYING TO FORGET, YOU SAY YOU'RE COMING BACK TO SEE ME...
OH, LILA, YOU'RE GOING TO DRIVE ME CRAZY!!
BOOT!
SCHULZ

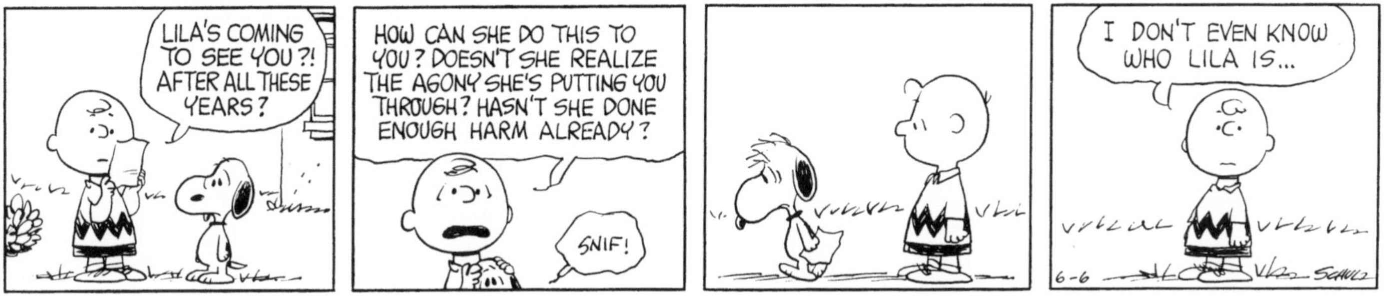
LILA'S COMING TO SEE YOU?! AFTER ALL THESE YEARS?
HOW CAN SHE DO THIS TO YOU? DOESN'T SHE REALIZE THE AGONY SHE'S PUTTING YOU THROUGH? HASN'T SHE DONE ENOUGH HARM ALREADY?
SNIF!
I DON'T EVEN KNOW WHO LILA IS...
6-6
SCHULZ

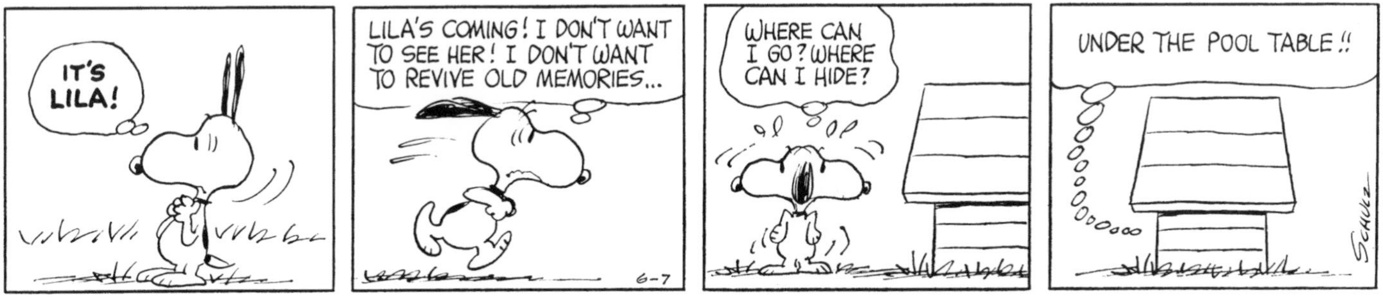
IT'S LILA!
LILA'S COMING! I DON'T WANT TO SEE HER! I DON'T WANT TO REVIVE OLD MEMORIES...
6-7
WHERE CAN I GO? WHERE CAN I HIDE?
UNDER THE POOL TABLE!!
SCHULZ

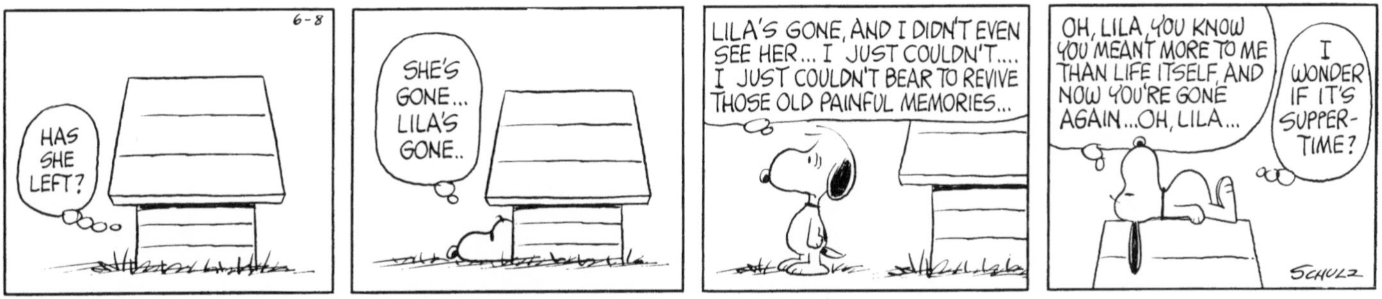
6-8
HAS SHE LEFT?
SHE'S GONE... LILA'S GONE..
LILA'S GONE, AND I DIDN'T EVEN SEE HER... I JUST COULDN'T.... I JUST COULDN'T BEAR TO REVIVE THOSE OLD PAINFUL MEMORIES...
OH, LILA, YOU KNOW YOU MEANT MORE TO ME THAN LIFE ITSELF, AND NOW YOU'RE GONE AGAIN...OH, LILA...
I WONDER IF IT'S SUPPER-TIME?
SCHULZ

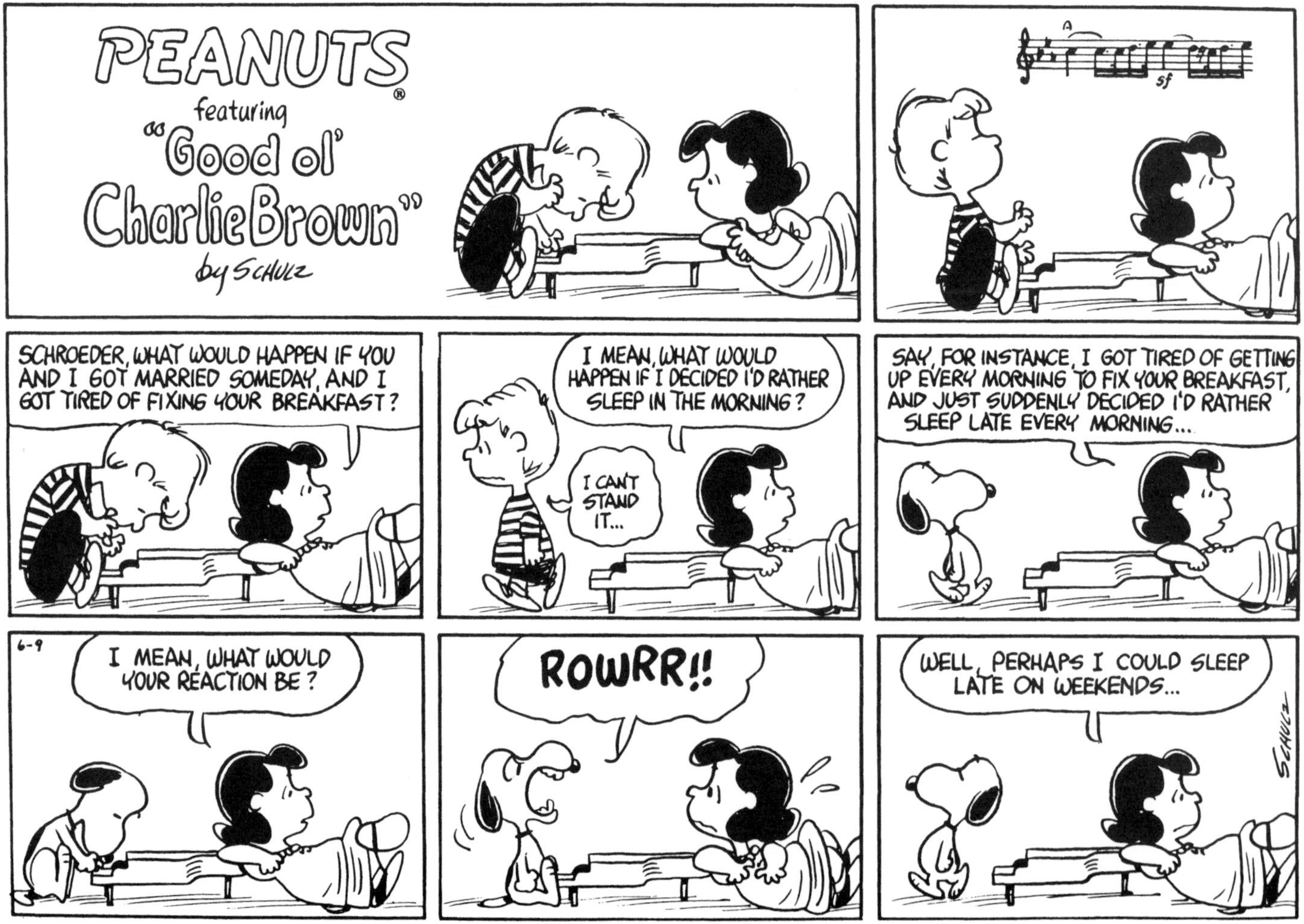
PEANUTS®
featuring
"Good ol' Charlie Brown"
by SCHULZ
SCHROEDER, WHAT WOULD HAPPEN IF YOU AND I GOT MARRIED SOMEDAY, AND I GOT TIRED OF FIXING YOUR BREAKFAST?
I MEAN, WHAT WOULD HAPPEN IF I DECIDED I'D RATHER SLEEP IN THE MORNING?
I CAN'T STAND IT...
SAY, FOR INSTANCE, I GOT TIRED OF GETTING UP EVERY MORNING TO FIX YOUR BREAKFAST, AND JUST SUDDENLY DECIDED I'D RATHER SLEEP LATE EVERY MORNING...
6-9
I MEAN, WHAT WOULD YOUR REACTION BE?
ROWRR!!
WELL, PERHAPS I COULD SLEEP LATE ON WEEKENDS...
SCHULZ

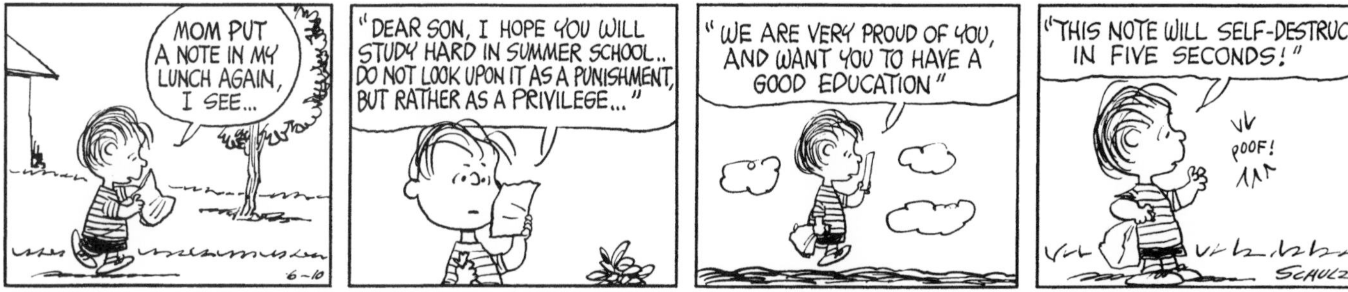
MOM PUT A NOTE IN MY LUNCH AGAIN, I SEE...
6-10
"DEAR SON, I HOPE YOU WILL STUDY HARD IN SUMMER SCHOOL.. DO NOT LOOK UPON IT AS A PUNISHMENT, BUT RATHER AS A PRIVILEGE..."
"WE ARE VERY PROUD OF YOU, AND WANT YOU TO HAVE A GOOD EDUCATION"
"THIS NOTE WILL SELF-DESTRUCT IN FIVE SECONDS!"
POOF!
SCHULZ

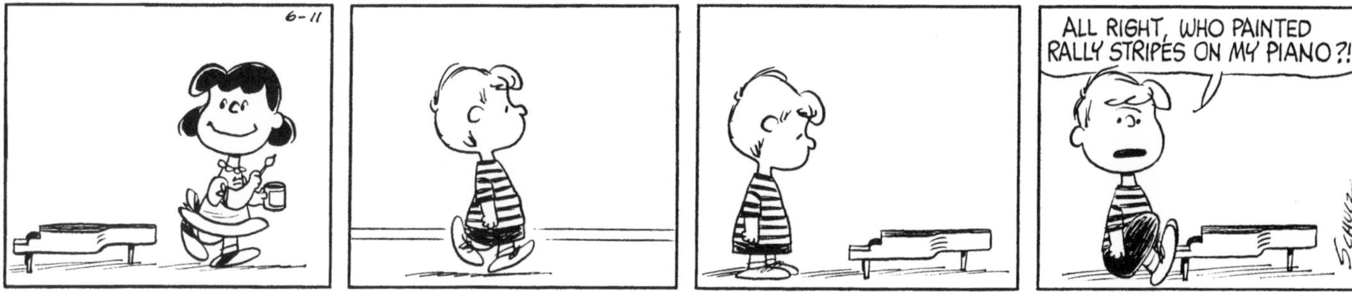
6-11
ALL RIGHT, WHO PAINTED RALLY STRIPES ON MY PIANO?!
SCHULZ

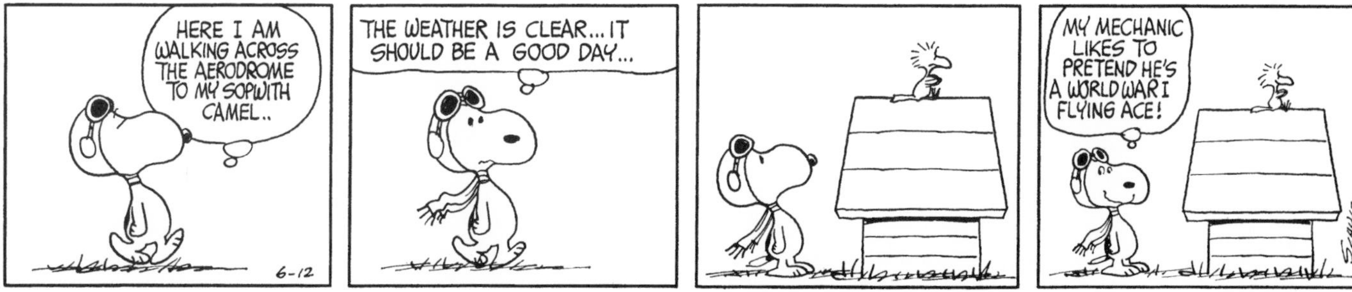
HERE I AM WALKING ACROSS THE AERODROME TO MY SOPWITH CAMEL..
6-12
THE WEATHER IS CLEAR... IT SHOULD BE A GOOD DAY...
MY MECHANIC LIKES TO PRETEND HE'S A WORLD WAR I FLYING ACE!
SCHULZ

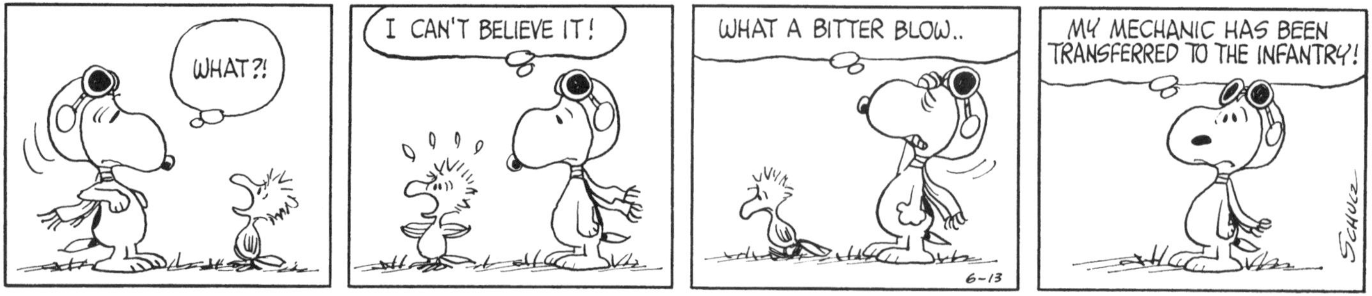
WHAT?!
I CAN'T BELIEVE IT!
WHAT A BITTER BLOW..
6-13
MY MECHANIC HAS BEEN TRANSFERRED TO THE INFANTRY!
SCHULZ

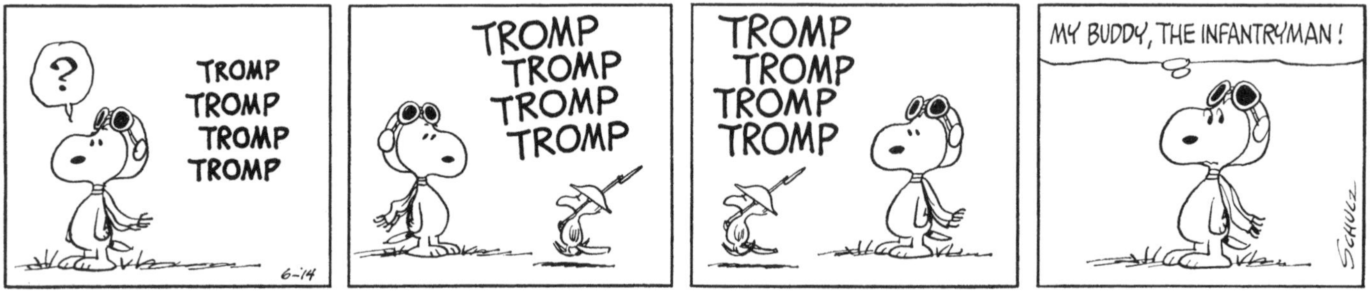
?
TROMP TROMP TROMP TROMP
6-14
TROMP TROMP TROMP TROMP
TROMP TROMP TROMP TROMP
MY BUDDY, THE INFANTRYMAN!
SCHULZ

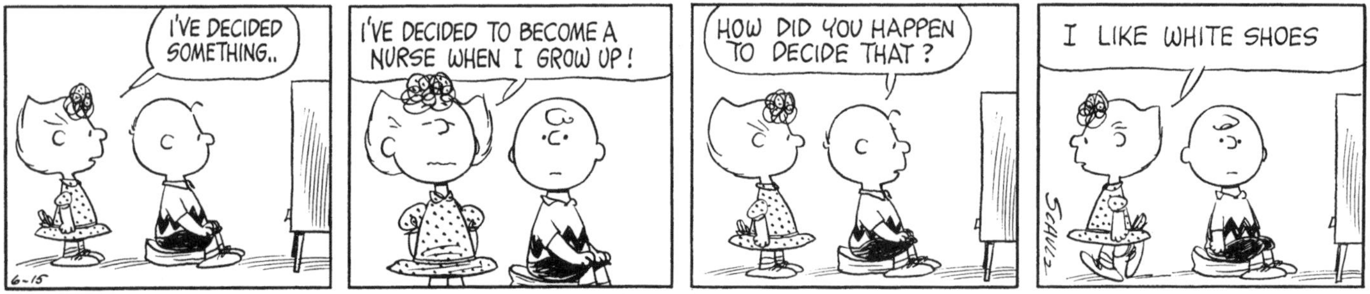
I'VE DECIDED SOMETHING..
6-15
I'VE DECIDED TO BECOME A NURSE WHEN I GROW UP!
HOW DID YOU HAPPEN TO DECIDE THAT?
SCHULZ
I LIKE WHITE SHOES

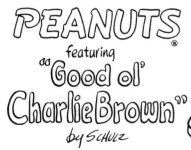

PEANUTS
featuring
"Good ol' Charlie Brown"
by Schulz

HAPPY FATHER'S DAY *from your rare gem.*

HI, ROY... I SUPPOSE YOU'RE WONDERING WHAT I'M DOING...

I'VE JUST MADE MY DAD A HAND-MADE FATHER'S DAY CARD..

6-16

EVERY NOW AND THEN MY DAD SAYS TO ME, "PEPPERMINT PATTY, DO YOU KNOW WHAT YOU ARE?" AND I ALWAYS SAY, "NO"...THEN HE SAYS TO ME, "YOU ARE A RARE GEM!" AND WE BOTH LAUGH...

SO YOU SEE, I'VE MADE A CARD FOR HIM... "HAPPY FATHER'S DAY FROM YOUR RARE GEM"

THAT'S VERY NICE..

THANK YOU.. I'LL PUT IT ON TOP OF HIS DRESSER WHERE HE'LL SEE IT...

ACTUALLY, ANYONE WHO GIVES HIS DAD A FATHER'S DAY CARD IS A RARE GEM...

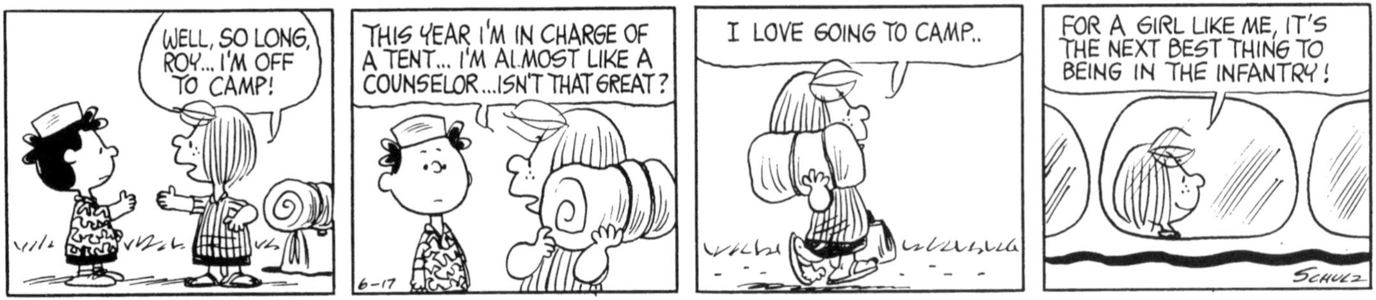
WELL, SO LONG, ROY... I'M OFF TO CAMP!
THIS YEAR I'M IN CHARGE OF A TENT... I'M ALMOST LIKE A COUNSELOR...ISN'T THAT GREAT?
6-17
I LOVE GOING TO CAMP..
FOR A GIRL LIKE ME, IT'S THE NEXT BEST THING TO BEING IN THE INFANTRY!
SCHULZ

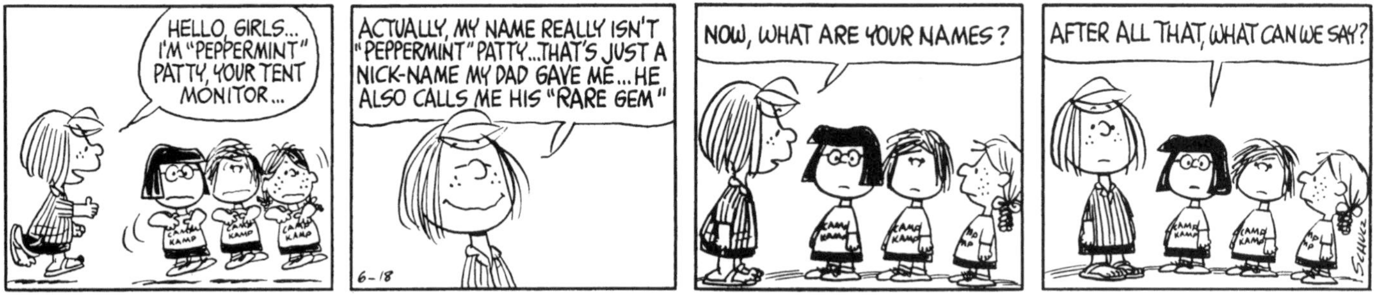
HELLO, GIRLS... I'M "PEPPERMINT" PATTY, YOUR TENT MONITOR...
ACTUALLY, MY NAME REALLY ISN'T "PEPPERMINT" PATTY...THAT'S JUST A NICK-NAME MY DAD GAVE ME... HE ALSO CALLS ME HIS "RARE GEM"
6-18
NOW, WHAT ARE YOUR NAMES?
AFTER ALL THAT, WHAT CAN WE SAY?
SCHULZ

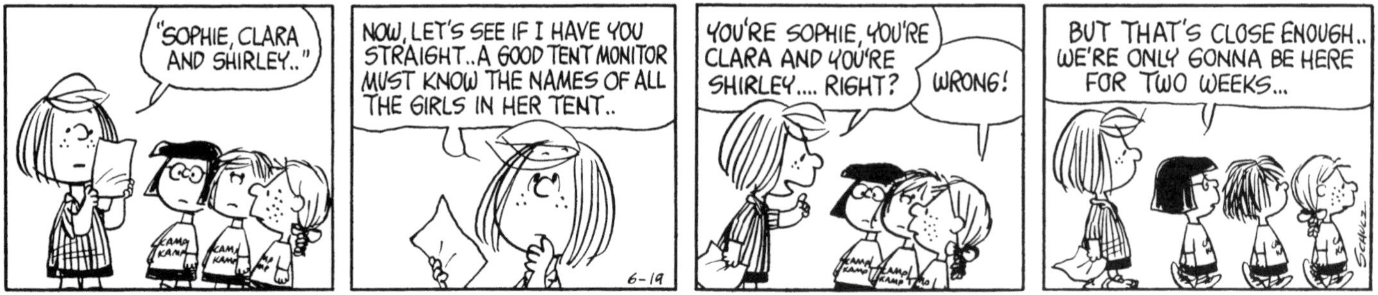
"SOPHIE, CLARA AND SHIRLEY.."
NOW, LET'S SEE IF I HAVE YOU STRAIGHT..A GOOD TENT MONITOR MUST KNOW THE NAMES OF ALL THE GIRLS IN HER TENT..
6-19
YOU'RE SOPHIE, YOU'RE CLARA AND YOU'RE SHIRLEY.... RIGHT?
WRONG!
BUT THAT'S CLOSE ENOUGH.. WE'RE ONLY GONNA BE HERE FOR TWO WEEKS...
SCHULZ

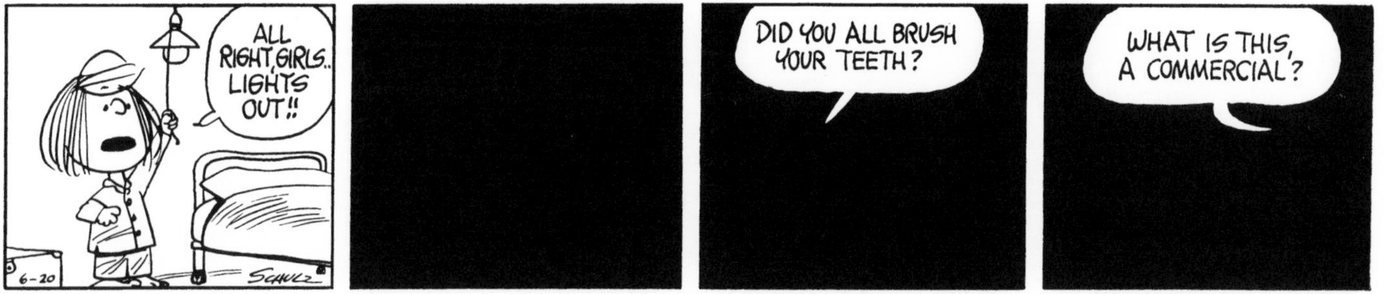
ALL RIGHT, GIRLS.. LIGHTS OUT!!
6-20
DID YOU ALL BRUSH YOUR TEETH?
WHAT IS THIS, A COMMERCIAL?

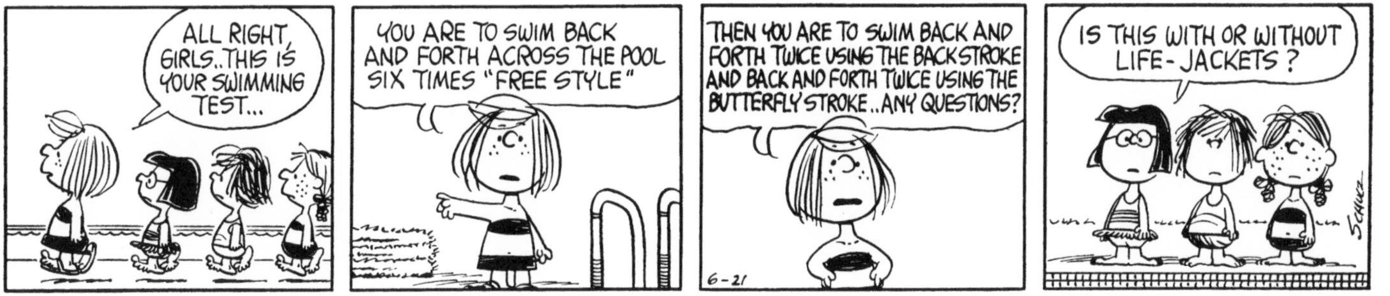
ALL RIGHT, GIRLS..THIS IS YOUR SWIMMING TEST...
YOU ARE TO SWIM BACK AND FORTH ACROSS THE POOL SIX TIMES "FREE STYLE"
THEN YOU ARE TO SWIM BACK AND FORTH TWICE USING THE BACKSTROKE AND BACK AND FORTH TWICE USING THE BUTTERFLY STROKE..ANY QUESTIONS?
6-21
IS THIS WITH OR WITHOUT LIFE-JACKETS?

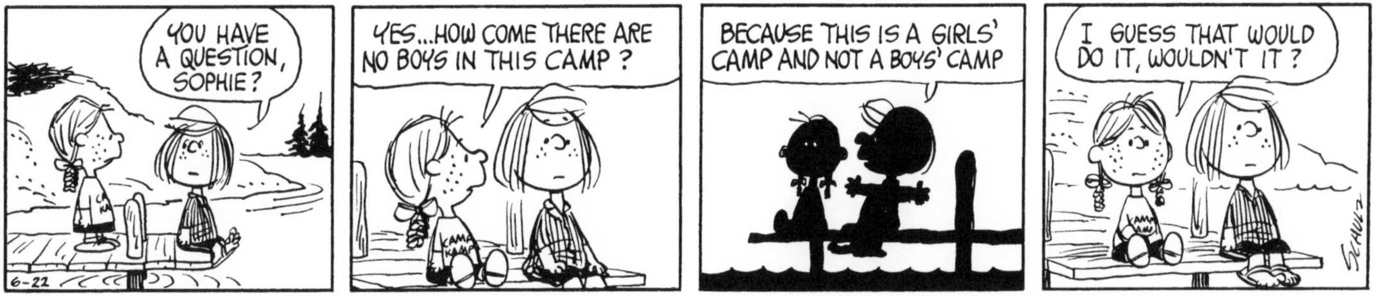
YOU HAVE A QUESTION, SOPHIE?
6-22
YES...HOW COME THERE ARE NO BOYS IN THIS CAMP?
BECAUSE THIS IS A GIRLS' CAMP AND NOT A BOYS' CAMP
I GUESS THAT WOULD DO IT, WOULDN'T IT?

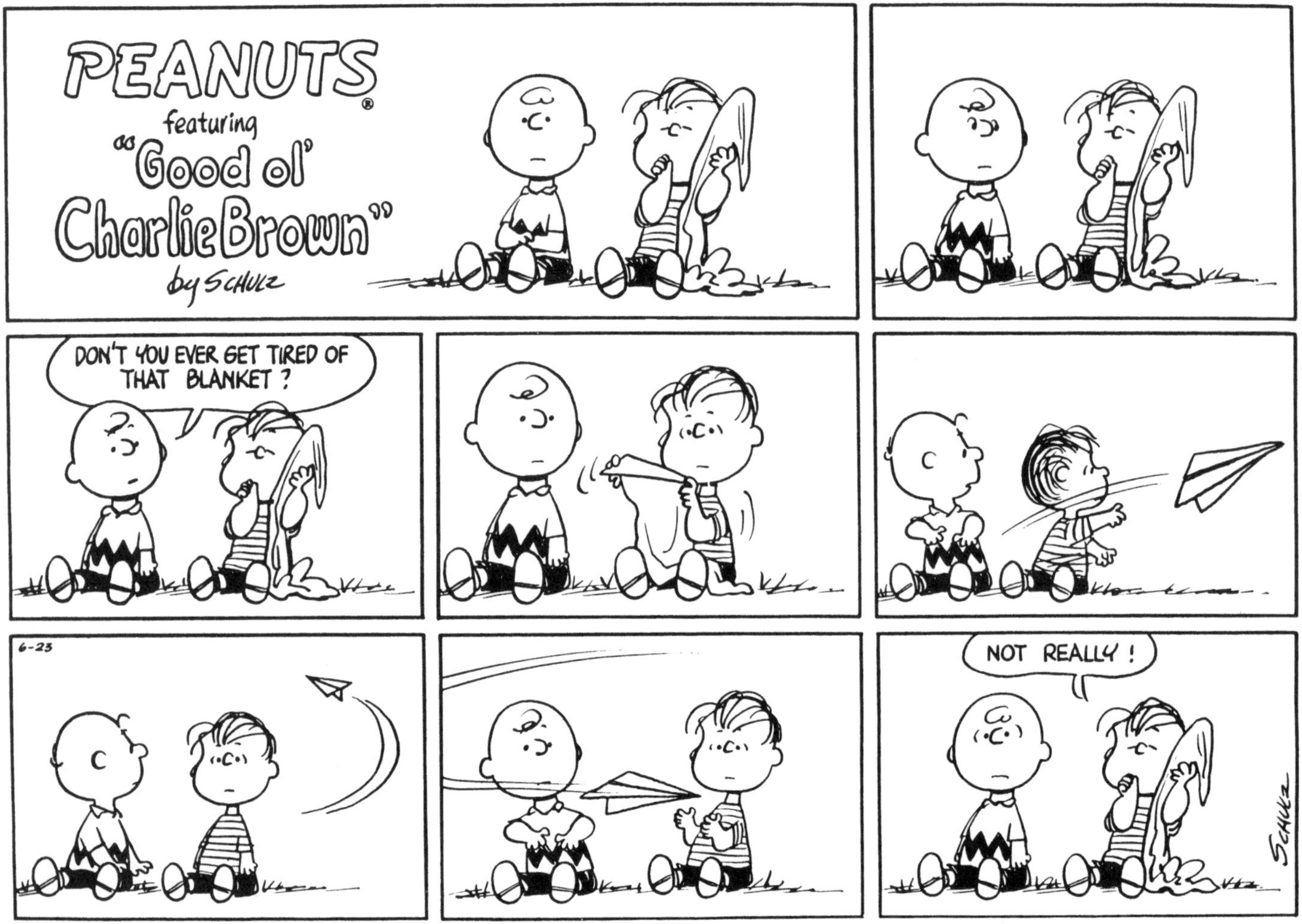
PEANUTS®
featuring
"Good ol' CharlieBrown"
by SCHULZ
DON'T YOU EVER GET TIRED OF THAT BLANKET ?
6-23
NOT REALLY !
SCHULZ

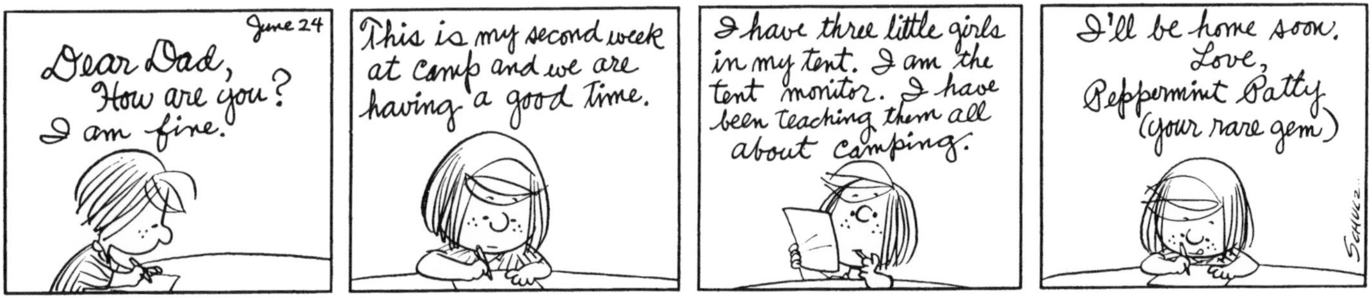
June 24
Dear Dad,
How are you?
I am fine.
This is my second week at camp and we are having a good time.
I have three little girls in my tent. I am the tent monitor. I have been teaching them all about camping.
I'll be home soon.
Love,
Peppermint Patty
(your rare gem)

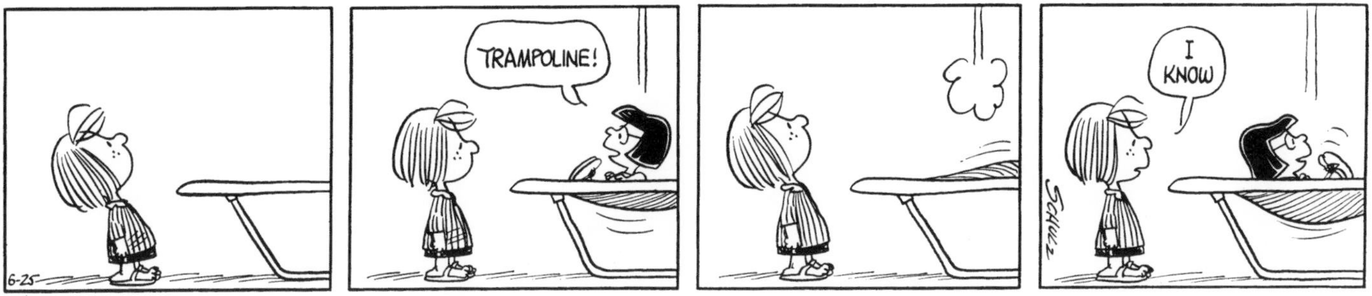
TRAMPOLINE!
I KNOW

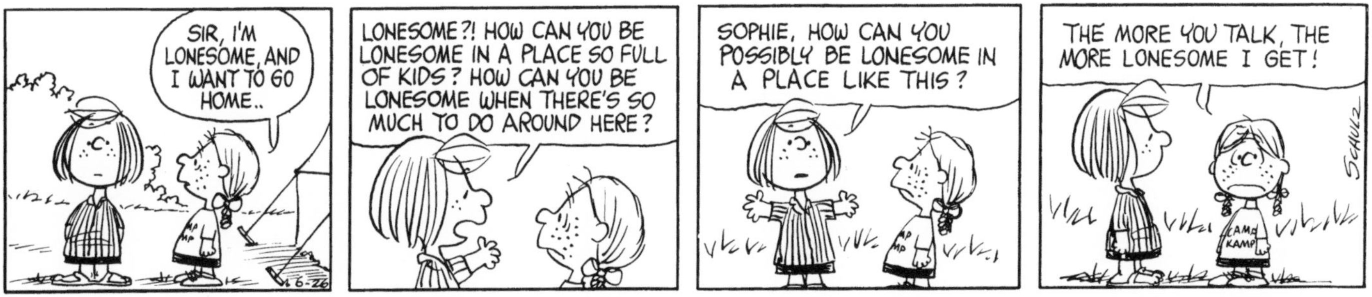
SIR, I'M LONESOME, AND I WANT TO GO HOME..
LONESOME?! HOW CAN YOU BE LONESOME IN A PLACE SO FULL OF KIDS? HOW CAN YOU BE LONESOME WHEN THERE'S SO MUCH TO DO AROUND HERE?
SOPHIE, HOW CAN YOU POSSIBLY BE LONESOME IN A PLACE LIKE THIS?
THE MORE YOU TALK, THE MORE LONESOME I GET!

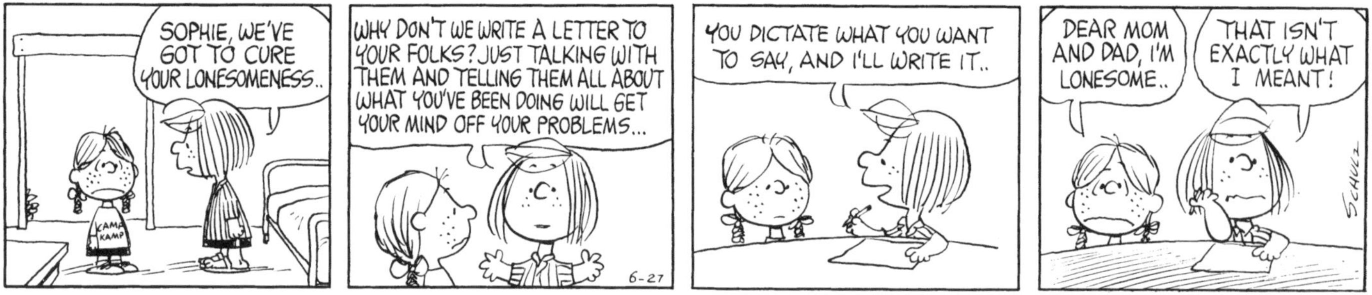
SOPHIE, WE'VE GOT TO CURE YOUR LONESOMENESS..
WHY DON'T WE WRITE A LETTER TO YOUR FOLKS? JUST TALKING WITH THEM AND TELLING THEM ALL ABOUT WHAT YOU'VE BEEN DOING WILL GET YOUR MIND OFF YOUR PROBLEMS...
6-27
YOU DICTATE WHAT YOU WANT TO SAY, AND I'LL WRITE IT..
DEAR MOM AND DAD, I'M LONESOME..
THAT ISN'T EXACTLY WHAT I MEANT!
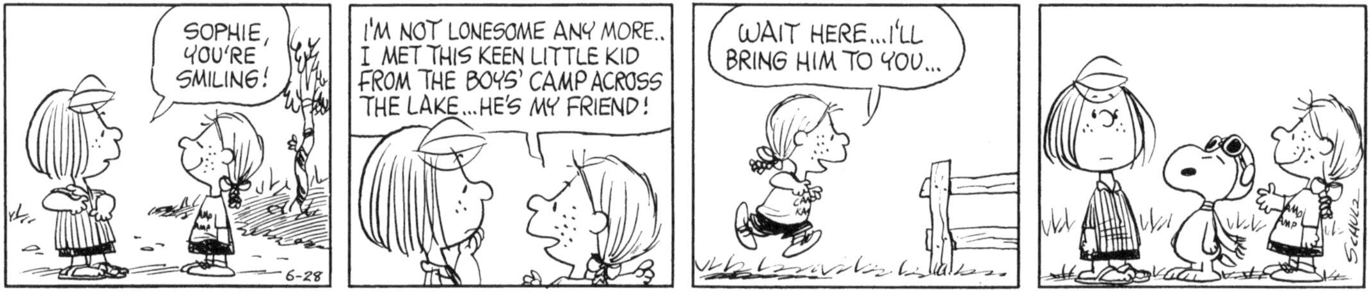
SOPHIE, YOU'RE SMILING!
6-28
I'M NOT LONESOME ANY MORE.. I MET THIS KEEN LITTLE KID FROM THE BOYS' CAMP ACROSS THE LAKE...HE'S MY FRIEND!
WAIT HERE...I'LL BRING HIM TO YOU...
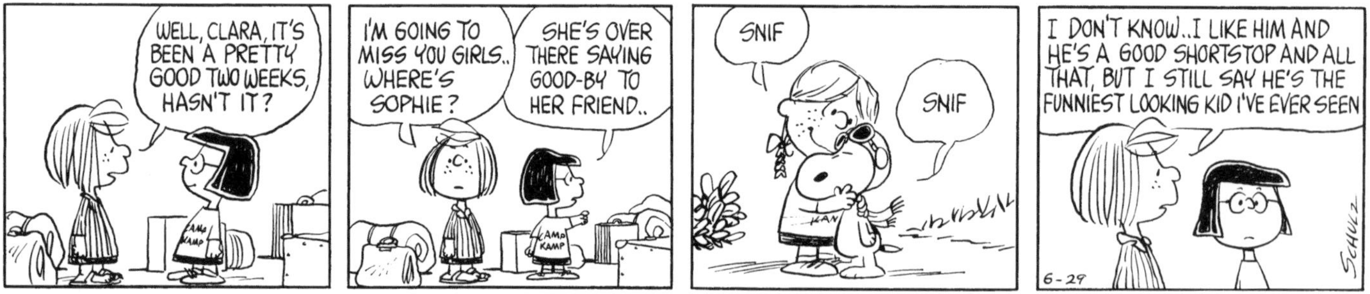
WELL, CLARA, IT'S BEEN A PRETTY GOOD TWO WEEKS, HASN'T IT?
I'M GOING TO MISS YOU GIRLS.. WHERE'S SOPHIE?
SHE'S OVER THERE SAYING GOOD-BY TO HER FRIEND..
SNIF
SNIF
I DON'T KNOW..I LIKE HIM AND HE'S A GOOD SHORTSTOP AND ALL THAT, BUT I STILL SAY HE'S THE FUNNIEST LOOKING KID I'VE EVER SEEN
6-29

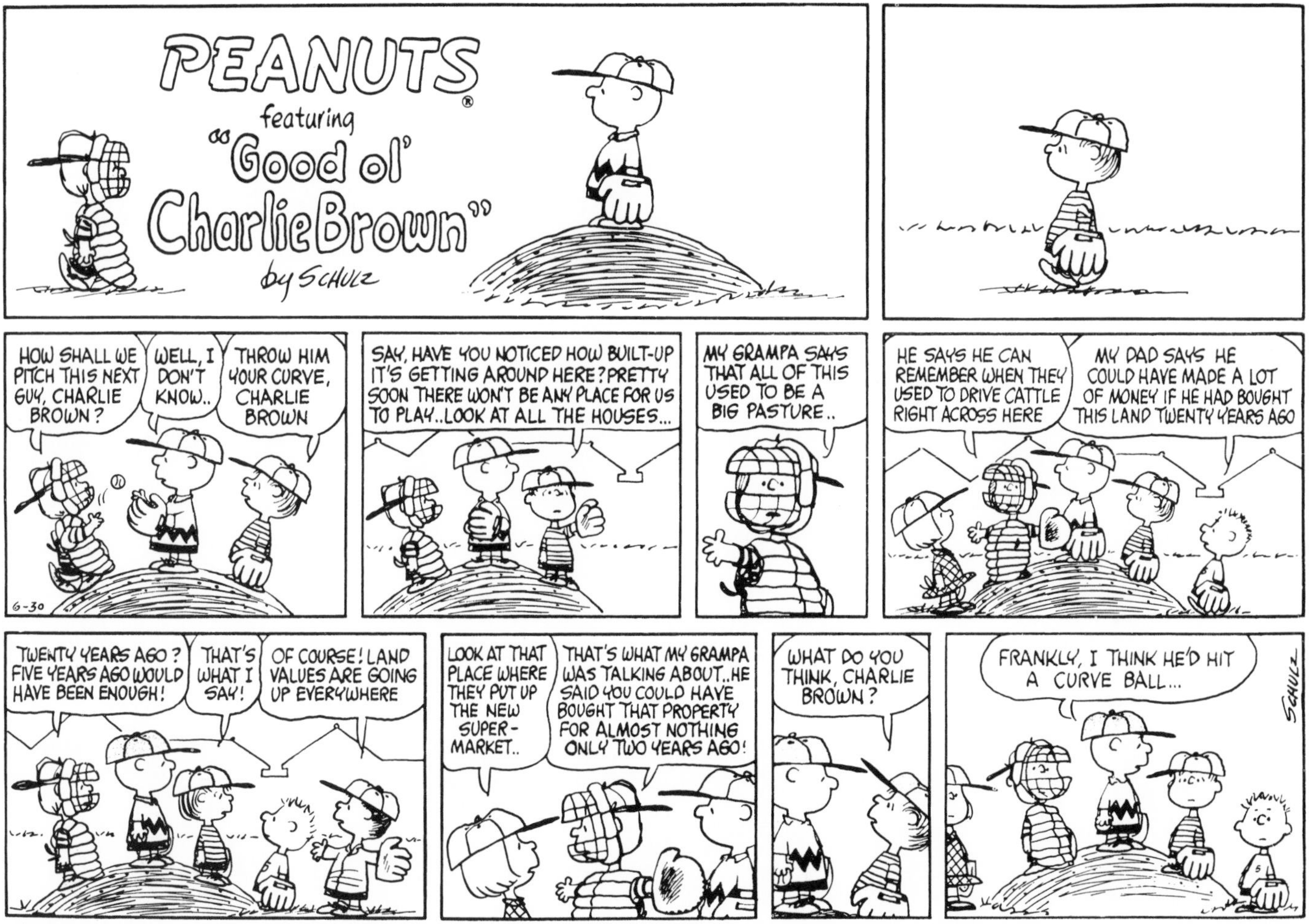
PEANUTS®
featuring
"Good ol' Charlie Brown"
by SCHULZ
HOW SHALL WE PITCH THIS NEXT GUY, CHARLIE BROWN?
WELL, I DON'T KNOW..
THROW HIM YOUR CURVE, CHARLIE BROWN
6-30
SAY, HAVE YOU NOTICED HOW BUILT-UP IT'S GETTING AROUND HERE? PRETTY SOON THERE WON'T BE ANY PLACE FOR US TO PLAY..LOOK AT ALL THE HOUSES...
MY GRAMPA SAYS THAT ALL OF THIS USED TO BE A BIG PASTURE..
HE SAYS HE CAN REMEMBER WHEN THEY USED TO DRIVE CATTLE RIGHT ACROSS HERE
MY DAD SAYS HE COULD HAVE MADE A LOT OF MONEY IF HE HAD BOUGHT THIS LAND TWENTY YEARS AGO
TWENTY YEARS AGO? FIVE YEARS AGO WOULD HAVE BEEN ENOUGH!
THAT'S WHAT I SAY!
OF COURSE! LAND VALUES ARE GOING UP EVERYWHERE
LOOK AT THAT PLACE WHERE THEY PUT UP THE NEW SUPER-MARKET..
THAT'S WHAT MY GRAMPA WAS TALKING ABOUT..HE SAID YOU COULD HAVE BOUGHT THAT PROPERTY FOR ALMOST NOTHING ONLY TWO YEARS AGO!
WHAT DO YOU THINK, CHARLIE BROWN?
FRANKLY, I THINK HE'D HIT A CURVE BALL...
SCHULZ

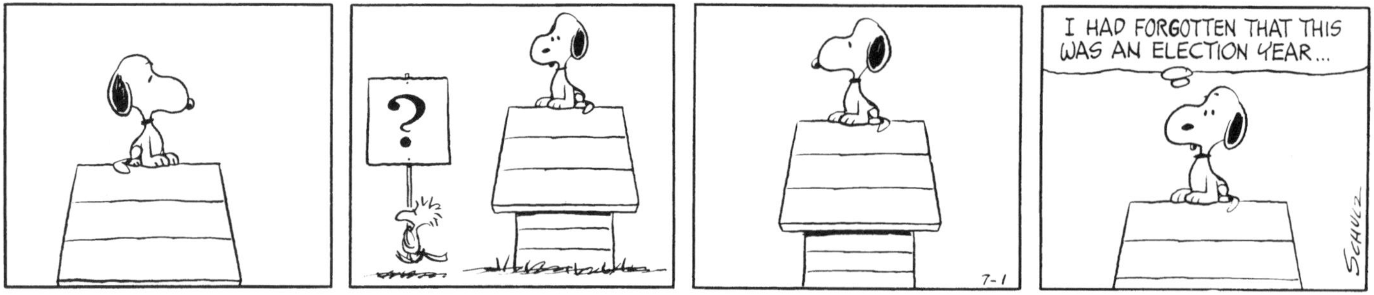
?
7-1
I HAD FORGOTTEN THAT THIS WAS AN ELECTION YEAR...
SCHULZ

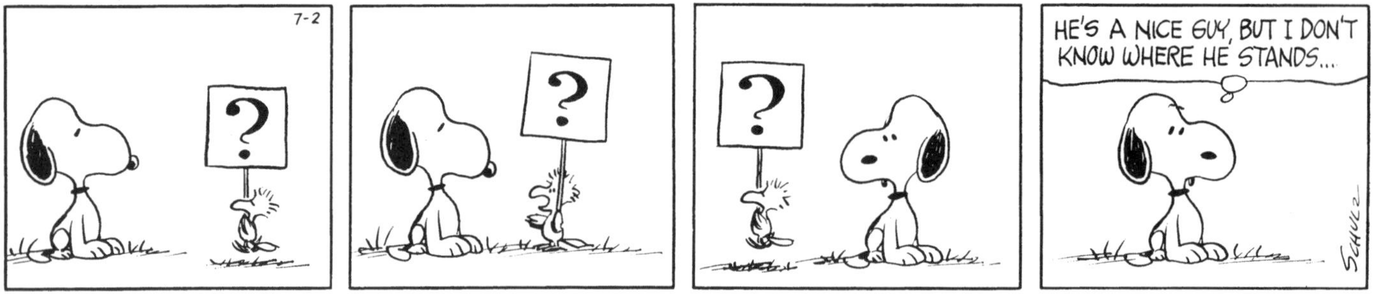
7-2
?
?
?
HE'S A NICE GUY, BUT I DON'T KNOW WHERE HE STANDS...
SCHULZ

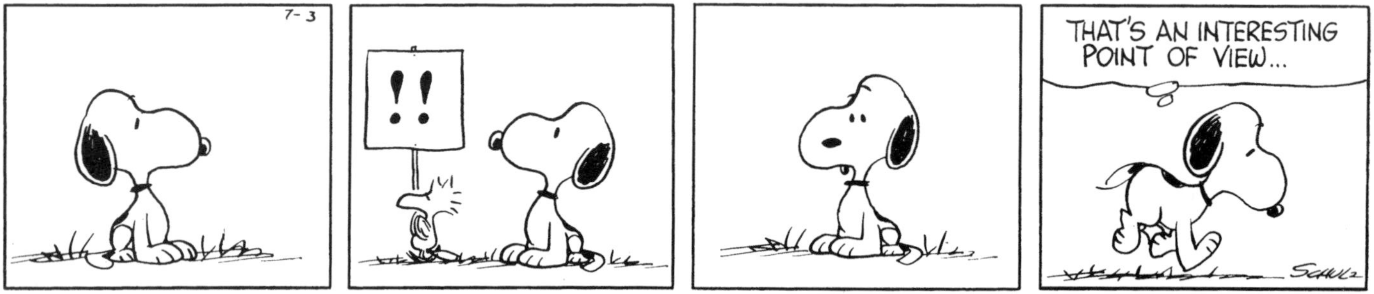
7-3
!!
THAT'S AN INTERESTING POINT OF VIEW...
SCHULZ

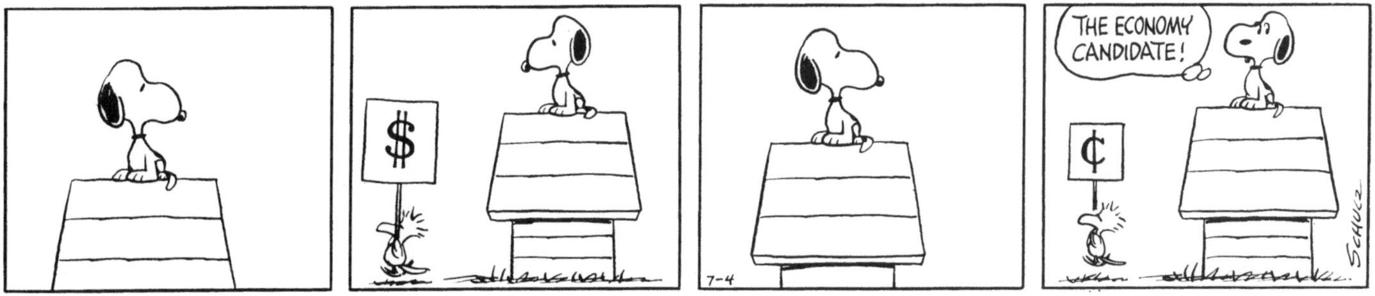
THE ECONOMY CANDIDATE!

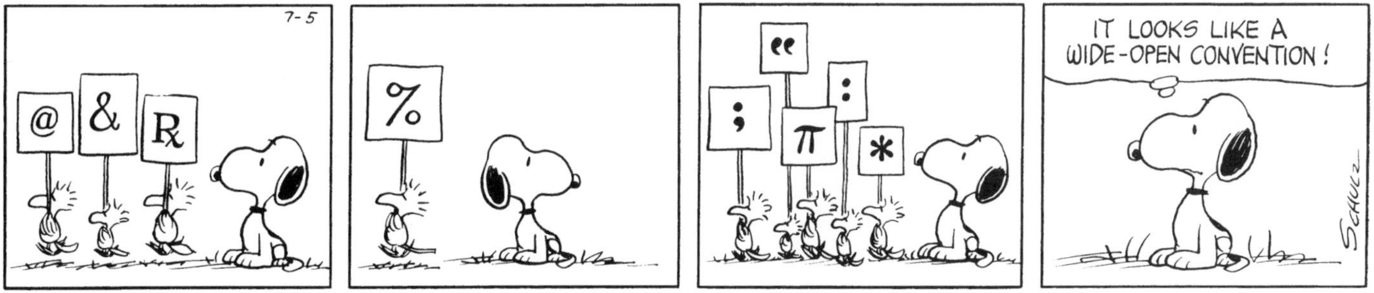
IT LOOKS LIKE A WIDE-OPEN CONVENTION!

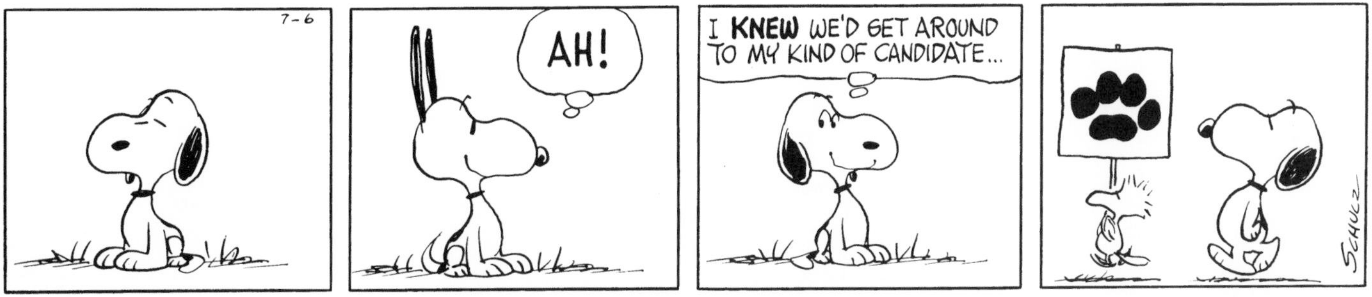
AH!
I **KNEW** WE'D GET AROUND TO MY KIND OF CANDIDATE...

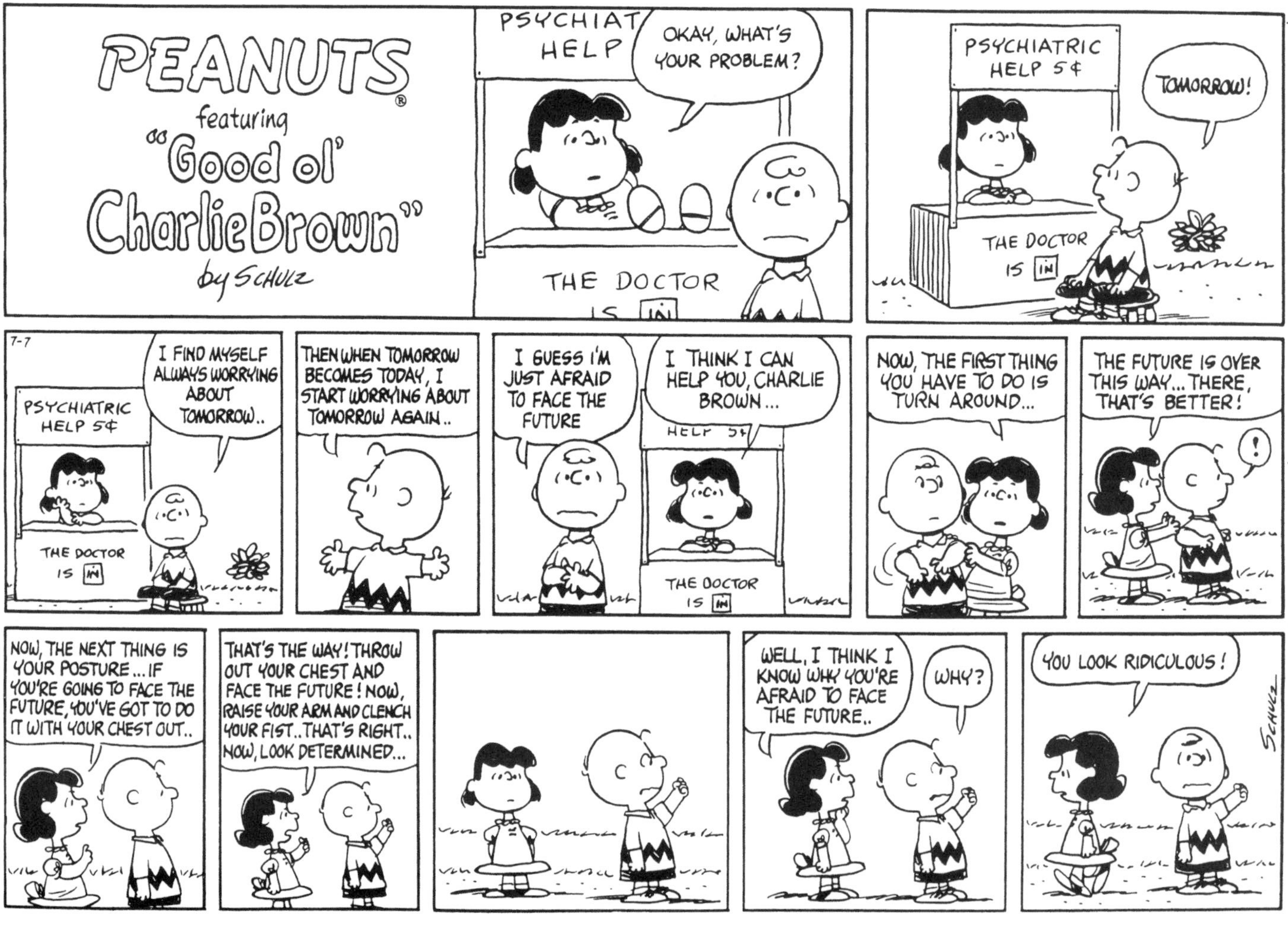
PEANUTS®
featuring
"Good ol' Charlie Brown"
by SCHULZ
PSYCHIAT HELP
OKAY, WHAT'S YOUR PROBLEM?
THE DOCTOR IS IN
PSYCHIATRIC HELP 5¢
TOMORROW!
THE DOCTOR IS IN
7-7
PSYCHIATRIC HELP 5¢
I FIND MYSELF ALWAYS WORRYING ABOUT TOMORROW..
THE DOCTOR IS IN
THEN WHEN TOMORROW BECOMES TODAY, I START WORRYING ABOUT TOMORROW AGAIN..
I GUESS I'M JUST AFRAID TO FACE THE FUTURE
I THINK I CAN HELP YOU, CHARLIE BROWN...
THE DOCTOR IS IN
NOW, THE FIRST THING YOU HAVE TO DO IS TURN AROUND...
THE FUTURE IS OVER THIS WAY... THERE, THAT'S BETTER!
!
NOW, THE NEXT THING IS YOUR POSTURE... IF YOU'RE GOING TO FACE THE FUTURE, YOU'VE GOT TO DO IT WITH YOUR CHEST OUT..
THAT'S THE WAY! THROW OUT YOUR CHEST AND FACE THE FUTURE! NOW, RAISE YOUR ARM AND CLENCH YOUR FIST.. THAT'S RIGHT.. NOW, LOOK DETERMINED...
WELL, I THINK I KNOW WHY YOU'RE AFRAID TO FACE THE FUTURE..
WHY?
YOU LOOK RIDICULOUS!
SCHULZ

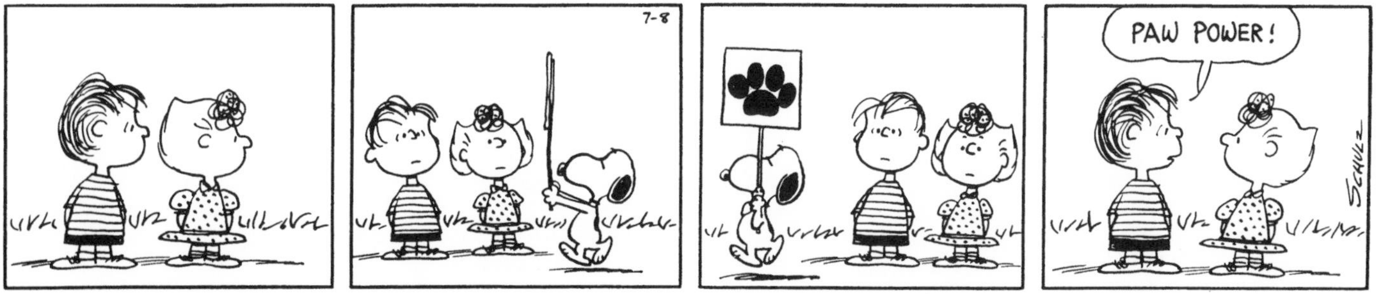
7-8
PAW POWER!
SCHULZ

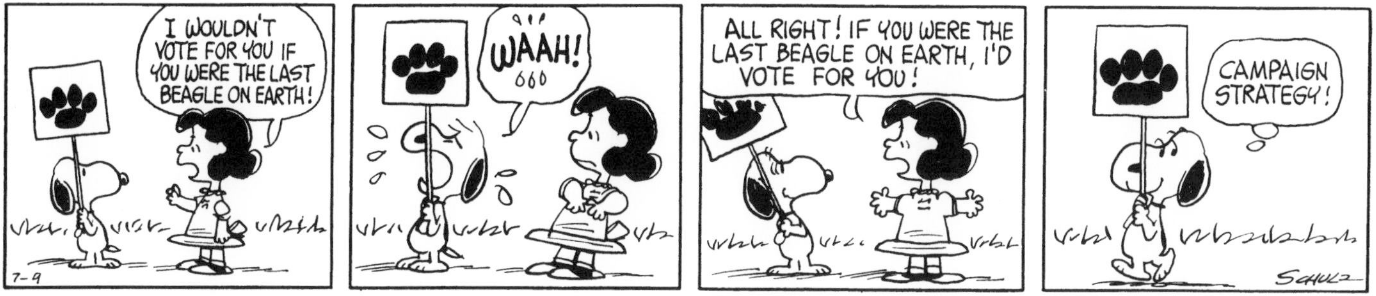
I WOULDN'T VOTE FOR YOU IF YOU WERE THE LAST BEAGLE ON EARTH!
7-9
WAAH!
ALL RIGHT! IF YOU WERE THE LAST BEAGLE ON EARTH, I'D VOTE FOR YOU!
CAMPAIGN STRATEGY!
SCHULZ

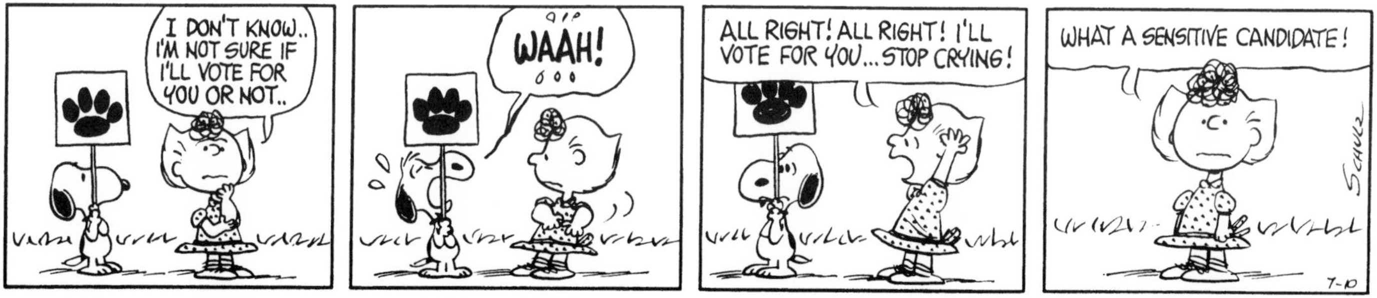
I DON'T KNOW.. I'M NOT SURE IF I'LL VOTE FOR YOU OR NOT..
WAAH!
ALL RIGHT! ALL RIGHT! I'LL VOTE FOR YOU... STOP CRYING!
WHAT A SENSITIVE CANDIDATE!
SCHULZ
7-10

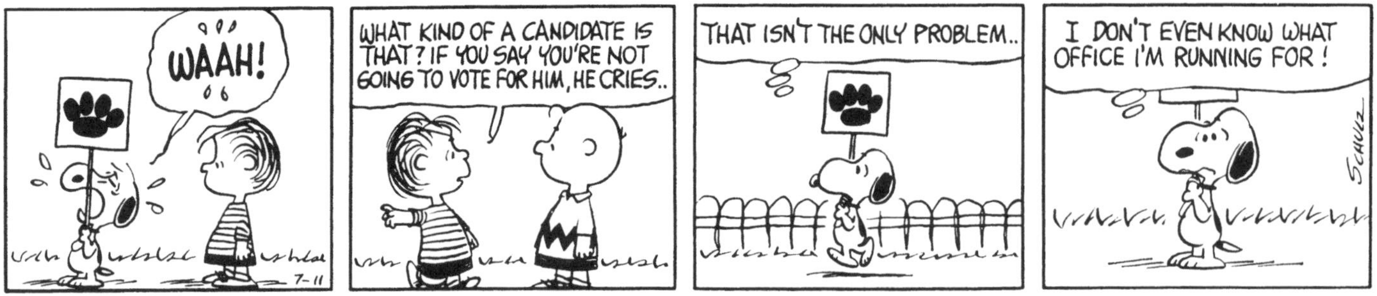
WAAH!
7-11
WHAT KIND OF A CANDIDATE IS THAT? IF YOU SAY YOU'RE NOT GOING TO VOTE FOR HIM, HE CRIES..
THAT ISN'T THE ONLY PROBLEM..
I DON'T EVEN KNOW WHAT OFFICE I'M RUNNING FOR!
SCHULZ

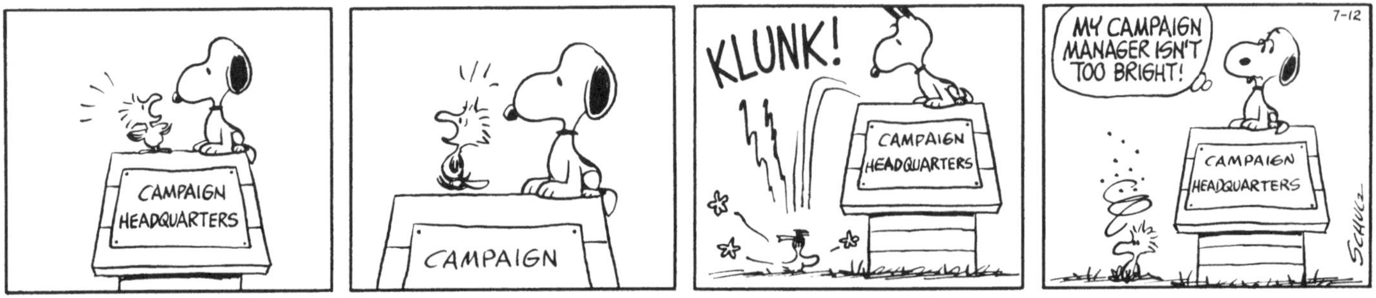
CAMPAIGN HEADQUARTERS
CAMPAIGN
KLUNK!
CAMPAIGN HEADQUARTERS
7-12
MY CAMPAIGN MANAGER ISN'T TOO BRIGHT!
CAMPAIGN HEADQUARTERS
SCHULZ

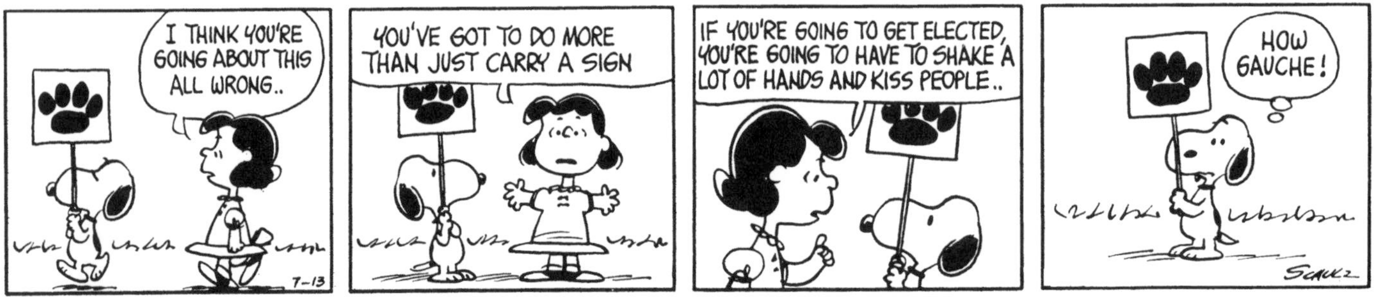
I THINK YOU'RE GOING ABOUT THIS ALL WRONG..
7-13
YOU'VE GOT TO DO MORE THAN JUST CARRY A SIGN
IF YOU'RE GOING TO GET ELECTED, YOU'RE GOING TO HAVE TO SHAKE A LOT OF HANDS AND KISS PEOPLE..
HOW GAUCHE!
SCHULZ

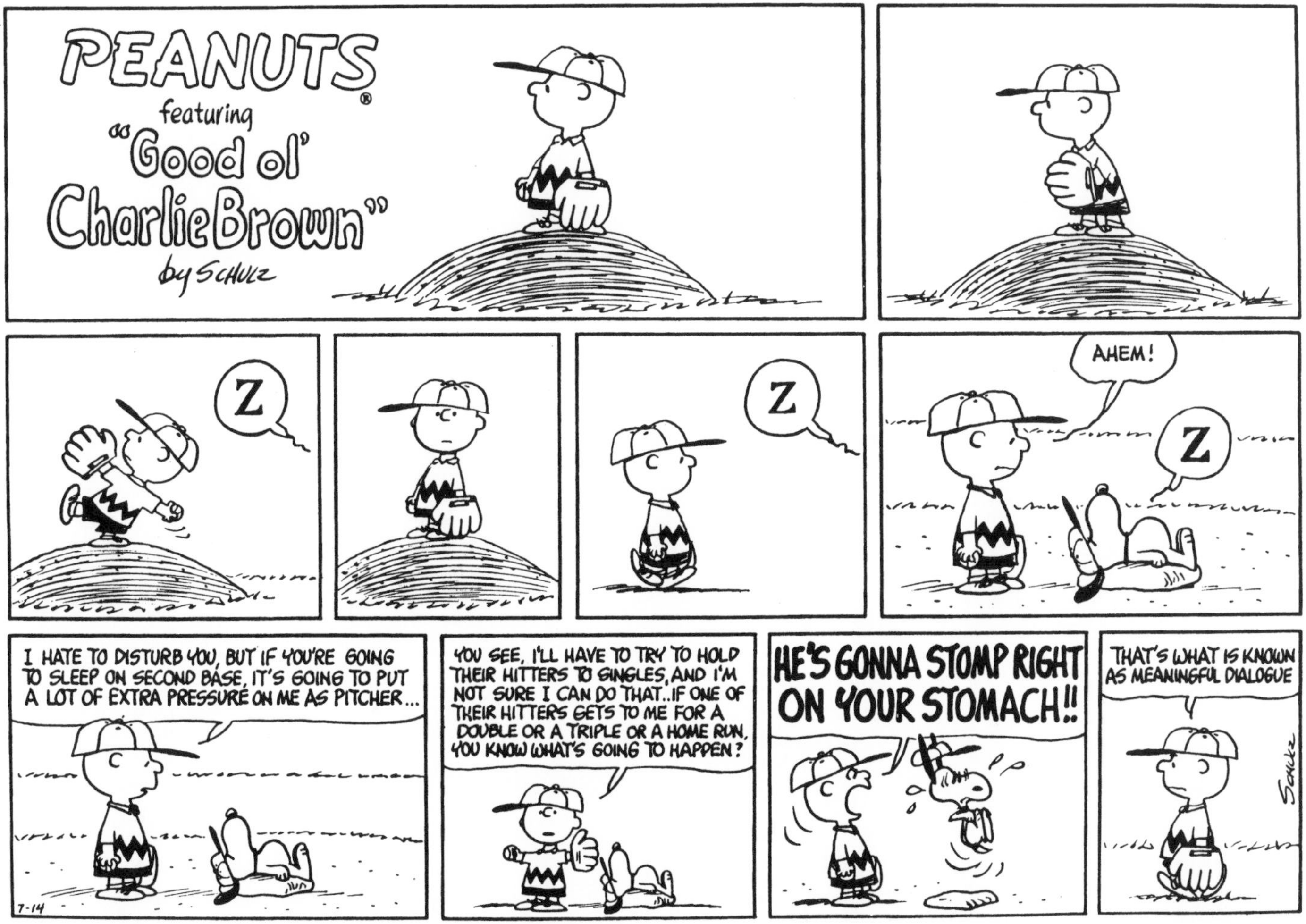
PEANUTS®
featuring "Good ol' Charlie Brown" by SCHULZ
Z
Z
AHEM!
Z
I HATE TO DISTURB YOU, BUT IF YOU'RE GOING TO SLEEP ON SECOND BASE, IT'S GOING TO PUT A LOT OF EXTRA PRESSURE ON ME AS PITCHER...
YOU SEE, I'LL HAVE TO TRY TO HOLD THEIR HITTERS TO SINGLES, AND I'M NOT SURE I CAN DO THAT..IF ONE OF THEIR HITTERS GETS TO ME FOR A DOUBLE OR A TRIPLE OR A HOME RUN, YOU KNOW WHAT'S GOING TO HAPPEN?
HE'S GONNA STOMP RIGHT ON YOUR STOMACH!!
THAT'S WHAT IS KNOWN AS MEANINGFUL DIALOGUE
SCHULZ
7-14

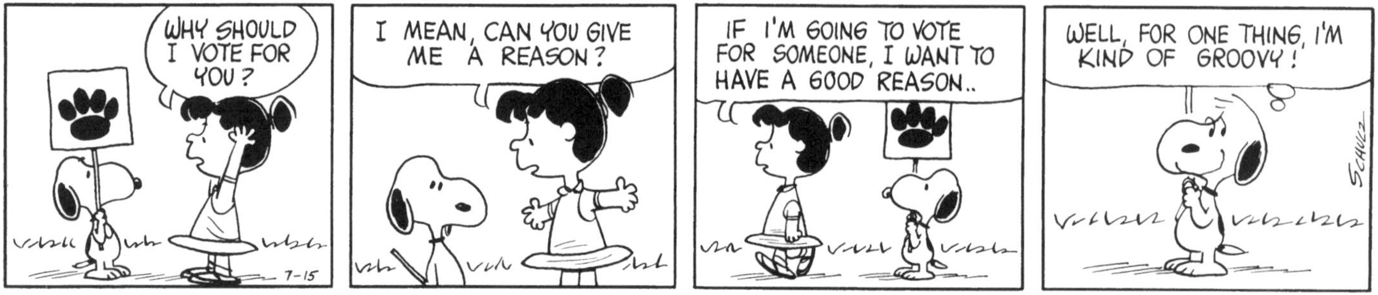
WHY SHOULD I VOTE FOR YOU?
7-15
I MEAN, CAN YOU GIVE ME A REASON?
IF I'M GOING TO VOTE FOR SOMEONE, I WANT TO HAVE A GOOD REASON..
WELL, FOR ONE THING, I'M KIND OF GROOVY!
SCHULZ

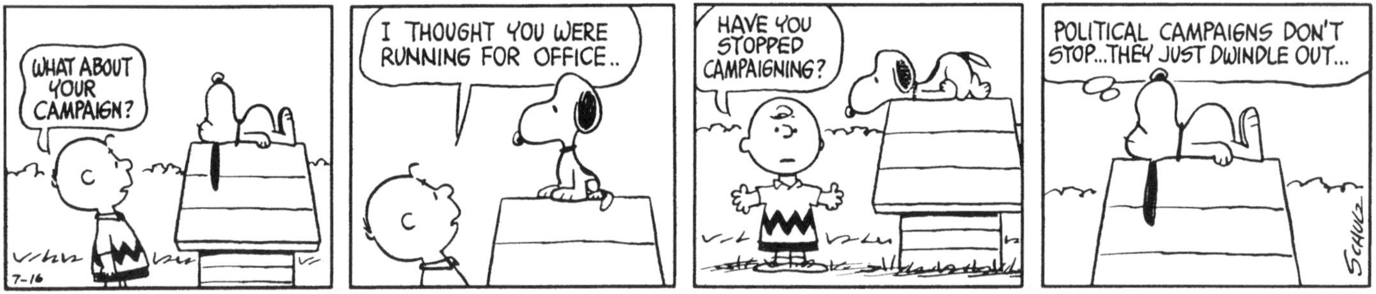
WHAT ABOUT YOUR CAMPAIGN?
7-16
I THOUGHT YOU WERE RUNNING FOR OFFICE..
HAVE YOU STOPPED CAMPAIGNING?
POLITICAL CAMPAIGNS DON'T STOP...THEY JUST DWINDLE OUT...
SCHULZ

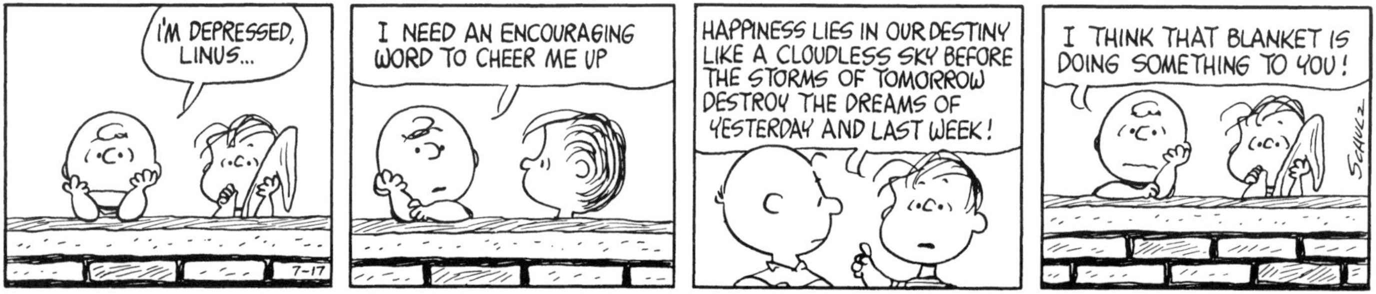
I'M DEPRESSED, LINUS...
7-17
I NEED AN ENCOURAGING WORD TO CHEER ME UP
HAPPINESS LIES IN OUR DESTINY LIKE A CLOUDLESS SKY BEFORE THE STORMS OF TOMORROW DESTROY THE DREAMS OF YESTERDAY AND LAST WEEK!
I THINK THAT BLANKET IS DOING SOMETHING TO YOU!
SCHULZ

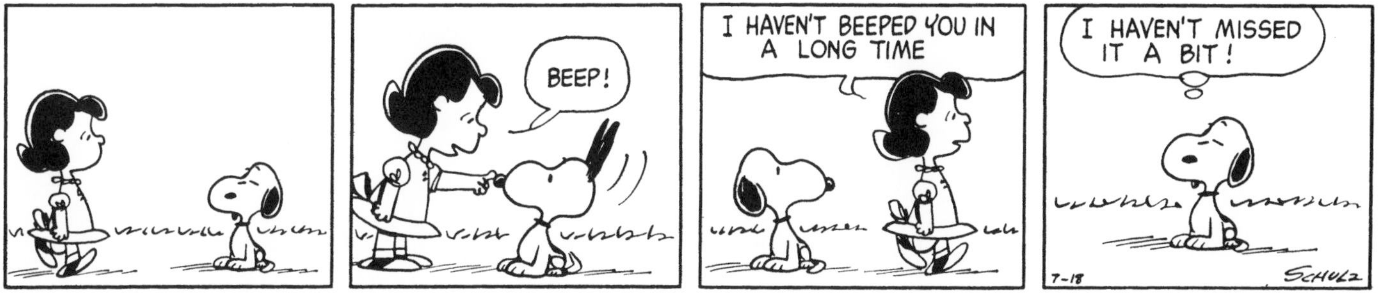
BEEP!
I HAVEN'T BEEPED YOU IN A LONG TIME
I HAVEN'T MISSED IT A BIT!
7-18
SCHULZ

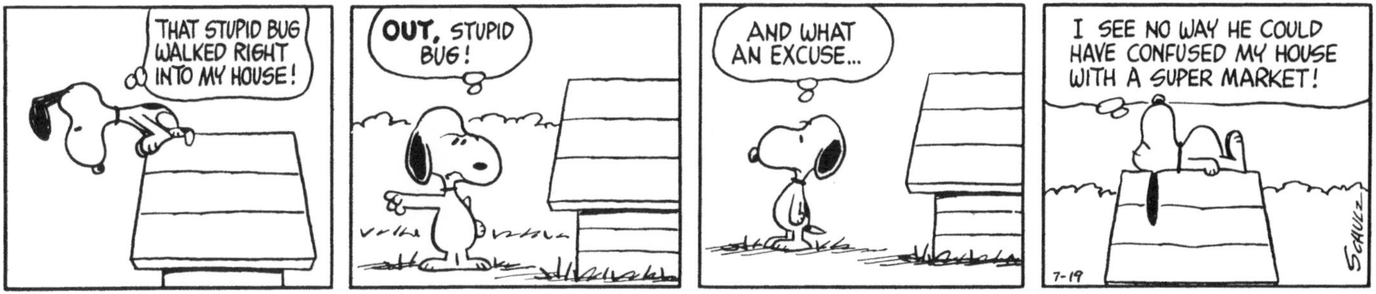
THAT STUPID BUG WALKED RIGHT INTO MY HOUSE!
OUT, STUPID BUG!
AND WHAT AN EXCUSE...
I SEE NO WAY HE COULD HAVE CONFUSED MY HOUSE WITH A SUPER MARKET!
SCHULZ
7-19

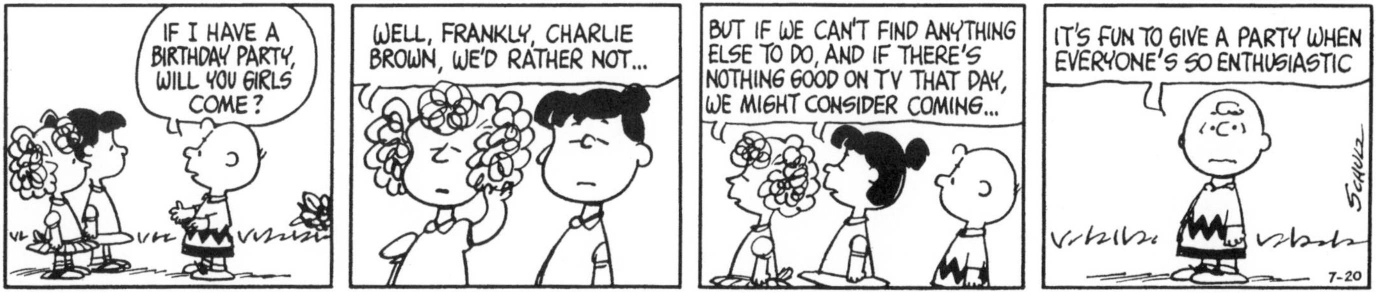
IF I HAVE A BIRTHDAY PARTY, WILL YOU GIRLS COME?
WELL, FRANKLY, CHARLIE BROWN, WE'D RATHER NOT...
BUT IF WE CAN'T FIND ANYTHING ELSE TO DO, AND IF THERE'S NOTHING GOOD ON TV THAT DAY, WE MIGHT CONSIDER COMING...
IT'S FUN TO GIVE A PARTY WHEN EVERYONE'S SO ENTHUSIASTIC
SCHULZ
7-20

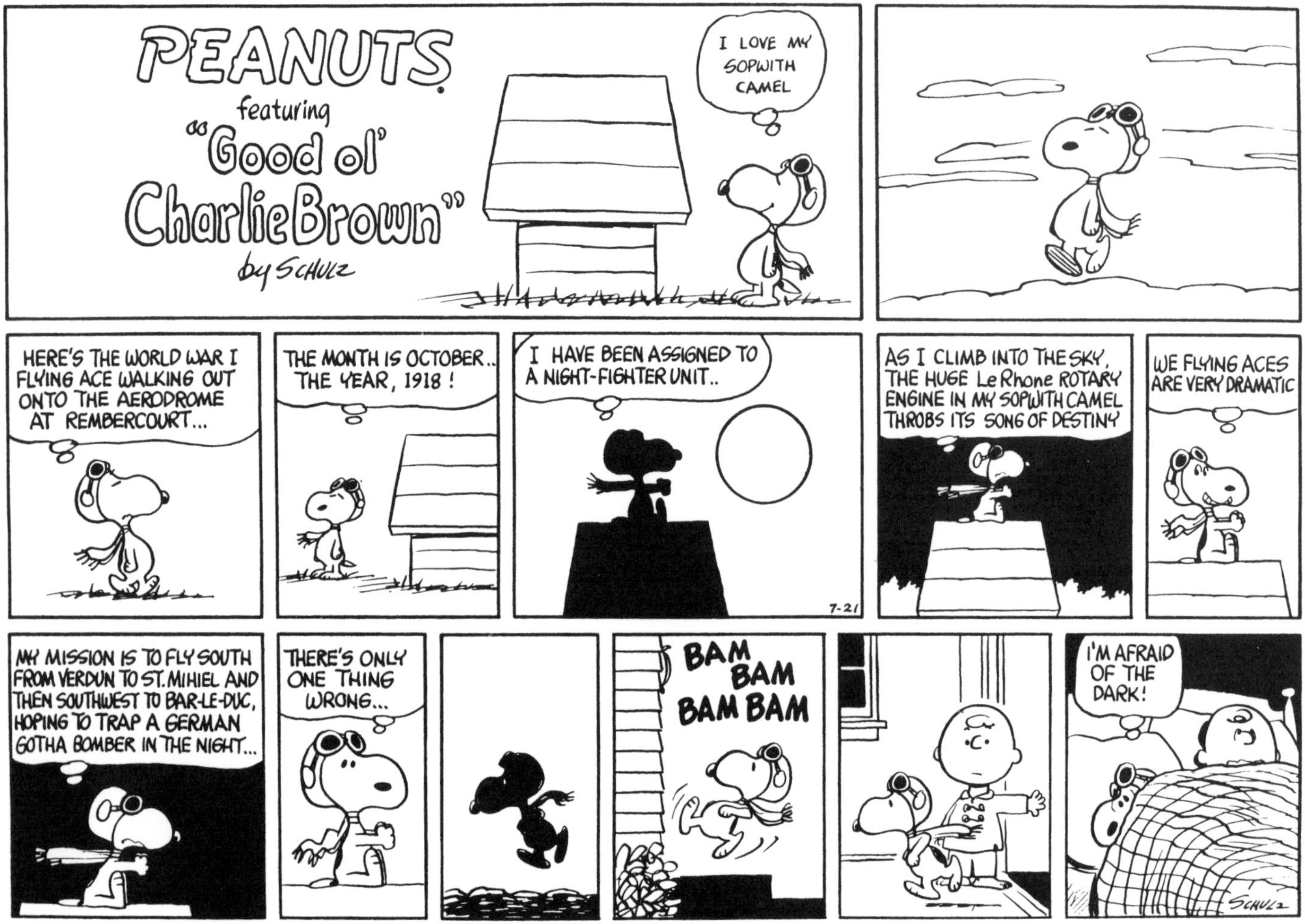
PEANUTS
featuring
"Good ol' CharlieBrown"
by SCHULZ
I LOVE MY SOPWITH CAMEL
HERE'S THE WORLD WAR I FLYING ACE WALKING OUT ONTO THE AERODROME AT REMBERCOURT...
THE MONTH IS OCTOBER.. THE YEAR, 1918 !
I HAVE BEEN ASSIGNED TO A NIGHT-FIGHTER UNIT..
7-21
AS I CLIMB INTO THE SKY, THE HUGE Le Rhone ROTARY ENGINE IN MY SOPWITH CAMEL THROBS ITS SONG OF DESTINY
WE FLYING ACES ARE VERY DRAMATIC
MY MISSION IS TO FLY SOUTH FROM VERDUN TO ST. MIHIEL AND THEN SOUTHWEST TO BAR-LE-DUC, HOPING TO TRAP A GERMAN GOTHA BOMBER IN THE NIGHT...
THERE'S ONLY ONE THING WRONG...
BAM BAM BAM BAM
I'M AFRAID OF THE DARK!
SCHULZ

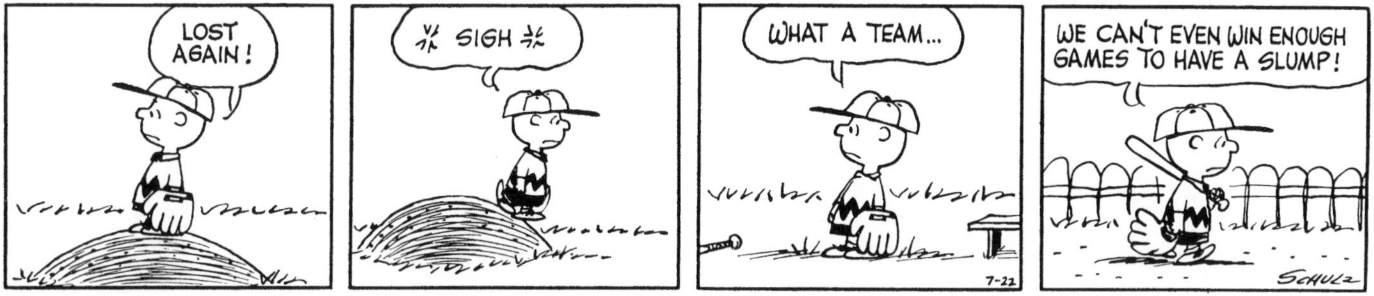

LOST AGAIN!
SIGH
WHAT A TEAM...
7-22
WE CAN'T EVEN WIN ENOUGH GAMES TO HAVE A SLUMP!
SCHULZ

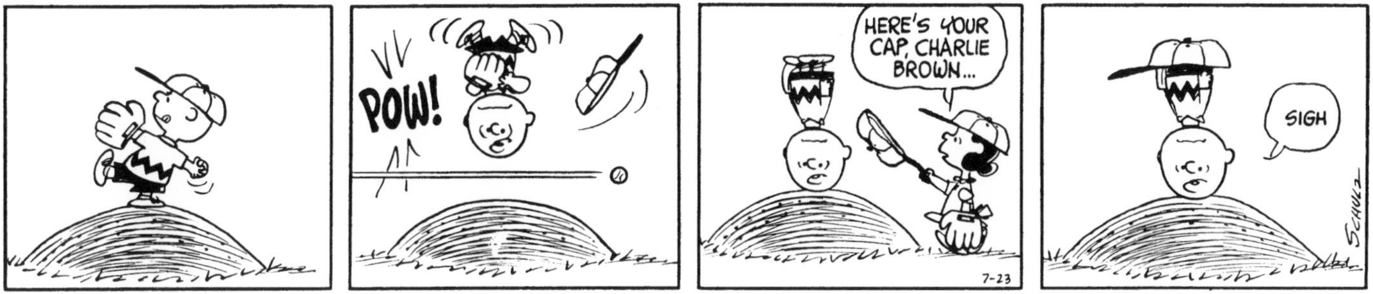

POW!
HERE'S YOUR CAP, CHARLIE BROWN...
7-23
SIGH
SCHULZ

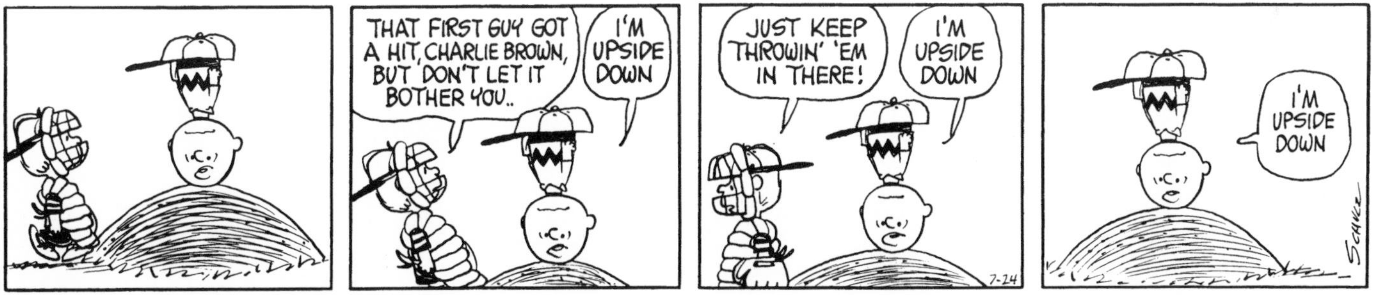

THAT FIRST GUY GOT A HIT, CHARLIE BROWN, BUT DON'T LET IT BOTHER YOU..
I'M UPSIDE DOWN
JUST KEEP THROWIN' 'EM IN THERE!
I'M UPSIDE DOWN
7-24
I'M UPSIDE DOWN
SCHULZ

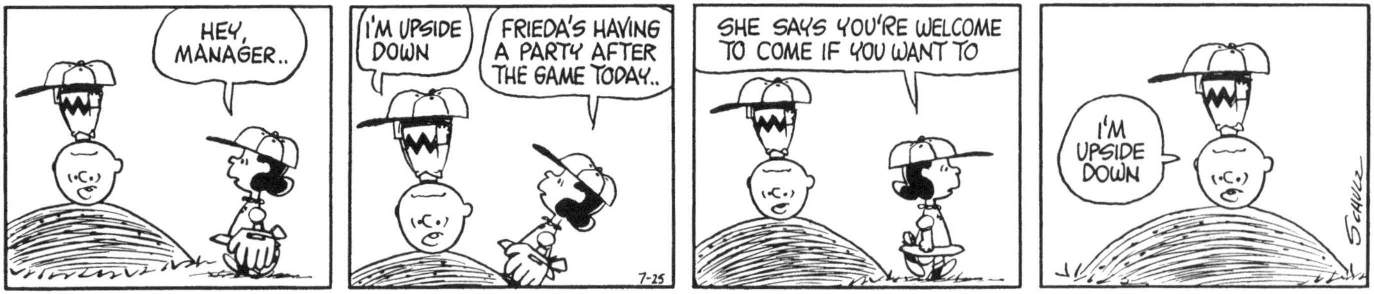
HEY, MANAGER..
I'M UPSIDE DOWN
FRIEDA'S HAVING A PARTY AFTER THE GAME TODAY..
7-25
SHE SAYS YOU'RE WELCOME TO COME IF YOU WANT TO
I'M UPSIDE DOWN
SCHULZ

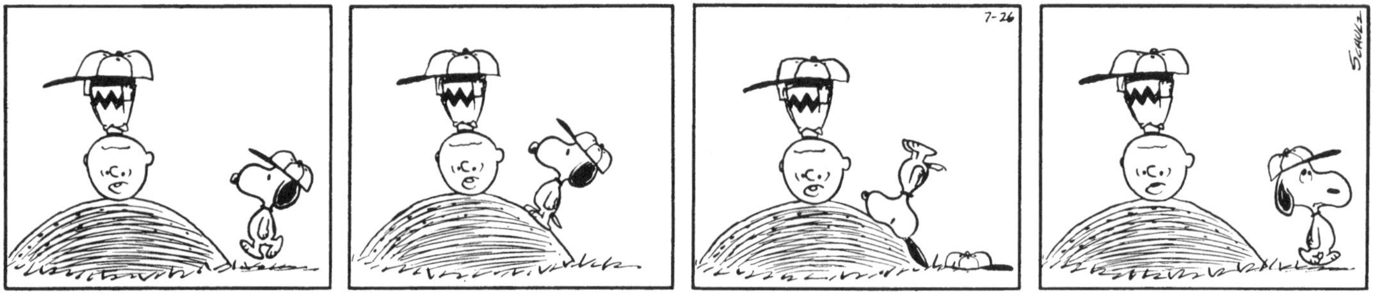
7-26
SCHULZ

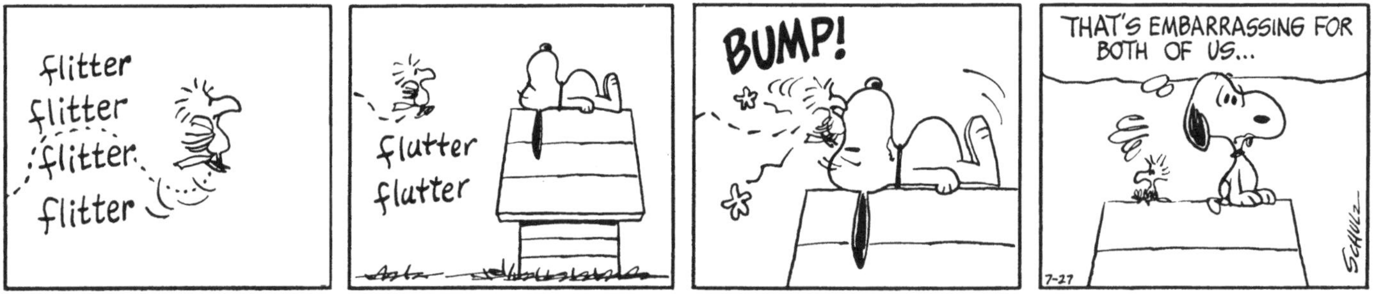
flitter
flitter
flitter
flitter
flutter
flutter
BUMP!
THAT'S EMBARRASSING FOR BOTH OF US...
7-27
SCHULZ

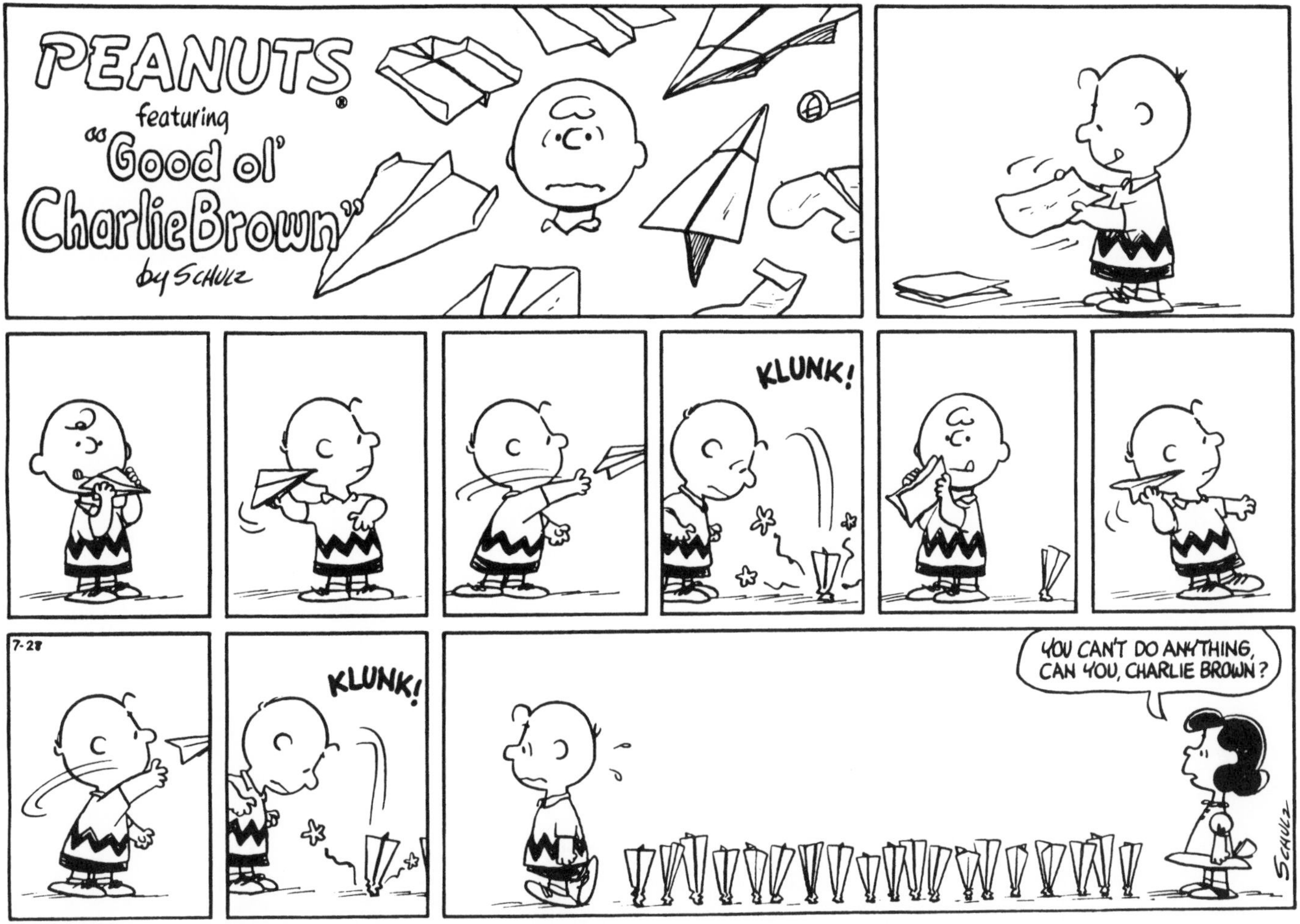
PEANUTS®
featuring
"Good ol' Charlie Brown"
by SCHULZ
KLUNK!
7-28
KLUNK!
YOU CAN'T DO ANYTHING, CAN YOU, CHARLIE BROWN?
SCHULZ

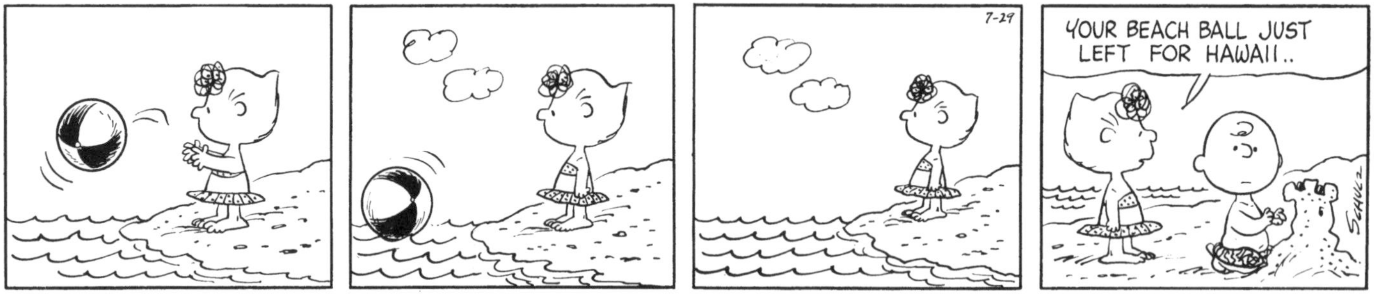
7-29
YOUR BEACH BALL JUST LEFT FOR HAWAII..

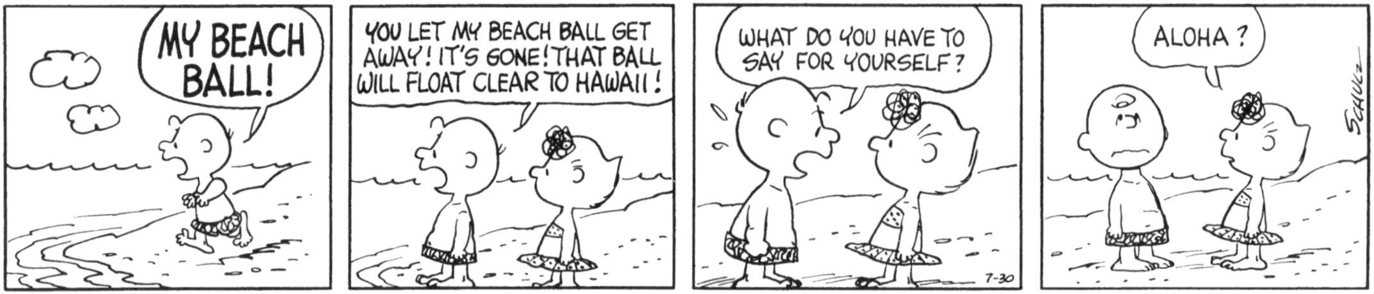
MY BEACH BALL!
YOU LET MY BEACH BALL GET AWAY! IT'S GONE! THAT BALL WILL FLOAT CLEAR TO HAWAII!
WHAT DO YOU HAVE TO SAY FOR YOURSELF?
7-30
ALOHA?

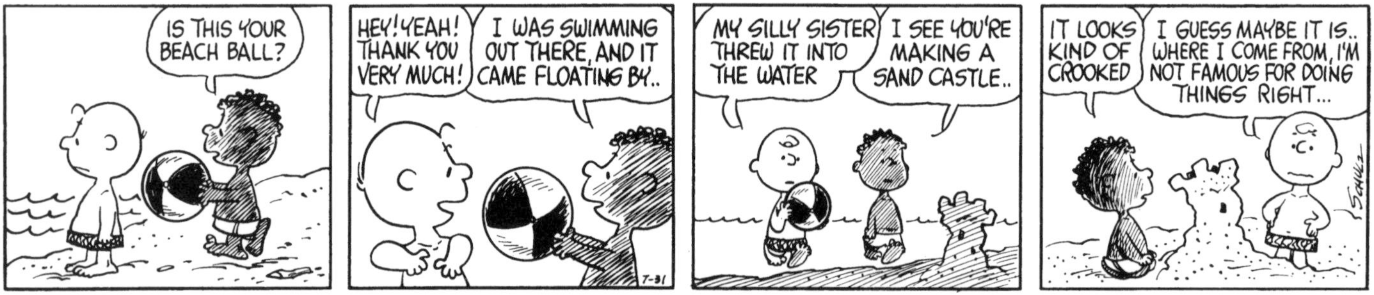
IS THIS YOUR BEACH BALL?
HEY! YEAH! THANK YOU VERY MUCH!
I WAS SWIMMING OUT THERE, AND IT CAME FLOATING BY..
7-31
MY SILLY SISTER THREW IT INTO THE WATER
I SEE YOU'RE MAKING A SAND CASTLE..
IT LOOKS KIND OF CROOKED
I GUESS MAYBE IT IS.. WHERE I COME FROM, I'M NOT FAMOUS FOR DOING THINGS RIGHT...

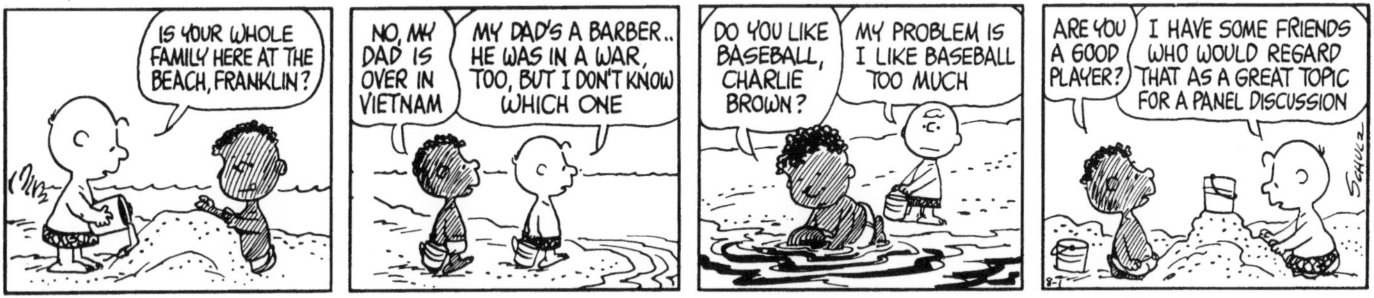
IS YOUR WHOLE FAMILY HERE AT THE BEACH, FRANKLIN?
NO, MY DAD IS OVER IN VIETNAM
MY DAD'S A BARBER.. HE WAS IN A WAR, TOO, BUT I DON'T KNOW WHICH ONE
DO YOU LIKE BASEBALL, CHARLIE BROWN?
MY PROBLEM IS I LIKE BASEBALL TOO MUCH
ARE YOU A GOOD PLAYER?
I HAVE SOME FRIENDS WHO WOULD REGARD THAT AS A GREAT TOPIC FOR A PANEL DISCUSSION
SCHULZ
8-1

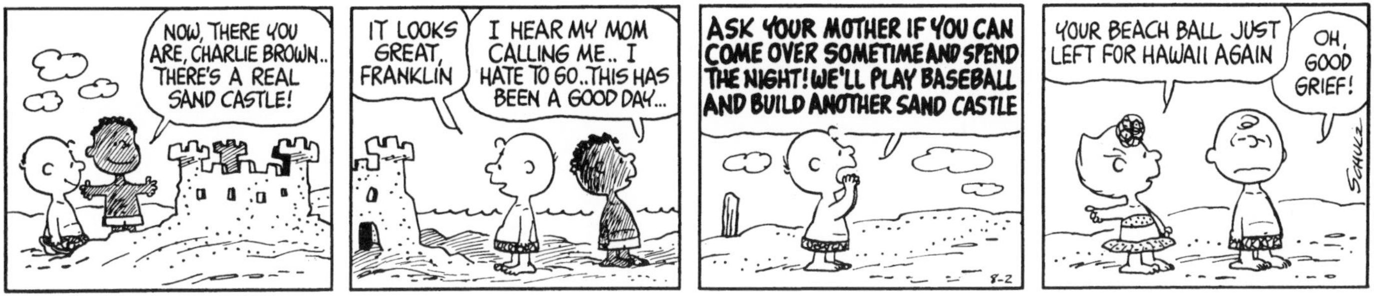
NOW, THERE YOU ARE, CHARLIE BROWN.. THERE'S A REAL SAND CASTLE!
IT LOOKS GREAT, FRANKLIN
I HEAR MY MOM CALLING ME.. I HATE TO GO..THIS HAS BEEN A GOOD DAY...
ASK YOUR MOTHER IF YOU CAN COME OVER SOMETIME AND SPEND THE NIGHT! WE'LL PLAY BASEBALL AND BUILD ANOTHER SAND CASTLE
8-2
YOUR BEACH BALL JUST LEFT FOR HAWAII AGAIN
OH, GOOD GRIEF!
SCHULZ

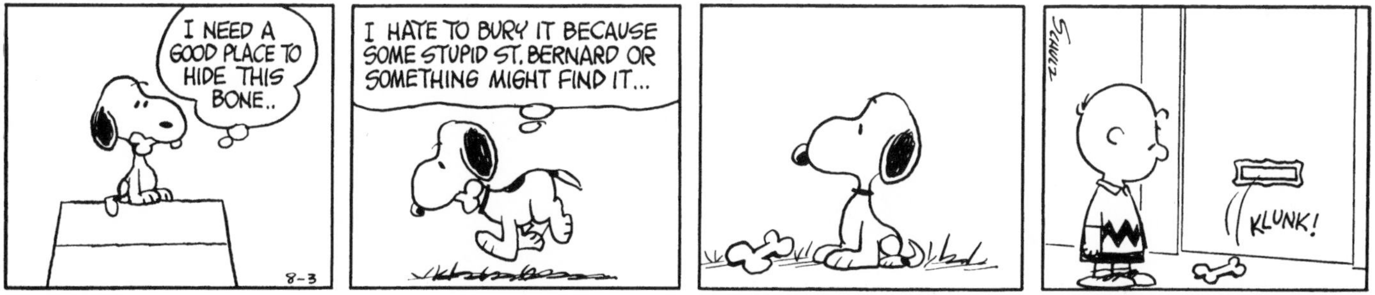
I NEED A GOOD PLACE TO HIDE THIS BONE..
8-3
I HATE TO BURY IT BECAUSE SOME STUPID ST. BERNARD OR SOMETHING MIGHT FIND IT...
SCHULZ
KLUNK!

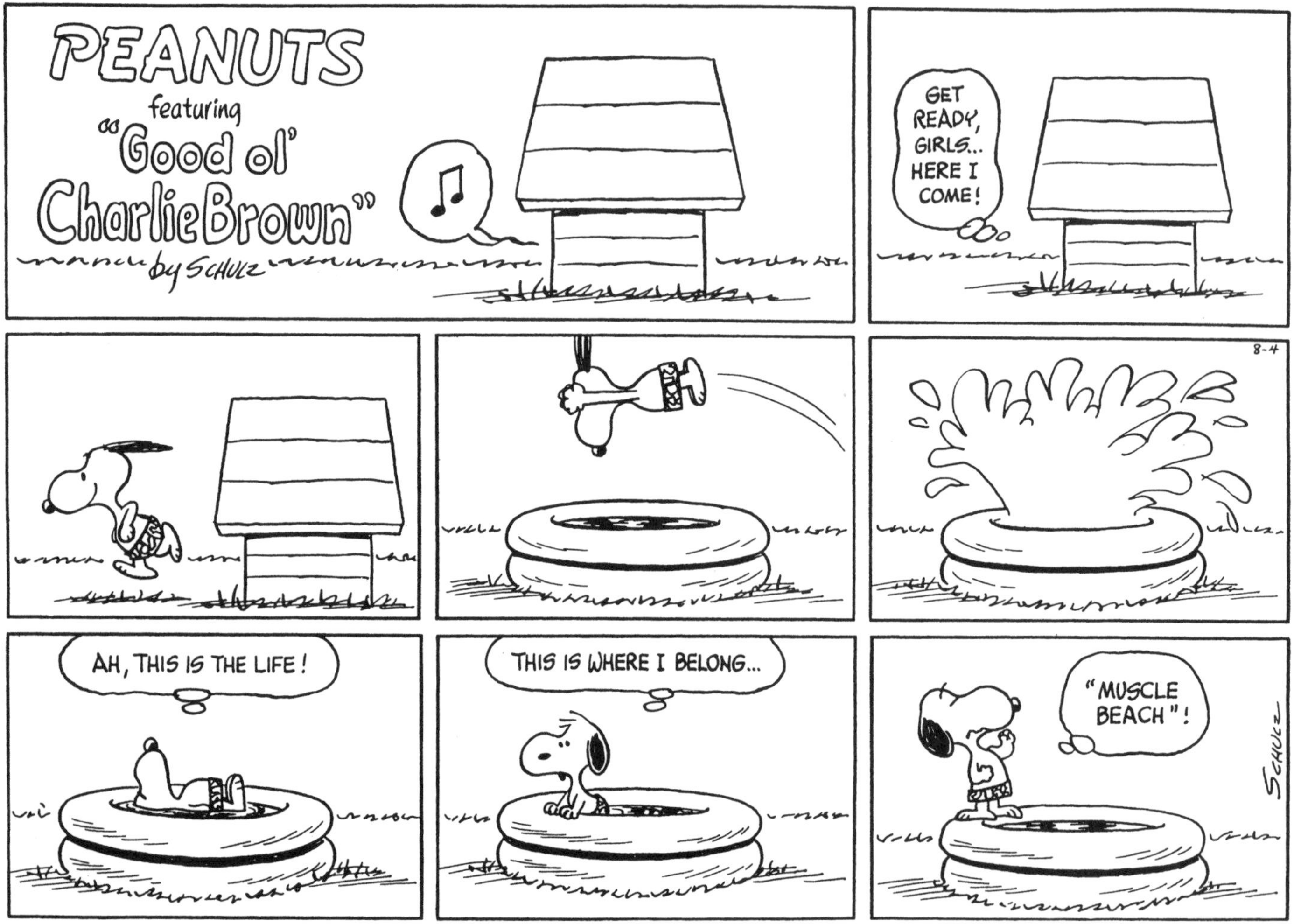
PEANUTS
featuring "Good ol' CharlieBrown"
by SCHULZ
GET READY, GIRLS... HERE I COME!
8-4
AH, THIS IS THE LIFE!
THIS IS WHERE I BELONG...
"MUSCLE BEACH"!
SCHULZ

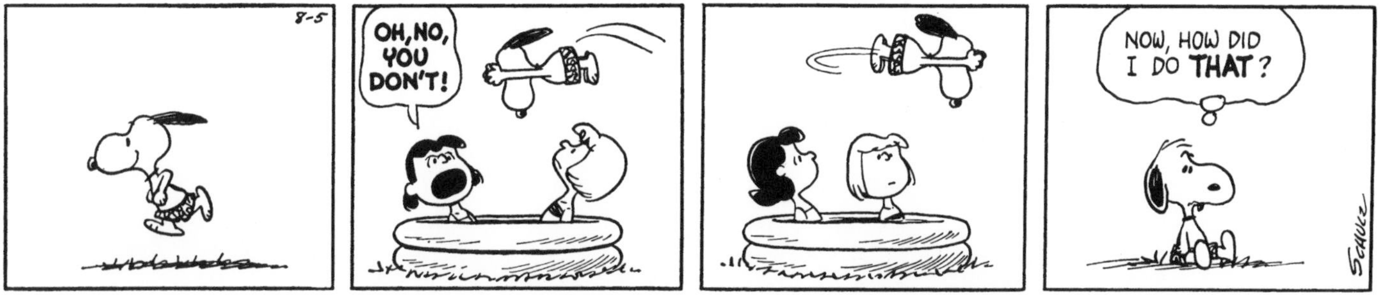
OH, NO, YOU DON'T!
NOW, HOW DID I DO THAT?

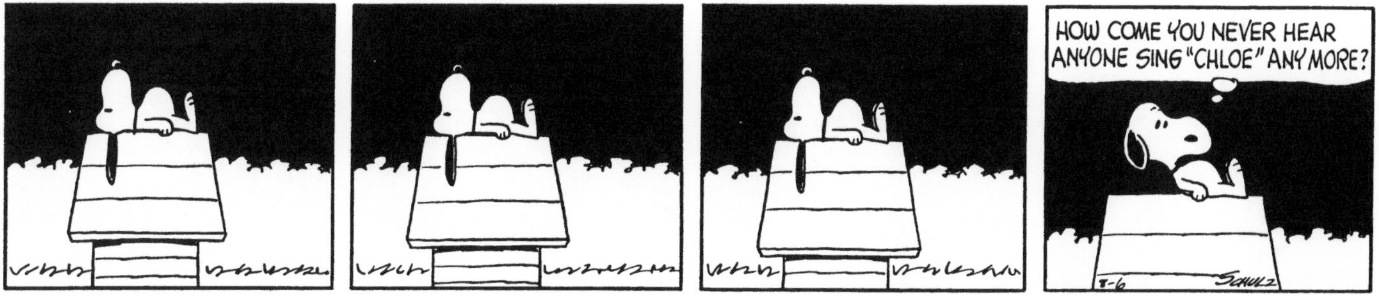
HOW COME YOU NEVER HEAR ANYONE SING "CHLOE" ANY MORE?

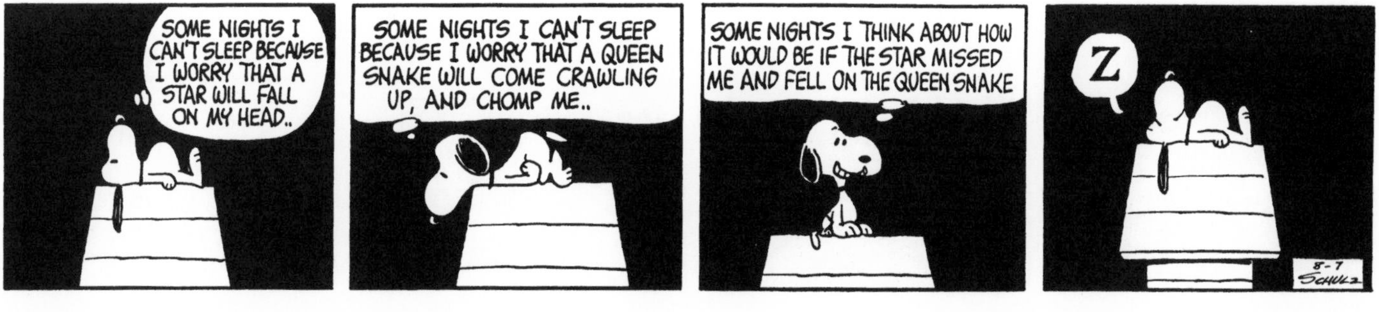
SOME NIGHTS I CAN'T SLEEP BECAUSE I WORRY THAT A STAR WILL FALL ON MY HEAD..
SOME NIGHTS I CAN'T SLEEP BECAUSE I WORRY THAT A QUEEN SNAKE WILL COME CRAWLING UP, AND CHOMP ME..
SOME NIGHTS I THINK ABOUT HOW IT WOULD BE IF THE STAR MISSED ME AND FELL ON THE QUEEN SNAKE
Z

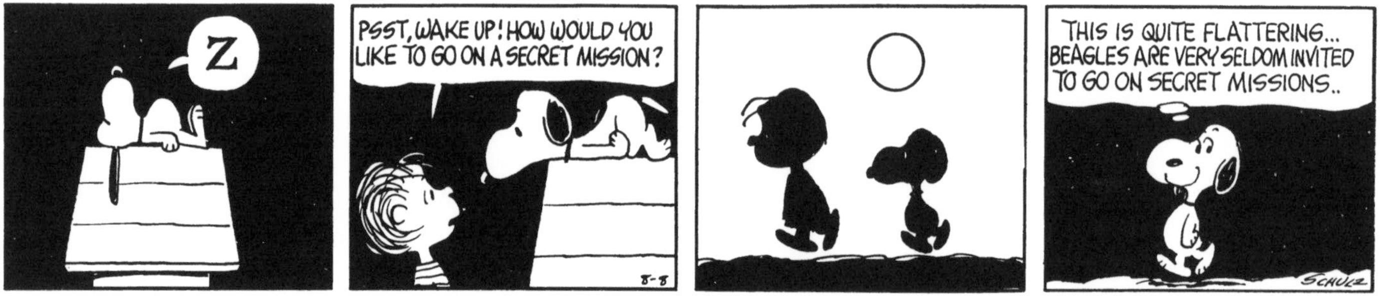
Z
PSST, WAKE UP! HOW WOULD YOU LIKE TO GO ON A SECRET MISSION?
8-8
THIS IS QUITE FLATTERING... BEAGLES ARE VERY SELDOM INVITED TO GO ON SECRET MISSIONS..
SCHULZ

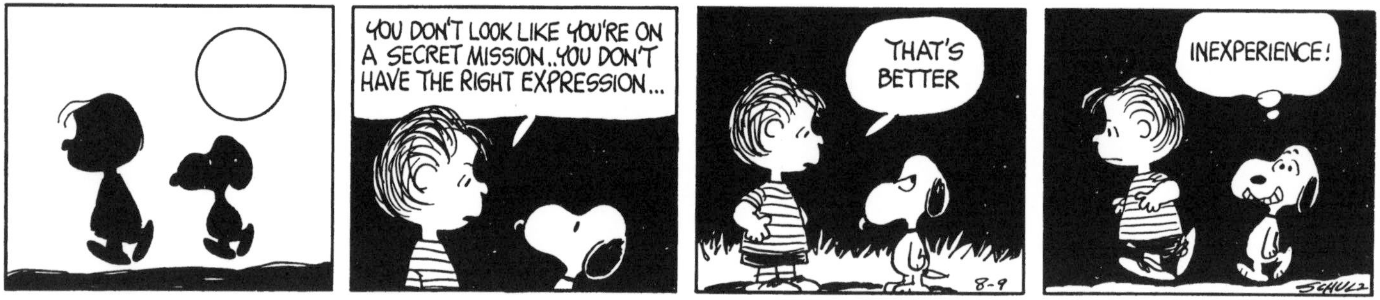
YOU DON'T LOOK LIKE YOU'RE ON A SECRET MISSION..YOU DON'T HAVE THE RIGHT EXPRESSION...
THAT'S BETTER
8-9
INEXPERIENCE!
SCHULZ

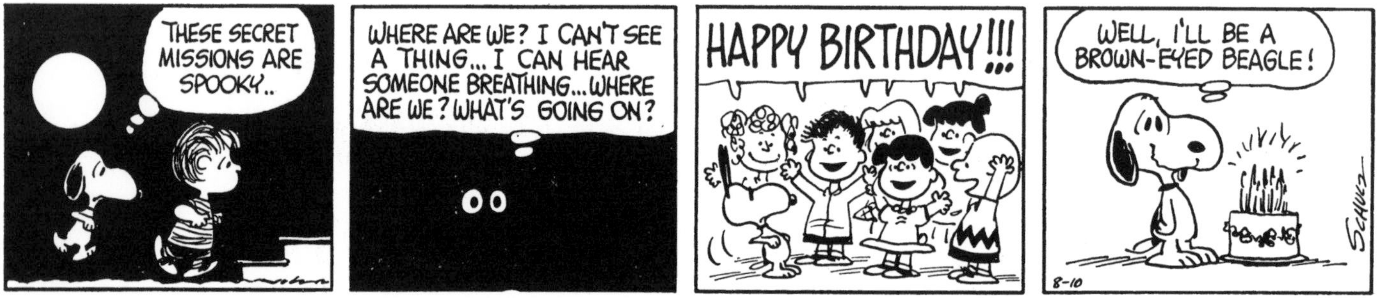
THESE SECRET MISSIONS ARE SPOOKY..
WHERE ARE WE? I CAN'T SEE A THING... I CAN HEAR SOMEONE BREATHING...WHERE ARE WE? WHAT'S GOING ON?
HAPPY BIRTHDAY!!!
WELL, I'LL BE A BROWN-EYED BEAGLE!
8-10
SCHULZ

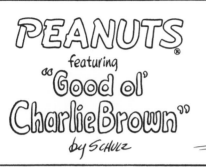

PEANUTS featuring "Good ol' CharlieBrown" by Schulz

PSYCHIATRIC HELP 5¢

THE DOCTOR IS [IN]

I'VE BEEN THINKING ABOUT YOUR CASE A LOT LATELY...

THAT'S VERY GRATIFYING..

THE DOCTOR IS [IN]

PSYCHIA... HELP...

YOU KNOW WHAT YOUR TROUBLE IS, CHARLIE BROWN?

THE DOCTO... IS...

YOU DON'T HAVE A PERSONAL PHILOSOPHY...

YOU NEED TO DEVELOP A PHILOSOPHY THAT WILL CARRY YOU THROUGH TIMES OF STRESS... CAN YOU DO THAT?

CAN YOU DEVELOP A PERSONAL PHILOSOPHY? THINK, CHARLIE BROWN! THINK HARD!

THE DOCTOR IS [IN]

"LIFE IS LIKE AN ICE CREAM CONE... YOU HAVE TO LEARN TO LICK IT!"

8-11

HELP 5¢

THE DOCTOR

THAT'S THE MOST STUPID PHILOSOPHY I'VE EVER HEARD!

THE DOCTOR IS [IN]

I CAN'T DO ANYTHING FOR SOMEONE WHO HAS A PHILOSOPHY LIKE THAT! YOU'RE HOPELESS, CHARLIE BROWN!

TH...

IT'S HARD TO DEVELOP A REAL PERSONAL PHILOSOPHY IN LESS THAN TWENTY MINUTES..

Schulz

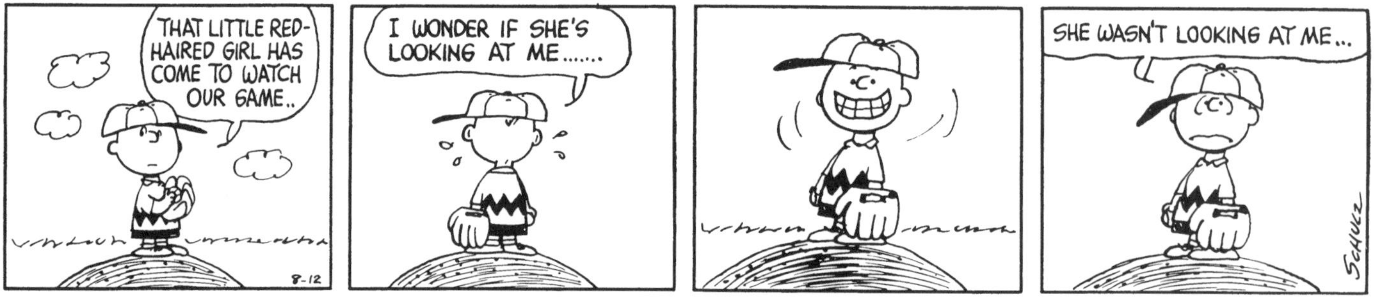
THAT LITTLE RED-HAIRED GIRL HAS COME TO WATCH OUR GAME..
8-12
I WONDER IF SHE'S LOOKING AT ME.......
SHE WASN'T LOOKING AT ME...
SCHULZ

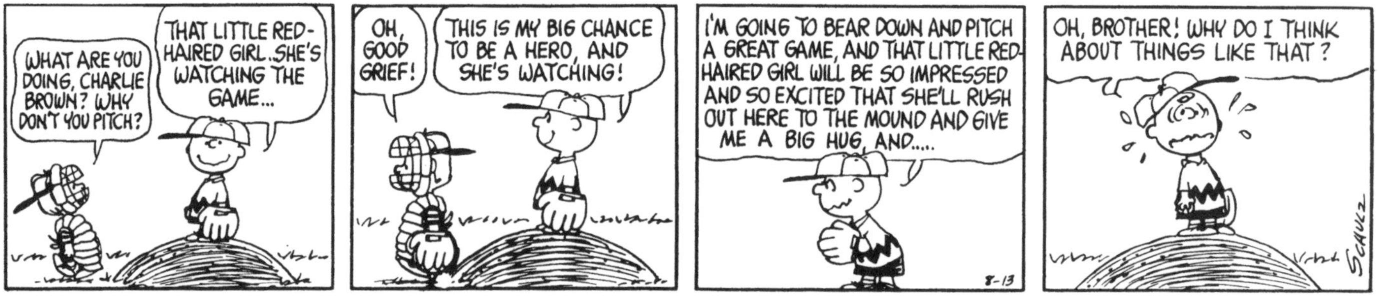
THAT LITTLE RED-HAIRED GIRL..SHE'S WATCHING THE GAME...
WHAT ARE YOU DOING, CHARLIE BROWN? WHY DON'T YOU PITCH?
THIS IS MY BIG CHANCE TO BE A HERO, AND SHE'S WATCHING!
OH, GOOD GRIEF!
I'M GOING TO BEAR DOWN AND PITCH A GREAT GAME, AND THAT LITTLE RED-HAIRED GIRL WILL BE SO IMPRESSED AND SO EXCITED THAT SHE'LL RUSH OUT HERE TO THE MOUND AND GIVE ME A BIG HUG, AND.....
8-13
OH, BROTHER! WHY DO I THINK ABOUT THINGS LIKE THAT?
SCHULZ

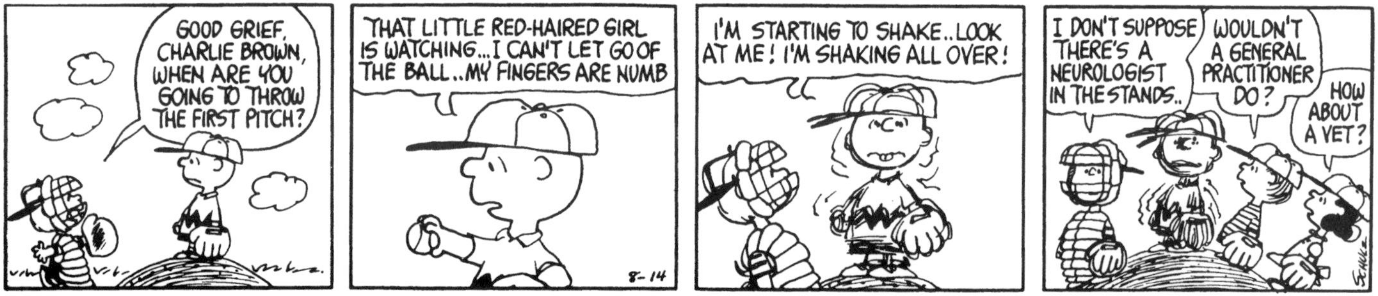
GOOD GRIEF, CHARLIE BROWN, WHEN ARE YOU GOING TO THROW THE FIRST PITCH?
THAT LITTLE RED-HAIRED GIRL IS WATCHING... I CAN'T LET GO OF THE BALL..MY FINGERS ARE NUMB
8-14
I'M STARTING TO SHAKE..LOOK AT ME! I'M SHAKING ALL OVER!
I DON'T SUPPOSE THERE'S A NEUROLOGIST IN THE STANDS..
WOULDN'T A GENERAL PRACTITIONER DO?
HOW ABOUT A VET?
SCHULZ

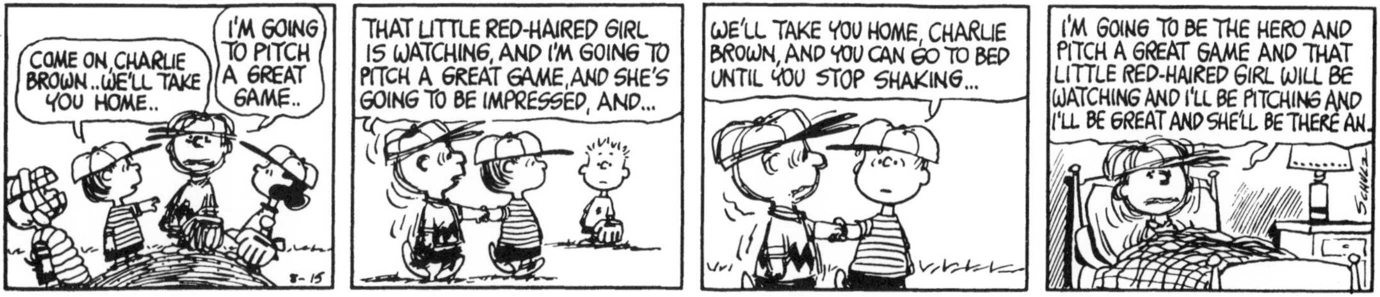
COME ON, CHARLIE BROWN.. WE'LL TAKE YOU HOME..
I'M GOING TO PITCH A GREAT GAME..
8-15
THAT LITTLE RED-HAIRED GIRL IS WATCHING, AND I'M GOING TO PITCH A GREAT GAME, AND SHE'S GOING TO BE IMPRESSED, AND...
WE'LL TAKE YOU HOME, CHARLIE BROWN, AND YOU CAN GO TO BED UNTIL YOU STOP SHAKING...
I'M GOING TO BE THE HERO AND PITCH A GREAT GAME AND THAT LITTLE RED-HAIRED GIRL WILL BE WATCHING AND I'LL BE PITCHING AND I'LL BE GREAT AND SHE'LL BE THERE AN.
SCHULZ

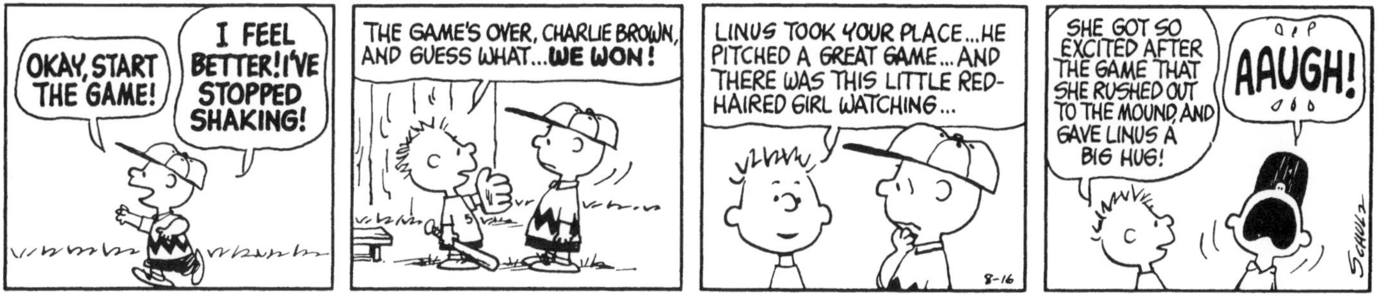
OKAY, START THE GAME!
I FEEL BETTER! I'VE STOPPED SHAKING!
THE GAME'S OVER, CHARLIE BROWN, AND GUESS WHAT... WE WON!
LINUS TOOK YOUR PLACE... HE PITCHED A GREAT GAME... AND THERE WAS THIS LITTLE RED-HAIRED GIRL WATCHING...
8-16
SHE GOT SO EXCITED AFTER THE GAME THAT SHE RUSHED OUT TO THE MOUND, AND GAVE LINUS A BIG HUG!
AAUGH!
SCHULZ

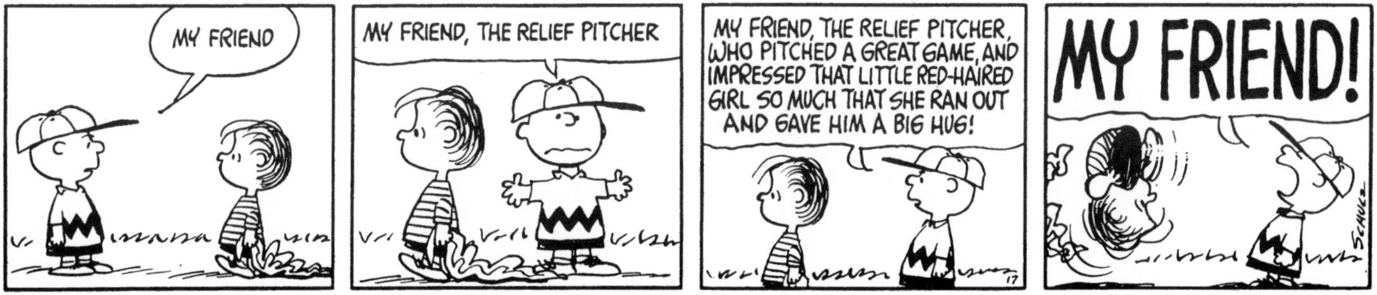
MY FRIEND
MY FRIEND, THE RELIEF PITCHER
MY FRIEND, THE RELIEF PITCHER, WHO PITCHED A GREAT GAME, AND IMPRESSED THAT LITTLE RED-HAIRED GIRL SO MUCH THAT SHE RAN OUT AND GAVE HIM A BIG HUG!
17
MY FRIEND!
SCHULZ

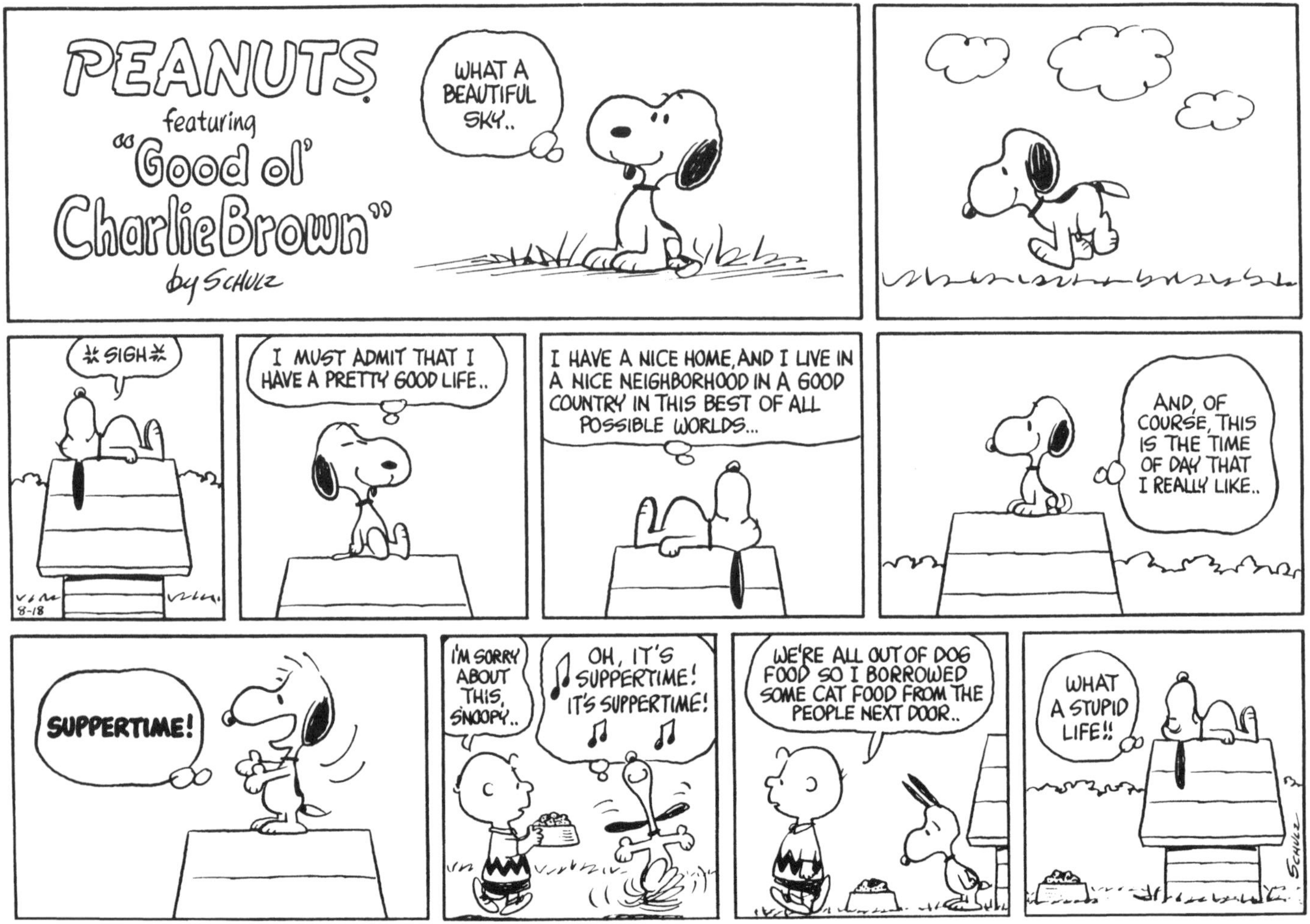
PEANUTS
featuring
"Good ol' CharlieBrown"
by SCHULZ
WHAT A BEAUTIFUL SKY..
SIGH
I MUST ADMIT THAT I HAVE A PRETTY GOOD LIFE..
I HAVE A NICE HOME, AND I LIVE IN A NICE NEIGHBORHOOD IN A GOOD COUNTRY IN THIS BEST OF ALL POSSIBLE WORLDS...
AND, OF COURSE, THIS IS THE TIME OF DAY THAT I REALLY LIKE..
SUPPERTIME!
I'M SORRY ABOUT THIS, SNOOPY..
OH, IT'S SUPPERTIME! IT'S SUPPERTIME!
WE'RE ALL OUT OF DOG FOOD SO I BORROWED SOME CAT FOOD FROM THE PEOPLE NEXT DOOR..
WHAT A STUPID LIFE!!
SCHULZ

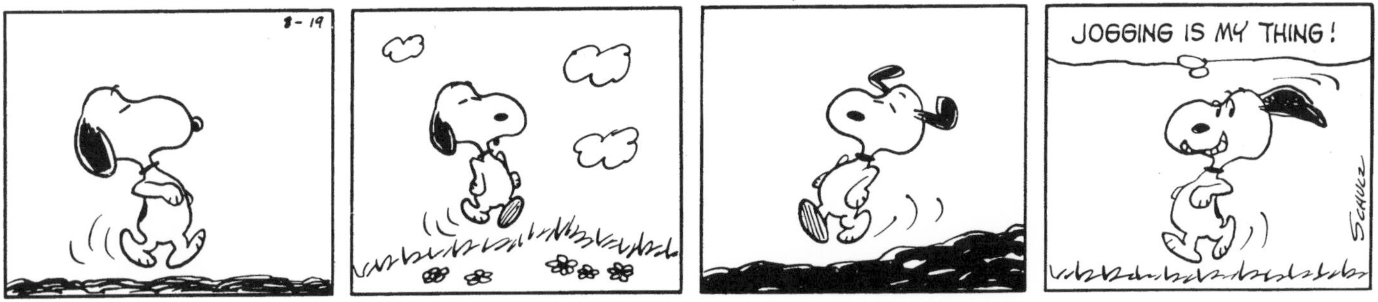
8-19
JOGGING IS MY THING!
SCHULZ

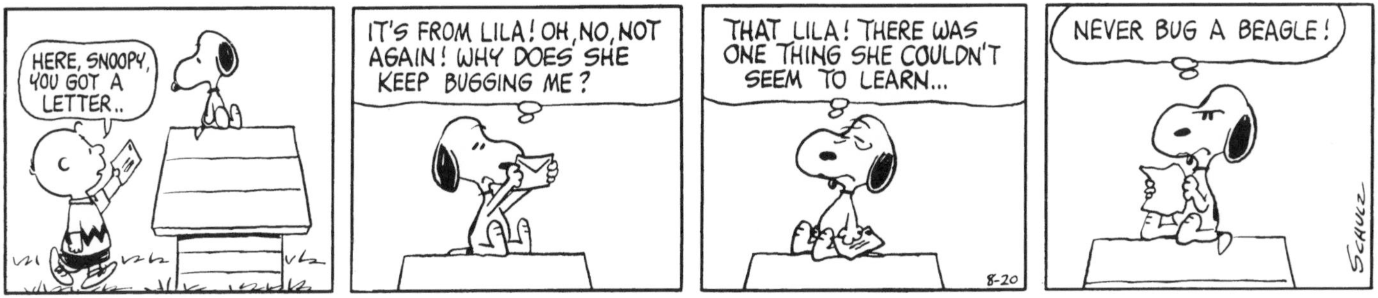
HERE, SNOOPY, YOU GOT A LETTER..
IT'S FROM LILA! OH, NO, NOT AGAIN! WHY DOES SHE KEEP BUGGING ME?
THAT LILA! THERE WAS ONE THING SHE COULDN'T SEEM TO LEARN...
8-20
NEVER BUG A BEAGLE!
SCHULZ

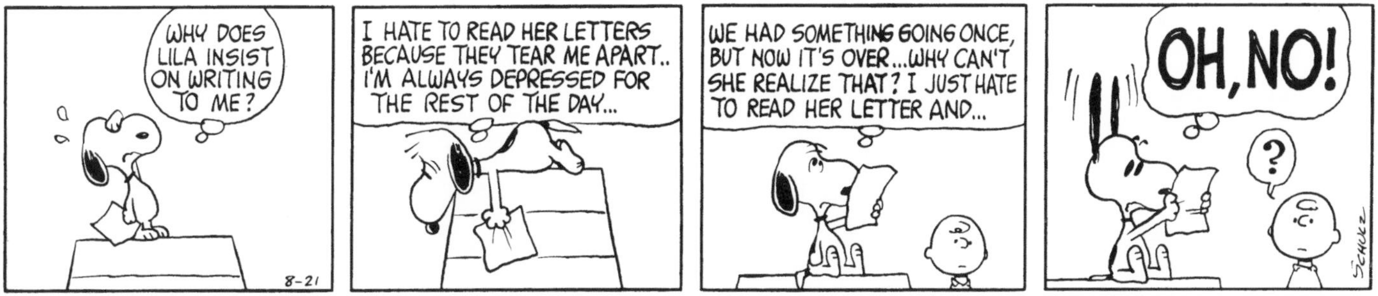
WHY DOES LILA INSIST ON WRITING TO ME?
8-21
I HATE TO READ HER LETTERS BECAUSE THEY TEAR ME APART.. I'M ALWAYS DEPRESSED FOR THE REST OF THE DAY...
WE HAD SOMETHING GOING ONCE, BUT NOW IT'S OVER...WHY CAN'T SHE REALIZE THAT? I JUST HATE TO READ HER LETTER AND...
OH, NO!
?
SCHULZ

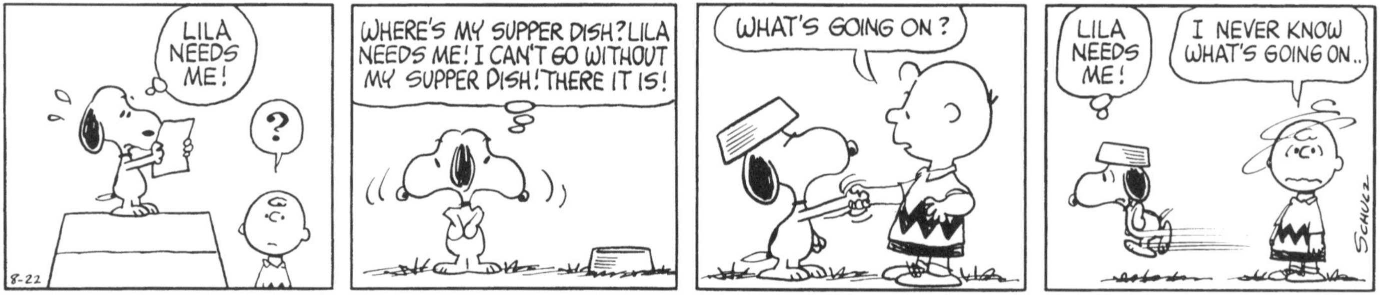
LILA NEEDS ME!
?
8-22
WHERE'S MY SUPPER DISH? LILA NEEDS ME! I CAN'T GO WITHOUT MY SUPPER DISH! THERE IT IS!
WHAT'S GOING ON?
LILA NEEDS ME!
I NEVER KNOW WHAT'S GOING ON..
SCHULZ

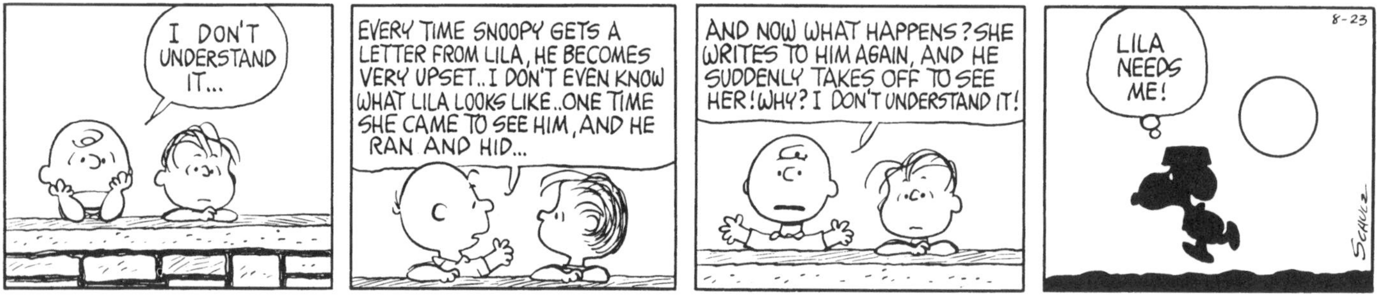
I DON'T UNDERSTAND IT...
EVERY TIME SNOOPY GETS A LETTER FROM LILA, HE BECOMES VERY UPSET.. I DON'T EVEN KNOW WHAT LILA LOOKS LIKE.. ONE TIME SHE CAME TO SEE HIM, AND HE RAN AND HID...
AND NOW WHAT HAPPENS? SHE WRITES TO HIM AGAIN, AND HE SUDDENLY TAKES OFF TO SEE HER! WHY? I DON'T UNDERSTAND IT!
8-23
LILA NEEDS ME!
SCHULZ

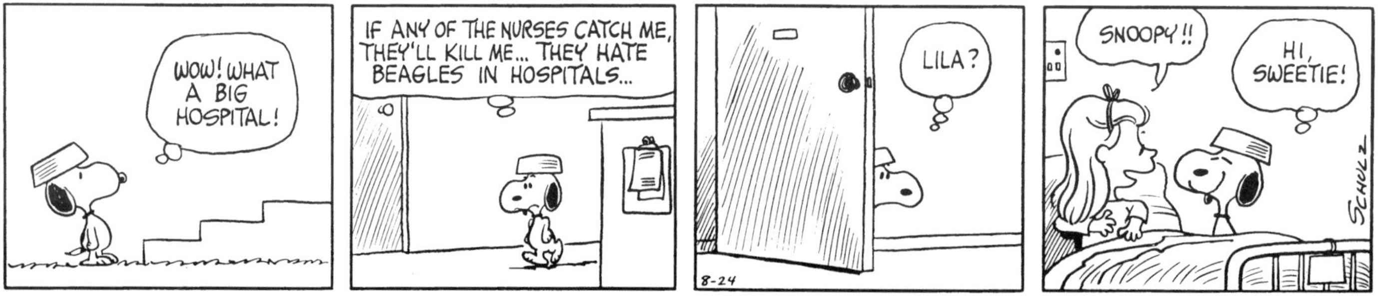
WOW! WHAT A BIG HOSPITAL!
IF ANY OF THE NURSES CATCH ME, THEY'LL KILL ME... THEY HATE BEAGLES IN HOSPITALS...
LILA?
8-24
SNOOPY!!
HI, SWEETIE!
SCHULZ

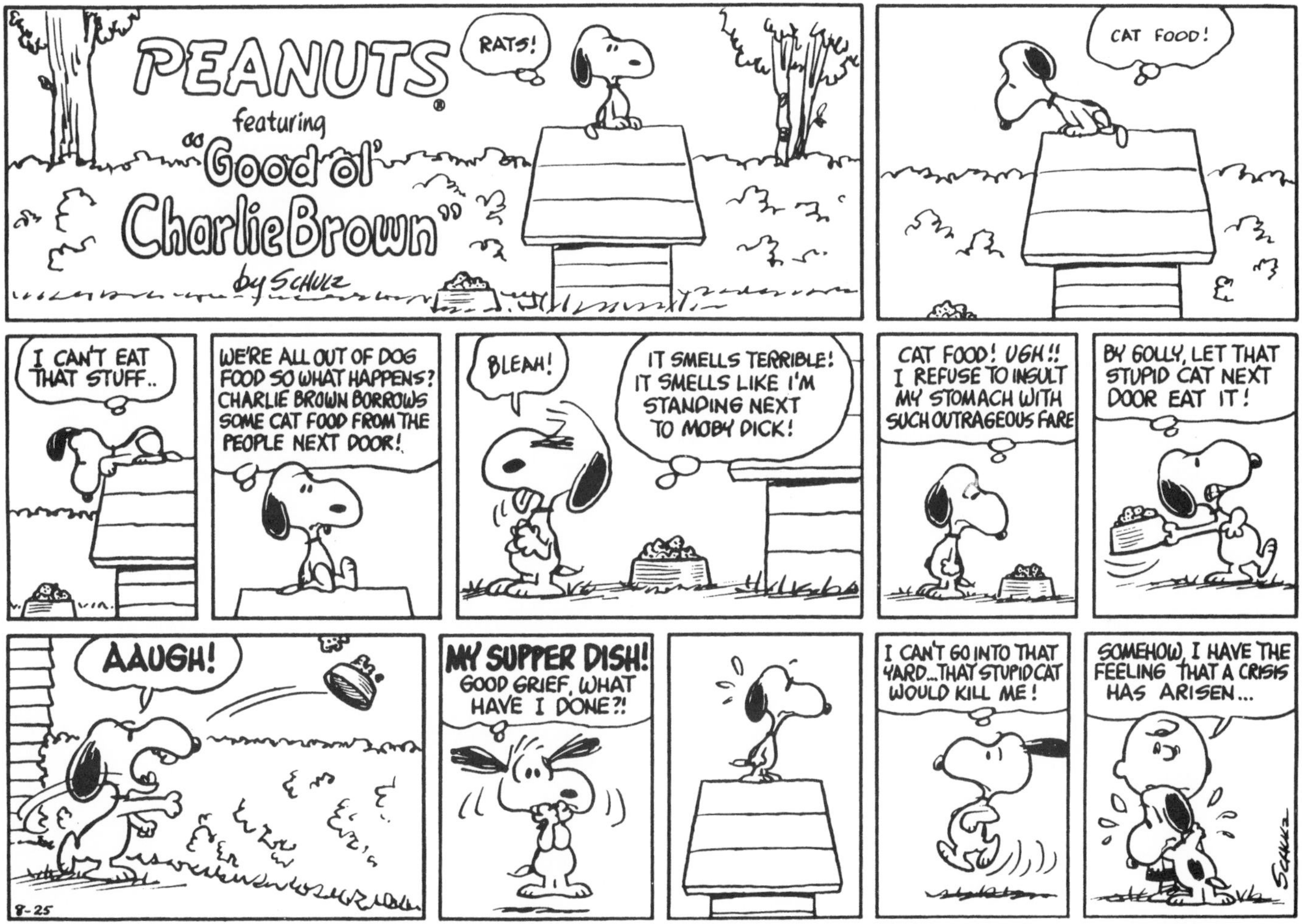
PEANUTS®
featuring "Good ol' Charlie Brown"
by SCHULZ
RATS!
CAT FOOD!
I CAN'T EAT THAT STUFF..
WE'RE ALL OUT OF DOG FOOD SO WHAT HAPPENS? CHARLIE BROWN BORROWS SOME CAT FOOD FROM THE PEOPLE NEXT DOOR!
BLEAH!
IT SMELLS TERRIBLE! IT SMELLS LIKE I'M STANDING NEXT TO MOBY DICK!
CAT FOOD! UGH!! I REFUSE TO INSULT MY STOMACH WITH SUCH OUTRAGEOUS FARE
BY GOLLY, LET THAT STUPID CAT NEXT DOOR EAT IT!
AAUGH!
8-25
MY SUPPER DISH! GOOD GRIEF, WHAT HAVE I DONE?!
I CAN'T GO INTO THAT YARD...THAT STUPID CAT WOULD KILL ME!
SOMEHOW, I HAVE THE FEELING THAT A CRISIS HAS ARISEN...
SCHULZ

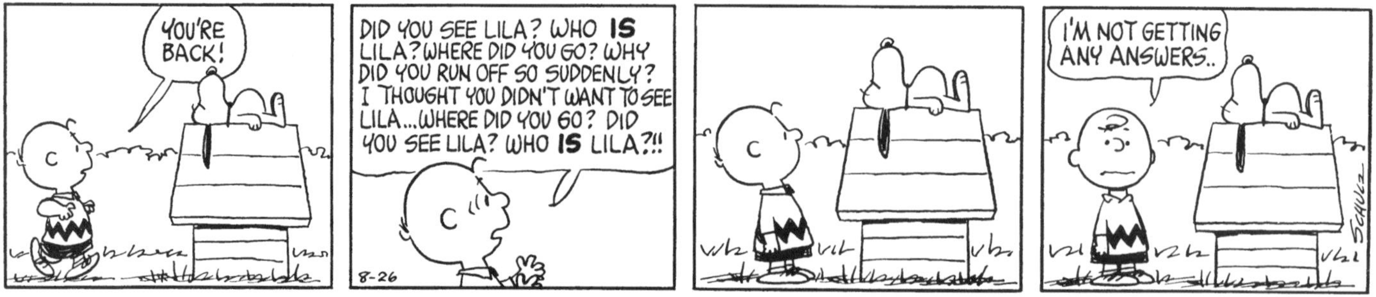
YOU'RE BACK!
DID YOU SEE LILA? WHO IS LILA? WHERE DID YOU GO? WHY DID YOU RUN OFF SO SUDDENLY? I THOUGHT YOU DIDN'T WANT TO SEE LILA...WHERE DID YOU GO? DID YOU SEE LILA? WHO IS LILA?!!
8-26
I'M NOT GETTING ANY ANSWERS..
SCHULZ

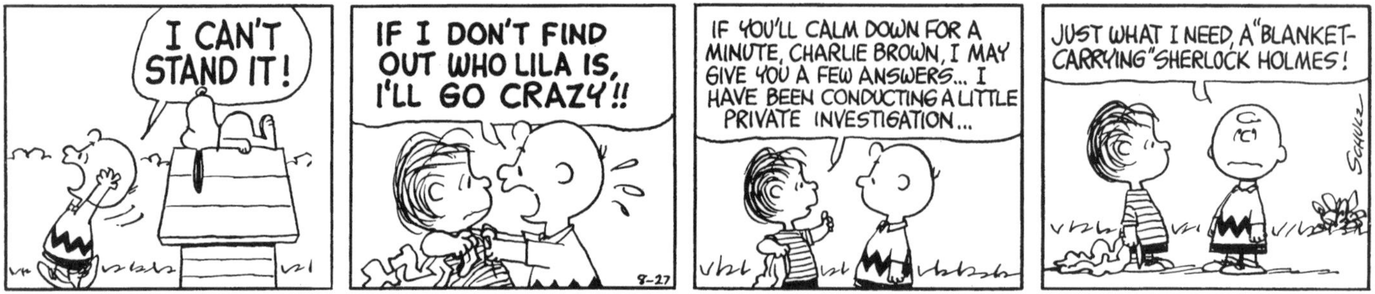
I CAN'T STAND IT!
IF I DON'T FIND OUT WHO LILA IS, I'LL GO CRAZY!!
8-27
IF YOU'LL CALM DOWN FOR A MINUTE, CHARLIE BROWN, I MAY GIVE YOU A FEW ANSWERS... I HAVE BEEN CONDUCTING A LITTLE PRIVATE INVESTIGATION...
JUST WHAT I NEED, A "BLANKET-CARRYING" SHERLOCK HOLMES!
SCHULZ

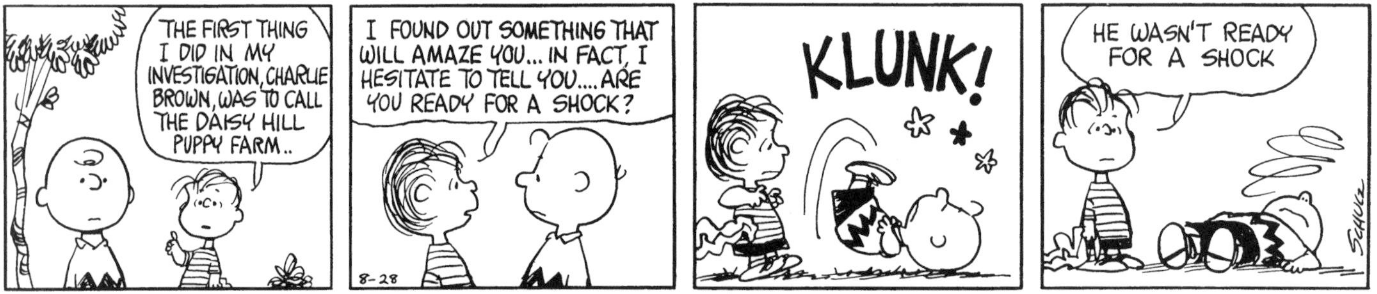
THE FIRST THING I DID IN MY INVESTIGATION, CHARLIE BROWN, WAS TO CALL THE DAISY HILL PUPPY FARM..
I FOUND OUT SOMETHING THAT WILL AMAZE YOU... IN FACT, I HESITATE TO TELL YOU.... ARE YOU READY FOR A SHOCK?
8-28
KLUNK!
SCHULZ
HE WASN'T READY FOR A SHOCK

WHAT HAPPENED?

HOW CAN I TELL YOU SOMETHING THAT WILL SHOCK YOU IF YOU PASS OUT BEFORE I CAN TELL YOU?

I'M SORRY... I'VE BEEN HYPERVENTILATING A LOT LATELY...

WELL, ANYWAY, HERE'S WHAT I FOUND OUT WHEN I CALLED THE DAISY HILL PUPPY FARM... YOU ARE **NOT** SNOOPY'S ORIGINAL OWNER!

8-29

KLUNK!

OH, GOOD GRIEF!

YOU BOUGHT SNOOPY IN THE MONTH OF OCTOBER, RIGHT?

ACCORDING TO THE RECORDS AT THE DAISY HILL PUPPY FARM, SNOOPY WAS BOUGHT BY ANOTHER FAMILY IN AUGUST... THIS FAMILY HAD A LITTLE GIRL NAMED LILA...

8-30

SNOOPY AND LILA LOVED EACH OTHER VERY MUCH, BUT THEY LIVED IN AN APARTMENT, AND THE FAMILY DECIDED THEY JUST COULDN'T KEEP SNOOPY SO THEY RETURNED HIM...

YOU GOT A USED DOG, CHARLIE BROWN!

NOW, I SEE WHY THOSE LETTERS FROM LILA WOULD UPSET SNOOPY SO MUCH

SURE, HE WAS TRYING TO FORGET HER, BUT WHEN HE FOUND OUT SHE WAS IN THE HOSPITAL, HE RAN OFF TO SEE HER...

8-31

I'LL BET HE WISHES HE WAS STILL HER DOG INSTEAD OF MINE...

I DOUBT IT, CHARLIE BROWN.. HE WOULDN'T HAVE BEEN HAPPY IN AN APARTMENT

HERE'S THE WORLD WAR I FLYING ACE ZOOMING THROUGH THE AIR IN HIS SOPWITH CAMEL!

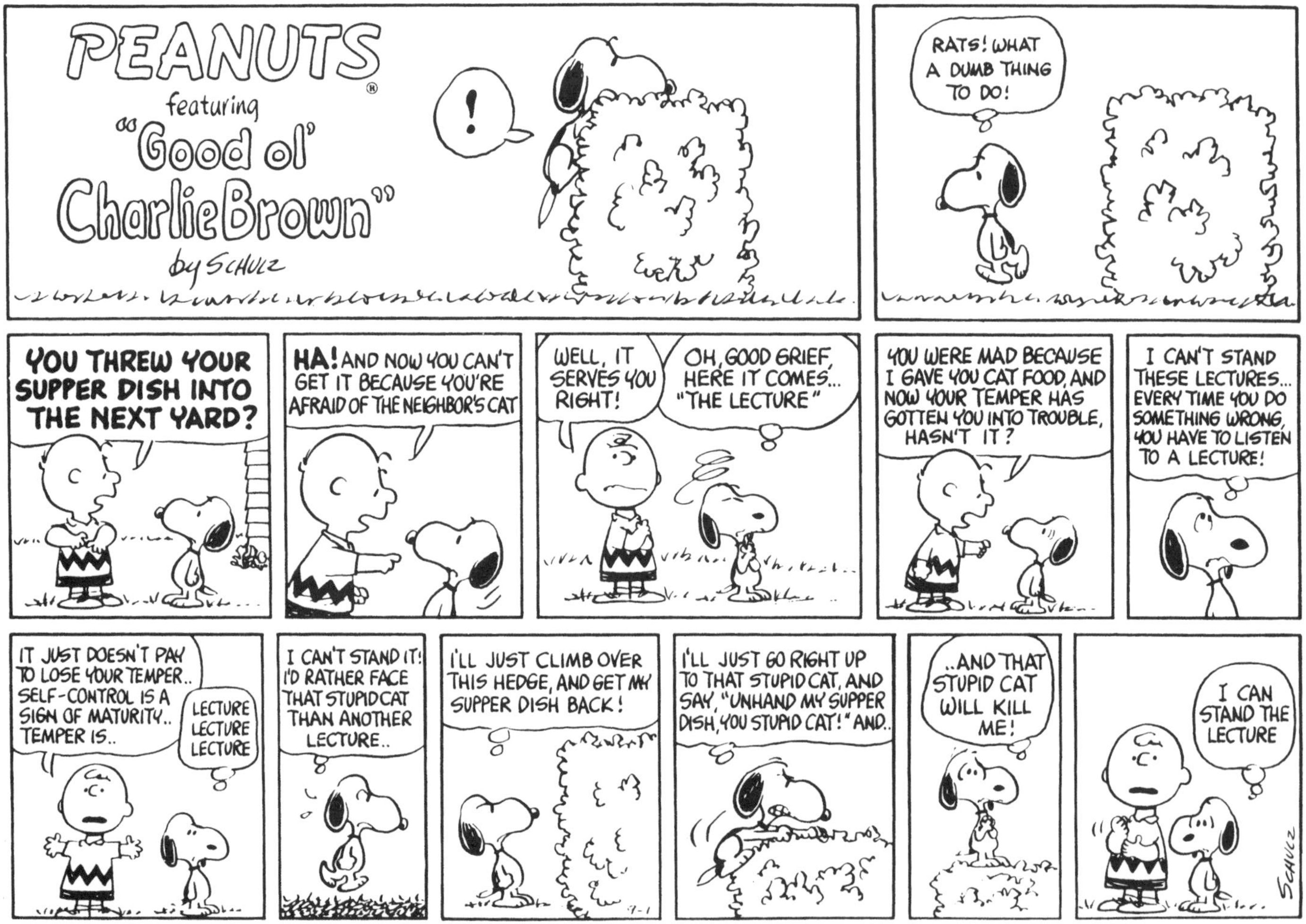
PEANUTS®
featuring
"Good ol' Charlie Brown"
by SCHULZ
!
RATS! WHAT A DUMB THING TO DO!
YOU THREW YOUR SUPPER DISH INTO THE NEXT YARD?
HA! AND NOW YOU CAN'T GET IT BECAUSE YOU'RE AFRAID OF THE NEIGHBOR'S CAT
WELL, IT SERVES YOU RIGHT!
OH, GOOD GRIEF, HERE IT COMES... "THE LECTURE"
YOU WERE MAD BECAUSE I GAVE YOU CAT FOOD, AND NOW YOUR TEMPER HAS GOTTEN YOU INTO TROUBLE, HASN'T IT?
I CAN'T STAND THESE LECTURES... EVERY TIME YOU DO SOMETHING WRONG, YOU HAVE TO LISTEN TO A LECTURE!
IT JUST DOESN'T PAY TO LOSE YOUR TEMPER.. SELF-CONTROL IS A SIGN OF MATURITY.. TEMPER IS..
LECTURE LECTURE LECTURE
I CAN'T STAND IT! I'D RATHER FACE THAT STUPID CAT THAN ANOTHER LECTURE..
I'LL JUST CLIMB OVER THIS HEDGE, AND GET MY SUPPER DISH BACK!
I'LL JUST GO RIGHT UP TO THAT STUPID CAT, AND SAY, "UNHAND MY SUPPER DISH, YOU STUPID CAT!" AND..
..AND THAT STUPID CAT WILL KILL ME!
I CAN STAND THE LECTURE
SCHULZ

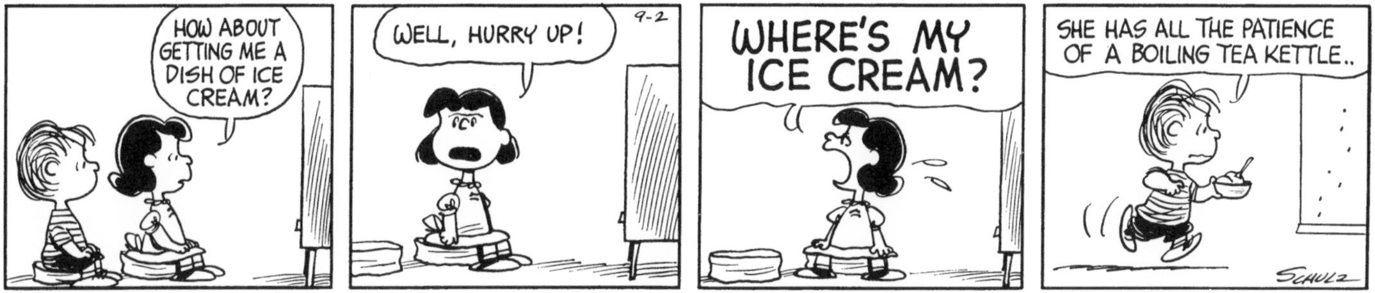
HOW ABOUT GETTING ME A DISH OF ICE CREAM?
WELL, HURRY UP!
WHERE'S MY ICE CREAM?
SHE HAS ALL THE PATIENCE OF A BOILING TEA KETTLE..

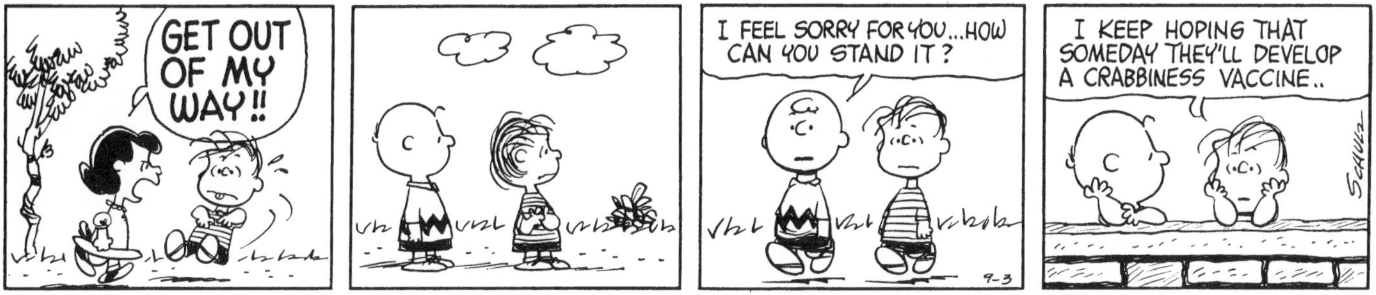
GET OUT OF MY WAY!!
I FEEL SORRY FOR YOU...HOW CAN YOU STAND IT?
I KEEP HOPING THAT SOMEDAY THEY'LL DEVELOP A CRABBINESS VACCINE..

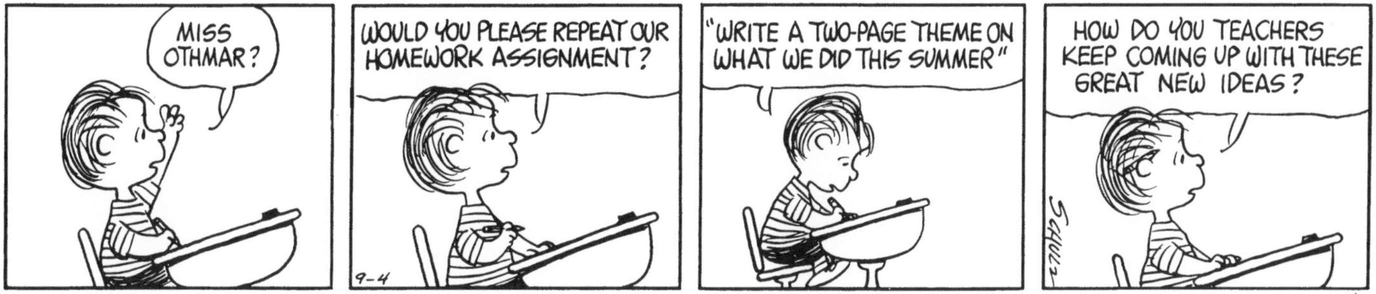
MISS OTHMAR?
WOULD YOU PLEASE REPEAT OUR HOMEWORK ASSIGNMENT?
"WRITE A TWO-PAGE THEME ON WHAT WE DID THIS SUMMER"
HOW DO YOU TEACHERS KEEP COMING UP WITH THESE GREAT NEW IDEAS?

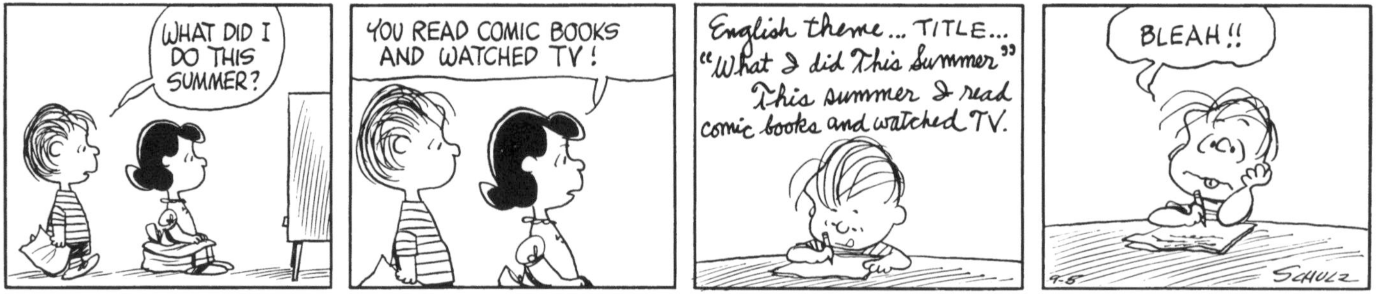
WHAT DID I DO THIS SUMMER?
YOU READ COMIC BOOKS AND WATCHED TV!
English theme... TITLE... "What I did This Summer" This summer I read comic books and watched TV.
BLEAH!!
9-5
SCHULZ

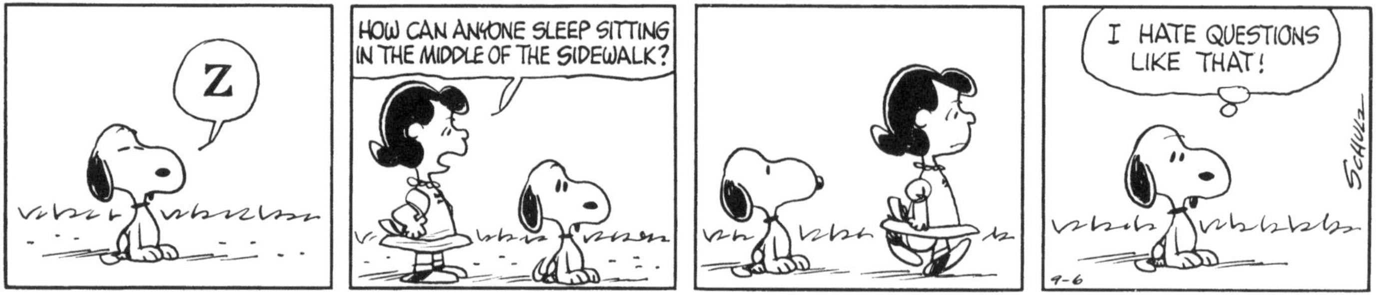
Z
HOW CAN ANYONE SLEEP SITTING IN THE MIDDLE OF THE SIDEWALK?
I HATE QUESTIONS LIKE THAT!
SCHULZ
9-6

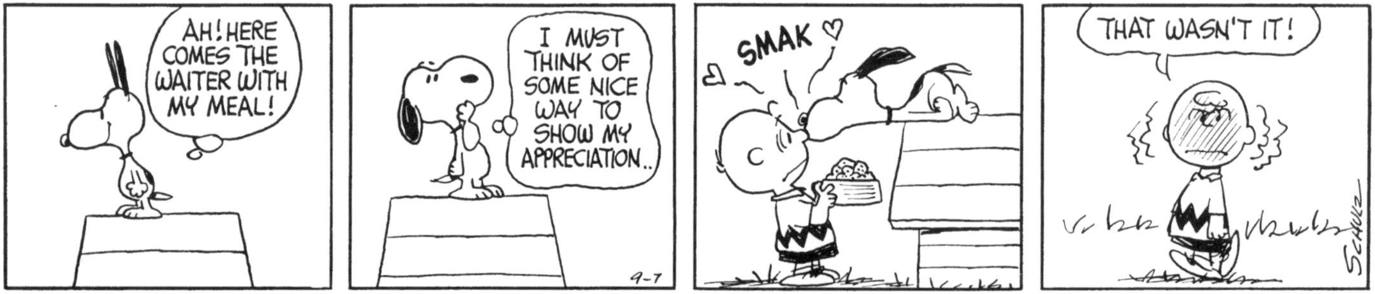
AH! HERE COMES THE WAITER WITH MY MEAL!
I MUST THINK OF SOME NICE WAY TO SHOW MY APPRECIATION..
9-7
SMAK
THAT WASN'T IT!
SCHULZ

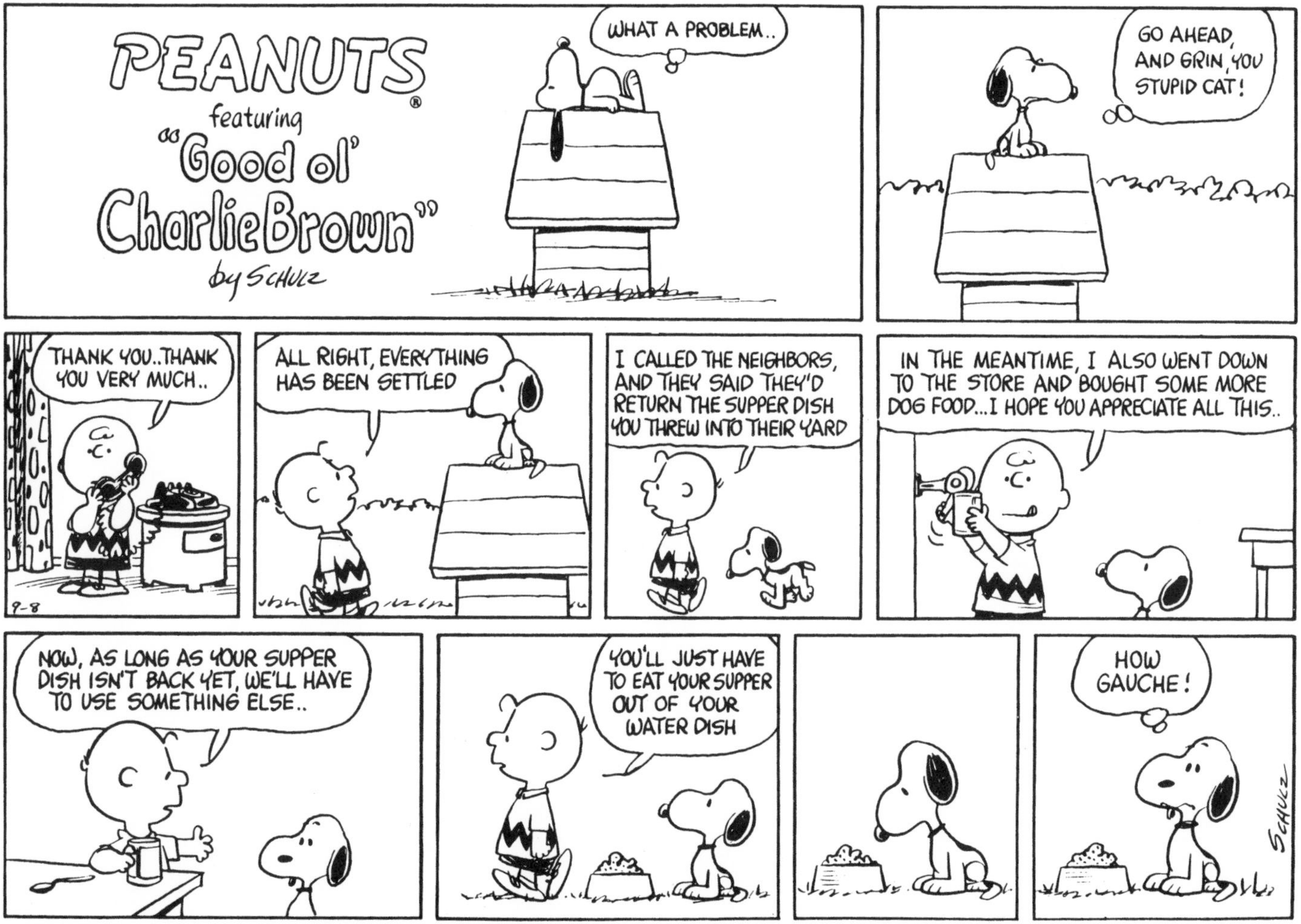
PEANUTS®
featuring
"Good ol' CharlieBrown"
by SCHULZ
WHAT A PROBLEM..
GO AHEAD, AND GRIN, YOU STUPID CAT!
THANK YOU..THANK YOU VERY MUCH..
9-8
ALL RIGHT, EVERYTHING HAS BEEN SETTLED
I CALLED THE NEIGHBORS, AND THEY SAID THEY'D RETURN THE SUPPER DISH YOU THREW INTO THEIR YARD
IN THE MEANTIME, I ALSO WENT DOWN TO THE STORE AND BOUGHT SOME MORE DOG FOOD...I HOPE YOU APPRECIATE ALL THIS..
NOW, AS LONG AS YOUR SUPPER DISH ISN'T BACK YET, WE'LL HAVE TO USE SOMETHING ELSE..
YOU'LL JUST HAVE TO EAT YOUR SUPPER OUT OF YOUR WATER DISH
HOW GAUCHE!
SCHULZ

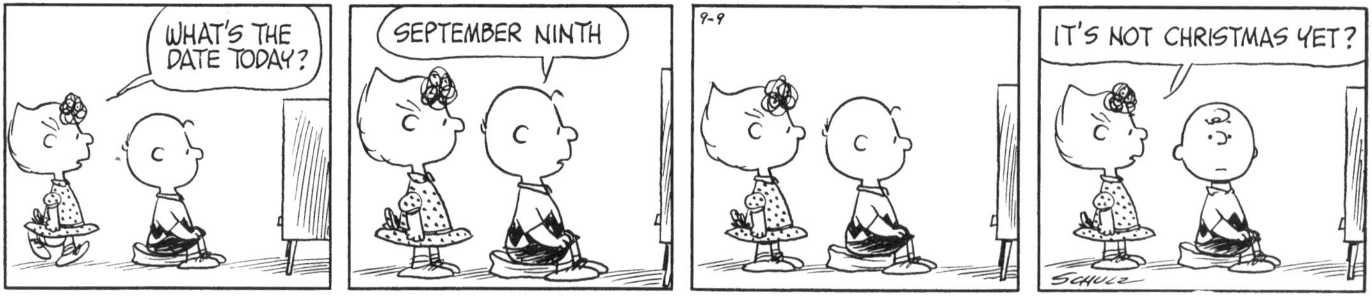
WHAT'S THE DATE TODAY?
SEPTEMBER NINTH
9-9
IT'S NOT CHRISTMAS YET?
SCHULZ

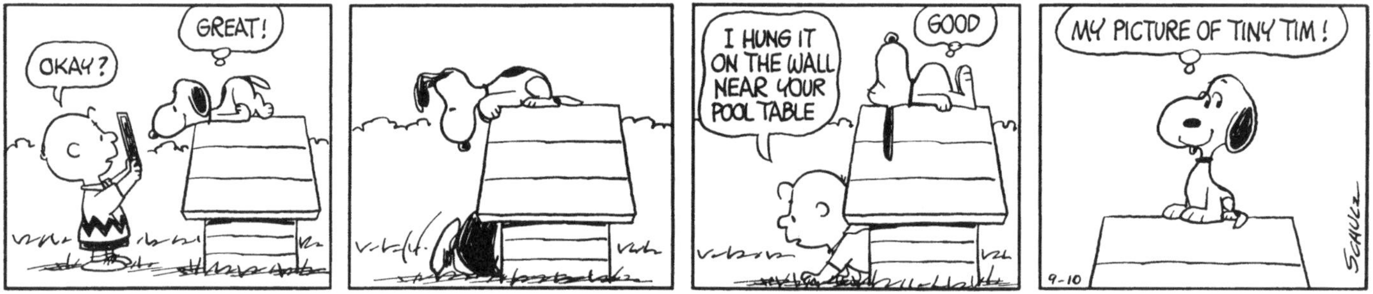
OKAY?
GREAT!
I HUNG IT ON THE WALL NEAR YOUR POOL TABLE
GOOD
MY PICTURE OF TINY TIM!
9-10
SCHULZ

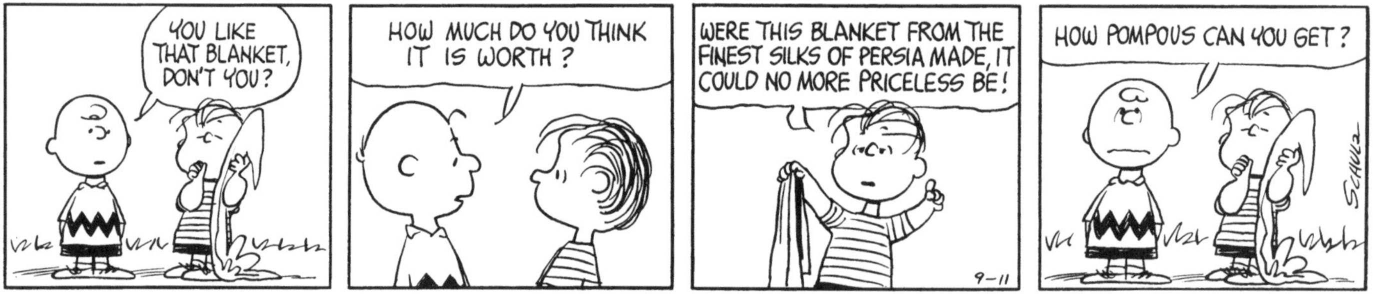
YOU LIKE THAT BLANKET, DON'T YOU?
HOW MUCH DO YOU THINK IT IS WORTH?
WERE THIS BLANKET FROM THE FINEST SILKS OF PERSIA MADE, IT COULD NO MORE PRICELESS BE!
9-11
HOW POMPOUS CAN YOU GET?
SCHULZ

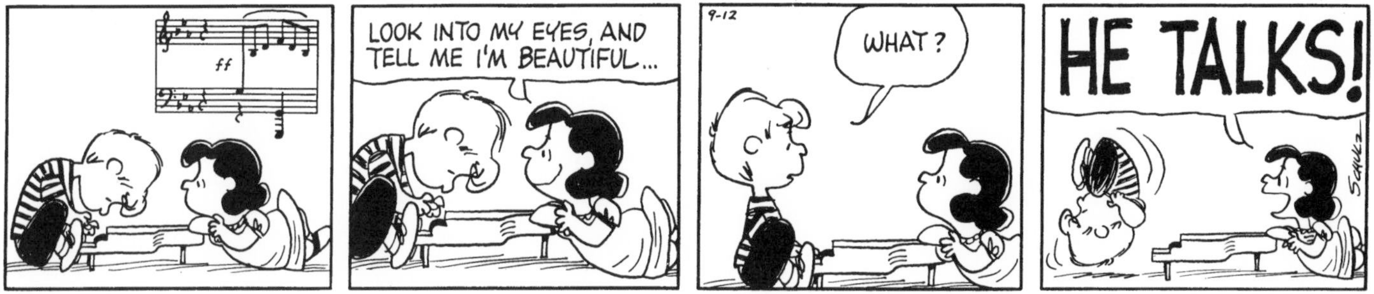
LOOK INTO MY EYES, AND TELL ME I'M BEAUTIFUL...
WHAT?
HE TALKS!

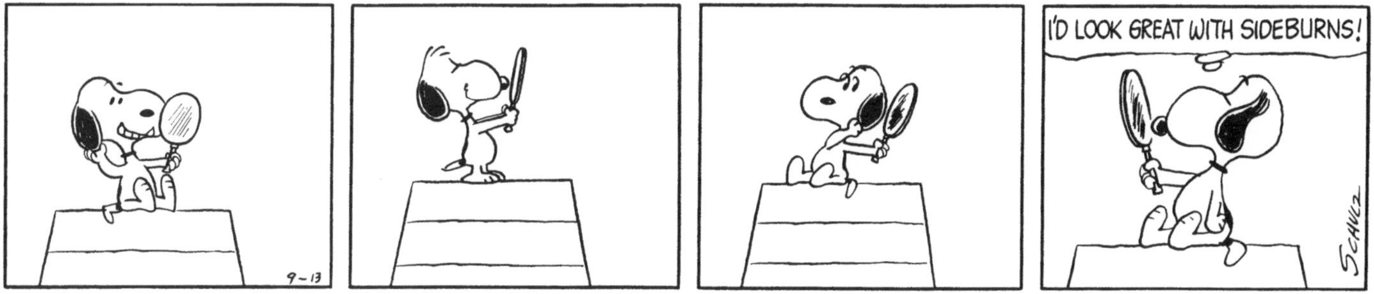
I'D LOOK GREAT WITH SIDEBURNS!

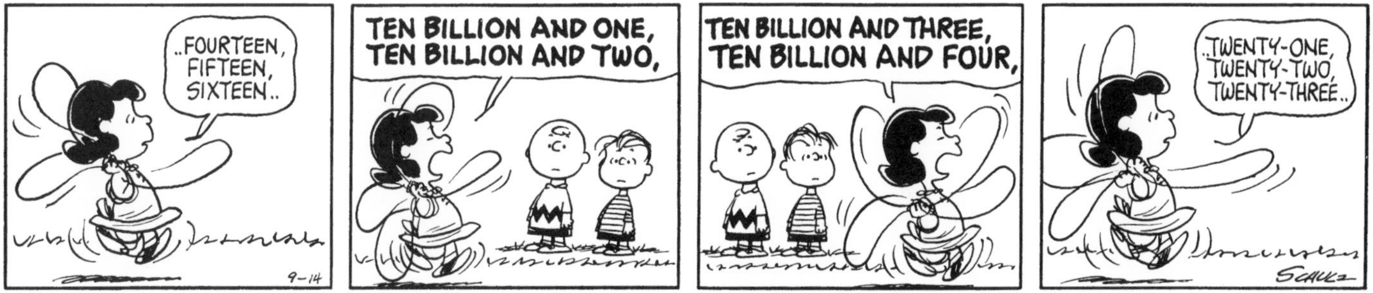
..FOURTEEN, FIFTEEN, SIXTEEN..
TEN BILLION AND ONE, TEN BILLION AND TWO,
TEN BILLION AND THREE, TEN BILLION AND FOUR,
..TWENTY-ONE, TWENTY-TWO, TWENTY-THREE..

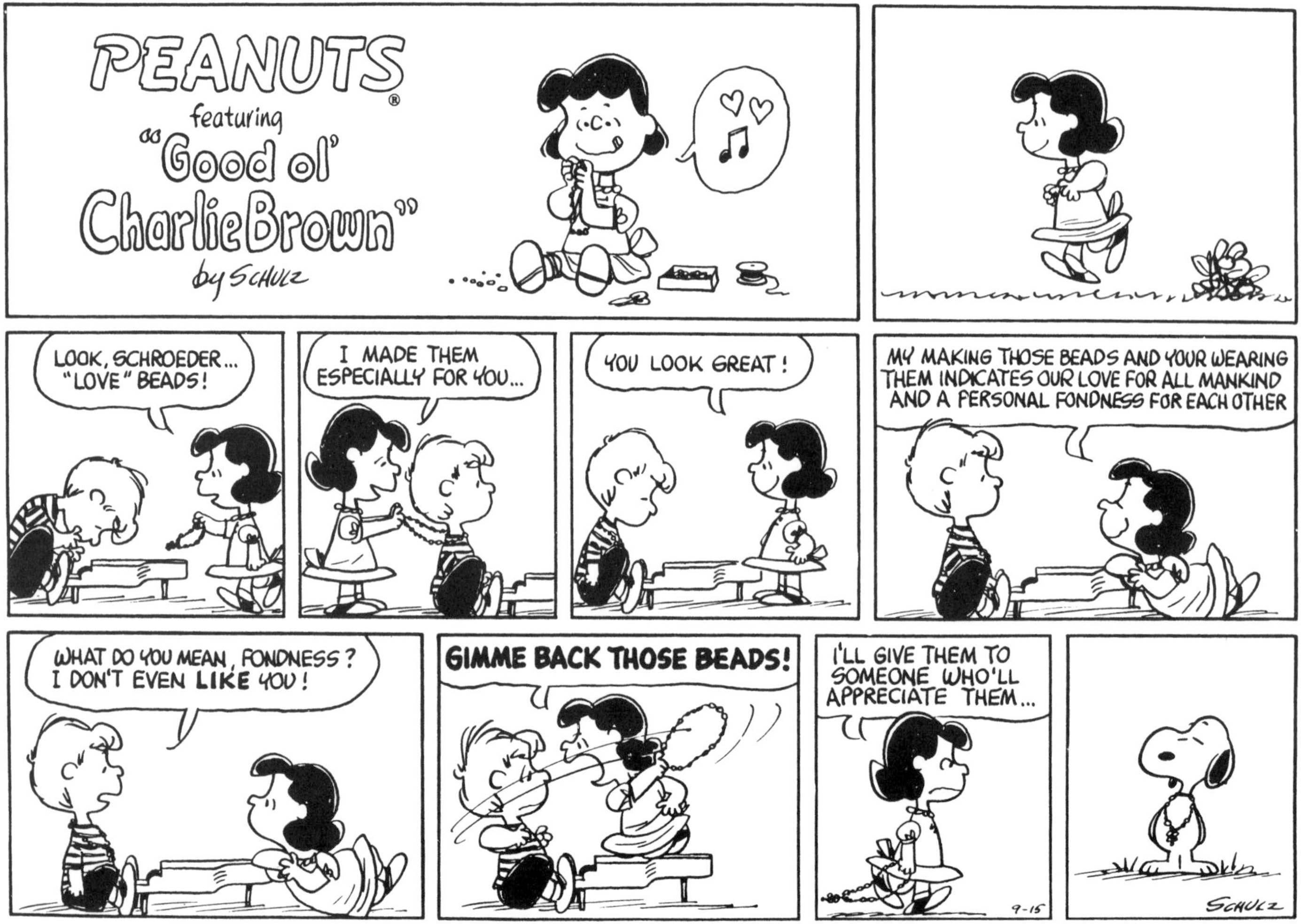
PEANUTS®
featuring "Good ol' Charlie Brown"
by SCHULZ
LOOK, SCHROEDER... "LOVE" BEADS!
I MADE THEM ESPECIALLY FOR YOU...
YOU LOOK GREAT!
MY MAKING THOSE BEADS AND YOUR WEARING THEM INDICATES OUR LOVE FOR ALL MANKIND AND A PERSONAL FONDNESS FOR EACH OTHER
WHAT DO YOU MEAN, FONDNESS? I DON'T EVEN **LIKE** YOU!
GIMME BACK THOSE BEADS!
I'LL GIVE THEM TO SOMEONE WHO'LL APPRECIATE THEM...
9-15
SCHULZ

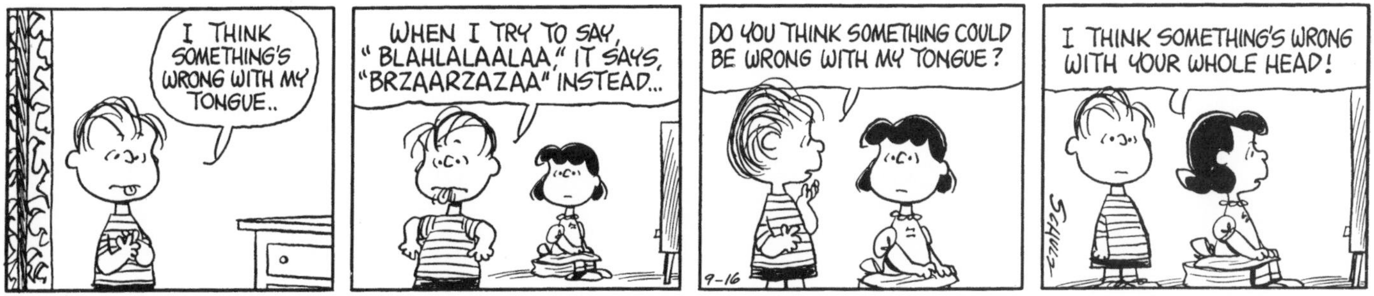
I THINK SOMETHING'S WRONG WITH MY TONGUE..
WHEN I TRY TO SAY, "BLAHLALAALAA," IT SAYS, "BRZAARZAZAA" INSTEAD...
DO YOU THINK SOMETHING COULD BE WRONG WITH MY TONGUE?
9-16
I THINK SOMETHING'S WRONG WITH YOUR WHOLE HEAD!
SCHULZ

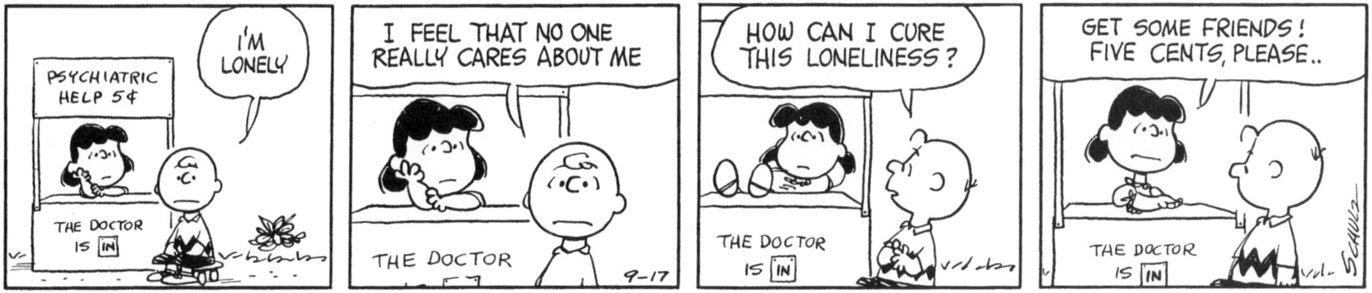
PSYCHIATRIC HELP 5¢
THE DOCTOR IS IN
I'M LONELY
I FEEL THAT NO ONE REALLY CARES ABOUT ME
THE DOCTOR
9-17
HOW CAN I CURE THIS LONELINESS?
THE DOCTOR IS IN
GET SOME FRIENDS! FIVE CENTS, PLEASE..
THE DOCTOR IS IN
SCHULZ

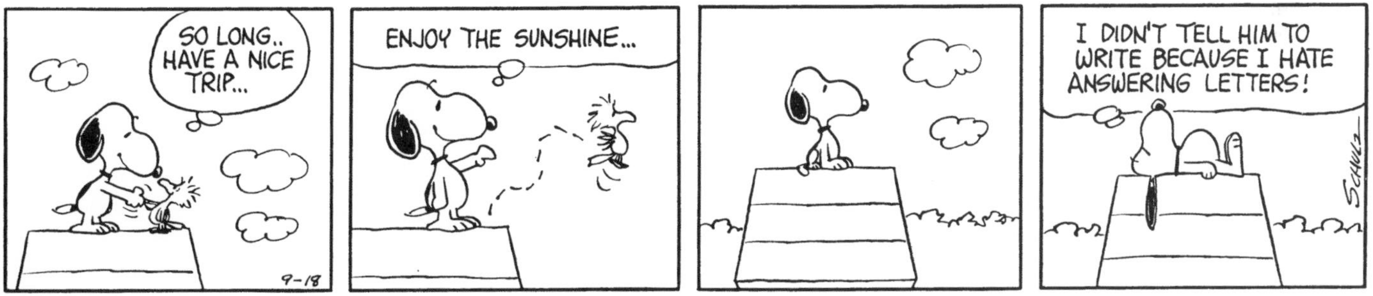
SO LONG.. HAVE A NICE TRIP...
9-18
ENJOY THE SUNSHINE...
I DIDN'T TELL HIM TO WRITE BECAUSE I HATE ANSWERING LETTERS!
SCHULZ

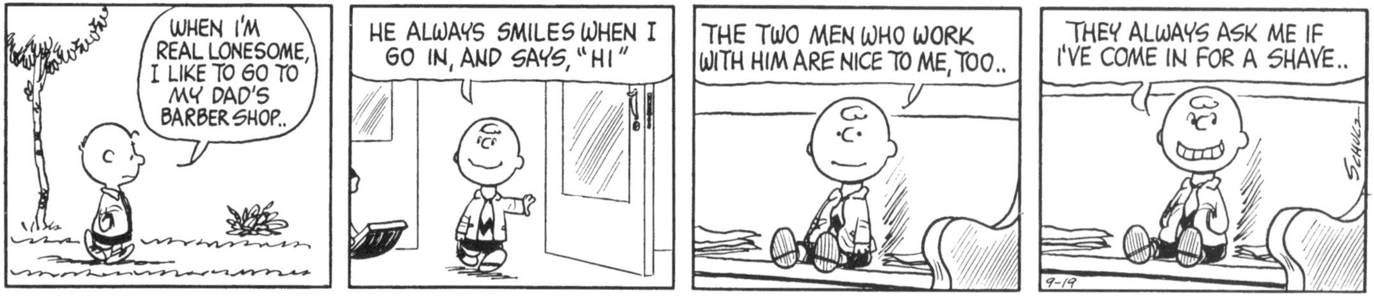
WHEN I'M REAL LONESOME, I LIKE TO GO TO MY DAD'S BARBER SHOP..
HE ALWAYS SMILES WHEN I GO IN, AND SAYS, "HI"
THE TWO MEN WHO WORK WITH HIM ARE NICE TO ME, TOO..
THEY ALWAYS ASK ME IF I'VE COME IN FOR A SHAVE..

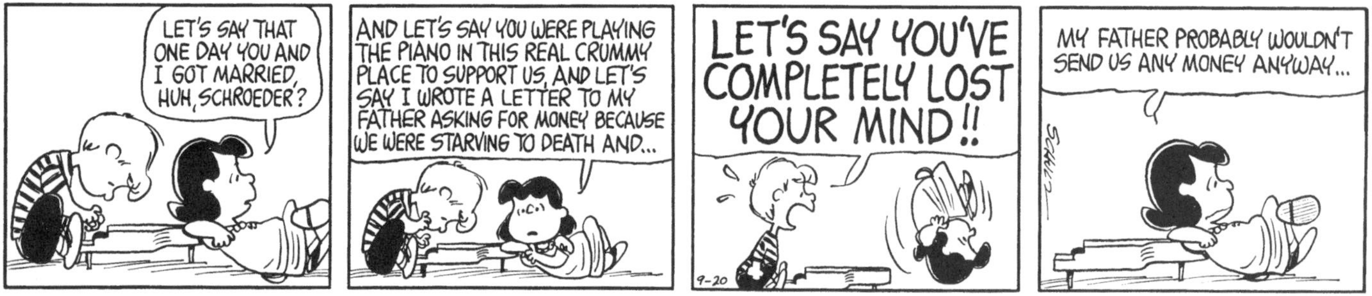
LET'S SAY THAT ONE DAY YOU AND I GOT MARRIED, HUH, SCHROEDER?
AND LET'S SAY YOU WERE PLAYING THE PIANO IN THIS REAL CRUMMY PLACE TO SUPPORT US, AND LET'S SAY I WROTE A LETTER TO MY FATHER ASKING FOR MONEY BECAUSE WE WERE STARVING TO DEATH AND...
LET'S SAY YOU'VE COMPLETELY LOST YOUR MIND!!
MY FATHER PROBABLY WOULDN'T SEND US ANY MONEY ANYWAY...

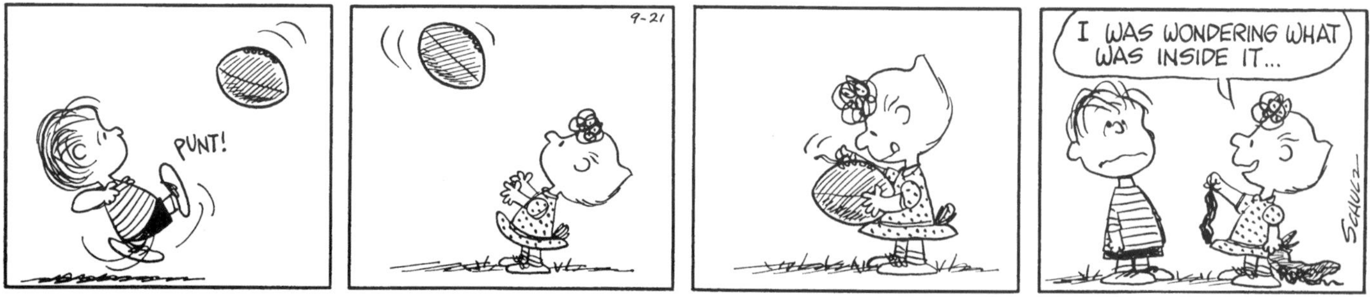
PUNT!
I WAS WONDERING WHAT WAS INSIDE IT...

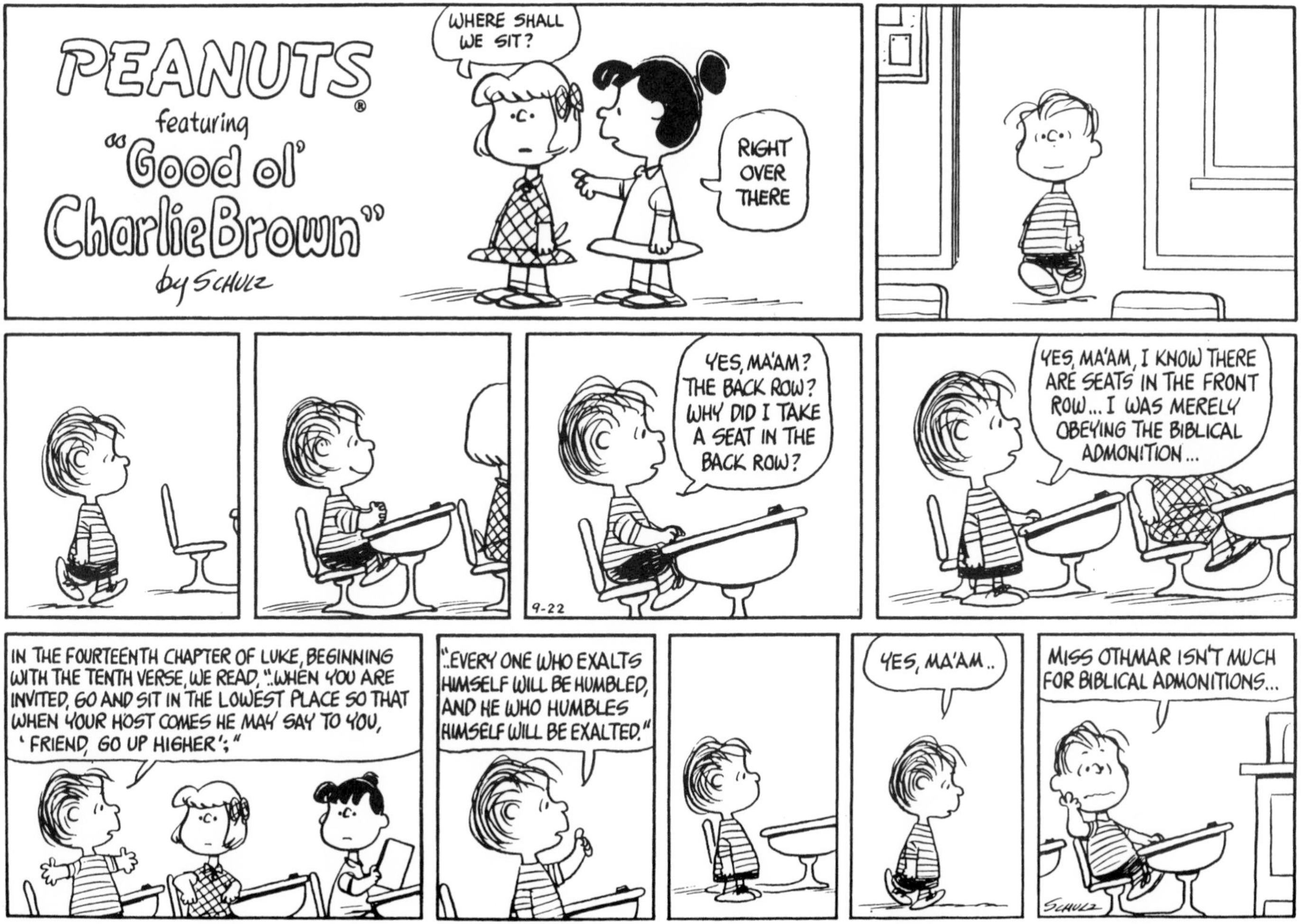
PEANUTS®
featuring
"Good ol' Charlie Brown"
by SCHULZ
WHERE SHALL WE SIT?
RIGHT OVER THERE
YES, MA'AM? THE BACK ROW? WHY DID I TAKE A SEAT IN THE BACK ROW?
9-22
YES, MA'AM, I KNOW THERE ARE SEATS IN THE FRONT ROW... I WAS MERELY OBEYING THE BIBLICAL ADMONITION...
IN THE FOURTEENTH CHAPTER OF LUKE, BEGINNING WITH THE TENTH VERSE, WE READ, "..WHEN YOU ARE INVITED, GO AND SIT IN THE LOWEST PLACE SO THAT WHEN YOUR HOST COMES HE MAY SAY TO YOU, 'FRIEND, GO UP HIGHER';"
"..EVERY ONE WHO EXALTS HIMSELF WILL BE HUMBLED, AND HE WHO HUMBLES HIMSELF WILL BE EXALTED."
YES, MA'AM..
MISS OTHMAR ISN'T MUCH FOR BIBLICAL ADMONITIONS...
SCHULZ

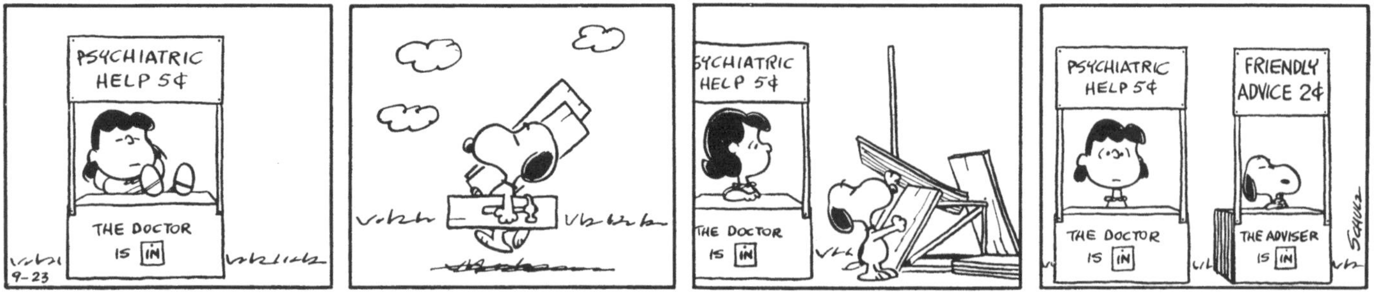
PSYCHIATRIC HELP 5¢
THE DOCTOR IS IN
9-23
SYCHIATRIC HELP 5¢
THE DOCTOR IS IN
PSYCHIATRIC HELP 5¢
THE DOCTOR IS IN
FRIENDLY ADVICE 2¢
THE ADVISER IS IN
SCHULZ

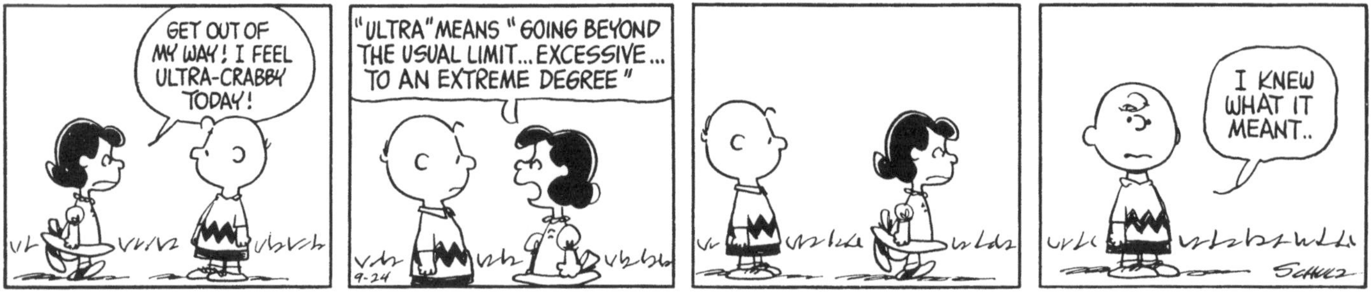
GET OUT OF MY WAY! I FEEL ULTRA-CRABBY TODAY!
"ULTRA" MEANS "GOING BEYOND THE USUAL LIMIT... EXCESSIVE... TO AN EXTREME DEGREE"
9-24
I KNEW WHAT IT MEANT..
SCHULZ

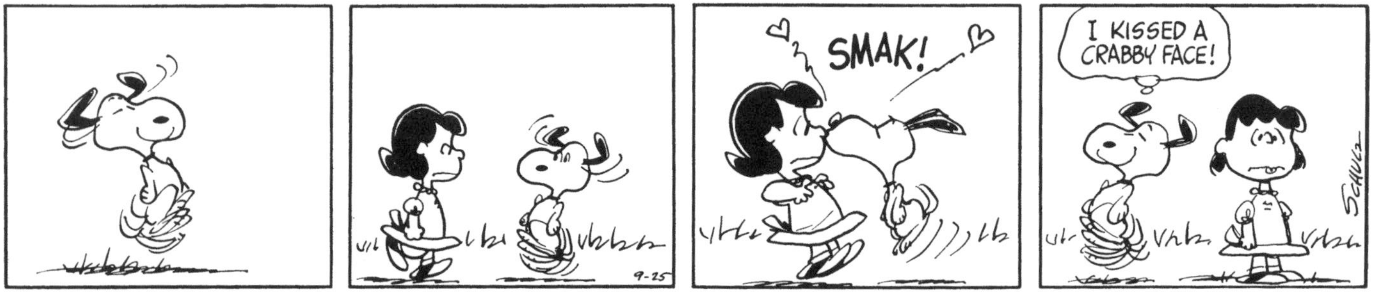
9-25
SMAK!
I KISSED A CRABBY FACE!
SCHULZ

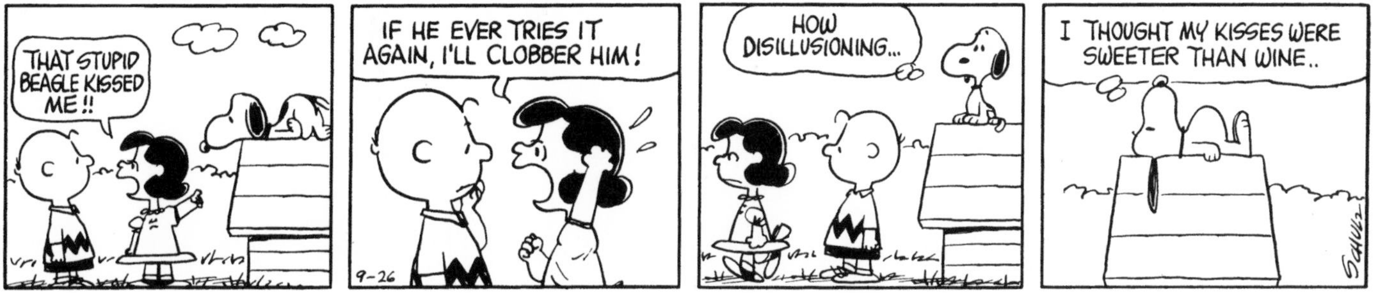
THAT STUPID BEAGLE KISSED ME!!
IF HE EVER TRIES IT AGAIN, I'LL CLOBBER HIM!
9-26
HOW DISILLUSIONING...
I THOUGHT MY KISSES WERE SWEETER THAN WINE..
SCHULZ

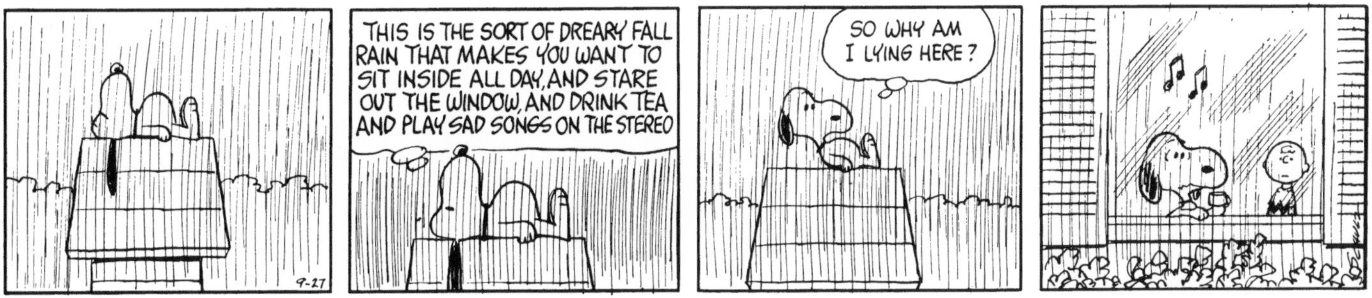
9-27
THIS IS THE SORT OF DREARY FALL RAIN THAT MAKES YOU WANT TO SIT INSIDE ALL DAY, AND STARE OUT THE WINDOW, AND DRINK TEA AND PLAY SAD SONGS ON THE STEREO
SO WHY AM I LYING HERE?
SCHULZ

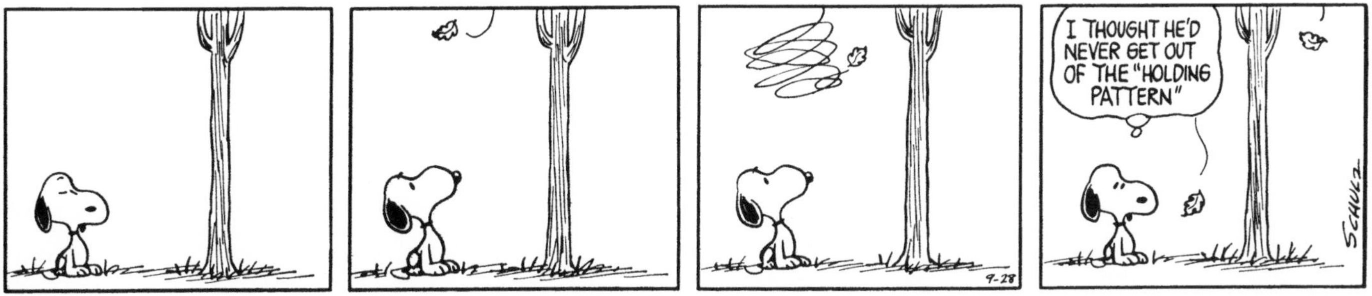
9-28
I THOUGHT HE'D NEVER GET OUT OF THE "HOLDING PATTERN"
SCHULZ

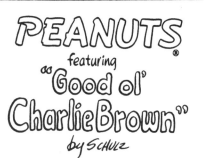

PEANUTS®

featuring "Good ol' Charlie Brown"

by Schulz

CHARLIE BROWNNNNN ♪♫

I CAN'T BELIEVE IT...SHE MUST THINK I'M THE MOST STUPID PERSON ALIVE...

COME ON, CHARLIE BROWN..I'LL HOLD THE BALL, AND YOU KICK IT...

HOLD IT? **HA!** THAT'S A LAUGH! YOU'LL PULL IT AWAY, AND I'LL KILL MYSELF!

WHY, CHARLIE BROWN, HOW CAN YOU SAY THAT? DON'T I HAVE A FACE YOU CAN TRUST? DON'T I HAVE AN INNOCENT LOOK ABOUT ME?

LOOK AT THE INNOCENCE IN MY EYES...

SHE'S RIGHT... IF A GIRL HAS INNOCENT-LOOKING EYES, YOU SIMPLY HAVE TO TRUST HER...

THIS TIME I'M GONNA KICK THAT FOOTBALL CLEAR TO THE MOON!

9-29

AAUGH

WUHAM!

WHAT YOU HAVE LEARNED HERE TODAY, CHARLIE BROWN, WILL BE OF IMMEASURABLE VALUE TO YOU FOR MANY YEARS TO COME

SIGH!

SCHULZ

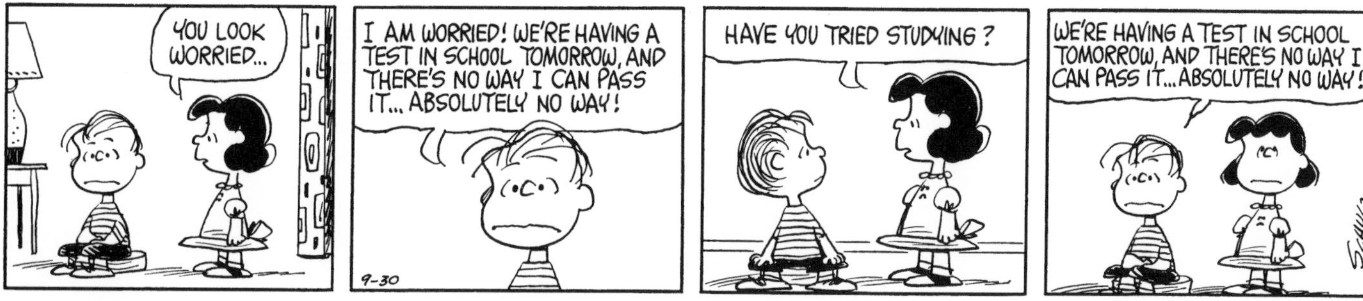
YOU LOOK WORRIED...
I AM WORRIED! WE'RE HAVING A TEST IN SCHOOL TOMORROW, AND THERE'S NO WAY I CAN PASS IT... ABSOLUTELY NO WAY!
9-30
HAVE YOU TRIED STUDYING?
WE'RE HAVING A TEST IN SCHOOL TOMORROW, AND THERE'S NO WAY I CAN PASS IT... ABSOLUTELY NO WAY!
SCHULZ

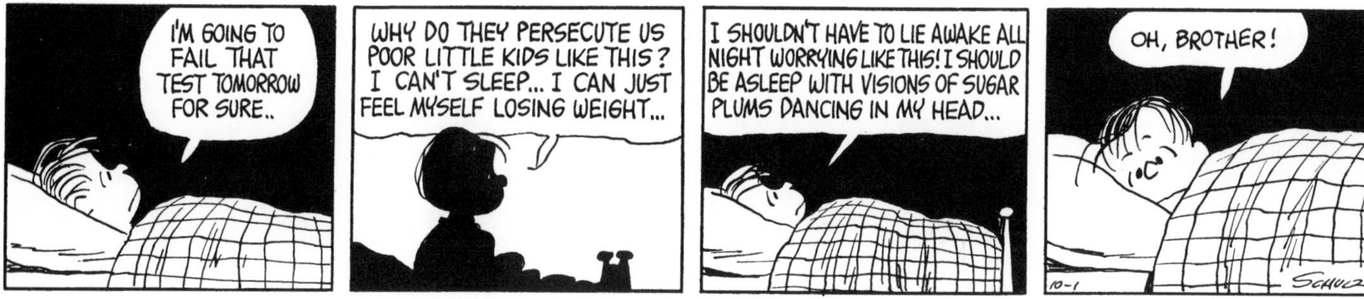
I'M GOING TO FAIL THAT TEST TOMORROW FOR SURE..
WHY DO THEY PERSECUTE US POOR LITTLE KIDS LIKE THIS? I CAN'T SLEEP... I CAN JUST FEEL MYSELF LOSING WEIGHT...
I SHOULDN'T HAVE TO LIE AWAKE ALL NIGHT WORRYING LIKE THIS! I SHOULD BE ASLEEP WITH VISIONS OF SUGAR PLUMS DANCING IN MY HEAD...
OH, BROTHER!
10-1
SCHULZ

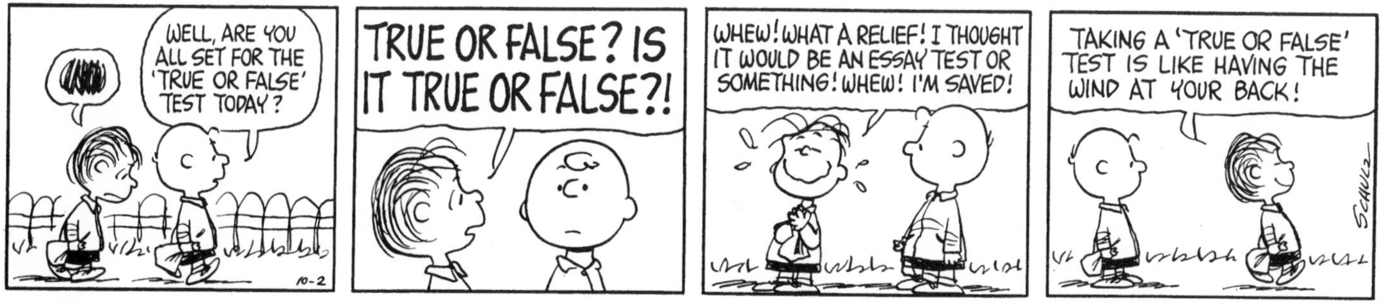
WELL, ARE YOU ALL SET FOR THE 'TRUE OR FALSE' TEST TODAY?
10-2
TRUE OR FALSE? IS IT TRUE OR FALSE?!
WHEW! WHAT A RELIEF! I THOUGHT IT WOULD BE AN ESSAY TEST OR SOMETHING! WHEW! I'M SAVED!
TAKING A 'TRUE OR FALSE' TEST IS LIKE HAVING THE WIND AT YOUR BACK!
SCHULZ

LET'S SEE NOW... IN A TRUE OR FALSE TEST, THE FIRST QUESTION IS ALMOST ALWAYS 'TRUE'...

THAT MEANS THE NEXT ONE WILL BE FALSE TO SORT OF BALANCE THE TRUE ONE..THE NEXT ONE WILL ALSO BE FALSE TO BREAK THE PATTERN..

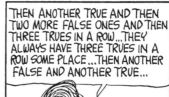

THEN ANOTHER TRUE AND THEN TWO MORE FALSE ONES AND THEN THREE TRUES IN A ROW...THEY ALWAYS HAVE THREE TRUES IN A ROW SOME PLACE...THEN ANOTHER FALSE AND ANOTHER TRUE...

IF YOU'RE SMART, YOU CAN PASS A TRUE OR FALSE TEST WITHOUT BEING SMART!

10-3

HOW DID YOU DO ON YOUR TEST?

DON'T ASK ME...IT WAS A DISASTER..

COULDN'T YOU EVEN PASS A TRUE OR FALSE TEST? WHAT HAPPENED?

10-4

I FALSED WHEN I SHOULD HAVE TRUED!

WELL, I HOPE YOU LEARNED A LESSON

YOU FAILED THAT TRUE OR FALSE TEST BECAUSE YOU DIDN'T STUDY

NO, I THINK I MERELY MISCALCULATED...

IF I HAD STARTED WITH A FALSE INSTEAD OF A TRUE, THEN THE THREE TRUES WOULD HAVE BEEN FALSES, AND THE FALSE THAT FOLLOWED THE TRUE WOULD HAVE...

OH, GOOD GRIEF!

10-5

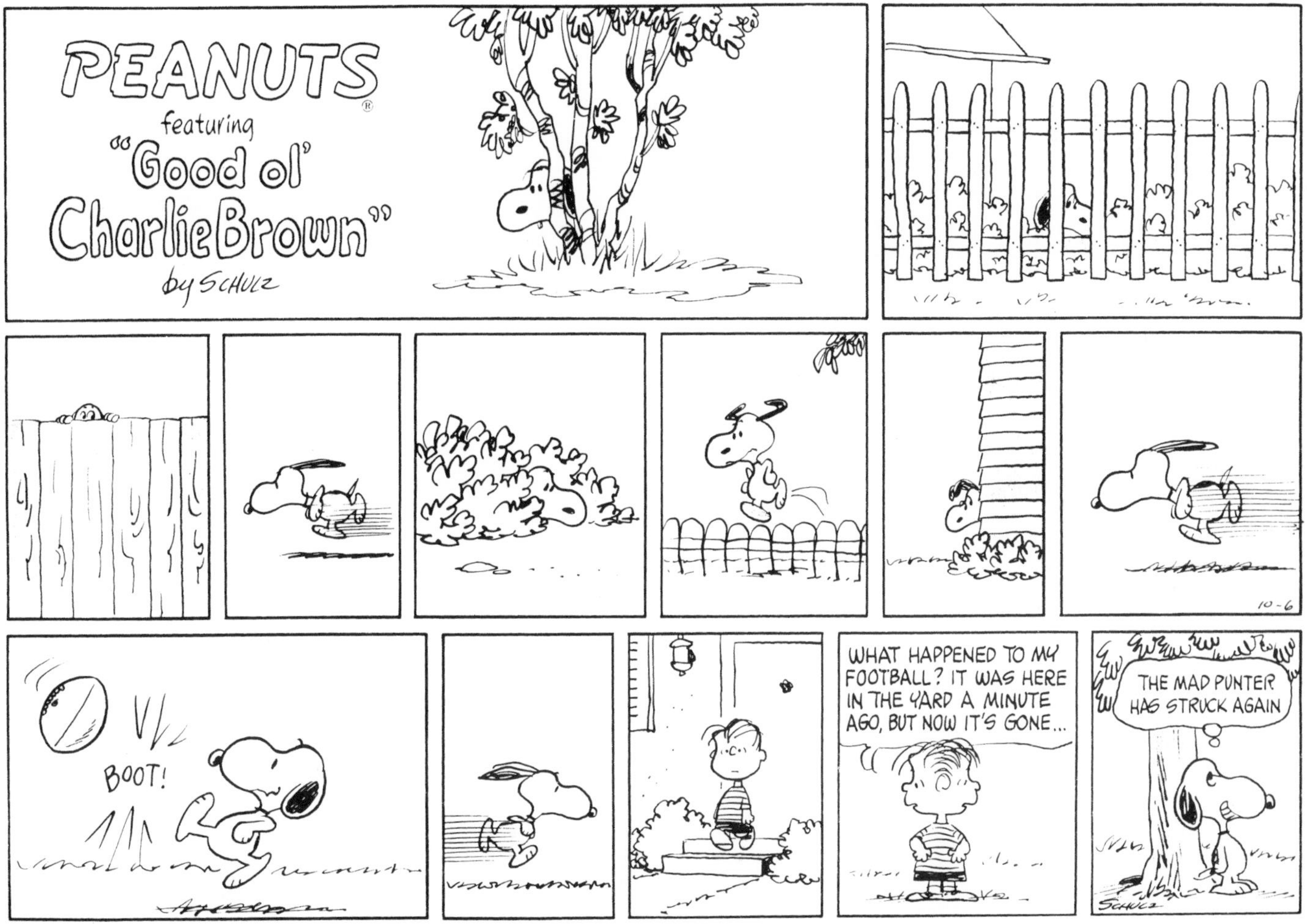
PEANUTS
featuring
"Good ol' CharlieBrown"
by SCHULZ
10-6
BOOT!
WHAT HAPPENED TO MY FOOTBALL? IT WAS HERE IN THE YARD A MINUTE AGO, BUT NOW IT'S GONE...
THE MAD PUNTER HAS STRUCK AGAIN
SCHULZ

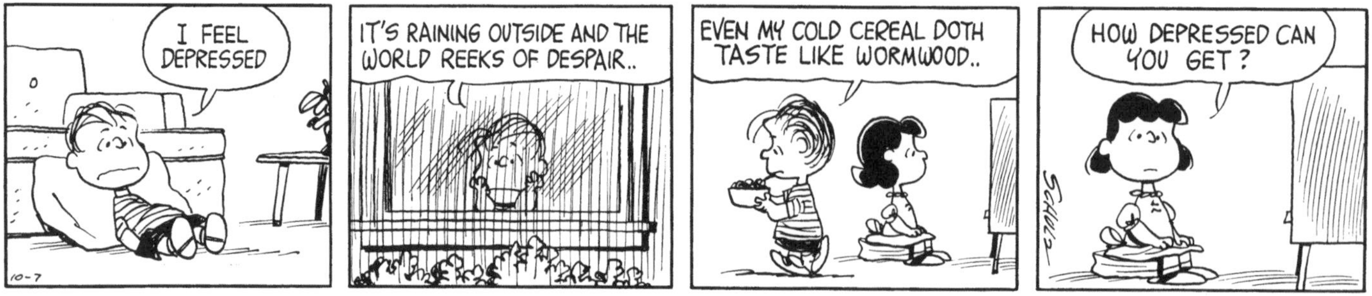
I FEEL DEPRESSED
10-7
IT'S RAINING OUTSIDE AND THE WORLD REEKS OF DESPAIR..
EVEN MY COLD CEREAL DOTH TASTE LIKE WORMWOOD..
HOW DEPRESSED CAN YOU GET?
SCHULZ

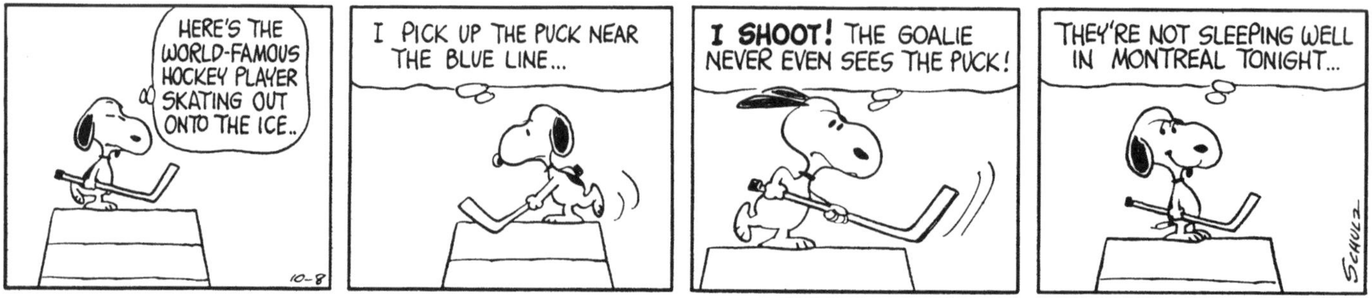
HERE'S THE WORLD-FAMOUS HOCKEY PLAYER SKATING OUT ONTO THE ICE..
10-8
I PICK UP THE PUCK NEAR THE BLUE LINE...
I SHOOT! THE GOALIE NEVER EVEN SEES THE PUCK!
THEY'RE NOT SLEEPING WELL IN MONTREAL TONIGHT...
SCHULZ

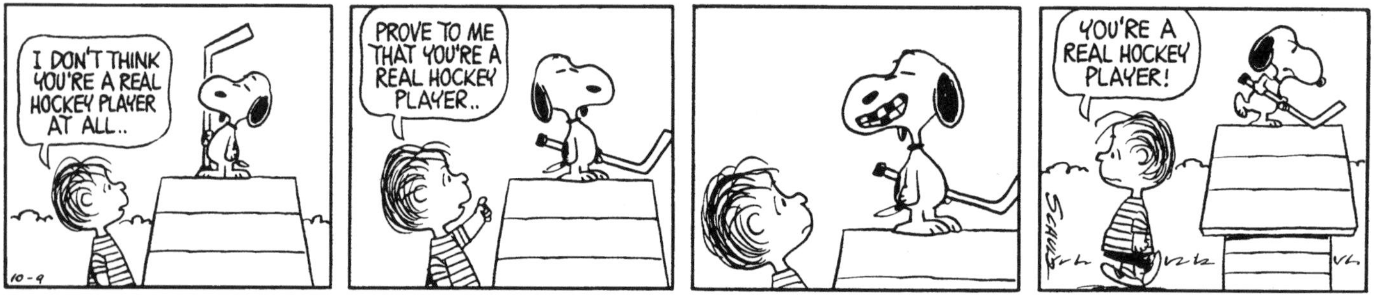
I DON'T THINK YOU'RE A REAL HOCKEY PLAYER AT ALL..
10-9
PROVE TO ME THAT YOU'RE A REAL HOCKEY PLAYER..
YOU'RE A REAL HOCKEY PLAYER!
SCHULZ

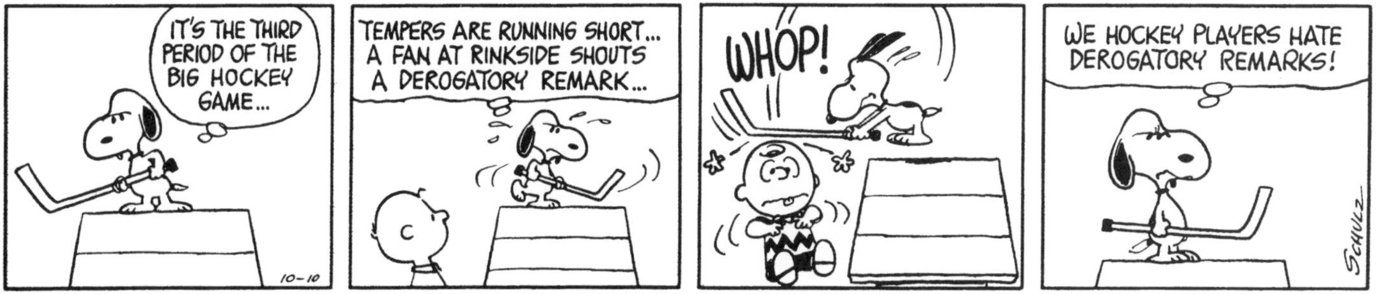
IT'S THE THIRD PERIOD OF THE BIG HOCKEY GAME...
10-10
TEMPERS ARE RUNNING SHORT... A FAN AT RINKSIDE SHOUTS A DEROGATORY REMARK...
WHOP!
WE HOCKEY PLAYERS HATE DEROGATORY REMARKS!
SCHULZ

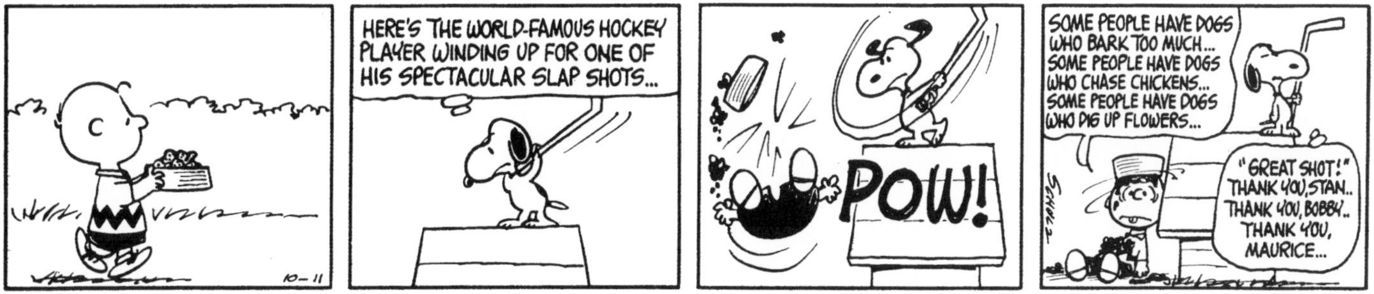
10-11
HERE'S THE WORLD-FAMOUS HOCKEY PLAYER WINDING UP FOR ONE OF HIS SPECTACULAR SLAP SHOTS...
POW!
SOME PEOPLE HAVE DOGS WHO BARK TOO MUCH... SOME PEOPLE HAVE DOGS WHO CHASE CHICKENS... SOME PEOPLE HAVE DOGS WHO DIG UP FLOWERS...
SCHULZ
"GREAT SHOT!" THANK YOU, STAN.. THANK YOU, BOBBY.. THANK YOU, MAURICE...

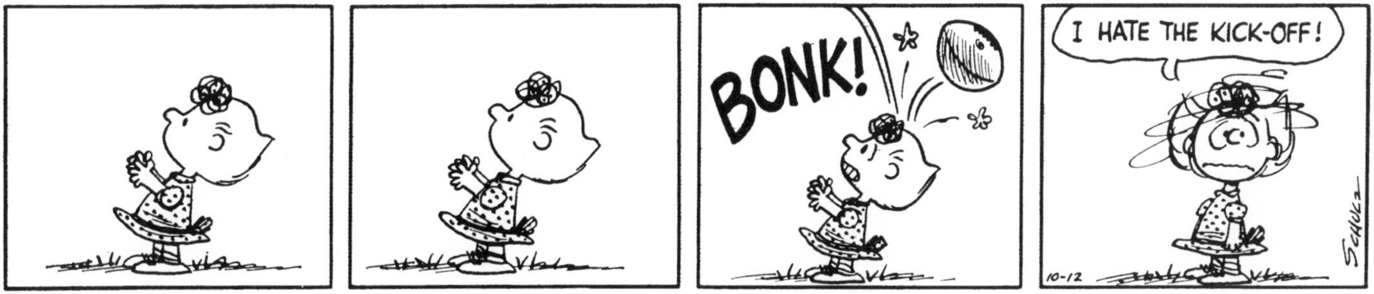
BONK!
I HATE THE KICK-OFF!
10-12
SCHULZ

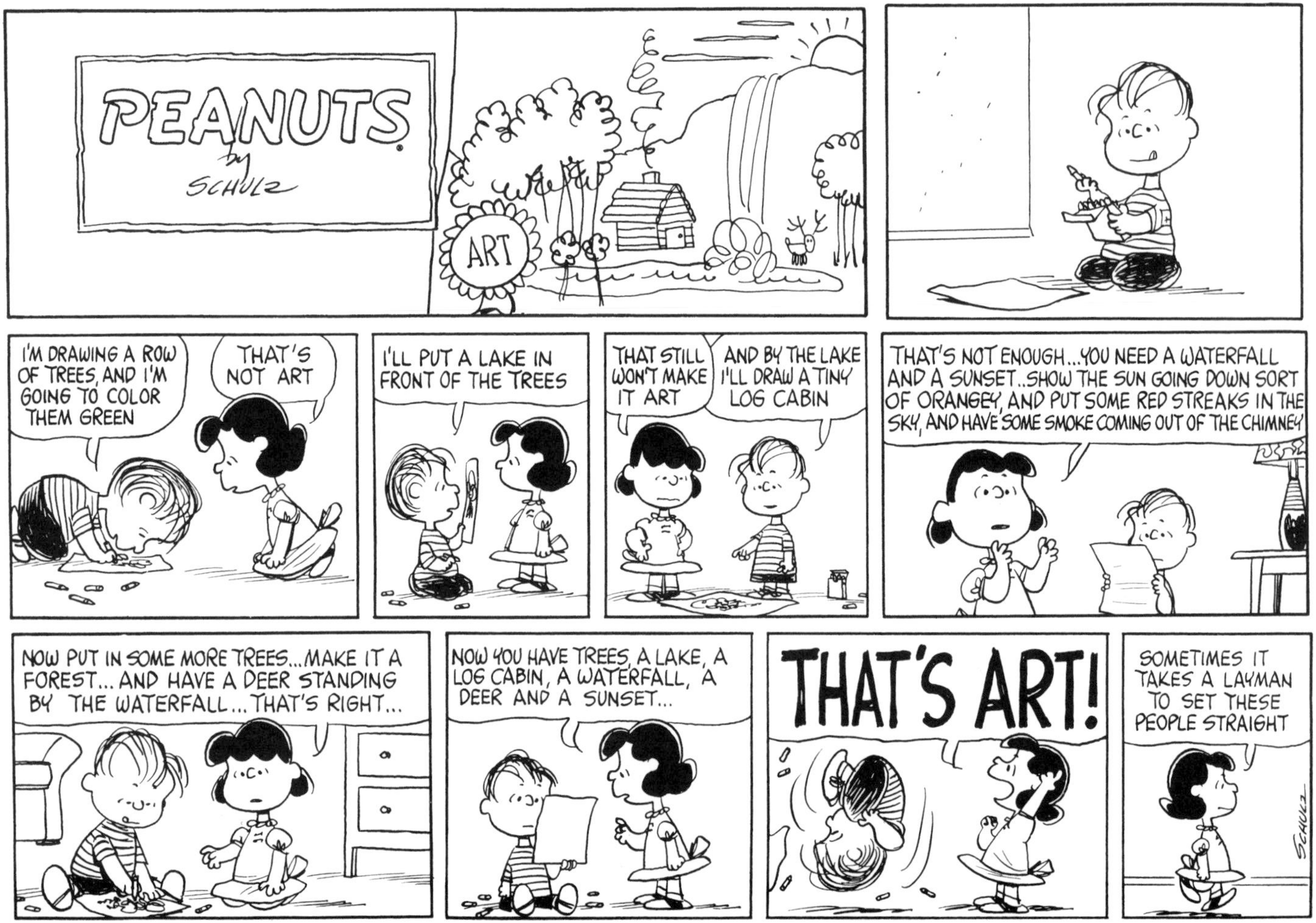
PEANUTS
by SCHULZ
ART
I'M DRAWING A ROW OF TREES, AND I'M GOING TO COLOR THEM GREEN
THAT'S NOT ART
I'LL PUT A LAKE IN FRONT OF THE TREES
THAT STILL WON'T MAKE IT ART
AND BY THE LAKE I'LL DRAW A TINY LOG CABIN
THAT'S NOT ENOUGH...YOU NEED A WATERFALL AND A SUNSET..SHOW THE SUN GOING DOWN SORT OF ORANGEY, AND PUT SOME RED STREAKS IN THE SKY, AND HAVE SOME SMOKE COMING OUT OF THE CHIMNEY
NOW PUT IN SOME MORE TREES...MAKE IT A FOREST... AND HAVE A DEER STANDING BY THE WATERFALL... THAT'S RIGHT...
NOW YOU HAVE TREES, A LAKE, A LOG CABIN, A WATERFALL, A DEER AND A SUNSET...
THAT'S ART!
SOMETIMES IT TAKES A LAYMAN TO SET THESE PEOPLE STRAIGHT
SCHULZ

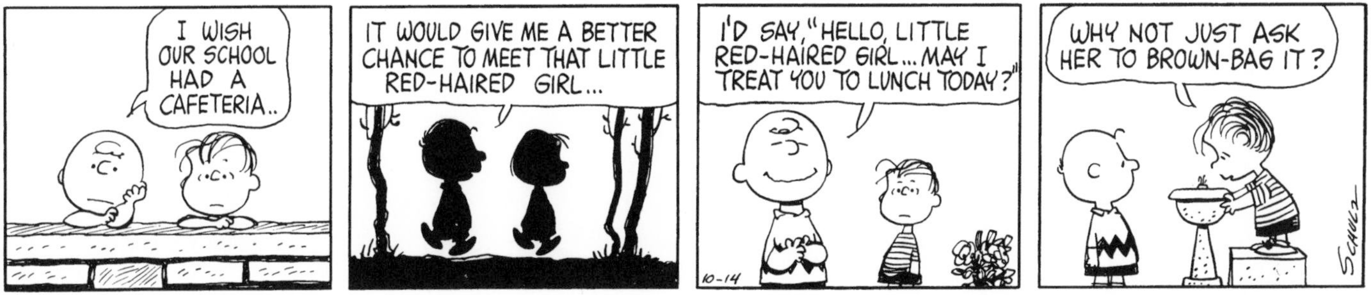
I WISH OUR SCHOOL HAD A CAFETERIA..
IT WOULD GIVE ME A BETTER CHANCE TO MEET THAT LITTLE RED-HAIRED GIRL...
I'D SAY, "HELLO, LITTLE RED-HAIRED GIRL... MAY I TREAT YOU TO LUNCH TODAY?"
10-14
WHY NOT JUST ASK HER TO BROWN-BAG IT?
SCHULZ

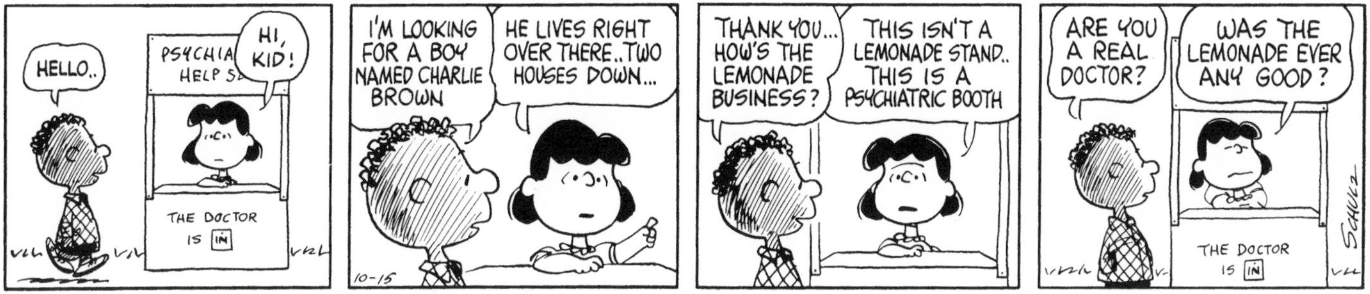
HELLO..
HI, KID!
THE DOCTOR IS IN
I'M LOOKING FOR A BOY NAMED CHARLIE BROWN
HE LIVES RIGHT OVER THERE..TWO HOUSES DOWN...
10-15
THANK YOU... HOW'S THE LEMONADE BUSINESS?
THIS ISN'T A LEMONADE STAND.. THIS IS A PSYCHIATRIC BOOTH
ARE YOU A REAL DOCTOR?
WAS THE LEMONADE EVER ANY GOOD?
THE DOCTOR IS IN
SCHULZ

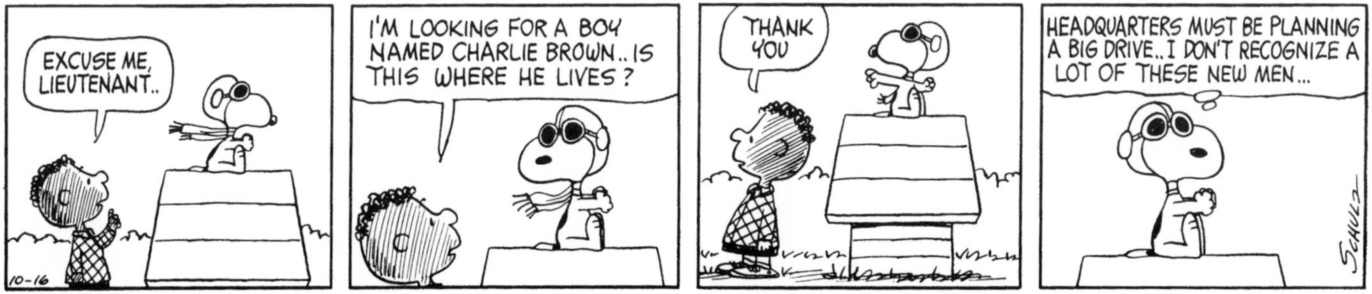
EXCUSE ME, LIEUTENANT..
10-16
I'M LOOKING FOR A BOY NAMED CHARLIE BROWN.. IS THIS WHERE HE LIVES?
THANK YOU
HEADQUARTERS MUST BE PLANNING A BIG DRIVE.. I DON'T RECOGNIZE A LOT OF THESE NEW MEN...
SCHULZ

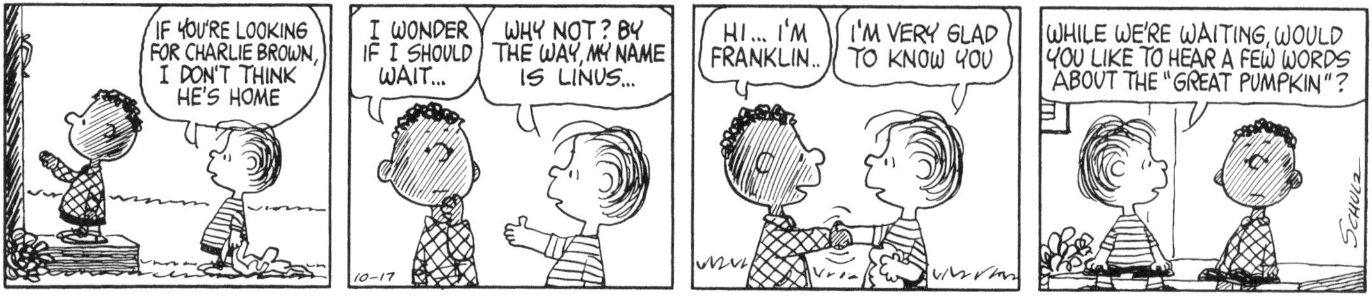
IF YOU'RE LOOKING FOR CHARLIE BROWN, I DON'T THINK HE'S HOME
I WONDER IF I SHOULD WAIT...
WHY NOT? BY THE WAY, MY NAME IS LINUS...
10-17
HI... I'M FRANKLIN..
I'M VERY GLAD TO KNOW YOU
WHILE WE'RE WAITING, WOULD YOU LIKE TO HEAR A FEW WORDS ABOUT THE "GREAT PUMPKIN"?
SCHULZ

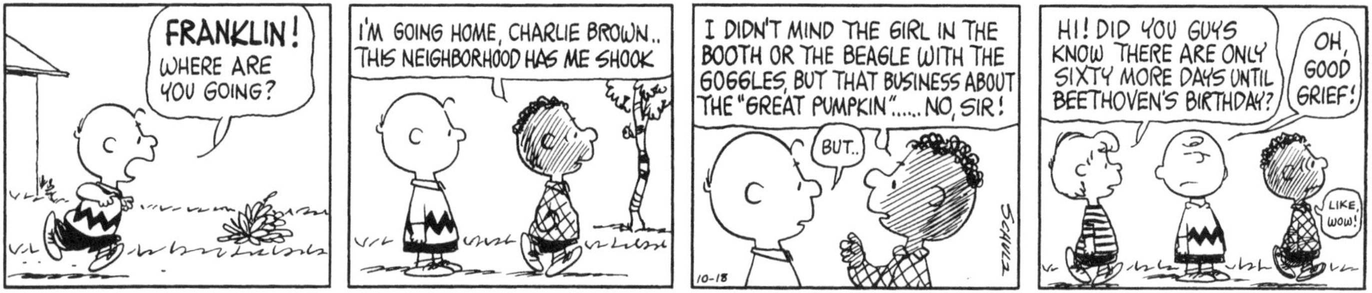
FRANKLIN! WHERE ARE YOU GOING?
I'M GOING HOME, CHARLIE BROWN.. THIS NEIGHBORHOOD HAS ME SHOOK
I DIDN'T MIND THE GIRL IN THE BOOTH OR THE BEAGLE WITH THE GOGGLES, BUT THAT BUSINESS ABOUT THE "GREAT PUMPKIN"..... NO, SIR!
BUT..
10-18
SCHULZ
HI! DID YOU GUYS KNOW THERE ARE ONLY SIXTY MORE DAYS UNTIL BEETHOVEN'S BIRTHDAY?
OH, GOOD GRIEF!
LIKE, WOW!

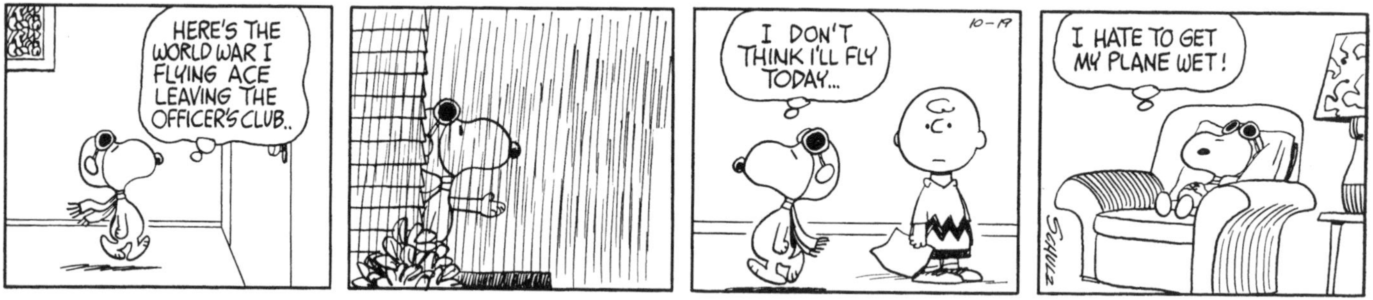
HERE'S THE WORLD WAR I FLYING ACE LEAVING THE OFFICER'S CLUB..
I DON'T THINK I'LL FLY TODAY...
10-19
I HATE TO GET MY PLANE WET!
SCHULZ

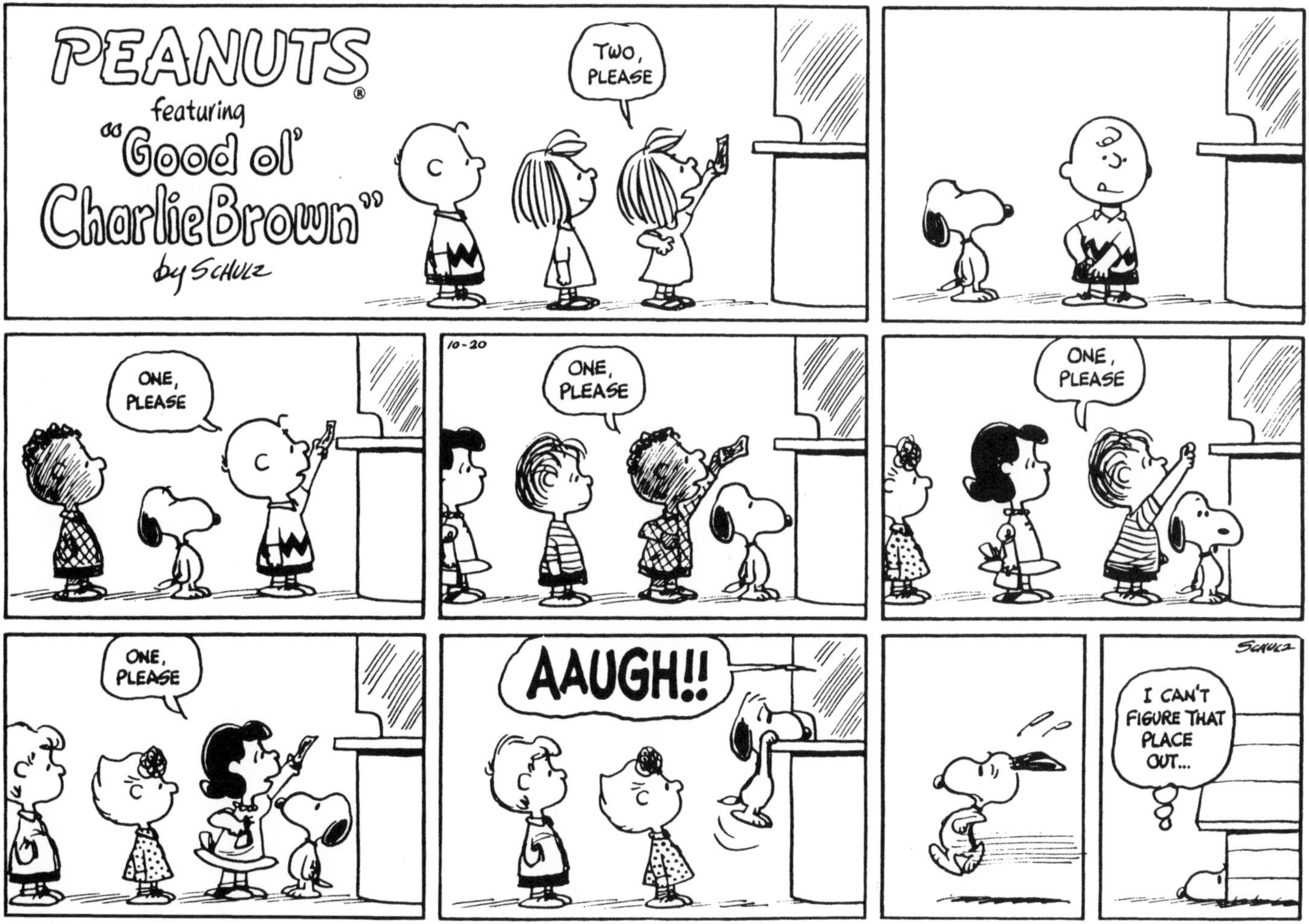
PEANUTS
featuring
"Good ol' Charlie Brown"
by SCHULZ
TWO, PLEASE
ONE, PLEASE
10-20
ONE, PLEASE
ONE, PLEASE
ONE, PLEASE
AAUGH!!
SCHULZ
I CAN'T FIGURE THAT PLACE OUT...

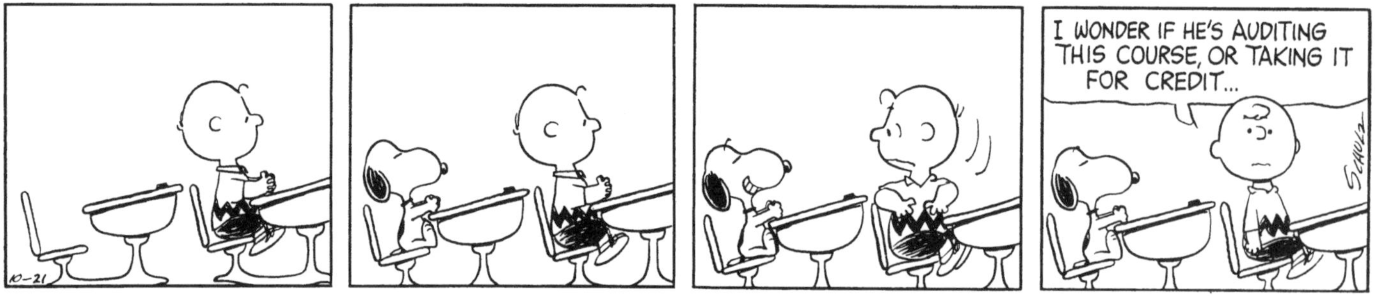
I WONDER IF HE'S AUDITING THIS COURSE, OR TAKING IT FOR CREDIT...

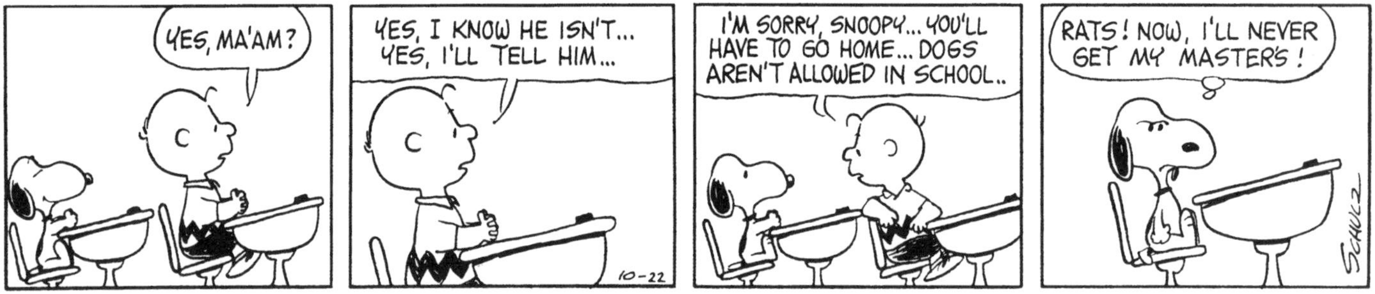
YES, MA'AM?
YES, I KNOW HE ISN'T... YES, I'LL TELL HIM...
I'M SORRY, SNOOPY... YOU'LL HAVE TO GO HOME... DOGS AREN'T ALLOWED IN SCHOOL..
RATS! NOW, I'LL NEVER GET MY MASTER'S!

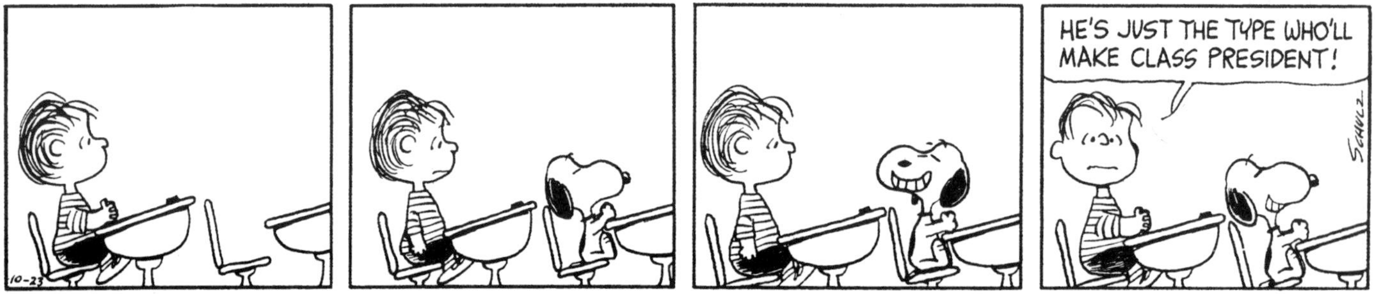
HE'S JUST THE TYPE WHO'LL MAKE CLASS PRESIDENT!

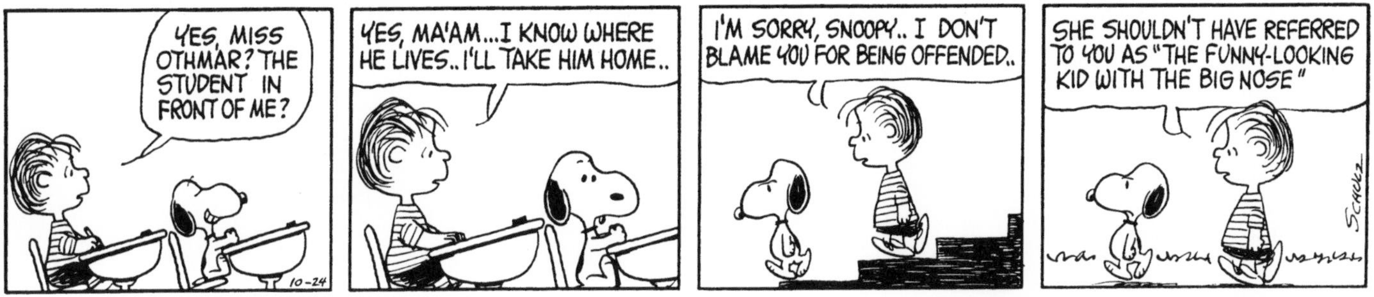
YES, MISS OTHMAR? THE STUDENT IN FRONT OF ME?
YES, MA'AM...I KNOW WHERE HE LIVES.. I'LL TAKE HIM HOME..
I'M SORRY, SNOOPY.. I DON'T BLAME YOU FOR BEING OFFENDED..
SHE SHOULDN'T HAVE REFERRED TO YOU AS "THE FUNNY-LOOKING KID WITH THE BIG NOSE"

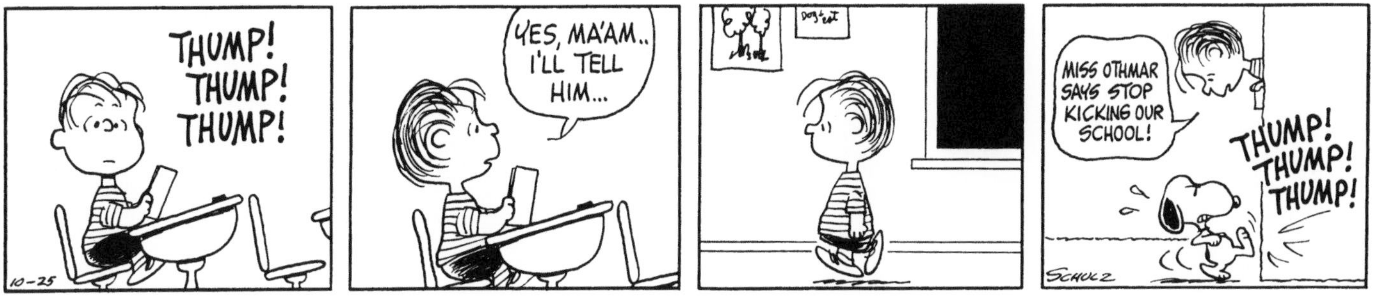
THUMP! THUMP! THUMP!
YES, MA'AM.. I'LL TELL HIM...
MISS OTHMAR SAYS STOP KICKING OUR SCHOOL!
THUMP! THUMP! THUMP!

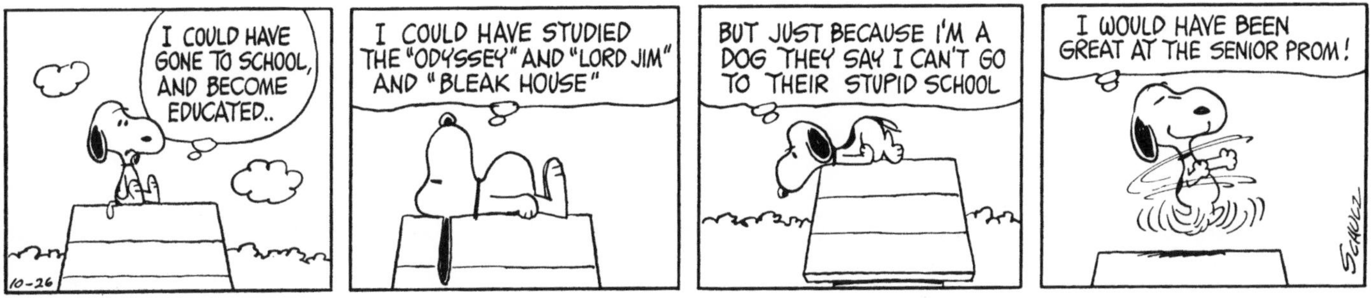
I COULD HAVE GONE TO SCHOOL, AND BECOME EDUCATED..
I COULD HAVE STUDIED THE "ODYSSEY" AND "LORD JIM" AND "BLEAK HOUSE"
BUT JUST BECAUSE I'M A DOG THEY SAY I CAN'T GO TO THEIR STUPID SCHOOL
I WOULD HAVE BEEN GREAT AT THE SENIOR PROM!

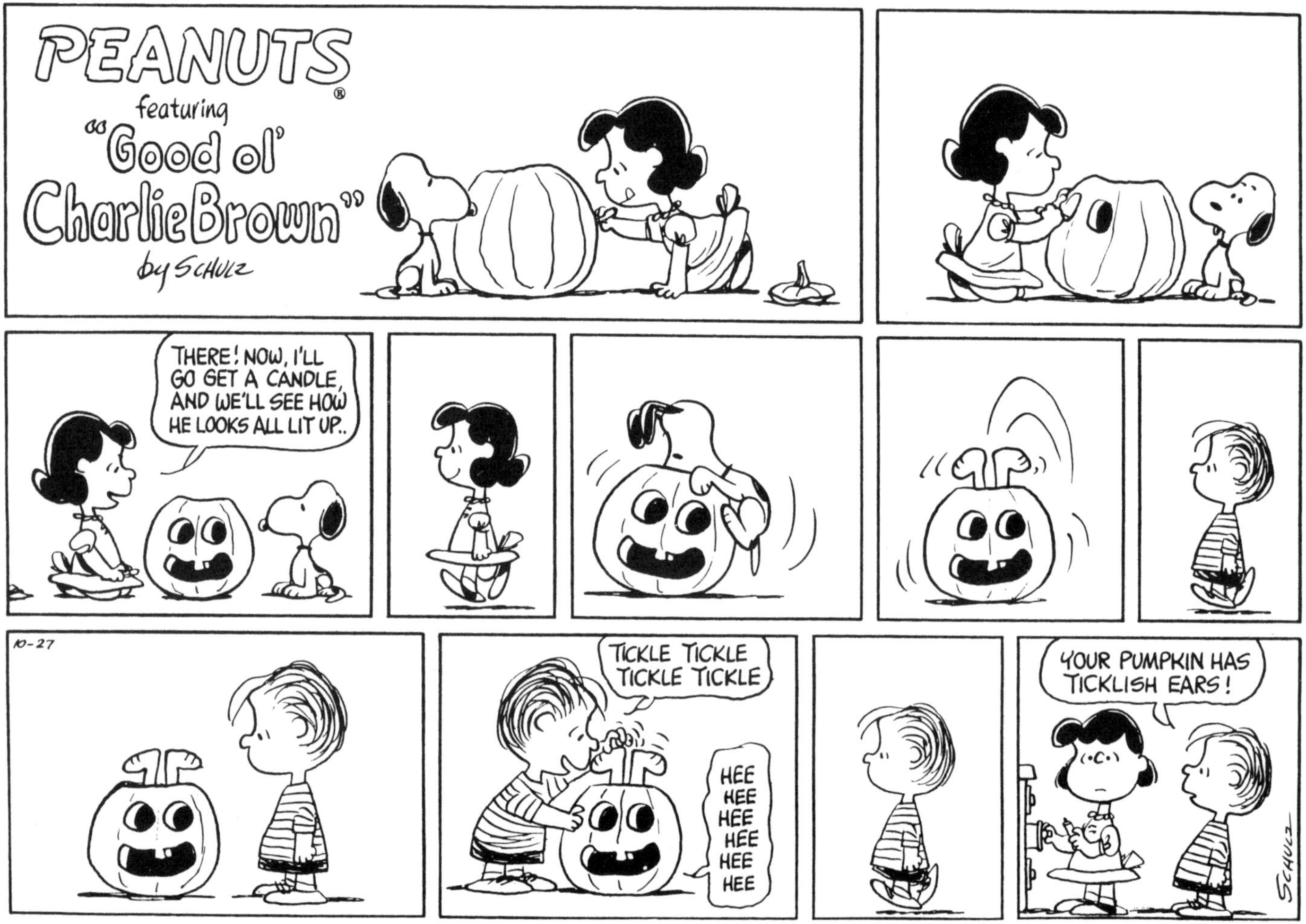
PEANUTS®
featuring
"Good ol' Charlie Brown"
by SCHULZ
THERE! NOW, I'LL GO GET A CANDLE, AND WE'LL SEE HOW HE LOOKS ALL LIT UP..
10-27
TICKLE TICKLE TICKLE TICKLE
HEE HEE HEE HEE HEE HEE
YOUR PUMPKIN HAS TICKLISH EARS!
SCHULZ

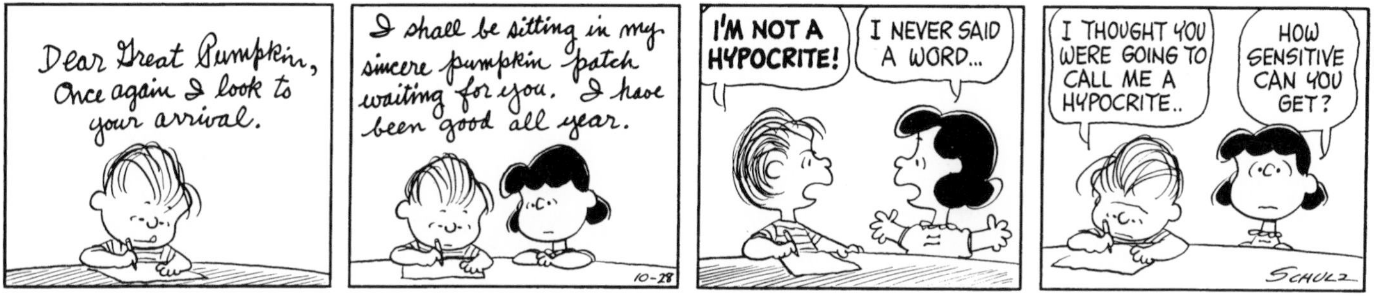
Dear Great Pumpkin, Once again I look to your arrival.
I shall be sitting in my sincere pumpkin patch waiting for you. I have been good all year.
10-28
I'M NOT A HYPOCRITE!
I NEVER SAID A WORD...
I THOUGHT YOU WERE GOING TO CALL ME A HYPOCRITE..
HOW SENSITIVE CAN YOU GET?
SCHULZ

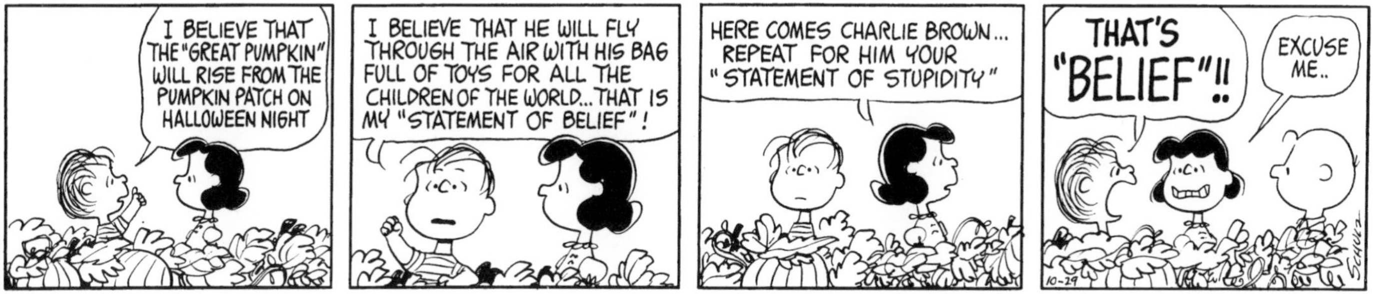
I BELIEVE THAT THE "GREAT PUMPKIN" WILL RISE FROM THE PUMPKIN PATCH ON HALLOWEEN NIGHT
I BELIEVE THAT HE WILL FLY THROUGH THE AIR WITH HIS BAG FULL OF TOYS FOR ALL THE CHILDREN OF THE WORLD... THAT IS MY "STATEMENT OF BELIEF"!
HERE COMES CHARLIE BROWN... REPEAT FOR HIM YOUR "STATEMENT OF STUPIDITY"
THAT'S "BELIEF"!!
EXCUSE ME..
10-29
SCHULZ

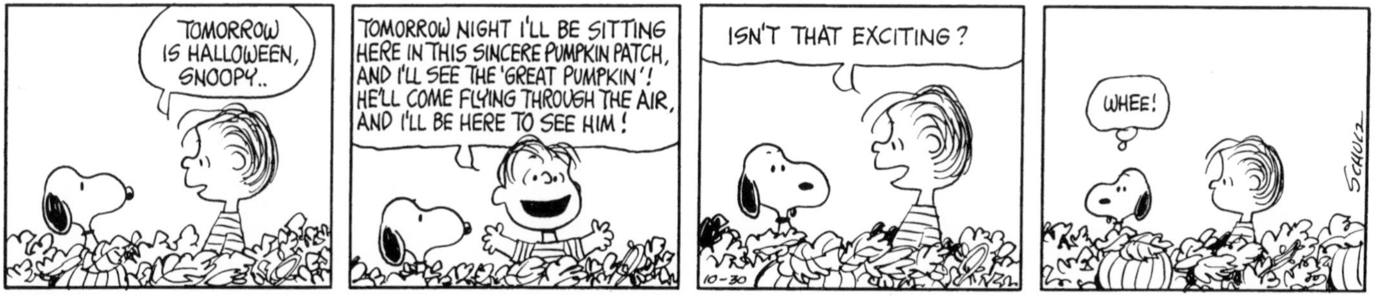
TOMORROW IS HALLOWEEN, SNOOPY..
TOMORROW NIGHT I'LL BE SITTING HERE IN THIS SINCERE PUMPKIN PATCH, AND I'LL SEE THE 'GREAT PUMPKIN'! HE'LL COME FLYING THROUGH THE AIR, AND I'LL BE HERE TO SEE HIM!
ISN'T THAT EXCITING?
10-30
WHEE!
SCHULZ

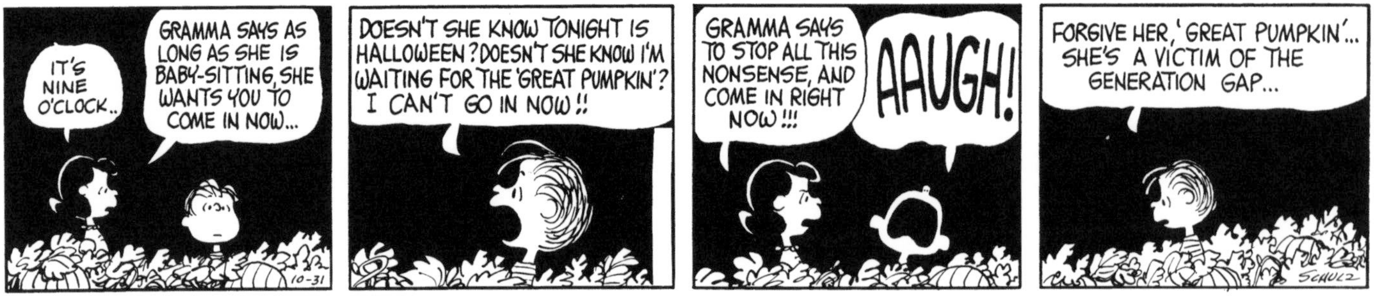
IT'S NINE O'CLOCK..
GRAMMA SAYS AS LONG AS SHE IS BABY-SITTING, SHE WANTS YOU TO COME IN NOW...
DOESN'T SHE KNOW TONIGHT IS HALLOWEEN? DOESN'T SHE KNOW I'M WAITING FOR THE 'GREAT PUMPKIN'? I CAN'T GO IN NOW!!
GRAMMA SAYS TO STOP ALL THIS NONSENSE, AND COME IN RIGHT NOW!!!
AAUGH!
FORGIVE HER, 'GREAT PUMPKIN'... SHE'S A VICTIM OF THE GENERATION GAP...

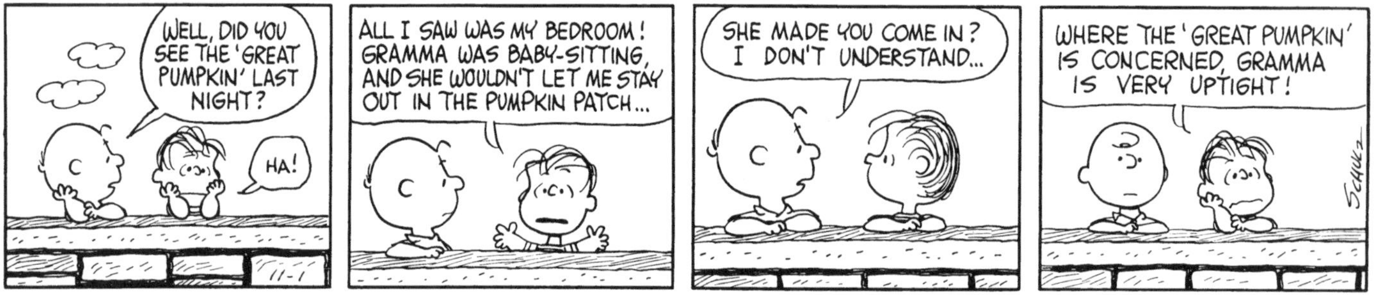
WELL, DID YOU SEE THE 'GREAT PUMPKIN' LAST NIGHT?
HA!
ALL I SAW WAS MY BEDROOM! GRAMMA WAS BABY-SITTING, AND SHE WOULDN'T LET ME STAY OUT IN THE PUMPKIN PATCH...
SHE MADE YOU COME IN? I DON'T UNDERSTAND...
WHERE THE 'GREAT PUMPKIN' IS CONCERNED, GRAMMA IS VERY UPTIGHT!

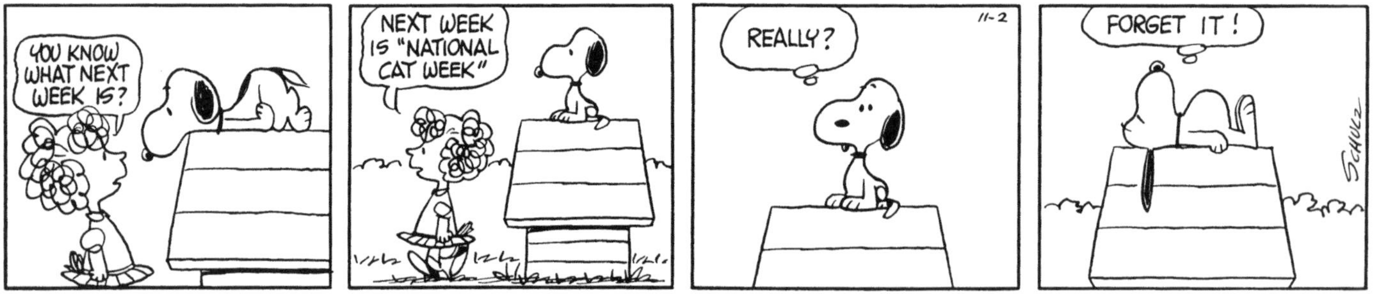
YOU KNOW WHAT NEXT WEEK IS?
NEXT WEEK IS "NATIONAL CAT WEEK"
REALLY?
FORGET IT!

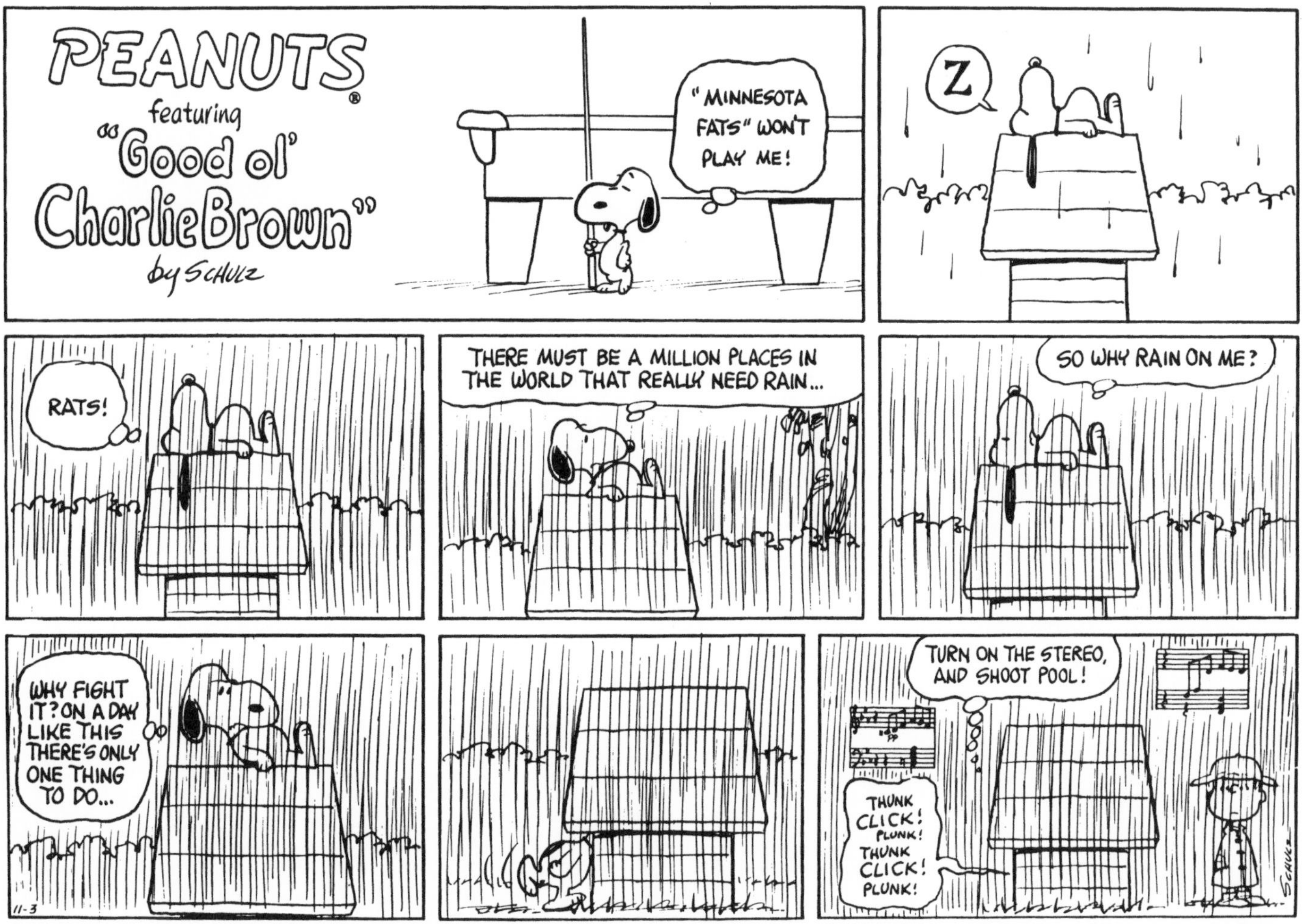
PEANUTS
featuring
"Good ol' CharlieBrown"
by SCHULZ
"MINNESOTA FATS" WON'T PLAY ME!
Z
RATS!
THERE MUST BE A MILLION PLACES IN THE WORLD THAT REALLY NEED RAIN...
SO WHY RAIN ON ME?
WHY FIGHT IT? ON A DAY LIKE THIS THERE'S ONLY ONE THING TO DO...
11-3
TURN ON THE STEREO, AND SHOOT POOL!
THUNK CLICK! PLUNK! THUNK CLICK! PLUNK!
SCHULZ

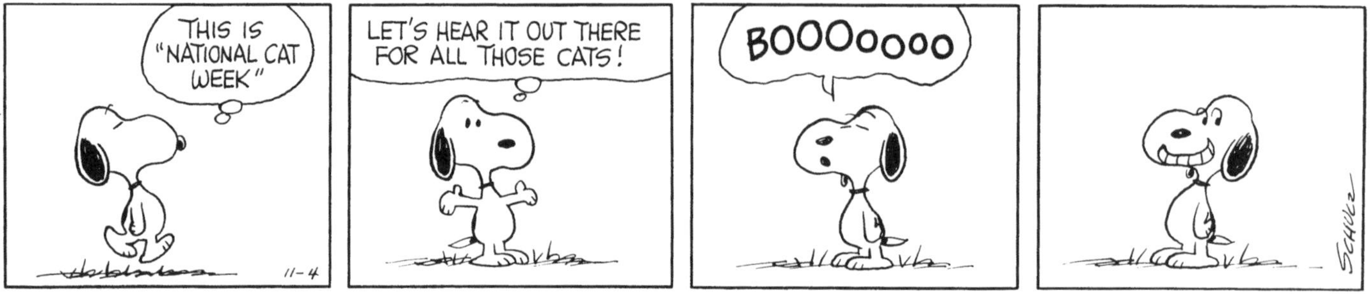
THIS IS "NATIONAL CAT WEEK"
11-4
LET'S HEAR IT OUT THERE FOR ALL THOSE CATS!
BOOOoooo
SCHULZ

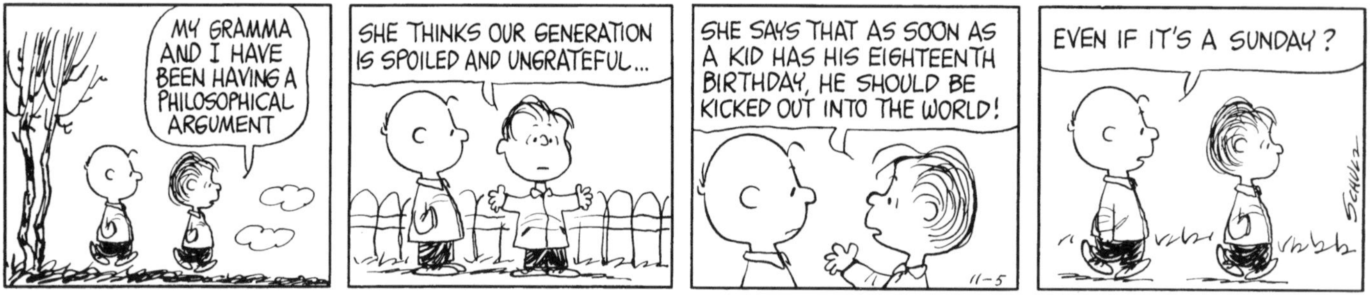
MY GRAMMA AND I HAVE BEEN HAVING A PHILOSOPHICAL ARGUMENT
SHE THINKS OUR GENERATION IS SPOILED AND UNGRATEFUL...
SHE SAYS THAT AS SOON AS A KID HAS HIS EIGHTEENTH BIRTHDAY, HE SHOULD BE KICKED OUT INTO THE WORLD!
11-5
EVEN IF IT'S A SUNDAY?
SCHULZ

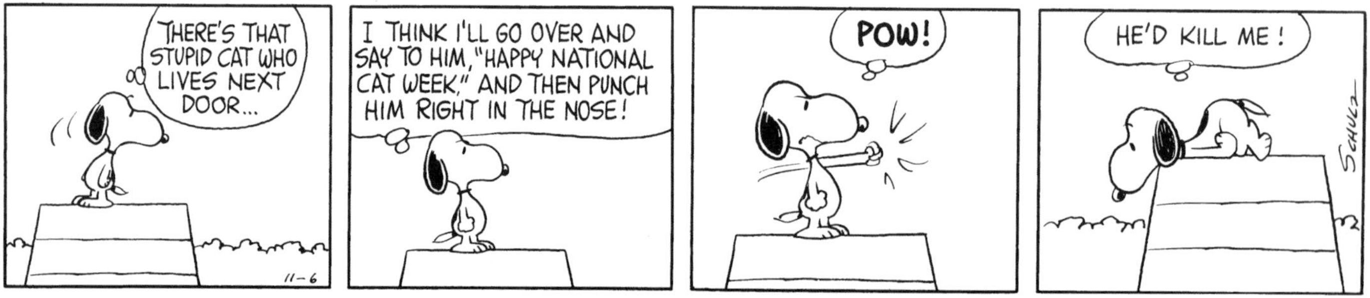
THERE'S THAT STUPID CAT WHO LIVES NEXT DOOR...
11-6
I THINK I'LL GO OVER AND SAY TO HIM, "HAPPY NATIONAL CAT WEEK," AND THEN PUNCH HIM RIGHT IN THE NOSE!
POW!
HE'D KILL ME!
SCHULZ

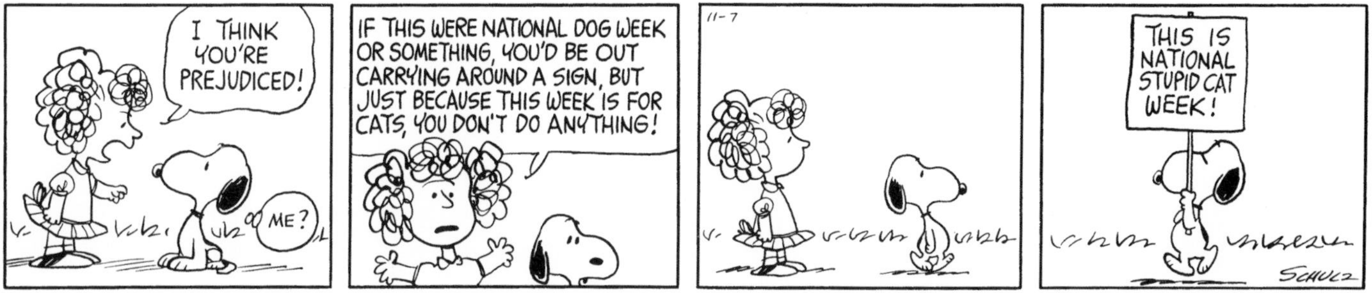
I THINK YOU'RE PREJUDICED!
ME?
IF THIS WERE NATIONAL DOG WEEK OR SOMETHING, YOU'D BE OUT CARRYING AROUND A SIGN, BUT JUST BECAUSE THIS WEEK IS FOR CATS, YOU DON'T DO ANYTHING!
11-7
THIS IS NATIONAL STUPID CAT WEEK!
SCHULZ

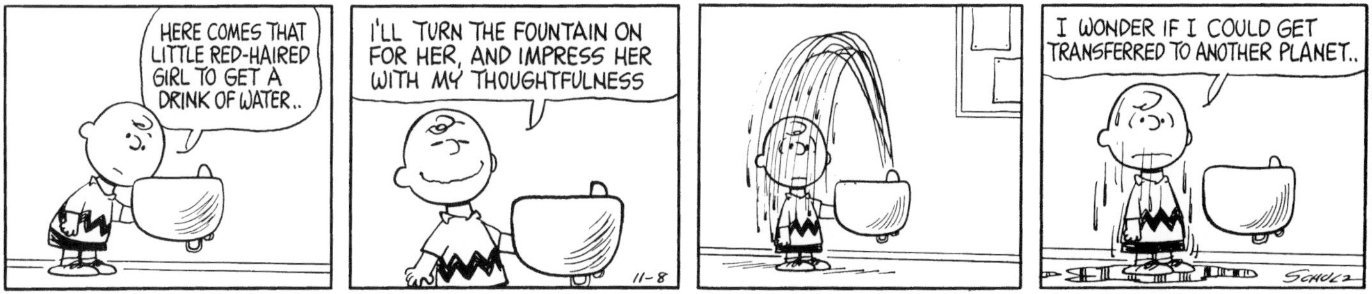
HERE COMES THAT LITTLE RED-HAIRED GIRL TO GET A DRINK OF WATER..
I'LL TURN THE FOUNTAIN ON FOR HER, AND IMPRESS HER WITH MY THOUGHTFULNESS
11-8
I WONDER IF I COULD GET TRANSFERRED TO ANOTHER PLANET..
SCHULZ

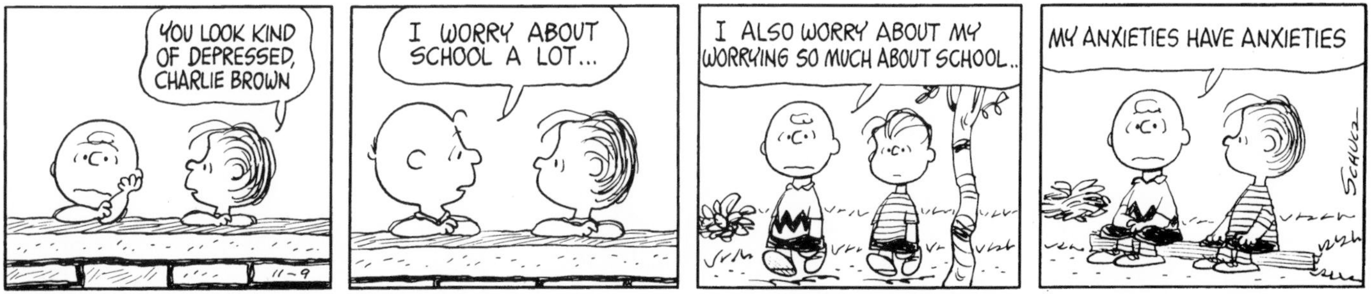
YOU LOOK KIND OF DEPRESSED, CHARLIE BROWN
11-9
I WORRY ABOUT SCHOOL A LOT...
I ALSO WORRY ABOUT MY WORRYING SO MUCH ABOUT SCHOOL..
MY ANXIETIES HAVE ANXIETIES
SCHULZ

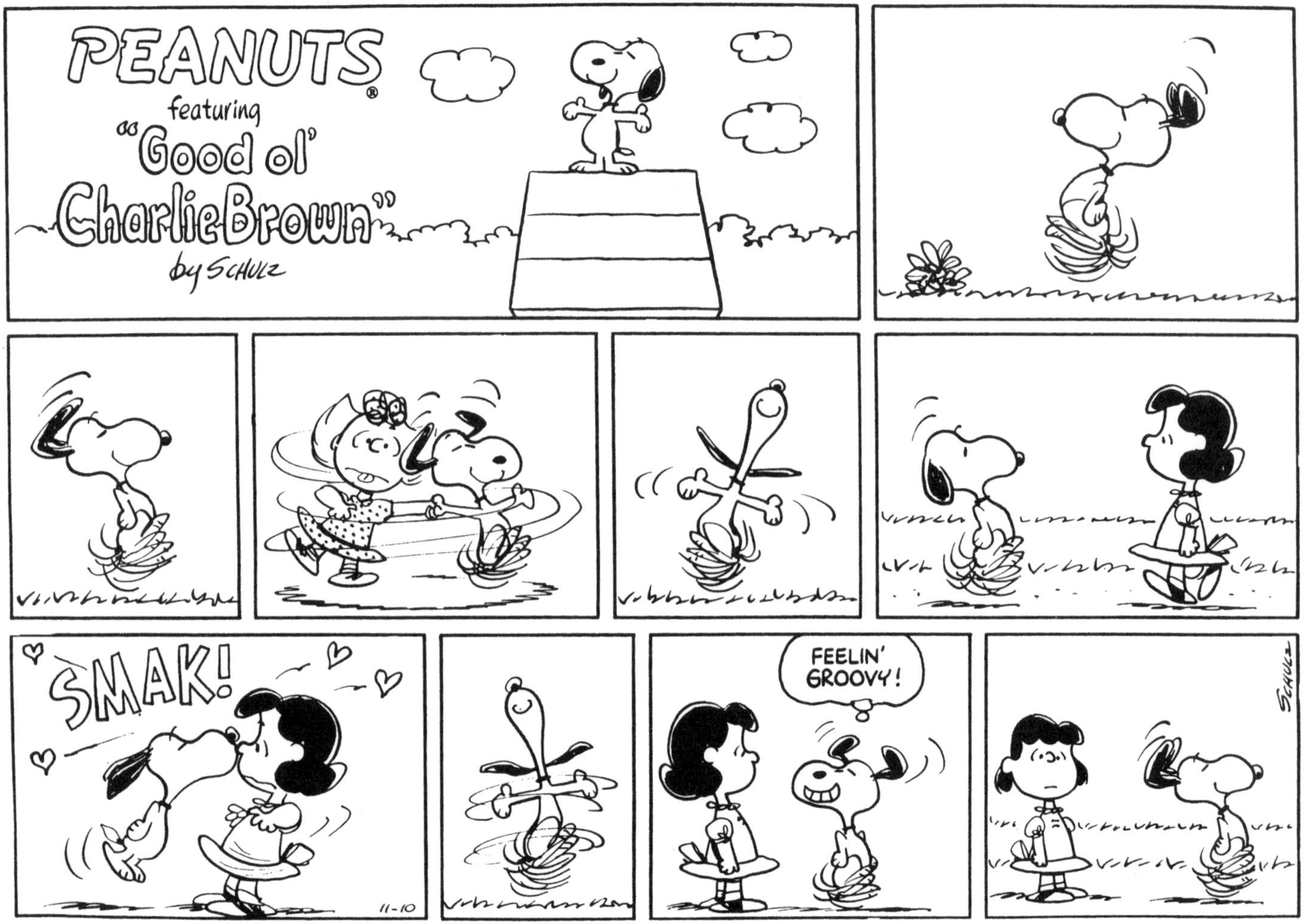
PEANUTS®
featuring "Good ol' Charlie Brown"
by SCHULZ
SMAK!
11-10
FEELIN' GROOVY!
SCHULZ

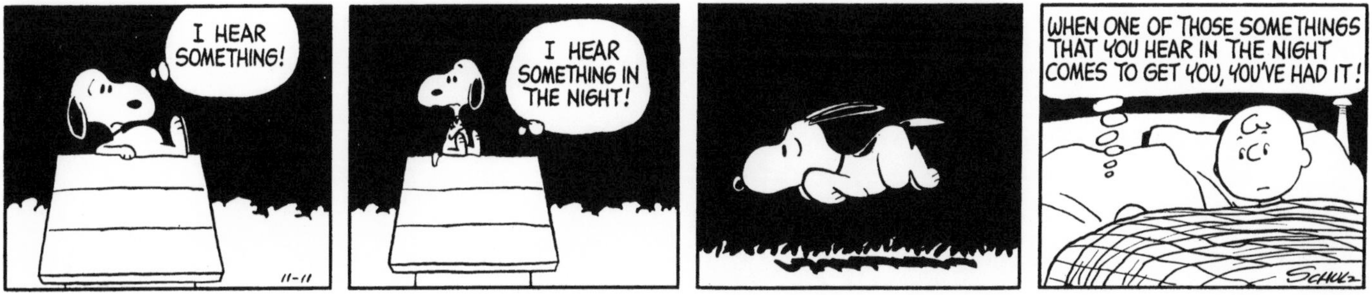
I HEAR SOMETHING!
I HEAR SOMETHING IN THE NIGHT!
WHEN ONE OF THOSE SOMETHINGS THAT YOU HEAR IN THE NIGHT COMES TO GET YOU, YOU'VE HAD IT!

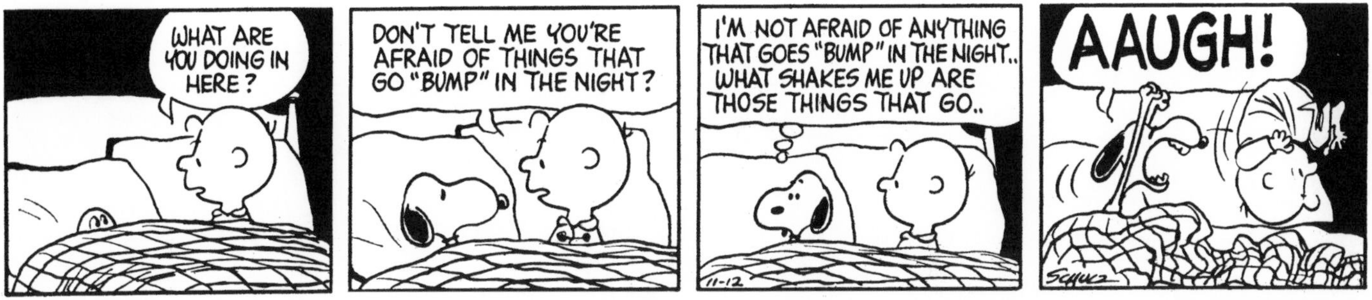
WHAT ARE YOU DOING IN HERE?
DON'T TELL ME YOU'RE AFRAID OF THINGS THAT GO "BUMP" IN THE NIGHT?
I'M NOT AFRAID OF ANYTHING THAT GOES "BUMP" IN THE NIGHT.. WHAT SHAKES ME UP ARE THOSE THINGS THAT GO..
AAUGH!

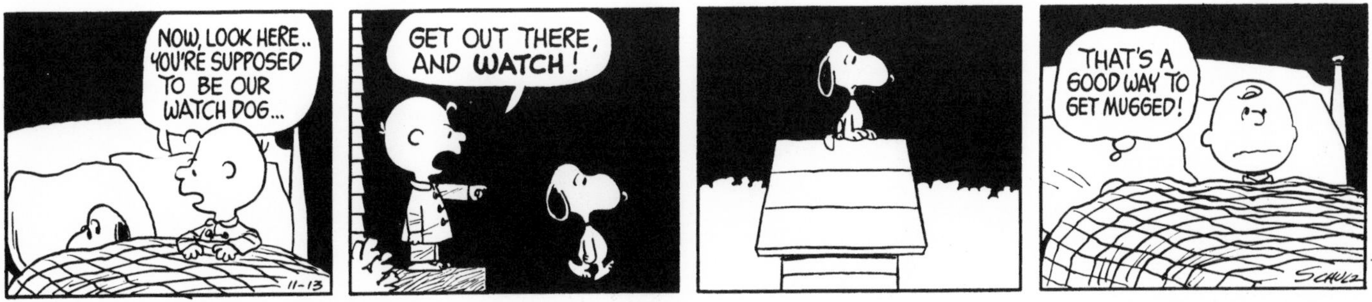
NOW, LOOK HERE.. YOU'RE SUPPOSED TO BE OUR WATCH DOG...
GET OUT THERE, AND WATCH!
THAT'S A GOOD WAY TO GET MUGGED!

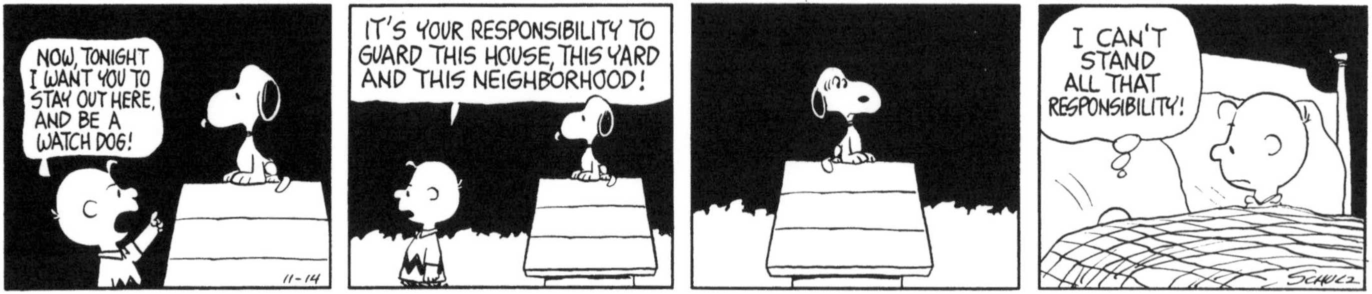
NOW, TONIGHT I WANT YOU TO STAY OUT HERE, AND BE A WATCH DOG!
11-14
IT'S YOUR RESPONSIBILITY TO GUARD THIS HOUSE, THIS YARD AND THIS NEIGHBORHOOD!
I CAN'T STAND ALL THAT RESPONSIBILITY!
SCHULZ

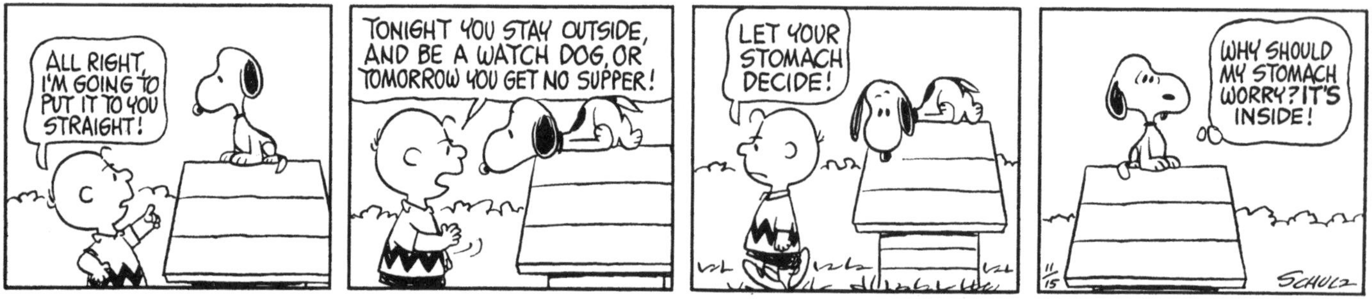
ALL RIGHT, I'M GOING TO PUT IT TO YOU STRAIGHT!
TONIGHT YOU STAY OUTSIDE, AND BE A WATCH DOG, OR TOMORROW YOU GET NO SUPPER!
LET YOUR STOMACH DECIDE!
WHY SHOULD MY STOMACH WORRY? IT'S INSIDE!
11/15
SCHULZ

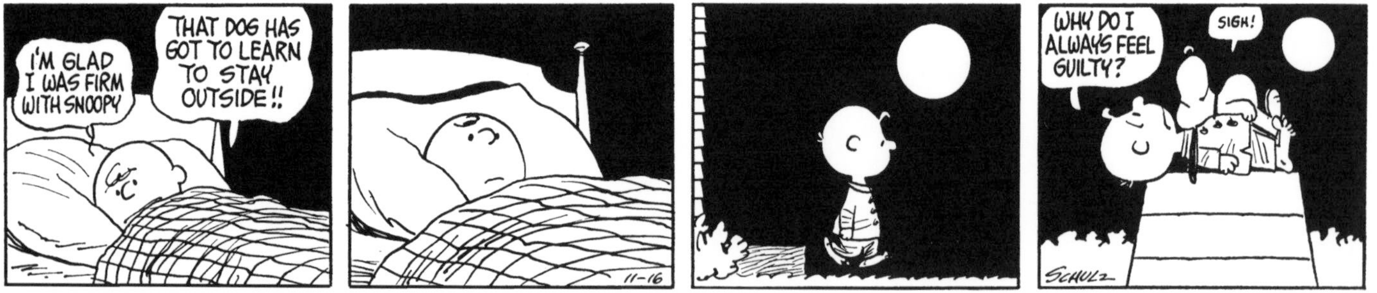
I'M GLAD I WAS FIRM WITH SNOOPY
THAT DOG HAS GOT TO LEARN TO STAY OUTSIDE!!
11-16
WHY DO I ALWAYS FEEL GUILTY?
SIGH!
SCHULZ

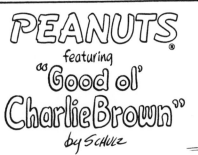

PEANUTS
featuring
"Good ol' CharlieBrown"
by Schulz

IT'S TEN MINUTES TO ELEVEN... EXACTLY!

AND NOW IT'S NINE AND ONE-HALF MINUTES TO ELEVEN... EXACTLY!

NEW WATCH!

NEW WATCH!

11-17

SLURP

YOU LICKED MY WATCH!

HE'S FOGGED UP THE CRYSTAL! IT'LL RUST! IT'LL TURN GREEN! HE'S RUINED IT! IT'LL WARP!!

I THOUGHT IT WOULD HAVE BEEN IMPOLITE NOT TO TASTE IT!

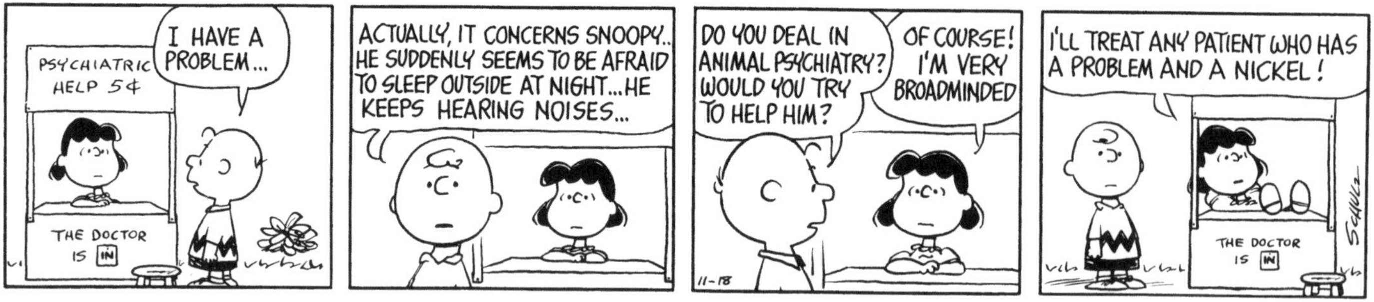
PSYCHIATRIC HELP 5¢
I HAVE A PROBLEM...
THE DOCTOR IS IN
ACTUALLY, IT CONCERNS SNOOPY.. HE SUDDENLY SEEMS TO BE AFRAID TO SLEEP OUTSIDE AT NIGHT...HE KEEPS HEARING NOISES...
DO YOU DEAL IN ANIMAL PSYCHIATRY? WOULD YOU TRY TO HELP HIM?
OF COURSE! I'M VERY BROADMINDED
11-18
I'LL TREAT ANY PATIENT WHO HAS A PROBLEM AND A NICKEL!
THE DOCTOR IS IN
SCHULZ

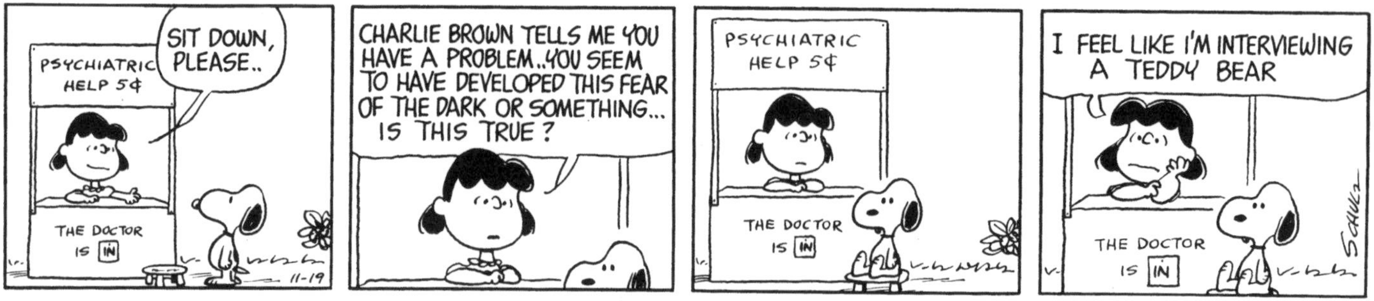
PSYCHIATRIC HELP 5¢
SIT DOWN, PLEASE..
THE DOCTOR IS IN
11-19
CHARLIE BROWN TELLS ME YOU HAVE A PROBLEM..YOU SEEM TO HAVE DEVELOPED THIS FEAR OF THE DARK OR SOMETHING... IS THIS TRUE?
PSYCHIATRIC HELP 5¢
THE DOCTOR IS IN
I FEEL LIKE I'M INTERVIEWING A TEDDY BEAR
THE DOCTOR IS IN
SCHULZ

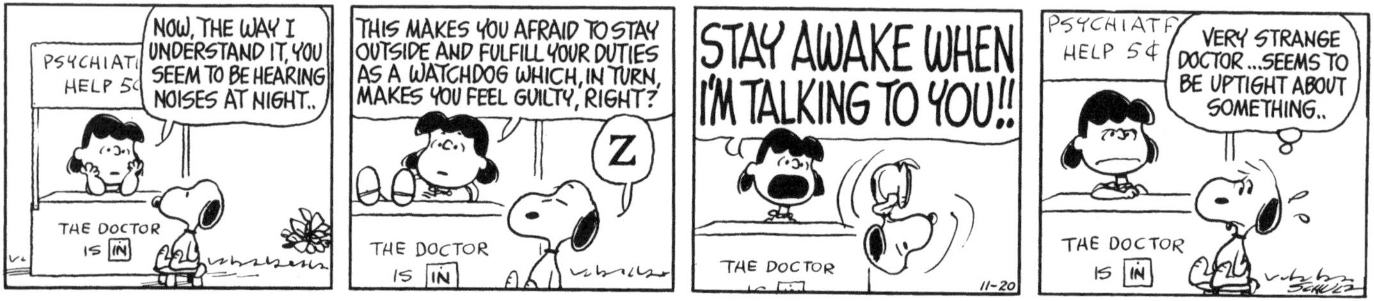
PSYCHIATI HELP 5¢
NOW, THE WAY I UNDERSTAND IT, YOU SEEM TO BE HEARING NOISES AT NIGHT..
THE DOCTOR IS IN
THIS MAKES YOU AFRAID TO STAY OUTSIDE AND FULFILL YOUR DUTIES AS A WATCHDOG WHICH, IN TURN, MAKES YOU FEEL GUILTY, RIGHT?
Z
THE DOCTOR IS IN
STAY AWAKE WHEN I'M TALKING TO YOU!!
THE DOCTOR
11-20
PSYCHIATF HELP 5¢
VERY STRANGE DOCTOR...SEEMS TO BE UPTIGHT ABOUT SOMETHING..
THE DOCTOR IS IN
SCHULZ

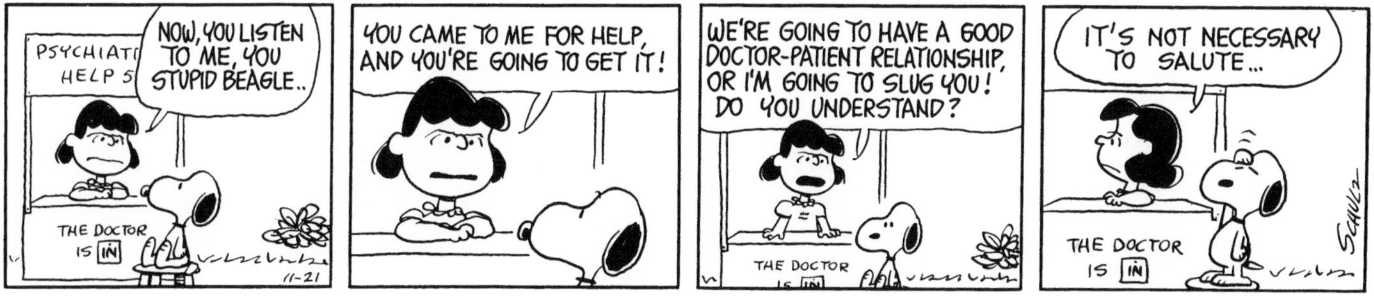
PSYCHIATI
HELP 5
NOW, YOU LISTEN TO ME, YOU STUPID BEAGLE..
THE DOCTOR IS IN
11-21
YOU CAME TO ME FOR HELP, AND YOU'RE GOING TO GET IT!
WE'RE GOING TO HAVE A GOOD DOCTOR-PATIENT RELATIONSHIP, OR I'M GOING TO SLUG YOU! DO YOU UNDERSTAND?
THE DOCTOR
IT'S NOT NECESSARY TO SALUTE...
THE DOCTOR IS IN
SCHULZ

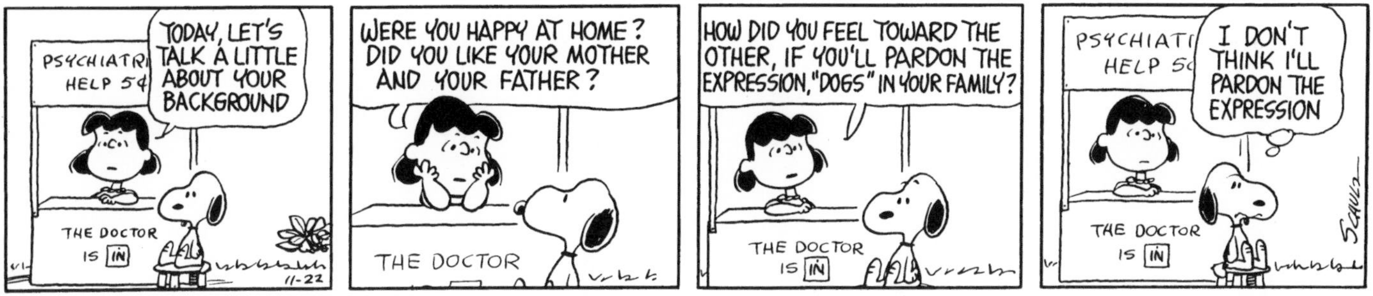
PSYCHIATRI
HELP 5¢
TODAY, LET'S TALK A LITTLE ABOUT YOUR BACKGROUND
THE DOCTOR IS IN
11-22
WERE YOU HAPPY AT HOME? DID YOU LIKE YOUR MOTHER AND YOUR FATHER?
THE DOCTOR
HOW DID YOU FEEL TOWARD THE OTHER, IF YOU'LL PARDON THE EXPRESSION, "DOGS" IN YOUR FAMILY?
THE DOCTOR IS IN
PSYCHIATI
HELP 5
I DON'T THINK I'LL PARDON THE EXPRESSION
THE DOCTOR IS IN
SCHULZ

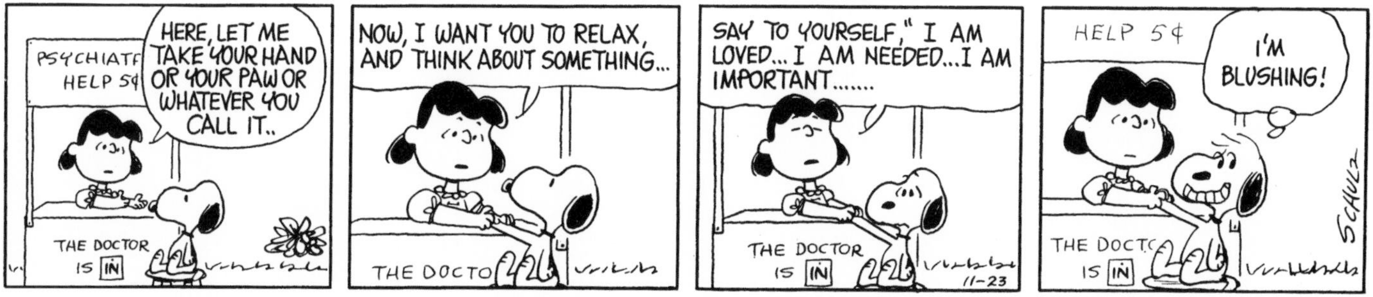
PSYCHIATI
HELP 5¢
HERE, LET ME TAKE YOUR HAND OR YOUR PAW OR WHATEVER YOU CALL IT..
THE DOCTOR IS IN
NOW, I WANT YOU TO RELAX, AND THINK ABOUT SOMETHING...
THE DOCTO
SAY TO YOURSELF, " I AM LOVED... I AM NEEDED... I AM IMPORTANT.......
THE DOCTOR IS IN
11-23
HELP 5¢
I'M BLUSHING!
THE DOCTO
IS IN
SCHULZ

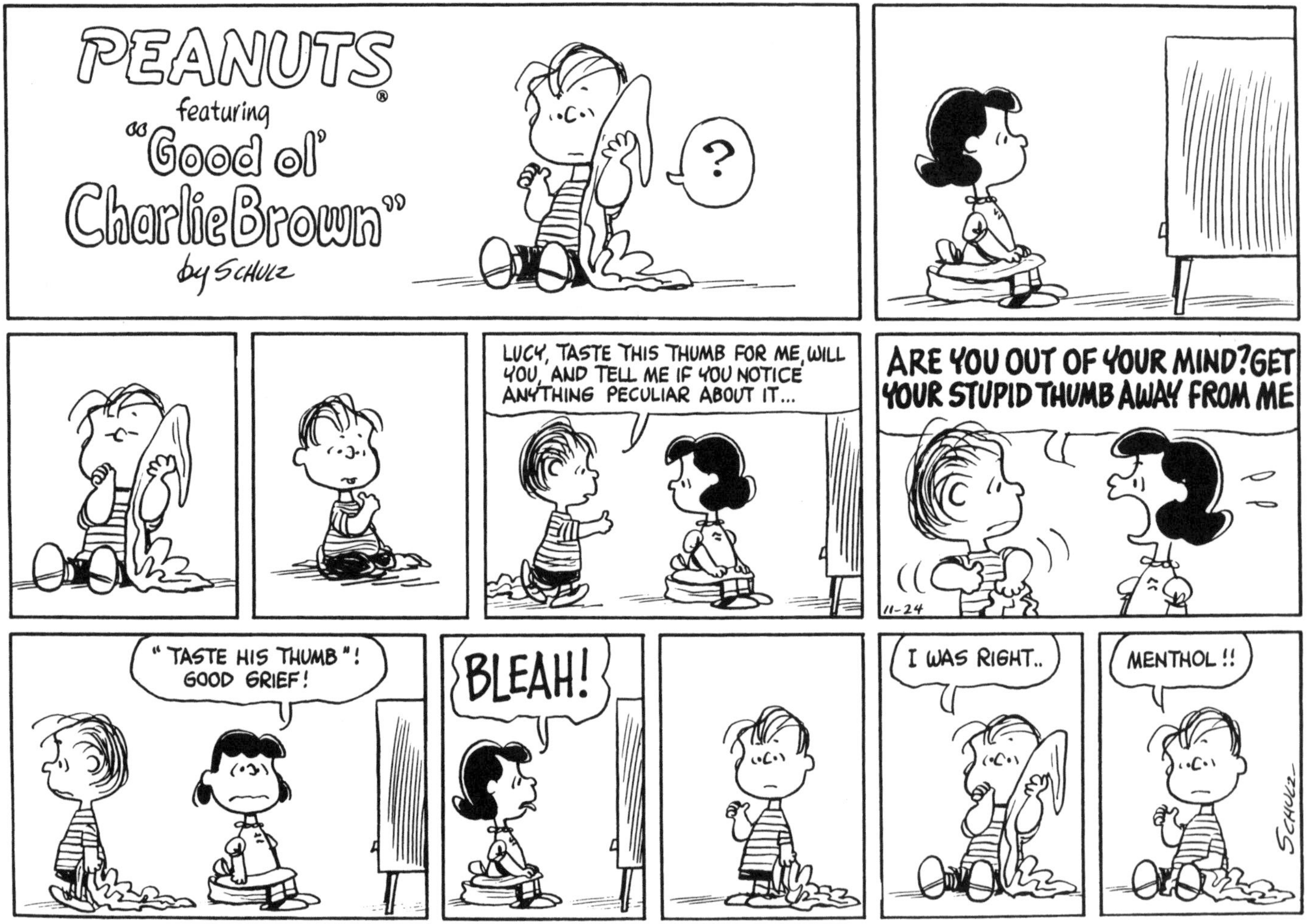
PEANUTS®
featuring "Good ol' Charlie Brown"
by SCHULZ
?
LUCY, TASTE THIS THUMB FOR ME, WILL YOU, AND TELL ME IF YOU NOTICE ANYTHING PECULIAR ABOUT IT...
ARE YOU OUT OF YOUR MIND? GET YOUR STUPID THUMB AWAY FROM ME
11-24
" TASTE HIS THUMB "! GOOD GRIEF!
BLEAH!
I WAS RIGHT..
MENTHOL !!
SCHULZ

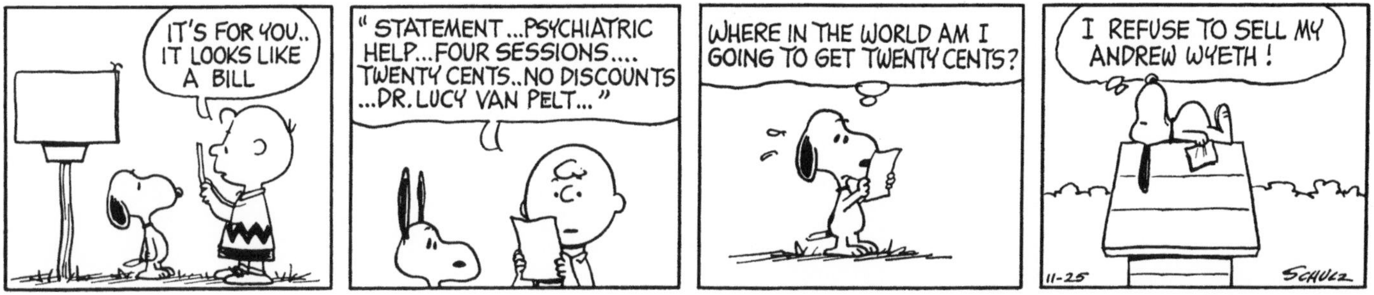
IT'S FOR YOU.. IT LOOKS LIKE A BILL
" STATEMENT...PSYCHIATRIC HELP...FOUR SESSIONS.... TWENTY CENTS..NO DISCOUNTS ...DR. LUCY VAN PELT... "
WHERE IN THE WORLD AM I GOING TO GET TWENTY CENTS?
I REFUSE TO SELL MY ANDREW WYETH!
11-25
SCHULZ

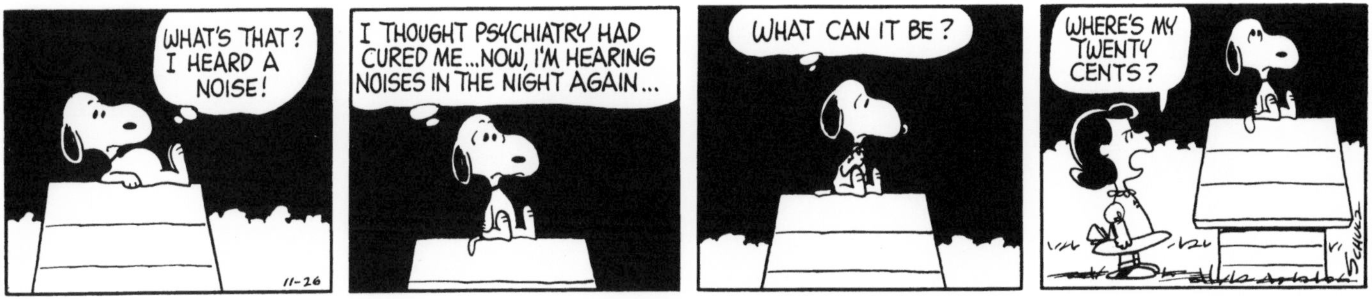
WHAT'S THAT? I HEARD A NOISE!
11-26
I THOUGHT PSYCHIATRY HAD CURED ME...NOW, I'M HEARING NOISES IN THE NIGHT AGAIN...
WHAT CAN IT BE?
WHERE'S MY TWENTY CENTS?
SCHULZ

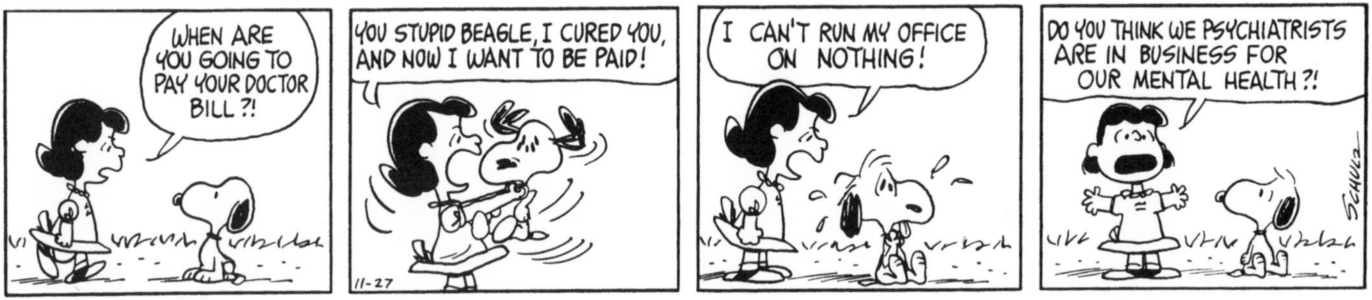
WHEN ARE YOU GOING TO PAY YOUR DOCTOR BILL?!
YOU STUPID BEAGLE, I CURED YOU, AND NOW I WANT TO BE PAID!
11-27
I CAN'T RUN MY OFFICE ON NOTHING!
DO YOU THINK WE PSYCHIATRISTS ARE IN BUSINESS FOR OUR MENTAL HEALTH?!
SCHULZ

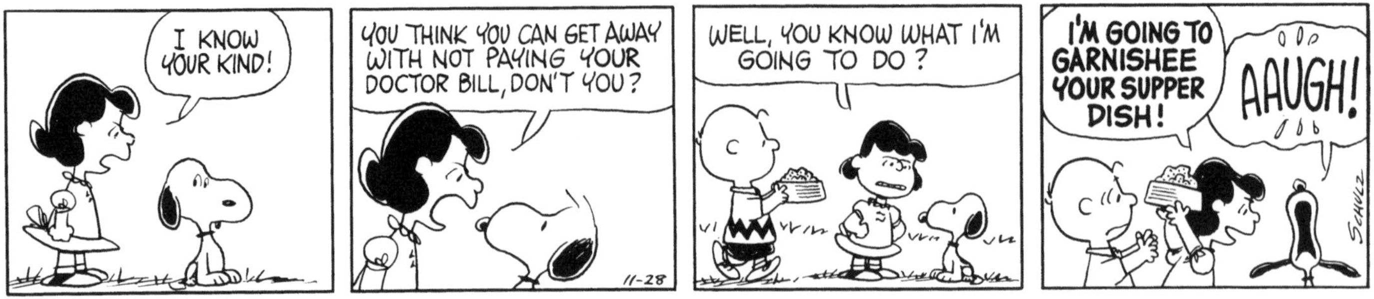
I KNOW YOUR KIND!
YOU THINK YOU CAN GET AWAY WITH NOT PAYING YOUR DOCTOR BILL, DON'T YOU?
11-28
WELL, YOU KNOW WHAT I'M GOING TO DO?
I'M GOING TO GARNISHEE YOUR SUPPER DISH!
AAUGH!
SCHULZ

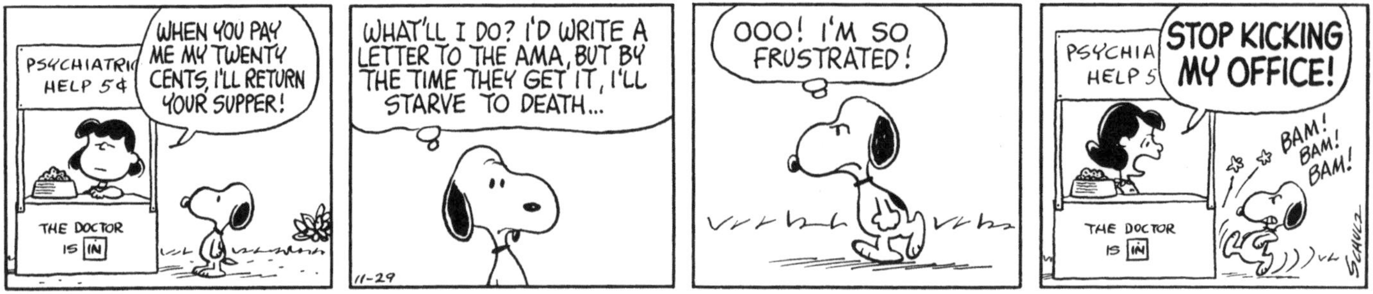
PSYCHIATRIC HELP 5¢
THE DOCTOR IS IN
WHEN YOU PAY ME MY TWENTY CENTS, I'LL RETURN YOUR SUPPER!
WHAT'LL I DO? I'D WRITE A LETTER TO THE AMA, BUT BY THE TIME THEY GET IT, I'LL STARVE TO DEATH...
11-29
OOO! I'M SO FRUSTRATED!
PSYCHIA HELP 5
THE DOCTOR IS IN
STOP KICKING MY OFFICE!
BAM! BAM! BAM!
SCHULZ

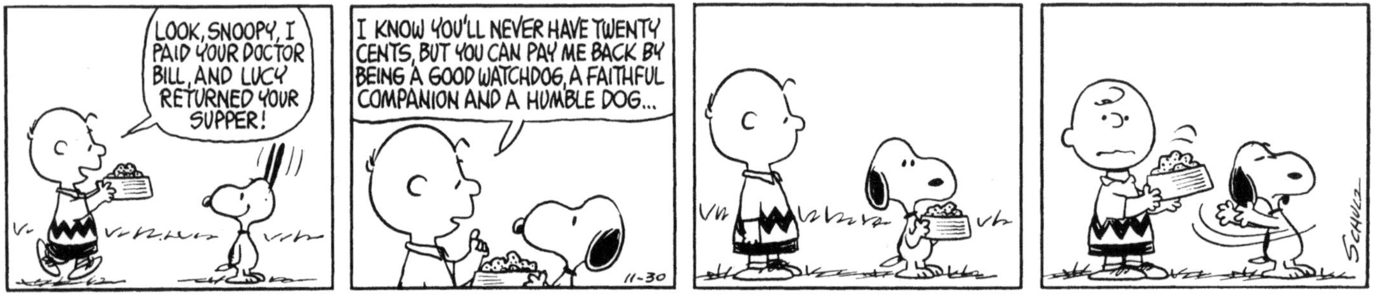
LOOK, SNOOPY, I PAID YOUR DOCTOR BILL, AND LUCY RETURNED YOUR SUPPER!
I KNOW YOU'LL NEVER HAVE TWENTY CENTS, BUT YOU CAN PAY ME BACK BY BEING A GOOD WATCHDOG, A FAITHFUL COMPANION AND A HUMBLE DOG...
11-30
SCHULZ

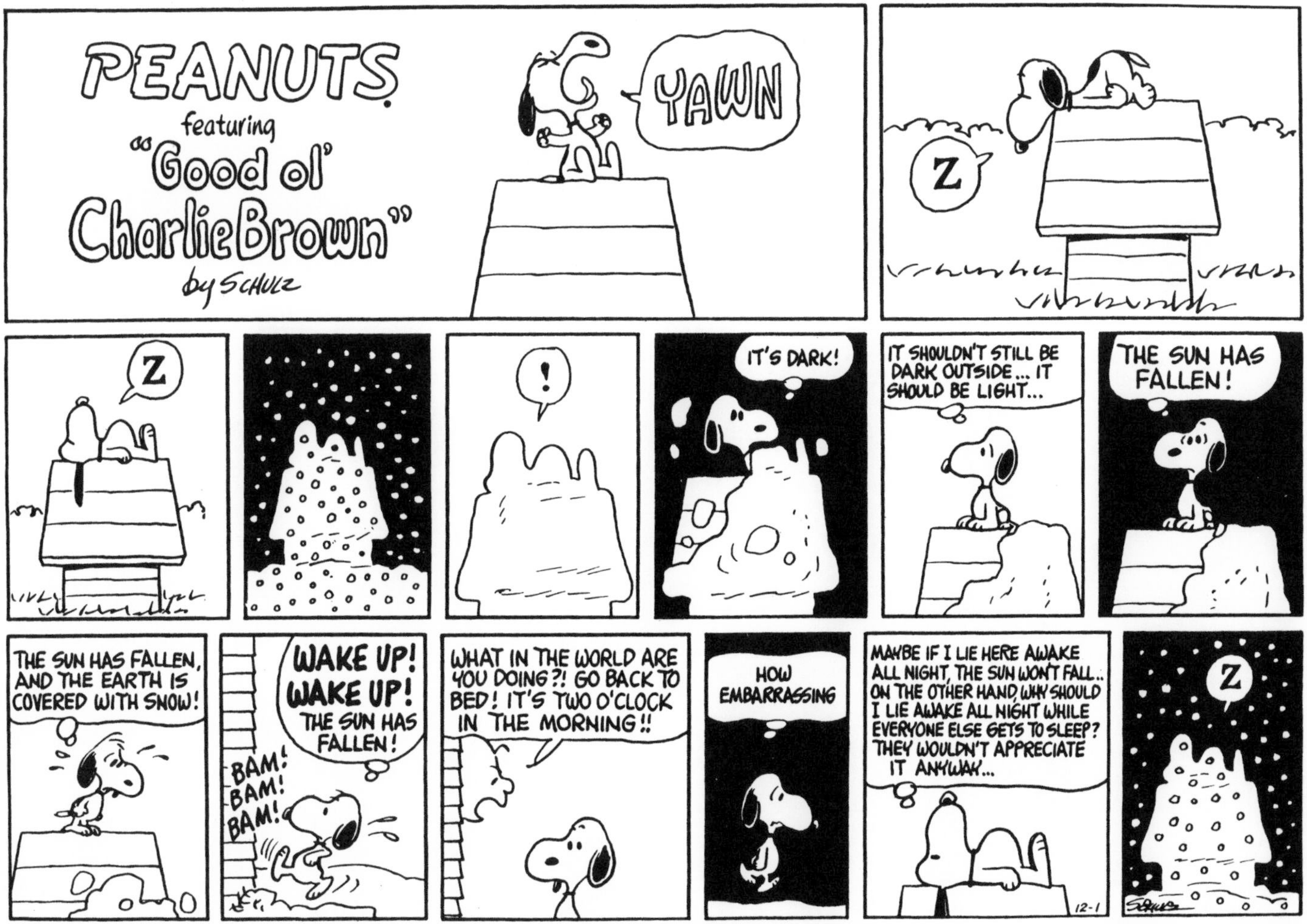
PEANUTS
featuring
"Good ol' Charlie Brown"
by SCHULZ
YAWN
Z
Z
!
IT'S DARK!
IT SHOULDN'T STILL BE DARK OUTSIDE... IT SHOULD BE LIGHT...
THE SUN HAS FALLEN!
THE SUN HAS FALLEN, AND THE EARTH IS COVERED WITH SNOW!
WAKE UP! WAKE UP! THE SUN HAS FALLEN!
BAM! BAM! BAM!
WHAT IN THE WORLD ARE YOU DOING?! GO BACK TO BED! IT'S TWO O'CLOCK IN THE MORNING!!
HOW EMBARRASSING
MAYBE IF I LIE HERE AWAKE ALL NIGHT, THE SUN WON'T FALL... ON THE OTHER HAND, WHY SHOULD I LIE AWAKE ALL NIGHT WHILE EVERYONE ELSE GETS TO SLEEP? THEY WOULDN'T APPRECIATE IT ANYWAY...
12-1
Z
SCHULZ

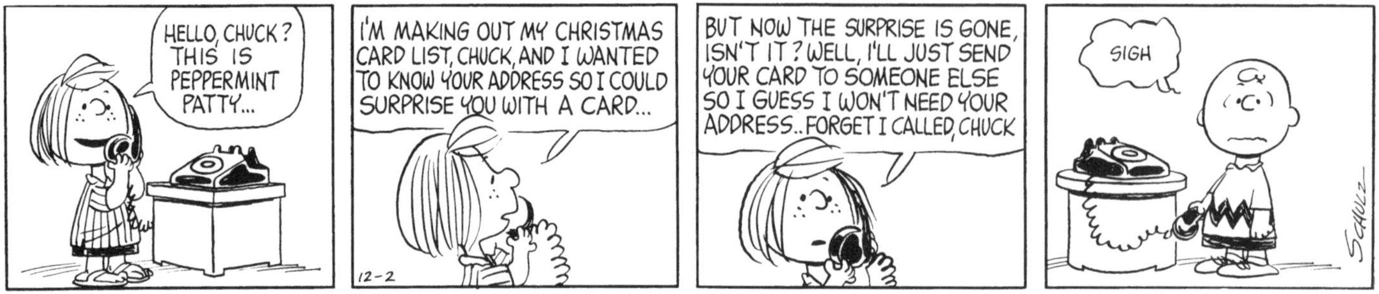
HELLO, CHUCK? THIS IS PEPPERMINT PATTY...
I'M MAKING OUT MY CHRISTMAS CARD LIST, CHUCK, AND I WANTED TO KNOW YOUR ADDRESS SO I COULD SURPRISE YOU WITH A CARD...
12-2
BUT NOW THE SURPRISE IS GONE, ISN'T IT? WELL, I'LL JUST SEND YOUR CARD TO SOMEONE ELSE SO I GUESS I WON'T NEED YOUR ADDRESS.. FORGET I CALLED, CHUCK
SIGH
SCHULZ

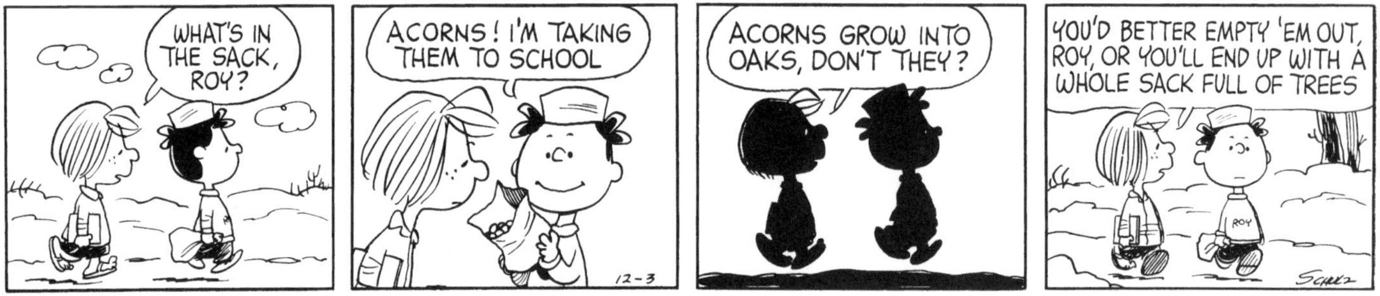
WHAT'S IN THE SACK, ROY?
ACORNS! I'M TAKING THEM TO SCHOOL
12-3
ACORNS GROW INTO OAKS, DON'T THEY?
YOU'D BETTER EMPTY 'EM OUT, ROY, OR YOU'LL END UP WITH A WHOLE SACK FULL OF TREES
ROY
SCHULZ

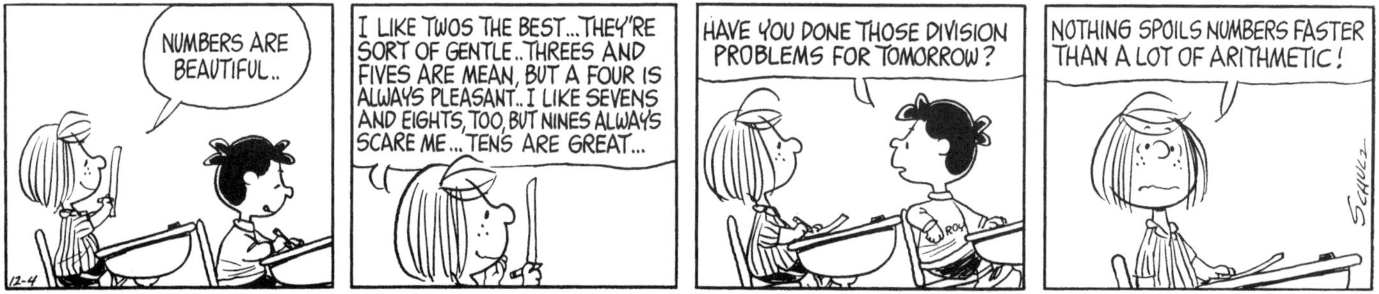
NUMBERS ARE BEAUTIFUL..
12-4
I LIKE TWOS THE BEST...THEY'RE SORT OF GENTLE..THREES AND FIVES ARE MEAN, BUT A FOUR IS ALWAYS PLEASANT..I LIKE SEVENS AND EIGHTS, TOO, BUT NINES ALWAYS SCARE ME...TENS ARE GREAT...
HAVE YOU DONE THOSE DIVISION PROBLEMS FOR TOMORROW?
ROY
NOTHING SPOILS NUMBERS FASTER THAN A LOT OF ARITHMETIC!
SCHULZ

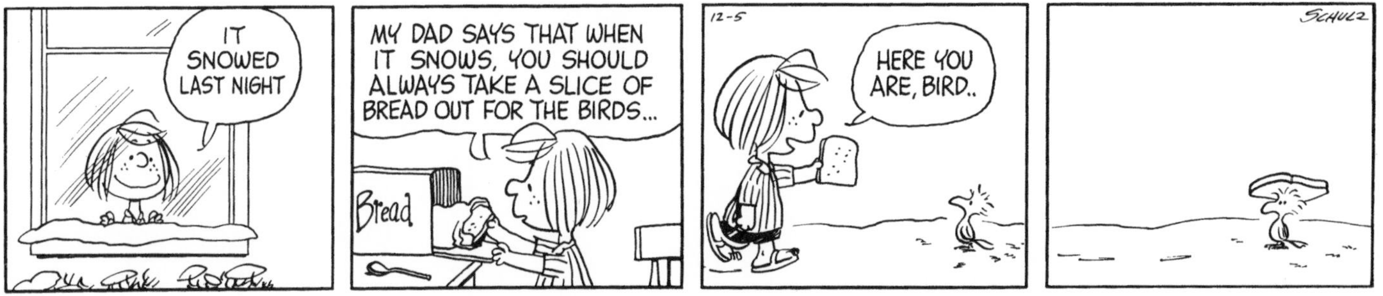
IT SNOWED LAST NIGHT
MY DAD SAYS THAT WHEN IT SNOWS, YOU SHOULD ALWAYS TAKE A SLICE OF BREAD OUT FOR THE BIRDS...
Bread
12-5
HERE YOU ARE, BIRD..
SCHULZ

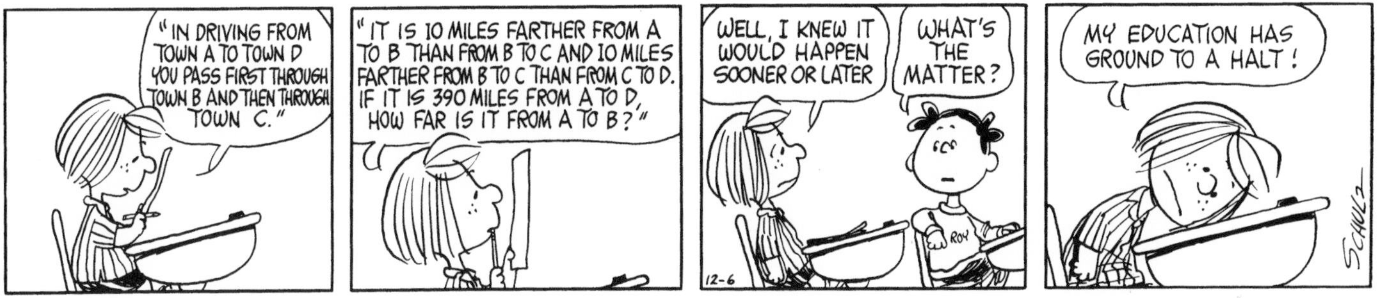
"IN DRIVING FROM TOWN A TO TOWN D YOU PASS FIRST THROUGH TOWN B AND THEN THROUGH TOWN C."
"IT IS 10 MILES FARTHER FROM A TO B THAN FROM B TO C AND 10 MILES FARTHER FROM B TO C THAN FROM C TO D. IF IT IS 390 MILES FROM A TO D, HOW FAR IS IT FROM A TO B?"
WELL, I KNEW IT WOULD HAPPEN SOONER OR LATER
WHAT'S THE MATTER?
ROY
12-6
MY EDUCATION HAS GROUND TO A HALT!
SCHULZ

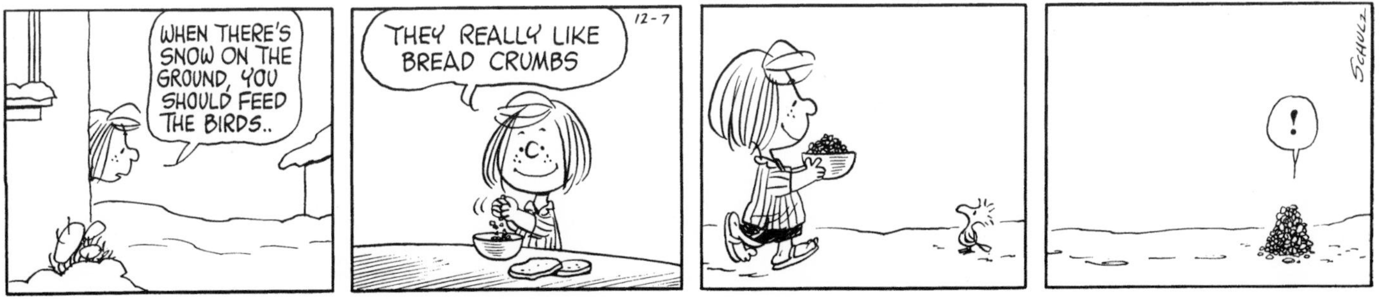
WHEN THERE'S SNOW ON THE GROUND, YOU SHOULD FEED THE BIRDS..
12-7
THEY REALLY LIKE BREAD CRUMBS
SCHULZ
!

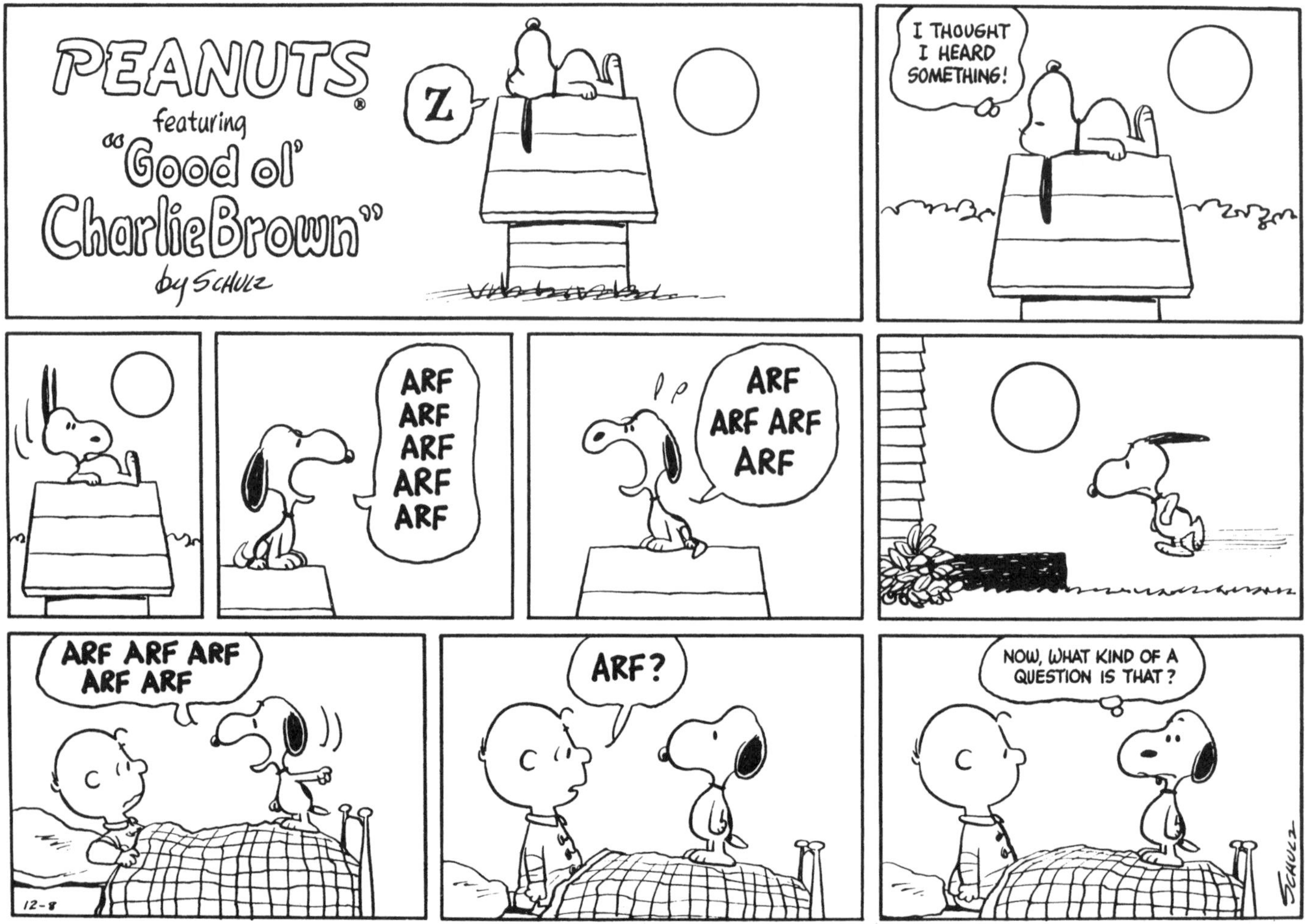
PEANUTS®
featuring
"Good ol' Charlie Brown"
by SCHULZ
Z
I THOUGHT I HEARD SOMETHING!
ARF ARF ARF ARF ARF
ARF ARF ARF ARF
ARF ARF ARF ARF ARF
ARF?
NOW, WHAT KIND OF A QUESTION IS THAT?
12-8
SCHULZ

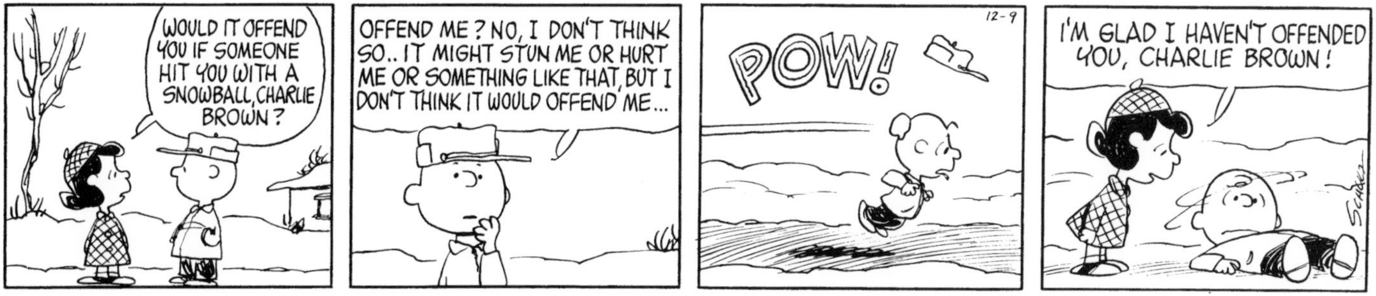
WOULD IT OFFEND YOU IF SOMEONE HIT YOU WITH A SNOWBALL, CHARLIE BROWN?
OFFEND ME? NO, I DON'T THINK SO.. IT MIGHT STUN ME OR HURT ME OR SOMETHING LIKE THAT, BUT I DON'T THINK IT WOULD OFFEND ME...
POW!
I'M GLAD I HAVEN'T OFFENDED YOU, CHARLIE BROWN!

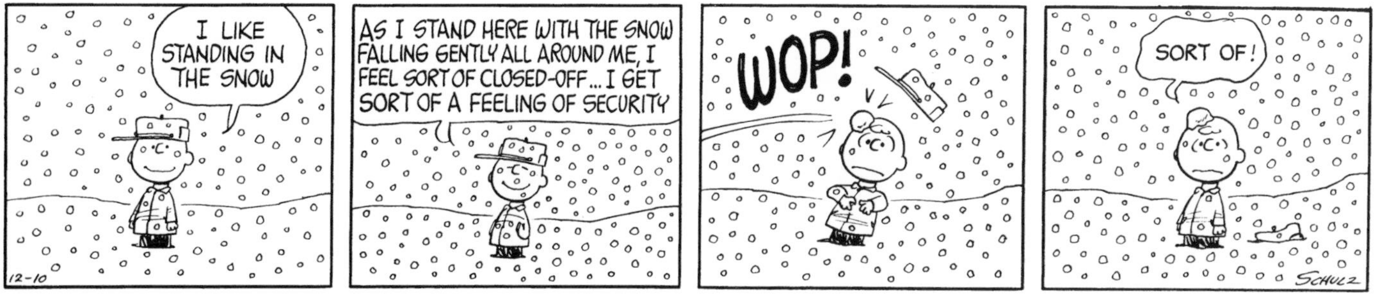
I LIKE STANDING IN THE SNOW
AS I STAND HERE WITH THE SNOW FALLING GENTLY ALL AROUND ME, I FEEL SORT OF CLOSED-OFF... I GET SORT OF A FEELING OF SECURITY
WOP!
SORT OF!

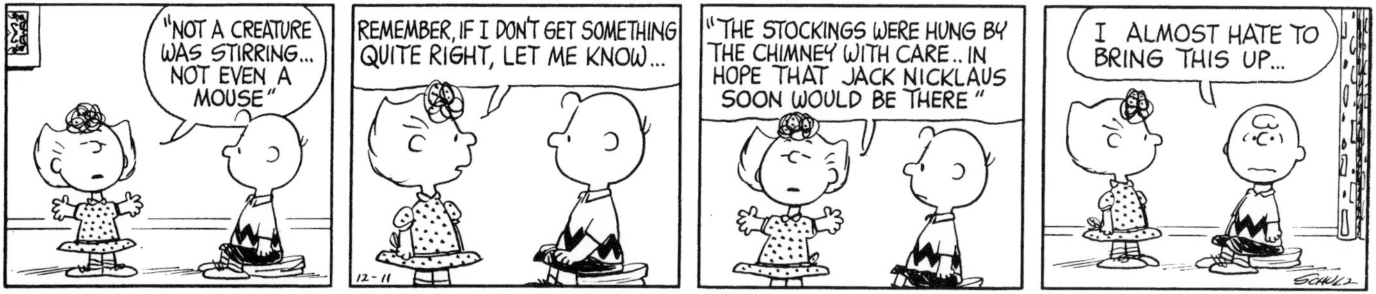
"NOT A CREATURE WAS STIRRING... NOT EVEN A MOUSE"
REMEMBER, IF I DON'T GET SOMETHING QUITE RIGHT, LET ME KNOW...
"THE STOCKINGS WERE HUNG BY THE CHIMNEY WITH CARE.. IN HOPE THAT JACK NICKLAUS SOON WOULD BE THERE"
I ALMOST HATE TO BRING THIS UP...

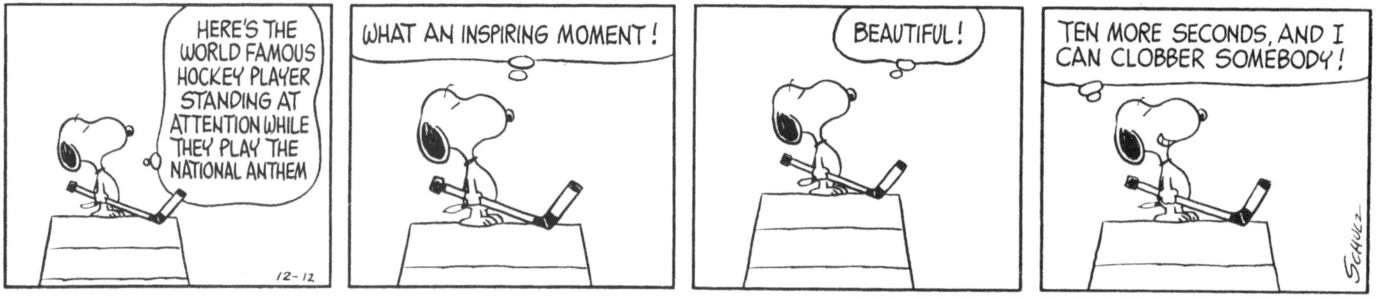
HERE'S THE WORLD FAMOUS HOCKEY PLAYER STANDING AT ATTENTION WHILE THEY PLAY THE NATIONAL ANTHEM
12-12
WHAT AN INSPIRING MOMENT!
BEAUTIFUL!
TEN MORE SECONDS, AND I CAN CLOBBER SOMEBODY!
SCHULZ

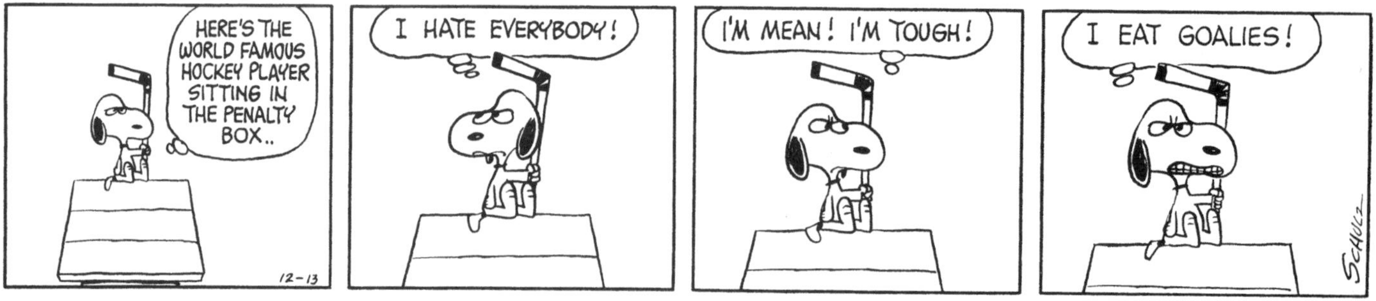
HERE'S THE WORLD FAMOUS HOCKEY PLAYER SITTING IN THE PENALTY BOX..
12-13
I HATE EVERYBODY!
I'M MEAN! I'M TOUGH!
I EAT GOALIES!
SCHULZ

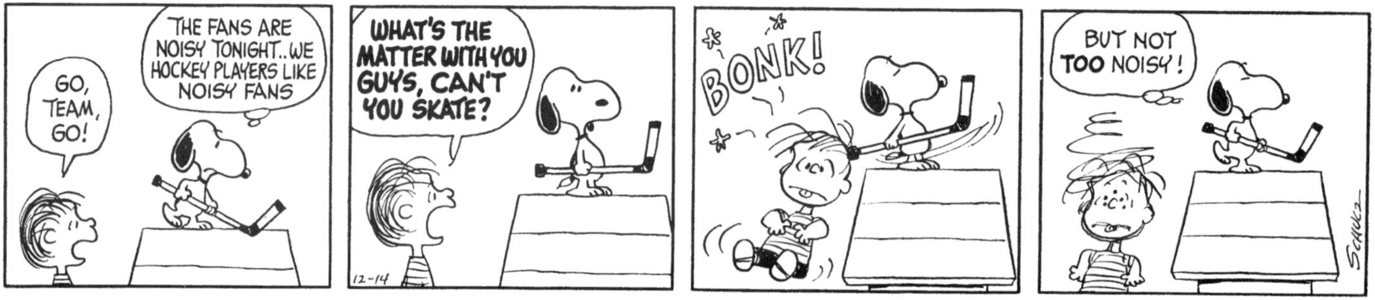
GO, TEAM, GO!
THE FANS ARE NOISY TONIGHT..WE HOCKEY PLAYERS LIKE NOISY FANS
WHAT'S THE MATTER WITH YOU GUYS, CAN'T YOU SKATE?
12-14
BONK!
BUT NOT TOO NOISY!
SCHULZ

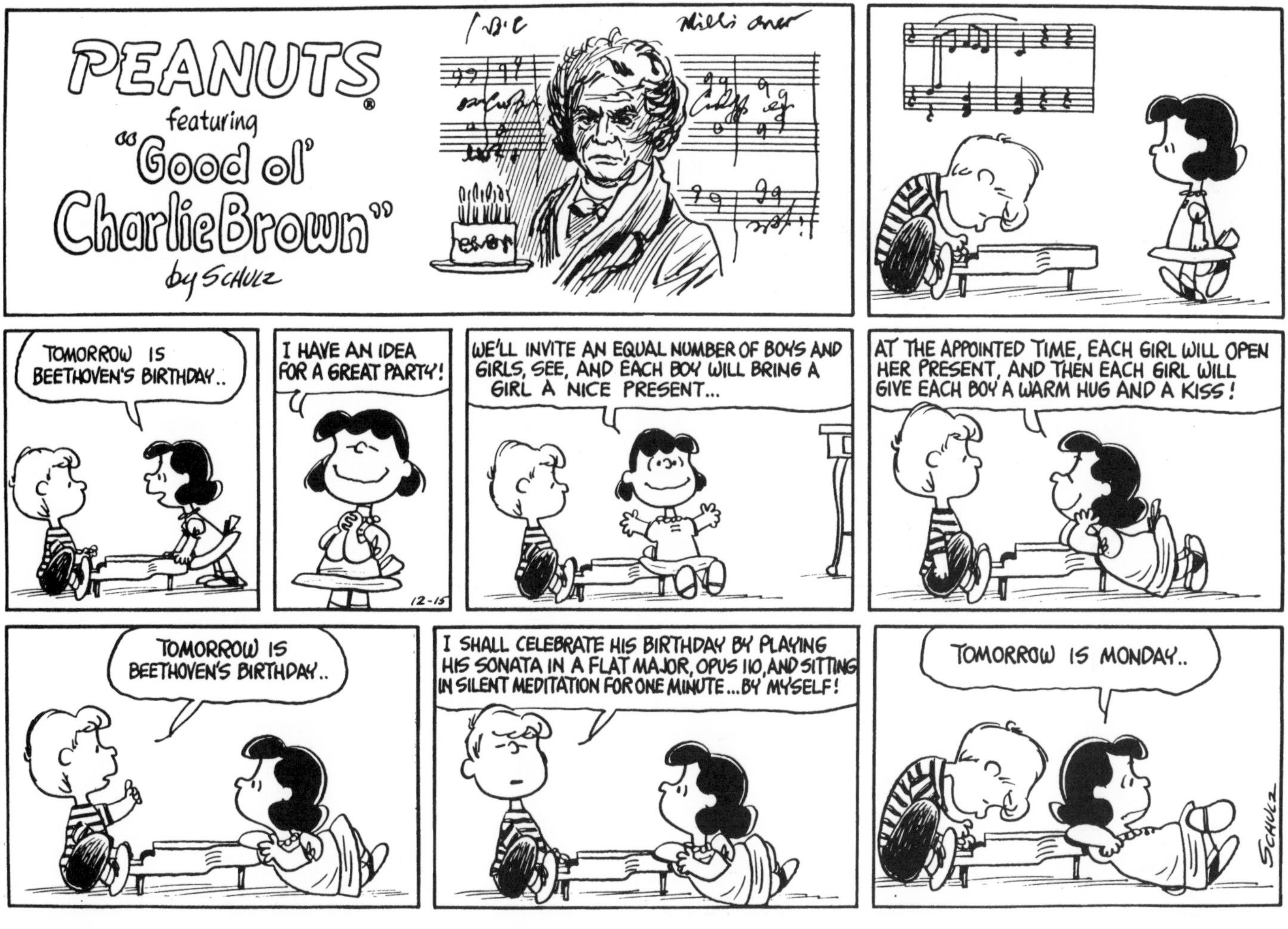

PEANUTS®
featuring "Good ol' Charlie Brown"
by SCHULZ
TOMORROW IS BEETHOVEN'S BIRTHDAY..
I HAVE AN IDEA FOR A GREAT PARTY!
WE'LL INVITE AN EQUAL NUMBER OF BOYS AND GIRLS, SEE, AND EACH BOY WILL BRING A GIRL A NICE PRESENT...
12-15
AT THE APPOINTED TIME, EACH GIRL WILL OPEN HER PRESENT, AND THEN EACH GIRL WILL GIVE EACH BOY A WARM HUG AND A KISS!
TOMORROW IS BEETHOVEN'S BIRTHDAY..
I SHALL CELEBRATE HIS BIRTHDAY BY PLAYING HIS SONATA IN A FLAT MAJOR, OPUS 110, AND SITTING IN SILENT MEDITATION FOR ONE MINUTE... BY MYSELF!
TOMORROW IS MONDAY..
SCHULZ

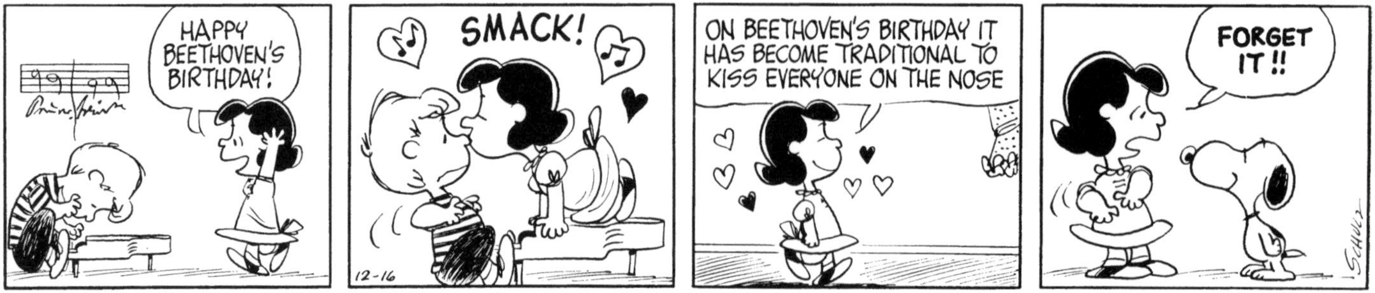
HAPPY BEETHOVEN'S BIRTHDAY!
SMACK!
12-16
ON BEETHOVEN'S BIRTHDAY IT HAS BECOME TRADITIONAL TO KISS EVERYONE ON THE NOSE
FORGET IT!!
SCHULZ

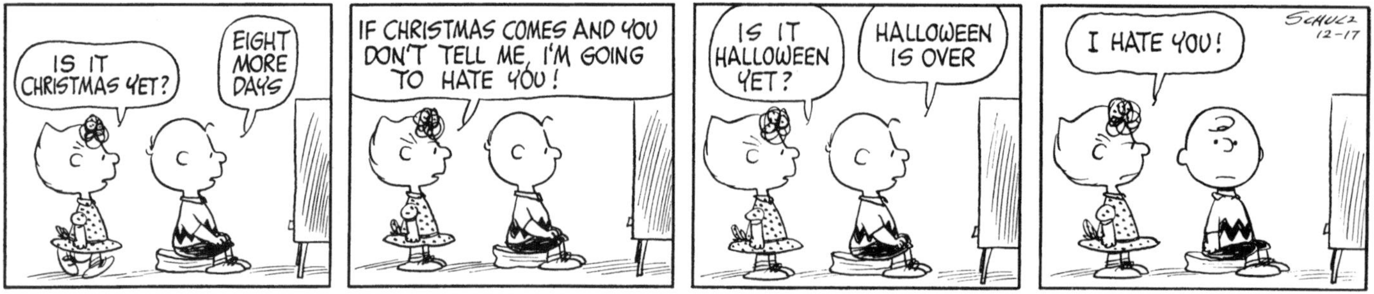
IS IT CHRISTMAS YET?
EIGHT MORE DAYS
IF CHRISTMAS COMES AND YOU DON'T TELL ME, I'M GOING TO HATE YOU!
IS IT HALLOWEEN YET?
HALLOWEEN IS OVER
SCHULZ 12-17
I HATE YOU!

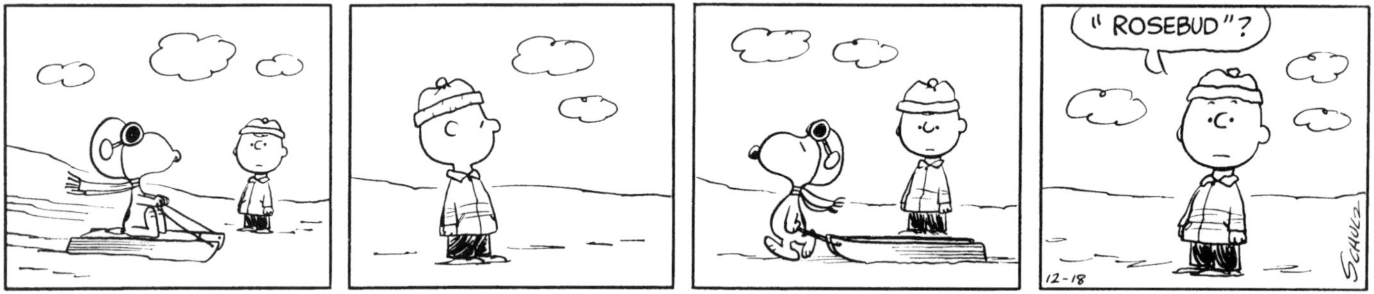
"ROSEBUD"?
12-18
SCHULZ

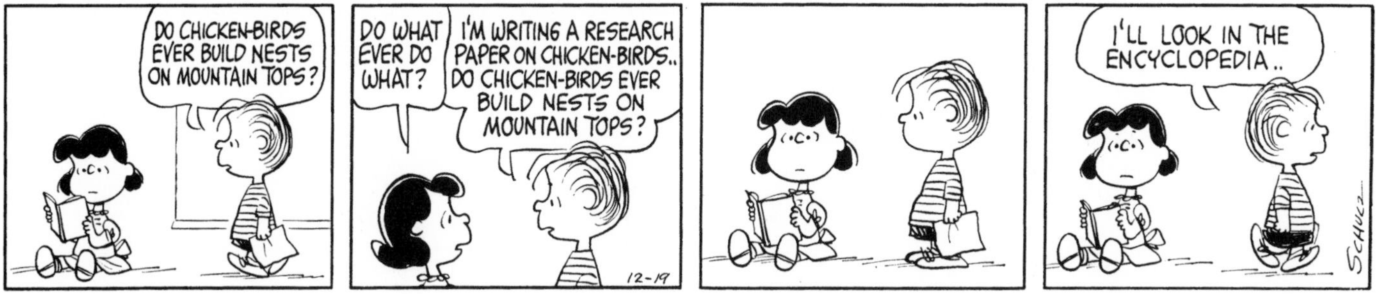
DO CHICKEN-BIRDS EVER BUILD NESTS ON MOUNTAIN TOPS?
DO WHAT EVER DO WHAT?
I'M WRITING A RESEARCH PAPER ON CHICKEN-BIRDS.. DO CHICKEN-BIRDS EVER BUILD NESTS ON MOUNTAIN TOPS?
12-19
I'LL LOOK IN THE ENCYCLOPEDIA..
SCHULZ

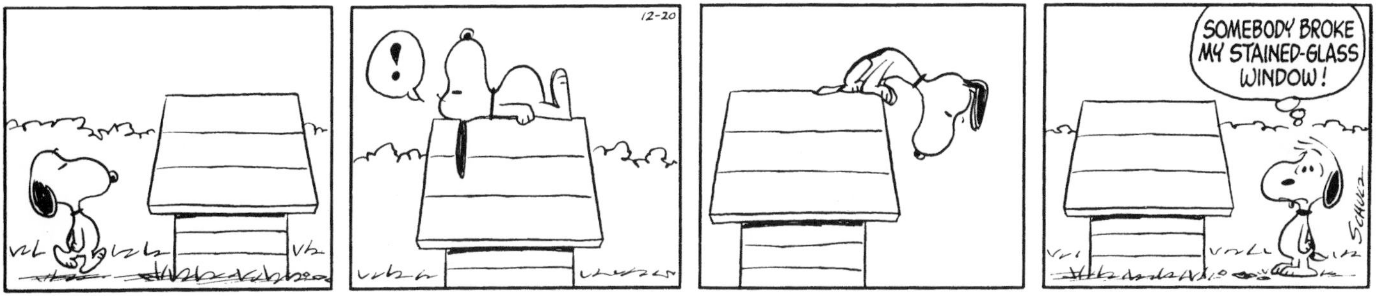
12-20
!
SOMEBODY BROKE MY STAINED-GLASS WINDOW!
SCHULZ

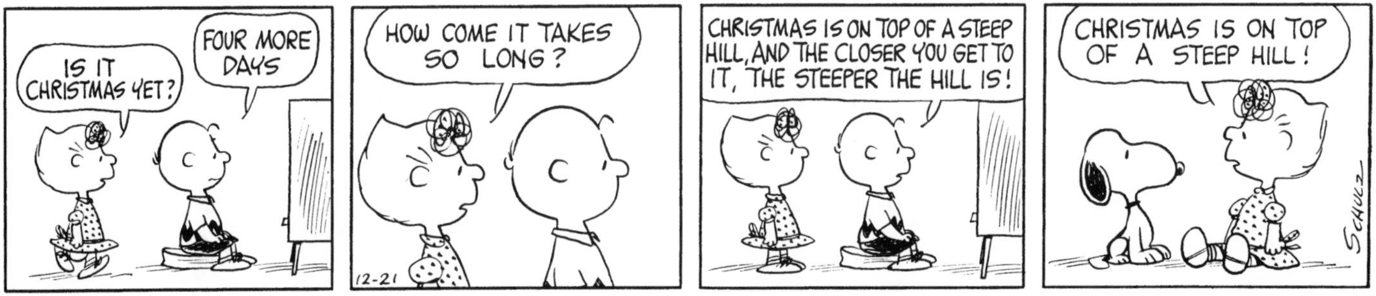
IS IT CHRISTMAS YET?
FOUR MORE DAYS
HOW COME IT TAKES SO LONG?
12-21
CHRISTMAS IS ON TOP OF A STEEP HILL, AND THE CLOSER YOU GET TO IT, THE STEEPER THE HILL IS!
CHRISTMAS IS ON TOP OF A STEEP HILL!
SCHULZ

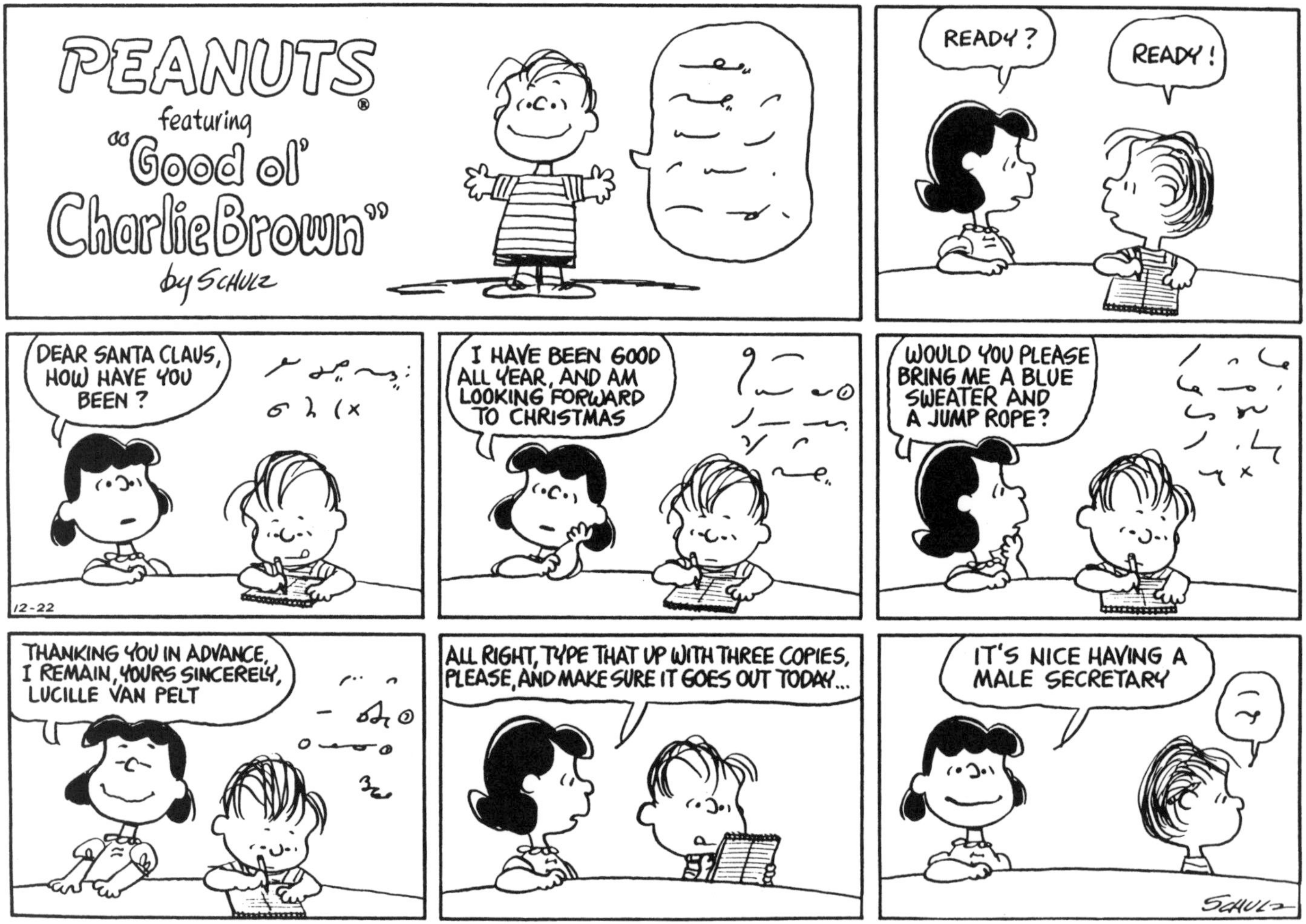
PEANUTS®
featuring "Good ol' Charlie Brown"
by SCHULZ
READY?
READY!
DEAR SANTA CLAUS, HOW HAVE YOU BEEN?
12-22
I HAVE BEEN GOOD ALL YEAR, AND AM LOOKING FORWARD TO CHRISTMAS
WOULD YOU PLEASE BRING ME A BLUE SWEATER AND A JUMP ROPE?
THANKING YOU IN ADVANCE, I REMAIN, YOURS SINCERELY, LUCILLE VAN PELT
ALL RIGHT, TYPE THAT UP WITH THREE COPIES, PLEASE, AND MAKE SURE IT GOES OUT TODAY...
IT'S NICE HAVING A MALE SECRETARY
SCHULZ

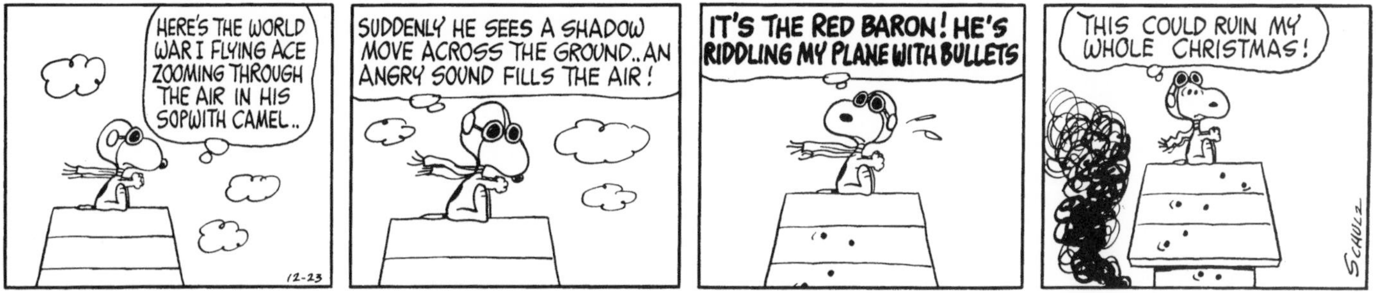
HERE'S THE WORLD WAR I FLYING ACE ZOOMING THROUGH THE AIR IN HIS SOPWITH CAMEL..
12-23
SUDDENLY HE SEES A SHADOW MOVE ACROSS THE GROUND..AN ANGRY SOUND FILLS THE AIR!
IT'S THE RED BARON! HE'S RIDDLING MY PLANE WITH BULLETS
THIS COULD RUIN MY WHOLE CHRISTMAS!
SCHULZ

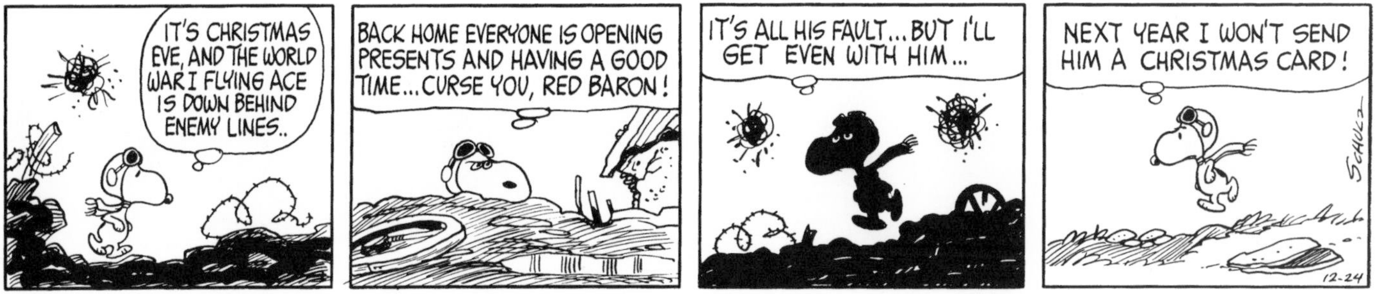
IT'S CHRISTMAS EVE, AND THE WORLD WAR I FLYING ACE IS DOWN BEHIND ENEMY LINES..
BACK HOME EVERYONE IS OPENING PRESENTS AND HAVING A GOOD TIME...CURSE YOU, RED BARON!
IT'S ALL HIS FAULT...BUT I'LL GET EVEN WITH HIM...
NEXT YEAR I WON'T SEND HIM A CHRISTMAS CARD!
SCHULZ
12-24

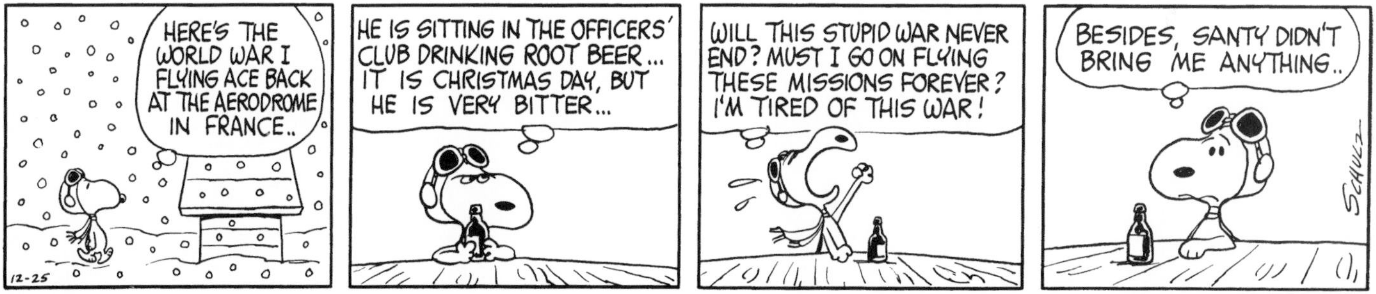
HERE'S THE WORLD WAR I FLYING ACE BACK AT THE AERODROME IN FRANCE..
12-25
HE IS SITTING IN THE OFFICERS' CLUB DRINKING ROOT BEER... IT IS CHRISTMAS DAY, BUT HE IS VERY BITTER...
WILL THIS STUPID WAR NEVER END? MUST I GO ON FLYING THESE MISSIONS FOREVER? I'M TIRED OF THIS WAR!
BESIDES, SANTY DIDN'T BRING ME ANYTHING..
SCHULZ

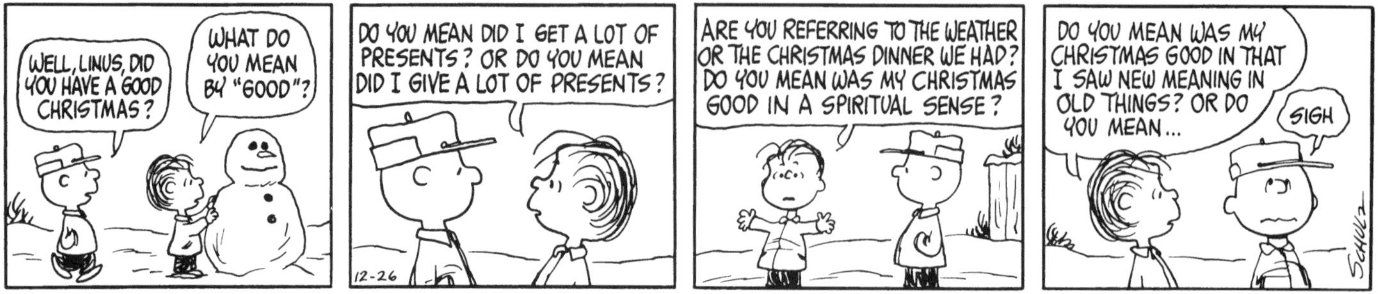
WELL, LINUS, DID YOU HAVE A GOOD CHRISTMAS?
WHAT DO YOU MEAN BY "GOOD"?
DO YOU MEAN DID I GET A LOT OF PRESENTS? OR DO YOU MEAN DID I GIVE A LOT OF PRESENTS?
12-26
ARE YOU REFERRING TO THE WEATHER OR THE CHRISTMAS DINNER WE HAD? DO YOU MEAN WAS MY CHRISTMAS GOOD IN A SPIRITUAL SENSE?
DO YOU MEAN WAS MY CHRISTMAS GOOD IN THAT I SAW NEW MEANING IN OLD THINGS? OR DO YOU MEAN...
SIGH
SCHULZ

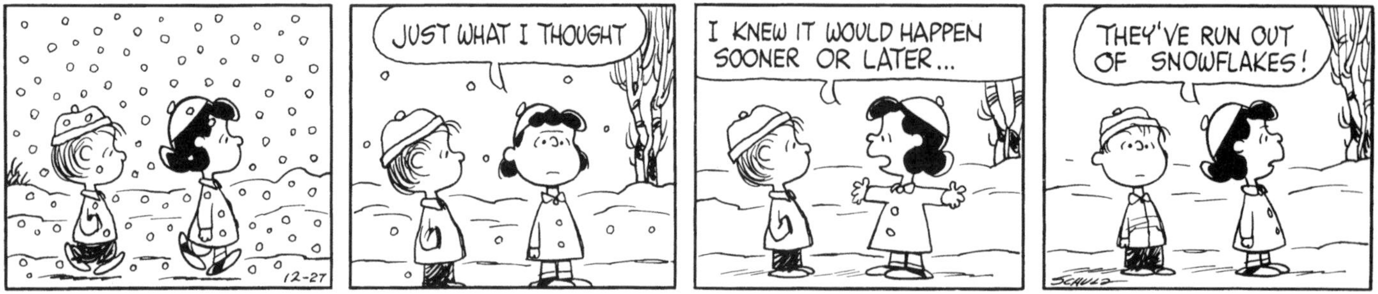
12-27
JUST WHAT I THOUGHT
I KNEW IT WOULD HAPPEN SOONER OR LATER...
THEY'VE RUN OUT OF SNOWFLAKES!
SCHULZ

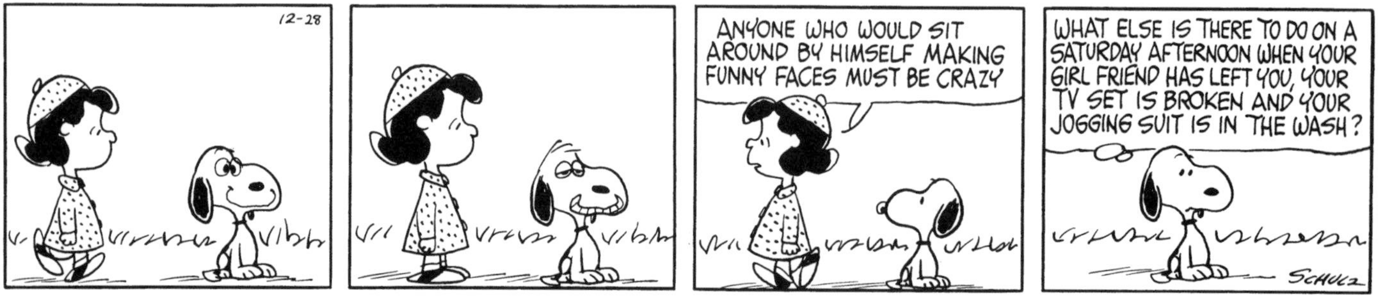
12-28
ANYONE WHO WOULD SIT AROUND BY HIMSELF MAKING FUNNY FACES MUST BE CRAZY
WHAT ELSE IS THERE TO DO ON A SATURDAY AFTERNOON WHEN YOUR GIRL FRIEND HAS LEFT YOU, YOUR TV SET IS BROKEN AND YOUR JOGGING SUIT IS IN THE WASH?
SCHULZ

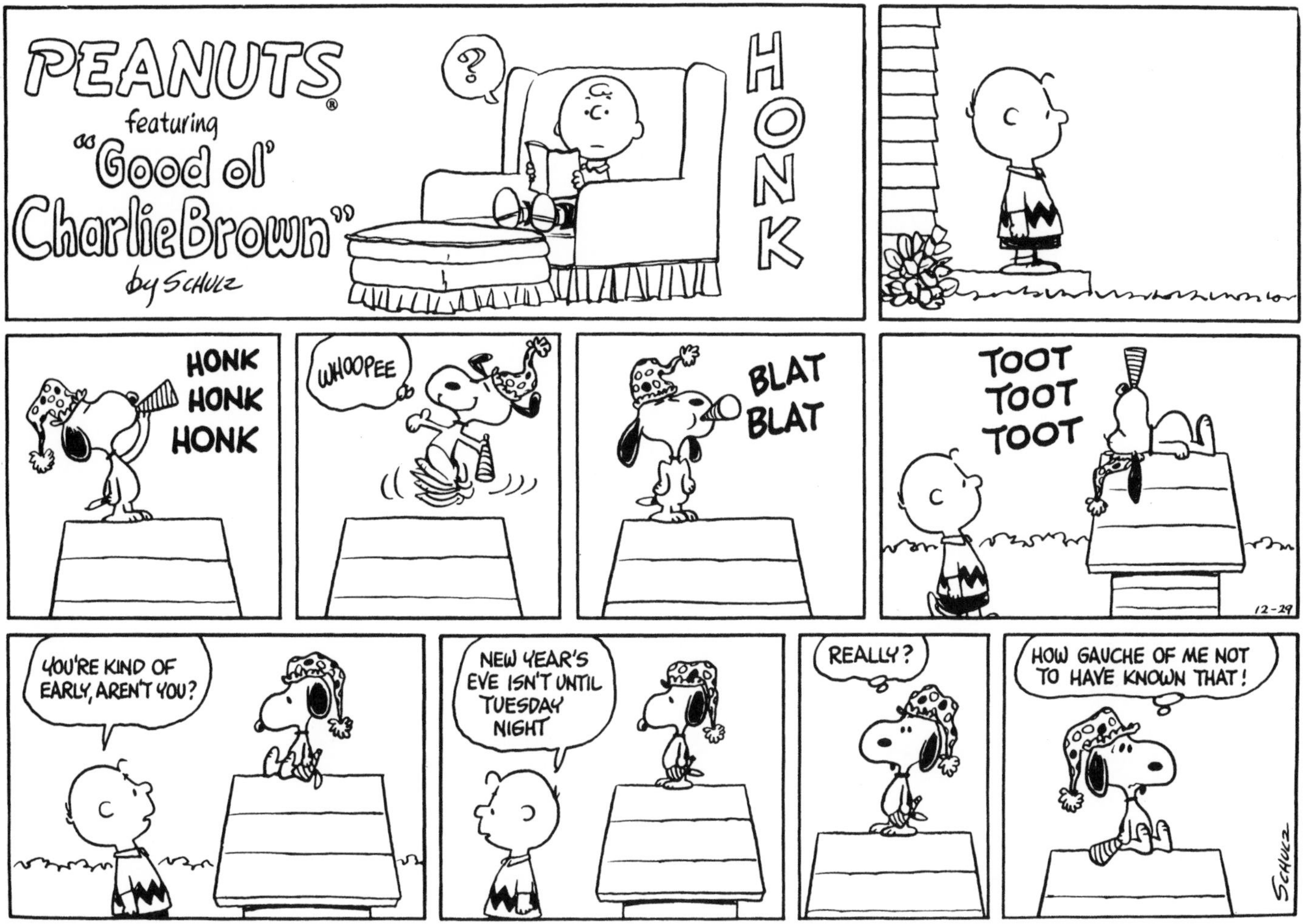
PEANUTS®
featuring "Good ol' CharlieBrown"
by SCHULZ
?
HONK
HONK
HONK
HONK
WHOOPEE
BLAT
BLAT
TOOT
TOOT
TOOT
12-29
YOU'RE KIND OF EARLY, AREN'T YOU?
NEW YEAR'S EVE ISN'T UNTIL TUESDAY NIGHT
REALLY?
HOW GAUCHE OF ME NOT TO HAVE KNOWN THAT!
SCHULZ

12-30

WELL, THIS IS IT..
THE LAST DAY OF THE YEAR, AND I DID IT AGAIN
DID WHAT ?
I BLEW ANOTHER YEAR!
SCHULZ
12-31

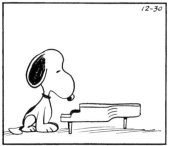

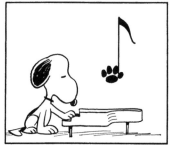

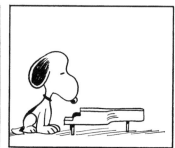

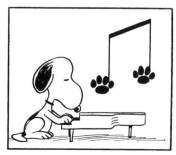

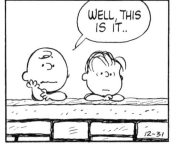

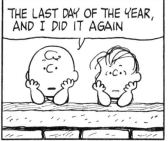

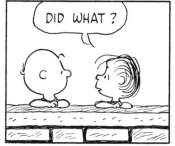

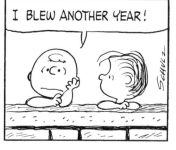

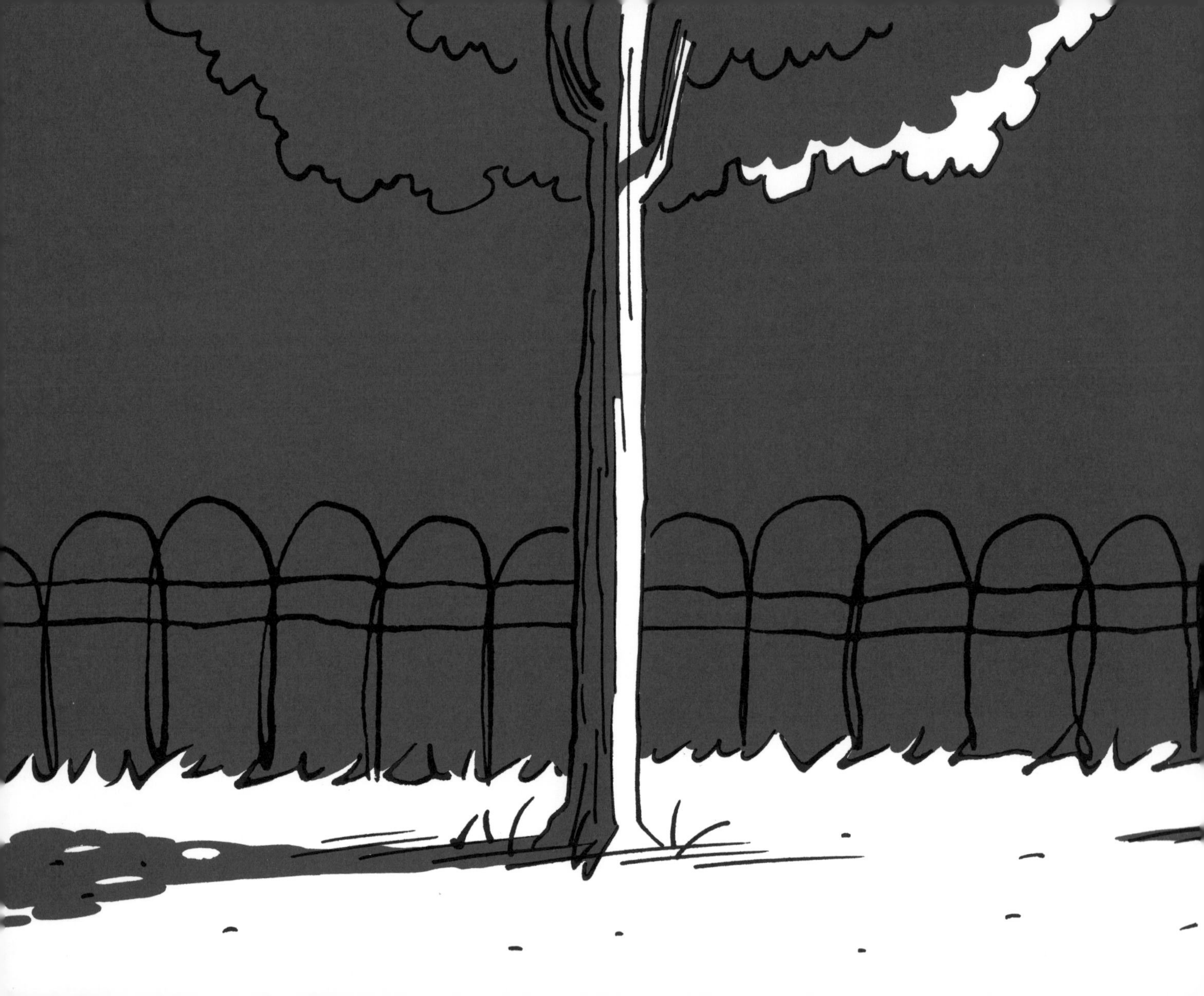

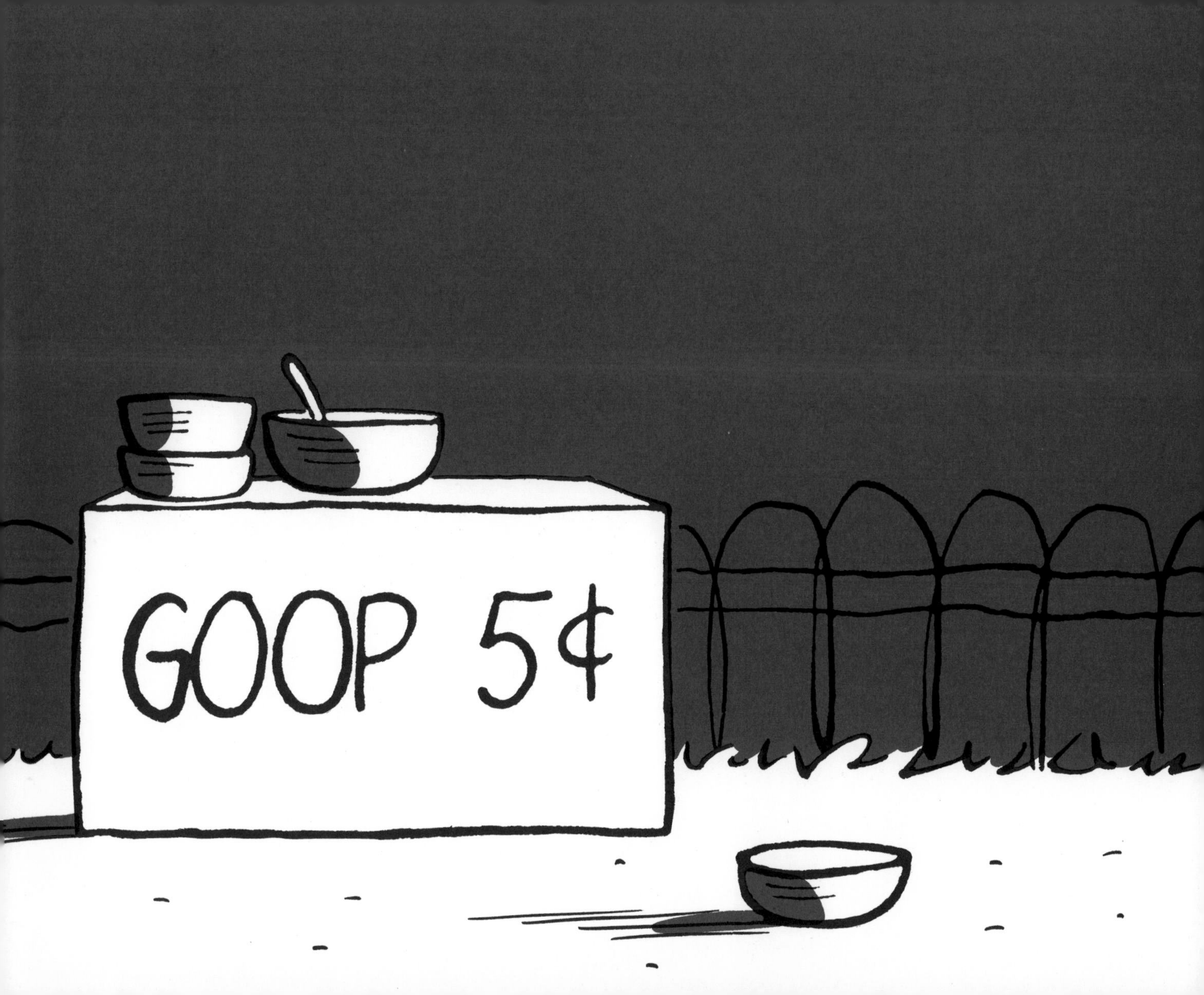
GOOP 5¢

INDEX

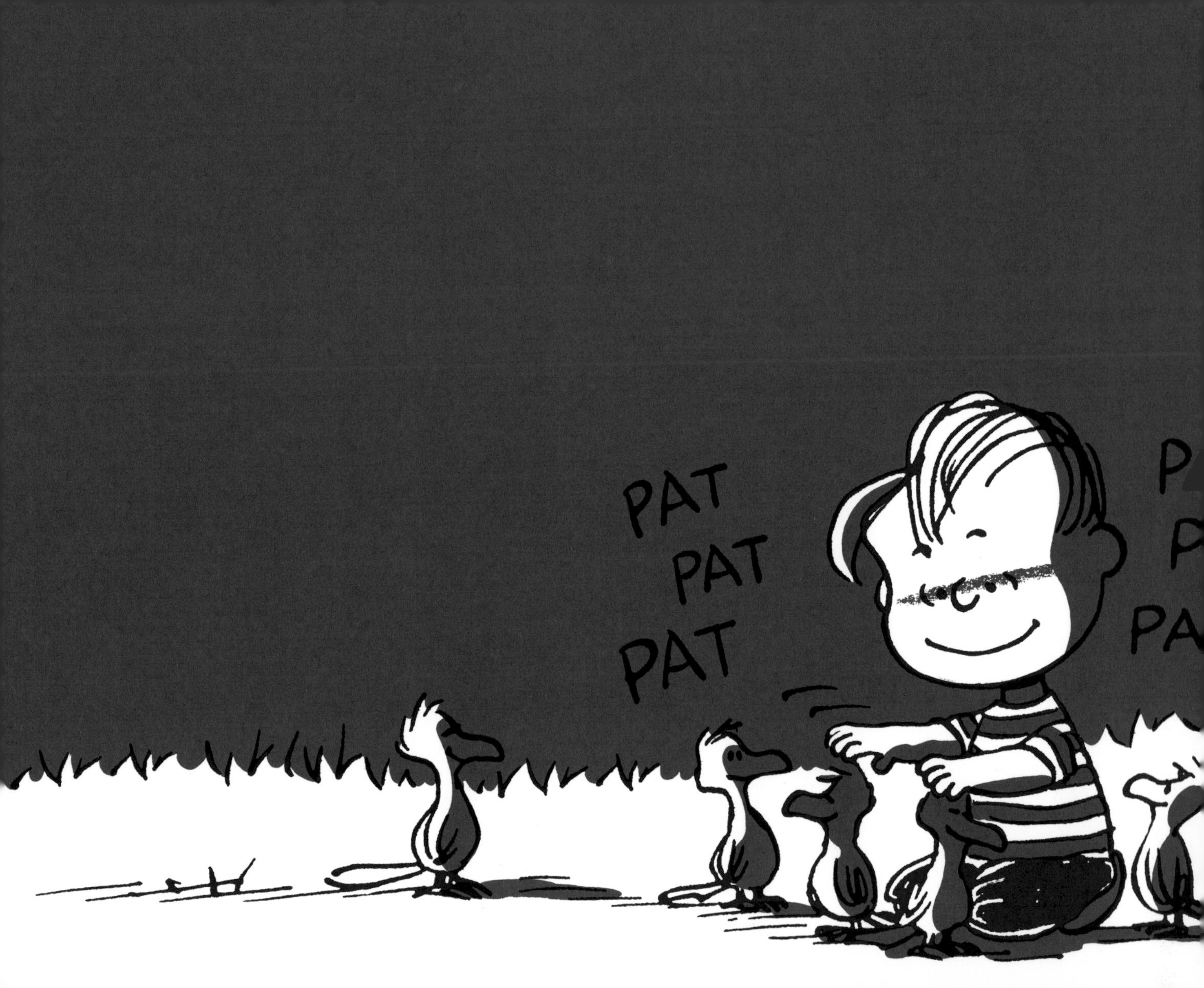
PAT
PAT
PAT

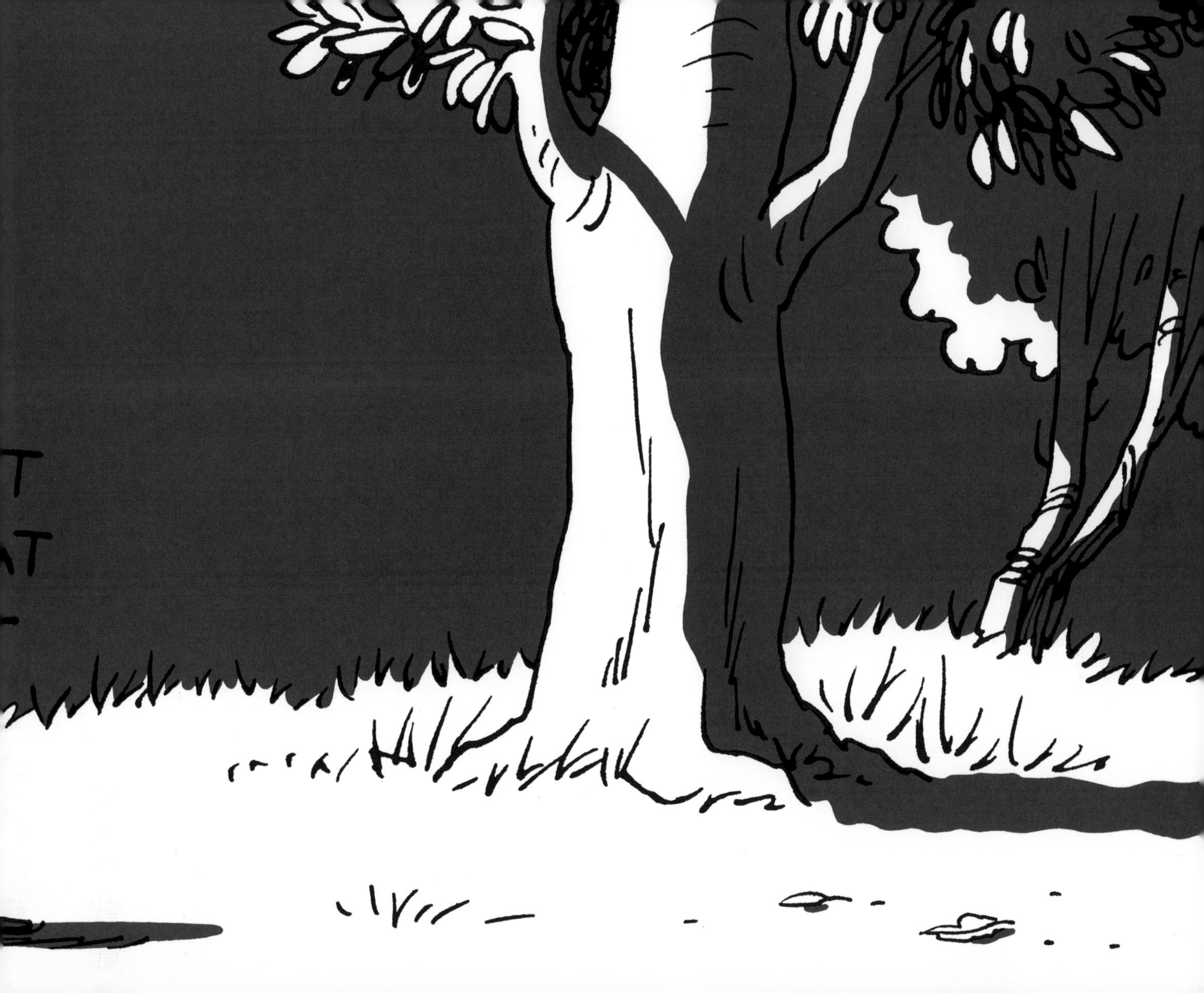

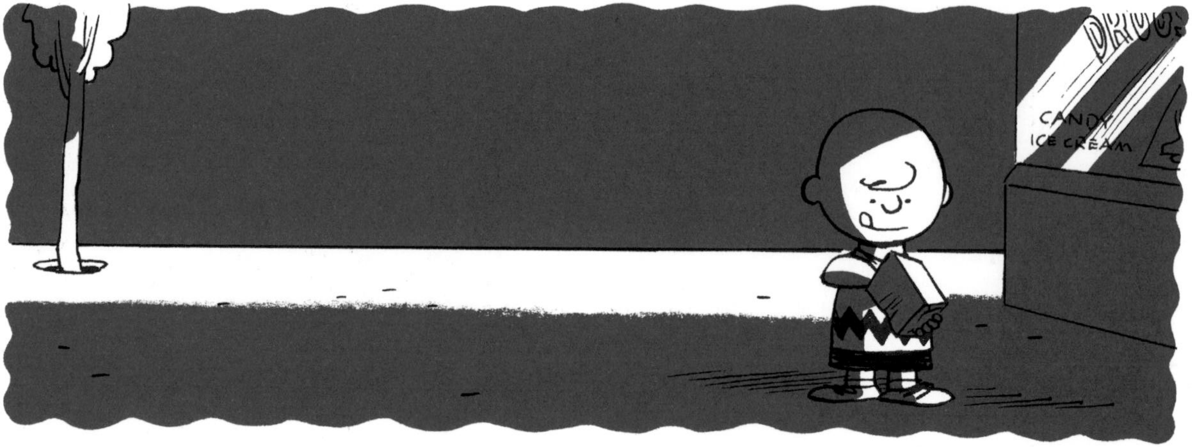
CANDY
ICE CREAM

CHARLES M. SCHULZ · 1922 TO 2000

Charles M. Schulz was born November 25, 1922 in Minneapolis. His destiny was foreshadowed when an uncle gave him, at the age of two days, the nickname Sparky (after the racehorse Spark Plug in the newspaper strip *Barney Google*).

Schulz grew up in St. Paul. By all accounts, he led an unremarkable, albeit sheltered, childhood. He was an only child, close to both parents, his eventual career path nurtured by his father, who bought four Sunday papers every week — just for the comics.

An outstanding student, he skipped two grades early on, but began to flounder in high school — perhaps not so coincidentally at the same time kids are going through their cruelest, most status-conscious period of socialization. The pain, bitterness, insecurity, and failures chronicled in *Peanuts* appear to have originated from this period of Schulz's life.

Although Schulz enjoyed sports, he also found refuge in solitary activities: reading, drawing, and watching movies. He bought comic books and Big Little Books, pored over the newspaper strips, and copied his favorites — *Buck Rogers*, the Walt Disney characters, *Popeye, Tim Tyler's Luck*. He quickly became a connoisseur; his heroes were Milton Caniff, Roy Crane, Hal Foster, and Alex Raymond.

In his senior year in high school, his mother noticed an ad in a local newspaper for a correspondence school, Federal Schools (later called Art

Instruction Schools). Schulz passed the talent test, completed the course and began trying, unsuccessfully, to sell gag cartoons to magazines. (His first published drawing was of his dog, Spike, and appeared in a 1937 *Ripley's Believe It Or Not!* installment.)

After World War II had ended and Schulz was discharged from the army, he started submitting gag cartoons to the various magazines of the time; his first breakthrough, however, came when an editor at *Timeless Topix* hired him to letter adventure comics. Soon after that, he was hired by his alma mater, Art Instruction, to correct student lessons returned by mail.

Between 1948 and 1950, he succeeded in selling 17 cartoons to the *Saturday Evening Post* — as well as, to the local *St. Paul Pioneer Press*, a weekly comic feature called *Li'l Folks*. It was run in the women's section and paid $10 a week. After writing and drawing the feature for two years, Schulz asked for a better location in the paper or for daily exposure, as well as a raise. When he was turned down on all three counts, he quit.

He started submitting strips to the newspaper syndicates. In the Spring of 1950, he received a letter from the United Feature Syndicate, announcing their interest in his submission, *Li'l Folks*. Schulz boarded a train in June for New York City; more interested in doing a strip than a panel, he also brought along the first installments of what would become *Peanuts* — and that was what sold. (The title, which Schulz loathed to his dying day, was imposed by the syndicate). The first *Peanuts* daily appeared October 2, 1950; the first Sunday, January 6, 1952.

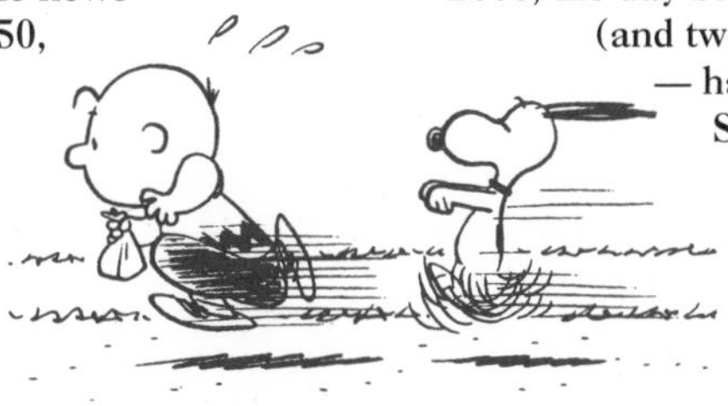

Prior to *Peanuts*, the province of the comics page had been that of gags, social and political observation, domestic comedy, soap opera, and various adventure genres. Although *Peanuts* changed, or evolved, during the 50 years Schulz wrote and drew it, it remained, as it began, an anomaly on the comics page — a comic strip about the interior crises of the cartoonist himself. After a painful divorce in 1973 from which he had not yet recovered, Schulz told a reporter, "Strangely, I've drawn better cartoons in the last six months — or as good as I've ever drawn. I don't know how the human mind works." Surely, it was this kind of humility in the face of profoundly irreducible human question that makes *Peanuts* as universally moving as it is.

Diagnosed with cancer, Schulz retired from *Peanuts* at the end of 1999. He died on February 12th 2000, the day before his last strip was published (and two days before Valentine's Day) — having completed 17,897 daily and Sunday strips, each and every one fully written, drawn, and lettered entirely by his own hand — an unmatched achievement in comics.

—Gary Groth

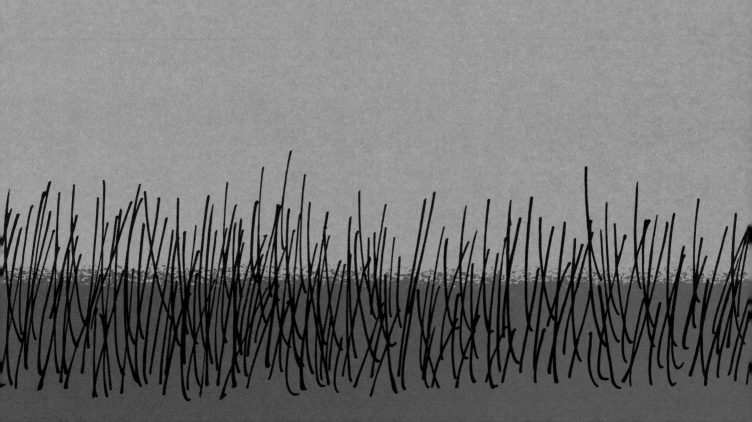

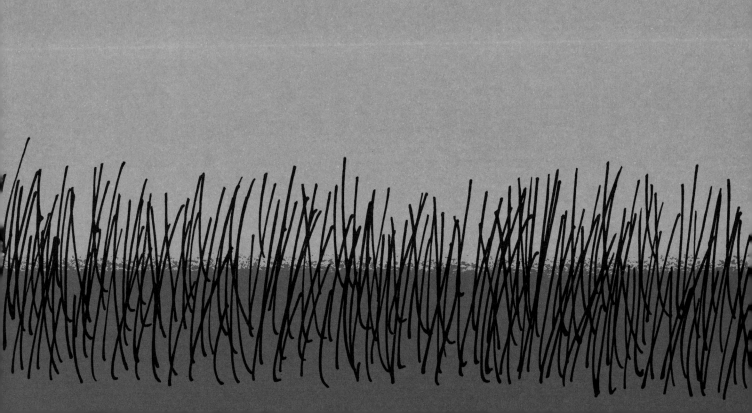

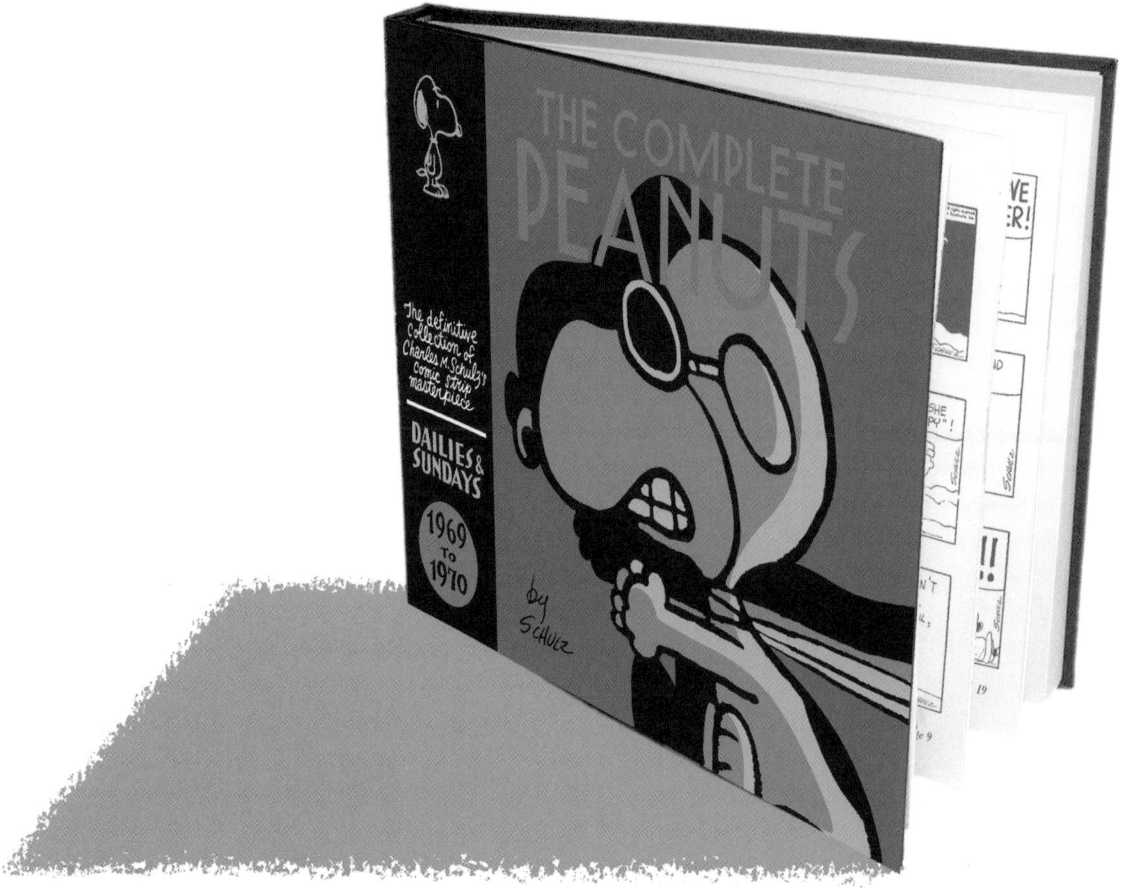
THE COMPLETE PEANUTS
The definitive collection of Charles M. Schulz's comic strip masterpiece
DAILIES & SUNDAYS
1969 TO 1970
by SCHULZ

COMING IN *THE COMPLETE PEANUTS: 1969-1970*

The 1960s wind down as Peppermint Patty runs afoul of her school's dress code, Lucy declares herself a "New Feminist," and Snoopy's Daisy Hill Puppy Farm speaking engagement climaxes in a riot...and a new love found amidst the teargas. Also in this volume, The Head Beagle, Miss Othmar on strike, Snoopy on the Moon, dinner with Joe Shlabotnik, kite-eating tree vs. piano, and (oh no!) the Little Red-Haired Girl moves away...

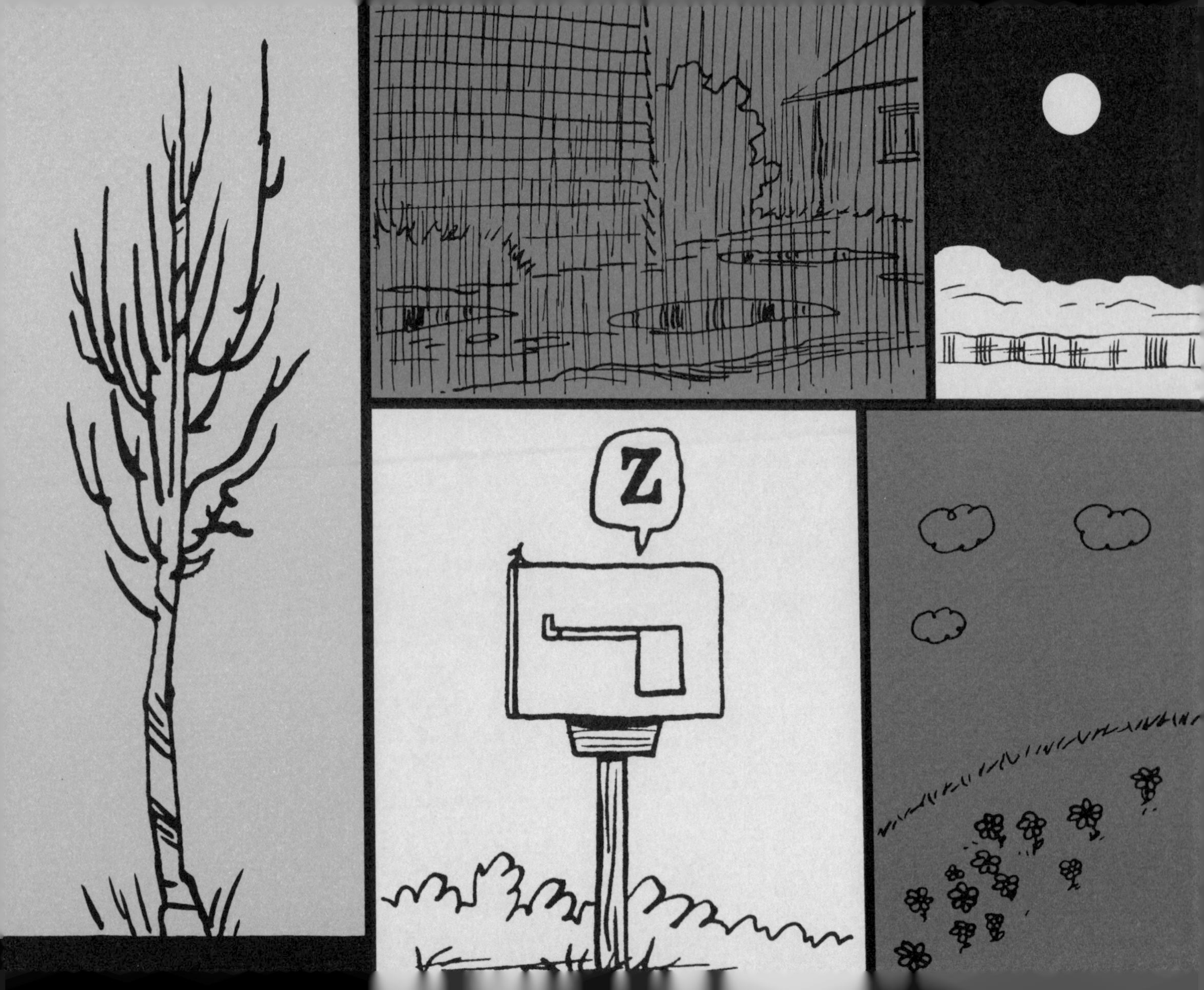
Z